Streetwise

We dedicate this book to all the authors over the years who have enabled *The Journal of Portfolio Management* to make a contribution to the theory of finance and to that theory's many powerful applications in the real world.

Peter L. Bernstein and Frank J. Fabozzi

Streetwise
The Best of *The Journal of Portfolio Management*

Peter L. Bernstein
and Frank J. Fabozzi, Editors

Princeton University Press
Princeton, New Jersey

"Challenge to Judgment," by Paul A. Samuelson © 1974 Institutional Investor, Inc.

"The Dividend Puzzle," by Fischer Black © 1976 Institutional Investor, Inc.

"The Capital Asset Pricing Model and the Market Model," by Barr Rosenberg © 1981 Institutional Investor, Inc.

"Factors in New York Stock Exchange Security Returns, 1931–1979," by William F. Sharpe © 1982 Institutional Investor, Inc.

"What Hath MPT Wrought: Which Risks Reap Rewards?" by Robert D. Arnott © 1983 Institutional Investor, Inc.

"Persuasive Evidence of Market Inefficiency," by Barr Rosenberg, Kenneth Reid, and Ronald Lanstein © 1985 Institutional Investor, Inc.

"What Moves Stock Prices?" by David M. Cutler, James M. Poterba, and Lawrence H. Summers © 1989 Institutional Investor, Inc.

"The Complexity of the Stock Market," by Bruce I. Jacobs and Kenneth N. Levy © 1989 Institutional Investor, Inc.

"Beta and Return," by Fischer Black © 1993 Institutional Investor, Inc.

"Performance Evaluation and Benchmark Errors," by Richard Roll © 1980 Institutional Investor, Inc.

"The Trouble with Performance Measurement," by Robert Ferguson © 1986 Institutional Investor, Inc.

"How to Detect Skill in Management Performance," by Mark Kritzman © 1986 Institutional Investor, Inc.

"The Implementation Shortfall: Paper versus Reality," by André F. Perold © 1988 Institutional Investor, Inc.

"Continuously Rebalanced Investment Strategies," by Mark Rubinstein © 1991 Institutional Investor, Inc.

"A New Route to Higher Returns and Lower Risks," by Gary L. Bergstrom © 1975 Institutional Investor Inc.

"A Global Approach to Money Management," by François Garrone and Bruno Solnik © 1976 Institutional Investor, Inc.

"How to Win at the Loser's Game," by Edward M. Miller, Jr. © 1978 Institutional Investor, Inc.

"A New Paradigm for Portfolio Risk," by Robert H. Jeffrey © 1984 Institutional Investor, Inc.

"Latané's Bequest: The Best of Portfolio Strategies," by Richard W. McEnally © 1986 Institutional Investor, Inc.

"The Fundamental Law of Active Management," by Richard C. Grinold © 1989 Institutional Investor, Inc.

"The Sharpe Ratio," by William F. Sharpe © 1994 Institutional Investor, Inc.

"The Invisible Costs of Trading," by Jack L. Treynor © 1994 Institutional Investor, Inc.

"Real Estate: The Whole Story," by Paul M. Firstenberg, Stephen A. Ross, and Randall C. Zisler © 1988 Institutional Investor, Inc.

"Breaking Tradition in Bond Portfolio Investment," by Madeline W. Einhorn © 1975 Institutional Investor, Inc.

"The Dividends from Active Bond Management," by Kenneth R. Meyer © 1975 Institutional Investor, Inc.

"Duration as a Practical Tool for Bond Management," by Richard W. McEnally © 1977 Institutional Investor, Inc.

"Goal Oriented Bond Portfolio Management," by Martin L. Leibowitz © 1979 Institutional Investor, Inc.

"The Challenge of Analyzing Bond Portfolio Returns," by Peter O. Dietz, H. Russell Fogler, and Donald J. Hardy © 1980 Institutional Investor, Inc.

"The Art of Risk Management in Bond Portfolios," by G. O. Bierwag, George G. Kaufman, Robert Schweitzer, and Alden Toevs © 1981 Institutional Investor, Inc.

"The Uses of Contingent Immunization," by Martin L. Leibowitz and Alfred Weinberger © 1981 Institutional Investor, Inc.

"Bond Indexation: The Optimal Quantitative Approach," by Christina Seix and Ravi Akhoury © 1986 Institutional Investor, Inc.

"Why Invest in Foreign Currency Bonds," by Kenneth Cholerton, Pierre Pieraerts, and Bruno Solnik © 1986 Institutional Investor, Inc.

"Duration Models: A Taxonomy," by G. O. Bierwag, George G. Kaufman, and Cynthia M. Latta © 1988 Institutional Investor, Inc.

"Convexity and Exceptional Return," by Ronald N. Kahn and Roland Lochoff © 1990 Institutional Investor, Inc.

"Non-Parallel Yield Curve Shifts and Immunization," by Robert R. Reitano © 1992 Institutional Investor, Inc.

"Bond Yield Spreads: A Postmodern View," by Chris P. Dialynas and David H. Edington © 1992 Institutional Investor, Inc.

"Options Can Alter Portfolio Return Distributions," by Richard Bookstaber and Roger Clarke © 1981 Institutional Investor, Inc.

"Option Portfolio Risk Analysis," by Jeremy Evnine and Andrew Rudd © 1984 Institutional Investor, Inc.

"The Use of Options in Performance Structuring," by Richard Bookstaber © 1985 Institutional Investor, Inc.

"Futures and Alternative Hedge Ratio Methodologies," by Alden L. Toevs and David P. Jacob © 1986 Institutional Investor, Inc.

"Hedging Corporate Bond Portfolios," by Robin Grieves © 1986 Institutional Investor, Inc.

Published by Princeton University Press, 41 William Street, Princeton, New Jersey 08540

In the United Kingdom: Princeton University Press, Chichester, West Sussex

All Rights Reserved

Library of Congress Cataloging-in-Publication Data

Streetwise : the best of the Journal of portfolio management / Peter L. Bernstein and Frank J. Fabozzi, editors.
    p.   cm.
    A selection of articles previously published in the Journal of portfolio management over a period of nearly 25 years.
    Includes bibliographical references.
    ISBN 0-691-01129-X (cl : alk. paper). — ISBN 0-691-01128-1 (pb : alk. paper)
    1. Portfolio management. 2. Investments. I. Bernstein, Peter L. II. Fabozzi, Frank J. III. Journal of portfolio management.
HG4529.5.S75 1997
332.6—dc21   97-15849

Princeton University Press books are printed on acid-free paper and meet the guidelines for permanence and durability of the Committee on Production Guidelines for Book Longevity of the Council on Library Resources

Printed in the United States of America

10 9 8 7 6 5 4 3 2 1

10 9 8 7 6 5 4 3 2 1
(Pbk.)

Contents

PART SIX: Options and Futures

Streetwise

Introduction

Peter L. Bernstein

In my introduction to Volume 1, Number 1, of *The Journal of Portfolio Management*, which appeared during the dark days of late 1974, I observed that "none of us can avoid being haunted by the academic diagnosis. . . . If all of this can add to our understanding of what it is we are actually doing, the less the possibilities will be of another round of agonies and disappointments such as those we have just been through."

Two additional quotations from contributors to that first issue offer conflicting views about what would be likely to happen next. In "The State of the Art in Our Profession," James Vertin, an early and persistent pioneer in the application of portfolio theory to hands-on management, cheered on his peers in the lead article with these words:

> [T]he full body of knowledge now available to our profession . . . can significantly improve our investment management product and our reputation. . . . Given the existing problems of the investment management community, such improvement seems well worth having. The means for obtaining it are at hand, are freely available to those who would make the effort to use them, and are usable *now*. Let's get on with it!

Nobel laureate Paul Samuelson, Professor of Economics, took a much dimmer view of the possibilities:

> [A] respect for evidence compels me to incline toward the hypothesis that most portfolio decision makers should go out of business—take up plumbing, teach Greek, or help produce the annual GNP by serving as corporate executives. Even if this advice to drop dead is good advice, it obviously is not counsel that will be eagerly followed. Few people will commit suicide without a push.

Samuelson's acclaimed forecasting skills were confirmed here: no portfolio manager I ever heard about followed his advice to commit professional suicide. Instead, a great many of them chose to follow Vertin's counsel to get on with it and proceeded to learn and apply the lessons of the academic diagnosis.

As a consequence, the profession of portfolio management has prospered. Armed with increasingly sophisticated tools for understanding capital market behavior, in all of its many manifestations across products and around the world, today's managers bear little resemblance to the go-go stock pickers of the 1960s or to the typical buy-and-hold sleepyheads who had dominated the fixed-income markets since the beginning of time. Since 1974, risk management has become the driving force in portfolio management, and the analysis of risk/return tradeoffs is what the modern investment process is all about. "How do you like the market?" remains a perennial inquiry for television interviews and newspaper quotes, but most organizations today appreciate the uncertainties that obscure any serious answer to that kind of question.

That is only the beginning. Twenty-five years ago, town and gown were two worlds that were not really on anything that could be described as speaking terms. Today, the two groups are in many ways indistinguishable, a development that my initiatives in founding *The Journal of Portfolio Management* explicitly promised to foster. Creative research by practitioners of the profession has opened important new fields of study for academics. Many scholars in finance, now often accompanied by scientists from other disciplines, have enthusiastically taken up the challenges of hands-on decision-making in the capital markets. On Wall Street today, M.B.A.'s rub shoulders with Ph.D.'s without either taking any notice of their differing backgrounds.

This fascinating and fruitful interchange was the primary inspiration for putting together this collection of articles from *The Journal of Portfolio Management*. Both finance theory and investment practice are at their best when they are directly addressing each other, and Frank Fabozzi and I had a plethora of material from which to make our selections.

There was nothing easy about the selection process. In compiling our list of candidates for inclusion in this volume, we both felt that we should focus on the classics in the collection—papers that may seem obvious or familiar from today's perspective but that in fact were laying out important new ideas for the very first time when we published them. We went through the material in constant astonishment at how many articles satisfied our criteria.

I was especially pleased to note how advanced we were in offering work in areas that today are taken completely for granted but that were only in their infancy at the time of publication. We carried our first articles on international investing, including a global approach, during the period 1975 to 1978. Half of our Spring 1975 issue was devoted to active fixed-income management; two of those six articles are reproduced here. An article on options trading appeared in our issue of Winter 1975, and we have included highly advanced successor articles in this volume, carrying dates as early as 1981 and 1984.

We had no choice but to exclude a large number of excellent papers because they did not qualify as "classics." For example, we published many important articles that presented or analyzed empirical data in original and useful ways but that fell short of offering an illuminating interchange between theory and practice. Passing commentaries on transitory events, even by distinguished authors, seemed inappropriate when space limitations were forcing us to include only the most outstanding of the approximately one thousand papers that we have published since the fall of 1974.

This book is therefore a history as well as an invitation to education. Too many of us use tools and concepts without any sense of where they came from, when they appeared, or why they were developed at that particular moment. I have discovered from my own research into the history of ideas that innovative notions are most exciting and most illuminating in their original versions. We learn far more by observing the pebble at the moment it strikes the water than we could ever discover by analyzing the ever-widening ripples that emanate from the event.

PART ONE
Market Behavior

The notion that managing risk is the primary task of portfolio management was a bitter pill for practitioners to swallow in the wake of the stock market disasters of 1972–1974. Even worse, how could anyone imagine that equations with Greek letters could begin to describe the rough-and-tumble of the marketplace? The very idea that there could be a *theory* of market behavior was almost impossible to grasp. But at that time even many academics were, like the professionals, wandering through foreign territory in the theory of finance, unsure as to where these revolutionary concepts were ultimately going to lead.

The early issues of *The Journal of Portfolio Management* contained a large number of articles that simply laid out the essential principles of modern portfolio theory. Some, like Paul Samuelson's article in the maiden issue, preached the new gospel—literally. Others, like Fischer Black's classic essay on the divi-

dend puzzle, raised questions and emphasized uncertainty. Soon, however, the practitioners joined in, and practical applications and explications appeared with increasing frequency, supplanting the more elementary papers. In time, contributors began to question the basic principles even as practitioners were finally beginning to accept them.

This opening section contains the papers that most effectively trace this history from the simple to the more complex and controversial. They are also the contributions that were the most innovative and ingenious in their presentations. Their authors explored the widening theoretical horizon, reflected the fascination with conflicting evidence about how things really do work, and examined the possibilities opened up by these concepts for transforming the management of investment portfolios from seat-of-the-pants to systematic quantitative methodologies.

Challenge to judgment

Perhaps there really are managers who can outperform the market consistently – logic would suggest that they exist. But they are remarkably well-hidden.

Paul A. Samuelson

Once upon a time there was one world of investment — the world of *practical* operators in the stock and bond markets. Now there are two worlds — the same old practical world, and the new world of the academics with their mathematical stochastic processes.

These worlds are still light-years apart: as far apart as the distance from New York to Cambridge; or, exaggerating a bit, as far apart as the vast width of the Charles River between the Harvard Business School and the Harvard Yard. Perhaps there has been in recent years some discernible rate of convergence between these disparate worlds. In any case, I would expect the future to show some further approach between them.

Indeed, to reveal my bias, the ball is in the court of the practical men: it is the turn of the Mountain to take a first step toward the theoretical Mohammed.

CAN ANYONE PERFORM?

Let me explain. If you oversimplify the debate, it can be put in the form of the question,

Resolved, that the best of money managers cannot be demonstrated to be able to deliver the goods of superior portfolio-selection performance.

Any jury that reviews the evidence, and there is a great deal of relevant evidence, must at least come out with the Scottish verdict:

Superior investment performance is unproved.

Let me not be misunderstood. The Morgan Bank people did do better in certain years than the average mutual fund. That is not in doubt. Nor is it denied that the T. Rowe Price organization achieved greater increments of wealth in certain years than did

many other organizations. And both of these may well turn out to perform better than the market as a whole in the future. Yet, recall that there were years when the Dreyfus Fund, or the Enterprise Fund, or Fidelity Funds seemed greatly to outperform the mob. And there were other years when they didn't.

What is at issue is not whether, as a matter of logic or brute fact, *there could exist a subset of the decision makers in the market capable of doing better than the averages on a repeatable, sustainable basis.* There is nothing in the mathematics of random walks or Brownian movements that (a) *proves* this to be impossible, or (b) *postulates* that it is in fact impossible.

The crucial point is that when investigators — like Irwin Friend, William Sharpe, Jack Treynor, James Lorie, Fischer Black, and Myron Scholes, or any Foundation treasurer of fair-minded and serious intent — look to identify those minority groups or methods endowed with sustainable superior investment prowess, they are quite unable to find them. The only honest conclusion is to agree that a loose version of the "efficient market" or "random walk" hypothesis accords with the facts of life. This truth, be it emphasized, is a truth about New York (and Chicago, and Omaha); and it is *as* true in New York as in Cambridge.

DEADWEIGHT TRANSACTION COSTS

This does not say that many people, or even most people, are not capable of frittering away the funds given them. To lose money, all you have to do is flip a coin, buying GM on heads and selling it on tails. That way you'll do worse than the averages, and worse even than holding GM or avoiding it. The money you lose — and the odds are overwhelmingly against you — will go to lower the losses of your hard-pressed broker. Similarly, the transaction vol-

7

ume generated by the non-random decisions of the vast majority of the big and small investors, who all *think* they have "flair" but do not demonstrably have it, serves only to suck economic resources out of useful GNP activities like osteopathy and rock singing into broker solicitations and bookkeeping.

This is not a condemnation of market activity: even if eight out of ten transactions are wasteful, who is to say which are the two that are not! It is, however, a useful hint to most pension and trust managers that their clients would in all likelihood be ahead if their turnover rates were halved and their portfolios were more broadly diversified. They also serve who only sit and hold; but I suppose the fees to be earned by such sensible and prosaic behavior are less than from essaying to give it that old post-college try.

EQUALITY OF AVERAGE AND ALL

What logic can demonstrate is that not everybody, nor even the average person, can do better than the comprehensive market averages. That would contradict the tautology that the whole is the sum of its parts.

What statistics can suggest is this: If you select at random a list of, say, 100 stocks and buy them *with weights proportional to their respective total outstanding market values*, although your sample's performance will not *exactly* duplicate that of a comprehensive market average, it will come close to doing so — closer than if you throw a dart at only one stock, but of course not quite as close as with a sample of 200, 300, or all the stocks available in the marketplace.

EUTHANASIA OF PERFORMERS

Do I really believe what I have been saying? I would like to believe otherwise. But a respect for evidence compels me to incline toward the hypothesis that most portfolio decision makers should go out of business — take up plumbing, teach Greek, or help produce the annual GNP by serving as corporate executives. Even if this advice to drop dead is good advice, it obviously is not counsel that will be eagerly followed. Few people will commit suicide without a push. And fewer still will pay good money to be told to do what it is against human nature and self-interest to do.

Emerson said that the world would beat a path to the door of the person who invented a better mousetrap. That showed what he knew about economics. Wells Fargo set out a trial balloon in the way of a sensible non-managed fund that embodied essentially the whole market. Batterymarch has done likewise. One of the American Express funds also experimented with such an outlet for pension fund money. The story is not yet over, but one is left with the impression that much underbrush has been growing up before the doors of these deviants into good sense.

At the least, some large foundation should set up an in-house portfolio that tracks the S & P 500 Index — if only for the purpose of setting up a naive model against which their in-house gunslingers can measure their prowess. Instead, most portfolio committees bolster their self-esteem by showing that they have done better than the Value Line 1500 Index. And no wonder: that being a geometric-mean index, I can outperform it merely by buying *its* stocks in its proportions; and can do so both in down markets and up markets — since money is only sophisticated enough to grow arithmetically, dollar on top of (algebraic!) dollar.

Perhaps CREF, which pioneered the variable annuity and the variable pension plan, can be induced to set up a pilot-plant operation of an unmanaged diversified fund, but I would not bet on it. I have suggested to my colleague, Franco Modigliani, who presumably will be President of the American Economic Association in 1976 (if there is a 1976), that economists might want to put their money where their darts are: the AEA might contemplate setting up for its members a no-load, no-management-fee, virtually no transaction-turnover fund along Sharpe-Mossin-Lintner lines. But there may be less supernumerary wealth to be found among 20,000 economists than among 20,000 chiropractors. For as Shaw should have said: "Those who have, don't know; those who know, don't have."

TEST OF PUDDINGS

How does one judge the validity of what I have been asserting? Certainly we don't want to replace old dogmas about "selectivity in search for quality" with new dogmas, however scientific their nomenclature. The sad truth is that it is precisely those who disagree most with the hypothesis of efficient market pricing of stocks, those who pooh-pooh beta analysis and all that, who *are least able to understand the analysis needed to test that hypothesis.*

First, they simply assert that it stands to common sense that greater effort to get facts and greater acumen in analyzing those facts will pay off in better performance somehow measured. (By this logic, the cure for cancer must have been found by 1955.)

Second, they always claim they know a man, a bank, or a fund that does do better. Alas, anecdotes are not science. And once Wharton School dissertations seek to quantify the performers, these have a tendency to evaporate into the air — or, at least, into statistically insignificant "t" statistics.

SUMMING UP

It is not ordained in heaven, or by the second law of thermodynamics, that a small group of intelligent and informed investors cannot systematically achieve higher mean portfolio gains with lower average variabilities. People differ in their heights, pulchritude, and acidity. Why not in their P.Q. or performance quotient? Any Sheik with a billion dollars has every incentive to track down organizations with such high P.Q. (But, paradoxically, it takes P.Q. to identify P.Q., so it is not easy to get off the ground.)

Anyone with special abilities earns a differential return on that flair, which we economists call a rent. Those few with extraordinary P.Q. will not give away such rent to the Ford Foundation or to the local bank trust department. They have too high an I.Q. for that. Like any race track tout, they will share it for a price with those well-heeled people who can most benefit from it.

It is a mistake, though, to think that *so much money* will follow the advice of the best talents *inevitably, as a matter of the logic of competitive arbitrage alone*, to leave everyone else facing a "white noise" random-dart situation, in which every security of the same expected variability has the same expected mean return. From the nature of the case, there must always be a measure of uncertainty and of doubt concerning how much of one's money one can entrust to an adviser suspected of having exceptional P.Q. Many academic economists fall implicitly into confusion on this point. They think that the truth of the efficient market or random walk (or, more precisely, fair-martingale) hypothesis is established by logical tautology or by the same empirical certainty as the proposition that nickels sell for less than dimes.

The nearest thing to a deductive proof of a theorem suggestive of the fair-game hypothesis is that provided in my two articles on why properly anticipated speculative prices do vibrate randomly.* But of course, the weasel words "properly anticipated" provide the gasoline that drives the tautology to its conclusion. As I pointed out at the conclusion of the second cited article, any subset in the market which has a better ex ante knowledge of the stochastic process that stocks will follow in the future is in effect possessed of a "Maxwell's Demon" who tells him how to make capital gains from his effective peek into tomorrow's financial page reports. To be sure those possessed of such special competence must stay a subset of the market; if they become big enough to dominate the process of present stock price formation, that will falsify the presumption that they are still possessed of differential, undiscounted, ex ante valuable knowledge.

What is interesting is the empirical fact that it is virtually impossible for academic researchers with access to the published records to identify any member of the subset with flair. This fact, though not an inevitable law, is a brute fact. The ball, as I have already noted, is in the court of those who doubt the random walk hypothesis. They can dispose of the uncomfortable brute fact in the only way that any fact is disposed of — by producing brute evidence to the contrary.

---

* P. A. Samuelson, "Proof That Properly Anticipated Prices Fluctuate Randomly," *Industrial Management Review* (now *Sloan Management Review*), 1965, 6, 41-49; reproduced as Chapter 198 in Samuelson, *Collected Scientific Papers, Volume III*, Cambridge, M.I.T. Press, 1967. See also my "Proof That Properly Discounted Present Values of Assets Vibrate Randomly," *Bell Journal of Economics and Management Science*, Autumn 1973, 4, 369-374.

The dividend puzzle

"The harder we look at the dividend picture, the more it seems like a puzzle, with pieces that just don't fit together."

Fischer Black

Why do corporations pay dividends? Why do investors pay attention to dividends? Perhaps the answers to these questions are obvious. Perhaps dividends represent the return to the investor who put his money at risk in the corporation. Perhaps corporations pay dividends to reward existing shareholders and to encourage others to buy new issues of common stock at high prices. Perhaps investors pay attention to dividends because only through dividends or the prospect of dividends do they receive a return on their investment or the chance to sell their shares at a higher price in the future.

Or perhaps the answers are not so obvious. Perhaps a corporation that pays no dividends is demonstrating confidence that it has attractive investment opportunities that might be missed if it paid dividends. If it makes these investments, it may increase the value of the shares by more than the amount of the lost dividends. If that happens, its shareholders may be doubly better off. They end up with capital appreciation greater than the dividends they missed out on, and they find they are taxed at lower effective rates on capital appreciation than on dividends.

In fact, I claim that the answers to these questions are not obvious at all. The harder we look at the dividend picture, the more it seems like a puzzle, with pieces that just don't fit together.

THE MILLER-MODIGLIANI THEOREM

Suppose you are offered the following choice. You may have $2 today, and a 50-50 chance of $54 or $50 tomorrow. Or you may have nothing today, and a 50-50 chance of $56 or $52 tomorrow. Would you prefer one of these gambles to the other?

Probably you would not. Ignoring such factors

as the cost of holding the $2 and one day's interest on $2, you would be indifferent between these two gambles.

The choice between a common stock that pays a dividend and a stock that pays no dividend is similar, at least if we ignore such things as transaction costs and taxes. The price of the dividend-paying stock drops on the ex-dividend date by about the amount of the dividend. The dividend just drops the whole range of possible stock prices by that amount. The investor who gets a $2 dividend finds himself with shares worth about $2 less than they would have been worth if the dividend hadn't been paid, in all possible circumstances.

This, in essence, is the Miller-Modigliani theorem.[1] It says that the dividends a corporation pays do not affect the value of its shares or the returns to investors, because the higher the dividend, the less the investor receives in capital appreciation, no matter how the corporation's business decisions turn out.

When we say this, we are assuming that the dividend paid does not influence the corporation's business decisions. Paying the dividend either reduces the amount of cash equivalents held by the corporation, or increases the amount of money raised by issuing securities.

IF A FIRM PAYS NO DIVIDENDS

If this theorem is correct, then a firm that pays a regular dividend equal to about half of its normal earnings will be worth the same as an otherwise similar firm that pays no dividends and will never pay any dividends. Can that be true? How can a firm that will never pay dividends be worth anything at all?

Actually, there are many ways for the stockholders of a firm to take cash out without receiving dividends. The most obvious is that the firm can buy

1. Footnotes appear at the end of the article.

back some of its shares. This has the advantage that most investors are not taxed as heavily on shares sold as they are on dividends received.

If the firm is closely held, it can give money to its shareholders by giving them jobs at inflated salaries, or by ordering goods from other firms owned by the shareholders at inflated prices.

If the firm is not closely held, then another firm or individual can make a tender offer which will have the effect of making it closely held. Then the same methods for taking cash out of the firm can be used.

Under the assumptions of the Modigliani-Miller theorem, a firm has value even if it pays no dividends. Indeed, it has the same value it would have if it paid dividends.

TAXES

In a world where dividends are taxed more heavily (for most investors) than capital gains, and where capital gains are not taxed until realized, a corporation that pays no dividends will be more attractive to taxable individual investors than a similar corporation that pays dividends. This will tend to increase the price of the non-dividend-paying corporation's stock. Many corporations will be tempted to eliminate dividend payments.

Of course, corporate investors are taxed more heavily on realized capital gains than on dividends. And tax-exempt investors are taxed on neither. But it is hard to believe that these groups have enough impact on the market to outweigh the effects of taxable individuals.

Also, the IRS has a special tax that it likes to apply to companies that retain earnings to avoid the personal taxation of dividends. But there are many ways to avoid this tax. A corporation that is making investments in its business usually doesn't have to pay the tax, especially if it is issuing securities to help pay for these investments.

If a corporation insists on paying out cash, it is better off replacing some of its common stock with bonds. A shareholder who keeps his proportionate share of the new securities will receive taxable interest but at least the interest will be deductible to the corporation. Dividends are not deductible.

With taxes, investors and corporations are no longer indifferent to the level of dividends. They prefer smaller dividends or no dividends at all.

TRANSACTION COSTS

An investor who holds a non-dividend-paying stock will generally sell some of his shares if he needs to raise cash. In some circumstances, he can borrow against his shares. Either of these transactions can be costly, especially if small amounts of money are involved. So an investor might want to have dividend income instead.

But this argument doesn't have much substance. If investors are concerned about transaction costs, the corporation that pays no dividends can arrange for automatic share repurchase plans, much like the automatic dividend reinvestment plans that now exist. A shareholder would keep his stock in trust, and the trustee would periodically sell shares back to the corporation, including fractional shares if necessary. The shareholder could even choose the amounts he wants to receive and the timing of the payments. An automated system would probably cost about as much as a system for paying dividends.

If the IRS objected to the corporation's buying back its own shares, then the trustee could simply sell blocks of shares on the open market. Again, the cost would be low.

Thus transaction costs don't tell us much about why corporations pay dividends.

WHAT DO DIVIDEND CHANGES TELL US?

The managers of most corporations have a tendency to give out good news quickly, but to give out bad news slowly. Thus investors are somewhat suspicious of what the managers have to say.

Dividend policy, though, may say things the managers don't say explicitly. For one reason or another, managers and directors do not like to cut the dividend. So they will raise the dividend only if they feel the company's prospects are good enough to support the higher dividend for some time. And they will cut the dividend only if they think the prospects for a quick recovery are poor.

This means that dividend changes, or the fact that the dividend doesn't change, may tell investors more about what the managers really think than they can find out from other sources. Assuming that the managers' forecasts are somewhat reliable, dividend policy conveys information.

Thus the announcement of a dividend cut often leads to a drop in the company's stock price. And the announcement of a dividend increase often leads to an increase in the company's stock price. These stock price changes are permanent if the company in fact does as badly, or as well, as the dividend changes indicated.

If the dividend changes are not due to forecasts of the company's prospects, then any stock price changes that occur will normally be temporary. If a corporation eliminates its dividend because it wants to save taxes for its shareholders, then the stock price might decline at first. But it would eventually go back to the level it would have had if the dividend had not been cut, or higher.

Thus the fact that dividend changes often tell us things about the corporations making them does not explain why corporations pay dividends.

HOW TO HURT THE CREDITORS

When a company has debt outstanding, the indenture will almost always limit the dividends the company can pay. And for good reason. There is no easier way for a company to escape the burden of a debt than to pay out all of its assets in the form of a dividend, and leave the creditors holding an empty shell.[2]

While this is an extreme example, any increase in the dividend that is not offset by an increase in external financing will hurt the company's creditors. A dollar paid out in dividends is a dollar that is not available to the creditors if trouble develops.

If an increase in the dividend will hurt the creditors, then a cut in the dividend will help the creditors. Since the firm is only worth so much, what helps the creditors will hurt the stockholders. The stockholders would certainly rather have $2 in dividends than $2 invested in assets that may end up in the hands of the creditors. Perhaps we have finally found a reason why firms pay dividends.

Alas, this explanation doesn't go very far. In many cases, the changes in the values of the stock and bonds caused by a change in dividend policy would be so small they would not be detectable. And if the effects are large, the company can negotiate with the creditors. If the company agrees not to pay any dividends at all, the creditors would presumably agree to give better terms on the company's credit. This would eliminate the negative effects of cutting the dividend on the position of the stockholders relative to the creditors.

DIVIDENDS AS A SOURCE OF CAPITAL

A company that pays dividends might instead have invested the money in its operations. This is especially true when the company goes to the markets frequently for new capital. Cutting the dividend, if there are no special reasons for paying dividends, has to be one of the lowest cost sources of funds available to the company.

The underwriting cost of a new debt or equity issue is normally several percent of the amount of money raised. There are no comparable costs for money raised by cutting the dividend.

Perhaps a company that has no profitable investment projects and that is not raising money externally should keep its dividend. If the dividend is cut,

the managers may lose the money through unwise investment projects. In these special cases, there may be a reason to keep the dividend. But surely these cases are relatively rare.

In the typical case, the fact that cutting the dividend is a low cost way to raise money is another reason to expect corporations not to pay dividends. So why do they continue?

DO INVESTORS DEMAND DIVIDENDS?

It is possible that many, many individual investors believe that stocks that don't pay dividends should not be held, or should be held only at prices lower than the prices of similar stocks that do pay dividends. This belief is not rational, so far as I can tell. But it may be there nonetheless.

Add these investors to the trustees who believe it is not prudent to hold stocks that pay no dividends, and to the corporations that have tax reasons for preferring dividend-paying stocks, and you may have a substantial part of the market. More important, you may have a part of the market that strongly influences the pricing of corporate shares. Perhaps the best evidence of this is the dominance of this view in investment advisory publications.

On the other hand, investors also seem acutely aware of the tax consequences of dividends. Investors in high tax brackets seem to hold low dividend stocks, and investors in low tax brackets seem to hold high dividend stocks.[3]

Furthermore, the best empirical tests that I can think of are unable to show whether investors who prefer dividends or investors who avoid dividends have a stronger effect on the pricing of securities.[4]

If investors do demand dividends, then corporations should not eliminate all dividends. But it is difficult or impossible to tell whether investors demand dividends or not. So it is hard for a corporation to decide whether to eliminate its dividends or not.

PORTFOLIO IMPLICATIONS

Corporations can't tell what dividend policy to choose, because they don't know how many irrational investors there are. But perhaps a rational investor can choose a dividend policy for his portfolio that will maximize his after-tax expected return for a given level of risk. Perhaps a taxable investor, especially one who is in a high tax bracket, should emphasize low dividend stocks. And perhaps a tax-exempt investor should emphasize high dividend stocks.

One problem with this strategy is that an investor who emphasizes a certain kind of stock in his portfolio is likely to end up with a less well-diversified portfolio than he would otherwise have. So he will probably increase the risk of his portfolio.

The other problem is that we can't tell if or how much an investor will increase his expected return by doing this. If investors demanding dividends dominate the market, then high dividend stocks will have low expected returns. Even tax-exempt investors, if they are rational, should buy low dividend stocks.

On the other hand, it seems that rational investors in high brackets will do better in low dividend stocks no matter who dominates the market. But how much should they emphasize low dividend stocks? At what point will the loss of diversification offset the increase in expected return?

It is even conceivable that investors overemphasize tax factors, and bid low dividend stocks up so high that they are unattractive even for investors in the highest brackets.

Thus the portfolio implications of the theory are no clearer than its implications for corporate dividend policy.

What should the individual investor do about dividends in his portfolio? We don't know.

What should the corporation do about dividend policy? We don't know.

---

[1] See Merton H. Miller and Franco Modigliani, "Dividend Policy, Growth, and the Valuation of Shares." *Journal of Business* 34 (October, 1961): 411-433. Also Franco Modigliani and Merton H. Miller, "The Cost of Capital, Corporation Finance, and the Theory of Investment: Reply." *American Economic Review* 49 (September, 1959): 655-669.

[2] This issue is discussed in more detail in Fischer Black and Myron Scholes, "The Pricing of Options and Corporate Liabilities." *Journal of Political Economy* 81 (May/June, 1973): 637-654.

[3] See Marshall E. Blume, Jean Crockett, and Irwin Friend, "Stockownership in the United States: Characteristics and Trends." *Survey of Current Business* 54 (November, 1974): 16-40.

[4] See Fischer Black and Myron Scholes, "The Effects of Dividend Yield and Dividend Policy on Common Stock Prices and Returns." *Journal of Financial Economics* 1 (May, 1974): 1-22.

The capital asset pricing model and the market model

"The concept of reward to equity market risk (or beta) is a theoretical insight that, in my view, is likely to endure."

Barr Rosenberg

Is Beta Dead?" (Wallace [1980]) and other recent articles have asked whether broad consequences, disastrous to modern investment technology, would result from misspecification of the Capital Asset Pricing Model (CAPM), or worse yet, from falsehood of the model. The criticisms have cited imprecise specification of the market portfolio as a misapplication of the CAPM, and have emphasized the difference between the "efficient portfolio" and the market portfolio when the CAPM is false. The purpose of this article is to evaluate these criticisms.

Many of the constructs of the "market model" are widely used in investment: "market portfolio," "systematic risk and return," "residual" or "diversifiable risk and return," "alpha," "beta." These ideas play an important role in the methods of "modern portfolio theory."

The Capital Asset Pricing Model of Sharpe, Lintner, and Mossin is the origin of these formal *constructs*. The constructs of the CAPM are important building blocks that retain validity in numerous applications, even where the CAPM fails. Sharpe's [1963, 1964] clear demonstration of the CAPM stimulated diverse quantitative methods in investment. Most of them, however, turn out to be justified by other arguments and not by the CAPM at all.

The CAPM is theory, but, paradoxically, the role of the CAPM as "theory" leading to application has been less important than its role in mobilizing attention and in defining constructs. We should keep in mind that the CAPM is not "true," since many of its assumptions are not exactly satisfied in the real world. Indeed, the CAPM rules out active management and investment research, and thus abolishes most applications at the stroke of a pen, by virtue of the unrealistic assumptions that it makes.

Some common applications do depend upon the correctness of the simple CAPM, or its extensions, in describing equilibrium returns. For these cases, one reaction to recent criticism can be paraphrased as follows: Is the CAPM true? *No.* Is imprecise knowledge of the market portfolio an important factor in this? *No.* Does the approximated market portfolio retain an important role in the reconstructed applications that emerge from recognition of the falsehood of the CAPM? In my judgment, *yes*, but there is controversy on this point (Ross [1977, 1978]). Hence, I would view the particular criticism centered upon imperfect knowledge of the market portfolio as a "red herring," distracting us from more useful criticisms that open out interesting paths of inquiry.

Applications of theory to active management, in contrast, can have meaning only if the CAPM is false! With regard to each application, the central questions are: Since the application does not depend on the CAPM, what is the justification? Does the market portfolio play an important role in the application? If so, how sensitive is the application to the kinds of error we are likely to make in specifying the market portfolio? Should we seek an "efficient portfolio," so as to do the application more wisely?

The conclusion seems to be that the market portfolio does play a natural role, and that likely specification errors are relatively unimportant. By contrast, the "true efficient portfolio" is not a useful construct: If we knew the efficient portfolio, the need for the application would disappear! Consequently, it is a logical contradiction to rely on a hypothetical efficient portfolio to improve application that is rendered void by that hypothesis.

In summary, I shall argue that criticisms of applications of theory that are based on imperfect knowledge of the market and the efficient portfolio are not very productive. Nevertheless, these critiques may have been fruitful since they have led to widespread discussion of subleties that might otherwise have been glossed over.

The plan of this article as as follows. The first section reviews the simple CAPM, its unrealistic assumptions, and its provocative implications. The second section progressively relaxes the assumptions in the direction of greater realism, and sketches some consequences.

The third section examines applications of the "market model" that depend upon the importance of the "market factor": market timing, performance attribution to market timing, research that breaks out market forecasts from forecasts of other components of return, studies of reward to market risk exposure, and representation of the market return in an asset-allocation decision. The fourth section considers applications in which the market portfolio is important because it is the average of investors' portfolios: Index funds, the "universal performance benchmark," and the idea of nonconsensus forecasts. The applications discussed through this point are not dependent on the CAPM, and are little affected by criticisms of the model.

The fifth section considers the extension of the CAPM into a multiple-factor context in which several factors may be rewarded, and the prediction of equilibrium rewards in this context. The sixth touches briefly upon the investment decision of the client who has, or considers having, multiple managers, and the requisites for performance analysis on behalf of such a client. The final section addresses applications where the falsehood of the CAPM is an important factor: the setting of risk-adjusted rates of return for security valuation, capital budgeting, and rate regulation.

THE ORIGINAL CAPITAL ASSET PRICING MODEL

Well before the CAPM, Markowitz [1959] pioneered the application of decision theory to investment. His was the crucial insight that portfolio optimization is characterized by a trade-off of the reward (expected return) of the individual security against the contribution of that security to portfolio risk. The key aspect of the security's risk is the contribution to *portfolio* risk, rather than its *own* risk. The optimal trade-off of expected reward against the contribution to portfolio risk is "the Markowitz condi-

tion;" this condition (and its extensions when investor goals are more complex) remains the central core of portfolio optimization. Indeed, portfolio optimization systems exist independently of the CAPM.

The CAPM studies a capital market in which all investors independently optimize and achieve the Markowitz condition for their portfolios. The CAPM characterizes the equilibrium condition of the market, when all individuals optimize their circumstances. The CAPM considers supply and demand in the capital market. It exploits the market-clearing condition that, at equilibrium, demand equals supply.

To obtain a neat equilibrium solution, the basic CAPM uses simplified assumptions: (1) All investors have identical expectations about security rewards; (2) all investors have identical expectations about security risks; (3) investors experience identical net returns (taxes and investment expenses are identical); (4) there are no investment constraints (no limits on borrowing or lending, no short-selling restrictions, no upper bounds on holdings); (5) there is a risk-free asset, which is borrowed or lent at identical rates; (6) all investors maximize mean/variance utility functions over a common investment horizon and are risk-averse; (7) investors experience risk only from the investment portfolio (there are no risky assets or liabilities excluded from the problem); (8) markets are perfect (each investor is a price-taker who does not believe he can influence price, there are no transaction costs and no costs of acquiring information).

Evidently, these statements rule out many aspects of diversity and assume away the process of information search and forecasting. The conclusions following from the assumptions are consequently clear-cut: (1) Each individual investor's porfolio satisfies the Markowitz condition; (2) each investor's portfolio of risky assets has the same composition as all other investors'; (3) the market portfolio, which is the aggregate of all portfolios, therefore has this same composition; (4) hence, the market portfolio is efficient for all investors, the unique "mutual fund" of all risky assets that exactly suits the needs of all investors; (5) since the market portfolio is efficient, any other portfolio of risky assets is inferior; (6) investors price each security in the market so that its expected reward compensates for its contribution to risk in the market portfolio (i.e. the equilibrium equation is the familiar "security market line," with expected excess security return being proportional to beta — in other words, alpha is zero for all securities); (7) hence, every portfolio also has an alpha of zero and every portfolio other than the market portfolio is inferior to the market portfolio because it has incremental diversifiable risk — not because it has a negative alpha.

THE TRANSITION FROM THE CAPM TO APPLICATION

If the CAPM were strictly true, there would be no active management. All investor expectations would be identical, and all investors would hold a single "consensus portfolio." The correct prices for assets would emerge magically as the consequence of costlessly materialized expectations. There would be no investment research.

We will find it interesting to trace a sequence of relaxations of the assumptions, which adds realism and consequently leads to more relevant and fruitful predictions. In what follows, I have tried to list successive relaxations in approximate order of importance, beginning with the most significant.

1. Investors actually experience different earned, after-tax returns due to differential tax law. Because different classes of investors face different tax laws, they hold grossly different portfolios. For example, municipal bonds are held by taxable investors, not by tax-exempt investors, and preferred stocks are held more by corporate investors than by individuals. Each investor favors those securities for which he has a comparative advantage (a lower tax, relative to other investors). Features of assets that are important to tax law, including the distribution of return between yield and capital gain, become important to each investor's portfolio decision. Therefore, these same features are important to aggregate demand and consequently figure in market equilibrium (Brennan [1970]).

2. Investors have diverse expectations, obtained by a research process and influenced by the actions of other investors in the market. Since expectations are diverse, there is no set of "true expectations" revealed to any market participant that he may use to define the true *ex ante* efficient portfolio. In practice, there is no such thing. Instead, the research process of each investor builds a set of expectations that constitute best judgment. The efficient portfolio of the investor, defined with respect to his or her expectations, is not efficient in any absolute sense. The market-clearing process now reflects, not "true expectations" as in the CAPM, but a "consensus expectation," which is an average of investors' expectations (Lintner [1969]).

The opportunity to do valuable research creates a competitive research contest among market participants. The need to evaluate diverse skill generates performance analysis. Since profit from research is gained through portfolio revision, transactions tend to dis-

close beliefs of market participants, which results in a competitive trading process.

Costs of information and research must be debited against investment returns, except in the case of the passive investor who accepts market prices as "fair" at all times. Securities with higher information costs per dollar invested hence require a higher return to compensate. For smaller companies, the magnitude of potential investment is so small that the investor may require a significant premium return to offset the minimum cost of effectively monitoring the security. This argument suggests that small companies may offer higher gross returns in equilibrium, before deduction of the information costs.[1]

3. A group of like securities, such as equities, is often styled as "the market" when it is actually only "a market" among multiple markets of risk assets. Analysis within one such market is actually only one component of a larger optimization problem: For example, when analyzing equities separately from bonds, or when separately analyzing individual countries in a multinational portfolio. Moreover, investors are exposed to risks arising from nonfinancial assets (claims on labor income and personal property). Such risks are tied to personal skills and preferences, the risks are often uninsurable, and the assets and liabilities may not even be marketable. These omissions can be classed as "excluded assets and liabilities" (Rudd and Rosenberg [1980]). Investors are concerned not only with the variance of their risky-asset portfolio within a "market," but also with the covariance of the risky-asset portfolio with other risky events in the economy. Investors' attitudes toward these factors of covariance are diverse and express a need to hedge within the capital market those individual risk exposures that are outside the capital market. Investors' holdings within the market differ for this reason. "Optimization" in any one market, ignoring excluded opportunities, is suboptimal.

4. There are constraints upon investment. Costs of borrowing and short positions are typically higher than the returns from lending or long positions. Moreover, widespread institutional barriers against short positions persist. Often, barriers against high concentration persist as well. The result is that any typical investor is a true "marginal investor" on only a fraction of issues; on other issues, the position is already at a constrained bound and is not altered by some changes in expected security return. The "consensus" appraisal of a security responds differently,

1. Footnotes appear at the end of the article.

16

and less sensitively, to changes in constrained investor expectations.

5. There are transaction costs arising from commissions and spreads as well as frequent and substantial transaction costs or benefits associated with tax effects and book-value accounting. As a result, many positions are "grandfathered," so that the investor requires a substantial change in expected reward to induce a trade. Transaction costs also influence equilibrium returns, because the investor must allow for the expected cost of transaction. There are also investment costs associated with custody of securities and accounting of returns. Securities having relatively high expected investment and transaction expenses must have higher equilibrium rewards to compensate. For example, there are higher transaction costs in the purchase and eventual sale of securities having illiquid markets; such securities will be traded less often, but since they must be traded occasionally, a higher gross return may be required in eqiuilibrium to amortize this expense.

There are unusually large surveillance and accounting costs when a security's trading is suspended due to extreme uncertainty or reorganization; hence, companies with higher probability of bankruptcy may exhibit higher equilibrium gross returns, to provide a cushion to cover possible expenses of this kind.

6. Unpredictable inflation causes assets with fixed nominal returns to have risky "real" returns (returns expressed in purchasing power). Unless inflation-indexed, default-free bonds exist, there is no true risk-free asset. This fact makes minimum-risk portfolios of risky asssts a more relevant investment vehicle.

7. Investors have diverse goals. We can approximate these moderately well by mean/variance utility functions defined over the return (or the logarithm of return) over a short holding period, but this "induced myopic utility function" cannot capture all of the subtleties of the multiperiod decision problem, particularly when returns are themselves serially dependent, as is the case for nominal returns on bonds, or when there are investment vehicles with highly assymetric distributions of returns, as is the case with options.

Also, some investors are obligatory holders of certain securities: The most prevalent causes are retention of voting control of the coporation and incentive compensation for management and employees. In some cases, large fractions of outstanding shares may be closely held and "disappear from the market" for extended periods.

8. When the theory calls for us to compute the portfolio of all outstanding assets, there are problems in specifying this portfolio. Since these problems are central to the ambiguity of the "market portfolio," it is important to go into them carefully. In the best of circumstances, a security is unambiguous in definition and publicly recorded: For example, a common stock registered with the SEC. Here, there may be problems in finding the number of securities outstanding, but such information is being steadily collected worldwide for most categories of financial assets. The difficulty here is to identify cross-ownership (one corporation owning another's stock); outstanding securities that are held as an asset of some other security should not be double-counted; fortunately, holdings of public companies in excess of 5% are registered in the U.S.

Other assets are unambiguous in definition, but hard to find. These include unregistered common stocks, privately placed debt, and nonfinancial assets (homogenous assets such as commodities are less of a problem than heterogeneous assets such as real estate and antiques).

Finally, there are assets that are ambiguous in their very definition, such as the present value of labor income (an unmarketable asset) and government debt. Government debt is an investors' asset that is offset by taxpayers' liability in the form of the obligation to pay future taxes. As we pursue the reasoning implied by the aggregate social balance sheet, more and more assets tend to be offset by liabilities, so that the risk associated with them is a risk of redistribution, rather than a risk to the society's aggregate portfolio. Redistributive risks arising from the political process are very difficult to model.

The response to these problems is to separate assets into broad homogeneous classes or "markets" and to use an index of approximate outstandings of more prominent securities in each market as a surrogate for the total market. Weaknesses of this solution are unrepresentativeness within the market, which we will argue is of small import, and exclusion of assets and liabilities, the problem mentioned above.

THE MARKET FACTOR

In view of the deficiencies of the simple CAPM, its great effect upon application must be explained through the vitality of its constructs and the manner of thinking that it has engendered.

One major contribution has been to call attention to the distinction between market-related and residual return. The "market model" expresses the return on every security as the sum of a systematic (market-related) component and a residual component that is uncorrelated with the market. The security's response to the market is its systematic risk coefficient, or beta. The mean and variance of the market return determine, through the beta coefficient, the systematic mean and variance of a security or portfolio. The expected value of the residual component and the residual variance are important properties of the security's residual return, and covariance among residual returns is important for portfolio residual variance.

The CAPM thus emphasizes the return on the market portfolio (or a surrogate for it). Empirical studies have shown that we can use the return on *any* stock market index to explain a large fraction of the variance of individual security returns and a still larger fraction of the variance of portfolio returns. This confirms long-standing recognition of "market movements."

Within each investment "market," such as equities, bonds, or real estate, securities tend to move up and down together. The statement, "The market is up," or "The market is down," would be meaningless otherwise. Numerous studies have since confirmed that in each market one "prominent factor" accounts for a far greater porportion of the variability of security returns than any other single factor, and that all — or almost all — security returns respond to the factor in the same direction. Following common parlance, this can be called the "market factor."

Studies in equity and bond markets confirm that broad-based indexes of returns within each market are highly correlated, even though the included securities and index weights are different. The correlation is so high because any widely based and correctly computed index tends to show up the prominent factor and becomes a surrogate for it.

Since this factor is so prominent, we should naturally take it into account in the investment process. Active investors almost universally attempt to forecast the movements of the market, although many do not make "market timing" an important element of their investment policy. In many organizations, "top-down" guides to security analysts are provided in the form of market forecasts; individual analysts forecast individual security returns conditional upon the market forecast.

We can use any widely based index to define the market. There are reasons, however, for using a "market portfolio" that is a capitalization-weighted average of all outstanding securities in the market. For one thing, investment return on this portfolio is the aggregate of return for all investors and therefore a natural variable in a macroeconomic model. Furthermore, since the market portfolio is the weighted average of all investors' holdings, weighted by their wealth, its value reflects a weighted average of all investors' valuations, or, in some sense, a "consensus valuation."

An important element of performance analysis is the attribution of return among various aspects of investment strategy. Because of the prominence of the market factor, strategy with respect to that factor is usually the first aspect to be emphasized, and Fama [1972] suggested that market timing be distinguished from selectivity of individual stocks as an element of performance, as did Rosenberg [1978]. This performance decomposition requires specification of a market return. The natural surrogate to use is the market index that is being forecast and with respect to which strategy is defined. Since the concern is to identify investment strategy, the index that is called for should be the index the investor is using.

The broad-based index, as market factor surrogate, is also important in historical studies of the reward to market factor risk exposure. Using any definition of the market factor, it is a legitimate question to ask how security returns have related to the security's exposure to that factor. Of course, this is only a pure test of the CAPM if the market-factor surrogate return is identical to the market portfolio return.

Putting aside such niceties, we can still consider the important question of the actual historical pattern of compensation. Several studies have shown that there has been higher historical average reward for higher beta stocks. Moreover, the comparative studies to date have found little change in the estimated amount of reward when we vary the definition of the market index among broad-based indexes. In other words, the exact definition of the market portfolio has not had an important effect upon the estimated reward for exposure to risk of the equity market factor.

Another important application of the "market factor" is as a surrogate for investment opportunities in that market, for consideration in a decision problem by an investor who is "allocating investment" across various markets. In this application, what is required is a representative index for each of several markets. Again, the "market portfolio" for each market is a natural index to use, since it is typical of all investors in the market.

As soon as the CAPM was publicized, research showed that securities had different degrees of responsiveness to the market factor (different betas). Later, we found that significant differences in beta could be consistently predicted. Of course, the exact definition of beta follows from the chosen surrogate for the market factor.

Precisely because of the great prominence of the

market factor in all broadly based indexes, however, substitution of one such index for another changes the definition of beta very little. What occurs is largely a change in the scale of betas (as from Fahrenheit to Centigrade), with little relative change in individual betas. Of course, real changes do emerge when one index is significantly biased relative to another, so as to have importantly different exposure to some secondary common factor in the market. On the other hand, these are second-order changes, because the market factor is so much the most prominent. Therefore, beta becomes a meaningful and predictable characteristic of a security.

In these applications, expected residual return is, by definition, that element of expected return that is not due to the market. Expected residual return is therefore a key description of the individual security in any investment process where we single out the market return. *The distinction between residual and market-related return is a consequence of the structure of the investment process (by virtue of the market return being a distinct construct), and not a result of the CAPM.* Since we express expected residual return conventionally in terms of the intercept of the security market line (zero-beta return) and the individual security's alpha, alpha is the natural way of describing the security's desirability for investment purposes, net of attractiveness arising from exposure through its beta to zero-beta and market returns. There is nothing mysterious about this alpha; it is simply an expression of judgment on the security's expected return. For the same reason as with beta, alpha changes little when one broad-based market index is substituted for another.

Note that none of the applications discussed in this section have been dependent upon the CAPM, nor are they importantly influenced by the exact definition of the market portfolio.

THE AGGREGATE OF INVESTORS' PORTFOLIOS

The CAPM rests upon the market-clearing condition that aggregate demand must equal aggregate supply. Aggregate demand is the sum of all investors' portfolios. Aggregate supply is the ensemble of securities, which, when viewed as the portfolio of all outstanding assets, is the market portfolio. Therefore the average of all investors' portfolios, weighted by the values of their investments, equals the market portfolio. The investment-weighted average of the returns on investors' portfolios similarly equals the market portfolio return. This simple relation, an accounting identity, has profound consequences.

One consequence is an argument for a passive investment strategy equal to the market portfolio. Such strategies have come to be called "index funds."

If carefully constructed, the fund earns a gross return equal to the market portfolio return. The net return is less, due to small costs of transactions and a small passive management fee. The market portfolio return is also the average of all investors' gross returns. Average net returns of all investors are lower due to transaction and management costs, and these expenses are significantly greater for active investors than for the passive fund.

Hence, the net return of the index fund is higher than the average net return of all investors. Moreover, since active investors' positions diverge from one another in the attempt to profit from diverse expectations, investors, on average, take more risk than is present in the market portfolio. Consequently, the passive "market portfolio" strategy earns an above-average net return at a below-average risk.

Imprecise specifications of the market portfolio can damage this argument only if the error causes a failure to capture the average return of investors. Since data on institutional investors' holdings are in the public domain, we can compute and approximate the average holdings of this population of investors. There seems little chance that the ambiguity of stock and bond market portfolios is a significant obstacle to attaining above-average net performance through a broadly based passive "market fund."

The CAPM asserts that the "market portfolio" is not just average in gross return, but also "efficient": The market-portfolio strategy is the perfect strategy for all investors. But the valid claim of above-average net return is more important than the problematic claim of *perfection.* My impression is that the CAPM-based argument of efficiency has been peripheral in the marketing of index funds. If it were crucial, surely there would have been efforts to adhere to the exact requirements of the CAPM by making equity index funds closely representative of the capitalization-weighted equity sector. Instead, the first passive fund followed an equal-weighted index, and most strategies since that time have matched conspicuous indexes such as the S&P 500 or the Dow Jones Industrials, rather than a broader index such as the NYSE.

Universal performance comparison with the market portfolio is another application that follows upon recognition that the market portfolio return is an average gross investor return. The market portfolio return defines the average gross payoff of the investment "game" in any market. In other words, average residual performance, relative to the market return, is zero. Comparison with the market portfolio defines a zero-sum game.

One widespread use of performance measurement is to array the accomplishments of many managers in competition with one another. For this purpose, there might seem to be no reason for the inclusion of the market portfolio return as a universal benchmark: After all, the managers' returns can simply be ranked in deciles. Nevertheless, an index that is a good surrogate for the market portfolio return is a desirable benchmark for several reasons.

First, the index does define the average gross return in the competition to the extent that average holdings of the investors approximate the weights of the index. Second, the index provides an unambiguous and unbiased benchmark. By contrast, percentiles of comparison populations tend to be biased, due to selective survivorship and due to retrospective inclusion of favorable past history of new entrants. Third, if passive funds track the index, the index represents a conspicuous investment alternative and is interesting for this reason.

Misunderstanding has been widespread to the effect that performance comparisons versus the market portfolio are undermined by the falsehood of the CAPM. According to this argument, it is the efficiency of the market portfolio that makes such comparison interesting, rather than its average character.

We must dispose of this misconception. In order to know the efficient portfolio (or the efficient frontier), one must have absolute foreknowledge of the true properties of all portfolios — both expected reward and risk. Computation of an estimate of those properties, based upon some performance numbers, is then a meaningless exercise: If the computations produce a different answer, this must be due to statistical noise. In short, knowledge of the efficient portfolio renders performance analysis meaningless. Nor can any paradigm for performance analysis be based upon hypothetical knowledge of the efficient portfolio, unless the purpose of the exercise is to reject that hypothesis, and by so doing, to deny meaning to the claim of efficiency.

Since the true efficient portfolio is unavailable and irrelevant to performance measurement, the next question is whether a benchmark that is believed to be more efficient that the average (market) portfolio is a meaningful possibility. For performance analysis by a single investor, reflecting his special circumstances, this is a valuable step, discussed below. As a device for universal comparison, however, any such benchmark destroys itself. Any candidate portfolio other than the average holding, which is believed to be more efficient for the average client, is intrinsically self-disfulfilling. As soon as the candidate portfolio is accepted as being more efficient, managers naturally attempt to move the average of their holdings away from the present average portfolio toward the candidate. As market

prices adjust to changing demand, the efficiency advantage of the candidate portfolio must erode; the process of adjustment cannot cease until the average portfolio becomes efficient and thereby supplants the candidate.

The self-destruction argument relies on disclosure of the candidate portfolio to all investors. If the portfolio is known in advance to some, but kept secret from most, it may not be self-disfulfilling, but then its usefulness in current universl comparison disappears. And if the portfolio is only arrived at *ex post*, its retrospective use is subject to all of the legitimate criticisms directed against hindsight, as well as to inevitable controversy over the fairness of a retrospective standard. In short, the return on the average portfolio is uniquely singled out as a benchmark for comparison in a universal population, and the idea of greater efficiency seems to have little relevance.

A third important application that follows from the "averageness" of the market portfolio is the concept of "nonconsensus" forecasts. For aggregate demand to equal aggregate supply, each security must be priced so that the "average marginal investor" will hold it. The security's price settles where it is "fairly priced," in the view of marginal investors. It follows that any one investor should favor a security to the extent that he finds reasons to believe that it is more desirable to him than to the marginal investors.

This line of reasoning demonstrates the usefulness of the information disclosed by market price. To the extent that manipulation is absent and all investors are just about as well informed as any one investor, market price discloses to that investor a meaningful consensus appraisal. Moreover, if the investor is typical of the marginal investors who hold the asset and if he finds no reason to differ from their judgments, then the correct position is probably the average of their holdings, which may be close to the proportion in the market portfolio. He can then justify deviation from the market proportion only by nonconsensus beliefs.

The first two applications discussed in this section, passive management and performance comparison, relied on the "averageness" of the market portfolio. The third application begins to rely on a more subtle property: The market portfolio, as an average of portfolios, is optimal with respect to a similar average of investor's expectations, or "consensus expectations." The nature of the averaging process is made precise below.

THE MARKET PORTFOLIO IN EXTENSIONS OF THE CAPITAL ASSET PRICING MODEL

As the CAPM assumptions are abandoned in favor of more realistic ones, multiple features of securities may influence expected returns at equilibrium. Features that enter into the tax law are one category. Features that determine correlations with risks outside the market are a second. Features influencing information and investment costs are a third.

Thus, equilibrium expected reward may depend upon several features. The next point is that the equilibrium reward for any particular feature may change, due to changes in the market environment; when a change occurs, there is a one-time windfall return on securities in proportion to the amount of that feature that they possess. Such windfalls constitute an uncertain factor in market return related to the feature. The expected reward and uncertain windfall are combined into a factor of return: Expected factor return rewards the feature, and risk of the factor introduces the uncertainty from possible changes in reward.

Moreover, asset features associated with likely rewards generally correlate with fundamental circumstances of the issuer. For example, a common stock's (1) yield, (2) size, (3) probability of bankruptcy, and (4) covariability with the bond market are not only technical features of the stock, which may be rewarded at equilibrium, but also relate strongly to the fundamental operating circumstances of the company and its industry. Outside economic events that produce returns in proportion to these circumstances therefore cause investment returns that align with the features, and which — when viewed as returns — become further variability of the factors.

The cumulative effect is an environment in which multiple features have associated common factors, with possibly nonzero rewards and definitely nonzero risk. There is a widespread misunderstanding that the market model implies a single-factor model that therefore rules out multiple factors. In fact, the distinction between market and residual return is quite separate from, and coexists with, the distinction between multiple common factors and specific return. A multiple-factor and specific-return model implies, for any given market portfolio, a market- and residual-return model that is superimposed upon the multiple-factor model (Rosenberg [1974]). For some applications of the basic multiple-factor model, there is no need to distinguish between market and residual return. In many other applications — in particular, all those where the market return is a distinct element in forecasting and strategy — we must distinguish the market factor, and we can then express other factors as residual factors.

When we admit heterogeneous expectations such a thing as "true expected return" no longer exists. Nevertheless, we can express the equilibrium for the capital market in terms of investment-weighted averages of expectations that thereby define "consensus expectations." Equilibrium continues to require that, in addition to the other multiple features that may be rewarded, covariance with the market portfolio, or systematic risk, is rewarded. Reward and covariance are here defined in terms of consensus expectations.

When we take into account restricted borrowing and lending and constraints on holdings, the averaging process that underlies equilibrium becomes more complex. In particular, some investors' attitudes toward some securities have no direct impact on those securities' prices, because the investors, constrained against adjusting their holdings, cease to be marginal investors. When the average is defined across those investors who are truly "marginal" for every security, however, it is again true in equilibrium that covariance with an average portfolio is rewarded in the consensus view.

It is difficult to imagine a market equilibrium in which covariance with the equity market portfolio, or some risk measure that is closely akin to this, would not be rewarded. A single, highly risky, prominent factor exists in the equity market and appears to constitute a societal risk rather than a redistributive risk. Covariance with the market portfolio is a surrogate for risk exposure to this factor and hence a conspicuous candidate for reward. Moreover, at equilibrium, the market must clear: Any element of risk must be compensated for, in aggregate, in proportion to that element's covariance with portfolios of investors who hold that security.

It is possible for the subset of investors holding a particular asset to have portfolios such that the covariance of that asset with their portfolios is different from its covariance with the market, but I have rarely seen plausible examples, and then only in cases of excluded risks. For almost all elements of risk, it does seem probable that the aggregate of portfolios exposed to that element will covary with it similarly to the market portfolio, so that the security's covariance with the market portfolio is a reasonable guide to investor's risk exposure that must be compensated. In sum, equilibrium considerations do suggest that market factor and market portfolio covariances are natural candidates for reward.

The historical studies of which I am aware tend to confirm the existence of reward for market index covariance, although smaller in magnitude than the CAPM would imply. Future studies will no doubt give more precise information on historical rewards to multiple factors, although factor variability inescapably obscures the historical expected reward. The fact remains that a historical study is exactly that — a *historical* study.

To expect predictive content for the future, one

must presume (1) that pricing relationships in the market are stable and (2) that pricing will not change as a result of the study. Stability suggests that the relation must be an equilibrium one. For disclosure of the study not to be self-disfulfilling, the factor compensations found by the study must be consistent with equilibrium. Thus, the task of predicting factor rewards cannot be separated from characterization of equilibrium factor rewards through economic analysis of market circumstances. The single most important tool of microeconomics has always been the insight that the market must clear; the market portfolio is the construct that implements this condition.

PERFORMANCE ANALYSIS

Performance analysis includes all aspects of the study of historical performance for the purpose of predicting managers' skill and usefulness in the future. Universal performance comparison is the simplest framework, with limited usefulness for the client's decision problem. The purpose of this section is to touch briefly on the roles of the market portfolio, market model, and efficient portfolio in the performance-analysis process. The approach taken here is quite different from recent literature (Roll [1978, 1979b], Mayers and Rice [1979], Cornell [1979]).

The money management client attempts to construct a best investment strategy, built upon the services of one or more money managers. Most large pools of funds now apportion their assets among multiple managers. The client's problem is to choose a portfolio of managers, just as an investor would construct a portfolio of securities. The client's decision has also additional dimensions because of the potential flexibility that the manager has to restructure the portfolio and management fee.

It is extremely useful, before tackling the question of performance measurement, to consider what would be the optimal portfolio for the client if management were completely passive. Passive management would make no use of special information but, instead, would consider only the relatively permanent aspects of the capital market — those aspects that characterize equilibrium. The client's equilibrium portfolio is shaded toward those assets that are relatively favorable for him, in comparison with the average investor. The client's goal, when constructing an optimal portfolio in a given market, may be atypical, due to special tax circumstances, excluded assets and liabilities not in that market, and multiperiod investment goals. The equilibrium portfolio reflects the unique circumstances of the investor but not the special information that is generated in the competitive research progress of active managers.

The outcome of this process is, at least, a spec-

ification of this equilibrium portfolio, a judgment as to equilibrium rewards of security features, and a specification of risk adversion for the client, not only with respect to the risk of the market factor, but also with respect to various other elements of risk that may have had special disutility, or even utility in hedging. In view of the best description of equilibrium in the capital markets available to the investor, this equilibrium portfolio is the efficient portfolio: It may coincide with the market portfolio, as the CAPM would suggest, but it may not.

There are several advantages to constructing the equilibrium portfolio. First, it is itself an investment alternative: The client can commit some funds to a passively managed equilibrium strategy, with low management fee, low transaction costs, and without active risk. The equilibrium portfolio exploits the disclosure of consensus expectations through the capital markets and takes into account the atypical needs of the client as well. Second, the equilibrium portfolio, in the client's judgment, gives the highest possible utility that can be achieved without superior expectations. Therefore, it is a benchmark for evaluation of managers' skill.

For example, for the typical tax-exempt investor, the equilibrium portfolio of equities may be shaded toward high-yielding stocks, according to the still controversial argument that this reflects the equilibrium distribution of equities between tax-exempt and taxable investors. This portfolio may be typical of the equilibrium portfolios of all tax-exempt investors, and, interestingly, one way of determining the equilibrium portfolio is to take the average of the portfolios of all investors with similar status; this presumes that the average of the peers have knowledgeably determined their investment strategy.

An equilibrium portfolio shaded toward high-yielding stocks is historically a slightly stiffer performance benchmark than the market portfolio. By advocating this equilibrium adjustment, the client asserts that, from the point of view of tax-exempt returns, market equilibrium permits one to outperform the market portfolio without superior information. (Conversely, from the taxable investor's point of view, one can outperform the market portfolio in after-tax return by shading toward low-yielding, growth-oriented stocks. The taxable investor would evaluate the after-tax, net performance of the manager, using a growth-shaded benchmark.) The equilibrium benchmark reflects the opportunities, built into market equilibrium, to maximally serve the client with consensus expectations.

Next, suppose, further, that the client is a highly levered financial company. The pension portfolio of the company is only one of the assets of the pension fund; the fund's main asset is the claim on contributions from the ongoing earnings of the company itself. This is an "excluded asset" in the problem of the beneficiaries. Because of the company's great exposure to the financial markets, the needs of the pension fund portfolio (and of the PBGC, as insurer) include the goal of hedging as much of the company's risk as possible within the pension portfolio. The resulting equilibrium portfolio may be quite atypical in its equity holdings of financial firms and in asset allocation.

Taken in isolation, this equilibrium portfolio is not efficient and constitutes a benchmark that is easier to beat than the market portfolio. When performance is correctly measured, however, allowing for the special disutility of covariance with the financial markets, the equilibrium portfolio is again the best portfolio employing only consensus judgments. The special circumstances of the client are implemented, not only by a special equilibrium portfolio, but also by computation of the disutility of risk appropriately for the client.

In studying the performance of any single manager, we can compute the utility contribution from the relative performance of that manager, compared to the equilibrium portfolio. This procedure is not identical to any of the classic procedures of performance analysis, even when the client's disutility for risk is homogeneous, but it is analogous. In a sense, the client's equilibrium portfolio takes the market portfolio's role: We substitute a more efficient portfolio (the client's equilibrium) for a less efficient one (the market portfolio — which is less efficient for this client).

The treatment of performance analysis is not yet fully developed, however. Each money manager's portfolio may differ from this equilibrium portfolio for two reasons. First, the normal investment emphasis of the manager may differ from the client's equilibrium portfolio. The manager's style, investment specialization, or accustomed habitat may cause the normal or neutral holdings of the manager to be atypical, and the equilibrium or neutral position of the client may be atypical also. This "normal difference," when the manager's norm and the client's equilibrium are compared, does not reflect the manager's judgment. Second, the actual portfolio of the manager differs from his normal by an "active portfolio," resulting from the current set of active judgments of the manager. The active portfolio (Treynor and Black [1973]) is a "hedge portfolio" (a portfolio with zero dollar value) that manifests the manager's skillful judgment.

The equilibrium portfolio is the ideal circumstance for the client if consensus expectations are correct. Yet, the client hopes to find managers whose expectations are superior to the consensus. The ability to develop superior expectations is the active advantage of the manager, which he reflects in the active portfolio; it thereby redounds to the benefit of the client. Clients should apply performance analysis to the active portfolios of managers — that is, to the performance difference between actual and normal portfolios.

When the active portfolio is studied, the manager's normal portfolio is functioning as a benchmark for his performance. The manager chooses his own benchmark, since the normal portfolio is his now *ex ante* description of his neutral point. The manager's normal portfolio thus plays another traditional role of the market portfolio, in parallel to the equilibrium portfolio.

This might seem to undermine performance analysis, since the manager can choose any benchmark. Since the client is informed of the normal portfolio in advance, however, the client uses this information to construct a stable of managers whose aggregate normal positions sum to the client's equilibrium. If necessary, a portion of the client's funds can be managed passively to bring the aggregate normal position in line, by compensating or hedging normal biases of active managers. In so doing, the client immunizes himself against the normal biases of the managers, which become irrelevant and disappear from the performance analysis. The greater the diversity among managers' normal positions and among clients' equilibrium portfolios, the greater is the need for treatment of normal bias.

The advantage of the normal benchmark is that it allows the manager's skill to be isolated and most accurately estimated. The active portfolio, in the manager's view, is the exact reflection of his judgments. The normal bias of the manager, which does not reflect an active decision, introduces incidental noise that is best eliminated.

The normal portfolio also plays a key role because it represents the "rest point" for the manager. The range of "variably aggressive" portfolios, beginning with a passive portfolio identical with the normal and moving out along the active frontier with increasing emphasis on active judgments, are all potential and valid outputs of the manager's production process. In principle, it is open to manager and client to determine the location along this frontier at which the client's portfolio is to be managed and the fee that will be charged. This open dimension is increasingly acknowledged in portfolio management. The active portfolio defines the character of the active frontier, something that is hidden in any analysis of the actual portfolio that omits a normal benchmark.

The performance of the active portfolio is evaluated so as to reflect the client's special disutilities for aspects of risk. The key problem is not just to compute historical performance; rather, it is to predict future performance. For this purpose, performance attribution to various aspects of investment strategy is valuable. As mentioned before, one important distinction is between market timing and selectivity, for managers whose investment process singles out the market forecast. When either the client's risk attitude toward the market factor is distinctive (presumably due to excluded assets that are correlated with this), or when the manager singles out this factor, the market factor (and hence the market portfolio as the natural surrogate for the factor) plays an important role in performance analysis of the active portfolio.

The client predicts future management skill based upon (1) past performance, (2) external evidence concerning the quality of the manager's investment process, and (3) prior skepticism derived from the competitive nature of the investment process. The last perspective arises because, if the manager's portfolio were the result of random selection within his normal universe (stratified so as to produce his normal portfolio on average), then skill (the advantage relative to consensus) would be zero. This is also the case when the manager, with the best of intentions, is not capable of improving upon consensus expectations. It is clear that the average manager does not outperform the consensus (which is the average). Hence, prior skepticism takes the form of expecting the performance of the manager to match the passive performance of his normal benchmark, implying an active expected return (akin to alpha) of zero. Use of the passive normal portfolio as benchmark causes the adjustment for prior skepticism to take this simple form. This is a third advantage of the normal benchmark.

Based upon much information, including past performance, the client constructs a portfolio — which may be an admixture of multiple active and passive management processes — that is believed to be efficient for the future. In doing this, the predicted active skills of managers are incorporated, so that the expected return of the portfolio is incremented to reflect superiority relative to the consensus.

The question of using a "more efficient portfolio" in performance analysis can not be reopened. The equilibrium portfolio is efficient for this client with respect to consensus expectations. Why not go a step further and use the existing aggregate portfolio — efficient with respect to active beliefs — as the comparison benchmark?

The answer to this question explains why it is an equilibrium portfolio, and not an active portfolio, that should be used in performance comparison. The equilibrium portfolio, being a reflection of the consensus, has stable properties that are not influenced by the active management of existing managers. In this sense, it is a stable prior perspective. Also, it implies a clear benchmark for prior skepticism. By contrast, when another manager is compared to the active portfolio, the prior expectation of alpha is negative, there is less reason to expect stability in the relative skill of a new candidate, and performance attribution is clouded by the presence of the investment strategies of existing active managers.

Finally, a new manager's pattern of active research and investment may well be related to and correlated with the active research and investment of one or more of the existing managers. If so, the existing portfolio should be reconstituted when the new manager is added (Rosenberg [1977], Sharpe [1980]), and the information needed to do this can only be established by analyzing all managers (existing and new) with respect to the equilibrium portfolio.

DISCOUNT RATES ADJUSTED FOR FEATURES

Valuation methods for financial securities based upon the discounting of expected future cash flows are common. For equities, there is the dividend-discount paradigm; for bonds, the computation of present value through the term structure of interest rates. These discount rates may vary with time and with the risk of the security.

The discount rate is also the required rate of return, since it translates future flows into present value. As such, it can serve the corporation for project valuation and as the "hurdle" in capital budgeting. The same discount rate is the "fair rate of return," a construct with an increasingly important role in rate regulation.

The CAPM asserts that the discount rate for a risky project equals the risk-free rate, plus beta times the excess return on the market portfolio. In practice, the "market portfolio" has been implemented as the S&P 500 or other broad equity market index. As we relax CAPM assumptions, the discount rate becomes a more complex function of security features.

The first natural extension is to free the "intercept" of the relationship, so that it is estimated from the data. This is done in fitting the *ex ante* capital market line and in historical studies of capital asset returns. Usually, the intercept is found to be higher than the risk-free rate, implying that the compensation for market risk is less than the full excess return on the market portfolio.

The next extension is to insert other features as candidates for reward. The security market line then becomes a "security market plane," with the slope along each axis being the reward for the corresponding feature. *Ex ante* security market planes have been estimated with rewards for several features, through the dividend-discount model. Historical studies of returns have estimated rewards to such features as specific risk, total risk, yield, co-skewness, and size.

The central problem is to forecast rewards for these features. We can draw these forecasts from current valuation of securities, solving for rates that equate discounted forecast cash flows to current price. *Ex ante* relationships fitted to forecasted dividends for a large population of stocks can come up with quite precise estimates of the co-efficients of the fitted plane, but this is only a true characterization of the *ex ante* security market plane to the extent that the input dividend forecasts are effective proxies for consensus forecasts. Predicted rewards can also be extrapolated from historical studies of equilibrium returns. Finally, by modeling investors' demand functions, rewards can be computed as the market-clearing conditions of a general equilibrium model. Whichever method(s) are used, there will inevitably be a large element of judgment in the predictions.

The question of rewards for factors other than equity market risk has been the subject of active study and controversy for a decade — and no doubt will continue to be so in the decades to come. Nevertheless, no one has refuted the existence of equilibrium reward for equity market risk; indeed, it has rarely been questioned, although the magnitude has been in doubt. The concept of reward to equity market risk (or beta) is a theoretical insight, that, in my view, is likely to endure.

---

[1] Smallness of the total company not effectively limit the holding of an individual investor, so the small investor might have a comparative advantage investing in small companies. Investors having personal dealings with the company may have an information advantage as well. Such investors might then become the dominant investors in small companies, due to their comparative advantage. The equilibrium returns of small companies would then reflect primarily the portfolio optimization of such investors, with respect to their expectations and wealth.

BIBLIOGRAPHY

Brennan, M. J. 1970. "Taxes, Market Valuation, and Corporate Financial Policy." *National Tax Journal* 23: 417-427.

Cornell, Bradford. 1979. "Asymmetric Information and Portfolio Performance Measurement." *Journal of Financial Economics* 7: 381-390.

Fama, Eugene. 1972. "Components of Investment Performance." *Journal of Finance* 27 (June): 551-567.

Lintner, John. 1969. "The Aggregation of Investor's Diverse Judgments and Preferences in Purely Competitive Security Marktets." *Journal of Financial and Quantitative Analysis*: 347-400.

Markowitz, Harry. 1959. *Portfolio Selection: Efficient Diversification of Investments*. New York: John Wiley and Sons.

Mayers, D., and Rice. E. M. 1979. "Measuring Portfolio Performance and the Empirical Content of Asset Pricing Models." *Journal of Financial Economics* 7: 3-28.

Roll, Richard. 1977. "A Critique of the Asset Pricing Theory's Tests." *Journal of Financial Economics*: 129-176.

——.1978. "Ambiguity When Performance Is Measured by the Securities Market Line." *Journal of Finance* 33: 1051-1069.

——. 1979a. "Sensitivity of Performance Measurement to Index Choice: Commonly-Used Indices." Conference on New Issues on the Capital Asset Pricing Model. Coeur 'dAlene, Idaho.

——. 1979b. "A Reply to Mayers and Rice." *Journal of Financial Economics* 7: 391-400.

Rosenberg, Barr. 1974. "Extra-Market Components of Covariance in Security Markets." *Journal of Financial and Quantitative Analysis*: 263-274.

——. 1977. "Institutional Investment with Multiple Portfolio Managers." *Proceedings of the Seminar on the Analysis of Security Prices.* University of Chicago.

——. 1978. "Performance Measurement and Performance Attribution." *Proceedings of the Seminar on the Analysis of Security Prices.* University of Chicago.

Ross, Stephan A. 1977. "Return, Risk and Arbitrage." In *Risk and Return in Finance*, Vol. 1. Edited by Irwin Friend and James L. Bicksler. Cambridge, Mass.: Ballinger, pp. 189-218.

——. 1978. "The Current Status of the Capital Asset Pricing Model (CAPM)." *Journal of Finance* 33: 885-890.

Rudd, Andrew, and Rosenberg, Barr. 1980. "The 'Market Model' in Investment Management." *Journal of Finance* 35, no. 2.

Sharpe, William F. 1963. "A Simplified Model for Portfolio Analysis." *Management Science* (January): 277-293.

——. 1964. "Capital Asset Prices: A Theory of Market Equilibrium Under Conditions of Risk." *Journal of Finance* 19: 13-37.

——. 1980. "Decentralized Investment Management." Research Paper No. 570. Graduate School of Business, Stanford University.

Treynor, Jack L., and Black, Fischer. 1973. "How to Use Security Analysis to Improve Portfolio Selection." *Journal of Business* 46, no. 1: 66-86.

Wallace, Anise. 1980. "Is Beta Dead?" *Institutional Investor*, (July) pp. 23-30.

Factors in New York Stock Exchange security returns, 1931-1979*

The analysis calls into question naive applications of the Capital Asset Pricing Model.

William F. Sharpe

In some months, high-yield ("value"?) stocks seem to do better than low-yield ("growth"?) stocks. In other months, the opposite situation seems to occur. Occasionally there seems to be no difference.

FACTOR MODELS

Figure 1 illustrates one way of providing substance for such statements. Each point represents one security. On the horizontal axis is a measure of yield.[1] On the vertical axis is the excess return (i.e. the return over and above a riskless rate) of the security in the following month.[2]

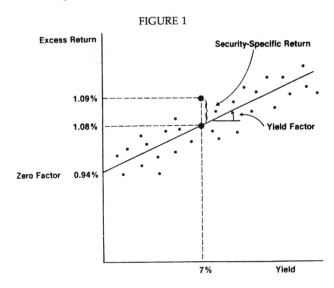

FIGURE 1

* An early version of this paper was presented at the Financial Analysts' Federation workshop at Princeton University in July 1981. Comments and suggestions from Peter Bernstein, Michael Gibbons, Robert Litzenberger, and Krishna Ramaswamy are gratefully acknowledged. This research was supported in part by the Stanford Program in Finance.

1. Footnotes appear at the end of the article.

In Figure 1, yield is an *attribute* of each security. The regression line fit to the data is an *ex post security market line* indicating the general relationship between this attribute and return over a subsequent period. We can describe the relationship as follows:

$$R_{it} - r_t = 1 \, F_{zt} + b_{i1t} F_{1t} + e_{it}, \qquad (1)$$

where:

R_{it} = the return on security i in period t;

r_t = the riskless interest rate for period t;

F_{zt} = the "zero" factor for period t;

b_{i1t} = the first *attribute* (here, yield) of security i at the beginning of period t;

F_{1t} = the first *factor* (here, the yield factor) for period t, and

e_{it} = security i's *security-specific* return in period t.

In Figure 1 the "zero" factor is .94% per month. This is the return on a "typical" security with zero yield. The "yield factor" is .02% per month. This indicates that, "in general," higher yield securities outperformed lower yield securities during the month, with (for example) the typical 4% yield stock outperforming the typical 3% yield stock by .02%. For the security plotted at point i, e_{it} was .01%: The stock's excess return was higher (by .01%) than the 1.08% "typical" for securities with its yield (b_{i1t}) of 7%.

In effect, Figure 1 and equation 1 *attribute* each security's excess return in each period to three elements:

$1 \, F_{zt}$: an effect common to all securities,

$b_{i1t} F_{1t}$: an effect that differs among securities, depending on their yields, and

e_{it}: an effect specific to each security.

26

Two statistics associated with regression analysis provide added information.

The *t-statistic* for factor 1 (the yield factor) indicates the *significance* of the value: The larger its (absolute) value, the more likely the relationship is "real." Assume, for example, that there was no "true" relationship between yield and excess return during the period in question. By chance a majority of securities with high yields might have had positive "true" security-specific returns, and a majority of those with low yields might have had negative "true" security-specific returns. The regression analysis would thus produce an erroneous positive yield factor with a t value that could, by chance, be large. A rough rule of thumb holds that a t value with an absolute value greater than 2.0 will obtain in roughly 5% of the months in which there is no "true" relationship.

The other statistic of interest is the *R-squared* of the regression. This indicates the proportion of the variance in security returns attributed to the factors. The smaller the scatter of points around the line, the greater the R-squared.

Yield is, of course, only one attribute of a security that may be related to return. In some months, stocks of large companies seem to outperform those of small companies; in other months, the opposite seems to occur. While we could investigate this relationship by repeating the procedure illustrated in Figure 1 with some measure of size on the horizontal axis, this has some drawbacks: Larger firms tend to provide higher dividends. Thus an investigation of yield alone (as in Figure 1) may attribute to yield some effects related to size, while an investigation of size alone may attribute to size some effects related to yield.

A better procedure uses *multiple regression*. Figure 2 provides an illustration. Each point represents a security, plotting both its attributes (b_{i1t} = yield and b_{i2t} = size) and its subsequent excess return. Regression analysis is used to fit an *ex post security market plane*. Its slope in the yield direction is the *yield factor* (F_{1t}), and its slope in the size direction is the *size factor* (F_{2t}). The intercept (the *zero factor*) indicates the return on a hypothetical security with zero yield *and* zero size. The distance of a security's point from the plane indicates its *security-specific return* (e_{it}), i.e. the portion not attributed to either the yield effect or the size effect.

The equation of the plane in Figure 2 can be written as:

$$R_{it} - r_t = 1 F_{zt} + b_{i1t} F_{1t} + b_{i2t} F_{2t} + e_{it}. \quad (2)$$

Multiple regression analysis produces t-statistics for each of the factors (which can be interpreted as before) and an R-squared value for the entire regression, indicating the proportion of the variance

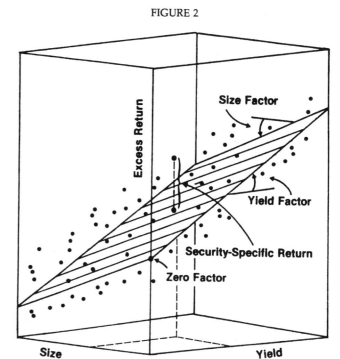

FIGURE 2

among security returns in the period that can be attributed to (all) the factors.

To extend the approach to more than two factors requires the abandonment of diagrams. Nevertheless, the concepts are the same. In effect, we fit an *ex post security market hyperplane* (the generalization of a plane) to the data using multiple regression analysis. If there are m attributes the equation can be written as:

$$R_{it} - r_t = 1 F_{zt} + b_{i1t} F_{1t} + b_{i2t} F_{2t} + \ldots + b_{imt} F_{mt} + e_{it}. \quad (3)$$

USES OF FACTOR MODELS

We can use a factor model for attribution of *ex post* portfolio performance. If X_{ipt} represents the proportion of portfolio p invested in security i at the beginning of period t, the return on the portfolio will be:

$$R_{pt} = X_{1pt} R_{1t} + X_{2pt} R_{2t} + \ldots + X_{npt} R_{nt}, \quad (4)$$

where n = the number of securities.

A little manipulation of equations (3) and (4) provides a formula for breaking the return on a portfolio into components:

$$R_{pt} = r_t + 1 F_{zt} + b_{p1t} F_{1t} + b_{p2t} F_{2t} + \ldots + b_{pmt} F_{mt}$$
$$+ (X_{1pt} e_{1t} + X_{2pt} e_{2t} + \ldots + X_{npt} e_{nt}), \quad (5a)$$

$$\text{where: } b_{pjt} = X_{1pt} b_{1jt} + X_{2pt} b_{2jt} + \ldots + X_{npt} b_{njt}. \quad (5b)$$

As indicated in (5b), each attribute of the portfolio (b_{pjt}) equals a weighted average of the corresponding values of the attribute for the securities in the portfolio, using the values of portfolio holdings as weights.

The terms in parentheses in (5a) represent the

27

effects of security-specific returns; each depends on the joint effect of the amount held (X_{ipt}) and the performance of the security *per se* (e_{it}). The terms not in parentheses represent the effects of factors. The first (r_t) is the riskless rate and the second ($1 F_{zt}$) an effect common to all securities. Each of the remaining terms involves the joint effect of an attribute of the portfolio (b_{pjt}) and the performance of the associated factor (F_{jt}).

Another use of factor models involves the comparison of two portfolios (e.g. an active portfolio and an index or an active portfolio and a "normal" set of holdings). Letting q represent a second portfolio, one can write an equation corresponding to (5a) for portfolio q, then subtract it from (5a) to get:

$$R_{pt} - R_{qt} = (b_{p1t} - b_{q1t})F_{1t} + (b_{p2t} - b_{q2t})F_{2t}$$
$$+ \ldots + (b_{pmt} - b_{qmt})F_{mt} + (X_{1pt} - X_{1qt})e_{it}$$
$$+ (X_{2pt} - X_{2qt})e_{2t} + \ldots + (X_{npt} - X_{nqt})e_{nt}. \quad (6)$$

In this case the *difference* between the returns on the portfolios is broken into components. Each of the initial m terms indicates the joint effect of the *difference* in the portfolios' attributes ($b_{pjt} - b_{qjt}$) and the performance of the related factor (F_{jt}). Each of the last n terms indicates the joint effect of the *difference* in the portfolios' holdings of a security ($X_{ipt} - X_{iqt}$) and its security-specific return (e_{it}).

Performance attribution is *ex post* in nature — it deals with the past. For decision-making one is concerned with *ex ante* values — values that will be realized in the future but must be predicted now. We can use factor models for predictive purposes as well.

One application concerns *expected values*. For example, does one expect high-yield stocks to outperform low-yield stocks, and if so, by how much (i.e. what is the expected value of the yield factor)? Does one expect General Motors to do especially well (i.e. what is the expected value of its security-specific return)?

An investment organization with a "bottom-up" approach might produce estimates of expected returns for each of many securities (perhaps using a dividend discount model). They can then use these *ex ante* expected returns in a multiple regression analysis (instead of *ex post* actual returns) to find implicit expected values for the various factors. After review, the firm might change some of the values (i.e. employ a bit of "top-down" decision-making).

A firm with a totally top-down approach might make estimates of expected factor values directly, with security analysts focusing on security-specific return (e.g. making *conditional* forecasts). Whatever procedure is employed, the goal is to estimate the *expected* position of the security market hyperplane and the *expected* distances of the points from it.

Expected values are, however, only part of the story. The actual hyperplane will undoubtedly turn out to be somewhere other than in its expected position, and at least some of the points will be in positions relative to it that are different from the expected ones. One thus needs to estimate the likely range within which the hyperplane might lie and the likely range within which each security-specific return might fall. Such estimates constitute a *risk model*. The needed ingredients are:

1. a measure of risk for each factor,
2. measures of the extent to which each factor is likely to move with each of the other factors, and
3. a measure of security-specific risk for each security.[3]

In practice, estimates of this type are usually obtained by assuming that *variations* around *average* values in the *past* provide good estimates concerning *risk* relative to *expected values* in the *future*. This is indeed an heroic assumption. In fact, it is difficult to defend the common practice of primary reliance on judgment for estimating expected values and the almost exclusive reliance on econometric analysis of past data to estimate components of risk, since risk and expected return are simply two summary descriptions of a (subjective) probability distribution. In time, both judgmental and econometric inputs will undoubtedly be employed for both purposes.

CALCULATING THE FACTOR MODEL

How many factors affect security returns? How can they be identified? One approach (factor analysis) relies solely on historic security returns to answer these questions. Present practice uses other information to *preselect* a set of attributes and the associated attribute values for securities. Whatever method is used, the goal is to obtain a model that will prove helpful for making the *predictions* needed for investment decisions.

We do not attempt to answer the difficult questions concerning selection of attributes and factors. Our goal is much more modest. We provide historic data over a long period for a model intended to be as similar as possible to those currently provided by consultants[4] and used by a number of investment organizations.

We follow standard practice by selecting a list of attributes (more or less *ex cathedra*) and then fitting an *ex post* security market hyperplane[5] for each of many months. A check on our selection of attributes is provided by the t-statistics. If a factor is significantly different from zero (i.e. the absolute value of the associated t-statistic exceeds 2.0), then in substantially more than 5% of the months we have at least some evidence that its inclusion in the model is desirable. As will be shown, all of our factors pass this test.

Since we compute a value for each factor for each of many months, it is a simple matter to compute the *average* value of a factor over the period examined, as well as its *variation* around that average over time.[6]

Commercial services typically employ a few "common factors" and a number of "industry factors." Moreover, a common factor may be related to a *composite attribute* that is, in turn, a function of a number of (simple) attributes. Models of this type have been fitted to data only from the last two or three decades, since the required detailed information is not available in appropriate form for earlier years.

Our goal is to provide a long view reaching back several decades. This requires a more parsimonious model.[7] Accordingly, we employ five simple "common" attributes and eight attributes representing "sectors" of the economy. There is an intentional correspondence between our common factors and those of presently-available commercial services, but it is, of necessity, less than perfect.[8]

TABLE 1

Attributes as of Dec. 1979
(1325 NYSE Stocks)

Attribute	Mean	Std. Dev.
Beta	1.336	0.555
Yield	4.781	3.204
Size	−0.698	0.653
Bond beta	1.323	0.686
Alpha	0.819	1.112

Attributes

Dividend *yield* is the first of the attributes. It is simply the prior twelve months' dividends paid common stockholders divided by the market value at the end of the prior month (expressed as percent yield per year).

The second attribute measures *size*. The value used is the logarithm (to base 10) of the market value (in billions of dollars) of the firm's equity at the end of the prior month. Thus a firm with $1 billion of equity has a "size" of 0, one with $10 billion a size of 1, one

TABLE 2

Sectors as of Dec. 1979
(1325 NYSE Stocks)

Sector	% of Stocks	% of Value
Basic Industries	9.97	9.34
Capital Goods	14.26	13.06
Construction	4.45	1.84
Consumer Goods	35.93	29.96
Energy	3.62	21.09
Finance	14.79	7.31
Transportation	5.66	3.47
Utilities	11.32	13.93

with $100 billion a size of 2, etc., while one with a $100 million has a size of −1 and one with $10 million a size of −2. This measure was adopted because returns correlate more closely with it than with the market value of equity *per se*.[9]

The remaining measures concern past performance. Following common practice, we regress the excess returns on a stock over the prior sixty months on those of Standard and Poor's stock index. The slope is the security's historic *beta* value; the intercept is its historic *alpha* value. Roughly, securities with high beta values were "aggressive" in the past, while those with low beta values were "defensive." Those with positive alpha values did well ("market-adjusted") and those with negative alpha values did poorly ("market-adjusted"). Alpha is measured in units of percent return per month.

The final attribute is obtained by regressing the excess returns on a stock over the prior sixty months on the excess returns on long-term government bond returns.[10] The slope coefficient is the security's historic *bond beta*. Roughly, securities with high bond betas were "bond-like" — due perhaps to the nature of their assets — while those with low bond betas were less "bond-like." Securities with negative bond betas tended to move counter to bonds in the past, perhaps because the firms had large amounts of financial leverage.

Significance of the Attributes

Are our attributes really relevant? Are security returns related to them often enough to warrant their examination (and prediction)? Tables 3 and 4 provide

TABLE 3

Percent of Months in Which a Common Factor Was Significant
[absolute value of t-statistic > 2]
1931-1979

Factor	% of Months
Beta	58.3
Yield	39.5
Size	56.5
Bond Beta	28.2
Alpha	43.5

TABLE 4

Percent of Months in Which a Sector was Significantly
Different from All Other Sectors
[absolute value of t-statistic > 2]
1931-1979

Sector	% of Months
Basic Industries	32.5
Capital Goods	18.7
Construction	15.3
Consumer Goods	39.3
Energy	36.9
Finance	16.3
Transportation	43.9
Utilities	35.0

some evidence. As described earlier, we would expect a truly irrelevant attribute to produce a t-statistic with an absolute value greater than 2.0 in about 5% of the 588 months. Every one of our attributes did so more often. While this is not a formal test, it provides presumptive evidence for including all our attributes in the analysis.[13]

Table 5 provides an indication of the extent to

TABLE 5

Average Cross-Section Fits of Models
588 Months, 1931-1979

Model	Average R^2	Diff.
Beta	.037	
		.042
Common Factors	.079	
		.025
Common and Sector Factors	.104	

which the attributes "explain" the variance among security returns. As indicated earlier, when a factor model is fitted to the returns for a month, the resulting R-squared value indicates the proportion of variance in security returns attributed to the associated factors. For our model, this was done 588 times. The *average* of the 588 R-squared values obtained in this manner was .104, as shown at the bottom of Table 5. In a typical month, about 10% of the variation in returns on *individual* securities could be attributed to our factors. While this may seem discouraging,[14] recall that security-specific returns are much less important for *portfolios* than for individual securities, and that a much higher R-squared value would typically be obtained if we were analyzing a group of diverse portfolios.

Table 5 also reports results obtained with two other models. The first uses only one attribute — historic beta. As shown, it explained only about one-third of the variance explained by the full model. The second approach used all five common attributes, but no sector information. The four additional attributes collectively added 4.2% to the 3.7% explained by beta alone. The eight sector attributes added another 2.5%. Historic beta is clearly an important attribute, but it is not the only one worth considering.[15]

Regression Procedures

All the results presented thus far were based on monthly regressions, with each security given equal weight. This was done to insure that the tests of significance and explanatory power would be difficult to pass. Both theory and practice show that better estimates can be obtained if relatively more attention is paid to data less likely to be subject to error.

For the remainder of the paper, we report results using a simple procedure similar to that em-

ployed by some of the commercial services. As described earlier, for each month a regression of the excess returns on a security over the prior sixty months on those of Standard and Poor's stock index was performed. The *standard error* of this regression measures the scatter of points around the resulting regression line — this is often termed the security's historic "non-market risk." The larger this value, the more likely it is that a security's return will reflect security-specific returns rather than factor effects. In the regressions designed to estimate factor effects, it makes sense to pay more attention to securities with less non-market risk. To do this, we weight each security by the reciprocal of this measure of historic non-market risk.[16]

Table 6 reports one set of results based on this procedure. For each month, the excess return on a stock can be broken into two parts — that attributed to the factors and that not so attributed (i.e. the security-specific return). Over the course of many months the excess return on the security will vary, and that variance can be compared with the variance of the two components. For example, if the variance of a stock's security-specific returns is 60% as great as the variance of its overall excess return, we say that the chosen factors "explained" 40% of the variance in the stock's excess return.[17]

TABLE 6

Average Time-Series Fit of Models
2197 stocks, 1931-1979

Model	Average R^2	Diff.
All Beta = 1	.250	
		.089
Beta	.339	
		.043
Common Factors	.382	
		.021
Common and Sector Factors	.403	

The percent of variance of returns explained by factors varied from security to security. In all, 2,197 securities entered the analysis at various times from 1931 through 1979.[18] Table 6 shows average values for the 2,197 stocks.

It is important to emphasize the difference between Tables 5 and 6. The former averages the results of cross-section analyses over 588 months, while the latter averages the results of time-series analyses over 2,197 stocks. Thus, Table 5 indicates the extent to which differences *among* stocks are explained in a "typical" month, while Table 6 indicates the extent to which we can explain differences in the returns of a "typical" stock *over time*.

The bottom line in Table 6 indicates that we can attribute about 40% of the variance in return for the typical stock to our factors. The other lines report results for other factor models. A model using only historic beta explained about 34% of the average variance in return, while one with all five common factors explained about 38%.

The first line in the table reports results for a model in which each security was assigned a beta of 1.0.[19] As shown, the performance of the overall stock market is important, although differences in security attributes are well worth attention.

These values are larger than those in Table 5 and comparable values for most portfolios would typically be larger still.[20]

FACTOR PERFORMANCE

Table 7 provides summary data concerning the

TABLE 7

Annualized Values
588 Months: 1931-1979

Factor	Avg.	Std. Dev.
SP500 ER	8.295	20.969
LT Govt ER	0.518	5.760
Beta	5.355	18.376
Yield	0.237	1.043
Size	−5.563	7.804
Bond Beta	−0.118	2.719
Alpha	−2.001	4.639
Basic Industries	1.653	7.974
Capital Goods	0.155	5.720
Construction	−1.589	8.862
Consumer Goods	−0.180	5.173
Energy	6.282	11.042
Finance	−1.478	5.247
Transportation	−0.570	9.492
Utilities	−2.622	9.425

performance of the factors over time. In this case, each of the 588 months was given equal weight. The first column indicates the average value for a factor, the second its standard deviation over time. For comparison, two additional rows are included. The first summarizes the excess returns on Standard and Poor's stock index, the second the excess returns on long-term government bonds. For ease in interpretation the values in Table 7 are stated in terms of annualized monthly returns.[21]

As Table 7 shows, stocks outperformed Treasury bills by about 8.3% per year ("ER" means "excess returns"), but with considerable variability: The standard deviation was about 21% per year. Long-term government bonds outperformed Treasury bills by a much smaller amount, but with less variability.

Stocks with high historic betas outperformed those with low historic betas on average. Thus, stocks with betas of, say, 1.5 outperformed by over 5% per year other stocks similar in other respects but with betas of .5 — but not every year, as the standard deviation was over 18%.

High-yield stocks outperformed low-yield stocks by almost 24 basis points per year for each 1% difference in dividend yield. Nevertheless, the variability was substantial, with a standard deviation of over 100 basis points per year.

Large stocks underperformed smaller ones by a substantial amount. For each unit increase in size (i.e. ten-fold increase in market value of equity) average performance declined by 5.6% per year! While there was some variability — the standard deviation was 7.8% per year — the size factor was clearly negative most of the time.

The bond beta factor was relatively small and variable, but less important than the stock beta factor.

The alpha factor was negative on average, indicating that stocks with good historic non-market performance tended to do poorly (i.e. suffered a "reversal").[22] A portfolio of stocks with historic alphas of 1% per month might have underperformed, by about 2% per year on average, a portfolio similar in other respects but holding stocks with alphas of zero but with a standard deviation of more than 4%.

The sector factors indicate that, on average, energy stocks did especially well relative to the average sector (over 6% per year), and utility stocks did rather poorly (−2.6% per year). Although the energy sector factor showed the greatest variability, given the large average value, this sector clearly outperformed the average sector in most months.

Table 7 provides only one view of the data. To probe more deeply we need a method for displaying the behavior of a factor over time. To do so, we use the idea of the cumulative profit on a "factor play."

Figure 3 illustrates the procedure. Imagine that at the end of December 1930, one had purchased $1 worth of Standard and Poor's stock index and taken a short position in Treasury bills. At the end of January 1931, imagine that the long position outperformed the short position by $.02. The *cumulative profit* (undiscounted) would be $.02. Now imagine that, at the end of January 1931, the position was re-established, with $1 again invested in a long position in Standard and Poor's Index and a $1 short position taken in Treasury bills. Imagine that, at the end of February 1931, the long position underperformed the short position by $.05. The profit for the month would be −$.05 and the cumulative profit −$.03 (= $.02 − $.05).

Figure 3 shows the cumulative profit, month by month, for such a strategy with monthly adjustments in holdings. The curve goes up when Standard and Poor's index outperformed Treasury bills and goes down when Standard and Poor's index underperformed Treasury bills. Moreover, a given vertical distance represents the same magnitude in terms of the difference in returns, since the positions are revised to

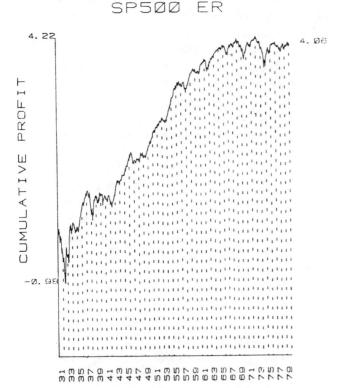

FIGURE 3

SP500 ER

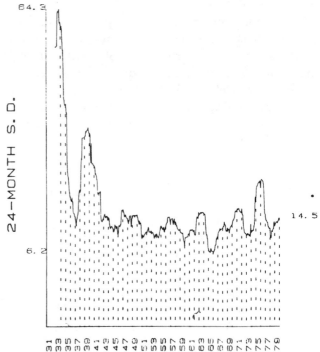

FIGURE 4

SP500 ER

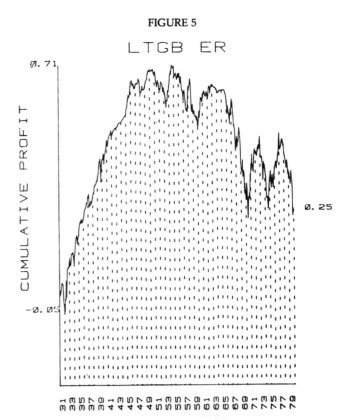

FIGURE 5

LTGB ER

be worth $1 each month. Thus the greater the slope of the curve, the greater the average difference: The greater the variability around a trend, the greater the variability of the difference in the two returns around the average.

One can easily assess the nature of average returns in a graph such as the one shown in Figure 3. In this case the flattening out in tl last two decades is depressingly obvious. Neverth ess, another representation is helpful to analyze changes in variability. Figure 4 plots the standard deviation of the difference in returns for the 24-month period from January 1931 through December 1932, then the standard deviation for the 24-month period from February 1931 through January 1933, etc. While the use of a 24-month "window" is arbitrary, the graph shows clearly that the stock market has been less variable in the last 40 years than it was in the 1930's.[23] A value-weighted index of all stocks on the New York Stock Exchange would show results close to those based on Standard and Poor's index.[24]

To display data efficiently, the figures have been scaled differently, so that vertical distances are not directly comparable from graph to graph. The range of values is shown on the left of each diagram and the ending value on the right to facilitate comparison.

Figures 5 and 6 are based on the difference between returns on long-term government bonds and those on Treasury bills. As Figure 5 shows, the first

and second halves of the period were different, with government bonds outperforming Treasury bills during much of the former period and underperforming them during much of the latter period. As Figure 6 shows, bond returns have also become more variable (not less, as have stock returns) over time.

FIGURE 6

LTGB ER

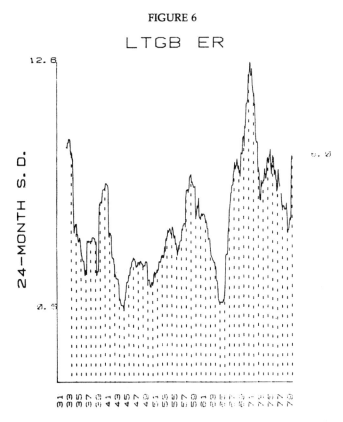

Figure 7 depicts the behavior of the beta factor. It is merely the cumulative value of the monthly factors; thus, the curve goes up in months when high-beta stocks outperformed low-beta stocks and down in months when high-beta stocks underperformed low-beta stocks. This graph can also be given a portfolio interpretation. Imagine a long position in a portfolio with an average beta of, say, 1.5 and a short position in a portfolio with an average beta of, say, .5, with each position worth $1. Assume that we construct these portfolios so that they are alike in all other attributes and that each is highly diversified.[25] The profit from such a strategy would be very close to the beta factor for the month. By re-adjusting the position each month, we could obtain a cumulative profit very close to that shown in Figure 7. A similar interpretation can be given for each of the other factors.

Not surprisingly Figure 7 bears a resemblance to Figure 3 — when the market went up, stocks with high historic betas tended to outperform those with low historic betas. The correlation between the beta factor and the excess return on Standard and Poor's stock index was in fact .814 over the period. This indicates that historic beta is a useful predictor of future beta. But it can be improved upon, as will be shown.

As Figure 8 shows, the pattern of the variability of the beta factor is similar to that of Standard and Poor's stock index.

Figures 9 and 10 provide information about the yield factor. As shown, high-yield stocks outperformed low-yield stocks on average, but there were extended periods during which they did not.

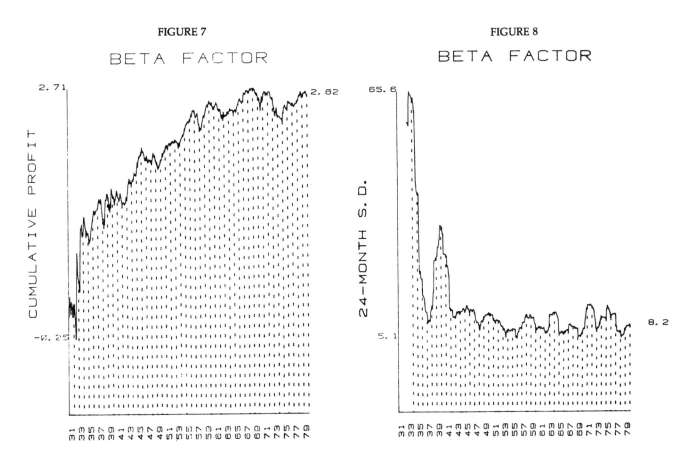

FIGURE 7

BETA FACTOR

FIGURE 8

BETA FACTOR

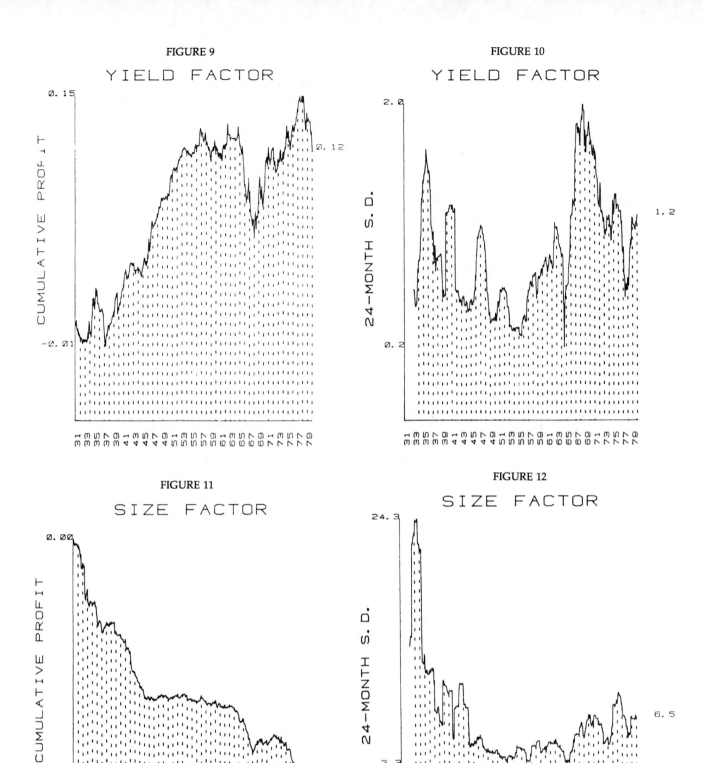

FIGURE 9

YIELD FACTOR

FIGURE 10

YIELD FACTOR

FIGURE 11

SIZE FACTOR

FIGURE 12

SIZE FACTOR

Figure 11 shows that the size factor has been negative most of the time. Moreover, the magnitudes are very large. Figure 12 shows the pattern of its variability.

Figures 13 and 14 show results for the bond beta factor. It is correlated with the excess return on government bonds, but not highly (the correlation coefficient was .154). Moreover, the magnitudes are relatively small.

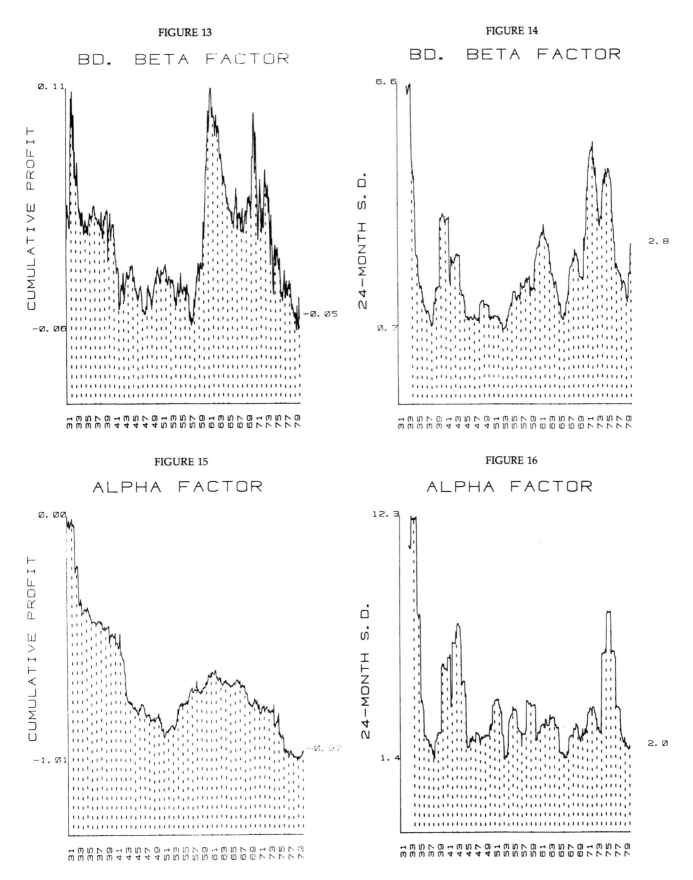

FIGURE 13

BD. BETA FACTOR

FIGURE 14

BD. BETA FACTOR

FIGURE 15

ALPHA FACTOR

FIGURE 16

ALPHA FACTOR

Figures 15 and 16 provide information about the alpha factor. Other things equal, an investor holding stocks with poor historic non-market performance would have done well overall except during the 1950's.

The remainder of the diagrams concern the sector factors (to save space, only the cumulative profit diagrams are shown). These results can also be given a portfolio interpretation. In this case, the strategy

35

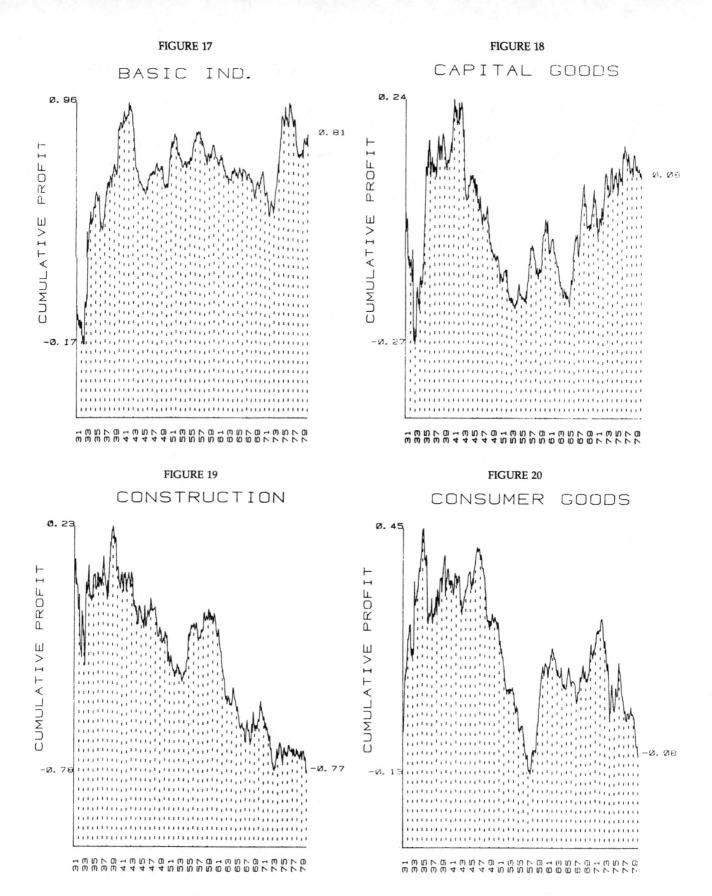

FIGURE 17

BASIC IND.

FIGURE 18

CAPITAL GOODS

FIGURE 19

CONSTRUCTION

FIGURE 20

CONSUMER GOODS

would involve a long portfolio of stocks in the sector in question and a short portfolio of stocks diversified across all sectors, with all other attributes equal in the two portfolios.

By far the most dramatic of these diagrams is that shown in Figure 21 for the energy sector. Not only is the magnitude large, but the graph is upward-sloping in most months.

FIGURE 21

ENERGY

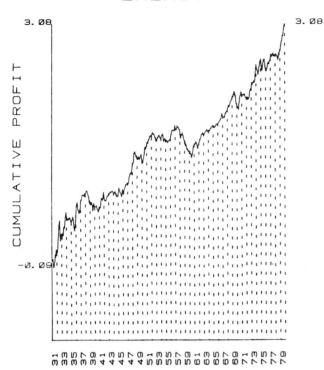

FIGURE 22

FINANCE

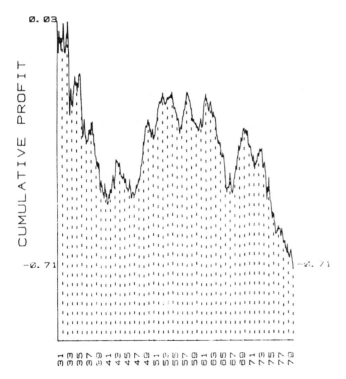

PREDICTING FUTURE BETA

The correlation between the beta factor and the excess return on Standard and Poor's stock index shows that "future beta" is definitely related to his-toric beta. With a factor model, however, one can go further. In fact, equation (3) implies directly that:

$$\beta(R_{it}) = \beta(F_{zt}) + b_{i1t}\beta(F_{1t})$$
$$+ b_{i2t}\beta(F_{2t}) + \ldots + b_{imt}\beta(F_{mt}) + \beta(e_{it}),$$

where (x) = the beta of x relative to some selected base (e.g. Standard and Poor's stock index). If the portfolio used as a base is well diversified, the betas of the security-specific returns will be very small. Thus:

$$\beta(R_{it}) \approx \beta(F_{zt}) + b_{i1t}\beta(F_{1t})$$
$$+ b_{i2t}\beta(F_{2t}) + \ldots + b_{imt}\beta(F_{mt}). \qquad (7)$$

Equation (7) provides a recipe for estimating the future beta of a security, given its attributes ($b_{i1t}, \ldots, b_{imt}$). All one needs (!) is the set of numbers $\beta(F_{zt})$, $\beta(F_{1t}), \ldots, \beta(F_{mt})$ for the equation.

Table 8 provides one set of such numbers,

TABLE 8

Beta Relative to SP500

Factor	Beta
Z (intercept)	.303
Beta (historic)	.745
Yield	−.014
Size	−.062
Bond Beta	−.009
Alpha	−.086
Basic Industries	.074
Capital Goods	−.014
Construction	.103
Consumer Goods	−.028
Energy	−.057
Finance	−.023
Transportation	.065
Utilities	−.047

based on the betas of each of the factors relative to Standard and Poor's stock index over the 1931-1979 period.[26] These values suggest that, other things equal:

— the higher a security's historic beta, the greater its future beta;
— the higher its yield, the smaller its future beta;
— the larger its size, the smaller its future beta;
— the more bond-like a security, the smaller its future beta, and
— the better its past non-market performance, the smaller its future beta.

Also, other things equal, basic industry, con-struction, and transportation stocks have substantially larger than average betas, while energy and utility stocks have substantially smaller than average betas.

AVERAGE FACTOR VALUES AND THE CAPITAL ASSET PRICING MODEL

An investment organization should be con-cerned with the *future* values of factors and security-

37

FIGURE 23

TRANSPORTATION

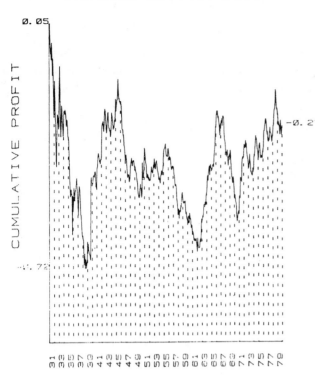

FIGURE 24

UTILITIES

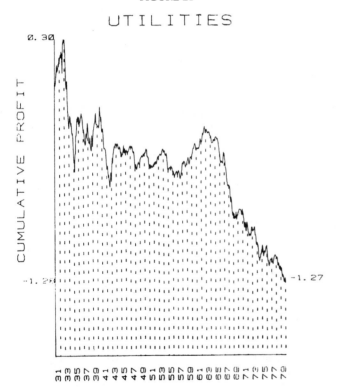

to key factors (in our notation, the b_{i1t}, b_{i2t}, . . . values). This theory, however, implies nothing about the signs or magnitudes of the expected values of the factors. Another theory, the original Capital Asset Pricing Model of Sharpe [5], Lintner [2], and Mossin [3], implies that expected returns will be related to predicted future beta values. For example, it implies:

$$\overline{R}_p - r = \beta_p(\overline{R}_m - r), \qquad (8)$$

where:

$\overline{R}_p$ = the expected return on portfolio or security p;

r = the riskless interest rate;

β_p = portfolio or security p's predicted beta relative to "the market portfolio," and

$\overline{R}_m$ = the expected return on the market portfolio.

As we have indicated, a "factor" can be thought of as the return on a portfolio. With this interpretation, the original Capital Asset Pricing Model implies that the expected value of each factor should equal its beta times the expected excess return on the market portfolio:

$$\overline{F}_{jt} = \beta(F_{jt}) (\overline{R}_m - r), \qquad (9)$$

where:

$\overline{F}_{jt}$ = the expected value of factor j at time t, and

$\beta(F_{jt})$ = the predicted beta of factor j at time t relative to the market portfolio.

A simple, though implausible, set of assumptions would hold that "true" expected returns and risks have been the same since 1931 and that the value-weighted index of New York Stock Exchange stocks is an adequate proxy for "the market portfolio." These assumptions, plus those of the original Capital Asset Pricing Model, would imply expected factor values equal to those shown in the second column of Table 9. For example, Table 8 showed that the yield

TABLE 9

Average Returns Versus CAPM Values

Factor	Avg.	CAPM	T-Diff
Z (intercept)	−0.24	2.51	−1.32
Beta	5.36	6.18	−0.31
Yield	0.24	−0.11	2.37
Size	−5.56	−0.51	−4.53
B. Beta	−0.12	−0.08	−0.11
Alpha	−2.00	−0.71	−1.94
Basic Ind.	1.65	0.61	0.91
Capital Gds.	0.16	−0.12	0.33
Construction	−1.59	0.85	−1.93
Consumer Gds.	−0.18	−0.23	0.07
Energy	6.28	−0.47	4.28
Finance	−1.48	−0.19	−1.72
Transptn.	−0.57	0.54	−0.82
Utilities	−2.62	−0.39	−1.66

specific returns. For example, what should one *expect* the yield factor to be? How much *risk* is associated with the projection?

One theory of market equilibrium, the *Arbitrage Pricing Theory* of Ross [4], holds that the expected return on a security will be related only to its sensitivities

factor had a beta of $-.014$, and Table 1 showed that the average excess return on the New York Stock Exchange index was 8.193% per year; the product, -0.11, is shown in Table 9.

The first column in Table 9 shows the actual average factor values. How significant are the differences from the values in the second column? The third column provides some answers. Given the variability of a factor, one can estimate the significance of the difference between actual and "expected" values. Using the usual standard (the absolute value of the t-statistic greater than 2.0), only three differences are large enough to command special attention. High-yield stocks did better, large stocks worse, and energy stocks better than would be expected, given these assumptions.

The data are thus inconsistent (but not pervasively so) with the *joint* hypothesis that includes (1) the original Capital Asset Pricing Model *and* (2) our very strong assumptions about stability of expected returns and risks and the adequacy of the New York Stock Exchange index to serve as as a market surrogate. Nevertheless, the data may be completely consistent with the implications of an expanded Capital Asset Pricing Model, a joint hypothesis involving changes in expectations and risks over time, or the use of an alternative measure of the return on the market portfolio.

Although these results do not confirm or reject the original Capital Asset Pricing Model as a description of reality, they do call into question naive applications in which expected returns are assumed to be related *only* to estimates of future betas based on past patterns of returns.

[1] E.g. dividends paid from March 1978 through February 1979, divided by the stock price at the end of February 1979.

[2] E.g. (1) the change in price from the end of February 1979 to the end of March 1979 plus dividends with ex-dates during March 1979, all divided by the price at the end of February 1979 minus (2) the return obtained by purchasing at the end of February a Treasury bill due to expire at the end of March.

[3] Factor models usually assume that security-specific returns are uncorrelated with the factors.

[4] In particular, Barra, Wells Fargo Investment Advisors, and Wilshire Associates.

[5] As indicated, this differs from factor analysis procedures that use return data to estimate (possibly unidentified) attributes directly. It also differs from procedures using forecasts (e.g. those employing scenarios).

[6] The correlation between the values of any two factors can be computed, as can the average value and variation in value for each security-specific return. These figures were computed but are not reported here.

[7] This may be desirable in its own right, since it may focus more on predictable regularities than on unpredictable anomalies.

[8] There are other differences between our approach and those of some of the commercial services. The relative merits of alternative procedures will not be considered here.

[9] Based on analyses not reported here; commercial services use a similar attribute.

[10] The Ibbottson/Sinquefield [1] data were used for bond, Treasury bills, and Standard and Poor's stock index returns.

[11] The codes used were those on the data base prepared by the Center for Research in Security Prices at the University of Chicago (this set of data was utilized for all the analyses). The ranges assigned to each of the eight sectors were:
Basic Industries:
  1000-1299, 1400-1499, 2600-2699, 2800-2829, 2870-2899, 3300-3399
Capital Goods:
  3400-3419, 3440-3599, 3670-3699, 3800-3849, 5080-5089, 5100-5129, 7300-7399
Construction:
  1500-1999, 2400-2499, 3220-3299, 3430-3439, 5160-5219
Consumer Goods:
  0000-0999, 2000-2399, 2500-2599, 2700-2799, 2830-2869, 3000-3219, 3420-3429, 3600-3669, 3700-3719, 3850-3879, 3880-3999, 4830-4899, 5000-5079, 5090-5099, 5130-5159, 5220-5999, 7000-7299, 7400-9999
Energy:
  1300-1399, 2900-2999
Finance:
  6000-6999
Transportation:
  3720-3799, 4000-4799
Utilities:
  4800-4829, 4900-4999

[12] In fact, the regression was actually performed using only seven of the eight attributes. The intercepts for the eight sectors were thus F_{zt}, $F_{zt} + F_{2t}$, $F_{zt} + F_{3t} \ldots$ and $F_{zt} + F_{8t}$, where F_{zt} represents the intercept and F_{2t} etc. the factor values obtained in the regression. These eight values were then averaged, with the difference between each one and the average value used as the corresponding sector factor.

[13] In other words, given the inclusion of all but one of the attributes, we should add the remaining one. On the other hand, all our results concern the extent to which our model *fits* historic data. More important questions concern the ability of a procedure using such a model to *predict* future risk and return. For this, one needs to define the precise manner in which results such as ours would be used for prediction — a task beyond the scope of this paper.

[14] Some commercial services fail to report the corresponding value for their models, perhaps because their principals are discouraged by them.

[15] It is important to point out that there is no inconsistency between the importance of other factors in explaining differences among *actual* security returns and the implication of the original Capital Asset Pricing Model that only *predicted* beta is relevant for explaining differences among *expected* security returns. The relationship between our results and the implications of the original Capital Asset Pricing Model is explored later in the paper.

[16] In principle one should use an estimate of *security-specific risk* based on the use of the full factor model over a period for this purpose. However, this requires more than sixty months of

data before a security can be included in the analysis. The cruder method described in the text was employed to use more of the data for fitting the factor model.

[17] This assumes (as does the model) that the security-specific return is uncorrelated with the factor values. The procedure does not guarantee this, but is likely to give results that are relatively uncorrelated. Each value in Table 6 equals one minus the ratio of the security-specific variance to the variance of the security's excess return.

[18] All securities with adequate prior data were included. This criterion might introduce a small amount of *ex post* selection bias, but any effects are likely to be minor (and of undetermined sign).

[19] In this case security-specific return was measured as:

$$(R_{it} - r_t) - (R_{mt} - r_t),$$

where R_{mt} is the return on the value-weighted index of all NYSE stocks in month t. As before, the R-squared value equals one minus the ratio of the variance of this security-specific return to that of the security's excess return.

[20] The figures in Table 6 were also larger than comparable values obtained using unweighted cross-section regressions.

[21] I.e. the average of the monthly values was multiplied by 12 and the standard deviation by the square root of 12; this is equivalent to multiplying each monthly return by 12, then taking the average and standard deviation of the resulting values.

[22] This borders on providing a statistically significant challenge to certain notions of market efficiency. An alternative approach would make predictions employing any serial correlation in factor or security-specific returns or (better yet) provide a detailed model of the time-series behavior of such returns.

[23] Interestingly, many users of commercial risk models assume a standard deviation for the stock market of approximately 20% (consistent with our 49-year average) but employ estimates of other risks based on the last two or three decades when the stock market risk was closer to 15%.

[24] The correlation between the two indices was .993.

[25] The latter assumption implies that the portion of each portfolio's return due to security-specific effects is very close to zero. In practice such portfolios might well require extreme positions (both long and short), with proceeds from short sales used to finance some of the long positions. Since such procedures are not feasible for most investors, and since no transactions costs have been assessed, our "portfolio interpretations" should be considered simply useful abstractions, and the figures should not be regarded as records of directly attainable investment outcomes.

[26] An alternative (and logically superior) method would use the assumed factor covariances and the *current* attributes of the base (and also take security-specific risk into account).

REFERENCES

1. Roger G. Ibbotson and Rex A. Sinquefield. *Stocks, Bonds, Bills and Inflation: Historical Returns.* The Financial Analysts Research Foundation, 1979.

2. John Lintner. "The Valuation of Risk Assets and the Selection of Risky Investments in Stock Portfolios and Capital Budgets." *Review of Economics and Statistics,* February 1965, pp. 13-37.

3. Jan Mossin. "Equilibrium in a Capital Asset Market." *Econometrica,* October 1966, pp. 768-783.

4. Stephen A. Ross. "The Arbitrage Pricing Theory of Capital Asset Pricing." *Journal of Economic Theory,* December 1976, pp. 341-360.

5. William F. Sharpe, "Capital Asset Prices: A Theory of Market Equilibrium Under Conditions of Risk." *Journal of Finance,* September 1964, pp. 425-442.

What hath MPT wrought: Which risks reap rewards?

Some risks do not correlate with systematic risks, so buy "risky" stocks and diversify.

Robert D. Arnott

The theories upon which Modern Portfolio Theory (MPT) is based have been under increasing attack of late. We have seen demonstrations that beta has little to do with return. This is further corroborated in this article. Many studies have suggested that the markets do not follow a random walk. Such factors as size, stock price variability, and P/E seem related to return, suggesting that security price behavior is not explained by the Random Walk Hypothesis. These results also are corroborated in this article.

Do we discard the theories that underly MPT? If so, do we throw out the tools that MPT has generated? The first of these two questions will be debated in the academic journals for years to come. To the second question, an emphatic "No" is appropriate. MPT tools can be of value whether or not the theories are accurate.

In fact, the purpose of this article is to examine precisely which elements of security risk the investment markets use in security pricing. This issue can be phrased in another way: While no one disputes the idea that the investment markets generally provide higher returns for higher risks, for which risks do investors require compensation? Furthermore, are these risks systematic or do they represent inefficiencies that

savvy participants in the marketplace can exploit?

The following analysis systematically examines these questions, using several measures of risks to accomplish this. The methodology will compare ex ante risk measures with subsequent security returns.[1] Two measures will evaluate the extent to which a given risk measure is associated with subsequent return. The first of these is the average annual information coefficient (IC);[2] the second is a measure of consistency, which we term the "stability t-statistic."[3]

IS BETA DEAD?

Beta is the most widely recognized risk measure in use in the investment community. Past studies[4] support the market beta as the single most significant contributor to stock price comovement. In short, beta has withstood all scrutiny to date as a legitimate measure of security behavior and risk and as an even more significant descriptor of portfolio behavior and risk.

Why, then, has there been so much controversy regarding the merits of beta? Logic dictates that investors will be risk averse and will expect more return for higher risk investments. Furthermore, logic suggests

1. Footnotes appear at the end of the article.

TABLE 1A.

1-YEAR INFORMATION COEFFICIENTS — ANNUAL SUMMARY

	1964	1965	1966	1967	1968	1969	1970	1971	1972	1973	1974	1975	1976	1977	1978	1979	1980	1981
TRUE BETA					+.17	−.09	−.29	+.25	+.22	−.28	−.32	+.38	+.19	−.13	+.23	+.36	+.47	−.15
EXP. BETA					+.17	+.02	−.31	+.21	.00	−.16	−.15	+.27	+.11	+.14	+.08	+.18	+.30	−.30
TRUE RISK					+.24	−.16	−.47	+.11	−.05	−.30	−.42	+.39	+.24	+.19	+.26	+.43	+.38	−.25
EXP. RISK					+.20	−.15	−.25	+.22	−.06	−.16	−.15	+.24	+.16	+.21	+.22	+.34	+.28	−.27
EPS UNCER.	+.22	+.25	+.16	+.21	+.16	−.28	+.14	−.11	−.10	+.01	+.27	+.25	+.42	+.19	+.09	+.19	−.20	+.11
CAPITALIZATION	+.19	+.29	+.08	+.43	+.34	−.08	+.07	+.15	+.05	−.02	+.16	+.35	+.40	+.44	+.24	+.24	−.01	+.22
TOTAL SALES	−.02	+.18	+.16	+.33	+.23	+.12	−.01	+.17	+.20	+.02	−.03	+.15	+.19	+.40	+.25	+.28	+.17	+.12
BOOK/PRICE	+.16	+.09	−.20	+.05	+.19	−.32	+.14	−.20	−.19	+.05	+.26	+.26	+.37	+.14	−.06	+.06	−.18	+.16
EARNINGS YIELD	+.24	+.11	−.10	+.15	+.23	−.23	+.21	−.03	−.08	+.03	+.26	+.16	+.29	+.16	−.01	−.12	−.14	+.13
RET. EPS YIELD	+.16	+.24	−.03	+.21	+.23	−.13	+.15	+.08	+.07	+.03	+.20	+.14	+.29	+.19	+.09	−.03	−.12	+.11

that rational investors will largely ignore elements of risk that they can eliminate through diversification.

These two ideas form the basis of the Capital Assets Pricing Model (CAPM). The CAPM suggests that the investor will be compensated for non-diversifiable risk and will not be compensated for diversifiable risk. This makes sense theoretically, but has failed to pass a blizzard of empirical tests.

Therein lies the problem. If investors are not compensated for accepting significant non-diversifiable risk, and if investors demand higher return for higher risk investments, then beta must not be the risk for which investors demand compensation! Indeed, it is not surprising that investors may focus on a risk other than beta. Investors will expect greater returns for those issues with greater perceived risk. This *perceived* risk need not bear any meaningful relationship with beta.

Table 1 summarizes the 1-year Information Coefficients for a number of potential risk measures. The first of these is "true beta."[5] Each information coefficient represents the correlation between true beta in a given year and total return for that year. In any given year there is typically a strong relationship between beta and return. This is only natural: High beta stocks should outperform low beta stocks in an up market, leading to a strong positive IC, and should underperform low beta stocks in a down market, leading to a strong negative IC.

The important item to note is that the mean IC is only 0.07, with a standard deviation of 0.26. This means that the estimated mean IC of 0.07 has a standard error of 0.07.[6] In other words, while beta is a significant descriptor of stock price behavior, we cannot assume with any confidence that the investor is compensated for this risk in the long run. The mean IC is not significantly different from zero.

In any case, no investor can know, ex ante, the true beta for a given year. We have nevertheless constructed an "expected beta," derived from historical data, that represents a good estimator for "true beta." This expected beta is derived from exponentially-weighted historical price behavior and is adjusted towards a beta of 1.0 using a Vasicek adjustment.[7] Table 2 shows that the expected beta has a correlation with the "true beta" of 0.53.

TABLE 2.

CORRELATIONS

	TRUE BETA	EXP. BETA	TRUE RISK	EXP. RISK	EPS UNCER.	CAP.	TOTAL SALES	BOOK/ PRICE	EPS YIELD
EXP. BETA	0.53								
TRUE RISK	0.61	0.54							
EXP. RISK	0.50	0.67	0.73						
EPS UNCER.	-0.01	0.00	0.19	0.18					
CAPITALIZATION	-0.02	0.00	0.35	0.37	0.36				
TOTAL SALES	0.00	0.01	0.31	0.31	-0.03	0.70			
BOOK/PRICE	0.01	-0.03	0.07	0.06	0.58	0.29	-0.14		
EARNINGS YIELD	0.02	-0.06	-0.09	-0.11	0.44	0.11	-0.17	0.32	
RET. EPS YIELD	0.01	-0.01	0.03	0.03	0.52	0.19	-0.06	0.27	0.77

If, however, we assume that this expected beta is typical of the ex ante estimates of beta that may have existed prior to each year (in fact, it is a better estimate than many beta estimates), we find more disappointing results. The mean IC of this expected beta measure is just 0.04, with a standard error of 0.05. These figures lack statistical significance and suggest that expected beta has a strikingly weak relationship with subsequent stock performance.

We might speculate that the long-term relationship between beta and return is stronger. This hypothesis is tested in Table 3, which shows the annual Information Coefficient for these same beta measures vis-à-vis 3-year total return results. The mean ICs are 0.03 and 0.06 for true beta (measured over the 3-year span) and expected beta (measured as before), respectively. Neither IC is very significant, although the figure for expected beta is marginally significant at the 90% level. In short, the relationship between beta and long-term returns hardly differs from the shorter term results.

Is beta dead? As a predictor of stock returns, we (and many others) have demonstrated that beta is of limited value at best. But beta is not dead. Beta's value is as a predictor of risk for the individual security and, more importantly, for portfolios.

STOCK PRICE RISK

If investors do not demand compensation for systematic risk, or beta, perhaps total price volatility is

TABLE 1B.

1-YEAR INFORMATION COEFFICIENTS —
OVERALL SUMMARY

	Mean IC	Std Dev	Std Err	Stab "t"
TRUE BETA	+.07	.26	.07	1.0
EXP. BETA	+.04	.19	.05	0.7
TRUE RISK	+.04	.30	.08	0.5
EXP. RISK	+.06	.23	.06	1.0
EPS UNCER.	+.11	.19	.04	2.6**
CAPITALIZATION	+.20	.18	.04	5.2***
TOTAL SALES	+.16	.12	.03	5.5***
BOOK/PRICE	+.04	.19	.04	1.0
EARNINGS YIELD	+.07	.16	.04	1.9*
RET. EPS YIELD	+.10	.12	.03	3.6***

* – Significant at the 90% level.
** – Significant at the 99% level.
*** – Significant at the 99.9% level.

3-YEAR INFORMATION COEFFICIENTS —
ANNUAL SUMMARY

	1964	1965	1966	1967	1968	1969	1970	1971	1972	1973	1974	1975	1976	1977	1978	1979
TRUE BETA					+.07	−.10	−.10	−.02	−.05	−.19	−.20	+.28	+.11	−.03	+.23	+.31
EXP. BETA					+.02	+.02	−.04	−.05	−.10	−.13	+.15	+.23	+.15	+.12	+.14	+.19
TRUE RISK					+.04	−.10	−.15	−.06	−.15	−.20	−.14	+.38	+.36	+.33	+.36	+.30
EXP. RISK					+.02	−.06	−.04	−.04	−.12	−.05	+.23	+.28	+.33	+.33	+.36	+.32
EPS UNCER.	+.24	+.28	+.26	+.11	+.05	−.11	−.01	−.01	+.16	+.25	+.45	+.36	+.32	+.26	+.16	+.09
CAPITALIZATION	+.25	+.34	+.42	+.36	+.25	+.09	+.12	+.08	+.10	+.18	+.38	+.48	+.43	+.40	+.30	+.27
TOTAL SALES	+.19	+.30	+.31	+.29	+.22	+.15	+.18	+.15	+.07	+.04	+.11	+.30	+.32	+.37	+.31	+.33
BOOK/PRICE	+.02	+.01	+.04	+.05	+.05	−.21	−.16	−.05	+.16	+.21	+.37	+.34	+.29	+.12	−.07	−.07
EARNINGS YIELD	−.02	+.02	+.18	+.10	+.18	−.07	−.05	−.02	−.01	+.14	+.37	+.20	+.20	+.06	−.07	−.15
RET. EPS YIELD	+.03	+.14	+.12	+.14	+.17	−.01	.00	+.07	+.03	+.09	+.38	+.23	+.24	+.15	+.04	−.04

TABLE 3B.

3-YEAR INFORMATION COEFFICIENTS —
OVERALL SUMMARY

	Mean IC	Std Dev	Std Err	Stab "t"
TRUE BETA	+.03	.17	.05	0.6
EXP. BETA	+.06	.12	.03	1.7*
TRUE RISK	+.08	.24	.06	1.2
EXP. RISK	+.13	.19	.05	2.3*
EPS UNCER.	+.18	.15	.04	4.7***
CAPITALIZATION	+.28	.13	.03	8.4***
TOTAL SALES	+.23	.10	.03	8.9***
BOOK/PRICE	+.07	.17	.04	1.6*
EARNINGS YIELD	+.07	.14	.03	1.9*
RET. EPS YIELD	+.11	.11	.03	4.1***

*   – Significant at the 90% level.
**   – Significant at the 99% level.
*** – Significant at the 99.9% level.

the perceived risk. We can test this hypothesis in the same way as the beta was tested.

The performance of "true risk" as a return measure also appears in Table 1. "True risk" is simply the standard deviation of stock price activity during the year in which return is tested. As is noted in Table 1B, the mean IC for "true risk" is only 0.04. With a standard error of 0.08, this IC is utterly insignificant. An examination of ex ante expected risk reveals marginally better results. This "expected risk" is determined by exponentially weighting past stock price volatility.[8] The mean IC is 0.06, with a standard error of 0.06.

Once again, it is appropriate to examine the relationship between volatility and longer term returns. As shown on Table 3, the 3-year performance of stocks is more strongly related to stock volatility than is the 1-year performance. The 3-year ICs relative to true risk (measured over the same 3-year span as return) and

relative to "expected risk" (as defined before) are 0.08 and 0.13, respectively. The IC for the "true risk" measure is not significant, but the IC for "expected risk" is significant at the 95% level.

All of the ICs associated with beta or risk measures are positive. This is consistent with the idea that the investment community demands greater return for greater stock price risk, both non-diversifiable and total. Only two of the ICs are significant, however; hence, this relationship must be considered a relatively weak one.

Note that the investment community appears more averse to the expected total stock price risk, demanding more return, than to the expected non-diversifiable portion of risk, or beta, which the CAPM would suggest is more important. It is also interesting that "expected risk" is apparently more strongly related to return than "true risk."

We would speculate that, if volatility exceeds expectations, investors would increase their required return and drop the price for a stock. This would reduce actual return and would weaken the relationship between true volatility and return.

Finally, it is interesting to note that the correlation between expected volatility and expected beta is 0.67, and that expected beta has ICs that are approximately two-thirds as strong as the ICs for expected volatility. This would suggest that any relationship between beta and return is predicated solely on volatility, and that the investment community requires no additional return for systematic risk except to the extent that systematic risk is related to stock volatility. Since none of these phenomena is statistically significant, however, a more detailed examination is not warranted without more extensive testing.

In short, the investment markets are remarkable insensitive to stock price risk. Yet, investors are almost universally risk averse. It is a rare investor or portfolio manager who would knowingly choose a "risky" investment over a "safe" investment without a substantial increase in expected return. But Tables 1 and 3 demonstrate that volatile or high beta issues do not generate appreciably more return than stable or low beta issues. Since it is clear that investors do not demand substantially more return for more price risk, price risk must differ sharply from *perceived* risk. In order to determine what constitutes perceived risk, let us now examine which investment characteristics *are* related to return.

EARNINGS UNCERTAINTY

Earnings do matter. Studies have demonstrated that, when earnings expectations change, the stock price responds, usually simultaneously,[9] that earnings surprises significantly affect prices even for some time after the surprise earnings have been announced,[10] and that uncertain earnings growth prospects lead to uncertain returns and stock volatility.[11] Since much investment community attention is focused on earnings, earnings uncertainty might be an element of *perceived* risk. In other words, investors may demand greater return on a stock with uncertain earnings than on a predictable "safe" stock.

For this test, we define earnings uncertainty by dividing the 7-year standard deviation in earnings per share by the stock price.[12] By taking a simple standard deviation, rather than a percent standard deviation around a trend, we eliminate any mathematical problems associated with negative earnings data. This approach does require some normalization to correct for discrepancies between high-price, high-earnings companies and low-price, low-earnings companies. We normalize by dividing by stock price, which once again avoids mathematical problems with companies with negative earnings data, while introducing a slight P/E effect.

Table 1 shows that ex ante earnings uncertainty does indeed correlate with return. The annual IC averages 0.11, with a standard error of just 0.04. Unlike the results for beta or price volatility, this result is mathematically significant at the 99% level. The longer term relationship between earnings uncertainty with subsequent 3-year total return is 0.18, which is significant at the 99.9% level.

Thus, we can confidently assert that earnings uncertainty is a major component of the *perceived* stock risk, for which greater return is required. Earnings uncertainty is related to stock price volatility with a correlation of 0.18-0.19, so stocks with high earnings uncertainty will be more volatile than stocks with stable earnings. Much of this risk is not systematic, however, and can be eliminated through diversification: Table 2 shows that there is essentially no correlation between earnings uncertainty and expected or actual beta.

THE SIZE EFFECT

A growing body of evidence supports the idea that small-capitalization stocks significantly outperform large-capitalization stocks.[13] This effect is so strong and so consistent that even advocates of the Efficient Markets Hypothesis have found no refutation of this effect. On the other hand, any non-systematic or diversifiable effect that exhibits a significant ex ante relationship with return clearly violates both the Efficient Markets Hypothesis and the CAPM.

The results presented in Tables 1 and 3 support the small stock effect,[14] even though our 700-stock test universe is heavily weighted toward larger issues and others have found this effect to be strongest for the very small issues that are absent from our study. Nonetheless, even in this universe of larger issues, the smaller stocks generate superior returns to a striking extent. The 1-year IC averages 0.20, with a standard error of only 0.04, while the 3-year IC averages a startling 0.28, with a standard error of just 0.03; both are significant at the 99.9% level. This small stock effect was evident in 15 of the last 18 years and never failed for any 3-year span.

Capitalization actually combines a size effect with a value effect. If we use total sales, net income, or book value as a measure of size, we find a size effect that is mathematically significant but not quite as great as the capitalization size effect. Tables 1 and 3 show the results for a size effect based on total sales.[15] The results for such a model are just as significant as the capitalization effect, but the ICs are lower. This occurs because a capitalization model can be viewed as a sales effect combined with a value effect based on the ratio of sales per share to stock price, or as a net income effect combined with an earnings yield effect, or a book value effect combined with a book to price ratio effect. Thus, if small companies generate better total returns than large companies, and if value measures such as an earnings yield are also correlated with subsequent total returns, then it is not surprising that capitalization is a stronger indicator of return than the internal measures of company size. Several value effects will be further reviewed in the next section.

If there is a size effect, why do we not see institutions stampede into smaller stocks and obliterate the size effect? The problem, once again, is one of perceived risk. Few investment practitioners would consider Maine Public Service to be safer than General Telephone, for example. Maine Public Service has hardly any institutional following, it is not widely understood, and it is illiquid (the stock moved almost 10% on just 10,000 shares of trading in three days in April 1982). Perhaps most important, a big loss in General Telephone is more likely to be forgiven by most clients than a big loss in Maine Public Service. Nonetheless, Maine Public Service is less volatile, has far less systematic risk (beta), and has generated more than 5% per annum more total return from 1975 through mid-1982 than General Telephone.

A second possible source of the small stock effect, which is related to perceived risk, is constituency: Who owns the stock, and what risks matter to them? The constituency of large stocks is usually dominated by institutional investors with well diversified portfolios. Institutional investors like to understand a company, so they want stocks covered by analysts; they like liquidity, so they favor the large companies on which block trades are easy; they are penalized by their clients for losing money on obscure bets, so they are encouraged to focus on large, good-quality, respectable stocks; their broad diversification means that only a modest expected return premium vis-à-vis potential non-stock investments is necessary to justify an investment, and, finally, the small size of the small issues precludes large investments, so there is a sense that these issues are "too small" to be worth the trouble. The constituency of small stocks is often individuals whose portfolios display little diversification; this includes small investors who cannot afford diversification and insiders with substantial undiversified holdings in their own company. These undiversified investors could be expected to require a larger expected return premium to justify their holdings in these small stocks.

This size effect, like the earnings uncertainty effect, is not meaningfully related to systematic risk. The correlation between size and either true beta or expected beta is effectively zero. As with the earnings uncertainty effect, however, the size effect is related to volatility. The correlation between size and volatility is 0.35, so small stocks are more volatile than large stocks. But, once again, this appears to be largely specific risk, which we can eliminate through diversification.

FUNDAMENTAL RISK

Fundamental ratios, such as P/E and the price to book ratio, are based on the consensus assessment by the investment community of the *fundamental* risk in a company. While P/E is not as tangible a measure of risk as beta, volatility, or even earnings uncertainty, it implies a judgment of the fundamental risk of a company. A high P/E suggests that the investment community believes that the company will grow quickly and predictably and that the risk of failing to achieve this growth is slight; a low P/E suggests an expectation of slow growth with substantial risk that growth will not be achieved. Thus, fundamental ratios of this sort

can be viewed as quantitative measures of qualitative consensus risk judgements.

Tables 1 and 3 summarize the results for three value measures:[16] the ratio of book value per share to stock price, the ratio of earnings per share to price (or earnings yield), and the retained earnings yield (earnings yield — dividend yield). Each shows positive correlation with subsequent returns, over both a 1-year and a 3-year span, with various levels of significance. The book to price ratio is not much better than the beta or volatility measures, with a 1-year IC averaging only 0.04 and a 3-year IC averaging only 0.07, and is sufficiently inconsistent that the 1-year results are not significant and the 3-year results are barely significant at the 90% level. Earnings yield is somewhat better than book-to-price, with 1-year and 3-year ICs both averaging 0.07. While these figures are similar to the ICs for beta and volatility, earnings yield is more consistently related to subsequent return than beta or volatility, so these results are both significant at the 90% level. Finally, retained earnings yield is substantially better than either of these, with 1-year and 3-year ICs of 0.10 and 0.11, respectively. These are consistent enough results that they are both significant at a 99.9% level.

It is reasonable to speculate that this retained earnings yield measures investor confidence that retained earnings will ultimately accrue to the shareholder. A high retained earnings yield suggests a lack of confidence in the likelihood that shareholders will ultimately benefit from the retained earnings, hence, a *risk* that the earnings are not meaningful or sustainable.

This evidence tells us that traditional value measures may be quantitative evidence of perceived qualitative risks. Many of these value measures are not particularly strong or consistent, but some are significant. For the most part, these value measures are not strongly correlated with systematic risk nor, surprisingly, with total volatility. Thus, once again, we find potential avenues for diversifiable risk, which may lead to superior returns.

YES, VIRGINIA, THERE IS A SANTA CLAUS

The market prices securities to reward risk. Investors willing to accept higher risk will reap greater returns. This idea is not new and has never been challenged. The key question is: Which risks are factored into the pricing mechanism of the market?

If the market were perfectly rational and efficient, some version of the CAPM would hold true, and returns would be directly related to non-diversifiable risk. But the market *is people*, and people are not perfectly rational. People expect greater return for greater *perceived* risk: They price securities in accordance with the consensus *perceived* risk. If the market is rational, this consensus perceived risk for a security will match the non-diversifiable risk of that security. *There is substantial evidence that this is not the case.*

Any of several strategies can be developed by exploiting the discrepancies between *perceived* risk and expected non-diversifiable risk. These strategies can lead to superior long-term performance without increased risk: Those elements of perceived risk that are diversifiable can, by definition, be eliminated through diversification.

What does any such strategy imply? To achieve superior results in the long run, one must invest in areas that are perceived by the consensus to be high-risk. By definition, this is a contrarian strategy. This implies the sale of "wonderful, safe" stocks and the purchase of the unloved "dogs," which are viewed as risky investments. Since such issues are demonstrated to have greater price volatility, this strategy will result in some spectacular flops that will typically be more than offset by spectacular gains. Finally, it is often more comfortable to fail conventionally than to succeed unconventionally; no portfolio manager was ever fired for buying IBM. This strategy, of necessity, forces the uncomfortable and unconventional decisions.

Can a strategy based on buying perceived risk that is not systematic risk backfire? Yes, two conditions can cause inferior performance. First, the perceived risk measure used in a strategy must be diversifiable. If the risk subsequently is found to be systematic, so that diversification does not reduce the risk for the portfolio, the exploitation of that risk may not result in superior performance. Second, if the aversion to some element of perceived risk increases over time (if there is a "flight to safety"), a strategy based on that element of perceived risk will fail. This second type of failure will be temporary but can cover an uncomfortable span of time. The two-tier market of 1969-1972 was an unpleasant time for managers using a value-oriented price to book strategy for this very reason. The use of a multidisciplinary strategy, focusing on several aspects of perceived risk, can avert both of these potential problems most of the time.

In short, there is a Santa Claus in the investment business who hands out superior performance without increased risk. This present is given only to those with the courage to ignore conventional wisdom and to buy the "risky" issues that do not add to true portfolio risk.

[1] The test universe for this study consists of some 700 issues on the Boston Company database, including all S&P 500 stocks and stocks on the Boston Company list of closely followed stocks. These tests were partially cross-checked against the full 4000-stock database (including dead stocks), to test for survivor bias. These tests revealed no meaningful differences vis-à-vis the 700-stock test.

[2] The information coefficient (IC) is simply the correlation between a selected return predictor and the subsequent total return. In most instances, a rank correlation is used. We use a simple correlation, since a simple correlation captures performance extremes better than a rank correlation. In practice, there is rarely any significant difference between these two correlation measures. The IC is widely used in the investment community in preference to an R^2 measure. One reason for this is the simplicity of the concept. A second reason is that an IC is directly and linearly related to the excess returns that a security selection strategy can achieve, while an R^2 is related to the potential value of a model in a more subtle way.

[3] We determine the "stability t-statistic" by computing annual ICs for each year in the study. A standard deviation of these annual IC measures is determined, and we then calculate the "stability t-statistic" by dividing the mean IC by the standard error in the estimate of mean IC. Clearly, a return forecasting model with an IC averaging 0.1 and a standard deviation of 0.1 is more consistent and useful than a model with an average IC of 0.1 and a standard deviation of 0.3. This "stability t-statistic" provides a simple measure of return forecasting model consistency, and, one can assume, the likelihood of a security selection model continuing to add value.

[4] See the following articles. James L. Farrell, Jr., "Analyzing Covariation of Returns to Determine Homogeneous Stock Groupings," *Journal of Business*, April 1974, pp. 186-207; Robert D. Arnott, "Cluster Analysis and Stock Price Co-movement," *Financial Analysts Journal*, Nov./Dec. 1980, pp. 56-62; Barr Rosenberg, "Extra-Market Components of Covariance in Security Returns," *Journal of Financial and Quantitative Analysis*, Vol. 9, pp. 263-274.

[5] "True beta" is determined by measuring the 52-week or 156-week regression coefficient of stock behavior relative to the S&P 500 Stock Index, over the same 1-year or 3-year span that is used for the total return calculation.

[6] The standard deviation of a series of data can be used to estimate the likely error in the mean; this likely error in the mean, or standard error, is simply:

$$\sqrt{\frac{\Sigma(x_i - x)^2}{n - 1}},$$

where n is the number of data samples.

[7] The expected beta is determined by regressing all available weekly behavior *prior to* the time span used for return measurement of a stock against the S&P 500 index, using an exponential weighting function of $e^{-0.99t}$ to emphasize more recent data. This historical beta is then adjusted toward 1.00, using a Vasicek adjustment, with the formula:

$$\text{expected beta} = 0.3 + 0.7 \times \text{historical beta}.$$

[8] The "expected risk" is determined by measuring the historical weekly standard deviation of stock price behavior, using all available weekly data *prior to* the time span used for return measurement, using an exponential weighting function of $e^{-0.98t}$ to emphasize more recent data.

[9] See the following articles. Edwin J. Elton, Martin J. Gruber,

and Mustafa Gultekin, "Earnings Expectations and Share Prices," *Management Science*, September 1981, pp. 975-987; Edwin J. Elton, Martin J. Gruber, and Sak Mo Koo, "Expectational Data: The Effect of Quarterly Reports," Working Paper, New York University.

[10] Henry A. Latané and Charles P. Jones, "Standardized Unexpected Earnings — 1971-77," *Journal of Finance*, June 1979, pp. 717-724.

[11] Tony Estep, Nick Hanson, and Cal Johnson, "Sources of value and risk in common stocks," *The Journal of Portfolio Management*, Summer 1983, pp. 5-13.

[12] A one-quarter lag was introduced to the ex ante test data to allow for reporting lags.

[13] See the following articles. R. W. Banz, "The Relationship Between Return and Market Value of Common Stocks," *Journal of Financial Economics*, Vol. 9, pp. 1-18; A. F. Ehrbar, "Giant Payoffs from Midget Stocks," *Fortune*, June 30, 1980, pp. 111-113.

[14] Our test is based on log-capitalization, or log (price x shares outstanding), at year-end immediately before the period over which returns are measured.

[15] Our test is based on log (total sales), using sales in the year preceding the period over which returns are measured. A one-quarter "reporting lag" is introduced to prevent the inclusion of data that might have been unavailable at the time.

[16] Many measures and strategies other than the ones shown here have been tested, particularly value-oriented approaches. These are representative of the kind of results we observe in our tests.

Persuasive evidence of market inefficiency

A book/price strategy and a "specific-return-reversal" strategy, subject to careful tests, lead to the "inescapable conclusion" that prices on the NYSE are inefficient.

Barr Rosenberg, Kenneth Reid, and Ronald Lanstein

This article reports the statistically significant abnormal performance of two strategies. One strategy is a "book/price" strategy. The strategy buys stocks with a high ratio of book value of common equity per share to market price per share and sells stocks with a low book/price ratio, where "book value" is common equity per share, including intangibles. The second strategy is a "specific-return-reversal" strategy. This strategy calculates the difference between the investment return for the previous month on the stock and a fitted value for that return based upon common factors in the stock market in the previous month. This differential return is the "specific return" that is unique to the stock. This strategy expects the specific return to reverse in the subsequent month. It therefore buys stocks having negative specific returns in the prior month.

We selected both strategies as interesting candidates for tests of market inefficiency based on data through 1980. We evaluated the prior performance of the strategies in 1980 and described them in speeches and articles in 1982 [6, 7, 10, 11]. Based on monthly returns since the completion of the prior study, both strategies have shown persuasive evidence of market inefficiency.

Despite the relatively short time span, the strategies have separately achieved t-statistics of 3.7 and 11.54, respectively, each implying that the null hypothesis of market efficiency can be rejected at a very high level of confidence. Further, both strategies produced performance in this evaluation period that was closely consistent with their prior performance. We obtained still higher t-statistics when the prior data

and the evaluation-period data were combined.

The two strategies are also expected to be statistically independent a priori, because the results have shown a negative and statistically insignificant correlation during the evaluation period. Thus, each study is an independent test of market inefficiency, which means that the confluence of the two results suggests still stronger evidence for market inefficiency.

We defined the strategies and singled them out for prospective study because we felt that they arose naturally as straightforward tests of market efficiency. Each strategy can be viewed as the result of using an "instrumental variable" for pricing error. To the extent that pricing errors, for whatever cause, are present in the U.S. stock market, we anticipated that these tests might show up that inefficiency by means of the instrumental variables (the book/price ratio and the prior month's specific return, respectively) that are used. We believe that this study leads to the inescapable conclusion that prices on the New York Stock Exchange are inefficient.

PROPERTIES OF THE STRATEGIES

We define each strategy by a set of weights, w_n, for each of the approximately 1400 stocks in a prospectively defined universe of large companies, called the HICAP universe. The set of weights is calculated as of the end of the previous month, based upon data available on or before that date. The outcome of the strategy, called the "return to the strategy" and denoted by "f," is the weighted average of the monthly returns for the stocks:

$$f = \Sigma w_n r_n,$$

where r_n is the rate of return on stock n.

The set of weights for each strategy has the following characteristics:

(1) The weights are both positive and negative, and the sum of the weights is zero. Consequently, the return to the strategy can be viewed as the return on a "pure hedge portfolio" with a zero investment value.

(2) The weights are constructed so that the sum of the weights is zero within each of 55 industry groups. Each strategy therefore takes both long and short positions in each industry, which average out to zero, and so is immunized against industry factors of return.

(3) The strategy is also constructed to be orthogonal to a set of "risk indexes," with which common factors of return are also associated. The weighted sum of each of the following risk indexes, weighted by the strategy weights, is zero:

1. *Variability in Markets.* Beta prediction based upon stock price behavior, option price, etc.
2. *Success.* Past success of the company, as measured by stock's performance and earnings growth.
3. *Size.* A size index based on assets and capitalization.
4. *Trading Activity.* Indicators of share turnover.
5. *Growth.* A predictive index for subsequent earnings per share growth.
6. *Earnings/Price.* Ratio of estimated current normal earnings per share to stock price.
7. *Earnings Variation.* Variability of earnings and cash flow.
8. *Financial Leverage.* Balance sheet and operating leverage of industrial companies.
9. *Foreign Income.* Proportion of income identified as foreign.
10. *Labor Intensity.* Ratio of labor cost to capital cost.
11. *Yield.* Predicted common stock dividend yield.

Consequently, the return to the strategy is immunized against any common factor returns associated with these stock characteristics.

(4) The book/price and specific-return-reversal strategies are orthogonal to one another. The two sets of weights have zero cross-product. Consequently, the return on each strategy is expected to be independent of the other one.

(5) Each strategy is standardized, so as to imply an exposure to the variable that is constant over time.

For the book/price strategy, the weighted sum of book/price ratios differs from the market average by one cross-sectional standard deviation of that ratio. In other words, the strategy is persistently located one standard deviation away from the capitalization-weighted mean value for all stocks. For the specific-return-reversal strategy, the sum of the positive weights is 1.0, and the sum of the negative weights is −1.0, so the return on the strategy corresponds to the difference between returns on a "buy portfolio" of stocks with negative prior specific returns and a "sell portfolio" of stocks with positive prior specific returns. (With respect to an "indicator variable" for the sign of the previous month's specific return, this strategy is positioned at two cross-sectional standard deviations away from the mean, so that it is, in a precise sense, twice as aggressive with respect to its instrumental variable as the book/price ratio strategy is with respect to its instrumental variable.)

(6) The set of weights for each strategy is calculated so as to minimize the variance of the strategy's return arising from the specific returns of the individual companies, subject to meeting the above five restrictions. In other words, the noise resulting from the random specific returns of the individual stocks is made as small as possible.

Because each strategy is a "pure hedge portfolio," we can view the return to the strategy as a potential incremental return that an investor can earn by adjusting an existing portfolio in the direction of the strategy.

Let h_n denote the investment proportions in an ordinary portfolio of common stocks. Let r_0 denote the investment rate of return on that portfolio. Then if the initial portfolio is adjusted in the direction of the hedged portfolio, so that the resulting investment weights are each $(h_n + w_n)$, then the rate of return on the adjusted portfolio will be $r_0 + f$. For this reason, statistically significant performance of the strategy — to the extent that that performance is uncorrelated with the return on the initial portfolio — implies that it is necessarily possible to improve the mean/variance characteristics of the initial portfolio by making the adjustment, and so suggests that the investor holding portfolio weights h_n would prefer to hold portfolio weights $h_n + w_n$; thus, good performance suggests an inefficiency in the marketplace.

THE TWO STRATEGIES AS INSTRUMENTS FOR MARKET INEFFICIENCY

Suppose that the market is in fact inefficient, in the sense that if v_n is the "fair value" of stock n, then the stock price p_n differs from the fair value by a pricing error e_n, i.e., $p_n = v_n + e_n$. The usual presumption is that the market price is unfair in the sense that the pricing error e will be reversed in the future. Consequently, the rate of return in the subsequent month, r_n, is negatively correlated with e_n. A variable, x_n, will serve as an "instrumental variable" for subsequent performance, r_n, if it is correlated with the initial pricing error, e_n. Therefore, to search for market inefficiency, we should search for a variable, x, which we expect to be negatively correlated with e, and therefore positively correlated with subsequent return, r. This variable will define the strategy that tests for the existence of the pricing error, by means of the test of subsequent returns.

One way to obtain an instrument for e is to find a variable that is correlated with the difference $v - p$, since $-e = v - p$. For a variable x to be positively correlated with $v - p$, x must increase when the value of the firm increases relative to the price of the firm.

Traditionally, ratios of the firm's activity to the stock price have been used for this purpose. In principle, any ratio, such as book/price, earnings/price, or dividend/price = yield, can be used. Nevertheless, the value of these financial ratios as instruments may be destroyed if they are used in the process of security analysis or as a quantitative screen by investors using quantitative techniques.

If an investor uses the variable x as an indication of the desirable stock quality, so that stock price is bid up in proportion to x, then x may acquire a positive correlation with p, over and above the indirect relationship with p, which x obtains through its link to underlying value, v. As the correlation with p increases (as the stocks with high x values are bid up in price and stocks with low x values are bid down in price), the result is to reduce the correlation of x with $v - p$ and eventually to destroy its usefulness entirely. Since substantial work had previously been done with yield as a criterion for investment, and since the earnings/price ratio was much emphasized in security analysis and had previously been studied in the finance literature by S. Basu, we felt that the book/price ratio was an intriguing candidate for study. Since it had not been heavily described in the quantitative literature, it might possibly serve as an as-yet unspoiled instrument.

Another approach to obtaining an instrumental variable is to attempt to find a variable x that is directly correlated with the pricing error e. The previous month's specific return, $u_{n,t-1}$, is a natural instrument for this purpose.

The explanation of this relationship is straight-forward. Suppose that a common-factor model is used to fit the most probable return for this stock in the previous month, by analogy with the returns with similar stocks. In other words, the common-factor model explains the returns on all stocks as a result of their characteristics, and so estimates factors of return associated with industry groups and with risk indexes. Then, to the extent that the stock's previous month's return differed from this fitted return, the difference was unique to that stock. If there is a pricing error for the stock, that error would probably show up as a component of this unique return.

In fact, we can consider the difference between the pricing error for the stock at the end of the prior month and the pricing error at the inception of that month as one of the components of the previous month's specific return. Therefore, in the absence of some adjustment to remove this relationship, we would expect that the previous month's specific return would be positively correlated with every one of its components and, particularly, with the component that was the change in the pricing error.

The final step in the argument is to notice that the pricing error at the end of the previous month is the starting point for the current month's return: A larger change in pricing error over the previous month implies, ceteris paribus, a likelihood of a larger pricing error at the end of the previous month.

The complete linkage is as follows: The previous month's specific return is positively correlated with its component, which is the change in the pricing error over the previous month, which is positively correlated with the magnitude of the pricing error at the end of the previous month. Therefore, the previous month's specific return is intrinsically positively correlated with the pricing error at the end of the previous month. Consequently, we can expect the negative of the specific return to be positively correlated with this month's investment return.

As in the case of the book/price variable, we must ask whether this correlation would be vitiated by use of the previous month's specific return by technicians as a transaction strategy. In other words, if market participants were actively seeking to profit from anticipated specific return reversals, the results would be to reduce, and even eliminate, the use of the instrumental variable.

There are two reasons, however, to think that the instrument might remain valid. First of all, because the strategy requires a high rate of turnover, the inhibition provided by transaction costs could leave a significant correlation even if the investment value of the strategy had been fully removed. Second, because of the strong bias toward market efficiency that has been present in academic circles, there might be skepticism about the use of such a simple, technical, quantitative rule for trading strategies.

For these reasons, we felt that the book/price (B/P) strategy and the specific-return-reversal (SRR) strategy were natural instruments to use in the search for market inefficiencies.

IMPLEMENTATION OF THE STRATEGIES AND CALCULATION OF THE RESULTS

We based the initial retrospective test of these strategies on a data base of monthly stock data from January 1973 through March 1980 for the B/P strategy, and on through December 1980 for the SRR strategy. For the retrospective study, we strove to assure that all data used in calculation of the weights in the strategies would have been available prior to the month for which the return was calculated. We also carefully screened the data base to remove as many errors as possible, so that the investment returns would be valid.

We based this analysis primarily upon the Standard & Poor's Compustat data base and the IBES Analytics data base. There was no retrospective bias in the latter, and retrospective bias in the former could be avoided by use of the Compustat Research Tape. As a result, we were able to avoid survivorship bias and retrospective inclusion bias.

For present purposes, the key concern is with the prospective tests, beginning with the endpoints of the retrospective studies. Strategy weights for every month were calculated, based upon data through to the prior month's close, and calculation of the strategy weights was usually completed by the second or third business day of the month. The sample was defined prospectively as the HICAP universe. The strategic returns calculated here are therefore a true test of the outcome of a predefined investment strategy.

PERFORMANCE OF THE BOOK/PRICE STRATEGY

The monthly strategy returns f_t can be analyzed for their relationships with the market returns by means of the time-series regression:

$$f_t = \alpha + \beta r_{Mt} + \epsilon_t, \; t = 1, \ldots, T \qquad (1)$$

where r_{Mt} is the excess return on the market (the monthly S&P 500 return minus the monthly 30-day Treasury Bill return), and ϵ_t is the unexplained return. The coefficient β gives the responsiveness of the strategy return to the market portfolio, and α is the average residual factor return. Let ω denote the standard deviation of the residual return, $\omega = $ std. dev. (ϵ).

Table 1 summarizes the results of this regres-

TABLE 1

Monthly Performance of the Book/Price Strategy

	1973.1-1980.3	1980.4-1984.9	1973.1-1984.9
α (basis points)	41	32	36
t-statistic	4.5	3.7	5.7
ω (basis points)	83	62	76
Number of months positive	64	38	102
Number of months negative	23	16	39
Number of months total	87	54	141

sion for the 87 months of the retrospective study, for the 54 months of the prospective study, and for the total sample of 141 months. Each panel provides the average residual return (α) for this strategy and the standard deviation of the residual return (ω), in basis points per month. For example, the average residual return for the entire period was $\alpha = 36$ basis points, or 0.36 percent per month, and the standard deviation of the monthly residual return was 76 basis points. The systematic risk coefficient, β, was indistinguishable from zero, so it is not reported in the table. The foot of Table 1 shows the number of monthly returns that were positive, negative, and the total for each subperiod and for the entire history.

The return to the B/P strategy was positive in 38 of the 54 months of the prospective evaluation. The mean residual return was 32 basis points and the standard deviation of monthly residual return was 62 basis points. This led to a t-statistic of 3.7, which permits us to reject the hypothesis that the mean residual return is zero at the 99.95% level of confidence. The performance of the B/P strategy in the evaluation period was consistent with the prior experience. Therefore, we are justified in combining the entire sample history into a single test of market efficiency.

Table 2 shows an intriguing aspect of the B/P returns for the 12 calendar months. The left-hand

TABLE 2

Seasonality of Book/Price Returns (Basis Points)

	1973.1-1980.3			1980.4-1984.9			1973.1-1984.9		
	μ	σ	t-stat	μ	σ	t-stat	μ	σ	t-stat
January	193	125	(4.39)	133	62	(4.29)	173	109	(5.58)
February	37	45	(2.31)	77	42	(3.67)	50	47	(3.70)
March	50	87	(1.63)	47	67	(1.39)	49	78	(2.18)
April	18	30	(1.63)	47	40	(2.64)	30	36	(2.88)
May	21	40	(1.40)	23	34	(0.85)	22	36	(2.15)
June	36	40	(2.43)	−17	53	(−0.72)	14	51	(0.97)
July	47	61	(2.05)	39	39	(2.22)	44	51	(2.97)
August	20	68	(0.78)	−13	86	(−0.33)	6	74	(0.25)
September	43	55	(2.07)	10	75	(0.30)	29	63	(1.61)
October	−28	69	(−1.08)	−16	23	(−1.39)	−24	55	(−1.45)
November	33	75	(1.16)	38	44	(1.75)	35	63	(1.85)
December	−13	42	(−0.81)	25	29	(1.71)	1	41	(0.05)

51

panel shows the mean and standard deviation of the returns over the historical sample. Both the mean (μ) and the standard deviation (σ) of the book/price return were much higher in January than in any other month. There appears to be a downward trend in μ over the course of the year. As the monthly t-statistics in the left-hand panel show, the mean return was highly significant in January (t-statistic = 4.39), and the t-statistic exceeded 2 in February, June, July, and September. We emphasized this seasonal pattern in our discussions of the strategy in 1982 [11].

The central panel of Table 2 displays the monthly means and standard deviations during the prospective evaluations. Again, the January mean stands out sharply and, again, there is an appearance of a downtrend in the mean values from January through December. Despite the brevity of the sample, the January and February means achieve high statistical significance, and the April and July means have t-statistics greater than 2.0.

The right-hand panel shows the seasonality for the entire eleven- and-three-quarter year sample. Here the downward trend from January through to the end of the year is pronounced, and the t-statistics for January, February, March, April, May, and July are each separately greater than 2.0.

PERFORMANCE OF THE SPECIFIC-RETURN-REVERSAL STRATEGY

The SRR strategy defined in the earlier paper [10] (Rosenberg and Rudd (1982)) used the negative of the previous month's specific return as the instrumental variable. Table 3 reports the strategy reported in the earlier paper, together with the subsequent performance of the strategy.

TABLE 3

Monthly Performance of Specific-Return-Reversal Strategy

	1973.5-1980.12	1981.1-1984.10	1973.5-1984.10
μ (basis points)	112	104	109
t-statistic	10.4	10.34	13.83
σ (basis points)	103	68	93
Number of months positive	83	43	126
Number of months negative	9	3	12
Number of months total	92	46	138

The performance in the prospective evaluation is similar to the historical study. The mean monthly return is smaller, but the time-series variability of the return is reduced even more, so that the strategy achieves even higher significance per unit time after the prospective evaluation. In fact, the results are pos-

itive 43 months out of 46. The result is a t-statistic of 10.3, which permits an essentially conclusive rejection of the null hypothesis that the actual mean return of the strategy is 0.0.

To provide a still clearer strategy, and to insulate the results from the effects of misrecorded prices, we considered an alternative strategy in which the instrumental variable is the sign of the previous month's specific return. In other words, the strategy is simplified to purchasing an equal-weighted "buy portfolio" of stocks whose previous month's specific returns were negative and selling short an equal-weighted portfolio whose previous month's specific returns were positive. The monthly return on that strategy is simply the difference between the monthly returns for the buy and sell portfolios, which coincides with the difference between the average return for the month on the stocks whose previous month's specific returns were negative and the average return in the month for the stocks whose previous month's specific returns were positive. The results of that strategy appear in Table 4. As the beta was significantly different from zero, we carried out the time-series regression on the market return (Equation 1) and report the alpha, beta, and residual standard deviation, omega, in the table. This strategy achieves an even higher level of statistical significance, with a t-statistic of 11.5 for the 46-month sample. The results are positive 45 months out of 46. Average January abnormal profits were 202 basis points, versus 129 basis points on average for the other eleven months of the year. This difference is intriguing, but it was not statistically significant.

TABLE 4

SRR Monthly Return (Basis Points)

α	β	ω
136	0.10	80
(11.54)	(3.65)	

t-statistics in parentheses.

TRADING THE STRATEGIES

Trading costs are an important aspect to be considered in applying these strategies. Trading costs include the direct expenses of commissions and taxes, plus the price effect of trading. Trading costs for an institutional investor utilizing the B/P strategy would almost certainly have had a negligible effect upon performance. Urgent trading of the B/P strategy is not necessary, because the B/P criterion variable is not timely; a round-trip trading cost of 100 basis points is probably an ample allowance. Portfolio turnover is less than 5% per month, so that the drain from trading costs would be less than 5 basis points per month, as against an average abnormal performance of 36 basis points per month for the entire history.

The performance of the SRR strategy, on the other hand, would be greatly reduced for an investor experiencing trading costs. The strategy relies on timely data, so that urgent trading is important. Since the SRR strategy reported in Table 4 involves holding one portfolio long and another portfolio short, and since approximately 50% of the stocks in each portfolio are switched each month, there is a trading cost drain equal to 100% of the round-trip trading cost each month. Therefore, a drain of 100 basis points or more against a monthly performance of 136 basis points is not unlikely.

Some investors would not be faced with these trading costs. Brokers and dealers, for example, might face trading costs that were a fraction of this. Also, the investor who had determined to trade for other reasons, and who was using the SRR strategy as a timing device, would face no incremental trading costs from exploiting it.

The abnormal return of 136 basis points per month reported in Table 4 for the SSR strategy may be unobtainable if an investor is unable to sell short the "sell portfolio" at the month-end closing prices.[1] We evaluated an alternate strategy where the investor takes a long position in the "buy portfolio" and sells short the S&P500 index.[2] The average residual return declines from 136 to 96 basis points per month. The long side of the SRR strategy, taken alone, provides most of the abnormal return.

MULTICOLLINEARITY OF MULTIPLE STRATEGIES

Multicollinearity of the strategy variables is another potential problem in studies of factors in market returns. When a variable is used in raw form to construct a strategy, without any attempt to immunize the strategy against other factors, the strategy weights are directly related to that variable. The mode of analysis corresponds to a simple regression on that variable, and we can define the results as a "simple factor" of return. When that approach is taken, the major potential criticism of our study is that that variable may have served as a surrogate for other variables more closely related to the subsequent abnormal returns.

In the present case, we have made each strategy orthogonal to the other strategy, to 55 industry groupings, and to 11 other "risk indexes," which are continuous variables characterizing the stocks. This

1. Footnotes appear at the end of the article.

approach is subject to the criticism that this orthogonalization of the strategy weights may create wildly variable weightings because of multicollinearity of these strategy variables with the other dimensions.

Fortunately, this is not a problem. We deliberately constructed the risk indexes so that multicollinearity would not be severe. As a matter of fact, the time-series standard deviation of the B/P strategy return discussed here is only 76 basis points, whereas the time-series variation of the simple B/P strategy return is 139 basis points. Both strategies have the same standardized exposure to the B/P ratio, so a reduction in the time-series variability can occur only if the risk reduction from immunizing the effects of other common factors has exceeded the risk increase due to higher specific variance from the wider variable weightings. In other words, the multiple-factor strategy has substantially lower time-series risk, which confirms the benefits from orthogonalizing the weights.

Another important question related to the two tests is the extent to which they are independent of each other. Since the weightings are orthogonal a priori, we should expect the strategies to show independent returns. The realized outcome was consistent with this: The correlation between the monthly residual returns on the B/P and SRR strategies was −.19 for the 45 overlapping months, which was insignificantly different from zero. A "super strategy" that exploited a portfolio of the two strategies would therefore have achieved an even higher t-statistic than either strategy separately.

The B/P and SRR strategies are independent in another important sense. The B/P strategy corresponds to a "slow idea," and the SRR strategy to a "fast idea." Specifically, the B/P strategy exploits a decision criterion having data that are one to four months out of date (depending upon the month in the calendar quarter), and stocks purchased based on that criterion tend to be held for more than a year, on average. The SRR strategy exploits timely data, with 50% of the stocks in the portfolio traded at the end of the month. The success of two such diverse strategies tends to confirm, in our minds, the existence of underlying pricing errors in the market, which can be imperfectly detected by either alternative instrument.

POSSIBLE BIAS

One potential problem in the study is a positive bias in the results due to errors in the recorded prices. The B/P and SRR strategies use instrumental variables for pricing error, and these will single out undervalued securities, whether the low price is a true market price or a problem in recording the price itself. There is a real potential that a pricing error will cause the stock to appear desirable by B/P or SRR criteria and that the correction of the pricing problem in a subsequent month will induce a spurious, favorable return. We have taken much care to eliminate this source of bias.

First, we screened the data base for errors in prices and adjustment factors. Second, we calculated the B/P variable only once at the inception of each quarter, and the market price used as the denominator is lagged one month prior to the beginning of the quarter. For example, the B/P strategy for the months of January, February, and March is based upon a value of B obtained from the Compustat tapes in mid-December and upon the closing market price P at the end of November. Since the vast majority of pricing errors in the U.S. common stock data bases are reversed within the following month, the one-month lag almost assures that there will be no spurious upward bias in returns due to errors in the denominator of the B/P ratio.

For the SRR strategy, timing is of the essence: It is detrimental to lag the month in which the specific return is calculated. Accordingly, we cannot use lagging to eliminate the potential upward bias from the reversal of the prior month's error during the current month.

We applied two modifications to the original strategy to minimize this bias, relying on the tendency of pricing errors in these data bases to be rare but large. Usual errors arise from mistyping or reversing the digits of the price or from mistiming a stock adjustment; in either instance, the error is likely to be more than 10%. Further, it is the large errors whose reversals have the potential to significantly bias the results in an upward direction. The SRR strategy reported in the previous paper [10] used the prior month's specific return itself as the instrument, and so undertook positions in stocks that were proportional to the prior month's specific return. This resulted in large weights on the few stocks with large errors, and so in substantial potential profit.

The SRR strategy reported here, in which the weight on the stock depends only on the sign of the prior month's specific return and not on the magnitude, is a natural adjustment to minimize the impact. Even if there is a 50% downward pricing error in the previous month, the weight on the stock in this month's buy portfolio will be only 1/700, so that the spurious positive return when the stock returns to the correct price in the current month will be only 1/700 of 100%, or 14 basis points. The results in Table 4 reflect this SRR strategy.

As a second check, we applied the SRR strategy only to those stocks with specific returns between −10% and +10% in the prior month. We deleted all stocks with specific returns beyond these boundaries. This caused more than 15% of the stocks to be ignored, and these were the stocks that would be most desirable according to the logic of the SRR instrument.

Evidently, this strategy is expected to perform less well than the strategy based on all stocks, but the key question is the extent of sacrificed return. If the original return were somehow due to undetected data errors, then we could expect that discarding the stocks with extreme prior specific returns to wipe out the effect. As Table 5 shows, exclusion of the prior returns does reduce the monthly productivity of this strategy from 136 basis points to 105 basis points, which is probably no more than would be expected in the absence of data error. The results for the truncated sample remain excellent, with a time-series t-statistic of 10.94 for the abnormal return.

TABLE 5

SRR Return Excluding Outlying Prior Returns
(Basis Points)

α	β	ω
105	0.08	66
(10.94)	(3.43)	

t-statistics in parentheses.

In short, we have been able to satisfy ourselves that the results reported here are not due to pricing error. Rather they reflect opportunities available when trading at the month-end market prices of U.S. common stocks.

Sample bias in favor of survivors is another potential problem in this sort of study. Both strategies single out stocks that have done poorly in the marketplace lately; they may not be as likely to survive as other companies. Any retrospective bias toward survivors would tend to reduce the losses of the strategies and so bias their performance upward. For the study through 1980, we took care to avoid retrospective sample biases, but it is possible that some crept in. For the evaluation since 1980, on the other hand, the sample was routinely defined in advance, and so no retrospective bias was possible.[3]

CONCLUSION

This study has evaluated two prospectively defined strategies for obtaining abnormal performance. Both strategies independently achieved highly significant results, which were consistent with their prior performance in the retrospective study. Therefore, we conclude that — for this universe of stocks during this time period — the actual market prices were inefficient. The universe of stocks consists of 1400 of the largest companies in the Computstat data base. The time period is from 1980 to 1984. The stocks are priced largely on the NYSE, and a few are priced on the ASE, other regional exchanges, or NASDAQ.

The success of two such diverse instrumental variables in detecting market inefficiency suggests that there are still larger potential profits to be made, provided that the security analyst can identify the valuation errors that correlate with these instruments.

[1] Investors can sell short only on up-ticks. It follows that in a declining market, the sell side of the SRR strategy would be difficult to implement in a timely fashion.

[2] This strategy could be implemented by selling S&P500 futures contracts.

[3] In an earlier version of the paper presented at the American Finance Association meeting (December 1984), we included only those stocks with a valid price within the last week of the month. We have since verified that the results also apply when all stocks which trade at any time within the month are included, with investment return calculated through to the last price.

REFERENCES

1. Fischer Black and Myron Scholes. "The Effects of Dividend Yield Policy on Common Stock Prices and Returns." *Journal of Financial Economics*, May 1974, pp. 1-22.

2. Sanjoy Basu. "Investment Performance of Common Stocks in Relation to Their Price-earnings Ratios: A Test of the Efficient Market Hypothesis." *Journal of Finance*, June 1977, pp. 663-682.

3. Eugene Fama. "Efficient Capital Markets: A Review of Theory and Empirical Work." *Journal of Finance*, May 1970, pp. 383-417.

4. Lawrence Fisher. "Some New Stock Market Indices." *Journal of Business*, January 1966, pp. 202-207.

5. Robert Litzenberger and Krishna Ramaswamy. "The Effect of Personal Taxes and Dividends on Capital Asset Prices." *Journal of Financial Economics*, June 1979, pp. 163-195.

6. Kenneth Reid. "Average Returns to Equity Characteristics." A paper presented at the Berkeley Program in Finance Seminar on *Recent Evidence Concerning Securities Market Efficiency*, March 1982.

7. ———. "Factors in the Pricing of Common Equity." Unpublished doctoral dissertation, Graduate School of Business, University of California, Berkeley, June 1982.

8. Marc Reinganum. "Misspecification of Capital Asset Pricing: Empirical Anomalies Based on Earnings' Yields and Market Values." *Journal of Financial Economics*, March 1981, pp. 19-46.

9. Barr Rosenberg and Vinay Marathe. "Common Factors in Security Returns: Microeconomic Determinants and Macroeconomic Correlates." *Proceedings of the Seminar on the Analysis of Security Prices*, May 1976, pp. 61-115.

10. Barr Rosenberg and Andrew Rudd. "Factor-related and Specific Returns of Common Stocks: Serial Correlation and Market Inefficiency." *Journal of Finance*, May 1982, pp. 543-554.

11. Barr Rosenberg, Kenneth Reid, and Ronald Lanstein. "Factor Portfolios and Studies of Reward to Equity Characteristics." A paper presented at the Quantitative Discussion Group, May 1982.

12. Michael Solt and Meir Statman. "A Stock Return Regularity Based on Tobin's Q-Ratio." Unpublished manuscript, Leavey School of Business, University of Santa Clara, Santa Clara, California, November 1984.

13. Timothy Sullivan. "A Note on Market Power and Returns to Stockholders." *Review of Economics and Statistics*, February 1977, pp. 108-113.

What moves stock prices?

Moves in stock prices reflect something other than news about fundamental values.

David M. Cutler, James M. Poterba, and Lawrence H. Summers

Financial economics has been enormously successful in explaining the relative prices of different securities, a process facilitated by the powerful intuition of arbitrage. On the other hand, much less progress has been recorded in accounting for the absolute level of asset prices.

The standard approach holds that fluctuations in asset prices are attributable to changes in fundamental values. Voluminous evidence demonstrates that share prices react to announcements about corporate control, regulatory policy, and macroeconomic conditions that plausibly affect fundamentals. The stronger claim that *only* information affects asset values is much more difficult to substantiate, however.

The apparent absence of fundamental economic news coincident with the dramatic stock market movements of late 1987 is particularly difficult to reconcile with the standard view. This paper explores whether the 1987 market crash is exceptional in this regard, or whether a large fraction of significant market moves are difficult to explain on the basis of information.

Several recent studies of asset pricing have challenged the view that stock price movements are wholly attributable to the arrival of news. Roll (1988) shows that it is difficult to account for more than one-third of the monthly variation in individual stock returns on the basis of systematic economic influences. Shiller's (1981) claim that stock returns are too variable to be explained by shocks to future cash flows or plausible variations in future discount rates argues

for other sources of movement in asset prices. French and Roll (1986) demonstrate that the variation in stock returns is larger when the stock market is open than when it is closed, even during periods of similar information release about market fundamentals.

The difficulty of explaining returns on the basis of information is not confined to equity markets. Frankel and Meese (1987) report similar findings in the foreign exchange market. Roll (1984) finds that news about weather conditions, the principal source of variation in the price of orange juice, explains only a small share of the movement in orange juice futures prices.

This paper estimates the fraction of the variation in aggregate stock returns that can be attributed to various types of economic news. The first section relates stock returns to the arrival of information about macroeconomic performance. We find that our news proxies can explain about one-third of the variance in stock returns.

To examine the possibility that the stock market moves in response to information that does not enter our definition of news, the next section analyzes stock market reactions to identifiable world news. While news regarding wars, the Presidency, or significant changes in financial policies affects stock prices, our results cast doubt on the view that "qualitative news" can account for all the return variation that cannot be traced to macroeconomic innovations. This finding is supported by the observation that many of the largest market movements in recent years

DAVID M. CUTLER is a graduate student and JAMES M. POTERBA is Professor of Economics at MIT in Cambridge (MA 02139). LAWRENCE H. SUMMERS is Nathaniel Ropes Professor of Political Economy at Harvard in Cambridge (MA 02138). The authors are grateful to Peter Bernstein, Eugene Fama, Kenneth French, and Andrei Shleifer for helpful comments, to the National Science Foundation for financial support, and to DRI for data assistance. This research is part of the NBER Programs in Economic Fluctuations and Financial Markets. A data appendix is available from the Interdisciplinary Consortium for Political and Social Research in Ann Arbor, MI.

have occurred on days when there were no major news events.

Our concluding section argues that further understanding of asset price movements requires two types of research. The first should attempt to model price movements as functions of evolving consensus opinions about the implications of given pieces of information. The second should develop and test "propagation mechanisms" that can explain why shocks with small effects on discount rates or cash flows may have large effects on prices.

THE IMPORTANCE OF MACROECONOMIC NEWS

Here we seek to determine whether unexpected macroeconomic developments can explain a significant fraction of share price movements. We analyze monthly stock returns for the 1926-1985 period, as well as annual returns for the longer 1871–1986 period.

For each data set, our analysis has two parts. First, we estimate regression models relating each macroeconomic variable to its own history and that of the other variables. We use these models (vector autoregressions) to identify the unexpected component of each time series and to consider the explanatory power of these news measures in explaining stock returns. Second, we adopt a less structured approach to the examination of macroeconomic news. After controlling for the influence of lagged economic factors on prices, we measure the incremental explanatory power of current and future values of our macroeconomic time series.

Structured Vector Autoregression Evidence

We begin by analyzing monthly stock returns for the 1926–1985 period, using seven measures of monthly macroeconomic activity, chosen to measure both real and financial conditions:[1]

1. The logarithm of real dividend payments on the value-weighted New York Stock Exchange portfolio, computed as nominal dividends from the Center for Research in Security Prices data base deflated by the monthly Consumer Price Index.
2. The logarithm of industrial production.
3. The logarithm of the real money supply (M1).
4. The nominal long-term interest rate, measured as Moody's AAA corporate bond yield.
5. The nominal short-term interest rate, measured as the yield on three-month Treasury bills.
6. The monthly CPI inflation rate.
7. The logarithm of stock market volatility, defined following French, Schwert, and Stambaugh (1987) as the average squared daily return on the Standard & Poor's Composite Index within the month.

To isolate the news component of these seven macroeconomic series, we fit vector autoregressions relating the current value of each to its own lagged values and those of the other six series. Each equation also includes a set of indicator variables for different months. We treat the residuals from these equations (denoted $\hat{\zeta}_{it}$) as macroeconomic news and use them as explanatory variables for stock returns:

$$R_t = \alpha_0 + \alpha_1 * \hat{\zeta}_{1t} + \alpha_2 * \hat{\zeta}_{2t} + \alpha_3 * \hat{\zeta}_{3t} +$$
$$\alpha_4 * \hat{\zeta}_{4t} + \alpha_5 * \hat{\zeta}_{5t} + \alpha_6 * \hat{\zeta}_{6t} + \alpha_7 * \hat{\zeta}_{7t} + \epsilon_t. \quad (1)$$

R_t is the real, dividend-inclusive return on the value-weighted NYSE index, and the seven variables on the right-hand side are the macroeconomic news variables. The $\bar{R}^2$ for Equation (1) measures the fraction of the return variation that can be explained by our right-hand side variables. In other words, it measures the importance of these types of macroeconomic news in explaining stock price movements.[2]

Table 1 reports estimates of Equation (1) using monthly data for both 1926–1985 and 1946–1985. Several conclusions emerge from this table. First, macroeconomic news as we have defined it explains only about one-fifth of the movement in stock prices. Increasing the number of lagged values included in the VARs does not substantially alter this finding. Second, most of the macroeconomic news variables affect returns with their predicted signs and statistically significant coefficients.[3] For the full sample period, an unexpected 1% increase in real dividends raises share prices by about one-tenth of 1%, while a 1% increase in industrial production increases share values by about four-tenths of 1%. Both inflation and market volatility have negative and statistically significant effects on market returns. An unanticipated 1% rise in volatility lowers share prices by slightly less than 0.025%, so a doubling of volatility would lower prices by about 2.5%. The other macroeconomic innovations appear to have a less significant effect on share prices.

We examine the robustness of our findings by performing similar tests for the 1871–1986 period. As monthly macroeconomic time series are unavailable for this extended period, we focus on annual returns. We measure R_t as the January-to-January return on the Cowles/Standard & Poor's stock price series. This series was developed by Robert Shiller and was used in Poterba and Summers (1988). Our macroeconomic variables include the logarithm of real dividend payments during the year, the logarithm of real GNP from Romer (1988), the logarithm of real M1, the nominal long-term interest rate, the six-month commercial paper rate, and the inflation rate for the NNP deflator (all from Friedman and Schwartz, 1982), and the logarithm of stock market volatility, defined as the sum of squared monthly returns on the Cowles/S&P Index within the year.

TABLE 1
Restricted VAR Evidence on Macroeconomic News and Stock Returns

				Coefficients on Macroeconomic News Variables				
Lags in VAR	Real Dividends	Industrial Production	Real Money	Interest Rates Long	Interest Rates Short	Inflation	Volatility	$\bar{R}^2$
1926–1986 Sample (Monthly Data)								
3	0.081 (.011)	0.427 (.112)	0.195 (.152)	−2.64 (1.57)	−0.682 (.638)	−0.079 (.071)	−0.022 (.003)	0.185
6	0.094 (.012)	0.398 (.113)	0.074 (.158)	−2.18 (1.62)	−0.586 (.654)	−0.123 (.073)	−0.023 (.003)	0.186
12	0.116 (.014)	0.373 (.121)	0.066 (.165)	−1.91 (1.73)	−0.967 (.079)	−0.111 (.079)	−0.023 (.003)	0.188
24	0.138 (.016)	0.382 (.133)	0.155 (.182)	0.41 (2.02)	−1.340 (0.824)	−0.138 (.088)	−0.025 (.004)	0.187
1946–1985 Sample (Monthly Data)								
3	0.050 (.012)	0.100 (.166)	0.180 (.355)	−2.15 (1.24)	−1.23 (.522)	−0.075 (.059)	−0.017 (.003)	0.149
6	0.051 (.013)	0.287 (.186)	0.081 (.206)	−2.15 (1.31)	−1.22 (.546)	−0.110 (.062)	−0.018 (.003)	0.144
12	0.068 (.016)	0.245 (.193)	0.017 (.482)	−1.92 (1.42)	−1.73 (.602)	−0.114 (.072)	−0.017 (.003)	0.155
24	0.078 (.020)	0.073 (.235)	−0.304 (.567)	0.352 (1.83)	−2.21 (.794)	−0.148 (.095)	−0.020 (.004)	0.126
1871–1986 Sample (Annual Data)								
2	−0.024 (.180)	0.738* (.483)	0.150 (.613)	−0.021 (3.83)	−4.91 (1.90)	−0.716 (.532)	−0.006 (.029)	0.064
3	−0.074 (.186)	0.875* (.450)	0.235 (.639)	0.175 (4.12)	−5.23 (2.10)	−0.814 (.591)	−0.004 (.030)	0.064
5	−0.066 (.220)	0.810* (.530)	0.146 (.729)	0.696 (5.07)	−6.04 (2.36)	−0.418 (.671)	0.004 (.034)	0.022

The dependent variable is the real return on value-weighted NYSE. Estimates correspond to Equation (1), with standard errors in parentheses. The news variables are the logarithms of real dividends, industrial production, and real money supply, nominal long-term and short-term interest rates, inflation, and the logarithm of volatility. All VARs and the return equation include a time trend.
*Industrial Production is real NNP for the long-term sample period.

The results for the longer sample period, presented in the bottom panel of Table 1, are similar to those for the post-1926 period. When two lagged values of the annual series are used in defining news components, the $\bar{R}^2$ in the returns equation is 0.064. Longer lags in the first stage reduce the extent to which the news can explain returns; with five lagged values, the $\bar{R}^2$ declines to 0.022. Using annual data for the post-1925 period, the $\bar{R}^2$ for the two-lag equation is −0.003, and that for the regression including five lags is −0.061. The estimated coefficients on the macroeconomic surprises for the 1871–1985 period resemble those for the post-1925 monthly return sample, adjusted for the annual rather than monthly span of the dependent variable, with one notable exception: the real dividend innovation has a negative coefficient for the long sample, although its large standard error also permits a wide range of positive values.

Unrestricted Regression Evidence

The foregoing method of defining macroeconomic news suffers from three potential problems.

First, it does not capture new information about future macroeconomic conditions that is revealed in period t but not directly reflected in that period's variables. Second, if the models for measuring news are misspecified, our estimated residuals may not reflect new information accurately. If market participants operate with an information set larger than the one we have considered, our residuals may overstate the news content of contemporaneous series. Finally, there are timing issues associated with the release of macroeconomic information. The Consumer Price Index for month t, for example, is announced during month t + 1, but market participants may have some information about this variable during month t. These considerations motivate our less-structured approach to identifying the importance of macroeconomic news.

We implement such an approach by first regressing stock returns on the lagged values of our macroeconomic time series and then including current *and future* values of these time series in the regressions. The incremental $\bar{R}^2$ associated with these additional variables measures the importance of macroeconomic news in explaining stock returns.

This approach is not without shortcomings. It may understate the true explanatory power of news, because we still omit changes in expectations about the distant future that are not reflected in macroeconomic variables in period t or the near future. Conversely, if stock market movements attributable to variables outside our information set affect future macroeconomic activity, our approach of including future macroeconomic realizations will overstate the role of expectational revisions.

Table 2 presents results using different numbers of lagged and led values of the macroeconomic variables for the 1926–1985 sample of monthly data. The findings are supportive of the results using the more structured VAR approach. Lagged values of the macroeconomic variables we consider can explain less than 5% of the variance of returns. Including the contemporaneous values of the seven macroeconomic time series significantly raises the explanatory power of these equations. With only one lagged value of the series included, the $\bar{R}^2$ rises to 0.14, and with twenty-four lags of each variable the $\bar{R}^2$ is 0.29. Including the one- and two-period led values of the macro variables raises the $\bar{R}^2$ even more, to 0.29 when only one lagged value of the series is included and as high as 0.39 when the longer lags are included. Results for the postwar period, presented in the middle panel of Table 2, are consistent with those for the longer sample

period. The lagged regressors have somewhat greater explanatory power in the more recent period.

We also applied our less structured approach to the 1871–1986 annual data sample. The explanatory power of the regressions with only lagged values of macroeconomic variables is greater for annual than for monthly data, ranging from 0.078 with one lag of each variable to a high of 0.124 with five lags. Adding the contemporaneous values of the macroeconomic series again raises the $\bar{R}^2$, with the largest gain an increase from 0.078 to 0.210 when only one lagged value is included. These results are similar to those obtained using monthly data.

Table 2 also reports the $\bar{R}^2$ for annual equations including lagged, contemporaneous, and one *led* value of the macroeconomic data series. The $\bar{R}^2$ exceeds 0.50, but this almost surely overstates the effect of macroeconomic news on share prices, because it also includes the effect of higher share prices on economic outcomes within the following year.[4] Fischer and Merton (1984) show that stock returns in year t can explain more than half of the variation in GNP growth in year t + 1, suggesting a strong correlation between returns and subsequent economic activity. While the same problem arises in our monthly analysis, the possibility of large feedback from the market to the economy is substantially greater with annual data.

Our results are broadly consistent with earlier studies, such as Fama (1981): a substantial fraction of return variation cannot be explained by macroeconomic news. The central question in interpreting this evidence is whether the unexplained return movements are due to omitted macroeconomic news variables and other information about future cash flows and discount rates, or to other factors that may not affect rational expectations of these variables. Below we present some evidence designed to distinguish these views.

BIG NEWS AND BIG MOVES: ARE THEY RELATED?

The foregoing analysis excludes a variety of important sources of information, besides macroeconomic developments, that could affect share prices. Political developments that affect future policy expectations and international events such as wars that affect risk premiums should also be important in asset pricing.

This section examines the importance of these other factors in two ways. First, we study the stock market reaction to major non-economic events such as elections and international conflicts. Neiderhoffer (1971) conducted a similar investigation for a wider sample of events during the 1960s. Second, we ana-

TABLE 2

Unrestricted VAR Evidence on Macro News and Stock Returns

Number of Lags in Specification	Lagged	Lagged and Current	Lagged Current, and Led
		$\bar{R}^2$ for Equations Including:	
1926–1985 Sample (Monthly Data)			
1	0.005	0.139	0.292
3	0.010	0.192	0.333
6	0.018	0.208	0.343
12	0.034	0.250	0.360
24	0.035	0.289	0.393
1946–1985 Sample (Monthly Data)			
1	0.060	0.194	0.318
3	0.087	0.254	0.332
6	0.080	0.259	0.327
12	0.065	0.267	0.327
24	0.136	0.355	0.396
1871–1986 Sample (Annual Data)			
1	0.078	0.210	0.515
2	0.122	0.149	0.509
3	0.113	0.162	0.511
5	0.124	0.102	0.534

Each entry reports the $\bar{R}^2$ from a regression of the real value-weighted NYSE return (Cowles return in annual data) on k lagged values, k lagged values and the current value, or k lagged, two led, and the current value, of the seven macroeconomic series noted in Table 1. Column 1 reports k. For the annual data, only one led value is included.

59

lyze the largest stock market movements of the last fifty years and review coincident news reports to identify, where possible, the proximate causes of these moves.

We begin by analyzing stock market reactions to non-economic events. We identified a sample of such events using the "Chronology of Important World Events" from the *World Almanac*. We first excluded events that we thought were unlikely to affect the stock market. We narrowed our set of events still further by considering only those events that the *New York Times* carried as the lead story, and that the *New York Times* Business Section reported as having affected stock market participants. Winnowing the events in this way biases our sample toward those news items that are likely to have had the largest impact on stock prices. This should bias our results toward finding a large stock market reaction to the forty-nine political, military, and economic policy events in our sample.

Table 3 lists these forty-nine events along with

TABLE 3

Major Events and Changes in the S&P Index, 1941-1987

Event	Date	Percent Change
Japanese bomb Pearl Harbor	Dec. 8, 1941	−4.37
US declares war against Japan	Dec. 9, 1941	−3.23
Roosevelt defeats Dewey	Nov. 8, 1944	−0.15
Roosevelt dies	Apr. 13, 1945	1.07
Atomic bombs dropped on Japan:		
Hiroshima bomb	Aug. 6, 1945	0.27
Nagasaki bomb; Russia declares war	Aug. 9, 1945	1.65
Japanese surrender	Aug. 17, 1945	−0.54
Truman defeats Dewey	Nov. 3, 1948	−4.61
North Korea invades South Korea	June 26, 1950	−5.38
Truman to send US troops	June 27, 1950	−1.10
Eisenhower defeats Stevenson	Nov. 5, 1952	0.28
Eisenhower suffers heart attack	Sep. 26, 1955	−6.62
Eisenhower defeats Stevenson	Nov. 7, 1956	−1.03
U-2 shot down; US admits spying	May 9, 1960	0.09
Kennedy defeats Nixon	Nov. 9, 1960	0.44
Bay of Pigs invasion announced;	Apr. 17, 1961	0.47
Details released over several days	Apr. 18, 1961	−0.72
	Apr. 19, 1961	−0.59
Cuban missile crisis begins:		
Kennedy announces Russian buildup	Oct. 23, 1962	−2.67
Soviet letter stresses peace	Oct. 24, 1962	3.22
Formula to end dispute reached	Oct. 29, 1962	2.16
Kennedy assassinated;	Nov. 22, 1963	−2.81
Orderly transfer of power to Johnson	Nov. 26, 1963	3.98
US fires on Vietnamese ship	Aug. 4, 1964	−1.25
Johnson defeats Goldwater	Nov. 4, 1964	−0.05
Johnson withdraws from race, halts		
Vietnamese raids, urges peace talks	Apr. 1, 1968	2.53
Robert Kennedy assassinated	June 5, 1968	−0.49
Nixon defeats Humphrey	Nov. 6, 1968	0.16
Nixon imposes price controls, requests Federal tax cut, strengthens dollar	Aug. 16, 1971	3.21
Nixon defeats McGovern	Nov. 8, 1972	0.55
Haldeman, Ehrlichman, and Dean resign	Apr. 30, 1973	−0.24
Dean tells Senate about Nixon cover-up	June 25, 1973	−1.40
Agnew resigns	Oct. 10, 1973	−0.83
Carter defeats Ford	Nov. 3, 1976	−1.14
Volcker appointed to Fed	July 25, 1979	1.09
Fed announces major policy changes	Oct. 6, 1979	−1.25
Soviet Union invades Afghanistan	Dec. 26, 1979	0.11
Attempt to free Iranian hostages fails	Apr. 26, 1980	0.73
Reagan defeats Carter	Nov. 5, 1980	1.77
Reagan shot, NYSE closes early;	Mar. 30, 1981	−0.27
Reopens next day	Mar. 31, 1981	1.28
US Marines killed in Lebanon	Oct. 24, 1983	0.02
US invades Grenada	Oct. 25, 1983	0.29
Reagan defeats Mondale	Nov. 7, 1984	1.09
House votes for Tax Reform Act of 1986	Dec. 18, 1985	−0.40
Chernobyl nuclear reactor meltdown;	Apr. 29, 1986	−1.06
Details released over several days	Apr. 30, 1986	−2.07
Senate Committee votes for tax reform	May 8, 1986	−0.49
Greenspan named to replace Volcker	June 2, 1987	−0.47
Important Events		
Average Absolute Return		1.46
Standard Deviation of Returns		2.08
All Days Since 1941		
Average Absolute Return		0.56
Standard Deviation of Returns		0.82

the associated percentage changes in the Standard & Poor's Composite Stock Index. Some of the events are clearly associated with substantial movements in the aggregate market. On the Monday after President Eisenhower's heart attack in September 1955, for example, the market declined by 6.62%. On the Monday after the Japanese attack on Pearl Harbor, the market fell 4.37%. The orderly presidential transition after President Kennedy was assassinated coincided with a 3.98% market uptick, while the actual news of the assassination reduced share values by nearly 3%. On the two days in 1985 and 1986 when passage of the Tax Reform Act of 1986, the most significant tax legislation in three decades, became much more likely, aggregate market reactions were less than one-half of 1%.[5] For the set of events we analyze, the average absolute market move is 1.46% in contrast to 0.56% over the entire 1941–1987 period.

These findings suggest a surprisingly small effect of non-economic news, at least of the type we have identified, on share prices. The standard deviation (variance) of returns on the news days we have identified is 2.08% (4.33%), compared with the daily average of 0.82% (0.67%) for the post-1941 period. This implies that the return on a typical event day in Table 3 is as variable as the cumulative return on 6.40 (4.33/0.67) "ordinary" days. If every day involved as much news as the forty-nine days in this sample, the standard deviation of annual returns would be 32% instead of the actual 13%. As most days do not witness information release as important as that on the days in Table 3, it may be difficult to explain the "missing variation" in stock returns with events of this kind.

An alternative strategy for identifying the importance of news is to examine large changes in share prices and related news developments. Table 4 lists the fifty largest one-day returns on the Standard & Poor's Composite Stock Index since 1946, along with the *New York Times* account of fundamental factors that affected prices.

It is difficult to link major market moves to release of economic or other information. On several of these days, the *New York Times* actually reported that there were no apparent explanations for the market's rise or decline. At the other extreme, some of the days clearly mark important information releases; the 1948 election outcome, President Eisenhower's heart attack, and the announcement of President Kennedy's success in rolling back the 1962 steel price increase are examples. On most of the sizable return days, however, the information that the press cites as the cause of the market move is not particularly important. Press reports on subsequent days also fail to reveal any convincing accounts of why future profits or discount rates might have changed. Our inability to identify the fundamental shocks that accounted for these significant market moves is difficult to reconcile with the view that such shocks account for most of the variation in stock returns.

CONCLUSIONS

Our results suggest the difficulty of explaining as much as half of the variance in aggregate stock prices on the basis of publicly available news bearing on fundamental values. The results parallel Roll's (1988) finding that most of the variation in returns for individual stocks cannot be explained using readily available measures of new information. Of course, it is possible that we have failed to consider some type of news that actually accounts for a significant fraction of asset price volatility. Although the hypothesis that stock prices move in response to news that is observed by market participants but not by investigators studying the market is irrefutable, we are skeptical of this

possibility. News important enough to account for large swings in the demand for corporate equities would almost surely leave traces in either official economic statistics or media reports about market movements.

The problem of accounting for price changes on the basis of fundamental values is not confined to the overall stock market. Studies of price behavior in settings where fundamental values can be measured directly have similar trouble in explaining prices. The classic example is closed-end mutual funds, discussed by Malkiel and Firstenberg (1978). These funds have traded at both discounts and premiums relative to their net asset value during the last twenty years. At any moment, the cross-sectional dispersion in discounts is substantial and difficult to link to fundamental factors. The widely documented patterns in stock returns over weekends, holidays, and different calendar periods, summarized in Thaler (1987a, 1987b), are also difficult to attribute to news about fundamentals, because fundamental values are not likely to move systematically over these periods.

The view that movements in stock prices reflect something other than news about fundamental values is consistent with evidence on the correlates of ex post returns. If prices were periodically driven away from fundamental values by something other than news but ultimately returned to fundamentals, one would expect a tendency for returns to be low when the market is high relative to some indicator of fundamental value, and high when the market is low relative to fundamental value. Such patterns emerge from studies of ex post returns that use the past level of prices, earnings, and dividends as indicators of fundamental value.[6]

Our results underscore the problem of accounting for the variation in asset prices. Throwing up one's hands and simply saying that there is a great deal of irrationality that gives rise to "fads" is not constructive. Two more concrete lines of attack strike us as potentially worthwhile. First, volatility may reflect changes that take place in average assessments of given sets of information regarding fundamental values as investors re-examine existing data or present new arguments. This view is suggested by French and Roll's (1986) finding that return volatility is greater when the market is open than when it is closed.

Second, it may be fruitful in accounting for volatility to explore propagation mechanisms that could cause relatively small shocks to have large effects on market prices.[7] "Informational freeloading" on observed asset prices may have something to do with market volatility. In a world where most investors accept prices as indicators of fundamental value, small changes in the supply of or demand for secu-

TABLE 4

Fifty Largest Post-War Movements in S&P Index and
Their "Causes"

	Date	Percent Change	New York Times Explanation*		Date	Percent Change	New York Times Explanation*
1	Oct. 19, 1987	−20.47	Worry over dollar decline and trade deficit, fear of US not supporting dollar.	28	Nov. 1, 1978	3.97	Steps by Carter to strengthen dollar.
2	Oct. 21, 1987	9.10	Interest rates continue to fall; deficit talks in Washington; bargain hunting.	29	Oct. 22, 1987	−3.92	Iranian attack on Kuwaiti oil terminal; fall in markets overseas; analysts predict lower prices.
3	Oct. 26, 1987	−8.28	Fear of budget deficits; margin calls; reaction to falling foreign stocks.	30	Oct. 29, 1974	3.91	Decline in short-term interest rates; ease in future monetary policy; lower oil prices.
4	Sep. 3, 1946	−6.73	"No basic reason for the assault on prices."	31	Nov. 3, 1982	3.91	Relief over small Democratic victories in House.
5	May 28, 1962	−6.68	Kennedy forces rollback of steel price hike.	32	Feb. 19, 1946	−3.70	Fear of wage-price controls lowering corporate profits; labor unrest.
6	Sep. 26, 1955	−6.62	Eisenhower suffers heart attack.	33	Jun. 19, 1950	−3.70	Korean War continues; fear of long war.
7	Jun. 26, 1950	−5.38	Outbreak of Korean War.				
8	Oct. 20, 1987	5.33	Investors looking for "quality stocks."	34	Nov. 18, 1974	−3.67	Increase in unemployment rate; delay in coal contract approval; fear of new mid-East war.
9	Sep. 9, 1946	−5.24	Labor unrest in maritime and trucking industries.	35	Apr. 22, 1980	3.64	Fall in short-term interest rates; analysts express optimism.
10	Oct. 16, 1987	−5.16	Fear of trade deficit; fear of higher interest rates; tension with Iran.	36	Oct. 31, 1946	3.63	Increase in commodity prices; prospects for price decontrol.
11	May 27, 1970	5.02	Rumors of change in economic policy. "The stock surge happened for no fundamental reason."	37	Jul. 6, 1955	3.57	Market optimism triggered by GM stock split.
				38	Jun. 4, 1962	−3.55	Profit taking; continuation of previous week's decline.
12	Sep. 11, 1986	−4.81	Foreign governments refuse to lower interest rates; crackdown on triple witching announced.	39	Aug. 20, 1982	3.54	Congress passes Reagan tax bill; prime rate falls.
13	Aug. 17, 1982	4.76	Interest rates decline.	40	Dec. 3, 1987	−3.53	Computerized selling; November retail sales low.
14	May 29, 1962	4.65	Optimistic brokerage letters; institutional and corporate buying; suggestions of tax cut.	41	Sep. 19, 1974	3.50	Treasury Secretary Simon predicts decline in short-term interest rates.
15	Nov. 3, 1948	−4.61	Truman defeats Dewey.	42	Dec. 9, 1946	3.44	Coal strike ends; railroad freight rates increase.
16	Oct. 9, 1974	4.60	Ford to reduce inflation and interest rates.	43	Jun. 29, 1962	3.44	"Stock prices advanced strongly chiefly because they had gone down so long and so far that a rally was due."
17	Feb. 25, 1946	−4.57	Weakness in economic indicators over past week.				
18	Oct. 23, 1957	4.49	Eisenhower urges confidence in economy.	44	Sep. 5, 1946	3.43	"Replacement buying" after earlier fall.
19	Oct. 29, 1987	4.46	Deficit reduction talks begin; durable goods orders increase; rallies overseas.	45	Oct. 30, 1987	3.33	Dollar stabilizes; increase in prices abroad.
20	Nov. 5, 1948	−4.40	Further reaction to Truman victory over Dewey.	46	Jan. 27, 1975	3.27	IBM wins appeal of antitrust case; short-term interest rates decline.
21	Nov. 6, 1946	−4.31	Profit taking; Republican victories in elections presage deflation.	47	Oct. 6, 1982	3.27	Interest rates fall; several large companies announce increase in profits.
22	Oct. 7, 1974	4.19	Hopes that President Ford would announce strong anti-inflationary measures.	48	Jul. 19, 1948	−3.26	Worry over Russian blockade of Berlin; possibility of more price controls.
23	Nov. 30, 1987	−4.18	Fear of dollar fall.				
24	Jul. 12, 1974	4.08	Reduction in new loan demands; lower inflation previous month.	49	Nov. 30, 1982	3.22	"Analysts were at a loss to explain why the Dow jumped so dramatically in the last two hours."
25	Oct. 15, 1946	4.01	Meat prices decontrolled; prospects of other decontrols.	50	Oct. 24, 1962	3.22	Krushchev promises no rash decisions on Cuban Missile Crisis; calls for US-Soviet summit.
26	Oct. 25, 1982	−4.00	Disappointment over Federal Reserve's failure to cut discount rates.				
27	Nov. 26, 1963	3.98	Confidence in Johnson after Kennedy assassination.				

*Per the financial section or front page.

rities can have large effects on prices.

Suppose, for example, that all investors desired to hold the market portfolio in order to achieve optimum diversification, except for one investor who wishes to concentrate holdings on a single security regardless of its price. The equilibrium price of this security would be infinite. This example, while extreme because speculators would intervene to sell an irrationally demanded stock well before its price approached infinity, makes an important point. If many investors accept market prices as indicators of value and so do not trade on the basis of their own assessment of values, market values will be more susceptible to those who trade on the basis of their own opinions.

The possibility that many investors do not formulate their own estimates of fundamental value is consistent with trading patterns surrounding the sharp stock market decline of October 1987.[8] Despite the market's dramatic drop, the vast majority of shares were not traded. This is only explicable if investors rely on market prices to gauge values, or if investors received information that led to significant downward revisions in fundamental values. It seems difficult to identify the information that would support the second explanation.

[1] Most of the monthly data series were drawn from the Data Resources, Inc., data base. Money supply data prior to 1960 come from Friedman and Schwartz (1963). More recent data are from various *Federal Reserve Bulletins*. Moody's corporate bond yield is from the Board of Governors of the Federal Reserve System, *Banking and Monetary Statistics: 1914-41 and 1941-70*, and various issues of the *Federal Reserve Bulletin*.

[2] We report $\bar{R}^2$ because it is a measure of goodness of fit that corrects for the expected explanatory power of additional regressors. While adding irrelevant regressors to an equation will raise the equation's R^2, it will not affect the expected value of the $\bar{R}^2 = (T-1)/(T-K)R^2 - (K-1)/(T-K)$, where T is the total number of observations, and K the number of degrees of freedom used in estimation.

[3] A related investigation by Chen, Roll, and Ross (1986) showed that various macroeconomic "factors" have positive prices. Their study is concerned with explaining the ex ante return on different securities, however, while ours considers the ex post movements in prices that result from macroeconomic innovations.

[4] The future dividend variable is the major source of the impressive fit when led values are included. The link between these series, however, is likely to be much stronger than would be the case if it reflected only information about t + 1 dividends that was released (and incorporated in prices) at t. In a model where dividends adjust to lagged share prices, as in Marsh and Merton (1987), future dividends are associated with current prices, but the principal causality is reversed.

[5] Cutler (1988) examines the events leading up to the Tax Reform Act in greater detail. The small aggregate market reaction on these days is matched by little abnormal cross-sectional variation in stock returns, despite the substantial differences in the law's likely impact across firms.

[6] Campbell and Shiller (1988), Cutler, Poterba, and Summers (1988), Fama and French (1988b), Poterba and Summers (1988), and Shiller (1984) find evidence consistent with this view. Models that explain the predictability of returns on the basis of trading by uninformed "noise traders" have been discussed by Black (1986) and DeLong, Shleifer, Summers, and Waldman (1987).

[7] Mandelbrot (1966) presents a rational model in which apparently small news releases can trigger large revaluations in expected future profits.

[8] Frankel (1989) suggests a number of stylized facts regarding foreign exchange markets, such as the short-term focus of most traders, that are consistent with the absence of independent assessment of fundamentals by most investors.

REFERENCES

Black, Fischer. "Noise." *Journal of Finance* 41 (July 1986), pp. 529-542.

Campbell, John Y., and Robert Shiller. "Stock Prices, Earnings, and Expected Dividends." *Journal of Finance* 43 (July 1988), pp. 661-676.

Chen, Nai-Fu, Richard Roll, and Stephen Ross. "Economic Forces and the Stock Market." *Journal of Business* 59 (July 1986), pp. 383-404.

Cutler, David M. "Tax Reform and the Stock Market: An Asset Price Approach." *American Economic Review* 78 (December 1988).

Cutler, David M., James M. Poterba, and Lawrence H. Summers. "Why Do Dividend Yields Forecast Stock Returns?" Massachusetts Institute of Technology, 1988.

DeLong, J. Bradford, Andrei Shleifer, Lawrence Summers, and Robert Waldman. "The Economics of Noise Traders." Harvard University, 1987.

Fama, Eugene. "Stock Returns, Real Activity, Inflation, and Money." *American Economic Review* 71 (1981), pp. 545-565.

Fama, Eugene, and Kenneth French. "Dividend Yields and Expected Stock Returns." Forthcoming in *Journal of Financial Economics*, 1988.

———. "Permanent and Transitory Components in Stock Prices." *Journal of Political Economy* 96 (April 1988), pp. 246-273.

Fischer, Stanley, and Robert Merton. "Macroeconomics and Finance: The Role of the Stock Market." *Carnegie-Rochester Conference Series in Public Policy* 21 (1984), pp. 57-108.

Frankel, Jeffrey. "Fixed Exchange Rates: Experience Versus Theory." *Journal of Portfolio Management*, Winter 1989, pp. 45-54.

Frankel, Jeffrey, and Richard Meese. "Are Exchange Rates Excessively Variable?" in S. Fischer, ed., NBER *Macroeconomics Annual 1987*. Cambridge: MIT Press, 1987, pp. 117-152.

French, Kenneth, and Richard Roll. "Stock Return Variances: The Arrival of Information and the Reaction of Traders." *Journal of Financial Economics* 17 (September 1986), pp. 5-26.

French, Kenneth, G. William Schwert, and Robert Stambaugh. "Expected Stock Returns and Stock Market Volatility." *Journal of Financial Economics* 19 (September 1987), pp. 3-30.

Friedman, Milton, and Anna Schwartz. *A Monetary History of the United States, 1867-1960*. Princeton: Princeton University Press, 1963.

———. *Monetary Trends in the United States and the United Kingdom*. Cambridge: Cambridge University Press, 1982.

Malkiel, Burton G., and Paul B. Firstenberg. "A Winning Strategy for an Efficient Market." *Journal of Portfolio Management*, Summer 1978, pp. 20-25.

Mandelbrot, Benoit. "Forecasts of Future Prices, Unbiased Markets, and Martingale Models." *Journal of Business*, 39 (Special Supplement, January 1966), pp. 242-255.

Marsh, Terry, and Robert C. Merton. "Dividend Behavior and the Aggregate Stock Market." *Journal of Business* 60 (January 1987), pp. 1-40.

Neiderhoffer, Victor. "The Analysis of World Events and Stock Prices." *Journal of Business* 44 (April 1971), pp. 193-219.

Poterba, James, and Lawrence Summers. "Mean Reversion in Stock Prices: Evidence and Implications." Forthcoming in *Journal of Financial Economics*, 1988.

Roll, Richard. "Orange Juice and Weather." *American Economic Review* 74 (December 1984), pp. 861-880.

——. "R²." *Journal of Finance* 43 (July 1988), pp. 541-566.

Romer, Christina. "The Prewar Business Cycle Reconsidered: New Estimates of Gross National Product, 1869-1908." Forthcoming in *Journal of Political Economy*.

Schwert, William. "Why Does Stock Market Volatility Change Over Time?" Working Paper GPB-8711, William Simon Graduate School of Management, University of Rochester, 1987.

Shiller, Robert. "Do Stock Prices Move Too Much to be Justified by Subsequent Dividends?" *American Economic Review* 71 (1981), pp. 421-436.

——. "Stock Prices and Social Dynamics." *Brookings Papers on Economic Activity* 1984:2, pp. 457-498.

Thaler, Richard. "Anomalies: The January Effect." *Journal of Economic Perspectives* 1 (Summer 1987), pp. 197-201.

——. "Anomalies: Weekend, Holiday, Turn of the Month, and Intraday Effects." *Journal of Economic Perspectives* 1 (Fall 1987), pp. 169-178.

The complexity of the stock market

". . . a web of interrelated return effects."

Bruce I. Jacobs and Kenneth N. Levy

Investment theory and practice have evolved rapidly and tumultuously in recent years. Many placed the Efficient Market Hypothesis (EMH) and the Capital Asset Pricing Model (CAPM) on pedestals in the 1970s, only to see them come crashing down in the 1980s. In explaining why such theories cannot represent the true complexity of security pricing, we suggest new approaches to coping with the market's complexity. To do so, we follow a taxonomy from the sciences.

Scientists classify systems into three types — ordered, complex, and random.[1] Ordered systems are simple and predictable, such as the neatly arranged lattice of carbon atoms in a diamond crystal. Similarly, Newton's Laws of Motion are a simple set of rules that accurately describe the movement of physical objects. At the other extreme, random systems are inherently unpredictable; an example is the random behavior, or Brownian Motion, of gas molecules.

Complex systems fall somewhere between the domains of order and randomness.[2] The field of molecular biology exemplifies complexity. The mysteries of DNA can be unraveled only with the aid of computational science. The human mind alone cannot cope with DNA's complexity, nor do simple theories suffice.

The stock market, too, is a complex system.[3] Security pricing is not merely random, nor are simple theories adequate to explain market operation. Rather, the market is permeated by a web of interrelated return effects. Substantial computational power is needed to disentangle and model these return regularities.

THE EVOLUTION OF INVESTMENT PRACTICE

Before the 1970s, the investment norm was security analysis and stock selection. In a traditional, compartmentalized approach, security analysts, technicians, and economists all funneled their insights to portfolio managers. The market was viewed as complex, in the sense that no single human mind could master all the knowledge needed for optimal decision-making. Coordinating the insights of multiple participants, however, is not a simple task. Needless to say, this approach has generally produced unsatisfactory results.

The EMH mounted a frontal assault on the traditional mode of investment management. In an efficient market, prices fully reflect all available information. With its flood of information and countless participants, the U.S. stock market was regarded by academicians as highly efficient. It was thought that no one could beat the market, with the possible exception of insiders. By the mid-1970s, the EMH had substantial empirical support, and was a central paradigm in finance.

The revolutionary concept of passive management was a natural outgrowth of the EMH. If security returns are random and unpredictable, then only a passive approach makes sense. Index funds that were introduced to the investment community in the mid-1970s soon blossomed in popularity.

BRUCE I. JACOBS and KENNETH N. LEVY are principals of Jacobs Levy Equity Management in Fairfield, N.J. (07006). An expanded version of this article is forthcoming in *Managing Institutional Assets*, edited by Frank Fabozzi, to be published by Ballinger Publishing, and it also forms the basis for *A Revolution in Common Stock Management: Exploiting Market Inefficiencies and Forecasting Security Returns*, by Jacobs and Levy, to be published by Dow Jones-Irwin.

Since the late 1970s, though, there has been a proliferation of empirical results uncovering security pricing patterns, or return regularities. In fact, many of these effects have long been part of market folklore. These include the low P/E, small-firm, and January effects.

Thomas Kuhn, the scientific historian, refers to such evidence of departure from conventional theory as "anomalies." In his words, "discovery commences with the awareness of anomaly, i.e., with the recognition that nature has somehow violated the paradigm-induced expectations that govern normal science" [1970, p. 52]. In recent years, investment theory has been undergoing such a process of discovery.[4]

At first, academics rallied to defend the EMH. Tests of market efficiency are joint tests of the effect studied and the validity of the asset pricing model used to adjust for risk. Perhaps anomalies were due solely to deficiencies in risk measurement. Yet anomalies have been shown to be robust to asset pricing models, including the CAPM and Arbitrage Pricing Theory (APT). By the early 1980s, there were undeniable chinks in the armor of the EMH.

Investors have also sought to benefit from market anomalies by using simple rules, such as buying low P/E stocks. Others have tilted toward smaller-size or higher-yielding stocks. These investors consider the stock market an ordered system; they believe that simple rules will provide consistent and predictable returns.

What has recently become evident, however, is that the market is not a simple, ordered system. In a number of instances, we have documented a pervasive and complex web of interrelated return effects. This web must first be disentangled to allow us to distinguish real effects from mere proxies. Moreover, some return effects do not produce consistent rewards. Thus, the optimal investment strategy is not as simple as tilting toward yesterday's anomalies.

Nevertheless, the indexers' nihilistic view of the market as a random system is unjustified. The market is not random, but rather complex. Computational systems can be designed to grapple with its complexity. Besides being objective and rigorous, such systems are also fully coordinated, unlike the more traditional compartmentalized approaches. Beneath the complexity of the market lie enormous inefficiency and substantial investment opportunity.

WEB OF RETURN REGULARITIES

Figure 1 displays some interrelated return effects. The various connections shown between pairs of effects have been reported by previous studies.[5] For example, the small-size effect and the January

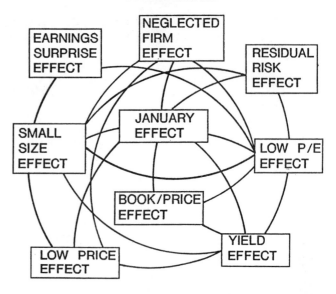

FIGURE 1

A WEB OF SOME INTERRELATED RETURN EFFECTS

effect are related, as it has been claimed that much of the annual outperformance of small stocks occurs in the month of January. The small-size and low P/E effects also are related. Because stocks with lower-than-average P/E ratios tend to be smaller in size, a natural question arises as to whether the size effect and P/E effect are two separate forces, or merely two different ways of measuring the same underlying phenomenon.

Many researchers have addressed this issue by examining two return effects jointly. Some conclude that the superior performance of small capitalization stocks relates to their tendency to have lower P/E ratios, while others find that low P/E stocks outperform simply because they are smaller in size. Still another viewpoint maintains that neglected securities outperform, and that low P/E and small size both proxy for this underlying effect.

While some previous academic studies have examined two or three return effects simultaneously, their findings often conflict with one another. This arises from the use of different methodologies, different time periods, and different company samples. But more fundamentally, conflicting results arise from failure to disentangle other related effects. Only a joint study of return effects in a unified framework can distinguish between real effects and illusory ones.

Consider the determinants of an individual's blood pressure. A medical researcher would not limit the analysis arbitrarily to just one or two explanatory variables, such as age and weight. More accurate evaluation can be obtained by including additional variables, such as exercise and diet. Of course, all these measures are somewhat correlated with one another.

But they may all have independent predictive content.

The same holds true for the stock market: Many forces affect stock returns; some of them may be correlated, but considering only a few can produce highly misleading results.

DISENTANGLING AND PURIFYING RETURNS

The standard approach to measuring a return effect, such as low P/E, first screens for a set of stocks below a given P/E ratio, or selects the lowest quintile of stocks as ranked by P/E. Portfolio returns are then calculated and compared to those of the universe. Any differences are ascribed to the low P/E effect. But, a low P/E portfolio by its nature will be biased unintentionally toward certain related attributes, such as higher yield, and show heavy representation in certain industries, such as utilities. Screening or quintiling procedures consider only one attribute at a time, while assuming that related effects do not matter at all. We refer to the returns produced by such methods as "naive."

The low P/E effect, measured naively, is contaminated by other forces. An oil price shock or an accident at a nuclear power plant, for instance, will have a major impact on utilities, which will be reflected in the returns of the low P/E portfolio. While fundamentals such as oil prices have no intrinsic relationship to the low P/E effect, they can confound its naive measurement.

In two papers we have introduced the alternative approach of disentangling and purifying return effects [ICFA, 1988, and FAJ, May/June 1988]. "Pure" return attributions result from a simultaneous analysis of all attribute and industry effects using multiple regression. Returns to each equity characteristic are purified by neutralizing the impact of all other effects. For example, the pure payoff to low P/E is disentangled from returns associated with related attributes, such as higher yield.

Conceptually, the pure return to low P/E arises from a lower P/E portfolio that is market-like in all other respects; that is, it has the same industry weights and the same average characteristics, such as yield and capitalization, as the market. Hence, any differential returns to such a portfolio must be attributable to the low P/E characteristic, because it is immunized from all other exposures that might contaminate returns.

ADVANTAGES OF DISENTANGLING

The pure returns that arise from disentangling eliminate the proxying problems inherent in naive returns. The unique insights from studying pure returns have many practical benefits for investment management.

When we distinguish between real effects and proxies, we find that some closely related effects are in fact distinct of one another. For instance, small size, low P/E, and neglect exist as three separate return effects in pure form. Each should be modeled individually, which provides greater explanatory power.

Conversely, some naive return effects merely proxy for one another, and vanish in pure form. Half of the outperformance of small stocks, for example, is reported to occur in January. But the small-firm effect, measured naively, arises from a bundle of related attributes. Smaller firms tend to be more neglected, and informational uncertainty is resolved at year-end as these firms close their books. This year-end reduction in uncertainty might induce a January seasonal return. Furthermore, smaller firms tend to be more volatile and are more commonly held by taxable investors, so they may be subject to heavier year-end tax-loss selling pressure. The abatement of selling pressure in January may lead to a price bounce-back.

We find the January small-firm seasonal vanishes when measured properly in pure form. Purifying the size effect of related characteristics, such as tax-loss selling, reveals the January size seasonal to be a mere proxy. The optimal investment approach models the underlying causes directly. Because not all small firms benefit from tax-loss rebound, a strategy that directs the purchase of smaller firms at year-end is only second-best.

While we find some return effects to be real, and others to be illusory, we also find the power of some pure return effects to exceed their naive counterparts by far. This is true, for example, of the return reversal effect. This effect represents the tendency of prices to overshoot and then correct, hence the term "reversal." Yet if a jump in price is due to a pleasant earnings surprise, the superior performance will persist and not reverse. Hence, disentangling return reversal from related effects, such as earnings surprise, results in a stronger, more consistent reversal measure.

Disentangling also reveals the true nature of the various return effects. For example, low P/E stocks are usually considered defensive. But pure returns to low P/E perform no differently in down markets than in up markets. The defensiveness of low P/E in naive form arises because it proxies for defensive attributes, such as high yield, and defensive industries, such as utilities. In fact, low P/E stocks are not the safest harbor in times of uncertainty. Rather, low P/E is an imperfect surrogate for truly safe havens, such as

67

higher yield.

Additionally, pure returns are more predictable than their naive counterparts. Pure returns possess cleaner time-series properties because they are not contaminated by proxying. For example, a time series of naive returns to the low P/E effect is buffeted by many extraneous forces, such as oil price shocks to low P/E utility stocks. In contrast, pure returns are immunized from such incidental forces, and thus can be predicted more accurately.

A major benefit of disentangling is that pure return effects avoid redundancies, and hence are additive. This allows us to model each return effect individually, and then to aggregate these attribute return forecasts to form predicted security returns. Moreover, by considering a large number of return effects, we obtain a very rich description of security pricing.

EVIDENCE OF INEFFICIENCY

Previous research on market anomalies taken one at a time has not added to the weight of evidence contravening market efficiency. That is, if the size, P/E, and neglect effects, all measured naively, proxy for the same underlying cause, they all represent "photographs" of the same anomaly taken from different angles. We have documented, however, the existence of many contemporaneous "pure" return effects. These separate photographs of many distinct anomalies, all taken from the same angle, constitute the strongest evidence to date of market inefficiency.

Calendar-related anomalies represent additional evidence of market inefficiency. We find that return patterns such as the day-of-the-week and January effects cannot be explained by considerations of risk or value, and thus cast further doubt on the EMH [FAJ, November/December 1988].

Return effects are also contrary to current asset pricing theories, such as the CAPM, the multi-factor CAPM, and the APT. For example, the CAPM posits that systematic risk, or beta, is the only characteristic that should receive compensation. Other considerations, such as a firm's size, or the month of the year, should be unrelated to security returns.

Figure 2 displays cumulative pure returns to beta in excess of market returns for the years 1978 through 1987. These returns derive from a one cross-sectional standard deviation of exposure to high beta, roughly equivalent to a sixteenth percentile ranking. While in the early years the beta attribute provided positive returns, its returns were negative thereafter. These pure returns may differ from other studies, because of our control for related attributes such as price volatility. The fact that pure returns to beta did

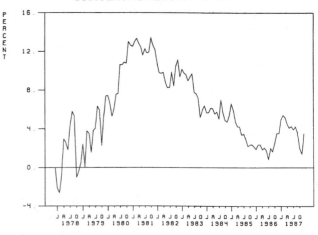

FIGURE 2
CUMULATIVE RETURN TO BETA

not accumulate positively over the period from July 1982 to August 1987, one of the strongest bull markets in history, casts serious doubt on the CAPM.

The existence of return effects also poses a challenge to the multi-factor CAPM.[6] Even the APT cannot account for the existence of several market anomalies. In fact, it appears doubtful that any meaningful definition of risk is as transient as some return effects. Thus, the weight of recent empirical evidence has buried the EMH. Also, while current asset pricing theories may contain elements of truth, none is fully descriptive of security pricing.

VALUE MODELING IN AN INEFFICIENT MARKET

In a reasonably efficient market, prices tend to reflect underlying fundamentals. An investor superior at gathering information or perceiving value will be suitably rewarded.

In an inefficient market, prices may respond slowly to new information and need not reflect underlying fundamentals. Given the substantial evidence of market inefficiency, the efficacy of value modeling is an open question. We have examined this issue by exploring the quintessential value model — the Dividend Discount Model (DDM) [FAJ, July/August 1988, and ICFA, 1989].

We find the DDM to be significantly biased toward stocks with certain attributes, such as high yield and low P/E.[7] In fact, some have argued that the only reason such attributes have positive payoffs is because they are highly correlated with DDM value. Further, they maintain that a properly implemented DDM will subsume these return effects.

We test this notion directly by incorporating a DDM in our disentangled framework. We find the DDM's return predictive power to be significantly weaker than that of many other equity attributes.

Hence, return effects such as P/E are not subsumed by the DDM. Rather, equity attributes emerge important in their own right, and the DDM is shown to be but a small part of the security pricing story.

The DDM embodies a particular view of the world, namely "going concern" value. But there are other sensible notions of value. For instance, current yield is an important consideration for endowment funds with restrictions against invading principal. Such endowments may be willing to pay up for higher-yielding stocks. And, in today's market environment, breakup value and leveraged buyout value have taken on increased significance. Thus, there are several competing and legitimate notions of value.

Also, we find the efficacy of value models varies over time, and often predictably. For instance, the effectiveness of the DDM depends on market conditions. Because the DDM discounts future dividends out to a distant horizon, it is a forward-looking model. When the market rises, investors become optimistic and extend their horizons. They are more willing to rely on DDM expectations. When the market falls, however, investors become myopic, and prefer more tangible attributes such as current yield.

In a price-inefficient market, the blind pursuit of DDM value is a questionable approach. Moreover, other value yardsticks clearly matter. We find that some rather novel implementations of value models offer substantial promise.

RISK MODELING VERSUS RETURN MODELING

While the existence of anomalies remains a puzzle for asset pricing theories, substantial progress has been made in the practice of portfolio risk control. In recent years, several equity risk models have become commercially available. Some are APT-based, and rely on factors derived empirically from historical security return covariances. These unnamed factors are sometimes related to pervasive economic forces.

Another, perhaps more common, approach relies on prespecified accounting and market-related data. Intuitive notions of risk, such as arise from company size or financial leverage, are first identified. Then, composite risk factors are formed by combining a number of underlying fundamental data items selected to capture various aspects of that type of risk. One well-known system, for instance, defines a successful firm risk factor in terms of historical price, earnings, dividend, and consensus expectational data.

Multi-factor risk models work quite well for risk measurement, risk control (portfolio optimization), and related tasks, such as performance analysis.

Both APT and composite factors are fairly stable over time. This is desirable, because meaningful definitions of a firm's risk do not change from day to day. Hence, such measures are eminently sensible for risk modeling purposes.

However, we find that the various components of composite factors often behave quite differently. For instance, each of the components of the successful company risk factor has a unique relationship to security returns. While historical relative price strength exhibits a strong January seasonal (because historical price weakness proxies for potential tax-loss selling), other fundamental components, such as earnings growth, have no seasonal pattern. Rather than combining these measures into one composite factor, we can model them more effectively individually.

Moreover, effects like return reversal and earnings surprise are ephemeral in nature, and thus unrelated to firm risk. Yet, they represent profitable niches in the market. These return-generating factors must be modeled individually, because their information content would be lost through aggregation. Hence, disaggregated measures are superior for return modeling. The use of numerous and narrowly defined measures permits a rich representation of the complexity of security pricing.

PURE RETURN EFFECTS

We find that pure returns to attributes can be classified into two categories. The distinction is best shown graphically. Figure 3 displays cumulative pure returns in excess of the market to the return reversal and small-size effects for the period 1978 through 1987.[8] Clearly, return reversal provides very consistent payoffs, while the small-size effect does not. Our classification system relates not only to the consistency of the payoffs, but also to the inherent nature of the attributes. This will become apparent shortly.

The pure payoff to return reversal is remarkably powerful. It provided a cumulative return, gross of transaction costs, of 257% in excess of the market, and "worked" in the right direction over 95% of the time. We refer to these market niches that produce persistent rewards as "anomalous pockets of inefficiency" (APIs), because they are anomalous to the EMH and represent instances of opportunity.

API strategies can require very high portfolio turnover, because the particular stocks exhibiting the desired characteristics change constantly. Such strategies include purchasing recent laggards to capture return reversal, or emphasizing stocks with recent pleasant earnings surprises.

We suggest exploiting these effects as trading overlays, because no additional transaction costs are

69

FIGURE 3
CUMULATIVE PURE RETURNS

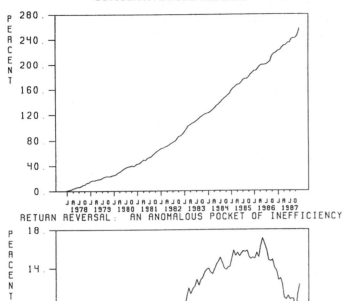

RETURN REVERSAL: AN ANOMALOUS POCKET OF INEFFICIENCY

SMALL SIZE: AN EMPIRICAL RETURN REGULARITY

ANOMALOUS POCKETS OF INEFFICIENCY

Return reversal relates to the concept of "noise" in security prices, that is, price movements induced by trading unrelated to fundamentals. The return reversal effect has psychological underpinnings. Investors tend to overreact to world events and economic news, as well as to company-specific information. Moreover, technical traders exacerbate price moves by chasing short-term trends. These types of behavior lead to overshooting and subsequent reversion in stock prices.

Another API relates to the earnings estimate revisions of Wall Street security analysts. We refer to this as the "trends in analysts' earnings estimates effect," for reasons that will soon become apparent. Upward revisions in a stock's consensus earnings estimates generally are followed by outperformance, as are downward revisions by underperformance.

The trends in estimates effect may be attributable in part to slow investor reaction to earnings estimate revisions. But it also relates to the psychology of Wall Street analysts, specifically to their herd instinct. When leading analysts raise their earnings estimate for a stock, clients will buy. Secondary analysts will then follow suit, and there will be more buying pressure.

Also, individual analysts tend to be averse to forecast reversals. Suppose an analyst had been forecasting $2 of earnings per share, but now believes the best estimate to be $1. Rather than admitting to a bad forecast, the analyst often shaves the estimate by a nickel at a time and hopes no one notices.

These psychological factors give a momentum to earnings revisions. Upward revisions tend to be followed by additional revisions in the same direction. The same is true for downgrades. This persistence of estimate revisions leads to a persistence in returns.

The earnings surprise effect closely relates to the trends in estimates effect. Stocks with earnings announcements exceeding consensus expectations generally outperform, and those with earnings disappointments underperform. This API relates to the tendency for earnings surprises to repeat in the following quarter. Also, we find evidence of anticipatory revisions in analysts' estimates up to three months ahead of an earnings surprise, and reactive revisions up to three months subsequent to a surprise, so there is an interplay between earnings revisions and earnings surprises.

Another analyst bias is a chronic tendency to overestimate the earnings of growth stocks. Such optimism leads, on average, to negative surprises, or "earnings torpedoes." Conversely, stocks with low

incurred if trades are to be made regardless. For instance, an investor purchasing energy stocks would benefit by focusing on recent laggards. Moreover, APIs such as return reversal can be exploited even more effectively with real-time trading strategies. APIs appear to be psychologically motivated, as we illustrate below.

The pure payoff to the smaller size attribute illustrates the second type of return effect. Unlike APIs, the payoffs to smaller size are not consistent. For instance, the pure returns were positive in 1983, but negative in 1986. While such effects are not regular to the naked eye, they are regular and predictable in a broader empirical framework, with the use of macroeconomic information. Hence, we refer to them as "empirical return regularities" (ERRs).

As characteristics such as size are fairly stable over time, directly exploiting ERRs requires less turnover than following an API strategy. Nonetheless, optimal exploitation of ERRs, such as the size effect, still requires portfolio turnover, because small stocks should be emphasized at times and large stocks at other times.

70

growth expectations tend, on average, to produce pleasant surprises. This analyst bias arises from cognitive misperceptions. Analysts place too much emphasis on recent trends, and consistently underestimate the natural tendency toward mean reversion. For instance, during the energy crunch in the early 1980s, many analysts predicted that oil prices would continue to rise unabated.

Year-end tax-loss selling pressure also has psychological underpinnings. We find evidence of tax-loss taking in depressed stocks near year-end, and the proceeds are often "parked" in cash until the new year. The abatement of selling pressure, combined with the reinvestment of the cash proceeds, produces a bounceback in January. Investors often defer selling winners until the new year, thereby deferring tax-gain recognition. This exerts downward pressure on winners in January.

But, waiting until year-end to take losses is not optimal. Before the 1986 Tax Reform Act, the optimal tax-avoidance strategy was to realize losses short-term throughout the year, prior to their becoming long-term, because short-term losses sheltered more taxable income. Yet investors are loath to admit mistakes and often defer loss-taking until year-end, when tax planning can be used as an excuse for closing out losing positions.

We find long-term tax-loss selling pressure to be stronger than short-term, which is surprising, given the greater tax-sheltering provided by short-term losses. But it is understandable in light of the investor disposition to ride losers too long in hopes of breaking even. Investor psychology thus leads to various predictable return patterns at the turn of the year.

The turn-of-the-year effect does not arise solely from tax-motivated trading. Institutional investors often dump losers and buy winners prior to year-end to "window-dress" their portfolio. Window-dressing is not sensible from an investment viewpoint, but may serve to deflect embarrassing questions at the annual review.

EMPIRICAL RETURN REGULARITIES

While APIs provide persistent payoffs, ERRs, like the size effect, do not. Nevertheless, we find these effects predictable in a broader framework, with the use of macroeconomic information.

Market commentators regularly discuss the "numbers that move the market." The focus in the early 1980s was on the money supply. Today, the emphasis is on the trade deficit and foreign exchange rates. Clearly, the stock market is driven by macroeconomic news. Moreover, macroeconomic events drive returns to some equity attributes.

Consider the linkage between foreign exchange rates and the size effect. The recent and substantial Japanese investments in U.S. stocks generally have been concentrated in more esteemed, bigger companies such as IBM and Coca-Cola. Fluctuations in the dollar/yen exchange rate alter the attractiveness of U.S. stocks to Japanese investors, which affects investment flows, thereby inducing a return differential between large and small companies.

The size effect is strongly linked to the default spread between corporate and government yields. The default spread, a business cycle indicator, widens as business conditions weaken and narrows as the economy strengthens. Smaller companies are especially susceptible to business cycle risk, as they are more fragile, less diversified, and have tighter borrowing constraints than larger firms. We find small stocks perform better when business conditions are improving; the converse is true as well. Hence, the default spread is a useful macro driver for predicting the size effect.

MODELING EMPIRICAL RETURN REGULARITIES

We can illustrate the predictability of ERRs by discussing the size effect in greater detail. We utilize pure returns to smaller size, thereby avoiding the confounding associated with other cross-sectional and calendar effects related to size.

We consider a variety of forecast techniques, as they pertain to the size effect, and utilize several statistical criteria for measuring "out-of-sample" forecast accuracy [FAJ, 1989]. That is, we estimate our models over a portion of the historical time series, leaving a more recent holdout sample for testing predictions. This differs fundamentally from "in-sample" data fitting.

We have categorized the size effect as an ERR, which suggests that predictive models should utilize macroeconomic drivers. Thus univariate forecasting techniques, which model only the historical returns to the size effect, are inappropriate.

Multivariate time series techniques can take explicit account of the macroeconomic forces that drive the size effect. Multivariate approaches, like vector autoregression (VAR), model a vector, or group, of related variables. A joint modeling permits an understanding of the dynamic relationships between the size effect and macroeconomic variables.

We constructed a monthly VAR model of the size effect using six economic measures as explanatory variables: 1) low-quality (BAA) corporate bond rate, 2) long-term Treasury bond rate, 3) Treasury bill rate, 4) S&P 500 total return, 5) Industrial Production

Index, and 6) Consumer Price Index. We chose these macro drivers because of their importance in security valuation. Other considerations, such as the dollar/yen exchange rate, may be helpful in modeling the size effect, but we limited our investigation to these six valuation variables.

While we found the VAR model to fit the size effect quite well in-sample, it provided poor forecasts out-of-sample. Because it has a large number of coefficients available to explain a small number of observations, a VAR model can explain historical data well. But it is likely to "overfit" the data. That is, it will fit not only systematic or stable relationships, but also random or merely circumstantial ones. The latter are of no use in forecasting, and may be misleading.[9]

One solution to the overfitting problem of vector time series approaches is to incorporate economic theory. Such structural econometric models include only those variables and relationships suggested by theory. Simple theories, however, are no more descriptive of the economy than they are of the stock market, and structural models generally have not performed well. An alternative solution involves a novel Bayesian technique.

BAYESIAN RANDOM WALK FORECASTING

Many economic measures are difficult to predict, but their behavior can often be approximated by a random walk. A random-walk model for interest rates assumes it is equally likely that rates will rise or fall. Hence, a random-walk forecast of next month's interest rate would be simply this month's rate of interest.

That it is difficult to predict stock returns is no secret. But stock prices, like other economic data, can be approximated by a random walk. As early as 1900, Bachelier proposed a theory of random walks in security prices. A random walk is thus an eminently sensible first approximation, or "prior belief," for modeling security returns.[10]

Prior beliefs about the coefficients of a forecast model can be specified in many ways. One Bayesian specification imposes a random-walk prior on the coefficients of a VAR model. This prior belief acts as a filter for extracting signals (meaningful relationships in the data), while leaving accidental relationships behind. Such a specification results in a powerful forecasting tool.

The results of modeling the size effect with a Bayesian random-walk prior belief are displayed in Figure 4. The upper chart shows cumulative pure returns to small size for the period January 1982 through December 1987. The lower chart shows "out-of-sample" return forecasts for one month ahead. The fore-

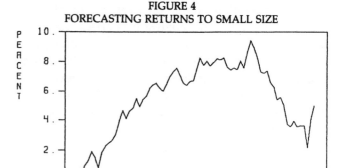

FIGURE 4
FORECASTING RETURNS TO SMALL SIZE

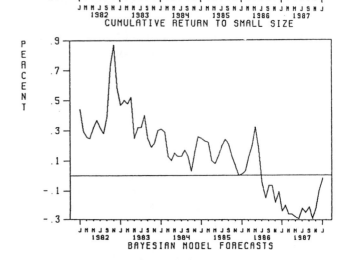

casts for small stocks are positive during the early years when small stocks performed well; they gradually decline and turn negative during the last two years, as small stocks faltered.

Moreover, the Bayesian model forecasts have statistically significant economic insight. Also, the results are quite intuitive. For instance, we find that smaller firms falter as the default spread between corporate and Treasury rates widens.

CONCLUSION

The stock market is a complex system. Simple rules, such as always buy smaller capitalization stocks, clearly do not suffice. At the same time, the nihilism of indexing is equally unjustified.

Proper study of the market requires the judicious application of computational power. Disentangling reveals the true cross-currents in the market. Only by exposing the underlying sources of return can we hope to understand them. And only through understanding can we hope to model and exploit them.

REFERENCES

Jacobs, Bruce, and Kenneth Levy. "Anomaly Capture Strategies." Presented at the Berkeley Program in Finance Seminar on The

Behavior of Security Prices: Market Efficiency, Anomalies and Trading Strategies, September 1986.

——. "Calendar Anomalies: Abnormal Returns at Calendar Turning Points." *Financial Analysts Journal*, November/December 1988, pp. 28-39.

——. "Disentangling Equity Return Regularities." In *Equity Markets and Valuation Methods*. Charlottesville: The Institute of Chartered Financial Analysts Continuing Education Series, 1988, pp. 36-46.

——. "Disentangling Equity Return Regularities: New Insights and Investment Opportunities." *Financial Analysts Journal*, May/June 1988, pp. 18-43.

——. "Forecasting the Size Effect." *Financial Analysts Journal*, May/June 1989.

——. "How Dividend Discount Models Can Be Used To Add Value." In *Improving Portfolio Performance With Quantitative Models*. Charlottesville: The Institute of Chartered Financial Analysts Continuing Education Series, 1989.

——. "Investment Management: Opportunities in Anomalies?" *Pension World*, February 1987, pp. 46-47.

——. "On the Value of 'Value'." *Financial Analysts Journal*, July/August 1988, pp. 47-62.

——. *A Revolution in Common Stock Management: Exploiting Market Inefficiencies and Forecasting Security Returns*. Homewood, IL: Dow Jones-Irwin, forthcoming.

——. "Stock Market Complexity and Investment Opportunity." In Frank Fabozzi, ed., *Managing Institutional Assets*. New York: Ballinger, forthcoming, 1990.

——. "Trading Tactics in an Inefficient Market." In Wayne Wagner, ed., *A Complete Guide to Securities Transactions: Controlling Costs and Enhancing Performance*. New York: John Wiley, 1989.

——. "Web of 'Regularities' Leads to Opportunity." *Pensions & Investment Age*, March 7, 1988, pp. 14-15.

Kuhn, Thomas. *The Structure of Scientific Revolutions*, 2nd edition. Chicago: University of Chicago Press, 1970.

Pagels, Heinz. *The Dreams of Reason: The Computer and the Rise of the Sciences of Complexity*. New York: Simon & Schuster, 1988.

Simon, Herbert. "Rationality in Psychology and Economics." In Hogarth and Reder, eds., *Rational Choice: The Contrast Between Economics and Psychology*. Chicago: University of Chicago Press, 1987.

[1] See Pagels [1988].

[2] The emerging field of catastrophe theory, or "chaos," should not be confused with randomness. Chaos theory has been applied to such diverse phenomena as the motion of smoke rings and the incidence of bank failures. In fact, chaos theory is a form of complexity. Ostensibly random behavior is sometimes well-defined by a series of non-linear dynamic equations.

An important characteristic of chaotic systems is that small changes in the environment can cause large, discontinuous jumps in the system. For instance, because the weather is chaotic, a butterfly stirring the air today in Japan can produce storms next month in New York.

[3] As Nobel laureate Herbert Simon has asserted, the emerging laws of economic behavior "have much more the complexity of molecular biology than the simplicity of classical [Newtonian] mechanics" [1987, p. 39].

[4] Science progresses through recurring cycles of a) conventional theory, b) discovery of anomalies, and c) revolution. Anomalies in the Newtonian dynamics model, for example, were resolved in 1905 by Einstein's revolutionary theory of relativity.

[5] See Table I in Jacobs and Levy [FAJ, May/June 1988] for a listing of previous studies on interrelationships.

[6] Time series regressions of pure returns to attributes on market excess (of Treasury bills) returns result in significant non-zero intercepts, indicating abnormal risk-adjusted payoffs. The non-zero intercepts could be due to non-stationary risk for these attributes, but we reject this explanation based on an examination of high-order autocorrelation patterns in the pure return series. Hence, these findings are anomalous in a multifactor CAPM framework.

[7] Such biases represent incidental side bets inherent in the DDM. We suggest various methods for controlling these biases in the 1989 ICFA article.

[8] It has often been reported that the small-size effect peaked in mid-1983. This observation is correct for naive small size, which is a bundle of several related attributes, including low price per share and high volatility. While these attributes peaked in 1983, the pure small-size effect continued to pay off positively until 1986.

[9] Vector autoregression-moving average (VARMA) models attempt to overcome the overfitting problem inherent in VAR models through a more parsimonious, or simpler, representation. But VARMA models are quite difficult to identify properly. As the number of explanatory variables increases, VARMA models face what statisticians call "the curse of higher dimensionality." In these cases, VARMA forecasting is not only extremely expensive, but also rather foolhardy.

[10] Technically, a random-walk model implies that successive price changes are independent draws from the same probability distribution. That is, the series of price changes has no memory and appears unpredictable. In fact, short-run stock returns are approximated well by a random walk. However, there is some evidence of a mean reversion tendency for longer-run returns.

Beta and Return

"Announcements of the 'death' of beta seem premature."

Fischer Black

FISCHER BLACK is a partner at Goldman, Sachs & Co. in New York (NY 10004).

ugene Fama says (according to Eric Berg of *The New York Times*, February 18, 1992) "beta as the sole variable explaining returns on stocks is dead." He also says (according to Michael Peltz of *Institutional Investor*, June 1992) that the relation between average return and beta is *completely* flat.

In these interviews, I think that Fama is misstating the results in Fama and French [1992]. Indeed, I think Fama and French, in the text of that article, misinterpret their own data (and the findings of others).

Black, Jensen, and Scholes [BJS, 1972] and Miller and Scholes [1972] find that in the period from 1931 through 1965 low-beta stocks in the United States did better than the capital asset pricing model (CAPM) predicts, while high-beta stocks did worse. Several authors find that this pattern continued in subsequent years, at least through 1989. Fama and French extend it through 1990.

All these authors find that the estimated slope of the line relating average return and risk is lower than the slope of the line that the CAPM says relates expected return and risk. If we choose our starting and ending points carefully, we can find a period of more than two decades where the line is essentially flat.

How can we interpret this? Why is the line so flat? Why have low-beta stocks done so well relative to their expected returns under the CAPM?

Black [1972] shows that borrowing restrictions

(like margin requirements) might cause low-beta stocks to do relatively well. Indeed, Fama and French refer often to the Sharpe-Lintner-Black (SLB) model that includes these borrowing restrictions. This model predicts only that the slope of the line relating expected return and beta is positive.

Fama and French claim to find evidence against this model. They say (for example, on p. 459) that their results "seem to contradict" the evidence that the slope of the line relating expected return and beta is positive.

This is a misstatement, in my view. Even in the period they choose to highlight, they cannot rule out the hypothesis that the slope of the line is positive. Their results for beta and average return are perfectly consistent with the SLB model.

Moreover, if the line is really flat, that implies dramatic investment opportunities for those who use beta. A person who normally holds both stocks and bonds or stocks and cash can shift to a portfolio of similar total risk but higher expected return by emphasizing low-beta stocks.

Beta is a valuable investment tool if the line is as steep as the CAPM predicts. It is even more valuable if the line is flat. No matter how steep the line is, beta is alive and well.

DATA MINING

When a researcher tries many ways to do a study, including various combinations of explanatory factors, various periods, and various models, we often say he is "data mining." If he reports only the more successful runs, we have a hard time interpreting any statistical analysis he does. We worry that he selected, from the many models tried, only the ones that seem to support his conclusions. With enough data mining, all the results that seem significant could be just accidental. (Lo and MacKinlay [1990] refer to this as "data snooping." Less formally, we call it "hindsight.")

Data mining is not limited to single research studies. In a single study, a researcher can reduce its effects by reporting all the runs he does, though he still may be tempted to emphasize the results he likes. Data mining is most severe when many people are studying related problems.

Even when each person chooses his problem independently of the others, only a small fraction of research efforts result in published papers. By its nature, research involves many false starts and blind alleys. The results that lead to published papers are likely to be the most unusual or striking ones. But this means that any statistical tests of significance will be gravely biased.

The problem is worse when people build on one another's work. Each decides on a model closely related to the models that others use, learns from the others' blind alleys, and may even work with mostly the same data. Thus in the real world of research, conventional tests of significance seem almost worthless.

In particular, most of the so-called anomalies that have plagued the literature on investments seem likely to be the result of data mining. We have literally thousands of researchers looking for profit opportunities in securities. They are all looking at roughly the same data. Once in a while, just by chance, a strategy will seem to have worked consistently in the past. The researcher who finds it writes it up, and we have a new anomaly. But it generally vanishes as soon as it's discovered.

Merton [1987, pp. 103-108] has an excellent discussion of these problems. He says (p. 108) "although common to all areas of economic hypothesis testing, these methodological problems appear to be especially acute in the testing of market rationality."

The "size effect" may be in this category. Banz [1981] finds that firms with little stock outstanding (at market value) had, up to that time, done well relative to other stocks with similar betas. Since his study was published, though, small firms have had mediocre and inconsistent performance.

Fama and French [1992] continue studying the small-firm effect, and report similar results on a largely overlapping data sample. In the period since the Banz study (1981-1990), they find no size effect at all, whether or not they control for beta. Yet they claim in their paper that size is one of the variables that "captures" the cross-sectional variation in average stock returns.

Fama and French also give no reasons for a relation between size and expected return. They might argue that small firms are consistently underpriced because they are "neglected" in a world of large institutional investors. But they do not give us that reason or any other reason. Lack of theory is a tipoff: watch out for data mining!

Fama and French also find that the ratio of

book value to the market value of the firm's equity helps capture the cross-sectional variation in average stock returns. They favor the idea that this ratio captures some sort of rationally priced risk, rather than market overreaction to the relative prospects of firms. But they say nothing about what this risk might be, or why it is priced, or in what direction.

They mention the possibility that this result is due to "chance," which is another way to describe data mining, but they don't consider that plausible, because the result appears in both halves of their period, and because the ratio predicts a firm's accounting performance.

I consider both those arguments weak. Given that an "effect" appears in a full period, we expect to find it in both halves of the period. We are not surprised when we do.

We know that when markets are somewhat efficient, stock prices react before accounting numbers to events affecting a firm's performance. Thus we are not surprised when firms with high ratios of book-to-market equity show poor subsequent accounting performance. I don't think this is evidence of a priced risk factor at all.

Thus I think it is quite possible that even the book-to-market effect results from data mining, and will vanish in the future. But I also think it may result in part from irrational pricing. The ratio of book-to-market equity may pick up a divergence between value and price across any of a number of dimensions. Thus the past success of this ratio may be due more to market inefficiencies than "priced factors" of the kind that Fama and French favor.

If the subsequent convergence of price and value is gradual, people seeking profit opportunities may not fully eliminate the effect. To capture the gains, they have to spend money on active management, and they must bear the risks of a less-than-fully diversified portfolio.

BETA THEORY

I think most of the Fama and French results are attributable to data mining, especially when they reexamine "effects" that people have discussed for years. Even they note that the ratio of book-to-market equity has long been cited as a measure of the return prospects of stocks.

I especially attribute their results to data mining when they attribute them to unexplained "priced factors," or give no reasons at all for the effects they find.

Strangely, the factor that seems most likely to be priced they don't discuss at all: the beta factor. We can construct the beta factor by creating a diversified portfolio that is long in low-beta stocks and short in smaller amounts of high-beta stocks, so that its beta is roughly zero. The returns to all such portfolios tend to be highly correlated, so we don't have to worry about the details of the "right" way to create the beta factor.

The empirical evidence that the beta factor had extra returns is stronger than the corresponding evidence for the small-stock factor or the book-to-market equity factor. The first evidence was published in 1972, and the factor has performed better since publication than it did prior to publication.

Moreover, we have some theory for the beta factor. Black [1972] showed that borrowing restrictions might cause low-beta stocks to have higher expected returns than the CAPM predicts (or the beta factor to have a higher expected return than interest at the short-term rate). Borrowing restrictions could include margin rules, bankruptcy laws that limit lender access to a borrower's future income, and tax rules that limit deductions for interest expense.

These restrictions have probably tightened in the United States in recent decades. Margin rules have remained in effect, bankruptcy laws seem to have shifted against lenders, and deductions for interest expense have been tightened. Many countries outside the United States seem to have similar restrictions. If they help explain the past return on the beta factor, they will continue to influence its future return.

Moreover, many investors who can borrow, and who can deduct the interest they pay, are nonetheless reluctant to borrow. Those who want lots of market risk will bid up the prices of high-beta stocks. This makes low-beta stocks attractive and high-beta stocks unattractive to investors who have low-risk portfolios or who are willing to borrow.

We can see some evidence for this in the market's reaction to a firm that changes its leverage. An exchange offer of debt for equity generally causes the firm's stock price to increase, while an offer of equity for debt causes it to decrease. This may be because of the tax advantages of debt; or because more debt transfers value from existing bondholders to stockholders; or because buying equity signals manager optimism.

I believe, though, that an important reason is reluctance to borrow: in effect, a firm that adds leverage is providing indirect borrowing for investors who are unwilling to borrow directly. These investors bid up its stock price.

BJS [1972] discuss another possible reason for beta factor pricing: mismeasurement of the market portfolio. If we use a market portfolio that differs randomly from the true market portfolio, stocks that seem to have low betas will on average have higher betas when we use the correct market portfolio to estimate them. Our betas are estimated with error (even in the final portfolio), and we select stocks that seem to have low betas. Such stocks will usually have positive alphas using the incorrect market portfolio. The portfolio method does not eliminate this bias.

Perhaps the most interesting way in which the market portfolio may be mismeasured involves our neglect of foreign stocks. World capital markets are becoming more integrated all the time. In a fully integrated capital market, what counts is a stock's beta with the world market portfolio, not its beta with the issuer country market portfolio. This may cause low-beta stocks to seem consistently underpriced. If investors can buy foreign stocks without penalty, they should do so; if they cannot, stocks with low betas on their domestic market may partly substitute for foreign stocks. If this is the reason the line is flat, they may also want to emphasize stocks that have high betas with the world market portfolio.

Can't we do some tests on stock returns to sort out which of these theoretical factors is most important? I doubt that we have enough data to do that.

We have lots of securities, but returns are highly correlated across securities, so these observations are far from independent. We have lots of days, but to estimate factor pricing what counts is the number of years for which we have data, not the number of distinct observations. If the factor prices are changing, even many years is not enough. By the time we have a reasonable estimate of how a factor was priced on average, it will be priced in a different way.

Moreover, if we try to use stock returns to distinguish among these explanations, we run a heavy risk of data mining. Tests designed to distinguish may accidentally favor one explanation over another in a given period. I don't know how to begin designing tests that escape the data mining trap.

VARYING THE ANALYSIS

While the BJS study covers lots of ground, I am especially fond of the "portfolio method" we used. Nothing I have seen since 1972 leads me to believe that we can gain much by varying this method of analysis.

The portfolio method is simple and intuitive. We try to simulate a portfolio strategy that an investor can actually use. The strategy can use any data for constructing the portfolio each year that are available to investors at the start of that year. Thus we can incorporate into our selection method any "cross-sectional" effects that we think are important.

However, the more complex our portfolio selection method is, the more we risk bringing in a data mining bias. I must confess that when we were doing the original BJS study, we tried things that do not appear in the published article. Moreover, we were reacting to prior work suggesting a relatively flat slope for the line relating average return to beta. Thus our article had elements of data mining too.

To minimize the data mining problem, BJS used a very simple portfolio strategy. We chose securities using historical estimates of beta, and we used many securities to diversify out the factors not related to beta.

But this method does have flaws. For example, beta is highly correlated with both total risk and residual risk across stocks. So what we call the "beta factor" might better be called the "total risk factor" or the "residual risk factor." I can't think of any reliable way to distinguish among these.

When doing the BJS study, we considered estimating the entire covariance matrix for our population of stocks, and using that to improve the efficiency of our test. We realized that this would require us to deal with uncertainty in our estimated covariances. We decided that the potential for improved efficiency was small, while the potential for error in our econometric methods was large. So we did not pursue that route.

Others have used different methods to update our study. My view is that in the presence of data mining and estimate error and changing risk premiums, none of these methods adds enough accuracy to warrant its complexity. I view most of these methods as our method expressed in different language.

For example, Fama and MacBeth [1973] start with cross-sectional regressions of return on beta, and

OVERALL PORTFOLIO RISK LOWERED.

look at the time series of regression intercepts. The time series is very similar to the BJS time series of returns on the beta factor. Stambaugh [1982] extends the analysis through 1976, and considers broader possible definitions of the market portfolio, but finds similar results. Lakonishok and Shapiro [1986] update the analysis to 1981, and include firm size to help explain average portfolio return. They conclude that the risk measures were unrelated to average return in the period 1962-1981.

Gibbons, Ross, and Shanken [GRS, 1989] contrast their "multivariate" tests with the series of univariate tests that they say BJS use. In fact, though, the key test in BJS is the portfolio method used to construct the beta factor. This method implicitly uses all the covariances that GRS estimate explicitly. The single BJS portfolio takes account of the covariances in a way that leaves relatively little scope for data mining. Thus I feel our portfolio method has about as much power as the GRS method, and may have less bias.

Malkiel [1990, pp. 238-248] studies the relation between beta and return for mutual funds in the 1980-1989 period. Stocks generally did well in this period, so we'd expect high-beta funds to outperform low-beta funds. But beta and fund performance seem utterly unrelated.

We can even interpret Haugen and Baker [1991] as showing for the 1972-1989 period that return and beta were not related as the CAPM leads us to expect. They say the market portfolio is not efficient, but the way it's inefficient is that low-risk stocks seem to have abnormally high expected returns.

Kandel and Stambaugh [1989] give a general mean-variance framework for likelihood ratio tests of asset pricing models, taking account of estimate error in both means and covariances, but assuming that the covariances are constant. In the real world, I doubt that their method adds precision to the single portfolio BJS test of the pricing of the beta factor.

Shanken [1992] has a comprehensive discussion of methods for estimating "beta-pricing models." He discusses such problems as estimate error in beta when using methods like Fama and MacBeth's [1973]. For some reason, he does not discuss the BJS and Black-Scholes [1974] portfolio method. Black and Scholes estimate beta for the final portfolio as they estimate alpha. Thus I believe they avoid the bias due to estimate error in beta.

EXHIBIT 1
Number of Stocks in the Sample

Year	Number of Stocks	Year	Number of Stocks	Year	Number of Stocks
1931	592	1951	954	1971	1182
1932	678	1952	979	1972	1238
1933	699	1953	1003	1973	1286
1934	693	1954	1011	1974	1363
1935	688	1955	1018	1975	1429
1936	685	1956	1009	1976	1479
1937	673	1957	1004	1977	1484
1938	699	1958	1010	1978	1470
1939	722	1959	1008	1979	1466
1940	752	1960	1033	1980	1452
1941	754	1961	1026	1981	1435
1942	767	1962	1034	1982	1405
1943	782	1963	1066	1983	1394
1944	784	1964	1089	1984	1400
1945	783	1965	1104	1985	1380
1946	798	1966	1128	1986	1361
1947	820	1967	1152	1987	1329
1948	847	1968	1152	1988	1325
1949	900	1969	1122	1989	1340
1950	934	1970	1126	1990	1415
				1991	1505

UPDATING THE BLACK-JENSEN-SCHOLES STUDY

I want to illustrate the portfolio method by updating the BJS [1972] study. I follow the BJS procedure closely, except that at the very end I adopt the Black-Scholes method of estimating portfolio beta, alpha, and residual risk at the same time.

I use monthly data from the Center for Research in Security Prices at the University of Chicago for the period 1926-1991. The portfolio method is especially useful when analyzing data over such a long period, since the stocks in the portfolio are constantly changing. Even when the stocks don't change, the portfolio method adapts in part to changes in their covariances.

I do not try to estimate changes in residual risk through time. In principle, this might let me improve the efficiency of the BJS "significance tests." But the significance tests are more seriously compromised by data mining than by heteroscedasticity, in my view. So I stick to the use of an average residual volatility for the whole period to keep the method simple.

I use New York Stock·Exchange listed stocks, as BJS did. Exhibit 1 shows the number of stocks in

EXHIBIT 2
Monthly Regressions: 1931 to 1965

Item	\multicolumn{11}{c}{Black-Jensen-Scholes Study Portfolio Number}
	1	2	3	4	5	6	7	8	9	10	M
1. β	1.56	1.38	1.25	1.16	1.06	0.92	0.85	0.75	0.63	0.50	1.00
2. α	-0.01	-0.02	-0.01	0.00	-0.01	0.00	10.01	0.01	0.02	0.02	
3. $t(\alpha)$	-0.43	-1.99	-0.76	-0.25	-0.89	0.79	0.71	1.18	2.31	1.87	
4. $\rho(\tilde{R}, \tilde{R}_m)$	0.96	0.99	0.99	0.99	0.99	1.98	0.99	0.98	0.96	0.90	
5. $\rho(\tilde{e}_t, \tilde{e}_{t-1})$	0.05	-0.06	0.04	-0.01	-0.07	-0.12	0.13	0.10	0.04	0.10	
6. $\sigma(\tilde{e})$	0.14	0.07	0.06	0.05	0.04	0.05	0.05	0.05	0.06	0.08	
7. μ	0.26	0.21	0.21	0.20	0.17	0.16	0.15	0.14	0.13	0.11	0.17
8. σ	0.50	0.43	0.39	0.36	0.33	0.29	0.25	0.24	0.20	0.17	0.31

Item	\multicolumn{11}{c}{Current Study Portfolio Number}
	1	2	3	4	5	6	7	8	9	10	M
1. β	1.53	1.36	1.24	1.17	1.06	0.92	0.84	0.76	0.63	0.48	1.00
2. α	-0.02	-0.02	-0.01	0.00	-0.01	0.00	0.01	0.01	0.02	0.03	
3. $t(\alpha)$	-0.78	-2.12	-1.30	-0.54	-1.38	0.55	0.72	1.64	1.74	2.21	
4. $\rho(\tilde{R}, \tilde{R}_m)$	0.97	0.99	0.99	0.99	0.99	0.99	0.98	0.98	0.96	0.90	
5. $\rho(\tilde{e}_t, \tilde{e}_{t-1})$	0.05	-0.06	0.00	-0.13	-0.11	-0.07	0.10	0.06	0.11	0.15	
6. $\sigma(\tilde{e})$	0.12	0.06	0.06	0.05	0.04	0.05	0.05	0.05	0.06	0.07	
7. μ	0.26	0.22	0.21	0.21	0.18	0.17	0.16	0.15	0.13	0.12	0.18
8. σ	0.49	0.43	0.39	0.37	0.33	0.29	0.27	0.24	0.20	0.17	0.31

my sample for each year in six decades plus a year. Because CRSP has corrected the data since the BJS study, the numbers differ slightly from the corresponding numbers in BJS.

Exhibit 2, panel 2, and Exhibit 5, line 2, replicate the BJS results for the BJS period. The results are similar, but not identical. Most studies that followed BJS emphasize the ten portfolios in Exhibit 2. But the essence of the portfolio method lies in constructing a single portfolio (in this case, the beta factor) as in Exhibit 5.

In Exhibit 2, the first two lines show the slope and intercept of a regression of portfolio excess return on an equally weighted market excess return. We chose the equally weighted market portfolio rather than the value-weighted portfolio for convenience

only. Line 3 shows a standard statistical measure of the "significance" of the intercept (compared with zero). But the data mining we did (along with the hundreds of other people looking at the same data) invalidates the significance test. I interpret the numbers in line 3 as roughly measuring the consistency of the positive intercept for low beta portfolios.

Line 4 shows the correlation between portfolio and market excess returns, while line 5 shows the estimated serial correlation of the residuals. Line 6 gives the estimated standard deviation of the residual. Lines 7 and 8 give the sample mean and standard deviation of portfolio excess return. Since means, correlations, and standard deviations are all changing, these are estimates of their averages through the period. Everything is expressed in annual terms, though BJS gave their

EXHIBIT 3
Monthly Regressions: 1931 through 1991

					Portfolio Number						
Item	1	2	3	4	5	6	7	8	9	10	M
1. β	1.52	1.34	1.22	1.14	1.05	0.93	0.85	0.76	0.64	0.49	1.00
2. α	-0.03	-0.02	-0.01	0.00	0.01	0.01	0.01	0.01	0.01	0.01	
3. $t(\alpha)$	-2.34	-2.25	-1.54	-0.62	-1.41	1.03	1.50	1.50	2.00	2.91	
4. $\rho(\tilde{R}, \tilde{R}_m)$	0.97	0.99	0.99	0.99	0.99	0.99	0.98	0.98	0.95	0.88	
5. $\rho(\tilde{e}_t, \tilde{e}_{t-1})$	0.02	-0.04	0.00	-0.08	-0.06	-0.03	0.05	0.05	0.10	0.13	
6. $\sigma(\tilde{e})$	0.11	0.06	0.05	0.04	0.04	0.04	0.05	0.05	0.06	0.07	
7. μ	0.17	0.17	0.16	0.14	0.14	0.13	0.11	0.11	0.10	0.09	0.14
8. σ	0.43	0.37	0.33	0.29	0.29	0.25	0.23	0.23	0.18	0.18	0.27

figures in monthly terms.

Exhibit 3 gives similar results for the entire period from 1926 through 1991. If anything, the pattern looks stronger than it did for the 1926-1965 period. (But keep in mind that if it looked weaker, I might not have written this article.) Low-beta stocks did better than the CAPM predicts, and high-beta stocks did worse.

In fact, as Exhibit 4 shows, the results since 1965 have been very strong. Over the entire twenty-six-year period, the market rose by normal amounts or more, but low-beta portfolios did about as well as high-beta portfolios. This is what Fama and French [1992] mean when they say the slope of the line relat-ing average return to beta is flat (though they usually control for firm size).

Exhibit 5 shows the results for the beta factor calculated the way BJS did it. We took the excess returns from the ten portfolios in Exhibits 2-4, and weighted them by $1 - \beta_i$, where β_i is the ith portfolio's beta. Thus we used positive weights on low-beta port-folios, and negative weights on high-beta portfolios. In effect, the beta factor is a portfolio that is long in low-beta stocks and short in high-beta stocks, with the largest long positions in the lowest-beta stocks, and the largest short positions in the highest-beta stocks.

Because low-beta stocks all tend to do well or badly at the same time, and because high-beta stocks

EXHIBIT 4
Monthly Regressions: 1966 through 1991

					Portfolio Number						
Item	1	2	3	4	5	6	7	8	9	10	M
1. β	1.50	1.30	1.17	1.09	1.03	0.95	0.87	0.78	0.67	0.51	1.00
2. α	0.00	-0.01	0.00	0.00	0.00	0.01	0.00	0.01	0.01	0.03	
3. $t(\alpha)$	-3.24	-0.93	-1.02	-0.24	-0.57	1.31	0.63	0.81	0.94	1.79	
4. $\rho(\tilde{R}, \tilde{R}_m)$	0.96	0.98	0.99	0.99	0.99	0.99	0.98	0.97	0.93	0.82	
5. $\rho(\tilde{e}_t, \tilde{e}_{t-1})$	-0.02	-0.02	0.00	0.04	0.06	0.02	-0.03	-0.02	0.09	0.12	
6. $\sigma(\tilde{e})$	0.08	0.05	0.04	0.03	0.03	0.03	0.03	0.04	0.05	0.08	
7. μ	0.06	0.08	0.08	0.08	0.08	0.08	0.07	0.07	0.07	0.06	0.08
8. σ	0.31	0.26	0.24	0.22	0.21	0.19	0.18	0.16	0.14	0.12	0.20

EXHIBIT 5

The Beta Factor

	Period	μ_z	σ_z	$t(\mu)$
BJS	1/31–12/65	0.04	0.15	1.62
1.	1/31–12/65	0.05	0.15	1.93
2.	1/31–12/91	0.05	0.14	2.94
3.	1/66–12/91	0.06	0.13	2.44

	Period	μ_z	σ_z	$t(\mu)$
1.	1/31–12/39	-0.07	0.22	-1.00
2.	1/40–12/49	0.06	0.15	1.17
3.	1/50–12/59	0.10	0.07	4.56
4.	1/60–12/69	0.06	0.11	1.67
5.	1/70–12/79	0.02	0.14	0.32
6.	1/80–12/91	0.14	0.12	3.90

all tend to do badly when low-beta stocks are doing well, this portfolio is not perfectly diversified. It has substantial variance. That's why we call it the "beta factor."

This portfolio captures the relative behavior of stocks with different betas. Since stocks that differ in beta also tend to differ in other ways, it combines the effects of all the characteristics correlated with beta. For example, high-beta stocks tend to be stocks with high return standard deviation, and issuers of high-beta stock tend to be high-leverage firms.

BJS did not, and I do not, try to isolate these characteristics. One reason is that it complicates the

EXHIBIT 6

The Beta Factor Using Only Prior Information

	Period	μ_e	σ_e	$t(\mu)$
BJS	1/31–12/65	0.04	0.15	1.62
1.	1/31–12/65	0.03	0.11	1.68
2.	1/31–12/91	0.04	0.10	2.69
3.	1/66–12/91	0.04	0.09	2.32

	Period	μ_e	σ_e	$t(\mu)$
1.	1/31–12/39	-0.05	0.17	-0.94
2.	1/40–12/49	0.03	0.10	1.06
3.	1/50–12/59	0.08	0.06	4.25
4.	1/60–12/69	0.03	0.07	1.32
5.	1/70–12/79	0.01	0.10	0.18
6.	1/80–12/91	0.09	0.08	3.90

analysis. Another is that it invites data mining.

Exhibit 5 summarizes the results in Exhibits 2-4, and divides them into approximate decades. We see that the beta factor had a negative excess return only in the first decade. Low-beta stocks did better after the BJS study period than during it. They did best of all in the most recent decade.

BJS, however, did not use a strict portfolio method. They chose stocks for the ten portfolios using only information that would have been available at the time (about five prior years of monthly data to estimate beta). But the weights on the ten portfolios use information that was not available.

Black and Scholes [1974] refine the portfolio method to eliminate this possible source of bias. The principle is simple. We select stocks *and* weight them using only information that would have been available at the time. This eliminates any bias, and generally makes it easier to understand and interpret the results. Since we revise the portfolio over time, it lets us adapt to changes in the stock list and in the covariances.

The "multivariate" testing methods that such researchers as Kandel and Stambaugh [1989] and Shanken [1992] have explored do not have these features. In effect, they require use of information on covariances that would not have been available to an investor constructing a portfolio. And I find formal statistical tests harder to interpret than a "portfolio test."

Exhibit 6 shows the beta factor using a strict portfolio test. We weight the ten portfolios using five-year historical betas rather than the realized betas. This takes out any bias due to use of unavailable information in creating portfolio weights. Then we regress the portfolio excess return on the market excess return, and figure the residual. This takes out any effects of market moves because the portfolio beta is not exactly zero. The story in Exhibit 6 is about the same as the story in Exhibit 5.

Is this article, like so many others, just an exercise in data mining? Will low-beta stocks continue to do well in the future, or will recognition of the pricing of the beta factor cause so many investors to change their strategies that the effect is eliminated (or reversed)? Are the effects of borrowing restrictions, reluctance to borrow, and a mismeasured market portfolio strong enough to keep it alive? If the flat line relating past return to beta steepens in the future, how much will it steepen?

Send me your predictions! I'll record them, and in future decades we can see how many were right. My prediction is that the line will steepen, but that low-beta stocks will continue to do better than the CAPM says they should.

CORPORATE FINANCE

Suppose you believe that the line relating expected return to beta will continue to be flat, or flatter than the CAPM suggests. What does that imply for a firm's investment and financing policy?

On the surface, you might think that the line for corporate investments will be flat or flatter too. You might think a corporation should use a discount rate when it evaluates proposed investments that does not depend very much on the betas of its cash flows. In effect, it should shift its asset mix toward high-risk assets, because its investors face borrowing restrictions or because they prefer high-risk investments.

But this conclusion would be wrong, because corporations can borrow so easily. They face fewer borrowing restrictions than individuals. The beta of a corporation's stock depends on both its asset beta and its leverage.

If the line is flat for investors, a corporation will increase its stock price whenever it increases its leverage. Exchanging debt or preferred for stock increases leverage, even when the debt is below investment-grade. Now that the market for high-yield bonds is so active, there is almost no limit to the amount of leverage a corporation can have. Some securities even let a firm increase its leverage without significantly increasing the probability of bankruptcy.

If today's corporations do not face borrowing restrictions, and if a corporation makes its investment decisions to maximize its stock price, the market for corporate assets should be governed by the ordinary CAPM. A firm should use discount rates for its investments that depend on their betas in the usual way.

On the other hand, I think many corporations act as if they do face borrowing restrictions. They worry about an increase in leverage that may cause a downgrade from the rating agencies, and they carry over the investor psychology that makes individuals reluctant to borrow.

This may mean that corporate assets are priced like common stocks. Low-beta assets may be underpriced, while high-beta assets are overpriced. The line relating expected return to beta for corporate assets may be flatter than the CAPM predicts.

If so, then any corporation that is free to borrow and that wants to maximize its stock price should again use the ordinary CAPM to value its investments, and should use lots of leverage. Low-beta investments will look attractive because they have positive alphas. Thus the corporation will emphasize low-risk assets and high-risk liabilities.

Just like an investor who is free to borrow, a rational corporation will emphasize low-beta assets and use lots of leverage. Even if the line is flat for both investors and corporations, beta is an essential tool for making investment decisions. Indeed, beta is more useful if the line is flat than if it is as steep as the CAPM predicts.

No matter what the slope of the line, a rational corporation will evaluate an investment using the betas of that investment's cash flows. It will not use the betas of its other assets or the betas of its liabilities.

Announcements of the "death" of beta seem premature. The evidence that prompts such statements implies more uses for beta than ever. Rational investors who can borrow freely, whether individuals or firms, should continue to use the CAPM and beta to value investments and to choose portfolio strategy.

ENDNOTE

The author is grateful to Russell Abrams and Jonathan Kelly for help with the calculations; and to Clifford Asness, John Bu, Wayne Ferson, Josef Lakonishok, Richard Roll, Barr Rosenberg, Jay Shanken, and Myron Scholes for comments on prior drafts.

REFERENCES

Banz, Rolf. "The Relationship Between Return and Market Values of Common Stock." *Journal of Financial Economics*, 9 (1981), pp. 3-18.

Black, Fischer. "Capital Market Equilibrium with Restricted Borrowing." *Journal of Business*, 45 (July, 1972), pp. 444-455.

Black, Fischer, Michael Jensen, and Myron Scholes. "The Capital Asset Pricing Model: Some Empirical Tests." In Michael C. Jensen, ed., *Studies in the Theory of Capital Markets*. New York: Praeger, 1972, pp. 79-121.

Black, Fischer, and Myron Scholes. "The Effects of Dividend Yield and Dividend Policy on Common Stock Prices and Returns." *Journal of Financial Economics*, 1 (May 1974), pp. 1-22.

Fama, Eugene F., and Kenneth R. French. "The Cross-Section of Expected Stock Returns." *Journal of Finance*, 47 (June 1992), pp. 427-465.

Fama, Eugene F., and James D. MacBeth. "Risk, Return, and Equilibrium: Empirical Tests." *Journal of Political Economy*, 81 (May/June 1973), pp. 607-636.

Gibbons, Michael R., Stephen A. Ross, and Jay Shanken. "A Test of the Efficiency of a Given Portfolio." *Econometrica*, 57 (September 1989), pp. 1121-1152.

Haugen, Robert A., and Nardin L. Baker. "The Efficient Market Inefficiency of Capitalization-Weighted Stock Portfolios." *Journal of Portfolio Management*, Spring 1991, pp. 35-40.

Kandel, Shmuel, and Robert F. Stambaugh. "A Mean-Variance Framework for Tests of Asset Pricing Models." *Review of Financial Studies*, 2 (1989), pp. 125-156.

Lakonishok, Josef, and Alan C. Shapiro. "Systematic Risk, Total Risk and Size as Determinants of Stock Market Returns." *Journal of Banking and Finance*, 10 (1986), pp. 115-132.

Lo, Andrew W., and Craig A. MacKinlay. "Data Snooping in Tests of Financial Asset Pricing Models." *Review of Financial Studies*, 10 (1990), pp. 431-467.

Malkiel, Burton G. *A Random Walk Down Wall Street*. New York: W.W. Norton & Co., 1990.

Merton, Robert C. "On the Current State of the Stock Market Rationality Hypotheses." In Rudiger Dornbusch, Stanley Fischer, and John Bossons, eds., *Macroeconomics and Finance: Essays in Honor of Franco Modigliani*. Cambridge, MA: MIT Press, 1987, pp. 93-124.

Miller, Merton, and Myron Scholes. "Rates of Return in Relation to Risk: A Re-examination of Some Recent Findings." In Michael C. Jensen, ed., *Studies in the Theory of Capital Markets*. New York: Praeger, 1972, pp. 47-78.

Shanken, Jay. "On the Estimation of Beta-Pricing Models." *Review of Financial Studies*, 5 (1992), pp. 1-33.

Stambaugh, Robert F. "On the Exclusion of Assets from Tests of the Two-Parameter Model: A Sensitivity Analysis." *Journal of Financial Economics*, 10 (November 1982), pp. 237-268.

PART TWO
Performance Measurement and Evaluation

For all of stock market history up until the early 1970s, investment performance was measured by realized and, on occasion, by unrealized capital gains. The word *performance* as an investment concept, in fact, came into use only in the late 1960s, carrying the special meaning of outstanding returns, not just returns.

In the ashes of the market collapse that followed those go-go years, investors finally awoke to the unhappy truth that the heroes of the late bull market were not so smart after all. They were just the big risk-takers of the era; like most big risk-takers, they had ended up paying the price of the outsized and not very carefully calculated risks they had taken.

At the same time, the Lorie-Fisher studies of overall market performance, which had originally appeared in 1964, now stimulated a fresh interest. First, they emphasized *total* return, which included dividends as well as the vagaries of capital values. Second, they demonstrated that a broad market index could serve as a benchmark against which to measure the results of active management.

Investors soon set about measuring performance by total return and then adjusting the raw figure for risk as proxied by beta. Although this was a big step forward from the old days, important questions remained unanswered. Was the benchmark in use the proper benchmark for the purpose? How well did beta measure portfolio risk? How could we distinguish performance due to luck from performance due to skill? How could managers develop a reliable gauge of the quality of their judgments? The five papers in this section provide innovative and lucid answers to these critically important questions.

Performance evaluation and benchmark errors (I)*

"True portfolio management ability is not indicated if the measured performance is due to the benchmark's own error."

Richard Roll

In portfolio performance evaluation, one compares the return obtained on a managed portfolio to the return expected on an unmanaged portfolio having the same risk. The benchmark is the expected return on the unmanaged portfolio. It should accurately reflect the risk associated with the managed portfolio during the evaluation period. However, since it is always difficult to measure the risk associated with a managed portfolio, there is always potential for error in the benchmark. The purpose of this paper is to analyze benchmark error, and I do so in the context of the current widespread practice of using the capital asset pricing model (CAPM) to measure risk. As we shall see, performance evaluations based on the CAPM are prone to systematic errors of various kinds.

Error in performance measurement can be ascribed to two sources. The first is random variation: The actual return is in part a function of unforeseeable events that cause parameter mis-estimation, events that tend to cancel each other's effects over repeated measurements. A second source of error is in the *ex ante* CAPM benchmark, an error that cannot be eliminated by repeated evaluations. Thus, *ex ante* benchmark errors are much more important than errors due to random causes; they make particular managers appear to "outperform" expectations when they fortuitously choose portfolios with negative errors in the benchmark, while managers unfortunate enough to choose portfolios with positive benchmark error will appear to do relatively poorly. We must remember that *true portfolio management ability is not accurately indicated if the measured performance reflects the benchmark's*

own error. Thus, the elimination of benchmark error is an extremely important practical problem for the evaluator.

BENCHMARK ERRORS OF THE CAPITAL ASSET PRICING MODEL (CAPM)

I have chosen to use the simplest version of the CAPM in this analysis of benchmark error. This version involves a linear relationship between the evaluator's expected return on a given asset or portfolio and the beta coefficient (which is supposed to measure the "systematic" risk of the asset[1]). This securities market line (SML), depicted in Figure 1, has an intercept equal to the risk-free rate of interest (E_F) and a slope equal to the difference between the evaluator's expected return (E_m) on the market index and the risk-free rate. I shall assume that a given market index has been selected for these evaluation procedures and that a nominal risk-free asset is available. My analysis assumes not that the simple CAPM is correct but only that it is used as a benchmark for performance evaluation.[2]

We can readily see from Figure 1 that an inaccurate assessment of risk will cause true performance to differ from measured performance. The measured performance is $\hat{\alpha}$, the vertical distance between the securities market line and the actual return (R_p) of the evaluated portfolio at the mis-assessed risk level ($\widehat{Risk_p}$). In this particular example, the performance is positive, because the observed return R_p lies above the securities market line at the assessed level of risk. The assessed risk level implies that the portfolio was expected to return $\hat{E}_p$. The actual performance (α) is negative, however, because the true risk associated

* This is the first part of an analysis of performance evaluation that will be continued in our issue of Winter 1981.

1. Footnotes appear at the end of the article.

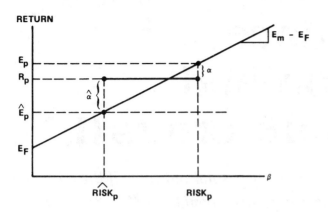

Figure 1. Mis-assessment of Performance Caused by Error in the Ex-ante Risk Measure. N.B.: the Risk Error is not Caused by Statistical Variation.

with this portfolio is larger than the measured risk. Thus, the true expected return of this portfolio is E_p, which lies above the observed return R_p.

In Figure 1 I illustrate benchmark error for the case in which one accurately assesses the position of the securities market line but inaccurately assesses the appropriate risk level for the portfolio. This error is *not* a statistical estimation error in the beta. It is possible to assess inaccurately the risk of a portfolio even if one knows the true expected returns and there is no statistical estimation problem at all.

How can this happen? It will occur if the market index is not on the evaluator's *ex ante* mean/variance efficient frontier; i.e., when the index is not an "optimized" portfolio. Unlike common estimation errors in statistics, one cannot eliminate this error in beta by using larger sample sizes. It will remain no matter how large the sample is. It is not an estimation error in the beta of the asset as measured against the market index *in use*. Instead, it is the difference between the measured beta and that beta which should have been calculated using an optimized index.

Figure 2 illustrates the situation in which the true and measured performances differ because the

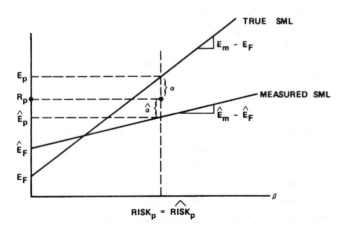

Figure 2. Mis-assessment of Performance Caused by Error in the Securities Market Line. This error is not due to statistical variation.

security market line's position is incorrect. The error in position is the result of two problems, neither of which is related to statistical variation: First, a non-optimized market index has been employed, an index whose expected return $\hat{E}_m$ differs from that (E_m) of the optimized index appropriate for the true risk-free asset. Second, the true risk-free asset has a return (E_F) that is different from the return on the nominal "riskless" asset used to measure $\hat{E}_F$. The net result is measured performance $\hat{\alpha}$ that differs from true performance α. As illustrated in Figure 2, the measured $\hat{\alpha}$ is positive, while the true performance α is negative. (R_p is the observed return.)

Figure 3 illustrates all possible non-statistical evaluation errors. It also introduces a number, π, that

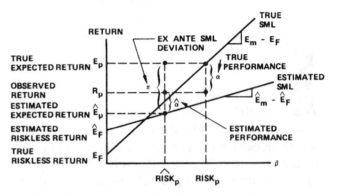

Figure 3. Mis-assessment of Performance Caused by Non-Statistical Errors in the Evaluation Benchmark, the Securities Market Line (SML).

measures the extent of these errors. In Figure 3, both the market index and the risk-free asset have been chosen incorrectly and in such a manner that the true risk of the portfolio is larger than the measured risk. Consequently, although the estimated performance is positive, the true performance is negative.

Before analyzing the ex-ante performance error that captures the essence of this problem, I must emphasize that true performance is an *ex post* quantity equal to the difference between the observed return and the *true* expected return. Of course, true performance is subject to statistical variation from one sample period to another. Clearly, the difference between an observed return and a true expected return consists of both random variation and true ability in portfolio management. On the other hand, if over time we repeatedly measure performance, we should find that the random variability tends to average out, leaving only true ability reflected in the average of such performance measurements. Notice, however, that repeated evaluations will not eliminate error in estimating the expected return, since the error will be present in the difference between the true performance and the estimated performance in *every one* of the evaluation periods.

The average performance evaluation error that remains as the number of evaluations grows large is equal to π, the deviation of the true expected return from the inaccurately assessed securities market line. This *ex ante* performance error is set forth algebraically in equation (1) and is derived formally in the footnote:[3]

$$\left.\begin{array}{l}\text{EX POST}\\ \text{PERFORMANCE}\\ \text{EVALUATION}\\ \text{ERROR IN}\\ \text{PERIOD } t\end{array}\right\} \; \hat{\alpha}_t - \alpha_t = \pi \left\{\begin{array}{l}\text{EX ANTE}\\ \text{SML}\\ \text{DEVIATION}\end{array}\right. \qquad (1)$$

The simple relationship in equation (1) makes it clear that the causes of deviation from the *ex ante* estimated securities market line are very important. If the evaluator could estimate such deviations independently, he could correct the traditional CAPM performance evaluations and thereby derive a more accurate assessment of true management ability.

THE CAUSES OF *EX ANTE* DEVIATIONS FROM THE SECURITY MARKET LINE

The entire error between true performance and estimated performance is due to deviation of the portfolio's position from the assessed securities market line. We shall now investigate why such deviations occur. Although it might seem that they could be caused by errors in assessing any of three components of the securities market line (the riskless rate of interest, the beta coefficient, or the expected return on the market index), we shall see that there is only one cause: failure to choose the proper optimized portfolio as the market index.

Figure 4 illustrates why the optimality or non-optimality of the chosen index is the critical ingredient for whether or not there are deviations from the securities market line. In the left panel of Figure 4, the il-

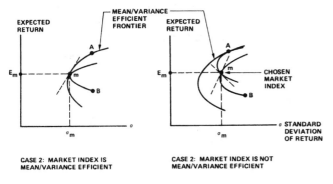

CASE 2: MARKET INDEX IS MEAN/VARIANCE EFFICIENT

CASE 2: MARKET INDEX IS NOT MEAN/VARIANCE EFFICIENT

Figure 4. The Slope of Portfolio Loci (Dotted Lines) when the Market Index is Optimal (left) and Non-optimal (right).

lustrated index (m) is an optimized portfolio and is therefore located on the *ex ante* mean/variance efficient frontier. Imagine forming a hybrid portfolio from an arbitrary asset and the market index. For example, if asset B were located as shown in the diagram, it could be combined in varying proportions with the market index to trace a locus of portfolios depicted by the

curve mB. Of course, points on the curve between m and B indicate some positive amounts invested in both m and B, whereas points outside this range indicate a short position either in m or in B. A similar locus can be created with m and any other asset; for example, with A. In this illustration, A is also an optimal portfolio.

The key principle in the diagram is: At the point where m is located, for any asset that is combined with m, the slopes of all such loci are equal to each other and to the slope of the efficient frontier at point m. This slope is indicated by the dotted line in the left hand panel.

In the right panel, I illustrate the second possibility. The chosen market index is not an optimized portfolio and therefore lies strictly inside the efficient frontier. Now, imagine combining assets with this index to generate a hybrid portfolio. The curve connecting m and B is again the locus of portfolios that can be generated by combining asset B with the market index. Similarly, the curve combining m and A indicates the portfolios that can be generated by combining the market index with A. Since m is strictly inside the efficient frontier, it is clear that the slope of these loci need not be equal at point m, unlike the case in which m is optimal. In fact, as the right panel in Figure 4 shows, the slope of the portfolio locus connecting m and A is negative at m, whereas the slope of the portfolio locus for m and B is positive.

It is possible to prove that there *must* be disagreements among these slopes when m is within the efficient frontier. Indeed, one correct definition of an optimized portfolio is that all slopes connecting any asset with the optimized portfolio are equal at the point where the optimized portfolio is located.

We can easily prove that in the general case the dotted lines in Figure 4 have slopes given by equation (2).[4]

$$\gamma_j = \frac{E_j - E_m}{\sigma_m(\beta_j - 1)} \qquad (2)$$

If E_j is the return expected on an arbitrary asset j and if β_j is its (true) beta computed against m, then E_m is the *true* expected return on the market index, and σ_m is the index's true standard deviation. Equation (2) gives the loci slope when the true market portfolio is not "optimized" as well as when it is "optimized" and located on the efficient frontier.

BRINGING IN THE CAPITAL MARKET LINE

We are now ready to introduce the final link in the chain connecting the position of the measured market index and the error in performance measurement. This final link is the estimated capital market line, the line between E_f and m in Figure 5. Since the

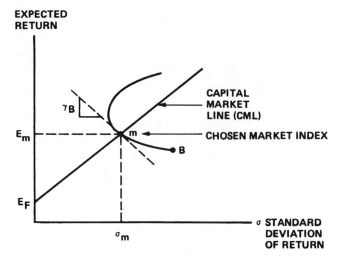

Figure 5. The Capital Market Line (CML) When the Market Index (m) is not optimized.

market index is not (necessarily) an optimal portfolio, the locus of portfolios formed from any asset, say B, and the market index may pass *through* the capital market line at m as shown in Figure 5. The estimated capital market line has a slope equal to

$$\frac{E_m - E_F}{\sigma_m}.$$

For the case illustrated in Figure 5, notice that the expected true return on asset B is less than the (true) expected return E_m on the market index. Since the slope of the locus of portfolios formed by combining m with B is negative at m, we infer from equation (2) that β_B must be greater than one. Comparing the slope of the locus of portfolios with the capital market line, we must have the following inequality:

$$\gamma_B = \frac{E_B - E_m}{\sigma_m(\beta_B - 1)} < \frac{E_m - E_F}{\sigma_m}. \qquad (3)$$

The standard deviation σ_m of the market index return is positive, and since $\beta_B > 1$, inequality (3) reduces to the following expression:

$$E_B < E_F + \beta_B(E_m - E_F). \qquad (4)$$

This is equivalent to the *ex ante* deviation from the securities market line being negative for asset B; i.e., it is equivalent to

$$\pi_B < 0. \qquad (5)$$

Thus, for any portfolio under evaluation, the *ex ante* deviation π from the securities market line depends upon three considerations. First, the index used in the evaluation must not be an optimized portfolio. Given this condition, the relationship between the position of the index and that of the portfolio under evaluation causes an *ex ante* securities market line deviation whose sign is dependent on two factors: (1) whether the measured beta is greater or less than unity and (2) whether the slope of the portfolio locus γ is

greater or less than the capital market line's slope.

The general relationship looks like a sharp-edged saddle and is depicted in Figure 6. Performance is judged to be better than it really is when β is less than one and γ is less than the slope of the capital market line or when β is greater than 1 and γ is greater than the slope of the capital market line. Performance

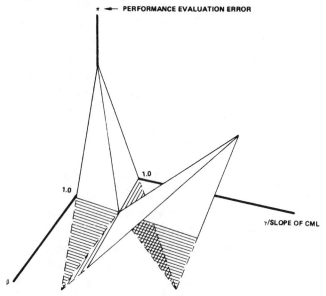

Figure 6. Non-Statistical Performance Evaluation Error as a Function of Beta (β) and Gamma(γ).

is better than it is assessed to be in the other two quadrants, when β is greater than 1 and γ is less than the slope of the capital market line or vice versa.

Equation (2) shows that γ depends on the difference between the true expected return of the portfolio under evaluation and the true expected return of the market index being employed. This permits a finer categorization of performance evaluation errors. Table 1 lists the six possibilities that produce positive or negative evaluation errors, and these possibilities are illustrated in the six panels of Figure 7. The letter corresponding to each of the six portfolios in Figure 7 is circled in the six panels of Table 1. Figure 7

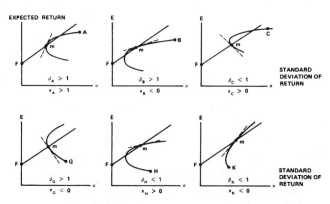

Figure 7. The Six Possible Configurations of Ex ante Deviations (π) from the Securities Market Line for Various Levels of Systematic Risk (β) and Expected Returns ($E_i - E_m$). The Dotted Line has a Slope Equal to $\gamma_i = (E_i - E_m)/[\sigma_m(\beta_i - 1)]$

TABLE 1

The Relationships Among Performance Evaluation Error π_p, Expected Return E_p, beta (β_p), and Portfolio Locus Slope (γ_p). Compare Figure 7. This tableau assumes $E_m > E_F$.

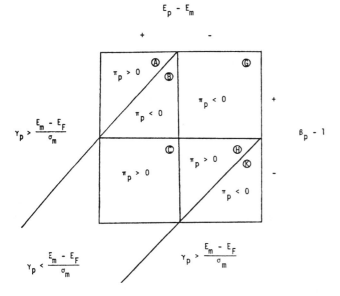

and Table 1 apply *only* in the "usual" case — when the CML has a positive slope or, equivalently, when $E_m > E_F$.

There are three cases in which performance may be evaluated as better than it actually is, and these are illustrated by portfolios A, C, and H. Of these three cases, two are associated with portfolios whose expected returns are larger than the market index's expected return. (These are portfolios A and C). Portfolios C and H have betas less than one, and portfolio A has a beta greater than 1. Thus, if the portfolio manager wants to appear to have more ability than he does have, he will choose a portfolio like A, C, or H. Given that the market index is not an optimized portfolio, any of these three cases will consistently produce "superior" results. Of course, this appearance is completely illusory, is due to benchmark error, and is not an indication of the portfolio manager's true ability.

Conversely, true ability will be offset by negative performance evaluation error if a manager is unfortunate enough to have chosen a portfolio such as B, G, or K. Of these three cases, two — G and K — are associated with portfolios whose expected returns are less than the market index. Portfolios B and G have betas greater than 1, and K has a beta less than 1.

Two of the six portfolios illustrated in Figure 7 — G and H — are dominated by the market index in the sense that the index has both a higher expected return and a lower variance of return. Such portfolios would be dominated by index funds that were successful in mimicking the market index. Nevertheless, though dominated by an index fund, the performance

evaluation benchmark would be negatively biased in the case of G and positively biased in the case of H. It is hard to imagine how any portfolio dominated by an index fund can be considered to be successfully managed. Yet, in the case of portfolio H, even if the manager had no ability whatsoever, he would be consistently judged to have superior ability, since the deviation π_H from the securities market line is positive.

On the other hand, the mirror image case is not possible: Provided that the market portfolio has a larger expected return than the risk-free interest rate (i.e., that the capital market line has a positive slope), no portfolio that dominates the market index can have a negative benchmark error. Thus, it is not possible for a managed portfolio that dominates an index fund to have consistently negative performance evaluations in the absence of ability.

ALTERATIONS IN THE CHOICE OF MARKET INDEX AND THE BENCHMARK ERROR

Frequently, the management performance evaluator is concerned with whether he would obtain a vastly different evaluation if he chose one market index rather than another. For example, would there be a major difference in the ranking of managed portfolios if one used, say, the Standard and Poor's 500 Index rather than the New York Stock Exchange Index? The purpose of this section is to show that a change in the market index need not produce a markedly different set of evaluations. But we will also show that this fact does not mitigate the basic benchmark error problem. Different indices can produce the same or similar benchmark errors. Agreement among evaluators who use different indices, therefore, does not imply that the evaluations are correct.

Suppose, for example, that a given portfolio has been evaluated with a particular market index m and that the evaluation contains a benchmark error, π_p. The relationship between the expected return on the portfolio, the beta, the risk-free asset, and the expected return of the market index is given by

$$E_p = \pi_p + E_F + \beta_p(E_m - E_F). \quad (6)$$

How does the benchmark error π_p change as a function of the choice of index? Let us consider, for example, an alternative index, say m', which need not fall on the securities market line produced by the original index. The expected return on the new index satisfies

$$E_{m'} = \pi_{m'} + E_F + \beta_{m'}(E_m - E_F) \quad (7)$$

where $\pi_{m'}$ is the benchmark error for the new index evaluated against the old one. By combining (6) and (7) we can eliminate the original market index and obtain an equation based on the new index that looks very much like a securities market line. The original benchmark error for portfolio p (the portfolio being evaluated) and the benchmark error for the new index are combined into the hybrid error in brackets:

$$E_p = [\pi_p - \pi_{m'}/\beta_{m'}] + E_F + (\beta_p/\beta_{m'})(E_{m'} - E_F). \quad (8)$$

The only difference between equation (8) and a securities market line (plus p's deviation) is that the beta for p computed with index m' may not be exactly equal to $\beta_p/\beta_{m'}$. It is quite easy to prove, however, that when the new and old indices are perfectly correlated, the new beta for portfolio p will be exactly equal to $\beta_p/\beta_{m'}$. In general, the new benchmark error will be $\pi_p - \pi_{m'}/\beta_{m'}$, plus some increment that depends on the indices' correlation. For high levels of positive correlation between the two indices, the new beta should be close to the ratio $\beta_p/\beta_{m'}$. Thus, the new benchmark error will be close to the old one plus the constant $-\pi_{m'}/\beta_{m'}$.

In Figure 8 we illustrate graphically how a change in the index affects benchmark error. The orig-

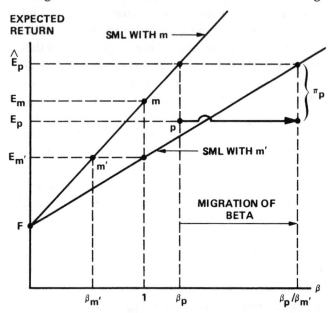

EXPECTED RETURN

$\hat{E}_p$

E_m

E_p

$E_{m'}$

SML WITH m

SML WITH m'

MIGRATION OF BETA

F

π_p

m

p

m'

$\beta_{m'}$ 1 β_p $\beta_p/\beta_{m'}$ β

Figure 8. Beta "Migration" and Constancy of Benchmark Error (π) with Change in Market Index (m to m').

inal securities market line with the original index m is the upper line, and the portfolio p being evaluated has a negative benchmark error with respect to that line. In this example, we assume the new index lies on the original securities market line at m', so that $\pi_{m'} = 0$.

When one uses the new rather than the old index, the evaluated portfolio's position will change; its beta will migrate to the right, as the arrow shows. If the old and new indices are perfectly correlated, the evaluated portfolio will maintain the distance under the new securities market line that it had under the old line. The benchmark error is constant because the beta has migrated from β_p to $\beta_p/\beta_{m'}$ with the index change.

Most of the commonly-used stock market indices, such as the Dow Jones Industrial Average, the New York Stock Exchange Index, and the Standard and Poor's 500, are very highly correlated. Although they are not perfectly correlated, the correlations are sufficiently high that the benchmark errors need not be significantly altered by using one index rather than another. However, as illustrated in Figure 8, this does *not* imply that there is no benchmark error. The benchmark errors are close to each other under alternative index choices, but the errors still exist and must be corrected if the evaluator is to obtain an accurate assessment of the manager's ability.

When a new index is associated with a non-zero benchmark error using the original securities market line (i.e., when $\pi_{m'} \neq 0$), the value of each new benchmark error will be different. Since the change in error, $-\pi_{m'}/\beta_{m'}$, is constant across evaluated portfolios, however, the *rankings* of estimated ability can remain unchanged. Thus, if with one index manager A has an algebraically larger benchmark error than manager B, he can also have a larger error with another index.

If there happen to be *no* differences in the evaluations produced by two indices, significant benchmark errors can still be present. The agreement in evaluations across indices does not guarantee that management ability has been properly assessed. On the other hand, if the old and new indices are not perfectly correlated, it is *possible* that substantial differences will occur in the benchmark errors produced by different indices. (See Roll [1978]).

To understand how a change in the market index can lead first to an alteration in benchmark error and then to a reversal of estimated management ability, consider the situation depicted in Figure 9. We

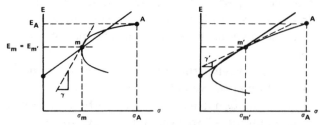

E E_A A

$E_m = E_{m'}$ m

γ

σ_m σ_A σ

E   A

m'

γ

$\sigma_{m'}$ σ_A σ

Figure 9. How the Benchmark Error of a Given Evaluated Portfolio (A) can Change Sign when the Index is Changed (from m to m').

evaluate a given portfolio, labeled A in both panels of the figure, against the CAPM benchmark. We use a given market index, m, in the left panel and a different index, m¹, in the right. To illustrate the nature of the evaluation process, we assume both indices have the same expected return and standard deviation of return. However, they are not perfectly correlated.

In this case, the evaluated portfolio has a β

greater than unity with both indices, *but* the degree of correlation is larger between portfolio A and index m' (on the right) than between A and index m (on the left). This difference in correlation results in the left-hand locus being more broadly curved, and, as a result, the γ for portfolio A, the dotted slope of the locus at m(m'), is larger (smaller) than the capital market line's slope for m(m'). As we have already seen, if the expected return on the evaluated portfolio exceeds the market index's expected return, if the β exceeds unity, and if γ exceeds the slope of the capital market line, the benchmark error will be positive. (See the top left panel in Figure 7.) Under the same circumstances for expected returns and β, if γ is less than the capital market line's slope, the benchmark error will be negative. (See the top center panel of Figure 7.)

The upshot? A change in the market index one uses in performance evaluation can result in a reversal of the benchmark error. In the absence of ability, this will cause a previously well-considered manager to fall into disfavor. The direction of change in esteem will be the same even if ability is present — the over-estimated manager will become under-estimated.

Figure 9 gives a special case because the means and variances of the two indices are identical, something that one cannot expect for most changes in index. For example, the NYSE index has a considerably lower variance than the AMEX index does. Such differences in mean or variance would serve to increase the possibility of changes in benchmark error, given the degree of correlation between the indices.

HOW TO DETECT AND CORRECT BENCHMARK ERROR

To detect and correct an error in the CAPM benchmark, the portfolio management evaluator must obtain an independent estimate of the error's two components, β and γ. (See Figure 6.) This is tantamount to obtaining independent estimates of the evaluated portfolio's expected return.[5]

One fairly straightforward method for obtaining such estimates is to apply the classification scheme of Table 1 (or Figure 7) to the individual securities approved for purchase by the portfolio manager. During some validation period (different from the period of management evaluation), each approved security would provide a sample estimate of β and γ from observed rates of return. These γ and β estimates must be calculated with the market index that will be used in performance evaluation.

One could proceed to form a qualitative judgment about the benchmark error for a given evaluated manager by noting whether he selected securities falling more heavily into the $\pi > 0$ cells of Table 1; i.e.,

whether he selected securities that had characteristics like those of portfolios A, C, or H in Figure 7. Selecting such securities would be evidence that he was attempting to "game" the evaluation by choosing securities with positive benchmark errors.

It is possible to be more precise and quantitative by estimating the *ex ante* SML deviation π_j for each approved security j. Then a quantitative benchmark error π_p would be simply an investment-weighted average of the π_j's constituting the portfolio. Unfortunately, some knotty statistical problems are associated with this procedure. During any validation period used to estimate the vector of approved π_j's, cross-sectional *dependence* will be present. Furthermore, since a vector is to be predicted, less familiar methods such as Stein-type estimators[6] should be employed. Although the expense of developing a satisfactory procedure may be substantial, the benefits will continue because the same mechanism can be employed to correct management evaluation in every period. For this reason, we should soon see such sophisticated correction methods put into practice.

An easy way to infer the existence of benchmark errors with the simple CAPM is to notice the ability of other variables to predict expected returns. Recently, such variables as dividend yield, price/earnings ratio, and firm size have been found to be useful return predictors,[7] and some have already received practical application.[8]

The very fact that such variables are useful implies the existence of ex ante deviations from the simple securities market line. Take the case of dividend yield: Although its importance is sometimes attributed to a tax differential between capital gains and ordinary income,[9] dividend yield is a surrogate, albeit a very imperfect one, for nominal expected return. Even with *no* effective tax differential,[10] "dividend tilt" could improve performance simply because high dividend yields are associated with positive benchmark errors (which also are related positively to nominal expected returns). To the extent that dividend yields are positively related to *beta* risk-adjusted nominal expected returns, they must be explaining benchmark errors in the simple no-tax CAPM. This implies that the tilting would become worthless if the market index currently in use were replaced by an "optimized" index.

SUMMARY

As a benchmark for evaluating portfolio management ability, the capital asset pricing model (CAPM) is subject to persistent error. This error is not due to statistical variation or estimation, and it will not average out over repeated manager evaluations. CAPM benchmark error is present whenever the market index is not "optimized"; i.e., whenever the index is not an ex ante mean/variance efficient portfolio. Whether a particular managed portfolio has a positive or negative benchmark error depends upon a complex set of factors, including the portfolio's expected return, beta, and variance of return. One can systematically categorize and correct benchmark errors by using additional sources of information concerning expected return.

It is possible for different market indices to produce different benchmark errors for the same managed portfolio. On the other hand, this need not happen. Agreement across indices in management evaluation implies neither the absence of benchmark error nor the validity of the evaluations.

The effectiveness of variables like dividend yield in explaining risk-adjusted returns is evidence of the presence of benchmark error.

[1] The "beta" for security j is

$$\beta_j \equiv \rho_{jm} \frac{\sigma_j}{\sigma_m}$$

where σ_j and σ_m are the standard deviations of returns on security j and the market index, respectively, and ρ_{jm} is the correlation coefficient between these returns.

[2] Sometimes researchers use more complicated versions of the CAPM. For example, if no risk-free asset exists, one can replace it with the expected return on a "zero-beta" portfolio. Because it is unclear which version of the asset pricing model is correct, such refinements introduce additional sources of error. However, since each version of the CAPM is prone to similar kinds of error, in this analysis I use the simplest capital asset pricing model for ease of exposition.

[3] For a given evaluation period t, the true and estimated performances are given by, respectively,

$$\alpha_t = R_{pt} - E_p$$
$$\hat{\alpha}_t = R_{pt} - \hat{E}_p.$$

So, the performance evaluation error is $\hat{\alpha}_t - \alpha_t = E_p - \hat{E}_p$.
Given the capital asset pricing model and the true risk of the portfolio, the true expected return is

$$E_p = E_F + \beta_p (E_m - E_F).$$

However, the *estimated* expected return is

$$\hat{E}_p = \hat{E}_F + \hat{\beta}_p (\hat{E}_m - \hat{E}_F),$$

where each component ($\hat{E}_F$, $\hat{E}_m$, and $\hat{\beta}_p$) of the estimated securities market line could be inaccurately assessed. If one does inaccurately assess these, the true expected return will deviate from the *estimated* SML on an *ex ante* basis, so that

$$E_p = \pi + \hat{E}_F + \hat{\beta}_p (\hat{E}_m - \hat{E}_F),$$

with $\pi \neq 0$. Thus, the performance evaluation error is given by

$$\hat{\alpha}_t - \alpha_t = E_p - \hat{E}_p = \pi.$$

[4] Let δ be the proportion invested in portfolio j (or in individual asset j) and $1 - \delta$ be invested in the market index m. This hybrid portfolio p then satisfies $E_p = \delta E_j + (1 - \delta) E_m$ and $\sigma^2_p = \delta^2 \sigma^2_j + (1 - \delta)^2 \sigma^2_m + 2\delta(1 - \delta)\sigma_{jm}$. It is easy to see that p's mean and variance change with δ. At $\delta = 0$ (100% invested in the market portfolio), the rate of trade-off between mean and standard deviation of p is given by $(\partial E_p / \partial \delta)/(\partial \sigma_p / \partial \delta)|\delta = 0 = (E_j - E_m)/\sigma_m(\beta_j - 1)$.

[5] Cornell [1980] argues forcefully for a portfolio management evaluation method based solely on independent estimates of expected return and not based on the CAPM or on any asset pricing model.

[6] See Efron and Morris [1975].

[7] See Litzenberger and Ramaswamy [1979], Basu [1977], Banz [1979], and Reinganum [1978].

[8] See W. F. Sharpe's excellent description [1978] of the Wells Fargo yield "tilt" portfolio management process.

[9] Litzenberger and Ramaswamy [1979].

[10] Miller and Scholes [1978] argue that there is no effective difference between the taxation rates of dividends and capital gains, since the former can be converted into the latter by appropriate financial planning.

REFERENCES

Rolf Banz, "On the Relationship Between the Market Value and the Return of Common Stocks," *Proceedings of the Seminar on the Analysis of Security Prices*, The Center For Research in Securities Prices, University of Chicago, Vol 24, No. 1, May 1979.

S. Basu, "Investment Performance of Common Stocks in Relation to Their Price-Earnings Ratios: A Test of the Efficient Market Hypothesis," *Journal of Finance*, 23, 1977, pp. 663-682.

Bradford Cornell, "Asymmetric Information and Portfolio Performance Measurement," *Journal of Financial Economics*, 7, December 1979, in press.

Bradley Efron and Carl Morris, "Data Analysis Using Stein's Estimator and Its Generalizations," *Journal of the American Statistical Association*," 70, June 1975, pp. 311-319.

Robert H. Litzenberger and Krishna Ramaswamy, "The Effect of Personal Taxes and Dividends on Capital Asset Prices: Theory and Empirical Evidence," *Journal of Financial Economics*, 7, June 1979, pp. 163-195.

Merton H. Miller and Myron S. Scholes, "Dividends and Taxes," *Journal of Financial Economics*, 6, December 1978, pp. 333-364.

M. R. Reinganum, "Misspecification of Capital Asset Pricing: Empirical Anomalies Based on Earnings Yields and Forecasts," Unpublished manuscript, Graduate School of Business, University of Chicago, 1978.

Richard Roll, "Ambiguity When Performance is Measured by the Securities Market Line," *Journal of Finance*, 33, September 1978, pp. 1051-1069.

William F. Sharpe, "Security Codings: Measuring Relative Attractiveness in Perfect and Imperfect Markets," Stanford University Working Paper No. 486, Graduate School of Business, November 1978.

The trouble with performance measurement

You can't do it, you never will, and who wants to?

Robert Ferguson

My message is short and simple. I hope it is also stimulating, entertaining, alarming, depressing, and nihilistic. If you finish the article thinking you are measuring investment performance only because you don't know of any better way to spend your time (remuneratively, of course), I will be a happy man.

I am going to tell you why:

1. Nobody knows how to measure investment performance;
2. Nobody ever will know how to measure investment performance, and
3. Nobody would want to measure investment performance even if they did know how.

NOBODY KNOWS HOW TO MEASURE INVESTMENT PERFORMANCE

Performance measurement consists of assigning numbers to portfolios. This does not matter if there is only one available portfolio to invest in, because then you have no choice. It does not matter if there is more than one available portfolio to invest in, either. But in that case it is not quite so clear why.

A few diehards still use return as a measure of performance. This is correct if all they care about is the portfolio's expected return. Since the expected returns of stocks differ, one stock will have the highest expected return. The implication is that a one-stock portfolio is the proper choice.

Most of the time, people who use return as a measure of performance do not have one-stock portfolios. This may be because they have a fragmented personality, or possible worse. I try to stay away from these people; they could be dangerous.

But perhaps I am being too hard on return. What about using long-term return as a measure of performance? I suppose the point is arguable if you are going to be around forever.[1]

Some people argue that long-term return is the proper definition of portfolio attractiveness for pension funds and other possibly immortal investors. I disagree for two reasons.

First, there are no immortal investors.[2]

My second reason is the important one. Only living people make decisions, and I believe that they try to make decisions that make them happy. The utility functions whose expected values are maximized in all of the textbooks are ours, not those of hypothetical people yet to be born. We place great importance on the short-term availability of funds for consumption and bequests.

Show me a pension fund manager who will take a 99% chance of losing almost everything in a year in order to maximize really long-term return and I will show you someone without a job.

The sophisticated measures of portfolio attrac-

1. Footnotes appear at the end of the article.

ROBERT FERGUSON is Senior Vice President of Leland O'Brien Rubinstein Associates in New York (NY 10028).

tiveness are adjusted returns. This makes more sense. If several portfolios are equivalent, taking into account everything but return, then it seems reasonable to compare them on the basis of their returns.

There are two problems with this approach. First, two portfolios are never precisely equivalent with respect to everything but return. Second, there are as many ways to define equivalence as there are investors.[3]

The Security Market Line (SML) was one of the ingenious attempts to define equivalence. This procedure can be characterized as follows:

1. Choose a reference portfolio, such as a broad stock market index.
2. Compute each managed portfolio's beta with respect to the reference portfolio.
3. Choose a relation between return and beta to serve as a measurement standard.
4. Use the relation to compute the return appropriate to each managed portfolio's beta.
5. Define the managed portfolio's performance as the difference between each managed portfolio's actual return and its appropriate return. This measure of performance usually is called an alpha.

My description of the SML procedure makes it sound arbitrary. Most descriptions make it sound like God's gift to the investment community. Actually, it *is* arbitrary. Both the reference portfolio and the measurement standard have to be chosen. I know of three popular measurement standards and a variety of commonly used reference portfolios. This choice gives the performance measurer some flexibility — enough, as it turns out, to get whatever result the measurer wants.

Richard Roll was the first person to point out how flawed is the SML approach.

The betas of securities depend upon the choice of the reference portfolio. The alphas of securities depend upon the betas. Different reference portfolios give rise to different betas and alphas for the managed portfolios. You can find a reference portfolio that will provide any desired ranking of the managed portfolios by alpha. Almost identical reference portfolios can result in radically different rankings.

The finance theory that motivated the SML procedure presumes that investors care only about single-period expected return and standard deviation of return. The emphasis is on having an efficient portfolio, one with the highest possible expected return for its level of standard deviation of return.

Wouldn't you know it — if the reference portfolio is efficient, the alphas of all securities and portfolios are zero.

If you start with a reference portfolio that is efficient and change it by even a tiny amount, then all of a sudden there will be alphas.[4] If you change the efficient reference portfolio in two different ways by a tiny amount, there will be two different sets of alphas for the managed portfolios. Depending upon the direction of the tiny changes in the efficient reference portfolio, the rankings of the managed portfolios will be different. I conjecture that there exist two reference portfolios with a correlation as close to 1.0 as you like that rank managed portfolios in the opposite direction.

Jack Treynor was the first person to note that focusing on alpha is just as bad as focusing on return. If adjusted return is the key to measuring performance, then you must also use an adjusted alpha. In Jack's view, the problem with the SML is in the way that it focuses on alpha and ignores the standard deviation of alpha. Jack showed that an investor who is concerned with only a portfolio's expected return and standard deviation of return will consider the ratio of alpha to standard deviation of alpha as the appropriate definition of portfolio attractiveness. If risk is relevant, an SML analysis is not. Jack called his definition of portfolio attractiveness the appraisal ratio.

The appraisal ratio never gained much popularity, even though it was *really* sophisticated.

After a while, Jack managed to communicate to me his ideas about the appraisal ratio. There was a consequence. I realized that Jack's appraisal ratio looked like the ratio of a mean to a standard deviation. This is the stuff of first-year statistics. These ratios can be associated with probabilities. And probabilities can be transformed to a scale of from 0 to 100. Everyone understands 0 to 100.[5]

My measure of portfolio attractiveness was the significance level of the portfolio's alpha. I simply treated the appraisal ratio as a "t" value in statistics, computed its cumulative probability, and scaled it by 100. If there was no indication of talent, you got 50. If everything you said was precisely correct, you got 100. If everything you said was exactly opposite to the truth, you got 0. People who got either 0 or 100 were, of course, equally valuable.

Time marched on and a variety of ever more sophisticated variants of the Capital Asset Pricing Model (CAPM) spawned ever more sophisticated definitions of portfolio attractiveness. Market Planes, Yield Alphas, and Appreciation Alphas were invented. Performance attribution came upon the scene.

Then I noticed that all of these sophisticated techniques used betas and alphas (of one sort or another) as an important element of their procedures. I remembered what Richard Roll had said, and I have rephrased it, slightly.

Betas and alphas depend upon the choice of a reference portfolio. Any definition of portfolio attractiveness that depends importantly on either alphas or betas will allow the measurer to rank the managed portfolios either arbitrarily or almost arbitrarily by choosing a suitable reference portfolio.

So much for all the sophisticated performance measurement systems used today.

One fundamental difficulty is that you need a theory to motivate the performance measurement procedure. One thing you can be sure of about any theory is that it isn't right. The important question is whether or not you really know where you are. In the case of Classical Physics, you do. Classical Physics is wrong, but its degree of approximation is known and it is sometimes very accurate. You use it where it is known to work. In the case of performance measurement, the degree of approximation of the motivating theory is not known. You do not really know where you are.

The perspective that I think is justified by the past is procedure after procedure, each with its own ranking of managed portfolios and its own problems. Of course, the problems are only appreciated after the fact. History offers no confidence in our ability to measure the relative attractiveness of portfolios. We have no reason to believe we are finally doing it right.

I hope that by this time you are convinced of the hopelessness of doing anything useful with performance measurement. If so, you should take pride in your ability to understand all the wonderfully subtle points I have made. You are certainly of above average intelligence.

Of course, there may be a few diehards among you who remain unconvinced despite my marvelous and insightful comments. To these individuals let me say two things.
1. When it comes right down to it, what I have said so far is interesting and entertaining but, in the grand scheme of things, irrelevant.
2. You had better pay particular attention from here on.

NOBODY EVER WILL KNOW HOW TO MEASURE INVESTMENT PERFORMANCE

The goal of performance measurement is to ascertain who knows how to invest best — for the future, of course. I shall now show you why this is not possible, theoretically, regardless of the distribution of talent in the investment community.

Some of you may take comfort, because my argument is a theoretical one. Probably you have all heard the phrase: Oh, well, that's only theory. If you are one of these people and are in the venture capital business, please contact me. I have a few product ideas I'd like to discuss with you.

Let us start off as simply as possible. Suppose that we could determine who is the best investor or, more accurately, who is going to be the best investor in the future. According to the performance measurement paradigm, everyone would want to invest with this person. As a result, everyone would have the same portfolio!

There are some important implications here. For one thing, there would be no further need for measuring performance. Everyone would have the same performance, but this is a minor point. There is something even more perverse going on.

Perhaps a little more *reductio ad absurdum* will clarify things. Once again, suppose it is possible to determine who will be the best investor in the future. Now suppose that this is done and that everyone knows who she is. Now let's add one wrinkle. Suppose it turns out that she is a perfect forecaster.

If this damsel wanted to buy 1000 XYZ from you at 35, would you sell it to her? Of course not. The last thing anyone would be willing to do would be to trade with a perfect forecaster at prices she is willing to trade at.

Assuming the current price of XYZ is 35, what will happen?

If the damsel thought that XYZ was worth 45, and nobody was willing to sell her stock at 35, she would raise her bid. She might offer to buy 800 XYZ at 38. No stock would be forthcoming at this price, either. She then might offer to buy 500 XYZ at 42.

You can see where this is leading. The higher the bid price, the less the number of shares she is willing to take. This makes sense. The size of the active position of XYZ in her portfolio should reflect the degree of undervaluation.

Eventually, the price of XYZ will settle at 45, but no transaction will have occurred. Everyone will have gained the benefit of the damsel's insight. The damsel will have outperformed no one.

A little reflection will convince you that matters are even worse than this. Everyone would insist on holding the same portfolio as the damsel. Consequently, everyone would have the same performance.

Here is the moral: If performance measurement can identify a perfect forecaster, there can be no performance.

In real life, it is hard to tell just how good investors are. Let us make our assumptions more realistic and see what the performance measurement equilibrium must be like.

Assume that performance measurement succeeds in designating one investor as superior but not perfect. The measurer concludes that the probability is 90% that the superior investor will be right if the two of you disagree. If she wants to buy 1000 XYZ from you at 35, would you sell it? Perhaps you would. This time around, the damsel could be wrong. After thinking about how big 90% is compared to 10%, however, you would be a fool not to try to protect yourself by asking for a higher price. Only by getting a higher price can you offset the losses you will incur on average due to her superiority. If the current price of XYZ is 35, you might offer to sell her 1000 XYZ at 42. Her response might be to take 200 XYZ at that price.

This hypothetical interchange suggests a way of determining what the damsel's notion of XYZ's fair price is. Nevertheless, I am unprepared[6] to follow through on this approach. Keep it simple and remember that no matter how depressing the conclusions, the true situation is bound to be far worse.

If the damsel is right, then she will have purchased 200 XYZ at 42 and will have seen it rise to 45. The stock trades somewhere between the current price of 35 and the final equilibirum price of 45. The damsel makes a 3-point profit. She outperforms you. There is performance, but it's small.

Now suppose that performance measurement suggests only a 10% chance that the damsel will be right if the two of you disagree. When she offers to buy 1000 XYZ from you at 35, you might counter with an offer to sell her 1000 XYZ at 38. You need less protection since you are more likely to be right. She might counter with an offer to buy 800 XYZ at 38.

If the damsel is right, then she will make a 7 point profit as XYZ rises to 45. This time her performance will be large.

Note the relationship among your confidence in the damsel's superiority, the price at which you are willing to trade with her, and the amount of the transaction. The more sure you are that she will prove to be right, the higher will be the price you demand and the lower will be the amount that is transacted and the lower her profit.

If the damsel's profit is lower, so will be her measured performance. Consequently, her signal-to-noise ratio will be smaller. It will be less clear that she is superior. The probability of her superiority will be smaller. Still, it is performance measurement that provides the probability of her superiority.

To the extent that we assume that performance measurement provides clear-cut evidence of superiority, to that extent it follows that performance is too low, or will be too low in the future, to provide clear-cut evidence of superiority. *Superior performance*

can be achieved by a superior investor only if the past record does not provide clear-cut evidence of that superiority.

This is the kind of bizarre circularity that I love. It is almost mystical! This is what I have always wanted — mystical nihilism!

Here are some of the consequences of what I have pointed out so far.

> 1. The more effective the statistical and other techniques used to measure performance, the lower must be the level of performance, both past and future.

This must be so, because the more effective the statistical techniques used to measure performance, the smaller the signal that can be detected in relation to the noise. Thus, a specific level of confidence in superiority can be established at a lower level of performance. At the same time, performance must be below the level at which clear superiority can be demonstrated.

> 2. It is not possible for any investor to acquire a record that makes superiority obvious.

The market forces that reduce perceived performance come into play smoothly, not suddenly. They strengthen as the record becomes clearer in the direction of superiority. Their very strengthening prevents the record from ever becoming clear enough to establish superiority with a high probability. There is a subtle negative feedback mechanism at work throughout an investor's career, analogous to a mechanical governor on an engine that controls its speed.

> 3. The amount of data required to begin to make an investor's superiority obvious is about the amount that can be accumulated during an individual's entire working life.

I am stretching it slightly here. I really do not expect superiority ever to be obvious, but, if it is just becoming obvious as retirement or, even better, death approaches, no significant damage will be done to my notions of sensible economic equilibrium.

Here is a realistic hypothetical example to illustrate the current state of affairs.

Let us focus on the increment to return that superiority can provide. An annual incremental return of 1.2%, net of the cost of achieving it, is exceedingly valuable. Think of it as an honest-to-God alpha of 1.2% annually. An optimistic level of standard deviation of alpha to associate with this is 5.0% annually.

The typical approach to determining whether or not performance is significant goes something like this:

1. Assume that the true alpha is 0.0% annually.
2. Compute the probability that an alpha as large as that observed would occur over the period of measurement.
3. If this probability is small enough, declare that the alpha is significant.

This process is called testing for statistical significance. The motivation is that, if you assume a state of nature that implies that the observed event is hardly possible, then perhaps an alternative assumption about the state of nature is preferable. For the most part, performance measurement services consider a probability of 5% or 1% as a definition of "hardly possible," assuming, of course, that they do any significance testing at all.

The smaller the choice of probability for "hardly possible," the less likely it is that the measurer will declare a managed portfolio to have performed if it did not. On the other hand, if it really did perform, but not by much, the more likely is the measurer to declare that it did not. One way of choosing an appropriate probability for the definition of "hardly likely" is to analyze the consequences, and their importance to the investor, of two kinds of possible errors. The first is declaring there is talent when there is none. The second is declaring there is no talent when there is some. Another way of choosing the probability for "hardly possible" is to cop out and use what seems to be popular at the moment or in the past. Needless to say, it is the latter method that people use, almost universally. This is where the 5% and 1% probabilities come from.

The significance test can be accomplished by collecting monthly alpha estimates and performing a "t" test. First collect the monthly alphas, average them, and then use the standard deviation of the monthly alphas to compute a quantity called "t." The formula is:

$$t = \frac{(R_b - U) \sqrt{N(N - 1)}}{\sqrt{\sum (R_i - R_b)^2}}$$

In this formula:

R_i = the alpha observed in month i;

R_b = the average monthly alpha;

N = the number of observed monthly alphas, and

U = the assumed level of alpha (0, in this case).

This formula can be thought of as the ratio of two quantities. The numerator is the difference between the observed average monthly alpha and the assumed monthly alpha. To the extent there is talent, the average monthly alpha will exceed the assumed monthly alpha and the numerator will be relatively large and positive. The denominator is the estimated standard deviation of the numerator. Thus "t" is very much like the standard normal variates discussed in first-year statistics courses.

In effect, "t" measures the number of standard deviations of the observed average monthly alpha from the assumed monthly alpha. If this is large and positive, then either the measurer has observed an improbable event or his assumption about the average monthly alpha is wrong and there is talent. If "t" is small, the observed average monthly alpha is consistent with the assumed monthly alpha. Nothing suggests the existence of talent. The measurers then determine what levels of "t" correspond to probabilities of 5% and 1% and declare significance at these probabilities if the computed "t" values exceed these levels.

In our example, all the quantities in the formula are known except for the number of months of data to obtain the desired levels of significance. An examination of the formula shows that the greater the number of observations, the larger is "t." There is some number of observations just large enough to make "t" just large enough to exceed the level required for a declaration of significance.

As it turns out, you need about 47 years of monthly data to obtain statistical significance at the 5% level and about 94 years of data for significance at the 1% level. Since 5% levels of significance are the most widely used, I conclude that the normal working life of a professional investor is about 47 years. This is in good agreement with the theory discussed earlier. Perhaps there is something to this theory after all.

By now I am sure that all of you are convinced that there is no future in measuring investment performance. We have seen that it does not work in practice and that it cannot work in principle. Need I say more? Well, perhaps just two more points should be made:

1. When it comes right down to it, what I have said so far is fascinating, insightful, and entertaining but, in the grand scheme of things, irrelevant.
2. You better pay particular attention from here on.

NOBODY WOULD WANT TO MEASURE INVESTMENT PERFORMANCE EVEN IF THEY DID KNOW HOW

Performance measurement is supposed to rank managed portfolios in order of attractiveness. But then what is the investor to do? Is the investor supposed to allocate all funds to the top-ranked portfolio? If so, then performance measurement makes sense. But I submit that no rational investor will want to do this.

Think about securities for a moment. How many portfolio managers do you know who construct one-stock portfolios? None! Why is this?

Portfolios contain many securities because real life investors like portfolios with particular blends of characteristics. If investors like expected return and dislike standard deviation of return, they will hedge and diversify risk in order to achieve a high reward/risk ratio. Hedging and diversification enable the portfolio manager to manage risk in a way that makes it possible to increase a portfolio's reward/risk ratio far beyond what is attainable from a single security.

A rational investor faced with the opportunity to invest in a number of managed portfolios will think of them in the same way that a portfolio manager thinks of securities. The investor will want to know how to allocate the available funds among the managed portfolios, not which one to invest in.

Long ago Jack Treynor showed that, if short sales are allowed, maximizing an investor's ratio of expected return to standard deviation of return requires an active position in every available security. The only questions are the size of the position and whether the position is long or short.

What's more, the correct position in each security depends upon the characteristics of that security in relation to the characteristics of all of the other securities.

Similarly, the proper allocation of an investor's funds to a particular managed portfolio depends upon the characteristics of all of the managed portfolios that are available to him. But the numbers assigned to managed portfolios by a performance measurement ranking do not reflect all of these characteristics. Since they do not, they are useless to investors.

Some of you may think that someone can develop a performance measurement scheme that does reflect the characteristics of all of the available portfolios. If there is one, however, it won't be recognizable as a performance measurement scheme: It won't rank portfolios, but it will provide allocation proportions. These will be a function of the available managed portfolios. A particular managed portfolio may receive a high allocation in one application and a low allocation in another. To repeat: It won't be a performance measurement system; it will be a portfolio allocation system.

So much for performance measurement. Let's spend our time doing something useful.

I wonder if it is possible to forecast the characteristics of securities. If so, perhaps we could build, and use, that portfolio allocation system.

[1] I'm a short timer myself, and by cosmological standards, so are all of you. Infinite is different from a measly 40 years or so.

[2] According to modern physics, the nature of the Universe in the not too distant future (again, by cosmological standards) is inconsistent with their survival. If the Universe is constantly expanding, then existence becomes more and more tenuous (pardon the pun). Pension funds cannot exist in an environment where everything is in the form of an extremely low-density gas, although some would argue that that is precisely the case now. If the Universe cycles through Big Bangs, well — I haven't run across any survivors from the previous Bangs. Have you? Check out the third law of thermodynamics and get back to me if you see a way out.

[3] All investors — past, present, and future.

[4] This is sort of like God and the "Let There Be Light" routine. It makes you feel like somebody.

[5] Now I could be sophisticated, too.

[6] And will be for the indefinite future.

How to detect skill in management performance

You won't find it by using conventional portfolio performance measurement techniques.

Mark Kritzman

The purpose of this paper is to propose a methodology to detect skill from performance that appears random or insignificant. The methodology focuses on seeking evidence of conduct. This approach parallels the concept of the "perfect failure," which implies that it is better to perform correctly and fail because the outcome was influenced by random events than it is to perform incorrectly and succeed for the same reason.

Each year billions of dollars of pension assets are distributed among the professional investment management community on the basis of summary results that reflect very little about the managers' conduct. The typical criteria for manager evaluation are comparison to an index such as the Standard & Poor's 500 Stock Composite and ranking within some universe of competing managers.

Comparison to an index is considered appropriate, because the performance of the index can be achieved inexpensively by a mechanical process. Relative ranking is considered worthwhile, because a broad universe of managers would be expected to generate a normal distribution of returns with an average *active* return[1] of slightly less than zero (due to the cost of transacting). Therefore, by omitting managers with poor relative performance, one might expect the remaining managers to produce an active return that, on average, exceeds the result that would be achieved from an index fund.

1. Footnotes appear at the end of the article.

Both of these evaluation approaches are flawed. In particular, the relative ranking argument is sophistical, in that poor managers should not be expected to perform worse than average before transaction costs. Even if they have no information or skill, they should be wrong only half the time; otherwise one could profit by reversing their decisions.

Also, both approaches suffer from style bias. Managers' styles, which are not part of their discretionary active management, may be the most important determinant of their return or universe ranking. For example, equity managers who concentrate in small capitalization companies may outperform the index and the average equity manager over some periods. These managers, however, should not be credited for the favorable performance attributable to this exposure, since it does not reflect an "active judgment" on their part.

Part of this style bias can be overcome by comparing only managers with similar styles. A more direct approach, though, is to construct a normal portfolio[2] for each manager and to use it as the benchmark against which to measure active return.

The use of normal portfolios should help to correct the style bias that contaminates historical performance results, but a more serious problem remains. Investment returns are highly random or noisy. This problem may be characterized by the concept, "signal-to-noise ratio." Signal-to-noise ratio is an engineering term that refers to the ratio of a radio signal that is received compared to the noise that is

MARK KRITZMAN is Vice President in the Investment Management Group at Bankers Trust in New York (NY 10015). He benefited by comments from Stephen Brown, Dean D'Onofrio, Eric Lobben, and Krishna Ramaswamy.

introduced by the receiving system. The term is loosely applied here to refer to the ratio of return caused by manager conduct relative to that part of return resulting from the random movement of security prices.

The signal-to-noise ratio in security prices is low because most relevant information about security prices arrives randomly and cannot be anticipated but, nonetheless, causes prices to fluctuate. Most information that does not arrive randomly is anticipated and, hence, does not cause prices to change. On the other hand, signals of investment skill are related to information that arrives non-randomly and is not yet impounded in the price. This type of information is relatively scarce.

DETECTING INVESTMENT SKILL

Just how difficult is it to detect skill with confidence by examining summary measures of performance such as total return or active return? Confidence that a return is non-random is a function of the ratio of return to risk (in this case, active return and active risk):

$$\text{Confidence} = \text{function} \left(\frac{\text{Active Return}}{\text{Active Risk}} \right).$$

Since returns increase with time while risk increases with the square root of time, confidence after n years is a function of:

$$\frac{\text{Active Return} \times \text{Time}}{\text{Active Risk} \times \sqrt{\text{Time}}}.$$

By arranging terms, we can see that:

$$\text{Time} = \text{function} \left(\frac{\text{Confidence} \times \text{Active Risk}}{\text{Active Return}} \right)^2.$$

If active return equals 1% and active risk equals 2%, for example, 15 years of evidence are required before one could be 95% confident that the active return was, in fact, causally produced and not randomly generated, assuming returns are normally distributed.

If we were to take the partial derivative of time with respect to active return, active risk, and confidence, we would find that the length of the period required to demonstrate skill is a negative function of return and a positive function of risk and confidence level.[3]

Although this exercise may be sobering to some, it does not necessarily imply an industry-wide absence of investment skill. It simply underscores the limitations of relying on summary measures of performance to detect skill.

It is perhaps true that skill exists at a particular

type of decision for some investment managers, even in the presence of a low signal-to-noise ratio for total active return. Therefore, let us partition active return and risk and examine the signal-to-noise ratio associated with each decision separately. This decomposition of the investment results may begin to provide insight about manager conduct that could reduce the time required to detect skill in some cases.

For example, if we assume that security returns are linearly related to a series of factors, then value added by decisions relating to a particular factor can be measured as:

$$V_i = \beta_i(F_{i,p} - F_{i,m}),$$

where:

V_i = value added by exposure to factor i,

β_i = marginal return to factor i from cross-sectional regression of security returns on security factor values,

$F_{i,p}$ = portfolio's factor i value, and

$F_{i,m}$ = market's factor i value.

Therefore:

$$F_{i,p} - F_{i,m} = \text{active exposure to factor i.}$$

The risk inherent in a particular factor can be measured as:

$$\sigma_i = \left[\frac{\sum_{j=1}^{n} (\beta_{i,j} - \bar{\beta}_i)^2}{n} \right]^{1/2},$$

where:

σ_i = historical standard deviation of marginal returns to factor i,

$\beta_{i,j}$ = marginal return to factor i in period j, and

$\bar{\beta}_i$ = average marginal return to factor i.

Therefore, the risk incurred by exposure to a particular factor equals:

$$S_i = [\sigma_i^2(F_{i,p} - F_{i,m})^2]^{1/2}.$$

The framework described above is general. In applying this framework, we must normalize the results to an appropriate benchmark.

BROWNIAN MANAGEMENT[4]: A CASE STUDY

The following analysis illustrates how we might apply this approach to extract signals from noisy data. It is based on a particular multiple factor model that assumes a return generating process consisting of a market factor, eight common factors, and 10 market sector factors. The unexplained component of return is attributed to company-specific factors.[5] Implicit in this factor model is an investment management process that includes four reasonably distinct types of decisions: a market timing decision, a common factor exposure decision, a market sector weighting decision, and a security selection decision.

The context in which noise is presented is a confidence interval based on an expected contribution of 0.0% (absence of skill) and the standard deviation associated with each type of decision. The standard deviation is the sum of the risk incurred by exposure to the relevant factors recognizing covariance between factors. The value added is the sum of the returns achieved by exposure to the relevant factors. The results are cumulative and annualized so that different periodicities are comparable.[6]

This framework implies that a manager with no skill over a short period of time may produce a return substantially different from zero due to the random movement of security prices. As time passes, however, the cumulative annualized return should converge toward zero. The cumulative annualized confidence interval should also converge toward zero monotonically with the square root of time if risk remains constant.

The first chart for our sample manager, Brownian Management, seems to confirm this expected pattern. Although the first few quarters indicate that total

CHART 1

CONFIDENCE INTERVAL — TOTAL ACTIVE RETURNS

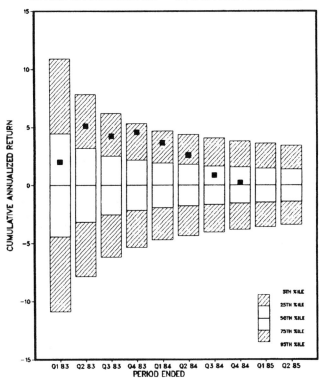

active return was significantly positive (the square plots), the return converged toward zero as the periodicity was extended to eight quarters. We would

be inclined to infer from these results that Brownian Management did not demonstrate very much skill, although it incurred significant active risk. The confidence intervals without plots show the returns required for significance in subsequent periods if risk remains consistent with the average risk incurred thus far.

The second chart suggests that Brownian Management's active timing decisions contributed neutrally to total active return, which is to be expected given the minimal degree of risk incurred by exposure to the market factor. In effect, Brownian Management does not time the market — which may reflect recognition on their part that they lack skill in this area.

CHART 2

CONFIDENCE INTERVAL — MARKET TIMING RETURNS

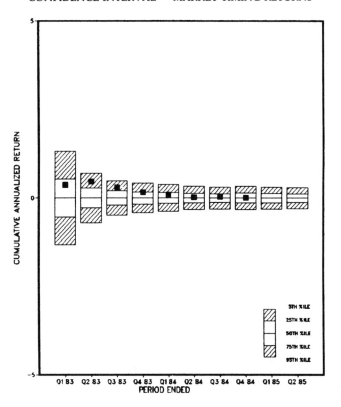

On the other hand, the next chart (Chart 3) shows that the value added by exposure to common factors suggests extraordinary skill. In a strict statistical sense, there is less than a one in a hundred chance that the value added after eight quarters could have occurred by random process.

Nonetheless, the statistics may overstate the true confidence we should have in the results in the following sense. Over a relatively short period of time, such as two years, a particular factor could produce a return that on average is very high or very low, and the manager could be consistently over- or under-exposed to it. The implied confidence in this

103

CHART 3

CONFIDENCE INTERVAL — COMMON FACTOR RETURNS

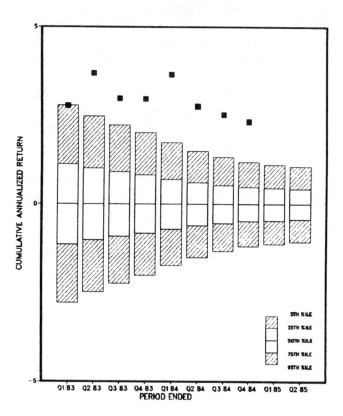

situation would be very high, but it would be based only on one event. Since a manager can just as well flip a head as easily as a tail, the implied confidence overstates the true significance of the results.

Therefore, when we observe a high return-to-risk ratio, we should explore further to determine how many decisions the manager actually made. For example, if the factor return reverses itself several times in the measurement period while the manager remains consistently overexposed to it, the anecdotal evidence would be less indicative of skill than when the manager's exposure corresponded with the reversals. This evidence of conduct could be measured directly by regressing the time series of factor returns with the time series of factor exposure changes.

It is important to look at the time series of decisions rather than the cross-sectional decisions because the factors could be co-linear. If the factors are co-linear, one decision could produce a favorable result across several factors so that the implied confidence is still dependent upon only one event.

The market sector results (Chart 4) are also encouraging. Brownian Management produced significantly positive results, and the trend seems to suggest that these results could persist. It is interesting to note that Brownian Management apparently increased its active exposure to market sector factors in the second

quarter of 1984, since the confidence intervals converge non-monotonically.

The security selection results in Chart 5 show that Brownian Management's company-specific de-

CHART 4

CONFIDENCE INTERVAL — MARKET SECTOR RETURNS

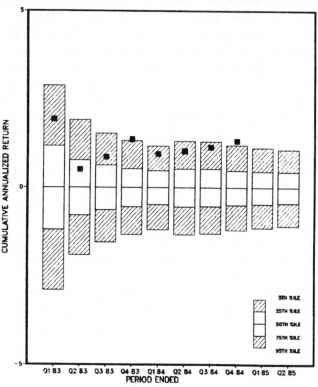

CHART 5

CONFIDENCE INTERVAL — SECURITY SELECTION RETURNS

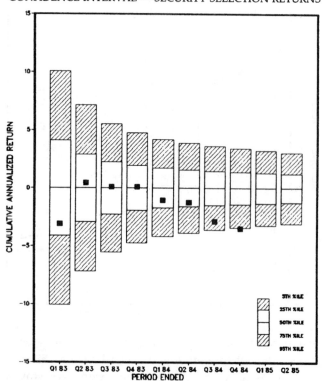

cisions contributed negatively to total active return, yet they exposed the portfolio to a significant amount of specific risk. In fact, they incurred more risk in security selection decisions — where they should have the least confidence — than with any other type of decision.

Nevertheless, these results are somewhat perverse, because they suggest that Brownian Management was wrong more than half the time. If they are indeed consistently wrong, they could serve as an excellent reverse indicator. One possibility is that Brownian Management consistently acquires valuable information that is especially perishable. Or, perhaps, its investment process may not be sufficiently responsive, so that the valuable company-specific information perishes before it can act on it, thus producing a drag on performance. It is more likely, however, that the measurement period is simply too short.

The foregoing analysis illustrates the difficulty in detecting skill from summary measures of performance such as total active return and risk. A more detailed examination of the value added by specific types of decisions, however, shows that Brownian Management is probably skillful at common factor and market sector decisions. Unfortunately, this skill was completely obscured by the risk incurred from company-specific decisions.

CONCLUSION

This paper suggests that the industry standard for measuring investment performance typically provides very little insight about superior managers because it focuses on summary results rather than on evidence of conduct. Evidence of a manager's conduct is more likely to be uncovered within the following context.

- The results of each management organization should be normalized to an appropriate benchmark in order to eliminate any systematic biases that may result from the particular style of each.
- Risk and return should be partitioned to correspond to the manager's decisions, so that potential skill is not obscured by risk emanating from unskilled decisions.
- The number of events that underlie the confidence measure should be determined so as to provide confirmatory evidence of skillful conduct.

[1] Active return is that portion of return attributable to active management; that is, deviations from a normal portfolio. It can be thought of as value added.

[2] The normal portfolio represents the portfolio a manager would hold in the absence of any judgments. It is the manager's neutral portfolio.

[3] Assume μ = return, σ = risk, t = confidence, and n = time.

Then:

$$n = \sigma^2 \mu^{-2} t^2$$

and

$$\frac{\partial n}{\partial \mu} = -2\mu \sigma^2 t^2$$

$$\frac{\partial n}{\partial \sigma} = 2\sigma \mu^{-2} t^2$$

$$\frac{\partial n}{\partial t} = 2t \sigma^2 u^{-2}.$$

[4] These results are from an actual equity portfolio with no cash covering the period from December 31, 1982 through December 31, 1984. The manager's name has been changed.

[5] The eight common factors are: a discount factor, earnings/price ratio, financial risk, growth in assets, historical success, sales sensitivity, size, and yield. The 10 market sectors are: consumer durables, consumer non-durables, finance and building, health care, capital goods, energy related, basic industry, transportation, utility, and a miscellaneous sector.

[6] The standard deviation used to estimate the cumulative annualized confidence intervals is calculated as follows:

$$S_{i,ca} = \left[\left(\sum_{k=1}^{n} S_{i,k}^2 / n^2 \right) * 12^2 \right]^{1/2},$$

where:

$S_{i,ca}$ = cumulative annualized risk incurred by exposure to factor i,

$S_{i,k}^2$ = variance of monthly marginal returns to factor i up to month k adjusted for active exposure as of month k, and

n = number of months in period.

The cumulative value added is calculated as follows:

$$V_{i,ca} = \left[\left(1 + \left(\frac{\sum_{k=1}^{n} V_{i,k}}{n} \right) \right)^{12} - 1 \right] * 100,$$

where:

$V_{i,ca}$ = cumulative annualized value added by exposure to factor i,

$V_{i,k}$ = value added in kth month by exposure to factor i, and

n = number of months in period.

The implementation shortfall: Paper versus reality

Reality involves the cost of trading and the cost of not trading.

André F. Perold

After selecting which stocks to buy and which to sell, "all" you have to do is implement your decisions. If you had the luxury of transacting on paper, your job would already be done. On paper, transactions occur by mere stroke of the pen. You can transact at all times in unlimited quantities with no price impact and free of all commissions. There are no doubts as to whether and at what price your order will be filled. If you could transact on paper, you would always be invested in your ideal portfolio.

There are crucial differences between transacting on paper and transacting in real markets. You do not know the prices at which you will be able to execute, when you will be able to execute, or even whether you will ever be able to execute. You do not know whether you will be "front-run" by others. And you do not know whether having your limit order filled is a blessing or a curse — a blessing if you have just extracted a premium for supplying liquidity, a curse if you have just been bagged by someone who knows more than you do. Because you are so much in the dark, you proceed carefully, and strategically.

In the end, your actual portfolio looks different from your ideal portfolio. It also performs differently. If the differences in performance were small, the problems of implementation would be minor. The evidence, however, says the difference in performance can be very big. And implementation can be a major problem.

If you are looking for evidence that paper portfolios consistently outperform real portfolios, you probably need go no further than to your own investment shop. How often have you tested an investment strategy on paper, found it to perform superbly, only to discover mediocre performance when it goes live? How often have directors of research been able to show that paper portfolios based on their analysts' recommendations outperform the firm's actual portfolios?

Perhaps the best known example of this phenomenon, and the one with the longest publicly available record, is the Value Line ranking system. The Value Line funds that make use of the system have excellent long-term track records, but none has done as well as the paper portfolios based upon the Value Line rankings. For example, over the period 1965-1986, the Value Line Fund has outperformed the market by 2.5% a year, while the paper portfolio based upon the Value Line rankings with weekly rebalancing has outperformed the market by almost 20% a year.[1,2]

THE BASIC APPROACH

This article proposes a way to assess the drag on performance caused by the problems of implementation. The proposal is for you to run a paper portfolio alongside your real portfolio. The paper portfolio should capture your "wish list" of decisions just before you try to implement them. You should manage this paper portfolio within the same restrictions and guidelines as the real portfolio with respect to diversification and riskiness. The performance of

ANDRÉ F. PEROLD is Associate Professor of Business Administration at the Harvard Graduate School of Business Administration in Boston (MA 02163). He wishes to thank Jay Light and Robert Salomon for thought-provoking discussions on the subject, and Fischer Black, Paul Samuelson, Evan Schulman, and Wayne Wagner for their comments.

this paper portfolio will tell you a lot about your skill at selecting stocks that outperform. The difference between your performance on paper and in reality is what we call the *implementation shortfall* (or just "shortfall"). The implementation shortfall measures the degree to which you are unable to exploit your stock selection skill.

We shall see that the shortfall measures not only what are traditionally thought of as "execution costs," but also the opportunity costs of not transacting. Measuring the shortfall in conjunction with execution costs therefore allows you to separate out opportunity costs. To reduce the shortfall, you have to improve how you manage the trade-off between execution costs and opportunity costs. Minimizing execution costs alone may be no good if it results in unacceptably high opportunity costs. Minimizing opportunity costs will not be worthwhile if it leads to execution costs that are too high.

While they can measure certain types of execution cost, outsiders generally cannot reconstruct the shortfall after the fact by working with only transaction data. The paper portfolio must be managed internally and in real time. Depending on the investment process, its management may require great care and diligence.

We should note also that a large implementation shortfall is not bad per se. If your overall performance is good, a large shortfall may be a necessary cost of doing business. On the other hand, a small shortfall is not necessarily good — it is no help if your overall performance is bad.

The point of this article is that monitoring the shortfall will enable you to measure and better understand the sources of drag on your investment performance. You will be able to separate bad research from poor implementation. If you can improve your understanding of performance drag, you can better control it.

HOW TO CALCULATE THE IMPLEMENTATION SHORTFALL

To calculate the shortfall, you must calculate the performance of both your real and paper portfolios. The performance of your real portfolio will obviously be net of brokerage commissions, transfer taxes, and any other charges incremental to your investment decisions. The result should not include management fees, whether fixed or incentive in nature.

To calculate the performance of the paper portfolio, you use the principle that on paper you transact instantly, costlessly, and in unlimited quantities. For example, if you would like to buy 50,000 shares at current prices, simply look at the current bid and ask, and consider the deal done at the average of the two. The same applies if you want to sell.

Using the average of the prevailing bid and ask means that you get the same price whether you are buying or selling. If you bought at the ask and sold at the bid, you would be incurring transaction costs. These occur only in real world implementations, not on paper.

WHAT IS THE SHORTFALL MEASURING?

The shortfall measures the degree to which you have been unable to exploit your stock selection skills. Just how it measures this will depend on your implementation strategy. In some situations — such as trading on the basis of an impending earnings announcement — you may want to execute quickly by means of a block trade and may be quite willing to move the market to do so. In other situations, your only concern may be to transact at the "right price," and you may be willing to wait "forever" if necessary. Here, you may wish to place a limit order, either explicitly, or implicitly by indicating interest at your chosen price. If the order does not execute, you may later be willing to pay a higher price to get the execution. Generally, your implementation strategy will involve combinations of these and other approaches.[3]

The implementation shortfall has two basic components. The first, *execution cost*, relates to the transactions you actually execute. The second, *opportunity cost*, relates to the transactions you fail to execute. The shortfall is the sum of these two. The derivation of this relationship is given in Appendix B.

Execution cost measures all the obvious costs such as brokerage commissions and transfer taxes. This follows directly from the way the implementation shortfall is calculated. Opportunity cost (the cost of not transacting) simply measures the paper performance of the buys and sells you did not execute.

Execution cost also measures price impact. For the purposes of this discussion, let us define price impact to be the difference between the price you could have transacted at on paper (the average of the bid and ask at the time of the decision to trade) and the price you actually transacted at, whether immediately following the decision to trade or later. For example, if you buy at the ask (or sell at the bid) prevailing at the time of the decision to trade, your price impact will be half the bid–ask spread.

Price impact may occur because you have to move the market temporarily away from its current price in order to induce someone to supply the liquidity you are seeking. From time to time, there may be negative price impact, because you are able to take advantage of someone on the other side who needs the liquidity more than you do. When the price impact is purely a liquidity effect, the price of the stock will usually return to the level it was at before you traded.

Price impact may occur also because the market suspects you know something. Think of the block trader who has to find the other side of the trade for you. If you often show up with "soiled merchandise," he is going to go out of business if he always accommodates you at current prices and bags his clients on your behalf. More likely, he will adjust the price somewhat. The smarter he thinks you are, the bigger the adjustment. Once you have traded, the price may not return to its previous level because the cat is now out of the bag. In that case, part of the price impact will be permanent.

Included in the shortfall is something called the cost of *adverse selection*.[4] Typically, some of the transactions that execute on paper but not in the real portfolio do not execute because you choose not to incur the price impact; some, particularly limit orders, do not execute because the market chooses not to execute them. When you place a limit order to buy, you are giving the market a free put option, and when you place a limit order to sell, you are giving the market a free call option.[5]

The market will often exercise these options strategically. If the order executes, it is because you are offering the best price — your price is better than "fair value." Thus, to some extent, your real portfolio tends to get stuck with stocks you are paying top dollar for, even though you are executing at your limit price. You will tend not to own the stocks the market decides it likes better than your limit price. Meanwhile, your paper portfolio owns both the ones the market likes and the ones it does not like.

Thus, the shortfall measures the cost of adverse selection through the opportunity cost represented by the trades the market chooses not to execute. To the extent that you later transact at a less advantageous price after your limit order has expired unexecuted, this is still a cost that can be attributed to adverse selection, but it will show up under execution cost under the general heading of price impact.

You could not begin to measure opportunity costs without the paper portfolio. Execution costs, on the other hand, are regularly measured in practice. The methods employed are usually different from the component of the shortfall that we have labeled execution cost. In part, this is because of the lack of access to prices prevailing at the time of the decision to trade. The methods used in practice can give you information that is valuable, particularly when you use them in conjunction with the implementation

shortfall. Accordingly, Appendix A discusses how these methods fit within the framework of this paper.

PACE OF TRADING AS THE KEY DETERMINANT OF EXECUTION AND OPPORTUNITY COSTS

What determines the amount of your execution costs and opportunity costs? In general, there will be many factors, including how smart a trader you are or how well you manage your relationships with the Street. The chief factor, however, is how quickly you trade.

If you trade quickly and aggressively, you will tend to pay a bigger price to transact. It is much harder to find the other side over the next hour than over the next week. When you are in a hurry, you also indicate your need to get in or out, which in turn may signal valuable information to others. Hence, the faster you trade, the larger your execution costs will be. On the other hand, you will have more of your ideal portfolio in place, and your opportunity costs consequently will be lower.

If you trade slowly and patiently, your execution costs will tend to be lower. For example, if you execute a large order in deliberate piecemeal fashion, you will not disturb the market very much. Alternatively, if you do not break up the order but bide your time until the other side shows up in size, then you may even reap a premium to market. Nevertheless, although your execution costs will be lower, your opportunity costs will be higher. For the more slowly you trade, the more you will be forgoing the fruits of your research, and the more you will become prone to adverse selection (which shows up mostly in opportunity cost). The longer you are out there, the more time others have to act strategically against you.

USING THE SHORTFALL TO FOCUS MANAGEMENT EFFORT

Once you know what the shortfall in performance is relative to your ideal paper portfolio, how might you use this knowledge to focus your management concerns and effort? Is your time best spent on improving the investment process? Or should you pay greater attention to implementation?

The easy case occurs when the shortfall is small. Implementation is not a significant problem, and the greatest payoff will be derived from directing your efforts toward improving the investment process.

If the shortfall is large, then implementation is obviously significant. To say more, you need to separate how much of the shortfall is due to execution cost and how much to opportunity cost.[6] If the bulk of the shortfall is execution cost, then you are being hurt chiefly by price impact. Your efforts should go toward trading less aggressively. To the extent that this strategy lowers price impact by more than it increases opportunity cost, you will have been successful in reducing the shortfall.

If the shortfall is mostly opportunity cost, then you are being hurt by trading too slowly. You should focus on speeding up execution. Your shortfall will be lower to the extent that you can constrain the resulting increase in price impact to be less than the reduction you achieve in opportunity cost (and adverse selection).

IMPLEMENTATION SHORTFALL AND ASSET MANAGEMENT CAPACITY

An important problem for asset managers is how to assess the capacity of their investment operations. Managers with good performance usually have little difficulty attracting new business. All too often, as they grow, their investment performance deteriorates, even though larger firms have greater resources that should provide a competitive advantage over smaller firms.

The reasons for a slowdown in performance are many, including the increased focus of investment "stars" on business rather than investment matters. The key reason is that increased size brings increased inefficiency in implementation. It is harder to execute an investment decision swiftly when you need to seek peer approval and persuade committees. It is harder to execute million-share purchases than 50,000-share purchases.

Faced with these realities, large firms try to adapt their investment operations. They offer alternative investment products, sometimes managed in decentralized fashion. At some point they may curtail asset growth within a particular discipline. If firms fail to take this step themselves, clients will eventually take it for them.

How do you know when you have grown too big? One indicator is the performance of your paper portfolio relative to that of your real portfolio. If your paper portfolio continues to do well as assets grow, but your real portfolio does not, you may be growing too large. That is, good performance on paper coupled with a growing implementation shortfall reflects increased inefficiencies in executing investment decisions. These inefficiencies may be due either to organizational inefficiencies or to increased frictions arising from trying to execute larger transactions, or both.[7]

On the other hand, if your shortfall is not growing but your performance on paper is deteriorating, then probably it is not asset growth that is causing the implementation problem. Rather, your problem lies with the investment process.

Managing a paper portfolio along with your real portfolio is the best way to separate the effect on performance of operational inefficiencies from a weakening of your investment process.

SUMMARY AND CONCLUSIONS

Implementing investment decisions can be costly. The costs arise both in executing decisions (execution cost) and in failing to execute decisons (opportunity cost). These costs lead to a shortfall in performance. You can measure the shortfall by managing a paper portfolio that reflects the output of your investment process, then comparing the performance of this portfolio with that of your real portfolio. The amount of the shortfall will depend on the type of decisions you are trying to implement and how good you are at implementing them.

Execution costs and opportunity costs are at opposite ends of a seesaw. Lowering one generally will increase the other. To reduce the shortfall, you must lower one by more than you increase the other.

Through ongoing monitoring of the shortfall, you can assess how much of your research effort is being diluted in the process of implementation. You can also separate research-related problems from implementation-related problems, with implications on how to best focus your management concerns and efforts. These distinctions are particularly important to large managers who have to cope with greater organizational complexity as well as the increased frictions that flow from transacting in large amounts.

APPENDIX A: A COMPARISON OF APPROACHES TO MEASURING EXECUTION COSTS

Most services that measure execution costs do so with the use of transaction data. They compare the prices at which you transacted to various measures of "fair value." One measure of fair value is tonight's closing price. Another might be tomorrow night's closing price, or next week's closing price, or some price prevailing after you have finished trading in the stock. Yet another measure of fair value may be the average of the high and the low for the day, or some (weighted) average of all prices at which market participants transacted during the day, and so on. These measures of fair value usually are adjusted to reflect overall market moves, industry moves, and other kinds of moves. In the end, if on average you buy at prices higher than "fair value," and sell at prices lower than "fair value," you will record positive execution costs.

Just how execution costs should be measured is a controversial subject. The debate usually concerns at least the following:

1. Should fair value be based on prices that existed prior to any market disturbance caused by you? Or should it be

109

based on prices that fully reflect whatever impact your trading may have had? Or, might it suffice to use prices prevailing while you were still in the market?

2. If traders know they are being measured under a particular method, can they game the system so as to look good under that method?

3. What are you not measuring when you restrict yourself to using only transaction data?

The discussion can be made most concrete by considering the commonly used "after trade" execution cost measure (see Beebower and Priest, 1980, and Beebower and Surz, 1980). This measure of execution cost is the difference between the price at which you actually transact and some price prevailing after you have finished transacting. Also add in the easy-to-measure costs of transacting such as commissions.

Now compare this after-trade measure with the execution cost we discussed earlier. Ours is a "before trade" measure, as the paper portfolio involves comparing the actual transaction price to the paper price, that is, the price prevailing at the time of the decision to trade.[8]

First, and most important, execution costs are calculated only with actual transaction data, so neither the before-trade nor the after-trade measure tells us anything about the opportunity cost of not transacting.

Second, the after-trade execution cost measures only temporary price impacts, because it is measuring how much the price rebounds after you transact. To the extent that your attempts to transact signal the value of your research to the market, and thereby adjust prices permanently (before you can put your position in place), this will not be measured by an after-trade execution cost measure. The extreme case is that of the smart manager whom the block traders have come to know well. Whenever she tries to trade, they move the price against her — permanently — to reflect the full value of her research. Her research effort is thus completely wasted. This manager will measure a zero execution cost after the fact because she trades at fair prices. Fair, that is, taking into account her research. Of course, she will register a big before-trade execution cost, because she can trade on paper without communicating with others.

Third, the after-trade execution cost does measure the cost of adverse selection. To the extent the market chooses to transact with you because yours is the best price given what it knows about where the stock is going, then you are transacting at "unfair" prices. This is by definition an after-trade execution cost.

The before-trade execution cost does not measure the full cost of adverse selection, because you find out only after the fact whether you were selected against or not. As we discussed in the body of the article, the before-trade execution cost measures only that portion of adverse selection cost that shows up when, having failed to get your preferred price, you "chase the market" to execute anyway. The balance of the adverse selection cost is captured in the implementation shortfall through the opportunity cost.

The way in which the implementation shortfall measures adverse selection cost is the mirror image of the way in which the after-trade execution cost measures adverse selection. The latter does so by looking at the trades the market chooses to execute, while the former does so by looking at the trades the market chooses *not* to execute. Statistically, and over many transactions, the differences between these two approaches to measuring adverse selection will be small.

Fourth, if we ask whether execution cost measures can be gamed against, the answer surely is yes for all of them. All you need to do is execute nothing but the obviously "easy" trades. Then your execution cost will be negligible, no matter how it is measured. Short of executing only the easy trades, however, the after-trade execution cost basically cannot be gamed even though the before-trade execution cost can. If you know you are being measured on a before-trade basis, you simply wait a while. Then you buy the stocks on your order list whose prices have fallen (since receipt of the order), and sell the stocks whose prices have risen. You dismiss the other orders as being "too expensive" to execute.

If you are being measured by the implementation shortfall, on the other hand, there is no way to game it. By definition, your yardstick of performance is the paper portfolio — one that reflects perfect implementation. If you try to get an artificially low execution cost by executing only the "easy" trades, you will measure a high shortfall because of the opportunity cost. If you minimize your opportunity cost by trading aggressively, you may still measure a high shortfall because of a large execution cost. The only way to obtain a low implementation shortfall is to have both a low execution cost and a low opportunity cost.[9]

Taken all together, we can say that the implementation shortfall, made up of the opportunity cost plus the before-trade execution cost, measures what after-trade execution costs measure plus two things: the opportunity cost incurred when you choose not to transact, and the cost that arises when your attempt to trade signals valuable information to the market. For most managers, the opportunity cost will represent the great bulk of the difference.

[1] Sources: *The Value Line Investment Survey* and *Barron's*.

[2] These numbers should be interpreted with some caution. The Value Line Fund on occasion has had fairly substantial holdings in debt securities. And mutual funds generally maintain cash balances to facilitate transactions. This causes a drag on performance in up markets. Value Line's fund managers also have had to compete for trades with subscribers to the *Value Line Investment Survey*. These likely explain at least part of the shortfall in performance. If the need to hold cash balances and competition for trades are sources of performance drag, however, they represent some of the very problems of implementation that concern us here.

[3] See Cuneo and Wagner (1975) and Treynor (1981) for discussions of implementation strategy.

[4] Treynor (1981) theorizes that nearly all of the shortfall is due to adverse selection.

[5] For a further discussion, see Copeland and Galai (1983).

[6] You can do this using the formulas given in Appendix B.

[7] In certain circumstances, transactions in the real portfolio may subsidize the performance of the paper portfolio, and so may overstate the "true" amount of the shortfall. For example, you can look good on paper merely by selling immediately after having forced prices up with a large real buy order. This is something you can and should monitor,

and, if necessary, you should make allowance for it when interpreting the performance of the paper portfolio.

[8] It is harder to be as explicit about just what you are measuring when the calculation of fair value is based on prices prevailing during the period of trading (e.g., the average of the high and low of the day, or the volume-weighted price as described in Berkowitz and Logue, 1986). Absent gaming considerations, these methods should be roughly equivalent to averaging the before-trade and after-trade measures.

[9] As footnote 7 notes, playing games with the paper portfolio can make it possible to overstate the shortfall but not to understate it artificially.

APPENDIX B: DERIVATION OF THE BREAKDOWN OF IMPLEMENTATION SHORTFALL

This appendix shows formally how the shortfall breaks down into its execution cost and opportunity cost components. The breakdown is helpful if you wish to calculate the components separately.

We will measure the shortfall over periods of no trading in the paper portfolio. For example, if changes are made in the paper portfolio on a weekly basis, then we will measure the shortfall weekly. The length of the measurement period is unimportant. It need not be regular. The only requirement is that the period lie between transactions in the paper portfolio.

At the beginning of a measurement period, the paper portfolio will be assumed to have the same value of assets as the real portfolio. At the end of the period, they will differ in value by the shortfall.

Trading in the real portfolio can occur at any time.

Suppose there are N securities in total, and that one of these is a cash account.

Let n_i denote the number of shares of security i in the paper portfolio (held throughout the measurement period).

Let m_i^b be the number of shares of security i held in the real portfolio at the beginning of the period, and m_i^e the number of shares held at the end of the period. m_i^e will differ from m_i^b by the net shares traded in security i during the period.

Denote by $j = 1, \ldots, K$ the times (during the period) at which trades occur in the real portfolio. Denote by t_{ij} the number of shares you trade of security i at time j. t_{ij} is positive if you are buying and negative if you are selling. If you do not trade in security i at time j, then t_{ij} is zero. The end-of-period shareholding in security i is given by

$$m_i^e = m_i^b + \Sigma t_{ij},$$

where the summation is over $j = 1$ to K.

Denote by p_{ij} the prices at which transactions take place. The p_{ij} are assumed net of incremental costs such as commissions and transfer taxes.

Let the paper price of security i at the beginning of the period be p_i^b, and at the end of the period be p_i^e.

For simplicity, we will assume there are no net cash flows into or out of the real portfolio. Hence, all transactions in the real portfolio are financed with proceeds of other transactions. That is, at each time j, $\Sigma t_{ij} p_{ij}$ is zero when

summed over $i = 1$ to N. We can do this because one of the securities is a cash account.

Let the value of the paper and real portfolios at the beginning of the period be V_b:

$$V_b = \Sigma n_i p_i^b = \Sigma m_i^b p_i^b.$$

Let the end-of-period values of the real and paper portfolios be V_r and V_p, respectively:

$$V_p = \Sigma n_i p_i^e, \text{ and } V_r = \Sigma m_i^e p_i^e.$$

The performance of the paper portfolio is $V_p - V_b$, and the performance of the real portfolio is $V_r - V_b$. The implementation shortfall is the difference between the two.

The performance of the real portfolio can be expanded as

$$\Sigma(m_i^e p_i^e - m_i^b p_i^b),$$

which may be rewritten as

$$\Sigma m_i^e(p_i^e - p_i^b) - \Sigma p_i^b(m_i^e - m_i^b).$$

In turn, this can be shown to be equal to

$$\Sigma m_i^e(p_i^e - p_i^b) - \Sigma\Sigma(p_{ij} - p_i^b)t_{ij}.$$

The performance of the paper portfolio can be expanded as

$$\Sigma n_i(p_i^e - p_i^b).$$

Subtracting real performance from paper performance gives the desired result:

Implementation Shortfall $= \Sigma\Sigma(p_{ij} - p_i^b)t_{ij} + \Sigma(p_i^e - p_i^b)(n_i - m_i^e)$

$$= \text{Execution cost} + \text{Opportunity cost}.$$

This can be interpreted as follows: The term $(p_{ij} - p_i^b)$ is the cost of transacting at p_{ij} instead of at p_i^b. t_{ij} is the number of shares with respect to which you incur this cost. The product of the two, summed over j, is the before-trade execution cost incurred in achieving a position of m_i^e shares in security i. The term $(p_i^e - p_i^b)$ is the paper return on security i over the period. The term $(n_i - m_i^e)$ is the position in security i that remains unexecuted by the end of the period. The product of the two is the opportunity cost of the unexecuted position in security i.

REFERENCES

Beebower, Gilbert L., and William Priest. "The Tricks of the Trade." *Journal of Portfolio Management*, Winter 1980, pp. 36-42.

Beebower, Gilbert L., and Ronald J. Surz. "Analysis of Equity Trading Execution Costs." Center for Research in Security Prices Seminar, November 1980, pp. 149-163.

Berkowitz, Stephen A., and Dennis Logue. "Study of the Investment Performance of ERISA Plans." Prepared for U.S. Department of Labor, Office of Pension and Welfare Benefits, by Berkowitz, Logue & Associates, Inc., July 1986.

Copeland, Thomas E., and Dan Galai. "Information Effects on the Bid-Ask Spread." *Journal of Finance*, Vol. 38, No. 5, December 1983, pp. 1457-1469.

Cuneo, Larry L., and Wayne H. Wagner. "Reducing the Cost of Stock Trading." *Financial Analysts Journal*, November-December 1975, pp. 35-44.

Treynor, Jack L. "What Does It Take to Win the Trading Game?" *Financial Analysts Journal*, January-February 1981, pp. 55-60.

Continuously rebalanced investment strategies

"The long run may be long indeed."

Mark Rubinstein

How long must an investor be prepared to wait before the probability becomes high that an all-stock portfolio will outperform an all-bond portfolio?

Following an article by Leibowitz and Krasker [1988], which gives only numerical results, this article provides the elegant mathematical arguments behind them, along with further numerical evidence including results on continuously rebalanced stock-bond portfolios. It provides in addition a simple proof of the well-known capital-growth theorem, which says that the probability that the logarithmic utility strategy will outperform any other continuously rebalanced strategy approaches 1 as time approaches infinity. Logarithmic utility strategies are important in financial economics because they can help in deciding how much of a portfolio to allocate between safe and risky assets.

The article also offers new evidence that, while the capital-growth theorem is true, to be 95% sure of beating an all-cash strategy will require 208 years; to be 95% sure of beating an all-stock strategy will require 4700 years — much, much longer than one might have guessed from reading the literature on this subject.

STOCKS VERSUS BONDS

Under the conditions envisioned by Leibowitz and Krasker, it is possible to derive a simple expression for the probability that a stock portfolio will outperform a bond portfolio that investors may find useful. Here is the theorem:

Assume that all available assets collectively follow a stationary random walk in continuous time.[1] Let X and Y be the values after elapsed time $t > 0$ from following two strategies (with equal initial total investment), each being the result of continuously rebalancing a portfolio to maintain constant proportions in the available assets. Then:

$$\text{prob}(X > Y) = N\{[(\mu_x - \mu_y)\sqrt{t}]/[\sigma_x^2 - 2\rho\sigma_x\sigma_y + \sigma_y^2]^{1/2}\}$$

(1)

where X and Y are jointly lognormally distributed with

$$
\begin{aligned}
\mu_x t &\equiv E(\ln X), & \mu_y t &\equiv E(\ln Y), \\
\sigma_x\sqrt{t} &\equiv \text{std}(\ln X), & \sigma_y\sqrt{t} &\equiv \text{std}(\ln Y), \\
\rho &\equiv \text{correlation}(\ln X, \ln Y), \text{ and}
\end{aligned}
$$

$N(\ )$ is the standard normal distribution function.[2]

Notice that we can also write the result as:

$$\text{prob}(X > Y) = N(a\sqrt{t}), \text{ where } a \equiv (\mu_x - \mu_y)/[\sigma_x^2 - 2\rho\sigma_x\sigma_y + \sigma_y^2]^{1/2}$$

(2)

As the horizon lengthens, other things equal, a remains unchanged, and this probability increases as a function of $\sqrt{t}$. Note also that the sign of $a\sqrt{t}$ is the same as the sign of $\mu_x - \mu_y$.

MARK RUBINSTEIN is Professor of Finance at the University of California at Berkeley (94720).

Leibowitz and Krasker compare an all-stock portfolio (X) with an all-bond portfolio (Y). They assume that $\mu_x - \mu_y = 0.025$, $\sigma_x = 0.18$, $\sigma_y = 0.10$, and $\rho = 0.4$.[3] In that case, a = 0.148, and we can derive the following:

t (years)	prob(X > Y)
10	0.681
20	0.747
30	0.792
40	0.826
50	0.853
123	0.950

That is, after twenty years, the probability that the stock portfolio will outperform the bond portfolio is about 75%. Or, phrased another way, the probability that the stock portfolio will underperform the bond portfolio is about 25%. It will take 123 years to reduce this probability of underperformance to less than 5%. This table would be little changed if the bond portfolio were riskless ($\sigma_y = 0$), because then a = 0.137.

In this first application of our theorem, the portfolios are trivially rebalanced between stocks and bonds because they are continuously 100% invested in one or the other. Let us now consider a wider class of strategies where portfolios are rebalanced continuously to a constant proportion, possibly intermediate between 0% and 100%.

To take a simple example, suppose we restrict ourselves to portfolios X and Y, each involving continuous rebalancing between two assets. In particular, suppose that μ (σ^2) is the expectation (variance) of the natural logarithm of 1 plus the rate of return of the risky asset, and r is 1 plus the riskless rate of return. Let $\alpha \geq 0$ ($\beta \geq 0$) be the proportion of the total investment in the risky asset for strategy X (Y). It can be shown that:

$$\text{prob}(X > Y) = N\{(\sqrt{t}/\sigma)[\mu - (\ln r) + \tfrac{1}{2}\sigma^2(1 - \alpha - \beta)]\text{sgn}(\alpha - \beta)\} \quad (3)$$

That is, given the market parameters (μ, σ, r) and the target proportions (α, β) of two portfolio strategies, this formula can be used to show how the probability that strategy X will outperform strategy Y depends on the length of time these strategies are pursued.[4]

Considering Y as a benchmark strategy, one case is of particular interest: the benchmark of all cash ($\beta = 0$). Ask now, for various target proportions α, how long it will take to have a probability of at least 0.95 of outperforming the all-cash benchmark. Continuing to use the Leibowitz-Krasker estimates ($\mu - \ln r = 0.025$ and $\sigma = 0.18$):

α	(years)
0.5	80.8
1.0	142.1
1.5	313.0

LOGARITHMIC UTILITY STRATEGY

Suppose we want to choose a strategy that has a probability greater than one-half of beating any other (continuously rebalanced) strategy we might set against it. The best such strategy can easily be inferred from our original expression for prob(X > Y). By this criterion, if strategy X is to beat strategy Y, then the argument of N must be positive. In turn, the argument will be positive if and only if $\mu_x > \mu_y$, which implies that the best strategy by our criterion is the one that maximizes μ_x. This is none other than the strategy that maximizes the expected logarithmic return (logarithmic utility).

To use the logarithmic utility strategy as a benchmark, we would choose β to maximize μ_y. A little calculus shows this to be:[5]

$$\beta^* = \tfrac{1}{2} + (\mu - \ln r)/\sigma^2$$

Staying with the Leibowitz-Krasker estimates ($\mu - \ln r = 0.025$, and $\sigma = 0.18$), the logarithmic utility investor would choose $\beta^* = 1.267$. With this benchmark, substituting β^* for β in Equation (3) for prob(X > Y):

$$\text{prob}(X > Y) = N\{-\tfrac{1}{2}\sigma\sqrt{t} \,|\, \beta^* - \alpha\,|\}$$

Now, after five years, what is the probability that an alternative rebalancing strategy (X) will outperform the logarithmic strategy (Y)?

α	prob(X > Y)
0	0.399
0.5	0.439
1.0	0.479
1.5	0.481
2.0	0.441
2.5	0.402

This analysis suggests that, the longer we wait, the better the logarithmic strategy will do. Indeed, we have now arrived quite easily at a key well-known result of financial economics:

As $t \to \infty$, the probability that the logarithmic utility strategy will outperform any other continuously rebalanced strategy goes to 1.

To see this, if X is the result of maximizing the expected logarithmic return, and Y is the result of any other different strategy, then a > 0. As t → ∞, then a√t → ∞; so that prob(X > Y) = N(a √t) → 1.

This result about logarithmic utility can be useful. Many gambling and market situations involve an opportunity to make repeated bets at similar favorable odds, where the bettor successively reinvests the original capital and accumulated profits at each stage. Frequently, the bettor's problem is to determine what fraction of the accumulated capital to commit to the bet at each stage and what fraction to hold in reserve.

A bettor who bets too much at each stage might lose all the capital by a short series of adverse outcomes. One betting too little may be likely to end up ahead, but capital would accumulate slowly. An attractive intermediate strategy would minimize the chance of bankruptcy while at the same time causing capital to grow as rapidly as possible.

The logarithmic utility strategy has this property. As we have shown above, this strategy at any one stage will probably outperform any other strategy set against it. Therefore, it is hardly surprising, as we have also shown, that over time after many stages, this short-run advantage amasses in the long run to a near certainty of outperforming any other strategy. It can also be shown that a bettor following the logarithmic strategy never risks ruin.

As a final property, it can be shown that the expected time E(t) to reach any prespecified target return, a, greater than the interest rate, is (ln a)/μ_x. As the logarithmic utility strategy maximizes μ_x, it perforce minimizes the expected time to reach the target. For example, under our empirical assumptions, for the logarithmic utility strategy with α = 1.267, the expected time to double your money is E(t) = (ln 2)/0.1072 = 6.47 years.

HOW GOOD IS THE STRATEGY?

So how long will it take for the logarithmic utility strategy to have at least a 0.95 probability of outperforming alternative strategies?

α	t (years)
0	208
0.5	569
1.0	4700
1.5	6136
2.0	621
2.5	220

Although the logarithmic utility strategy will almost surely in the long run outperform any other different strategy set against it, the long run may be long indeed. To be even 95% sure of beating an all-

cash strategy, an investor must be prepared to wait 208 years (about the time since George Washington was president). To be at least 95% sure of beating an all-stock strategy will take 4700 years (about the time from the unification of Lower and Upper Egypt to the present).

We should not become too enamored of the logarithmic utility strategy. In particular, we might be tempted to think that relative to a fixed-return benchmark, the logarithmic strategy has a higher probability of outperforming that benchmark than any other strategy. This would be a serious mistake.

So let us ask: After a prespecified horizon, how does the logarithmic utility strategy perform relative to other strategies in beating a low or high fixed-return benchmark? To answer this question, standardize the initial investment to $1, and let Y (now a constant) be the level of the fixed return. The problem is to calculate:

$$\text{prob}(X > Y) = N\{[(\alpha\mu + (1-\alpha)\ln r + \tfrac{1}{2}\alpha(1-\alpha)\sigma^2)t - (\ln Y)]/[\alpha\sigma\sqrt{t}]\}$$

Here we will need to specify both μ and ln r separately to make the calculation. Again following Leibowitz and Krasker, set μ = 0.106 and ln r = 0.081. Say our horizon is t = 5 years. To get a feel for how we might expect to do, if we used an all-cash strategy, the value of our portfolio at the horizon would be 1.09^5 = 1.54.

Let us look at fixed targets Y that are about one-half and five times this amount:

α	prob(X > 0.5)	prob(X > 5)
0	1.000	0.000
0.5	1.000	0.000
1.0	0.999	0.004
1.267	0.992	0.018
1.5	0.979	0.037
2.0	0.930	0.083
2.5	0.864	0.117

Logarithmic utility strategy is underlined.

This shows that the criterion of choosing a strategy that is likely to beat any other strategy set against it is not the same as choosing the strategy with the highest probability of beating a particular prespecified benchmark.

For example, suppose the benchmark strategy were a fixed return equal to 0.5 after five years. The all-stock strategy (α=1) has a higher probability of outperforming this benchmark than the logarithmic strategy. This illustrates a general proposition about strategies. Say we compare three strategies X, Y, and

114

Z (think of X as the logarithmic strategy, Y as the all-stock strategy, and Z as the fixed-return benchmark):

If prob(X > Y) > $\frac{1}{2}$, it *does not* follow that prob(X > Z) > prob(Y > Z).

Thus, there is a kind of intransitivity in an investment criterion that relies solely on the probability of outperforming alternative strategies, as Samuelson [1963] contends in a similar argument.

[1]We also need the technical assumption that the return variances of the individual assets and their paired return covariances are finite numbers.

[2]Here is a quick proof. Prob(X > Y) = prob(ln X > ln Y) = prob(ln X - ln Y > 0). It is well known that, under the conditions stated, a continuously rebalanced portfolio will be lognormally distributed over any finite time interval. Thus X and Y are jointly lognormally distributed. Therefore, ln X and ln Y are jointly normally distributed, and their difference is also normally distributed. The probability that the normally distributed random variable z ≡ ln X - ln Y is greater than 0 is $N(\mu/\sigma)$, where (μ, σ) are the mean and standard deviation of z. Therefore, prob(X > Y) = $N(\mu/\sigma)$. The result follows because $\mu = \mu_x t - \mu_y t$ and $\sigma^2 = \sigma_x^2 t - 2\rho\sigma_x\sqrt{t}\sigma_y\sqrt{t} + \sigma_y^2 t$.

[3]This logarithmic differential is derived from assumed expected *arithmetic* annual returns of 0.13 and 0.09 for X and Y using the formulas:

$$\mu_x = (\ln 1.13) - \frac{1}{2} \times 0.18^2 \quad \text{and} \quad \mu_y = (\ln 1.09) - \frac{1}{2} \times 0.10^2.$$

[4]To see this, suppose that one asset is risky with return r_1 and the other is riskless with return r. It follows from Cox and Leland [1981] that:

$$\ln r_x = \alpha\ln r_1 + (1 - \alpha)\ln r + \frac{1}{2}\alpha (1 - \alpha)\sigma^2$$

$$\ln r_y = \beta\ln r_1 + (1 - \beta)\ln r + \frac{1}{2}\beta(1 - \beta)\sigma^2$$

where σ ($\equiv$ std(ln r_1)) is the (logarithmic) volatility of the risky asset, and μ ($\equiv$ E(ln r_1)) is the expected (logarithmic) return of the risky asset. Taking expectations, we have:

$$\mu_x = \alpha\mu + (1 - \alpha)\ln r + \frac{1}{2}\alpha(1 - \alpha)\sigma^2, \qquad \sigma_x = \alpha\sigma,$$

$$\mu_y = \beta\mu + (1 - \beta)\ln r + \frac{1}{2}\beta(1 - \beta)\sigma^2, \qquad \sigma_y = \beta\sigma,$$

and $\rho = 1$. Substituting these expressions into our earlier result for prob(X > Y) leads to the result in the text.

In a more general case, where rebalancing takes place with two risky assets and one riskless asset:

$$\ln r_x = \alpha_1\ln r_1 + \alpha_2\ln r_2 + (1 - \alpha_1 - \alpha_2)\ln r + [\frac{1}{2}\alpha_1(1 - \alpha_1)\sigma_1^2 - \alpha_1\alpha_2\rho\sigma_1\sigma_2 + \frac{1}{2}\alpha_2(1 - \alpha_2)\sigma_2^2]$$

where (r_1, r_2) are the two risky asset returns, (σ_1, σ_2) are the two risky asset volatilities, and (α_1, α_2) are the target proportions invested in the two risky assets.

[5]This solution requires that the expected rate of return of the risky asset be greater than the interest rate.

REFERENCES

Cox, John, and Hayne Leland. "On Dynamic Investment Strategies." Paper presented to the American Finance Association, New York, December 1981.

Leibowitz, Martin, and William Krasker. "The Persistence of Risk: Stocks versus Bonds over the Long Term." *Financial Analysts Journal*, November-December 1988.

Samuelson, Paul. "Risk and Ambiguity: A Fallacy of Large Numbers." *Scientia*, April-May 1963.

PART THREE
Portfolio Strategy

Although portfolio strategies for active management abound, the basic principles of modern portfolio theory have formed the foundation for most strategies developed since the early 1970s. Diversification—the search for low covariance—is a central theme. The linkage between risk and expected return is a dominant consideration, the variety in strategies having sprung primarily from the many differing approaches to measuring risk—especially the role of volatility in the process—and to improving return forecasts. All of this takes place in a setting that pays appropriate respect to the efficiency of the market: nothing is easy even when it looks easy, high-quality information is critical, interpretations of the information are not always obvious, transaction costs matter, and the discipline of quantitative methods is essential.

The eight papers in this section are not a collection of get-rich-quick applications of modern portfolio theory (we are unaware of any such thing!). They appear here because they represent important and original demonstrations of how theory and practice intertwine: all eight have a clearly hands-on character, but it is inconceivable that any of them could have been written before the introduction of modern portfolio theory into the daily practice of portfolio management.

A new route to higher returns and lower risks

Securities of foreign companies tend to offer higher average returns than ours — but international diversification simultaneously lowers volatility of returns

Gary L. Bergstrom

In recent years, a number of scholarly articles and research papers have emphasized the theoretical possibilities for reducing portfolio risk and/or increasing the return on common stock portfolios by diversifying holdings internationally. The empirical analyses in several of these studies suggest that the potential benefits are substantial — perhaps a 20 to 40% reduction in portfolio variability or risk without sacrificing return, or commensurately enhanced performance without increased portfolio volatility. Although both the conceptual and numerical arguments advanced in favor of international diversification appear articulate and persuasive, thus far the U.S. investment community has reacted with a great collective yawn. The level of disinterest in foreign securities is evidenced by the less than 2% of equity portfolios currently invested outside of North America by U.S. institutional investors. Apparently there is little present inclination to increase this exposure. Yet in a capitalization-weighted world stock market index, non-North American issues would currently account for as much as 40% of total value.

This paper has three primary goals. First, it reviews some of the more important theoretical and empirical research findings regarding the benefits of international portfolio diversification. Second, it describes some of the pragmatic operational considerations facing the U.S. institutional investor who wishes to diversify his equity holdings internationally. Third, it shows the actual investment results attained by certain internationally diversified portfolios over the past four years.

THE THEORY OF DIVERSIFICATION

To appreciate fully the arguments advanced in favor of international portfolio diversification, it is useful to have some knowledge of modern portfolio theory. Those readers familiar with Professor Markowitz' seminal contribution need little further introduction to this subject. For others, it is useful to start with a brief theoretical overview of the effects of combining investments in two stock markets into an international portfolio. Two key relationships describe the return and the variability of return or "risk" of an international portfolio:

1. The expected return on a two-market international portfolio (assuming for the moment we own the index in each country) is simply the expected return in each market weighted by the fraction invested in that market.

2. The variability of returns for this international portfolio is slightly more complex since it depends both upon the variability of each of the two markets held *and* the degree of co-movement or correlation between them. If S_1 and S_2 are the measures of respective market variability (i.e., their standard deviations) and r is the correlation coefficient between the two markets (an r of +1.0 means the markets move together in perfectly synchronized fashion, while −1.0 means they always move in exactly contra-cyclical fashion), it can be shown that the total variance of an international portfolio, when X_1 and X_2 are the fractions invested in markets one and two respectively, equals:

$$X_1^2 S_1^2 + X_2^2 S_2^2 + 2 X_1 X_2 S_1 S_2 r[1]$$

Taking the square root of this expression yields the standard deviation of portfolio return.

TWO EXAMPLES

Our domestic stock market as measured by the

---

[1] See Lorie and Hamilton, "The Stock Market Theories and Evidence," p. 179 for a derivation of this formula.

S & P 500 Index during the post World War II period can be roughly approximated in risk-return terms as follows:

Return = 10% per annum

Variability of Return = 16% per year
(standard deviation)

By holding a U.S. "index" fund over this period, an investor could have achieved investment results quite close to these two numbers. A simple alternative strategy, however, would be to invest half of one's portfolio in a foreign stock market, while keeping the other half in our domestic market. (As subsequently will be seen, most foreign equity markets have actually experienced superior investment performance versus the U.S. market in recent years.) Nevertheless, presume for the moment that a foreign market is available with exactly the same risk-return characteristics as the U.S. market. Let us also assume that this foreign equity market has a zero correlation with the U.S. stock market, implying on average no association between price moves in the U.S. market and the foreign market. As both markets are assumed to have the same return, this two-market international portfolio would earn the same 10% per annum return as a portfolio totally invested in the U.S. market.

Its *variability of return*, however, would be quite different. Using the formula previously developed, the standard deviation of return for the international portfolio can be calculated to be 11.3% per year versus 16% per year for the 100% domestic portfolio.[2] Therefore, in this example, one achieves almost a 30% reduction in variability of returns without any sacrifice in expected portfolio performance! Or, conversely, of course, one could achieve higher long-term returns with the same risk as owning the U.S. market through a more aggressive investment posture in each market or through borrowing to purchase securities.

SOME NUMERICAL FINDINGS

Thus far, we have talked only in hypothetical terms about returns, variability of returns, and correlations between stock markets. What does the empirical evidence show?

Let's look first at correlation coefficients. A priori, it would seem reasonable to expect the equity markets of countries whose economies and business cycles are closely interrelated because of geography, well-developed financial linkages, and extensive trade relationships to show relatively high correlations. This surmise, in fact, appears to be a reasonably accurate first order description of international stock market relationships.

In 1968, the *American Economic Review* published the first quantitative paper on "Internationally Diversified Portfolios" by Herbert Grubel. He calculated rates of return and standard deviations of return for many world equity markets as well as the correlations between them. Using monthly data from 1959 through 1966, Grubel estimated the correlation coefficients between the U.S. and other major stock markets (see Table I). The Canadian and U.S. markets

TABLE I

CORRELATIONS VERSUS U.S. MARKET

Stock Market	Grubel (Published: 1968) (Data: 1959-1966)	Solnik (Published: 1973) (Data: 3/66-4/71)	Lessard (Published: 1975) (Data: 1/59-10/73)
Australia	.06	—	.23
Austria	—	—	.12
Belgium	.11	.47	.46
Canada	.70	—	.80
Denmark	—	—	.04
France	.19	.06	.25
Germany	.30	.22	.38
Italy	.15	.07	.21
Japan	.11	.19	.13
Netherlands	.21	.51	.61
Norway	—	—	.17
S. African Gold Mines	.16	—	—
Spain	—	—	.04
Sweden	—	.29	.33
Switzerland	—	.44	.49
United Kingdom	.24	.20	.29

had the closest relationship from 1959 through 1966 with a correlation coefficient of +.7, indicating that on average one could have explained about half of the price change in Toronto only by knowing what happened to quotations in New York during the same month.[3] Most of the major European markets and Japan fall in the range of +.1 to +.3, indicating that less than 10% of the price change in these markets was related to changes in the U.S. market during the same month.

In 1973, Bruno Solnik at Stanford University also computed similar estimates of the correlations between many of these same stock markets using monthly data for the period March, 1966 through April, 1971. Solnik's results are found in the second column of Table I. One of the most comprehensive and

[2] $S_p = \sqrt{X_1^2 S_1^2 + X_2^2 S_2^2 + 2X_1 X_2 S_1 S_2 r}$

and, therefore, in this example

$S_p = \sqrt{(.5)^2(16)^2 + (.5)^2(16)^2 + (.5)(.5)(16)(16)(0)}$

and since the third term equals zero, $S_p = 11.3\%$ per year

[3] The correlation coefficient squared (the R-squared) is a statistical measure of the degree to which one variable "explains" another. In this case, (.7)(.7) equals 49%.

recent estimations of the correlation structure between world stock markets is found in a paper by Professor Donald Lessard of the Sloan School of Management at M.I.T. He used monthly market indices computed by Capital International Perspective, Geneva, Switzerland, as his primary source of stock market data.

While these three sets of correlation numbers are not in perfect agreement, they certainly suggest a considerable degree of stability in inter-market relationships over time, especially after allowing for the use of different market indices and time periods by each of these three authors.

What empirical evidence exists on the variability of returns in various world stock markets? Professor Solnik also calculated the standard deviation of return for a number of world stock markets during the period 1967-1971. As his results in Table II indicate, most foreign stock markets with the exception of Belgium were more volatile than the U.S. over this period.

TABLE II

Country	Ratio of Standard Deviation of Return to Standard Deviation of NYSE Composite Index Solnik March 1967-April 1971
Belgium	.67
France	1.29
Germany	1.06
Italy	1.03
Japan	.98
Netherlands	1.00
Sweden	1.14
Switzerland	1.17
United Kingdom	1.37

Surprisingly, there is a paucity of performance information on foreign equity markets. To my knowledge, little total returns data for foreign equity markets have been published by either academics or practitioners. To fill this void, we have collected an extensive data file enabling us to estimate long-term historical rates of return on twenty major world stock markets. Investment results for these twenty markets have been computed using Capital International indices in most cases. Estimated dividends have been reinvested in each market index, and all results have been currency adjusted to U.S. dollar terms. These numbers are quite startling. As can be seen from Table III, on a total return basis, the U.S. market ranked number seventeen out of twenty markets over the 6½ year period from 1968 through the first half of 1975. Only three bourses declined over this period, Italy, the U.K., and Australia. The NYSE Index showed a nominal rise of 5%, while most other world markets

TABLE III

Stock Market Returns

Stock Market	Estimated 6½ Year Total Return to June 30, 1975 (in U.S. dollars)	Compounded Total Returns (Percent per Year)
Italy	− 30%	− 5.3%
Australia	− 14%	− 2.3%
United Kingdom	− 13%	− 2.2%
U.S. (NYSE Composite Index)	+ 5%	+ .7%
Netherlands	+ 23%	+ 3.3%
Canada	+ 30%	+ 4.1%
France	+ 53%	+ 6.7%
Switzerland	+ 63%	+ 7.8%
Sweden	+ 81%	+ 9.6%
Germany	+ 83%	+ 9.7%
Singapore (a)	+ 106%	+ 11.8%
Belgium	+ 115%	+ 12.5%
Denmark	+ 123%	+ 13.1%
Austria	+ 162%	+ 15.9%
Spain	+ 168%	+ 16.4%
Norway	+ 222%	+ 19.6%
Japan	+ 225%	+ 19.8%
South Africa (Gold Shares)	+ 261%	+ 21.8%
Hong Kong (c)	+ 310%	+ 24.1%
Brazil (b)	+ 740%	+ 38.5%

With certain noted exceptions, index data is from Capital International Perspective, Geneva, Switzerland. All returns are after reinvestment of estimated dividends and are currency adjusted to U.S. dollar terms.
(a) Straits Times Industrial Index — Base 1966 = 100
(b) Source: The Rate of Return to Investors in Brazilian Shares, 1955-1971, Walter L. Ness, Jr., New York University IVB Index is a total value index.
(c) Hang Seng Index — Base 1964 = 100

achieved significant gains. Brazil, Hong Kong, South African Golds, and Japan were the strongest performers, each being up well over 200% during these years.

We also computed total return results for the 16½ year period from the end of 1958, when the Capital International data become available, through the first six months of 1975 (Table IV). Market index data for the Hong Kong and Singapore exchanges are not available before 1964 and 1966, respectively, thereby restricting their computations to these shorter intervals. Once again we see performance of the NYSE Index lagging sixteen of twenty foreign exchanges. Only Italy and France evidenced distinctly inferior performance versus the U.S. market, while markets such as Japan, Spain, and Brazil rose dramatically.

MORE RAPID GROWTH ABROAD?

Is this long-term pattern of more rapid growth in foreign stock markets likely to persist into the future? Those who believe that corporate earnings growth is the prime determinant of long-term stock market growth should first note that the rate of real economic growth in many foreign countries is likely to

121

continue to be considerably higher than that in the United States.

TABLE IV

Stock Market Returns

Stock Market	Estimated 16½ Year Total Return to June 30, 1975 (in U.S. dollars)	Compounded Total Return (Percent per Year)
Italy	+ 36%	+ 1.9%
France	+ 175%	+ 6.3%
Canada	+ 190%	+ 6.7%
U.S. (NYSE Composite)	+ 194%	+ 6.8%
United Kingdom	+ 211%	+ 7.1%
Netherlands	+ 239%	+ 7.7%
Australia	+ 240%	+ 7.7%
Belgium	+ 306%	+ 8.9%
Denmark	+ 349%	+ 9.5%
Switzerland	+ 482%	+ 11.3%
Germany	+ 490%	+ 11.4%
Sweden	+ 504%	+ 11.5%
Norway	+ 566%	+ 12.2%
Spain	+ 598%	+ 12.5%
Austria	+ 625%	+ 12.7%
Japan	+ 884%	+ 14.9%
Hong Kong (c) (10 yrs. 11 mos. only)	+ 354%	+ 14.9%
Singapore (a) (9 yrs. only)	+ 249%	+ 14.9%
South Africa (Gold Shares)	+ 1003%	+ 15.6%
Brazil (b)	+ 2565%	+ 22.0%

Of course the reasons why some countries achieve more rapid economic growth than others are complex. Population attributes, including cultural and social goals, the availability of specific entrepreneurial, managerial, and technical skills and the general level of motivation toward economic achievement among the populace are obviously important factors. Sufficient investment capital, incentives for capital formation, and a stable government which actively encourages economic development through tax structure and other policy mechanisms are significant prerequisites for rapid growth. However, the availability of natural resources and energy has probably not been as critical to the process as once was assumed (although it may be more critical in the future). The extraordinary postwar growth of the Japanese economy is an excellent example of what may be accomplished with relatively limited domestic natural resources.

Those countries that have achieved extremely rapid stock market growth over the past 16½ years such as Japan, Spain, and Brazil have, not surprisingly, experienced extremely high rates of real GNP growth over the same period. For the decade 1960 to 1970, Brazil's real GNP grew at 6.0% per annum, Spain's at 7.5%, and Japan's at 11.0%. Among other major industrialized countries, France's GNP grew at 5.8% per annum, and Germany and Canada both

achieved a 4.9% growth rate. In contrast, real GNP in the United States increased by only 4.0% per year over this decade, and, according to an OECD study, we ranked number eighteen out of twenty developed economies.

Another perspective on foreign growth rates is provided by an examination of the foreign component of the earnings of U.S. corporations. Although there is a lack of complete data, most analysts would agree that foreign earnings of U.S. multi-national corporations have grown significantly faster than domestic earnings in recent years. For example, in the last ten years, IBM's net income grew 10.8% per annum domestically and 23.2% per annum abroad. Looking at the drug industry as another case, over the past five years, Upjohn's domestic earnings grew 15% per annum while foreign earnings increased over 18%. Merck's foreign earnings growth of over 22% was more than double its domestic growth rate; Eli Lilly's domestic earnings grew about 10% per annum while the foreign component increased in excess of 30%.

PRACTICAL CONSIDERATIONS

While the theoretical framework just offered looks highly encouraging, there are a host of pragmatic problems that must be resolved before a typical institution can implement an international investment program. Many of these issues have already been addressed elsewhere; for example, in an excellent recent article in this *Journal* by Roger Cass. Therefore, the objective here is only to provide an overview of a few of the most crucial considerations.

Perhaps the first question typically raised by U.S. investment professionals concerns the lack of detailed information and analysis on foreign companies. It can be a serious if not fatal handicap to U.S. investors who are oriented towards traditional "information based" stock trading. Unfortunately, it is not easy even for the large U.S. institutional investor to obtain access to timely, high quality research on some foreign securities.

It is also intriguing to note that thus far there have been only a few systematic studies of what economists and random walkers call the "efficiency" of foreign stock markets. The very limited evidence available seems to indicate that the Tokyo and London exchanges are close to ours in efficiency while the French and German markets harbor inefficiencies which are of significant practical importance after transactions costs. All of this suggests that there is a strong role for the security analyst in evaluating European companies with documentable opportunities to outperform the overall markets through diligent research and judicious company selection.

But analysts — and research directors — should not delude themselves into thinking they can compete and win against local investors on the basis of a casual commitment to European research. Sending a domestic analyst on a periodic ten-day blitz across the continent is simply insufficient, because even the most basic ground rules of company evaluation are significantly different. Accounting standards, financial reporting procedures, and taxation systems all vary widely between countries within the E.E.C. community. Depreciation techniques in particular often differ widely from those encountered among U.S. companies. To cite some notable examples, the accounting employed by Japanese non-life insurance companies is a classic illustration of the use of reserve accounts to significantly decrease reported earnings relative to U.S. accounting standards. Brazilian accounting can be especially bewildering to the outsider because of the unique calculations performed to systematically adjust corporate earnings and assets for the effects of inflation. Moreover, the international security analyst must comprehend that the stock market regulatory environment abroad runs the gamut from countries like the United Kingdom and Japan, whose stringent market supervision compares favorably to our own exchanges, to some of the smaller developing markets where government supervision is virtually nonexistent and strict *caveat emptor* prevails.

Another potential concern is stock market liquidity. Certain foreign markets such as Norway and Denmark have only a handful of issues that enjoy substantial trading volumes by U.S. institutional standards. The Japanese market, however, has experienced months in recent years when total dollar volume has *exceeded* that on the New York Stock Exchange. To estimate aggregate marketability in major foreign stock markets, the dollar value of market turnover abroad was estimated, again utilizing data published by Capital International Perspective. For all of calendar year 1974, the twelve largest stock markets abroad together recorded 87% of the dollar trading volume of the New York Stock Exchange over this same period. For 1973, the comparable turnover figure for the ten largest markets outside the U.S. was 81% of the NYSE; for 1972, it was 88%. In light of such evidence, the often expressed view that U.S. institutions cannot invest abroad because of marketability limitations looks highly suspect.

The manager of an international equity portfolio must also be aware of the currency dimension in his security positions. If desired, holdings of securities denominated in most major currencies may be hedged against the dollar through forward market currency contracts. Naturally, such transactions have a cost

which can, over time, become significant. After the massive currency realignments that have occurred over the past four years, however, we may now be entering a period of relative quiet in foreign exchange markets where currency changes again become a second order factor in the performance of international portfolios.

The international investor must, of course, be aware of administrative restrictions and the tax treatment of nonresidents' security holdings in each country where he invests. The most common tax encountered is a source withholding, often at a rate of 15% of any dividends paid. A U.S. tax credit may often be claimed to totally or partially offset these levies, however. In certain extreme cases, such as Brazil at the moment, government policies and restrictive tax treatments interact to make it virtually impossible for the outside investor to participate directly in the local equity market. Even in Brazil, though, the government has recently authorized special investment funds for foreigners which are now being organized.

PERFORMANCE RESULTS

Investment professionals tend to be skeptical about claims for superior investment approaches, especially for those techniques predicated upon a new analytic methodology they may not totally comprehend. In the interest of dispelling some of this mystery, we will summarize Putnam's actual investment experience with international portfolios.

After extensive research and historical simulation studies, the Putnam Management Company began in early 1971 to manage a pilot portfolio using an internationally diversified management approach. Additional funds have been brought under management subsequently so that approximately $40,000,000 is now being invested in this manner. Over this four-year period, we have maintained as consistent an investment philosophy as possible. Its essence is as follows:

1. These international portfolios have remained as fully invested as possible at all times, consistent with sales and redemption requirements.
2. Portfolios have been constructed to take maximum advantage of the diversification possibilities across world stock markets. A modified Markowitzian type of portfolio selection model has been periodically employed in setting market-by-market investment objectives. Typically, investments have been held in seven to nine different national markets.
3. Within each country selected for investment, we have sought to maintain a diversified list of high quality companies. Whenever possible, sixty to

123

eighty different issues have been held in these portfolios.

Table V presents a statistical summary of the performance results achieved on an investment in these international diversified portfolios from early 1971 through the first six months of 1975. The cataclysmic events of the past four years — especially the Arab oil embargo, the most severe domestic bear market in forty years, and massive currency upheavals — have provided an extraordinarily severe testing period for an international management philosophy, but these numbers illustrate the favorable return and low-risk characteristics which can be achieved through an international diversification strategy. As an illustration of diversification possibilities, it is especially noteworthy that movements in the NYSE index only explain about a third of this portfolio's performance (R squared = .35); NYSE moves normally explain 80 to 95% of performance for typical U.S. equity portfolios.

FURTHER POSSIBILITIES

As almost everyone is now aware, the U.S. government's Interest Equalization Tax on foreign security purchases as well as the Federal Reserve Guidelines on foreign portfolio investment were abolished in early 1974. As a result, there are no U.S. governmental constraints on foreign portfolio investment by U.S. institutions at this time. Once a few intrepid investors begin exploiting and publicizing the gains possible through international investing, will the sophisticated U.S. investor be satisfied to keep all of his equity investments in our domestic stock market?

TABLE V

INTERNATIONAL PORTFOLIOS —
PERFORMANCE SUMMARY
March 24, 1971–June 30, 1975

Total International Portfolio Return	+30.8%
S & P 500 — Total Return	+11.6%
NYSE Composite — Total Return	+ 8.4%
U.S. Growth Funds Average (21 Funds)	− 6.8%
U.S. Common Stock Funds Average (24 Funds)	− 3.7%
Standard Deviation of International Portfolios	2.0% per week
Standard Deviation of NYSE Composite	2.7% per week
Total Portfolio Variability (S_p/S_{NYSE})	.7
Beta Coefficient versus NYSE Composite	.4
R^2 versus NYSE Composite	.35

BIBLIOGRAPHY

Grubel, Herbert G., "Internationally Diversified Portfolios: Welfare Gains and Capital Flows," *American Economic Review*, 58, no. 5, (December, 1968), p. 1299-1314.

Lessard, Donald R., "World, Country, and Industry: Relationships in Equity Returns," *Sloan School Working Paper*, (January, 1975), p. 766-775.

Lorie, James H., and Hamilton, Mary T., *The Stock Market: Theories and Evidence*, Homewood, Illinois: Richard D. Irwin, Inc., 1973.

Solnik, Bruno H., *European Capital Markets: Towards a General Theory of International Investment*, Lexington, Massachusetts: D.C. Heath and Company, 1973.

A global approach to money management

Here "global" means more than you think, time emerges as a hero, and history provides portfolio management techniques.

François Garrone and Bruno Solnik

In recent years a vast amount of empirical research has led scholars to believe that the capital market was efficient or nearly so. It simply recognized the intense competition between skillful analysts and investors and the rapidity of stock price adjustment to any new information. Similarly, some portfolio managers came to the conclusion that it was difficult and costly to beat the market consistently. This leads to the development of "index" funds or at least a change in portfolio management strategy where the short-term speculation attitude is replaced by a long-term perspective. Similarly, the risk-return, efficient market analysis coupled with recent dramatic swings in the market implied a shift of emphasis from the search for go-go return to improved risk diversification and protection against inflation.

The purpose of this paper is to present a global approach to money management and its application by the second largest private commercial bank in France. This bank has a century of experience in international investment and money management.

The first part of the paper will briefly present some elements of empirical evidence and theoretical arguments, and what seems to be their operational implications. The application to an integrated system of financial analysis and money management is sketched in part II. While the conclusions presented have been derived in the French environment, they apply to a highly diversified international portfolio and should be relevant for everyone; besides, comparable empirical results are presented for the American investor.

WHAT HAVE WE LEARNED FROM THE PAST?

Market experience and theory would agree that asset prices reflect expectations, especially about future inflation and growth rates. Stock price fluctuations will be influenced by the continuous revision of forecasts of inflation and growth prospects made by investors. This is the definition of an efficient market where investors try to earn a positive return and *act* accordingly on a very frequent basis so that prices adjust rapidly to new anticipations.

In a risk-averse world, competent professionals are searching for new information and trying to earn positive (real) returns and therefore protect savings against money erosion. Investors will incorporate inflation in their discount rate, and in general, asset prices will adjust to provide a positive *expected* real return (the "risk premium" of the theory). But we all know that expectations might fail, especially in the short-run (risk). In periods of dramatic variations in the inflation rate (and inverse movements in the stock markets), we like to think of *risk* in terms of probability of not beating inflation and/or taking heavy losses.

The recent crisis has stressed again the importance of good protection against inflation. Europe is accustomed to fairly high inflation rates (especially France), and beating inflation has long been the objective for many portfolio managers on this side of the Atlantic.

An empirical analysis of the past leads to operational conclusions for money management: Charts I and II report the performance of a selected list of investment media over the past 25 years.[1] A quick look at the graphs and the statistical analysis which follows confirms that:

Conclusion 1: The performance of the various investment media is superior to the inflation rate over the very long-run. This is consistent with the theory that expectations are more likely to be realized over a longer time period.
(See Charts I and II)

1. Footnotes appear at the end of the article.

CHART I

COMPARATIVE PERFORMANCE IN FF OF VARIOUS FORMS
OF INVESTMENT FOR THE PERIOD 1950/1975

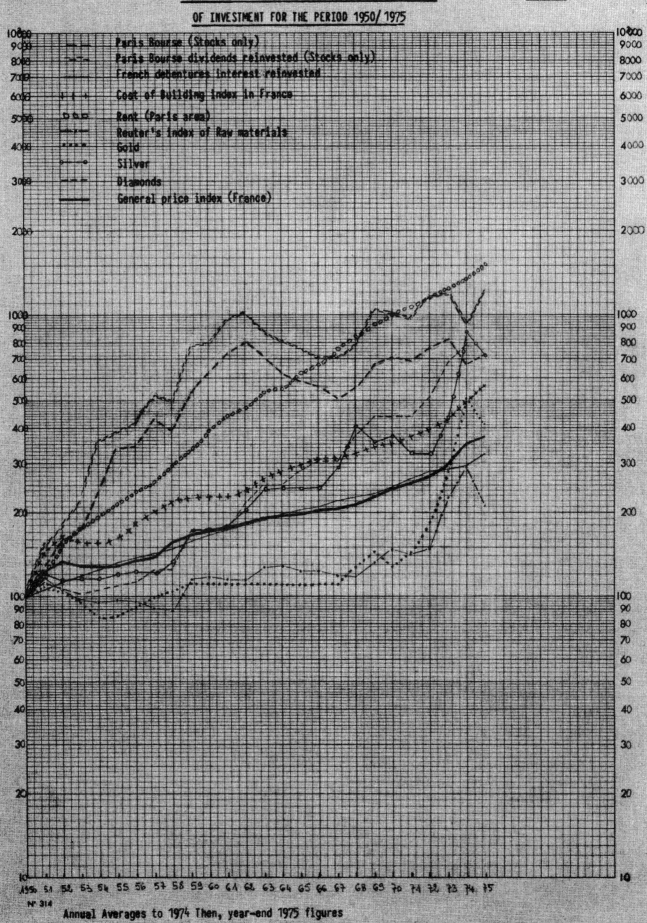

Paris Bourse (Stocks only)
Paris Bourse dividends reinvested (Stocks only)
French debentures interest reinvested
Cost of Building index in France
Rent (Paris area)
Reuter's index of Raw materials
Gold
Silver
Diamonds
General price index (France)

N° 314
Annual Averages to 1974 Then, year-end 1975 figures

126

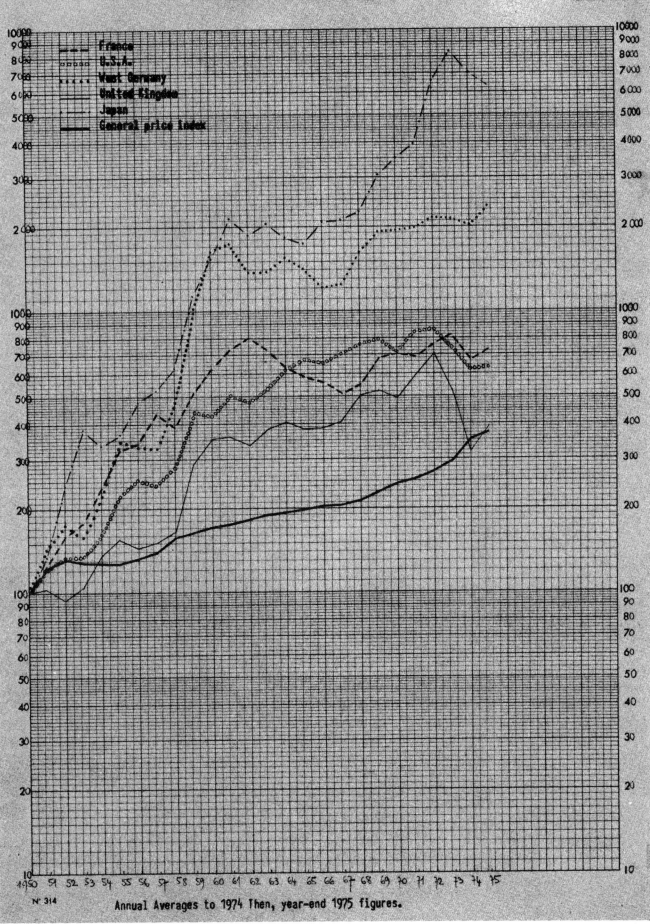

PERFORMANCE (IN FF) OF 5 MAJOR STOCK MARKETS RELATIVE TO GENERAL PRICE INDEX
IN FRANCE FOR THE PERIOD 1950/1975

CHART II

N° 314   Annual Averages to 1974 Then, year-end 1975 figures.

127

Conclusion 2: Over shorter periods of time, asset prices exhibit large price variability (risk). One cannot be assured that an investment medium or a stock market will beat inflation over a period of a few years (see for example Chart III, which gives the performance of various stock markets in 1969-1975).

Conclusion 3: Although risk can never be fully eliminated, it diminishes with the length of the time horizon (time diversification).[2]

Conclusion 4: Asset diversification will reduce the amplitude of the portfolio price fluctuations.

This last conclusion simply extends the well-known principle of diversification to all investment media. Indeed, the value of a portfolio diversified over all media is much less volatile (risky) than each individual investment. Media diversification is all the more important since it is so hard to make reliable long-term return forecasts on individual stock markets and media; with few exceptions (bonds, bills), past performances over 25 years do not exhibit statistically significant differences.

Before studying the practical implementations of these conclusions, it might be useful to study in a more detailed fashion the relationship between the price behavior of some of these media and inflation. Such a study would provide useful insights for portfolio management.

ASSET PRICES AND INFLATION

Besides common stocks, very few investment media have been subjected to a thorough statistical analysis because of a lack of interest and reliable data. Studies on some specific media usually ignore inflation and the portfolio context[3]. Our purpose is to analyse the various assets as inflation hedges and derive implications for portfolio management.

In Table I we report the mean geometric return and standard deviation of returns for the period 1950-1975 (from the French investor viewpoint). The squares of the correlation coefficient of individual asset prices with the price index are also given in the fourth column (more about column 3 presently). They indicate the proportion of variability of returns or prices which can be associated with inflation (the minus sign (−) indicates a negative relationship). Table II gives similar statistics on a smaller number of investment media for an American investor. Comments will be made on the first set of results; American results will be discussed only when they differ from the French one.

As one would expect, according to all economic theories, the nominal return on most investments has been larger than inflation rate in the postwar period.

However, the *fluctuations* in nominal returns have also been much larger (a standard deviation of 20 to 40% per annum for stocks and gold as opposed to 5.7% for the inflation rate). Bonds and Treasury bills are the only assets to have a lower volatility of returns, but, on the average, they performed poorly compared to inflation. The same conclusions apply for a U.S. investor except that bond returns have been somewhat more volatile and short-term money investment slightly more profitable.

An indication of the degree to which an asset might be a good short-term hedge (i.e., annual hedge against inflation) is given by the third column. A large coefficient indicates that the return on the investment closely follows the inflation rate. Figures in the last column are an indication of the value of the asset as a long-term hedge against inflation.

It appears that few investment media are good short-term hedges. French Treasury bills have not been a good hedge, because the government strongly controlled short-term interest rates, preventing their adjustment to anticipated inflation. However, in the long-run, this vehicle was the most certain hedge against inflation (.98), despite the relatively low return. For the U.S., Treasury bill rates are more freely determined and therefore have followed more closely the inflation rate in the short-run ($R^2 = .70$) and yielded a slightly better return. It is also the most certain long-term protection. As expected, bonds are not a short-term hedge against inflation because of the negative relation between the value of a bond and the current long-term interest rates. However, in the long-run, the coupon effect is dominant, insuring a direct relation to inflation as long as long-term interest rates correctly anticipate future inflation. As mentioned previously, the average return on bonds has been slightly lower than inflation.

While stocks have performed very well in a very long period, their values seem negatively affected by the inflation rate. As professor Lintner indicated in his presidential address to the American Finance Association, all recent statistical analysis [4] has shown that stock nominal or real returns are negatively rather than positively related to inflation. Given the worldwide transfer of inflation, the same conclusion applies to foreign stock market investments.

Even in a five or ten-year period, one cannot be certain, if the past repeats itself, to beat inflation by investing in domestic stocks (R^2 of .6 to .9). In other words, there are long cyclical movements in stock markets. Therefore, international diversification will not protect investors against a sudden increase in the inflation rate if it is a worldwide phenomenon. However, to the extent that the long cyclical movements in

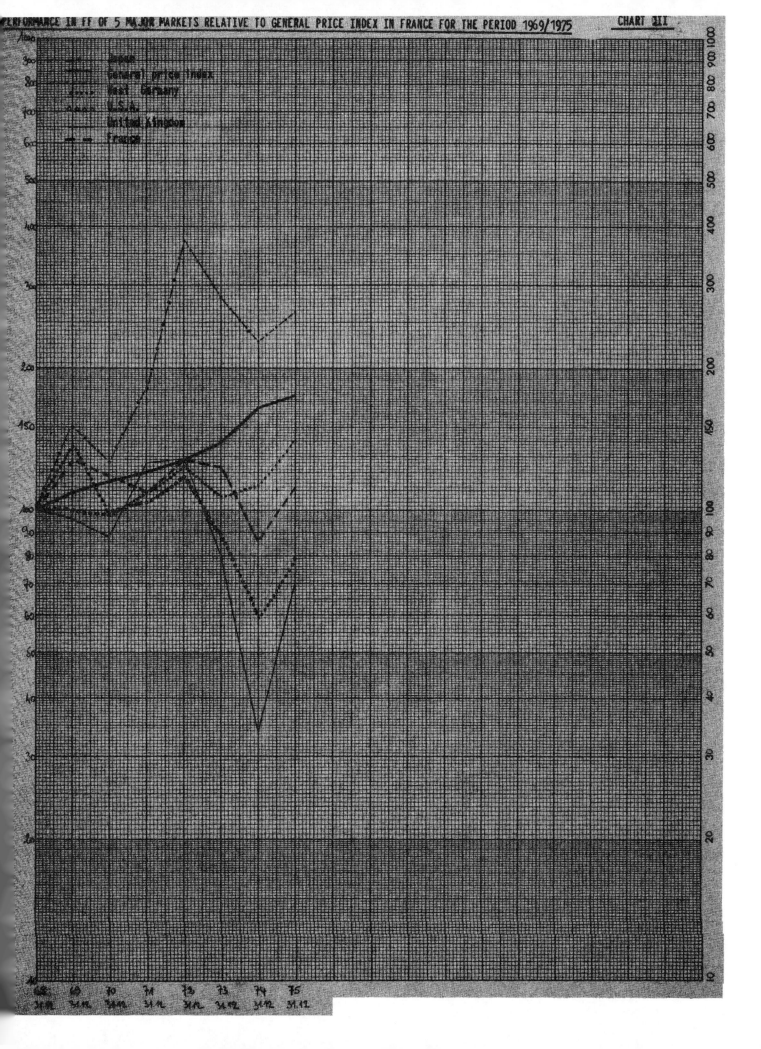

PERFORMANCE IN FF OF 5 MAJOR MARKETS RELATIVE TO GENERAL PRICE INDEX IN FRANCE FOR THE PERIOD 1969/1975   CHART III

various stock markets have been shown to be quite independent among countries, an internationally diversified portfolio will avoid these price fluctuations and give a lesser risk to underperform inflation on a long period (a few years).[5]

Gold seems to be a fairly good inflation hedge in the short-run. Gold is viewed by individuals in many countries as an extraordinary hedge or "store of value" because of its traditional ease of exchange for goods and services in those relatively infrequent but unhappy states of the world (political upheaval, economic crisis) when financial claims such as common stock lose value and liquidity. High inflation rates being often associated with economic or political uncertainty, the positive association between return on gold investments and the inflation rate is not surprising, especially in the short-run.

Commodity prices are one component of the general price index and as such commodities provide some natural protection against inflation. However, in the past, the average return on this type of investment has been low and the degree of protection quite small.

The results for real estate, metals, and precious stones are not surprising altogether and will not be discussed in detail. The source data for these investments need to be viewed with caution, and readers are cautioned against assuming a degree of precision in results not warranted by the data and methodology.

It is interesting to note that the realized depreciation of the French Franc (1.6%) has been fully anticipated by the short-term interest rate differential (1.6%). International investment media reported here will have the same risk premium or excess return in France and the U.S.

These results stress the importance of the time horizon considered. Some investments are good short-term inflation hedges but have a poor long-term performance, while other investments are a bad protection in the short-run but provide a positive excess return in the long-run.

PORTFOLIO STRATEGY

The conclusions derived previously will now be translated into some operational elements for a portfolio strategy.

Currents events have reemphasized that *beating inflation* should be a major objective. Our analysis clearly implies that:
1) given the efficiency of the financial markets, this objective is possible only over a very long-term and that, consequently,
2) a portfolio should be managed with *a very long-term perspective.*

While a long-term strategy might appear as a priority, short-term preoccupations should not be fully forgotten and advantage should be taken of possible exceptional profit opportunities and apparent temporary mispricing. However, such (hopefully profitable) short-term speculations and arbitrage should not confuse the basic, long-term strategy of the portfolio. Past experience in the bank leads to the recommendation of a strict separation of the total fund into two portfolios managed respectively according to long-term and short-term objectives.

Coming now to a description of a system that has been implemented at the CCF by one of the authors, it might be useful to first indicate the four elements of the management strategy. This system was evolved by the Bank from long experience in international investment, from the statistical analysis previously reported, and from some theoretical inputs.

Given the separation in two portfolios, the first step is to define, for each account, a proportion of long- and short-term investment. This will depend on the investment objectives of each client, his time horizon, and speculative attitude. Once these proportions have been determined, the following elements summarize the investment strategy. The first three refer to the long-term portfolio:

First Element: A long-term objective: beat inflation.

This is a "minimum" objective over the very long-run. Despite a tradition of high inflation in France, conclusion 1 indicates that stock markets, like most other investment media, have satisfied this objective with a nontrivial premium.

Second Element: Use all the investment media available.

Without exact knowledge about the future performance of each medium, the rule will be to *diversify* the long-term portfolio as much as possible across media[6] (stocks, real estate, precious metals and stones, paintings, etc. . .). Relative weights would be determined by economic factors, liquidity considerations, and relative performance forecast, if any. If necessary, the portfolio should be frequently rebalanced to maintain a good diversification between media and stock markets.

Third Element: A selective investment policy within each market.

The long-term horizon and extensive investment media diversification drastically reduce the risk of the portfolio. This allows the managers to invest in "growth" assets in each market. For a slight increase in short-term risk, it would increase the expected long-term performance. This is especially the case in all stock markets where diversified portfolios of growth stocks ought to provide a better margin over inflation.

Fourth Element: A short-term objective different from the long-term objective: Do as well as possible.

TABLE I - STATISTICS ON INVESTMENT ASSETS FOR A FRENCH INVESTOR (1) 1950-1975.

	Average return %	Standard deviation %	Correlation of returns R^2	Correlation of prices R^2
Price Index	5.4	5.7	1.00	1.00
Money rate	5.1	2.4	.29	.98
Bonds	4.6	1.5	.01	.94
French stocks.....	9.6	22.7	(-) .01	.66
U.S Stocks........	11.8	17.0	(-) .01	.82
Japanese stocks...	19.8	30.8	.00	.83
British stocks....	8.1	23.9	(-) .17	.65
German . stocks....	18.0	31.4	.01	.91
Constr. prices ...	6.8	13.3	.33	.94
Rent	11.6	5.2	.01	.96
Agric. land	10.4	5.2	.10	.97
Forest............	12.2	34.9	.03	.60
Gold	7.4	23.0	.32	.60
Gold mines	8.9	35.2	.23	.56
Silver	8.9	19.8	.24	.87
Diamonds	8.4	11.9	.01	.90
Emeralds	7.6	34.9	.03	.60
Commodities ...... (Reuter index)	3.8	13.3	.19	.80

TABLE II - STATISTICS ON INVESTMENT ASSETS FOR A U.S INVESTOR (2)

	Average return %	Standard deviation %	Correlation of returns R^2	Correlation of prices R^2
Price Index (CPI)..	3.0	2.8	1.00	1.00
U.S T. Bill	3.5	1.9	.70	.98
U.S Bonds	2.4	6.2	(-) .01	.81
U.S Stocks	10.2	15.2	(-) .37	.80
Japanese stocks....	18.2	30.6	(-) .22	.84
British stocks.....	6.5	22.2	(-) .42	.65
German stocks......	16.4	28.2	(-) .09	.90
French stocks......	8.0	22.4	(-) .15	.50
Gold	5.8	24.3	.52	.48
Gold mines.........	7.3	38.8	.40	.45
Silver	7.3	19.4	.37	.81
Diamonds	6.8	13.1	.02	.91
Emeralds	6.0	11.4	.07	.88
Commodities........	2.2	14.7	.13	.38

(1) All prices are expressed in French Francs. Money rate, bonds, forest, etc., refer to French assets.

(2) All prices are expressed in dollars. The dollar/French Franc exchange rate appreciated by 1.6% (average annual compounded rate). The first three series come from the IMF statistics and Ibbotson and Sinquefield "Stock, Bonds, Bills, and Inflation," CRSP Seminar, May, 1974.

The "short-term portfolio" is only a part of the overall portfolio, and it would be difficult to focus on inflation in an active trading strategy. The short-term strategy would be restricted to the very liquid markets on which we have expertise: short-term bills, bonds, and stock markets (and possibly gold for the French investor!). The objective would be to do as well as possible by either forecasting market and interest rate movements or outperforming the market in a skillful stock selection. This assumes some special skills and some market inefficiencies. The ex post performance measure would be to compare to the performance of the "best" market investment (bills, bonds, or stocks).

THE C.C.F.'S SYSTEM OF MANAGEMENT

This system of money management will be only very briefly sketched. It has four major characteristics:

1. It tends to translate directly in terms of the total portfolio every advice formulated by the research team; in other words to compare every new possibility of investment to all others, especially to those already included in the total portfolio. After comparison, a given percentage of the portfolio is allocated to each element. This is the definition of a *fully integrated method*.

2. The comparison among the different possibilities of investment is realized by evaluating the expected return of each possibility. For this purpose, valuation models are systematically used.

3. The allocation of a given percentage of the total portfolio to a certain number of the best "expected returns" realizes the diversification of the portfolio and is considered as the unique protection against risk. This active management method is theoretically supported, as explained in the first part of this paper, by the time diversification of the portfolio.

4. Evaluations of expected returns and diversification are realized on a continuing basis. By using the computer, both the new recommended portfolio structure and the state of the actual portfolio (consequence of the prior recommended portfolio + prices variations) are checked monthly.

This is necessary, since the most important name of the game, in this method, is perhaps *discipline*. The monthly checking by the computer will reveal the gaps between the recommended structure and the actual portfolio. These gaps have to be filled, normally; at least they are revealed and this indication leads the way to new decisions.

Practically, the system works through two sets of grids that represent the recommended structure of the portfolio at the different levels taken into account. Examples of these grids issued in the Bank in February, 1976 are given in the appendix.

The first set gives the breakdown by investment media for the long-term and short-term portfolio. It consists of two grids:

Grid I. Recommended *long-term structure* of the portfolio among investment media. In the grid given as example here is shown the case of a client having

GRID I

BREAKDOWN OF PORTFOLIO BY MAJOR INVESTMENT VEHICLES

	Very long term return	Very long term risk (1)	Medium term risk (2)	Liquidity	Portfolio Breakdown (3)		
					Long term 70% (in %)	Short term 6/18 months 30 % (in %)	TOTAL (in %)
Stocks	++	Average	High	+++	30	0/30	30/60
Bonds	0	Nil	Higher than average	+++	0	0/20	0/20
Property)					5	0	5
Real Estate)	++	Higher than average	Average	0	20	0	20
Precious Metals (Golds and vehicles related to gold ; silver)...........	+	Nil	Average	++	5	0	5
Precious stones ...	++	Higher than average	Average	0 +	5	0	5
Antiques, works of Arts	+++	Very high	High	0	5	0	5
Cash			Nil	++++	0	0/30	0/30
				TOTAL	70	30	100

(1) risk measured by the difficulty of diversifying sufficiently to obtain at least the average return of this investment media.
(2) risk measured by the price volatility.
(3) hypothetical breakdown for a French investor who wishes to keep 70% of his portfolio long term
30% of his portfolio short term.

	Common stocks	Bonds	Cash	Total by country (irrespective of relative importance of market)
U.S.A.	40 %	0 %	0 %	40 %
FRANCE (1)	30 % (1)	5 %	10 %	45 % (1)
UNITED KINGDOM	0 %	0 %	0 %	0 %
WEST GERMANY	0 %	5 %	0 %	5 %
NETHERLANDS	0 %	0 %	0 %	0 %
BELGIUM	5 %	0 %	0 %	5 %
SWITZERLAND	0 %	0 %	0 %	0 %
JAPAN	5 %	0 %	0 %	5 %
TOTAL BY CATEGORY OF INVESTMENT	80 %	10 %	10 %	100 %

(1) This portfolio breakdown is intended for french investors.

chosen a management of his assets 70% long-term, 30% short-term.

Grid II. Recommended *short-term structure* of the portfolio among stocks, bonds, and cash by country. Expected returns leading to these recommendations are derived from Grids II a/ and II b/, which evaluate the influence of economic conditions on stocks and bonds country by country.

This selection by expected returns is checked with indications given by other usual methods of market timing: a set of monetary and economic signals and technical analysis.

The second set gives the breakdown of investment within each media. Again, there will be one grid for the long-term part of the portfolio and one for the short-term part.

GRID II a/   FEBRUARY 1976

THEORETICAL RETURNS OF STOCK MARKETS

	U.S.A.	FRANCE	U. Kingdom	W. GERMANY	NETHERLANDS	BELGIUM	SWITZERLAND	JAPAN
GNP-Rate of growth 1976 (real terms) .... CCF E	4/6.5 4.5	5/1.5 3.5	- 0.5/2 1.5	4.5/2 3.5	1.5/2	0.5/2.5	1	4/6
Estimated annual rate of growth 1976/1985(real terms)	3.6/4.1	4.5/5	3.1/3.9	3/3.5	3.4/3.8	3.4/3.8	3/3.5	5/5.7
Estimated price increase 1976 (Retail prices).....	5.5/7	10	15	4.5/5	7/9	8.5/12	3/5	7/9 1/2
Estimated annual rate of price increase 1976/1985	6/8	7/9		4/6	6/8	6/8	5/7	7/9
Estimated wage increase 1976	7/8	10/12 (wage bill)	14	6	11	14	6	12
Estimated increase in productivity 1976	4	3	2/3	5	4	5	↗	↗
- Short term interest rates (end 1974)	9	11.75	12	8	8.50	11	8	6 3/4
2. 5.76	5	7	9 1/4	3.80	5 3/4	6.20	1 1/4	5 5/8
Tendency								
- Long term interest rates (end 1974)	9.25	11.90	18.50	10.09	9.50	11.18	8.60	8.77
2.5.76	8.84	10.75	14.57	8.44	8.43	10.70	6.56	7.37
Tendency	↓ 8.50	↓ 10		↓ 8	↓ 8	↓10	∼	∼
Forecast of evolution of profit margin 1976	↗	↗	↗	↗	↗	↗	↗	↗
Evolution of earnings Forecast for 1976	SP 500 :+17/+19 DJ : +14/+19	+ 120 %	+ 15/20 %	+ 20/+ 30 %	+ 5/ 10 %	+ 20/+ 25 %		+ 40/+ 50 %
Forecast of trend 76/85 ... (compound growth rate)	+ 7.5	+ 8	?	+ 5	+ 5	+ 6		+ 10/+ 15 ?
Stock market indices	DJ / SP500	(C.A.C.)	(F.T. 500)	(F.A.Z.)	ANP/CBS	Terme	SBS	ISE
12.31.74	616 / 68.6	59	68.4	177.2	77	108.8	206.3	278.4
2.10.76	968 / 100.5	78	173.6	244.4	103.5	131.7	293.9	334.1
	(+57%) (+46%)	(+32 %)	(+154 %)	(+38%)	(+33 %)	(+21%)	(44%)	(20 %)
P/E 76 (2.10.76)	10.1/ 11.2/ 11.3 12.6	11.8	9.5	10.3/11.2	5.9/7.2	12.7		11.7/12.8
Objective discounted 1976 P/E	13.5	13.5/14.3			13.5	6?/8 ?	12/13	17/18
Yield (2.10.76)	3.9%	6 %	5.4 %	3.6 %	5.1 %	5.2 %	2.8 %	1.9 %
Forecast of exchange rates relative to F (1976)	∼↗	=	↘	∼↗	∼↘	∼↘	∼↗	∼ ?
1976 theoretical stock index levels	1.150/1.250	90/95	200/220 ?	295/310	110/120	125/135	?	400/450 ?
Theoretical total return for 1976 as of 2.10.1976	+ 20/30 %	+20/25 %	+ 20/30 % ?	+20/30 %	+ 5/+20 %	+ 0/5 %	?	+20/30 %

133

	U.S.A.	FRANCE	UNITED KINGDOM	GERMANY	NETHER-LANDS	SWITZER-LAND	JAPAN	BELGIUM
Interest rates – end 1974 – 2.5.1976	9.25 8.84	11.90 10.75	18.50 14.57	10.09 8.44	9.50 8.43	8.60 6.56	8.77 7.37	11.18 10.70
Estimated 1976 rate decreases	8.50	10	?	8	8	6.50	7	10
Corresponding theoretical capital gains	+ 4	+ 5		+ 3	+ 3	∿	+ 2.5	+ 5
Theoretical total return in local currencies	+ 13	+ 16		+ 11.5	+ 11.5	+ 6.5	+ 10	+ 15.7
Forecast exchange rates relative to FF	∿			∿				

Taking stocks as one example, the grid for the recommended long-term structure of the portfolio is revised every semester. As explained, for this long-term part of the portfolio, the choice is restricted to growth stocks.

As far as stocks are concerned, a last grid, revised monthly, gives the recommended structure for the short-term part of the portfolio.

The method for building this grid is essentially similar to that used for Grid II:

1. Comparison of expected returns of the different stocks followed by the research team by using the valuation model;

2. Discussion of this first selection by evaluating influences for the short- to intermediate-term of economic and technical conditions of industries and individual stocks (determination of the development of the cycle of each industry, relative strength, relative earnings, relative P/E, β, technical analysis).

It is important to note that, for the short-term appreciation of the potential of an industry and of each stock, which is the objective of this grid, every assessment is made *relative to the market* (in other words, this grid is strictly dependent on Grid IIa).

In effect, as it is freely admitted, the method assumes that market performance is from far the most important factor of individual stock performance *for the short- to intermediate-term* (within each market cycle). On the contrary, as was explained, the method assumes that the earnings growth rate of each stock is almost the unique determinant of price development in the very long-run, and therefore stock selection is the unique tool for the long-term part of the portfolio.

[1] The analysis performed is based on a much larger sample and more detailed investigation including over thirty different types of investments.

[2] A simple statistical proof would go as follows: Let's call r_1 the yearly expected return for an investment and S_1 the standard deviation of this return, a measure of its dispersion and uncertainty. The return over n years (in percent per year) will be the compounded sum of returns. To simplify, assume that the expected return over n years, r_n, is also equal to r_1. Then statistics tell us that the standard deviation of r_n, i.e., the uncertainty or risk attached to the performance over n years is: $S_n = \dfrac{1}{\sqrt{n}} S_1$

It is a slowly decreasing function of time. A graphic representation of this phenomenon has been given by O'Brien in a recent article in *The Journal of Portfolio Management* (Summer 1975).

[3] The first application of portfolio management concepts to a number of investment media can be found in "Returns on Alternative Investment Media and Implications for Portfolio Construction" by A. Robichek, R. Cohn, and J. Pringle *Journal of Business* (July, 1972): they provide a good summary of previous work. Recently, studies on individual media have started to appear.

[4] J. Lintner, "Inflation and Security Returns," *Journal of Finance* (May, 1975). He reports works done on monthly or annual data for periods such as 1900-1970, 1934-1973, 1953-1972.

[5] G. Bergstrom has presented some evidence in a recent issue of *The Journal of Portfolio Management* (Fall 1975).

[6] Bonds are not taken into account for the diversification over the very long-term, since statistical studies clearly show that they were a poor hedge against inflation in the past (see Table I and II). On the contrary, bonds are played on a short- or medium-term strategy (one to five years).

How to win at the Loser's Game

Financial analysis can outperform random selection — but only in one direction!

Edward M. Miller, Jr.

Recently, the very idea of security analysis has been under attack: the stock market is such an efficient processor of information that it is virtually impossible to do better than the market averages and money spent on attempting to do so is simply wasted.

While the logic behind the random walk theory is unimpeachable, the necessary conditions to apply it to the New York Stock Exchange simply are not met. Nevertheless, the random walk theory can be modified to fit American institutions, and the modified theory does have implications for investment strategy.

THE LOGIC BEHIND RANDOM WALK

There are two ways to argue that all available information is promptly incorporated into stock prices. One is to argue that all investors are supermen, each of whom is capable of completely digesting and analyzing the full range of available information without ever making a mistake. The other is to argue that the market itself incorporates some mechanism that prevents particular stocks from being either over or undervalued.

Since all investors are not supermen, any realistic theory will have to allow for the existence of different types of investors, some knowledgeable and some uninformed. While obviously there is a smooth gradation of knowledge and ability among investors, this paper will assume only two types. (The author has discussed the case where there are many opinions about a stock elsewhere).[11]

One type will be assumed to be highly rational and aware of the publicly available information. We hope that most institutions will fall into this category. The remainder of investors will be assumed to be less well-informed, and to be at times ignorant of available information to which their attention has not been drawn. Many individual investors, untrained in se-

curity analysis, and with little time to devote to their investments, will be in this category.

THE MARKET AS SUPER-COMPUTER

If we reject the idea of all investors being supermen, support for the efficient market hypothesis must rest on the ability of the well-informed investors to keep market prices at levels where they fully incorporate all available information.[1] Given that ability, there cannot be undervalued securities, because the informed investors would have spotted the opportunities and bid the prices up until the securities were no longer undervalued. Likewise, there cannot be overvalued securities, because the informed investors would sell these stocks (going short if necessary), driving the price down to where the security was no longer overvalued. Thus, if securities can be neither undervalued nor overvalued, it follows that they must be correctly valued. Furthermore, if securities are always correctly valued, there would appear to be no role for security analysis (other than to select a portfolio that is diversified and provides the desired level of risk).

Before accepting this surprising conclusion, let us look more closely at the necessary conditions for such an efficient market. When this has been done, we will find that, although competition among informed investors eliminates opportunities to earn more than a "competitive" return, *this does not imply that securities must be correctly valued at all times,* or that such a competitive return can be earned without detailed and skilled security analysis.

We should accept the argument that there are unlikely to be undervalued securities promising more than a competitive return. Several million investors are looking for good buying opportunities, including a

1. Footnotes appear at the end of the article.

135

large number of institutional investors with full time managers. In addition, major brokerage firms with large staffs are also looking for undervalued securities. Company managements usually have a strong interest in a high stock price and can be expected to publicize any favorable information about the firm. Thus, the argument that competition will have eliminated the opportunity to earn returns above the competitive level can be accepted.

The other part of the argument is that selling by informed investors will prevent stocks from being bid up above their proper value. Yet, long selling by informed investors can be a restraint on the price of a stock only as long as these investors have stock to sell. Indeed, there are substantial numbers of stocks that the better informed investors do not hold; for example, the American Stock Exchange thought it worthy of note that more than half of the issues traded on their exchange were held by at least one institutional investor.[1] Obviously, selling by institutions cannot prevent a run up in the remaining stocks.

If the uninformed keep buying, there will eventually come a time when the better informed investors have "bought out" the others. Once this has happened, only short selling can keep the uninformed from bidding prices up to clearly unreasonable levels. Thus, it is necessary to look closely at how short sales are actually conducted. Once this has been done, it will appear that short selling as practiced in America is not the type of short selling that is needed for efficient security markets.

WHY THERE IS INEFFICIENCY ON THE SHORT SIDE

By definition, a short sale occurs when someone sells a stock he does not own (i.e., is short of). How can one sell what one does not have? Simple; one's brokerage firm borrows the stock certificate in order to make delivery to the buyer. Eventually, the short seller will close out the short sale by buying the stock and using the purchased stock certificate to repay the loan. Stock certificates are valuable pieces of paper, however, and owners are reluctant to lend them out without adequate security. To provide such security, the proceeds of the sale of the stock are deposited with the owner-lender, depriving the short seller of use of these funds. In current United States practice, the short seller does not even receive interest on the funds deposited with the lender of the stock.

Here, the real world differs from that assumed in the academic literature, whose short sellers are assumed to receive use of the proceeds of a short sale. Such an assumption is necessary to make sales of borrowed stock completely symmetrical with sales of owned stock. This "imperfection" in the short selling process is why real world markets need not be as efficient as predicted by academic theory.

When the lender of a stock certificate transfers it to the borrower for a short sale, he deprives himself of the dividends on the stock. Naturally, he is willing to do this only if the short seller reimburses him for the lost dividends. Thus, short sellers must pay dividends on the stock they sell short until they cover their positions.

A short sale of a dividend paying stock can only be profitable if the expected rate of return on the stock is below zero. To see this, imagine a stock with an annual dividend of d% of its selling price. Since someone selling the stock short will have to pay this dividend, he can show a profit only if the stock declines over the year more than d%. A stock declining in value at d% per year and paying a dividend of d% would have a total return of zero. Thus, short sellers can show a profit by selling an overvalued stock only if stock is so overvalued that its expected return is negative.

THE LIMITS TO AN EFFICIENT MARKET

So far, we have accepted the argument that well-informed investors will bid stocks up to the point where they promise no more than a competitive return (here called C). Keep in mind the additional argument that, by short selling, they will force overvalued stocks down in price until they promise a return of 0%. In both cases, the effects of risk are abstracted from. (They will be discussed later.) Thus, it appears that the actions of well-informed investors will limit the expected returns on stocks to the range 0 to C percent. Within this range, it is likely that most stocks will have expected returns of C, but, given the large number of part time and uninformed investors, there are likely to be some stocks with expected returns lower than C. These are stocks that badly-informed speculators have driven up in price causing well-informed investors to drop them from their portfolios.

In a market where some stocks have expected earnings of less than C, the average of the expected earnings of all stocks must be less than C. In particular, an index fund or broadly based stock average should show earnings of less than C. A well-informed investor should be able to avoid investing in stocks with a subnormal expected return, leaving him with a portfolio with an expected return of C. *Thus, investors doing good security analysis should be able to beat both the averages and the index funds.* The presence of extremely large numbers of very well-qualified analysts does not make above average performance impossible, contrary to the assertion of the proponents of the efficient market hypotheses. Such above average returns are made possible by the presence in the market of a large number of investors investing on either the basis of no security analysis or bad security analysis, and hence earning below average returns.

Since an investor can expect to earn average returns by random selection, it may be wondered what type of investment strategy will give below average returns. Diagram 1 shows how the expected return varies with the level of analysis. The lowest returns are earned by those who use naive analysis, such as buying the stock with the highest dividend rate or the lowest price/earnings ratio without understanding the reason why other investors are avoiding these stocks. Better results are obtained by those who use either random selection (or something close to it), or who employ very sophisticated analysis, trying to avoid holding the losers. Those at the low point of the curve, who consistently buy apparently undervalued stocks only to watch them decline further, are likely to change their strategy, moving towards one extreme or another. Thus, investors tend to separate themselves into two groups, those who are very well-informed, and those who are not. This provides a theoretical rationale for the assumption made at the beginning of the paper, namely that there were two classes of investors, knowledgeable and uninformed.

DIAGRAM 1

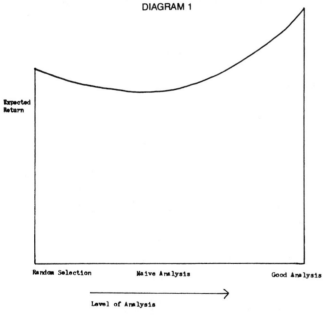

Of course, many who are not themselves able to do good analysis (typically because of lack of time) will attempt to purchase good analysis through advisory services, investment counselors, and mutual funds. Unfortunately, the investor who is unable to analyse individual companies in order to pick the best values may not be able to pick mutual funds or investment management firms any better.

Transactions costs of one form or the other may prevent investors from obtaining good analysis. For instance, in buying a mutual fund, the investor loses the opportunity to time his purchases and sales of individual issues for maximum tax advantage. The investor with a number of different issues in his portfolio, some with gains and some with losses, has a variety of tax techniques available to him. By selective selling of those stocks with losses, he can reduce his ordinary income by up to $3000 per year. Stocks with gains can either be held to retirement, given to charity, given to relatives in lower tax brackets, or sold during years when income is unusually low. Losses can be taken while they are still short term, while gains can be held until they become long term. Since a mutual fund normally pools gains and losses, its after tax return is likely to be lower than the before tax return of an investor taking advantage of the tax laws. Those that rely on investment counselors or purchased advice will have substantial fees to pay, and the improvement in performance may not cover these.

The question is sometimes asked, "If security analysts or investment advisors are so good, why aren't they rich, instead of living off selling their advice."[11] The previous analysis provides the answer. With large numbers of competent advisors around (plus some that are not so competent), the best that can be hoped for is a return that is only somewhat above average. The increase in rate of return possible is enough to justify paying for advice if large sums are to be managed, but not enough to permit the advisor to parlay his small personal grubstroke into a fortune. Thus, good investment analysts, like the rest of us, must work for a living.

THE ROLE OF THE SECURITY ANALYST

Under the assumption previously discussed, there will be a large number of properly valued stocks, and a smaller number of overvalued stocks. In such a market, the role of the security analyst is not to search for undervalued stocks that promise returns above the competitive level (for the competition is likely to be such that such securities will not exist), but to detect and avoid overvalued securities. As a practical matter, this means that the security analyst will spend his time looking for negative facts about particular stocks that are either not known to less informed investors, or whose significance has not been fully realized.

The previous argument has implications for how the security analyst goes about his business. With the traditional goal of looking for a few winners among many potential losers, a large number of stocks are given a quick analysis in the hope of finding the one stock that will double. Once it is realized that the goal is to avoid holding a bad stock, it becomes clear that having to examine large numbers of stocks requires that the examination of each one must be cursory. Such cursory examinations increase the probability of a mistake being made and an overvalued stock being included in the portfolio.

The optimal procedure for the security analyst starts with deciding how many stocks are required in the final portfolio to assure adequate diversification without incurring unnecessary transactions costs. A somewhat larger (but still small) sample of stocks is chosen for extensive analysis prior to inclusion in the portfolio. The initial selection of stocks could be random, but a better procedure would start by excluding stocks unsuited for the portfolio on the grounds of the wrong level of risk, or a dividend rate that was not suited for the tax status of the purchaser. A stratified sampling procedure (such as one stock from each industry) might then be used to assure the desired degree of diversification.

The preliminary set of stocks would then be subject to extensive analysis to determine if any were overvalued. The overvalued stocks would be dropped, and the remainder would be included in the portfolio after a final check to insure adequate diversification still existed. Such a strategy is designed to minimize the risk of purchasing a low total return stock while assuring adequate diversification and avoiding unnecessary expenses for analysis.

Once the portfolio had been selected, most of the manager's attention would be devoted to keeping it under review. From time to time there might be a speculative surge in the price of a stock, causing it to become overvalued. The stock would be sold. A tentative replacement would be selected based on maintaining the desired level of risk, and remaining diversified (i.e., the expected return of the new stock should have as little covariance with the expected return of the rest of the portfolio as practical). The proposed addition to the portfolio would be subjected to intensive analysis and would be bought if not overvalued. From time to time, other stocks might be sold to maintain the desired level of systematic risk, to reduce the proportion of the portfolio exposed to a particular risk (including a decline in one company or industry), or to eliminate securities no longer suited to the tax status of the portfolio owner.

IMPLICATIONS FOR INVESTOR PROTECTION

Only a small number of individuals need be overoptimistic about a stock for it to be bid up to an excessive price. Suppose the average naive investor who believes a story about a company with a million shares outstanding buys one thousand shares. It will be necessary for only a thousand investors, out of the millions that exist, to be deceived for the stock to be bid

up. Even if negative information is readily available, there are likely to be a thousand who have not taken the time to inform themselves.

This is the flaw in our current approach to investor protection through full disclosure. Even if the facts are readily available and known to the vast majority, the uninformed will still be numerous enough to bid stock up to unreasonable levels. An alternative approach would be to try to so organize the market that short selling prevented stocks from being bid to excessive heights. This would require establishing an institutional structure in which a short seller receives a market return on the proceeds from selling stocks short. One possibility would be to provide for him to receive interest at the market rate on the funds left with the lender of the certificate borrowed.

There are several reasons for believing a reasonably competent analyst should be able to uncover enough situations where stocks are overvalued to pay his salary. Most important, overvaluation can readily occur (as previously described) even where only a minority of investors are unaware of readily available information. While favorable information about a particular company is usually given wide distribution by the management of that company, unfavorable information will normally either be left unmentioned, or relegated to a footnote in the annual report. Although brokers spend much time distributing information about candidates for purchase, they devote very little attention to potentially overvalued companies that might be candidates for sale: any customer may generate commissions by buying a recommended stock but only those who already own a stock can respond to a sell recommendation (leaving aside the small minority who would consider a short sale). In addition, putting out sell recommendations could deprive an analyst of access to the information sources inside a company he needs to do his job and maintain his reputation, or could antagonize underwriting customers of his firm. Finally, in certain cases, sell recommendations could invite libel suits. (XYZ company should be sold because its President is a crook or a fool.)

R. E. Diefenbach,[4] in an article in the *Financial Analysts Journal,* reported that his mutual fund received 1,209 buy recommendations from 24 brokerage firms between November 17, 1967, and May 23, 1969 but only 46 sell recommendations. His experience was consistent with what would be expected from theory. Most of the sell recommendations proved profitable, showing that analysts can recognize an overvalued stock. On the other hand, only 47% of the buy recommendations outperformed the Standard and Poor's 425 Industrial Stock Average. While theory suggests that these recommendations would have done slightly better than average, the poor results are consistent with a market in which it is difficult to do appreciably better than the averages.

As additional evidence that it is possible to identify underperformers, Professor Fabozzi [15] has shown that 74% of the stocks criticized by one service ("The Quality of Earnings Report") for poor accounting subsequently underperformed the market. Presumably other close readers of corporate reports could also identify future underperformers.

More impressive confirmation of the inability of informed investors to select potential winners, combined with an ability to spot losers, was recently provided by Klemosky [8] He examined the price behavior during 1963 to 1972 of stocks that were subject to net buying or selling by institutions (presumably the better informed investors). He found that heavy institutional buying of a stock was typically followed by declines in the price of that stock. Stocks of which institutions were large net buyers typically declined (relative to the market) after the quarter in which the buying occurred. However, heavy sales of stocks by institutions were typically followed by declines in price, indicating that the institutions were able to spot (and sell) overvalued securities. An ability to spot losers but not winners is precisely what is predicted by the theory set out in this paper.

IMPLICATIONS FOR RANDOM WALK THEORY

If buying and selling by well-informed investors will limit the anticipated return on stocks to the range of 0% to C%, with most stocks expected to yield the competitive rate of C%, this implies that upper and lower limits will exist for the price of each stock, with the majority of stocks priced at the lower limit.

An illustration may make the argument clear. Suppose there is a mining company paying a dividend equal to 5% of its stock's selling price (a peculiar dividend policy that facilitates exposition) whose largest mine will be exhausted in ten years. This fact is in the public domain, but has not been given much publicity. The stock is held only by less informed investors who are not aware of this negative factor. The better informed investors have estimated that the value of the stock after exhaustion of the mine will be V.

Suppose the competitive rate of return is 10%, and the company is expected to pay a 5% dividend till then. To achieve the required 10% return from holding the stock, the investors will buy the stock only if its price can be expected to rise at 5% per year or more. Thus, in years before exhaustion of the mine, the lower limit to the price will be $(1.05)^{-n}V$. In the jargon of the technical analysts, this is the support price.

Since the stock pays a 5% dividend, it won't be profitable to sell the stock short unless its price is expected to decline at 5% per year or more. Thus, there will be an upper limit to the price which is $(1.05)^n V$. This might be referred to as the resistance level. In between the upper and lower levels, a well-informed long-term investor will find it profitable to neither buy nor sell the stock. Between these limits, the price of the stock is free to fluctuate up and down with the buying and selling of the stock by less informed investors. Ten years before exhaustion of the mine, this range of prices is from 61% of the value ten years hence to 163% of the value ten years hence (or, for a stock expected to sell at $10 in a decade, the current price can fluctuate from $6\frac{1}{8}$ to $16\frac{1}{4}$, a quite respectable range.)

The standard argument for the random walk theory is that, if the price of a stock displays any pattern other than a random walk, it will be possible for investors aware of the pattern to make money by buying or selling the stock. In turn, their buying or selling will raise or lower the price sufficiently to eliminate the non-random pattern. Although such an argument is valid where the seller immediately receives use of the proceeds of his sale, this condition is not met for the United States security market.

This can be seen by considering our mining stock. Suppose that if the stock rises during January, it will continue to rise at an annual rate of 4% per year for the next year. If it falls during January, it will decline for the next year at 4% per year. It is rather easy to construct a profitable trading rule: buy the stock if it rises during January and hold for a year; if it falls in January, don't buy the stock. Such a policy promises a return of 9% (4% in capital gains, and 5% in dividends) whenever the stock is bought.

Yet, a rational man upon being informed of this profit making opportunity would choose to ignore it. The reason? The 9% return promised is less than the 10% promised elsewhere. Since it is possible for profitable trading rules to exist but for investors to decline to take advantage of them, there is no theoretical reason for the price of a stock yielding a return between 0 and C to follow a random walk. There are a large number of non-random patterns of price movements whose existence is quite consistent with there being a large number of well-informed investors. (Of course, it is necessary for there to be some less informed investors in the stock, but a shortage of such individuals is not expected.)

Diagram 2 shows the price ranges within which such a stock may fluctuate. Whenever the price of the stock reaches either the upper or lower limit, further price changes are restrained by either buying or short selling by knowledgeable investors. A possible out-

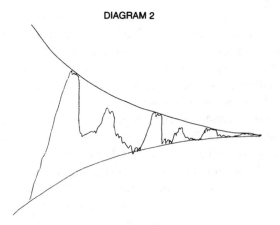

DIAGRAM 2

come would be for the stock to act as if it were restrained between "reflecting barriers."[3]

One strategy would be to buy stocks that were near their lower limit, arguing that a major decline would be prevented by smart investors buying on the fundamentals, while a surge of speculative interest could result in a large rise. A possible way to detect such situations would be to inspect charts of stock prices over time looking for resistance levels in volatile stocks. This provides a rationale for "technical analysis," which has frequently been regarded by academic writers as having no theoretical rationale. Of course, to actually detect "resistance" levels from charts, the fundamentals must stay put long enough for the lower limits to become apparent. In the real world this may not happen too often. (In fact, theory suggests that upper and lower levels should shift over time following a random walk with a trend.) An alternative strategy using fundamental analysis is to look for stocks that are properly priced based on their fundamentals, but that just might have a sudden run up based on speculative considerations.

INCLUSION OF RISK

For simplicity in presentation, risk has been ignored up to this point, with the result that for all stocks the upper limit on the expected rate of return is the same, C. Of course, investors will demand a higher expected return from the riskier stocks than they require from the less risky stocks. Thus, the competitive limit of C will depend on the risk of the stock. If investors are able to diversify their portfolios, the capital asset pricing model[14] can be extended to argue that the upper competitive limit on the rate of return should be a linear function of the systematic risk, such that the competitive limit is equal to the sum of the risk-free interest rate and the product of the beta coefficient of the stock and the price of systematic risk. However, as the author has pointed out elsewhere[13], the systematic risk of a stock depends on its covariance with the level of national income as well as its covariance with the stock market.

Investors will normally attempt to hold a well-diversified portfolio. This should not be a difficult task, since there will be a large number of stocks promising a competitive return from which to choose. One minor complication does exist. Investors might well attempt to have every major stock group represented in their portfolio in proportion to its total value on the stock exchange (attempting to approximate a market portfolio). Within each group, investors would concentrate on those stocks that promised a competitive return, avoiding those which had been bid up by less informed investors to unreasonable levels. One can conceive of a situation where most members of a popular speculative group (computers say) were overpriced. In order to obtain the diversification benefits of participation in this group, well-informed investors might be willing to pay a slight premium over the price that would be required by its expected return and beta. Thus, the price of particular securities would depend somewhat on industry group and other factors besides expected return and systematic risk.

The lower limit on the return, set by the possibility of short selling, would also depend on the risk. Because short selling is a way to hedge against a decline in the market, investors might very well accept a negative expected return from short selling in order to obtain the insurance value. Since the insurance value of a short position will depend on the systematic risk of that stock when held long, the minimum rate of return will be equal to the beta of the stock multiplied by the amount by which the market discounts price per unit of beta.

> Let r be the interest rate of risk-free obligations
> b be the beta of a stock
> and p be the reduction in price per unit of beta
> C be the upper limit on competitive returns
> L be the lower limit on competitive returns

Then $C = r + pb$ and $L = pb$ Thus, $C - L = r$

In other words, the width of the band within which the return on the stock fluctuates is equal to r, the rate of return on riskless investments and is independent of the systematic risk of the stock.

There remain several complications to be noted. The opportunities for selling stocks short profitably are much fewer than the opportunities for going long. This means that, if there are imperfections in the market such that individuals differ in their willingness to pay for insurance against a market decline, the price of systematic risk in the "short" market will be set by those willing to pay the most for insurance. This may make price of systematic risk in the "short" market higher than the value estimated in the long market.

THE ROLE OF SHORT SELLING

In the security markets, there is an asymmetry

between short and long sales, arising from the need to borrow certificates before they can be sold, and from the institutional arrangements for doing so. In markets for commodity futures and stock options, what is being traded are not items already in existence but contracts to make future delivery. Such contracts are as easily written on the long side as on the short side. Thus, it would appear that the institutional arrangements in the commodity and options markets would permit these markets to be efficient if there are sufficient numbers of well-informed speculators. Prices on such efficient markets would be expected to follow a random walk.

There is one important exception to the rule that the short seller does not receive use of the funds from the short sale, or even interest on them. If a brokerage firm, trading for its own account, takes a short position in a stock and is able to borrow the stock from the account of a client of the firm, the brokerage firm does have use of the proceeds of the sale. It can use these funds to reduce the amount that it needs to borrow from a bank to carry its customers' margin accounts. Because of this, a brokerage firm can show a profit from a short sale of a stock that rises in price but at a rate less than the rate of interest at which it borrows. Brokerage firms have a substantial advantage over other investors in their ability to profit from short selling. Thus, it is not surprising that brokers do a disproportionate amount of the short selling that is done. However, the total financial resources available to brokers are sufficiently small that this exception to the rule that short sellers do not receive use of the proceeds should not affect the validity of the argument of this paper.

The argument so far has been developed on the assumption that investors are just as willing to sell short as to buy long. This is probably not so. Most institutions, including pension funds, other trust funds, and mutual funds, cannot sell short as a matter of law. Large individual investors legally can go short, but there is a sufficient prejudice against doing so that such short sales are relatively rare. As noted earlier, brokers seldom put out sell recommendations, forcing the potential short seller to do his own analysis.

When an investor sells a stock short, he incurs a nonsystematic risk. The stock he sold short just may go up sharply giving him substantial losses. In theory this can be diversified against through holding a large number of long and short positions. Currently, short selling is a technique used primarily by individuals. Many individual portfolios are too small to completely diversify away the non-systematic risk incurred by going short. This will limit the extent to which such individuals take advantage of the insurance option provided by short sellings and may cause the floor to

be lower than it otherwise would be.

Because of the scarcity of potential short sellers, it is possible that there are unexploited opportunities for better than normal returns through short selling. The effect of this would be to decrease the lower limit on return below the product of a stock's beta and the price of systematic risk. A paucity of potential short sellers does not eliminate the concept of a competitively set lower limit to the return on a stock, it just lowers this limit. Whatever short sellers there are will presumably look for the most attractive opportunities, and by competing among themselves eliminate any opportunities for better than competitive returns on short sales.

AN EXPLANATION FOR MERGERS

Because of legal restrictions and investor prejudice, an increase in the price of stock frequently does not call forth an increase in the supply through short selling. However, the company itself may take advantage of this situation through issuing new stock since, unlike short sellers, it receives the proceeds of the sale. Sometimes this is done through selling new stock for cash which can then be invested in the business. This approach has the disadvantage that the additional stock may force the price down, and this result may not be in the interest of the company (or its owners, the original stockholders). Thus, as a rational monopolist, a company may be reluctant to take advantage of an overvalued stock by making additional stock sales.

Instead, many companies seek to discriminate in the market for their stock by using their overvalued stocks to purchase other companies. This minimizes the impact on a company's stock price by putting the additional stock in the hands of individuals who probably would not have normally considered purchasing the company's stock. Once they have received the stock as part of an exchange, they will frequently hold it through inertia, a desire to avoid brokerage commissions, or a desire to avoid capital gains taxes (where the stock exchanged in a tax free exchange had a tax basis far below the market price of the new stock). Purchases of companies with stock provide a way to dispose of overvalued stock with a minimal effect on the market for the stock. Thus, limitations on short selling are probably one of the major reasons for many of the mergers and takeovers that have been seen in recent years.

THE RATIONALITY OF INDEX FUNDS IN AN EFFICIENT MARKET

So far in this paper it has been argued that index funds are poor investments for pension funds because the stock markets are inefficient. However, should the stock market prove to be efficient, this logically implies pension funds should not invest in index funds or endeavor to assemble a portfolio that contained stocks in the same proportion as they were represented on the stock exchange. (Such a strategy has been described as trying to hold the "market basket" of securities.)

If investors properly utilized all publicly available information, they would take the difference in tax rates between capital gains and ordinary income into account. Individuals are taxed at only half of the normal rate (with some complications because of the minimum tax) on capital gains. Thus, rational tax paying investors should give preference in their portfolios to the securities expected to yield their return in the form of capital gain. In an efficient market, these will be the stocks paying either low dividends, or no dividends. Efforts by tax paying investors to acquire these stocks will raise their price, resulting in lower expected total returns before tax than can be earned on dividend paying stocks of a similar degree of risk. Investors not subject to the income tax, notably pension funds, would find that their best returns were achieved by investing primarily in high dividend paying stocks. Such a strategy should give an appreciably better return than a random sample of all stocks or index funds.

The possibility of increasing the dividend yield of a portfolio without incurring excessive market or non-market risk has been shown by Sharpe and Sosin.[19] Thus, if it is believed that the stock markets are efficient, managers of pension funds should avoid index funds,[2] choosing instead to invest preferentially in the dividend paying stocks avoided by individual investors in the higher tax brackets.

It is interesting that the banks managing the large pension funds appear to have been the greatest proponents of investing in the low dividend paying growth stocks expected to yield large capital gains. This is evidence that they at least do not believe the stock markets to be efficient.

---

[1] See Malkiel [10], Lorie and Hamilton [9], Black [2], Posner [16], Vasicek and McQuown [21].

[2] See Good, Ferguson, and Treynor [6] and Miller [12].

[3] See Jensen [7], Williamson [20], Friend, Blume, and Crockett [5], and Sharpe [18].

REFERENCES

1. American Stock Exchange, "162 Amex Issues Held by Ten or More Institutional Investors," *American Investor*, April, 1974.

2. Fischer Black, "Implications of the Random Walk Hypothesis for Portfolio Management," *Financial Analysts Journal*, Vol. 27 (March/April, 1971), No. 2, pp. 16-22.

3. Paul H. Cootner, "Stock Prices: Random vs. Systematic Changes," in Paul H. Cootner, Editor, *The Random Character of Stock Market Prices* (Cambridge, Massachusetts, MIT Press, 1964).

4. R. E. Diefenbach, "How Good is Institutional Brokerage Research," *Financial Analysts Journal*, January/February, 1972, pp. 54-60.

5. Irwin Friend, Marshall Blume, and Jean Crockett, *Mutual Funds and Other Institutional Investors, A New Perspective: A Twentieth Century Fund Study* (New York: McGraw-Hill Book Co., 1970).

6. Walter R. Good, Robert Ferguson, and Jack Treynor "An Investor's Guide to the Index Fund Controversy," *Financial Analysts Journal* (November/December, 1976), pp. 27-36.

7. Michael C. Jensen, "Risk, the Performance of Mutual Funds in the Period 1945-1964," *Journal of Finance*, Vol. 23 (May, 1968), No. 2, pp. 389-416.

8. Robert C. Klemosky, "The Impact and Efficiency of Institutional Net Trading Imbalances," *Journal of Finance*, March, 1977, pp. 79-86.

9. James H. Lorie and Mary T. Hamilton, *The Stock Market: Theories and Evidence* (Homewood, Illinois, Richard D. Irwin), pp. 70-112.

10. Burton Malkiel, *A Random Walk Down Wall Street* (New York, W. W. Norton & Co.), pp. 167-170.

11. Edward Miller, "Risk, Uncertainty, and Diversity of Opinion," *Journal of Finance*, September, 1977, pp. 1151-1168.

12. ———, "Index Fund Argument is Illogical: Market Averages Can Be Beaten," *Pensions and Investments*, June 5, 1975, p. 25.

13. ———, "Portfolio Selection in a Fluctuating Economy," *Financial Analysts Journal*, May/June, 1978, pp. 77-83.

14. ———, "A Simple Counter Example to the Random Walk Theory," forthcoming, *Financial Analysts Journal*.

15. Frank J. Fabozzi, "Quality of Earnings A Test of Market Efficiency," *Journal of Portfolio Management*, Fall, 1978.

16. Richard A. Posner, "The Prudent Investor's Powers and Obligations in an Age of Market (index) Funds," *Journal of Contempory Business*, Summer, 1976.

17. William F. Sharpe, "Capital Asset Prices: A Theory of Market Equilibrium Under Conditions of Risk," *Journal of Finance*, Vol. 19 (September, 1964), pp. 425-442.

18. ———, "Mutual Fund Performance" in *Security Prices: A Supplement, Journal of Business*, Vol. 39 (January, 1966), No. 1, Part 2, pp. 119-138.

19. ———, and Howard B. Sosin, "Risk Return and Yield: New York Stock Exchange Common Stocks, 1928-1969," *Financial Analysts Journal*, March/April, 1976.

20. Peter J. Williamson, "Measuring Mutual Fund Performance in the Period 1945-1964," *Journal of Finance* (November/December, 1972), pp. 78-82.

21. Oldrich A. Vasicek and John A. McQuown, "The Efficient Market Model," *Financial Analysts Journal*, Vol. 28 (September/October, 1972), No. 5, pp. 71-84.

A new paradigm for portfolio risk

Risk is a function of the cash-flow relationship between a portfolio's assets and its liabilities

Robert H. Jeffrey

Thomas Kuhn, in his landmark book, *The Structure of Scientific Revolutions*, describes the fall of a so-called "rational model" as a paradigm shift. "Scientists in any field and in any time," he writes, "possess a set of shared beliefs about the world, and for that time the set constitutes the dominant paradigm. . . . Experiments are carried on strictly within the boundaries of these beliefs and small steps toward progress are made." Citing the example of the Ptolemaic view of the universe with the earth at its center, Kuhn observes, "Elaborate mathematical formulas and models were developed that would accurately predict astronomical events based on the Ptolemaic paradigm" but it was not until Copernicus and Kepler discovered "that the formulae worked *more easily* [emphasis added]" when the sun replaced the earth as the center of the universe model that a "paradigm shift" in astronomy began and laid the foundation for even greater steps toward progress.[1]

The thrust of this paper is to put forth a similar proposition. I shall assert, on a more mundane level, that our portfolio management process should also "work more easily" and *rewardingly* if a paradigm shift were to occur in the "rational model" or "shared belief" that portfolio risk is strictly a function of the volatility of portfolio returns.

THE CASE IN BRIEF

This paper will suggest that the current paradigm is incomplete. More important, it is often misleading for a vast number of portfolio owners, because it fails to recognize that risk is a function of the characteristics of a portfolio's *liabilities* as well as of its assets and, in particular, of the cash-flow relationship between the two over time. Consequently, I shall offer a modification in the "rational model's" proxy for risk that, by including consideration of liabilities, which tend to be highly parochial, has the salutory effect of involving the portfolio *owner* more intimately in the risk determination process.

Finally, the paper will demonstrate how the acceptance of this modification in the definition of portfolio risk can naturally lead, in many cases, to the development of an asset mix policy tailored specifically to the particular, and often peculiar, needs of each portfolio owner. Such an asset mix is, after all, what "sophisticated" investors presumably seek but largely fail to achieve. The result is that most institutions have "look-alike" portfolios, even when the institutions themselves are markedly different.

Some of the ideas that I propose here have already been suggested, at least fragmentally, by others. In this Journal alone, Smidt, in discussing investment horizons and performance measurement, asks "How relevant are conventional risk/reward measures?"[2] and Trainer et al. state that the "holding period is the key to risk thresholds."[3] In fact, I have previously suggested that the holding periods or time horizons of a "major segment of institutional investors . . . (are) really infinity, at least as infinity is perceived by mortal beings."[4] Levy succinctly summarizes the concerns of those who are troubled by the current risk paradigm when he says that "time horizon is just as important as (return) variability in setting asset mixes" and suggests that "what is needed is an appropriate definition of risk."[5]

1. Footnotes appear at the end of the article.

143

While this Journal would seem to be read mostly by academics and practitioners, it is my hope that the messages of this paper may eventually reach portfolio owners, and, specifically, their chief executive officers and governing boards who, in the last analysis, are solely responsible for determining the measure of risk that is appropriate to their respective situations. On a more ambitious level, I suggest that the concepts here are relevant to *all* owners of assets, not just financial assets, and to all types of portfolios, not just those of institutions.

The conclusion that the acceptance of a new risk paradigm may prove rewarding for many portfolio owners stems from a belief that the current misunderstanding of what truly constitutes risk in a given situation often leads to portfolios with less than optimal equity contents and, therefore, lower long-term returns than might otherwise be achieved.[6] Furthermore, the failure to understand explicitly how much volatility risk can actually be tolerated in a given situation all too often encourages owners to dampen volatility by attempts to "time the market," which, as I — among others — have noted elsewhere, typically leads to mediocre long-term performance results.[7]

The utility of developing a concept of risk that is more intuitively understandable to portfolio owners and is universally applicable to *all* portfolio situations becomes more apparent when we accept the following three premises (of which only the third may be unfamiliar):

1. To the extent that the market *is* mostly efficient, we can expect only modest improvements in portfolio returns from active asset management.
2. To the extent that well diversified portfolio returns *do* vary directly with volatility over long periods of time, returns are indeed a function of risk as risk is presently defined.
3. Prudent portfolio owners, when confronted with *uncertainties* as to what constitutes an appropriate level of risk, will usually err on the side of accepting too little volatility rather than too much.

Given the first two premises, it follows naturally that the most effective way to enhance returns is to determine the extent to which volatility does indeed affect the portfolio owner's *true* risk situation, and to select a portfolio that provides the maximum level of *tolerable* volatility and thus the highest possible return, given the attendant risk. Since uncertainties concerning appropriate levels of risk usually result in overstatements of the impact of volatility, any change in the "rational model" that reduces portfolio owners' uncertainty of what truly constitutes risk in their particular situations should have a positive effect on future returns.

THE PROBLEM WITH VOLATILITY AS A PROXY FOR RISK

The problem with equating portfolio risk solely to the volatility of portfolio returns is simply that the proposition says nothing about what is being risked as a result of the volatility. For purposes of analogy consider the most common example of volatility in our daily lives, the weather. The risk implications of weather volatility are usually minimal for the vast majority of the population, who are not farmers or sailors or outdoor sports promoters or backpackers undertaking a winter hike in the mountains. Feeling "rewarded" by not having the daily burden of carrying a raincoat, many commuters are content to bear the nominal risk of occasionally getting slightly damp on their short walk to the office. On the other hand, on a long backpack in the mountains, where one of the "rewards" is clearly carrying as little weight as possible, prudent hikers will nonetheless hedge their risk of serious discomfort or worse by toting several pounds of raingear and perhaps a tent.

Volatility per se, be it related to weather, portfolio returns, or the timing of one's morning newspaper delivery, is simply a benign statistical probability factor that tells us nothing about risk until coupled with a consequence. Its measurement is useless until we describe that probability in terms of the "probability of what." If the "what" is of no concern to the given individual or group, then the probability of "what's" occurring is likewise of no concern, and vice versa, and vice all the gradations in between. As the editor of this Journal reminded his clients some years ago, "The determining question in structuring a portfolio is the *consequence* of loss; this is far more important than the *chance* of loss."[8]

What then is the specific *consequence* whose probable occurrence should concern us?

RISK IS THE PROBABILITY OF NOT HAVING SUFFICIENT CASH WITH WHICH TO BUY SOMETHING IMPORTANT

Since an investment *portfolio* is, etymologically, a collection of noncash pieces of paper (see footnote 9 for *portfolio's* literal meaning), and since nearly everything we buy or every obligation we retire requires outlays of cash, the real risk in holding a portfolio is that it might not provide its owner, either during the interim or at some terminal date or both, with the *cash* he requires to make essential outlays, including meeting payments when due. (In the case of pension funds, such purchases include deferred payments for services previously rendered.) As Smidt aptly points out, "Investors are ultimately interested in the future stream of *consumption* they will be able to obtain from their portfolios" by converting noncash assets into cash.[10]

Nevertheless, since a portfolio's "cash convertibility" varies so directly with the volatility of its returns that the two terms are typically used interchangeably, one might argue that this emphasis on cash requirements in no way affects the usefulness of volatility as a proxy for risk. To so argue, however, overlooks the critical fact that *different portfolio owners have different needs for cash*, just as the commuter and the backpacker have different needs for protective clothing.

Ability to purchase, which varies directly with portfolio volatility, should not be confused with *need* to purchase. The latter, d'être, as Smidt suggests, is the portfolio's raison d'être, and is, or should be, the governing factor in determining the division of the portfolio's asset mix of holdings between those that are readily convertible into predictable amounts of cash and those that are not. By developing a risk paradigm that places the emphasis on "need to purchase" rather than "ability to purchase," each *portfolio owner is encouraged to make a conscious decision as to whether or not to carry a raincoat (i.e., low volatile, "nearer to cash" assets). To carry a raincoat because others are carrying raincoats is simply being fashionable, and being fashionable in investment decisions typically leads to mediocre results, or worse.

From this, we can readily see that, strictly speaking, the widely used term "portfolio risk," standing by itself, is meaningless, because "the possibility of loss or injury," which is Webster's definition of risk, has no abstract significance. Like the weather, portfolios feel no pain; it is only *travelers* in the weather and *owners* of portfolios who bear whatever is the attendant risk. What then is "owner's risk"?

Owner's risk is measured by the degree of "fit" that appears when a portfolio's minimum projected cash flows from income and principal conversions into cash are superimposed by time period on the owner's maximum future cash requirements for essential payments. Such a juxtapositioning provides a continous series of pro forma cash flow statements. The periodic differences between the expected future cash conversion values of the assets, including their income flows, and the expected future cash requirements of the liabilities show up on the pro forma statements either as surpluses, connoting negative risk, or as deficits, connoting positive risk. As in all pro forma statements, however, the problem is not in the arithmetic, but rather in the accuracy of the assumptions used in projecting the cash flows.

A great deal of useful research has been done

on the predictability, over varying time frames, of the cash conversion values of various arrays of portfolio assets. In this context, "predictability" can be roughly translated as "volatility" and "cash conversion value" as "total return." What is typically left undone, however, is an equally thorough analysis of the liability side of the equation, i.e., of the essentiality, timing, magnitude, and predictability of the portfolio owner's future cash requirements.

In his excellent chapter on setting investment objectives, C.D. Ellis asserts that "the priority objective in investment management is to control risk, not to maximize returns."[11] Ellis says it is a "paradoxical fact that most investment managers devote most of their time, energy and ability in an apparently futile effort" to maximize returns when controlling risk would be "far, far easier" and much more effective.[12] Ellis's paradox, and his implied criticism of investment managers, is resolved in part by Smidt, who reminds us that "the risk of an asset or portfolio cannot be determined without knowing something about the characteristics of the investor."[13] I would say, instead, that this risk cannot be determined without knowing *a great deal* about the *future cash requirements* of the investor.

While the investment management community, and especially the consultants whose natural purview it should be, can perhaps be taken to task for devoting so little time to analyzing their client owners' cash liability structures, this analysis, for all practical purposes, can best be undertaken by the owners themselves for the simple reason that the essentiality, timing, magnitude, and predictability of each owner's future cash requirements are peculiar to his own particular situation. Said another way, the "expert from out of town" will bring few of the answers in his briefcase.

HOW DO YOU QUANTIFY "OWNER'S RISK"?

Because it is axiomatic that there is a direct relationship between risk and reward, it is not surprising that the theoreticians adopted volatility of asset returns as a universal proxy for portfolio risk. They were searching for a measurable proxy for risk to explain differences in portfolio returns. Return volatility is a readily available statistic, and, indeed, does seem to work nicely as a measure of "*portfolio* risk," which is to say the predictability of the future cash conversion value of the asset side of the portfolio equation. Did the theoreticians realize that "*portfolio* risk" becomes meaningful only when converted to "*owner's* risk" by superimposing on the former the cash requirements implicit in the owner's liabilities? I cannot answer this question, but, in any case, I am still confronted with the need to quantify the new and more meaningful risk proxy.

It would be helpful to support the new paradigm suggested in this paper with the familiar scatter chart showing risk on one axis and return on the other for a variety of portfolio owners' situations. As that is a practical impossibility, the best that I can offer at this point is an incomplete table of factors that affect an owner's risk.

FACTORS TENDING TO INCREASE "OWNER'S RISK"

	ASSET RELATED	LIABILITY RELATED
1. Large cash requirements relative to assets.	X	X
2. Large cash requirements relative to income.	X	X
3. Unpredictability of cash requirements.		X
4. High variability of owner's "emotional needs."		X
5. Small income stream relative to assets.	X	
6. High variability of income stream.	X	
7. High variability of total return.	X	
8. Near proximity of portfolio termination.		X
9. Absence of potentially available nonportfolio assets, including borrowing capacity.	X	

Using this table as a starting point, adding and discarding factors where necessary, and attempting to quantify the cash flow implications of each, the portfolio owner may eventually be able to tailor both the asset portfolio and the liability structure so that the projected cash inflows by period approximately equal the projected cash outflows. Short of this, he should be able to define with some precision the magnitude of the cash shortfalls that, using this approach, should now be at an irreducible minimum. This is admittedly a cut-and-fit process that does not easily lend itself to comparing one portfolio owner's results with another's. Nonetheless, careful consideration of these factors can provide a workable approach for determining the optimal portfolio for each owner's particular situation — that is, the portfolio that maximizes reward relative to the constraints imposed by the owner's needs for cash to meet essential payments.

KEY RISK FACTOR IS CASH REQUIREMENTS RELATIVE TO ASSETS

There should be little argument about the im-

portance of the first factor, large cash requirements relative to assets, since, *reductio ad absurdum*, an owner with zero future cash requirements bears no risk of having insufficient cash regardless of the choice of portfolio assets! Conversely, the owner whose entire asset stake is required to fund some essential outlay tomorrow is almost totally exposed to whatever may be the risk inherent in the portfolio's volatility. While the first parameter, having zero future cash requirements and no risk, is obviously absurd, the second parameter, which assumes that the *entire* portfolio must be converted into cash tomorrow, is almost equally unrealistic — *yet it is precisely this implicit assumption that owners make when they measure risk solely in terms of the volatility of portfolio returns.*

LARGE CASH REQUIREMENTS RELATIVE TO INCOME

While owners have been taught for 15 years or so that "total return is all that counts," the projected spread between a portfolio's cash income and the owner's cash expenditures (if negative) would seem to be far more significant than total return by itself. These cash shortfalls are precisely what determines the owner's actual exposure to the true risk of portfolio volatility. To the extent that an owner's cash requirements are (or could be) modest enough to be funded solely from a portfolio's income stream, and to the extent that this income stream might be expected to grow at roughly the same rate as the cash requirements, the volatility of the cash conversion value of the portfolio's assets ceases to be an economic consideration.

For example, since World War II the popular S&P 500 index has produced a stable income flow rising considerably faster than inflation,[14] and the investor could have purchased the index or its equivalent to yield 5% or more on frequent occasions. It is surprising, therefore, that more portfolio owners with inflation-related liabilities have not consciously sought to tailor their "cash requirement ratios" to assets and to income to take advantage of the very basic risk-reducing implications of "living within your income." There are, of course, some potential problems in following such a strategy, which I will discuss later.

This emphasis on cash requirements reinforces the common sense notion that, all other things being equal, rewards should tend to decrease as the owner's spending or consumption requirements increase. While this proposition may seem obvious, what seems to be less obvious is that, since spending decisions are determined not by portfolio managers but by portfolio owners, it is therefore the portfolio *owners* who, by their cash consumption habits, are determining their own risk tolerance to a large extent. Thus, they limit their portfolio returns. When Ellis says that "the priority objective in investment management is to control risk, not to maximize returns," he is speaking primarily to the owners and not to the "hired hands."

UNPREDICTABILITY OF FUTURE CASH REQUIREMENTS

If future cash requirements are in fact a major determinant of owner's risk, the owner can determine risk only to the extent that these cash requirements are predictable. Long-range planning or thinking of any sort is difficult because of the many variables involved, and is therefore too often left undone, but such an effort will serve to sort out those cash requirements that are, indeed, highly predictable from those that are not. Consequently, what initially seems to be a very large and complex forecasting problem can often be reduced to quite manageable proportions.

Furthermore, owners often bring this risk-enhancing problem on themselves unwittingly by entering into legal or tacit long-term commitments for future cash payments that later prove to be unpredictable. A case in point is the typical salaried pension plan whose cash requirements are based on salary levels many years hence. While "open-ended" contracts are probably unavoidable, such contracts do increase the uncertainty of future cash requirements, which in turn increases "owner's risk" and ultimately reduces portfolio returns. When new cash liabilities are being contemplated, this future "unpredictability" factor should be given important consideration by the portfolio owner, as it will ultimately have a material effect on his (or his successors') return.

VARIABILITY OF OWNER'S "EMOTIONAL" TOLERANCE FOR RISK

Ellis reminds us of the reality that "the risk tolerance of a fund . . . is the risk tolerance of a majority of the board of directors at the moment of most severe market adversity."[15] To the extent that high volatility of returns may indeed cause an owner to modify an earlier, well-thought-out economic assessment of risk, everything said thus far ceases to pertain. Given this circumstance, "owner's risk" reverts to being "portfolio risk," which we have already acknowledged to be a direct function of return volatility.

NONAVAILABILITY OF OTHER "NONPORTFOLIO" ASSETS

While, for various tax and legal reasons, endowment, foundation, and pension assets are segregated from the de facto owner's other assets, it is still the *owner*, and not the *portfolio*, who bears (at least the moral) risk of not being able to meet the future cash obligations for which the funds were established. Unfortunately, many owners seem to overlook the risk-reducing aspect of having assets outside the particular fund that might conceivably be called upon in an emergency to meet future cash requirements. A cash-rich corporation, for instance, can afford to maintain a portfolio with higher volatility (i.e., with many fewer near-to-cash assets) in its pension fund than a neighbor verging on bankruptcy. To the extent that the portfolio owner has other available resources to fund these obligations, such other resources should clearly be considered in determining "owner's risk."

USING "OWNER'S RISK" TO DETERMINE ASSET ALLOCATIONS

As previously noted, "owner's risk" is measured by the extent of the shortfalls that appear when the minimum expected cash inflows from income and asset conversions from a portfolio or other resources are superimposed by period on the owner's maximum expected cash outflows for essential payments. In the ideal but not necessarily imaginary situation where future cash inflows are always equal to or greater than the corresponding outflows, owner's risk is negative. In that case the owner has the option of increasing his future cash commitment liabilities, reducing his assets by deferring subsequent contributions, or carrying the "negative risk" forward as a cushion against any overly optimistic assumptions that may have crept into the cash flow analysis.

In the more common situation where some or most future cash outflows are greater than the corresponding inflows, making "owner's risk" positive, the owner is forced back to the drawing board to see if he can devise some rearrangement of the asset and/or liability structures that might solve or ameliorate the problem.

A few years ago, when interest rates were at record highs, many pension fund portfolio owners converted what were originally very large positive risk situations into negative risk situations overnight. They accomplished this by "dedicating" the known future cash inflows from principal and income of highly volatile long bond portfolios to meet the actuarially known future cash outflows to already retired and soon-to-retire employees. Such portfolio restructurings, whose unbelievably high interest rate assumptions have been given actuarial blessings by virtue of the dedications, are a classic case in support of the principal thesis of this paper, namely that risk is a function of the *matching of cash flows* and not the volatility of returns.

WHY NOT A "DEDICATED EQUITY PORTFOLIO"?

If a portfolio owner can disregard return volatility in a dedicated bond portfolio because the cash flows in and out are matched by period, can we apply the same principal to other kinds of portfolios? Chart I below suggests that, at least since World War II, inflation-related cash obligations could have been funded by the income stream from the S&P 500 with considerable cash left over. If the portfolio owner is comfortable with the notion that dividends will continue to be a good inflation hedge, and if he has sufficient resources relative to his present inflation-related cash requirements, why not fund these requirements with the income stream from a high-quality, diversified "dedicated *equity* portfolio" and forget about asset volatility entirely?

CHART I

S&P DIVIDENDS VERSUS THE CPI, 1945-1983

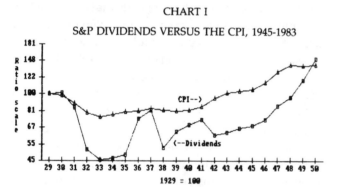

I can deal with the superficial reason for "why not" rather quickly, namely the *unconventionality* problem of an all-equity portfolio. While following convention is often an investor's opiate, the fact remains that the adoption of a totally dedicated portfolio strategy would rarely result in a 100% commitment to equities. Generally speaking, a proper dedication would lead to an all-equity portfolio only in situations where *all* of the portfolio owner's future cash obligations were inflation-related, a condition that might, at best, pertain to only a few immature pension plans, and, perhaps, an occasional endowment. Since most owners, particularly owners of mature pension plans, have extensive future cash obligations more or less fixed in both amount and time, whose requirements would best be matched with a dedicated bond portfolio, this dedicated matching of asset and liability cash flows would probably lead, in many cases, to overall asset mixes that would pass the "conventionality" test.

The key point here, of course, is not to suggest

a portfolio strategy that coincidentally gives rise to a conventional asset mix, but rather to argue that the dedication of cash flows automatically produces an asset mix that can be rationally explained, supported, and sustained in the face of adverse market conditions in terms of the owners's own particular and peculiar liability situation. The problem with conventional wisdom is not the 60/40 or 50/50 or 40/60 equity-to-debt asset mixes that generally arise; the problem is rather that conventional wisdom is transient, because it is typically based on irrational and irrelevant perceptions of risk that usually have little to do with the owner's own particular situation. Building the foundation for a long-term portfolio strategy on the "shifting sands" of conventional wisdom is obviously poor architecture.

The far more critical argument against relying on the income from a dedicated equity portfolio to meet future inflation-related cash obligations is the possibility that the dividend stream from such a portfolio might not always be as stable relative to inflation as it has been since World War II. Whereas the historical patterns shown on Chart I make the dedicated equity portfolio idea look eminently attractive from a cash-flow standpoint for those who have sufficient resources, such is anything but the case when we look at Chart II covering 1929-1950.

CHART II

S&P DIVIDENDS VERSUS THE CPI, 1929-1950

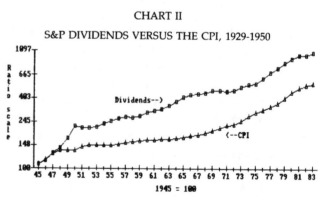

Because of the Great Depression's negative impact on corporate dividends during the 1930s, followed by wartime controls on dividends and postwar inflation, the cash flows from the S&P 500 dividend fell behind the Consumer Price Index after 1930 and did not catch up until 1950. A hypothetical portfolio owner, who commenced in 1929 to service $100,000 in annual inflation-related cash obligations with the income from a dedicated S&P 500 equity portfolio, would have found himself short over $500,000 on a cumulative basis by 1950, this being determined by the accumulated differences between the upper and lower lines on Chart II.

How much would it cost a 1984 portfolio

owner, adopting a dedicated equity portfolio strategy, to insure (or, more specifically, to self-insure) that sufficient cash would always be available to meet future obligations in the event of a similar economic debacle?

If we assume that the 1984 owner's current inflation-related cash requirements were $100,000 per year and that the S&P 500's yield were 4.5% at the time of inception, about $2.2 million would be required for the dedicated equity portfolio itself. In addition, the owner would need in his self-insurance subfund the *present value* of the assumed worst-case future cash shortfalls that, as noted above, total about $500,000 spread over 20 years. Assuming for simplicity that a dedicated bond portfolio of U.S. Treasury issues with appropriate maturities could be assembled in 1984 to yield 12% across the board, the required investment in the self-insurance fund would be $145,000.[16] If the portfolio owner's assets presently totaled $3 million, the additional capital investment required for the self-insurance fund would be roughly 5%.

Let us now assume that the existing $3 million portfolio is presently split equally between equities and fixed-income investments. Let us further assume a 6% equity risk premium. If, as a consequence of adopting this dedicated equity portfolio approach, the owner's commitment to equities were increased from $1.5 million to $2.2 million, the additional theoretical return would be $42,000 per year. If realized, this additional return would amortize the additional investment in 3.5 years.[17] The payout could be even shorter if the acceptance of this rational approach to the asset-mix question prevented the owner from making the classic mistake of bailing out of equities at market bottoms and buying in with everyone else when the market is soaring.

The portfolio owner need not make the move into an insured dedicated equity portfolio all at one time. As the arithmetic above would suggest, however, the ideal point to dedicate an equity portfolio (or a bond portfolio for that matter) is when equity yields and interest rates are high. At those times, the highest current income and the most insurance can be purchased at the lowest prices. Since the ideal market conditions under which to establish dedicated portfolios tend to arise infrequently and to be of short duration, owners would be well advised to have considered this matter in advance and to have made contingency plans for where and how they might obtain the additional funding when the opportunity arises.

Just as life and major medical insurance permit the owner with large family obligations to incur the risks of living more actively and therefore more re-

wardingly, so does the concept of insuring the income stream from a dedicated equity portfolio. Common sense tells us that, ideally, "living liabilities," — those that vary with inflation — should be matched with "living assets," such as equities, to the extent possible; but convention, on the other hand, suggests categorically that owners may not be able to tolerate the increased volatility risk. If this dilemma can be resolved by making a small investment (as it can in many cases) that obviates or minimizes the volatility problem, the higher long-term returns that should ensue would be well worth the cost.

I contend, in fact, that many portfolio owners are inadvertently over-insured against volatility by holding low-return, nearer-to-cash assets much of the time. And, to make matters worse, the insurance is too often cashed in just when the coverage is needed most. Owners would be well advised to rationally consider exactly what role "volatility insurance" might play in their respective situations, to invest accordingly to the extent that resources permit, and to continually reinforce the intellectual basis on which this decision was made. Inadvertence in critical policy decisions should have no placed in portfolio management.

SUMMARY: THE NEED FOR CASH DRIVES THE PROCESS

In the last analysis, risk is the likelihood of having insufficient cash with which to make essential payments. While the traditional proxy for risk, volatility of returns, does reflect the probable variability of the cash conversion value of a portfolio owner's assets, it says nothing about the cash requirements of his liabilities, or future obligations. Since fund assets exist solely to service these cash obligations, which vary widely from one fund to another in terms of magnitude, timing, essentiality, and predictability, portfolio owners are being seriously misled when they define risk solely in terms of the asset side of the equation.

Specifically, since both history and theory demonstrate that diversified portfolio returns historically and theoretically increase as return volatility increases, owners should be explicitly encouraged to determine *in their own particular situations* the maximum amount of return volatility that can be tolerated, given their own respective future needs for cash. While the theoreticians are presumably correct in directly relating volatility and returns, it is the owner's future *need for cash* that determines how much volatility he can tolerate and, therefore, the level of portfolio return that can theoretically be achieved.

My intention in emphasizing the *need for cash*

149

has been purposely to shift responsibility for the risk-determination process from the asset manager to the portfolio owner. As one author reminds us, "Spending decisions (and thus future needs for cash) are the one input to the portfolio management equation that is totally controllable by the owner."[18] Furthermore, the cumulative effect of the owner's prior spending decisions on future needs for cash can, in most cases, best be fathomed and thus planned for, conceivably modified, and insured against, within the owner's own shop and not by an outside agent.

Finally, by letting the need for cash drive the portfolio management process, the owner can make future spending decisions more wisely. Over time, he can develop and sustain an understandable and defendable asset mix policy that will provide him with an optimum portfolio return given his particular cash requirement situation. In one sentence, the traditional, narrow definition of portfolio risk based solely on volatility encourages owners to apply a universal risk-measurement standard, for which they themselves accept little personal responsibility, to what is essentially a highly parochial problem.

[1] T. Kuhn, *The Structure of Scientific Revolutions*, Chicago: University of Chicago Press, 1970, as quoted in T. J. Peters and R. H. Waterman, Jr., *In Search of Excellence*, New York: Harper & Row, 1982, p. 42.

[2] S. Smidt, "Investment horizons and performance measurement," *The Journal of Portfolio Management*, Winter 1978, p. 18.

[3] F. H. Trainer, Jr.; J. B. Yawitz; and W. J. Marshall, "Holding period is the key to risk threshholds," *The Journal of Portfolio Management*, Winter 1979, p. 48.

[4] R. H. Jeffrey, "Internal portfolio growth: The better measure," *The Journal of Portfolio Management*, Summer 1977, p. 10.

[5] R. A. Levy, "Stocks, bonds, bills, and inflation over 52 Years," *The Journal of Portfolio Management*, Summer 1978, p. 18.

[6] While presumably unnecessary for readers of this Journal, we note here (using Ibbotson and Sinquefield data through 1981) that the annualized total return of the S&P 500 from 1926-1983 was 9.6% versus 3.2% for 90-day Treasury bills.

[7] R. H. Jeffrey, "The Folly of Market Timing," *Harvard Business Review*, July-August 1984.

[8] P. L. Bernstein, "Management of Individual Portfolios," *Financial Analysts Handbook* (S. Levine, ed.), Homewood, Illinois: Dow Jones-Irwin, Inc., 1975, pp. 1373-1388.

[9] *Portfolio* derives from the Latin words *portare*, to carry, and *foglio*, leaf or sheet. Since the Romans had a perfectly good word for cash, *moneta*, which they could have used for "cashbox," we can thus infer that *foglio* refers to noncash forms of paper. Etymologically then, a "portfolio," or even a so-called "investment portfolio," is not and should not be confused with cash, a distinction that most investors fail to make in the "mark-to-market" world in which we live.

[10] Smidt, op. cit., p. 21

[11] C. D. Ellis, "Setting Investment Objectives," *Investment Manager's Handbook*, Homewood, Illinois: Dow Jones-Irwin, Inc., 1980, p. 66.

[12] Ibid., p. 61.

[13] Smidt, op. cit., p. 18.

[14] *Security Price Index Record*, New York: Standard & Poor's Corporation, 1980, pp. 134-137. From 1945 through 1982 the dividend on the S&P 500 has grown over tenfold, producing a compound annualized growth rate of 6.7% versus 4.6% for the Consumer Price Index. More important, in these 36 years the S&P 500 dividend has increased in every year but 4, and in all of the latter instances the declines were minimal.

[15] Ellis, op. cit., p. 67.

[16] The $145,000 present value of the 1930-1949 cash shortfalls is derived by discounting each year's shortfall by 12% for the corresponding number of years and summing the results.

[17] There is an additional but minor cost of insuring the income stream from a dedicated equity portfolio. Additional "premiums" must be paid each year as the future cash needs that are being insured increase with inflation. Resources would thus have to be found each year to increase the self-insurance fund accordingly, plus or minus any differences arising from changes in the discount factor applicable to the new investments.

[18] J. P. Williamson and H. A. D. Sanger, "Educational Endowment Funds," *Investment Manager's Handbook*, Homewood, Illinois: Dow Jones-Irwin, Inc., 1980, p. 839. The actual quotation is, "The spending rate is totally controllable."

Latané's bequest: The best of portfolio strategies

The geometric mean portfolio strategy is simple, flexible, comprehensible — and optimal.

Richard W. McEnally

The basic goal of many individual and institutional investors is to maximize the growth of portfolio value over the long run. For such investors, portfolio models that stress expected return and associated risk in a single period — such as the Markowitz model — are neither very appealing nor very relevant. The geometric mean portfolio strategy originally developed by Henry A. Latané should be more to their liking.[1]

As is suggested by two of its aliases — growth-optimal or wealth-maximization — this strategy seeks to maximize the probability that terminal portfolio value will exceed the value that would result from any other investment strategy. In the process, it provides practical guidance on such questions as the appropriate level of portfolio leverage. It does not involve consideration or analysis of utility or utility functions. And, despite its long-run orientation, it does not require that the investor look beyond the next decision period. For all these reasons, the geometric mean strategy deserves to be better known.

THE BASIC IDEA

Consider the investment alternatives labeled A and B in Table 1, where we see five holding period returns (HPR's) for each alternative, each return being equal to one plus a *rate* of return; for example, 1.10 means a 10% rate of return. For the moment, we can

1. Footnotes appear at the end of the article.

TABLE 1

Three Investment Alternatives

Period or State of Nature	HPR's for Alternative -		
	A	B	C
1	1.30	1.20	.70
2	1.10	1.10	1.40
3	1.20	1.00	1.50
4	.90	1.05	1.10
5	1.00	1.15	.90
Arithmetic Mean	1.100	1.100	1.120
Terminal Wealth Relative	1.544	1.594	1.455
Geometric Mean	1.091	1.098	1.078
Standard Deviation	.141	.071	.299
Variance	.020	.005	.089
Estimated Geometric Mean	1.091	1.098	1.079

regard these holding period returns as sequential in time — that is, for periods, 1, 2, and so on.

Now, which of these alternatives would be the more attractive investment? Looking at the summary statistics at the foot of the table, we can see that the arithmetic mean, or simple average, of the five holding period returns is the same for both. This equality of arithmetic means implies that the two investments would be equally rewarding over the five periods if one were to withdraw all gains (HPR > 1) and make up all losses (HPR < 1).

Many investors do not behave in this manner.

Richard W. McEnally is Mead Willis Professor of Investment Banking at the Graduate School of Business Administration, University of North Carolina at Chapel Hill (NC 27514). The author's obvious debt to Henry A. Latané, who died in 1984, and to William E. Avera is gratefully acknowledged.

151

Rather, they allow their gains or losses to cumulate over time. Such investors will be more interested in the terminal wealth relative, or its analogue, the geometric mean holding period return.[2]

The terminal wealth relative shows the number of dollars of value at the end of a run of periods per dollar of initial investment, assuming gains and losses are allowed to compound. It is simply equal to the product of the individual HPRs.

$$(1) \qquad \text{Terminal Wealth Relative} = \prod_{t=1}^{T} HPR_t,$$

where T is the number of compounding periods. The terminal wealth relative for alternative B, 1,594, is greater than the 1,544 for alternative A, so B is the preferred investment.

We can draw the same conclusion from the geometric means of the HPRs of 1.091 and 1.098 for A and B respectively. The geometric mean is simply the Tth root of the terminal wealth relative:

$$(2) \qquad \text{Geometric Mean across time}$$

$$= (\text{Terminal Wealth Relative})^{1/T} = \left(\prod_{t=1}^{t} HPR_t \right)^{1/T}.$$

Therefore,

$$\text{Terminal Wealth Relative} = (\text{Geometric Mean})^T,$$

and the geometric mean is equal to one plus the periodic rate of compounding or growth of portfolio value. Alternative B will return $1.59 after five periods for every initial dollar, which implies that funds invested in B will grow at an average rate of 9.8% per period.

Thus, we can say that, with reinvestment, the strategy of selecting the alternative with the higher geometric mean return across time is analogous to maximizing the growth rate of the portfolio or its terminal value.[3] Moreover, this is so even if all gains or losses are not reinvested, subject only to the proviso that the scheme of withdrawals or additions does not depend on the periodic performance of the portfolio.[4]

THE GEOMETRIC MEAN CRITERION AND PORTFOLIO RISK

Close readers of Table 1 will have noticed that alternative B has the smaller standard deviation or variance of returns. Therefore, B would also be chosen by the familiar Markowitz mean-variance criterion, since it has the smaller dispersion in the distribution of returns (or lower "risk"), whereas the arithmetic mean returns are identical.

Does this mean that the two approaches to portfolio selection will lead to the same decision? Not

necessarily, as examination of alternative C in Table 1 shows. This prospective investment has both a larger arithmetic mean and a larger standard deviation of holding period returns than either A or B. Therefore, when we use mean-variance criterion, we cannot say whether C is preferred to B. The answer would depend on the attitude of the investor towards return versus risk as reflected in the investor's utility function. But the geometric mean criterion has a clear answer: B is the preferred investment.

Nevertheless, the two approaches do have many similarities. These can be inferred from the following approximation to the geometric mean:

$$(3) \qquad (\text{Geometric Mean})^2$$

$$= (\text{Arithmetic Mean})^2 - (\text{Standard Deviation})^2,$$

which says that the square of the geometric mean is equal to the square of the arithmetic mean less the standard deviation squared (the variance).[5] The estimated geometric means in Table 1 show that this is a tolerable approximation.

Other things being equal, the larger the arithmetic mean, the larger the geometric mean will be, and the larger the standard deviation, the smaller the geometric mean will be. Therefore, an investor who seeks to maximize the rate of growth of a portfolio will prefer an investment with a high expected return and low variance of returns, just as the Markowitz model exhorts us to do. The difference is that the variance of returns is undesirable in the Markowitz model, because it is synonomous with risk. With the geometric mean criterion, variance is not liked simply because it lowers the rate of wealth accumulation.[6]

MAKING THE STRATEGY OPERATIONAL

The idea that we should pick the investment which will maximize the rate of growth of a portfolio may sound at this point like much advice from economists — laudable, but difficult or impossible to implement in practice because of the knowledge of the distant future it would require.[7]

At this juncture, Henry Latané made an original and insightful contribution. He showed that if, *in each period*, the investor chooses the alternative with the largest geometric mean across possible *outcomes* (rather than across periods), this strategy is almost certain to dominate all other strategies. That is, over many periods, the *geometric mean strategy* will almost surely result in larger wealth accumulation than any significantly different investment strategy; or, if the investor has a specific wealth target, the geometric mean strategy will minimize the expected time to attain the target.

Dominance in the first sense suggests that the

geometric mean strategy is appropriate for institutions attempting to maximize value of assets over either a specific time horizon or the indefinite long run. As Edward Thorpe has observed, dominance in the second sense means that the strategy is appropriate for an investor who has a set dollar portfolio goal; e.g., to be a millionaire.[8] These results obtain because maximizing the geometric mean of the distribution of holding period returns each period results in maximizing the probabilistic rate of asset growth over time.

The meaning of this last statement can be explored with the data in Table 1. Earlier we regarded the holding period returns for each alternative as sequential returns over five periods of time. Now think of them as possible outcomes in a single period under five different "states of nature" that have equal probability of occurring — State of Nature 1 might be strong economic growth with expansion in the money supply above 5%, State of Nature 2 might be moderate economic growth with expansion in the money supply below 5%, and so on. These five states of nature summarize our judgments as to all possible economic outcomes in the next period. The computations are similar to those used before. We simply take the geometric mean holding period return for each alternative across states of nature.

$$(4) \quad \text{Geometric Mean across states} = \left(\prod_{s=1}^{S} HPR_s \right)^{1/S}$$

where S is the number of states of nature.

The values of the geometric means are the same as those obtained previously, with alternative B having the largest geometric mean. Given our judgments as to return outcomes under different economic conditions in the coming period, the best course of action for us at the beginning of the period is to invest in alternative B. This is true even if our investment horizon extends much beyond the coming period.

SOME PROPERTIES OF THE GEOMETRIC MEAN STRATEGY

Myopia! The importance of the property implied by this last statement — that the geometric mean strategy only requires one to look one period ahead, even with a multi-period horizon — cannot be emphasized too strongly. Economists call it "myopia." In everyday life myopia, or shortsightedness, is not desirable either as a physical or business attribute. In portfolio management, circumstances are much different.

Here myopia means that, even with an investment horizon that extends over many periods, we need not look beyond the end of the coming period to make a decision that is optimal — the best that can be made knowing what is known. For example, even if we are investing for retirement thirty years hence, there is no need to worry now about conditions in twenty-nine or thirty years — if we are willing to revise our portfolio annually, we simply make the best possible portfolio decision for the coming year and repeat this process at the beginning of the following year. With respect to the geometric mean strategy, it should be emphasized that it is *not* necessary that the distribution of outcomes be identical from period to period; it is only necessary that the sequence of outcomes be independent — a characteristic that seems to correctly describe security returns.[9]

Conservatism! Suppose all outcomes are not equally likely? Table 2 will help us explore this situation and evaluate another property of the geometric mean strategy. Here there are also five states of nature

TABLE 2

Three Investment Alternatives

State of Nature	Probability	HPR's for Alternative –		
		X	Y	Z
1	.01	1.50	2.00	1.05
2	.24	1.25	1.00	1.05
3	.50	1.10	1.20	1.05
4	.24	.95	1.40	1.05
5	.01	.70	0.00	1.05
Arithmetic Mean (R)		1.100	1.196	1.050
Standard Deviation (SD)		0.118	0.200	0.000
Geometric Mean (G)		1.093	0.000	1.050

and three investment alternatives, with State 3 being most likely and States 1 and 5 not very likely to occur.[10] The geometric mean (G) for this case is given as:[11]

$$(5) \quad \text{Geometric Mean across states} = \prod_{s=1}^{S} (HPR_s)p_s$$

where p_s is the probability that state s will occur. For alternative X, for example,

$$G = (1.50)^{(.01)} (1.25)^{(.24)} (1.10)^{(.50)} (.95)^{(.24)} (.70)^{(.01)} = 1.093.$$

Notice that alternative Y, despite its high expected or arithmetic mean return, has a geometric mean holding period return that is zero. The reason is that, with a small probability — one in one hundred in state 5 — this alternative will result in the loss of all that is invested in it. And as we all know, when a series of numbers is multiplied together, the product is always zero if one value in the series is zero.

This example illustrates the basically conservative nature of the geometric mean strategy. It will never accept an investment that risks loss of the entire portfolio no matter how attractive the investment may be otherwise. Alternative Y is dominated by alternative Z — a risk-free investment that returns 5% regardless of the state of nature — and would also be dominated by the alternative of simply holding cash, which has a holding period return of 1.0. (If partial investment were permissible, we could combine Y and Z or Y and cash to obtain an alternative with a higher geometric mean than X.)

Asymptotic Dominance! Possibly it may be well to emphasize what should be evident in any event: The geometric mean strategy does not *guarantee* that the investor's wealth will be maximized after any finite number of periods. As a probabilistic strategy, it only insures that maximum terminal wealth is *more likely* with this strategy than with any other. There are two reasons for this reservation.

The first, which in practical situations will be the more important, is that we make errors in the forecasts of outcomes. Mistakes may be made in predicting outcomes under the various states of nature as well as in assessing the probabilities of the states themselves. Both types of errors might reduce the effectiveness of the geometric mean strategy as a means of generating maximum portfolio value. This reflects a weakness in return forecasting, however, not in the geometric mean strategy itself. Other strategies would be equally disadvantaged. The success of any portfolio model is dependent on the quality of the forecasts that enter into it.

A second potential difficulty is that there simply might be a run of adverse outcomes even though we have assessed the probabilities correctly. Under such conditions, alternatives with a lower geometric mean may actually give higher terminal portfolio value. This problem is apt to be most pronounced when the number of periods is small or when the alternatives are similar.

The data in Tables 3 and 4 give some insight into the gravity of this latter problem. Table 3 shows the probability distributions of outcomes for three pairs of alternatives. In each case, alternative 1 has the larger geometric mean. Table 4, which is based on computer simulation in which outcomes are randomly picked according to these probability distributions, shows the proportion of the time in 200 trials that alternative 1 actually produced the larger terminal portfolio value over 1, 4, 9, 16, and 25 holding periods.

The first pair of alternatives differs substantially. Alternative 1, which has a much larger geometric mean HPR, also has a larger arithmetic mean

TABLE 3

Probability Distributions of HPRs for Computer Simulation

	State of Nature. (Probability)					
	1 (.25)	2 (.50)	3 (.25)	R	SD	G
Pair R						
Alternative 1	1.0	1.2	1.4	1.20	.14	1.1916
Alternative 2	1.05	1.15	1.25	1.15	07	1.1478
Pair S						
Alternative 1	1.0	1.2	1.4	1.20	.14	1.1916
Alternative 2	.9	1.1	1.6	1.20	.26	1.1489
Pair T						
Alternative 1	1.0	1.2	1.4	1.20	.14	1.1916
Alternative 2	.7	1.25	1.8	1.25	.39	1.1845

TABLE 4

Results of Computer Simulation

Number of Periods	Percentage of Time Terminal Wealth Relative of Alternative 1 Exceeds Terminal Wealth Relative of Alternative 2		
	Pair R	Pair S	Pair T
1	70.0%	72.0%	21.0%
2	88.5	72.0	44.5
9	97.5	84.0	51.0
16	99.5	93.5	51.5
25	99.5	97.5	53.5

HPR and standard deviation of returns. Here alternative 1 was ahead 88.5% of the time after four periods, and its dominance increased with more periods, so that it produced the larger terminal wealth 99.5% of the time after twenty-five periods.

The second pair of alternatives is more alike. The arithmetic mean returns are equal, so alternative 1 has the larger geometric mean HPR only because its standard deviation is smaller. For this pair, domination by alternative 1 comes more slowly, but after twenty-five periods it is ahead 97.5% of the time.

The last pair illustrates the long-run properties of the geometric mean strategy especially effectively. Here alternative 2 actually has the larger expected return, and, with a probability of 0.75, it will have a holding period return in excess of alternative 1 in any single period. The difference in the geometric means is very small. In the simulations, alternative 1 is actually ahead only 21% of the time after one period. After nine periods, however, it dominates 51% of the time, and after 25 periods it is ahead 53.5% of the time. (William E. Avera, who conceived this example, has estimated via probability theory that after one thousand periods the first alternative would be ahead 98.8% of the time![12])

These examples all illustrate what is sometimes referred to as the asymptotic (meaning "becoming almost certain") dominance property of the geometric mean strategy. As the number of periods becomes

154

large, selection of the investment with the greatest geometric mean will almost surely result in more wealth than any other strategy.

THE GEOMETRIC MEAN STRATEGY VS. EXPECTED UTILITY MAXIMIZATION

The geometric mean strategy is a non-utility-based criterion for selecting among investment alternatives, but it leads to exactly the same decisions that a person would make who seeks to maximize expected utility and who has a "logarithmic" utility function — that is, whose utility is equivalent to the logarithm of his wealth.

This sameness is both fortunate and unfortunate. The economics profession has a strong predisposition toward maximization of expected utility as a paradigm or model of human behavior. Moreover, the logarithmic utility function has a long history in economics, and it is regarded as an ideal or "everyman's" utility function by many economists because of its simplicity and consistency with their priors regarding attitudes towards risk.[13] Thus, the strategy of picking the alternative with the highest likely growth rate of capital results in decisions that are acceptable to many economists on utility grounds. (To complicate matters even further, it has been shown that the geometric mean strategy produces behavior that closely approximates the behavior that would result from maximizing expected utility under many classes of utility functions other than the logarithmic!)[14]

On the other hand, some economists have criticized the geometric mean strategy because they incorrectly perceive it as endorsing logarithmic utility. Still others, including Paul Samuelson, have expressed doubts about the generality of its application, because it will lead to decisions that are clearly inappropriate for persons who maximize expected utility and who have utility functions that are much different than logarithmic.

Analysis of an example due to Samuelson may help clarify the issues raised by this criticism.[15] Consider the gamble on a fair coin that returns 170% of the wager (the HPR is 2.7) if a head turns up and loses 70% (HPR of 0.3) in the event of a tail. The geometric mean, G, of the probability distribution of outcomes is $(2.7)(0.3)^{1/2} = 0.9$. Since the participant always has the option of wagering nothing, a course of action with a geometric mean of 1.0, the geometric mean strategy suggests that the gamble not be taken. On the other hand, the arithmetic mean of the probability distribution, R, is $(2.7 + 0.3)/2 = 1.5$, which implies that on average for each dollar wagered the gambler would expect to gain 50% versus a gain of zero from no wager.

Most of us would have no hesitancy in making a small or infrequent wager on this gamble, suggesting that in this context our utility is directly related to the average or statistically "expected" outcome. How about wagering a large portion of our wealth over many trials? If we continue to maximize expected money wealth itself, we should feel equally comfortable in doing this. It can be shown that the expected terminal wealth per dollar initially wagered when gains and losses are allowed to cumulate is in general equal to R^n, where n is the number of trials or periods. If, for example, n is 24, then each dollar initially wagered is expected to grow to $(.15)^{24} = \$16,834.10$, a very impressive number indeed! On the other hand, had we followed the geometric mean strategy and wagered nothing, our wealth would not have been enhanced at all. The criticism that the geometric mean strategy can lead to inappropriate decisions for persons with certain utility functions is indeed so.

Before we abandon the geometric mean criterion, however, conclude we are expected wealth maximizers, and wager the family farm, let us take a better look at this gamble. Table 5 shows the probability distribution of outcomes from twenty-four tosses of the coin — the number of heads, probability of this number of heads, and terminal value of a dollar initially wagered if this number of heads comes up. We now see that the rewards are very high if we have long runs of heads, but the probabilities of this happening are very small.

For example, our dollar multiplies to $22,528,400,000 if we toss twenty-four heads, but the probability of this happening is only 0.0000000596. It is more sobering to see that there is only a 27% chance of the fourteen or more heads that must come up if we are to walk away with more money than we bring to the game. We also observe that the median or middle outcome from twenty-four trials is a return of only $0.08 for each dollar wagered initially; this value is equal to $(0.9)^{24}$. Just as the arithmetic mean raised to the n power is an estimate of expected terminal wealth, the geometric mean raised to the n power, G^n, is an estimate of median terminal wealth.[16] Half the time our terminal wealth will be this amount or less.

In short, the distribution of wealth outcomes is very skewed. When the statistically expected terminal wealth is computed, a few outcomes with very high payoffs but small probabilities of occurring offset many highly probable outcomes with small payoffs, making the sequence of gambles look very attractive, as indeed it would be to persons with certain types of utility functions. On the other hand, most serious investors would find this sequence of gambles un-

TABLE 5

Possible Outcomes fo 170% - 70% Coin toss

Number of Heads	Probability	Cumulative Probability	Terminal Value of Initial Wager	Probability X Terminal Value
24	.0000000596	.0000000596	$22,528,400,000	$1312.80
23	.00000143	.00000149	2,503,160,000	3580.80
22	.0000165	.0000179	278,129,000	4575.46
21	.000121	.000139	30,903,200	3728.16
20	.000633	.000712	3,433,680	2174.76
19	.00253	.00331	381,521	966.56
18	.00802	.01132	42,391	340.09
17	.0206	.03195	4,710	97.17
16	.0438	.07579	524	22.94
15	.0779	.15373	58.15	4.53
14	.117	.27063	6.46	.76
13	.149	.41941	.72	.11
12*	.161	.58159	.079	.01
11	.149	.72938	.0089	.00
10	.117	.84627	.00098	.00
9	.0779	.92421	.00011	.00
8	.0438	.96804	.000012	.00
7	.0206	.98867	.0000014	.00
6	.00802	.99670	.00000015	.00
5	.00253	.99923	.000000017	.00
4	.000633	.99986	.0000000018	.00
3	.000121	.99998	.00000000021	.00
2	.0000165	1.00000	.000000000023	.00
1	.00000143	1.00000	.0000000000025	.00
0	.0000000596	1.00000	.0000000000028	.00

Sum = Expected Value $16,834.10

* Median Outcome

satisfactory because of the high probability of an adverse final outcome. In fact, the property of asymptotic dominance still holds: The more the coin is tossed, the greater the probability that the outcome will be dominated by that of the strategy with a higher geometric mean, gambling nothing.[17]

IMPLEMENTING THE STRATEGY

The discussion up to this point has been mostly in terms of fairly abstract "investment alternatives" with an emphasis on the properties of the geometric mean strategy. The purpose of this section is to discuss the steps in implementing the strategy, with special emphasis on the all-important debt-equity decision.

Assuming security and portfolio returns are considered to be normally or lognormally distributed, the first two steps we take are similar to those encountered in implementing the Markowitz portfolio model.[18]

First, we must identify the set of "best" portfolios of risky securities — those portfolios with maximum expected returns for each level of standard deviation, or minimum standard deviation for each level of expected returns. This requirement implies that the portfolios will be efficiently or fully diversified. We can develop such identification via the Markowitz quadratic programming methodology, the Sharpe simplification, other mathematical methods, or simply through judgment. Insofar as the geometric mean strategy is concerned, the source of the portfolios is immaterial. The objective is simply to get the best combinations of expected returns and standard deviation of returns, because they raise and lower the geometric mean, respectively.

If the investor will hold only an all-equity portfolio, with investment in riskless debt securities and buying on margin excluded from consideration for policy or other reasons, the process is then substantially complete. It is only necessary to estimate the

FIGURE 1

Effects of Leverge on Returns

Panel A - Markowitz Model

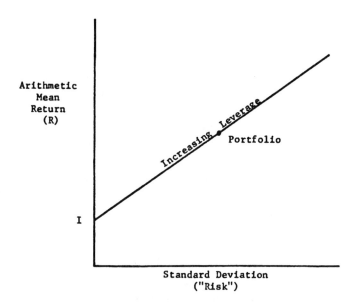

Panel B - Geometric Mean Strategy

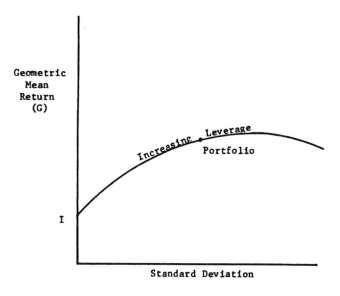

geometric mean for each portfolio in the set and then select the portfolio with the highest geometric mean. The approximation given in Equation 3 will be adequate for most well diversified portfolios, but we should introduce borrowing or lending into the investment package.

The second step is to identify the single best portfolio — that for which the excess returns per unit of standard deviation (in the Markowitz context, excess returns per unit of risk) is greatest. This is done by computing the ratio:

$$(6) \qquad (R - I)/SD,$$

where I is one plus the risk-free interest rate, and R and SD are, respectively, the arithmetic mean and standard deviation of the probabilistic HPR outcomes.[19]

At this point with the Markowitz or other expected utility maximization models, we are left with our own judgment. Panel A of Figure 1 represents the situation we face. We can raise our expected returns above those of the portfolio at the price of more risk by using leverage, or we can reduce our risk with some return sacrifice by placing a portion of our holdings in a riskless investment. Attitudes towards risk and return as reflected in our utility function determine which course we choose. Notice in particular that — under the admittedly unrealistic assumptions of no limits on leverage and a constant borrowing or lending rate — the risk-return tradeoff is linear and

there is no limit to how high the expected return can be levered up, provided the investor can stand the risk.

Panel B of Figure 1 illustrates the effect of leverage on the geometric mean holding period return, and it is much different. As riskless investment is reduced and leverage is increasingly employed, the geometric mean rises only to a point, beyond which it begins to decline as a consequence of increasing variability. Thus, there is an optimal level of leverage to maximize the growth rate of the investor's total portfolio. In the figure some leverage is optimal, but this is not a general result: The appropriate course of action might involve some riskless investment or 100% investment in the risky portfolio. The third and final step is to determine this optimal level of leverage.

For this purpose, a somewhat unusual measure of leverage, q, is useful, where:

(7)   q = (dollars of investment in risky portfolio)/

(dollars of investor's own resources).

In other words, q measures the proportion of the investor's equity placed in fluctuating return assets. If q is less than 1.0, $(1 - q)$ of the investor's resources are placed in riskless investment; $(q - 1)$ of the investor's resources are borrowed if q is greater than 1. For example, q = .5 implies 50% investment in the risky portfolio and 50% investment in riskless bonds; q = 2.0 means that every dollar of the investor's own re-

157

sources is matched by a borrowed dollar, both of which are invested in the risky portfolio.

Latané and Donald L. Tuttle[20] have shown that we can approximate the optimal q, which they call q*, as:

(8) $$q^* \approx (R - I)/SD^2,$$

which says that the optimal level of leverage is equal to the ratio of the expected excess return from the best risky portfolio (that is, the expected return over and above the interest rate) to the variance of returns (standard deviation squared) from the portfolio.[21]

Some implications of this formula appear in Table 6, which was prepared by Latané and Avera.

TABLE 6

Optimal Levels of Leverage (q*)

SD	.01	.015	.020	.025	.030	.035	.040	.045	.050	.055	.060	.065
.15	.44	.66	.88	1.11	1.33	1.55	1.77	2.00	2.22	2.44	2.66	2.88
.20	.25	.37	.50	.62	.75	.87	1.00	1.12	1.25	1.37	1.50	1.62
.25	.16	.24	.32	.40	.48	.56	.64	.72	.80	.88	.96	1.04
.30	.11	.16	.22	.27	.33	.38	.44	.49	.55	.61	.66	.72

The tabulation shows the optimal leverage as measured by q* at various levels of expected excess return and standard deviation. For example, if we expect the return from the risky portfolio to be .02 (2%) above the riskless rate and there is a standard deviation of .20 in the probability distribution of outcomes, then:

$$q^* = (.02)/(.20)^2 = .02/.04 = .5,$$

meaning that we should put half our funds in the portfolio and half in the riskless asset. On the other hand, if the expected excess return is .045 and the standard deviation is only .15, then:

$$q^* = (.045)/(1.5)^2 = .045/.0225 = 2.0,$$

and one dollar should be borrowed to buy the risky portfolio for every dollar of the investor's own resources.

The way optimal leverage changes within the table makes good practical sense. Given the standard deviation of returns, as the expected return on the portfolio rises relative to the risk-free rate, a more aggressive investment strategy is indicated; given the level of excess returns, an increase in the dispersion in possible outcomes suggests that a more conservative investment posture is appropriate.

We can also use these numbers to make some practical judgments about relative portfolio commitment to the overall stock market. This calculation might be of interest to, say, a pension sponsor investing in an index fund. Over a number of postwar years, the observed standard deviation of annual returns from the broad market indexes has run around 0.20. The market yield on 9-12 month Treasury bills is a good measure of the risk-free rate. From the table, we can see that an expected return from common stocks of 4 percentage points per annum in excess of this yield would be consistent with 100% investment in equities, assuming that this standard deviation is expected to persist. Greater pessimism or optimism about common stocks should be associated with a move into partial investment in fixed-income securities or into a leveraged position. On the other hand, if the stock market has become more volatile, as many suggest, fixed-income securities become more attractive. For example, if the standard deviation of returns rises to .25, a 25% increase, then, even with the same expectation of a 4-percentage-point excess return from equities, the optimal portfolio proportions become 64% equity and 36% debt; an excess return of 6.25% would then be required to justify 100% investment in equities.[20]

In an early exposition of the geometric mean portfolio strategy, Latané cited A. D. Roy to the effect that, "A man who seeks advice about his actions will not be grateful for the suggestion that he maximize expected utility."[22] The geometric mean strategy was developed in part to provide a non-utility basis for portfolio decisions. According to this strategy, the investor should pick, each period, that investment alternative with the largest geometric mean holding period return across possible outcomes.

Implementation will involve three steps, first, identify the set of "best" portfolios. Second, pick the single best portfolio. Third, determine the optimal amount of borrowing or lending to combine with this portfolio.

This strategy maximizes the probability of the investor's portfolio being more valuable than under any alternative strategy at the end of a run of periods. Like strategies that give explicit attention to risk-return tradeoffs — but for much different reasons — the geometric mean strategy will lead to portfolio diversification, and it will also trade off increasing dispersion of return outcomes for larger expected returns. Nevertheless, this strategy will never lead to acceptance of investment programs with a nonzero probability of total loss: It will also give explicit guidance as to the appropriate level of leverage to incorporate in the investment program. This feature should be particularly appealing to life insurance companies, pension funds, and other investors with a long horizon for whom short-term return fluctuation is a secondary consideration and the concept of expected utility maximization is difficult to implement.

[1] This strategy was first presented by Latané in a Cowles Foundation seminar, "The Choice between Risk and Certainty in Portfolio Management Assuming Reinvestment of All Returns" at Yale University, February 17, 1956. It was later developed in his Ph.D. dissertation, "Rational Decision Making in Portfolio Management," University of North Carolina, 1957, and in an article, "Criteria for Choice Among Risky Ventures," *Journal of Political Economy* 38 (April, 1959), pp. 145-155. An expanded version was presented by Latané and Donald L. Tuttle in "Criteria for Portfolio Building," *Journal of Finance* 22 (September, 1967), pp. 359-373. Independently, J. L. Kelly, Jr., developed the geometric mean strategy in a non-investment context about the same time as Latané; see J. L. Kelly, Jr., "A New Interpretation of the Information Rate," *Bell System Technical Journal* 35 (1956), pp. 917-926.

[2] Kelly provides an instructive gambling analogy. The geometric mean, he says, would be an appropriate criterion of choice for a man betting on the horses who knows his initial stake is all he'll ever have to bet; the arithmetic mean criterion would be appropriate for a man whose wife will give him a fixed amount to wager each week.

[3] Hence the name "growth-optimal" and "wealth-maximization" for this approach. In honor of Kelly, the strategy is sometimes referred to as the "Kelly criterion." It is also referred to as the "logarithmic" strategy because logarithms are used in necessary computations. For example, the natural logarithm of the holding period return is the continuously compounded rate of return, and the arithmetic mean of these logarithms is the rate of compounding expressed in continuous terms.

[4] For example, additions and withdrawals could be random in size and/or timing, or constant in size and timing, but one could not add capital following low HPRs and withdraw capital following high HPRs. See William E. Avera, "The Geometric Mean Strategy as a Theory of Multiperiod Portfolio Selection," Ph.D. dissertation, University of North Carolina, 1972.

[5] The basis for this and other approximations to the geometric mean is presented by William E. Young and Robert H. Trend, "Geometric Mean Approximations of Individual Security and Portfolio Performance," *Journal of Financial and Quantitative Analysis* 4 (June, 1969), pp. 179-199.

[6] It should be emphasized, however, that Harry Markowitz himself has been one of the strongest advocates of the geometric mean criterion. He devotes an entire chapter — Chapter 6, "Return in the Long Run," pp. 116-125 — to it in his classic monograph *Portfolio Selection: Efficient Diversification of Investments* (New York: John Wiley & Sons, Inc., 1959). More recently, he argues for the strategy in "Investment for the Long Run," Section Ten in *Risk and Return in Finance*, Volume I, Irwin Friend and James L. Bicksler, Editors (Cambridge, Massachusetts: Ballinger Publishing Company, 1977), pp. 219-244.

[7] The fact that wealth increases at the geometric mean of returns across time has long been known. It was presented by J. B. Williams in 1936 (see "Speculation and Carryover," *Quarterly Journal of Economics* 50 (May, 1936), pp. 436-455), and was no doubt recognized long before that time. Latané's contribution was in showing how to maximize this growth rate.

[8] Edward O. Thorp, "Portfolio Choice and the Kelly Criterion," Chapter 17 in *Investment Portfolio Decision-Making*, James A. Bicksler and Paul A. Samuelson, Editors (Lexington, Massachusetts: Lexington Books, 1974), pp. 253-270.

[9] The point that the distributions of outcomes need not be identical over periods has been proved by Richard Bellman and David Kalbba, "Dynamic Programming and Statistical Communication Theory," *Proceeding of the National Academy of Science* 48 (1957), pp. 749-751.

[10] All of the examples in this paper are in terms of discrete distributions for expositional purposes, but the geometric mean strategy is equally applicable to continuous distributions.

[11] Since the arithmetic mean or expected value and the standard deviation for discrete probability distributions may be unfamiliar, and because they will show up in the subsequent discussion, I show their computation at this point. The arithmetic mean or expected return (R) is:

$$R = \sum_{s=1}^{s} p_s(HPR_s),$$

and the standard deviation of returns (SD) is:

$$SD = \left[\sum_{s=1}^{s} p_s(HPR - R)^2 \right]^{1/2}.$$

For alternative X in Table 2,

$$R = (.01)(1.50) + (.24)(1.25) + (.50)(1.10) + (.24)(.95) + (.01)(.70) = 1.10$$

and

$$SD = [(.01)(.4)^2 + (.24)(.15)^2 + (.50)(.00)^2 + (.24)(.15)^2 + (.01)(.4)^2]^{1/2} = 0.118.$$

[12] Avera, "The Geometric Mean Strategy . . .," p. 67.

[13] In particular, the logarithmic utility function exhibits decreasing *absolute risk aversion* and constant *relative risk aversion*. These mean, respectively, that as wealth increases an investor is more willing to risk loss of a specific number of dollars, but the investor is neither more nor less willing to risk loss of a specific portion of wealth.

[14] Harry Markowitz, "Investment for the Long Run," . . .

[15] Paul A. Samuelson, "The 'Fallacy' of Maximizing the Geometric Mean in Long Sequences of Investing or Gambling," *Proceedings of the National Academy of Science* 68 (October, 1971), pp. 214-224; reprinted in *Investment Portfolio Decision-Making* (see Footnote 8). The fallacy to which Samuelson refers is concluding that, because the portfolio with the highest geometric mean will dominate all others over the long run, the geometric mean strategy must necessarily maximize expected utility.

[16] Nils H. Hakansson, "Multi-Period Mean-Variance Analysis: Toward a General Theory of Portfolio Choice," *Journal of Finance* 26 (July, 1971), pp. 857-884.

[17] For this and other reasons, some writers have gone as far as to argue that rational investors with long-run goals would be unlikely to have any utility function other than the logarithmic; see, for example, Nils H. Hakansson, "Multi-Period Mean-Variance Analysis. . . ." For a rejoinder to the Hakansson position, see Paul A. Samuelson and Robert C. Merton, "Generalized Mean-Variance Tradeoffs for Best Perturbation Corrections to Approximate Portfolio Decisions," *Journal of Finance* 39 (March, 1974), pp. 27-40.

18 This is a standard assumption in the Markowitz model and in many other portfolio modeling contexts. However, one of the advantages of the geometric mean strategy is that it is not limited to such normal distributions. In fact, the strategy will properly exploit any non-normal characteristics of security distributions such as skewness. While it is not possible to go directly from information on individual securities to exactly optimal geometric mean portfolios under these conditions, this can be done to a close approximation; see J. P. Evans, S. F. Maier, and D. S. Rubin, "Optimal Geometric Mean Portfolios," Technical Report #75-8 in Operations Research and Systems Analysis, University of North Carolina, September, 1976.

19 As is customary, for expositional purposes a single borrowing and lending rate is assumed. This assumption is amenable to relaxation with both the Markowitz model and the geometric mean strategy.

20 Latané and Tuttle, "Criteria for Portfolio Building," pp. 362-363.

21 A useful but somewhat different approach to the determination of overall portfolio parameters has been provided by Richard O. Michaud in "Risk Policy and Long-Term Investment," *Journal of Financial and Quantitative Analysis*, Vol. 16 (June, 1981), pp. 147-167. He shows that the level of overall portfolio "beta" risk which maximizes the expected growth of value over time is:

$$B = (R_M - I)r^2/(1 - 1/N)\sigma^2$$

where $(R_M - I)$ is the expected excess market return, r is the coefficient of correlation between the portfolio's returns and those of the market, N is the number of periods, and σ^2 is the variance of the market's returns. The overall portfolio beta, of course, reflects both the beta of the risky portfolio and the level of leverage. Providing the portfolio is well diversified ($r^2 \approx 1$) and N is large, this approach should yield the same level of portfolio leverage as that of Latané and Tuttle.

22 Latané, "Criteria for Choice . . .," p. 154, cited from A. D. Roy, "Safety First and the Holding of Assets," *Econometrica* 20 (1952), p. 433.

STATEMENT OF OWNERSHIP, MANAGEMENT AND CIRCULATION (Act of August 12, 1970: Section 3886. Title 39, United States Code)

1. *Title of publication:* The Journal of Portfolio Management
2. *Date of filing:* November 1, 1985
3. *Frequency of Issue:* Quarterly
4. *Location of known office of publication (not printers):* 488 Madison Avenue, New York, N.Y. 10022.
5. *Location of the headquarters or general business offices of the publishers (not printers):* Same as above
6. *Names and addresses of Publisher, Editor, and Managing Editor:* Publisher: Gilbert E. Kaplan, 488 Madison Avenue, New York, N.Y. 10022. Editor: Peter L. Bernstein, 509 Madison Avenue, New York, N.Y. 10022; Managing Editor: Frank J. Fabozzi, 10 Ingham Way, New Hope, Pa. 18938
7. *Owner (if owned by a corporation, its name and address must be stated and also immediately thereunder the names and addresses of stockholders owning or holding 1 percent or more of the total amount of stock. If not owned by a corporation, the names and addresses of the individual owners must be given. If owned by a partnership or other unincorporated firm, its name and address, as well as that of each individual must be given):* Capital Cities Communications, 24 East 51st Street, New York, N.Y. 10022.
8. *Known bondholders, mortgagees, and other security holders owning or holding 1 percent or more of total amount of bonds, mortgages or other securities (if there are none, so state):* None
9. Not applicable
10. *For completion by nonprofit organizations authorized to mail at special rates (Section 132.122, Postal Manual):* Not applicable
11. *Nature and extent of circulation:*

	Average number of copies of each issue during preceding 12 months	Actual number of copies of the single issue published nearest to filing date (Fall 1985)
A. Total number of copies printed (net press run)	3,464	3,293
B. Paid circulation:		
1. Sales through dealers and carriers, street vendors, and counter sales	0	0
2. Mail subscriptions	2,598	2,526
C. Total paid circulation	2,598	2,526
D. Free distribution by mail, carrier or other means,		
1. Samples, complimentary, and other free copies	291	292
2. Copies distributed to news agents, but not sold	0	0
E. Total distribution (sum of C and D)	2,889	2,818
F. Office use, leftover, unaccounted, spoiled after printing	575	475
G. Total (sum of E and F should equal net press run shown in A)	3,464	3,293

I certify that the statements made by me above are correct and complete.
Charles A. Raible, Vice President & Treasurer

The fundamental law of active management

Mc² is the Law, here as well as elsewhere.

Richard C. Grinold

S uppose you could start a new investment management firm. How would you do it? Imagine that your choices even include determining your own skills — not so much the level of skill, but that you can choose the "what," as in "skill at what." You could be an aggressive stock picker, a growth stock manager, a value-oriented manager, a rotating or cyclical manager, a quantitative manager, an economic sector manager, an index fund manager, or an extended/enhanced index fund manager, to mention just a few possibilities. Which style would you choose?

This paper tries to give some guidance to help you make those decisions. With a little reading between the lines, you can see how these insights might apply to your own investment management operations and allow you to exploit your own particular insights into the market.

We will be guided in this strategic thinking by "The Fundamental Law of Active Management." I can call it this with a reasonable amount of humility, because "The Law" was unearthed more than a decade ago under simpler assumptions (a diagonal model) and various other guises by William Sharpe, Jack Treynor and Fischer Black, Robert Ferguson, and Barr Rosenberg. These earlier authors, to a large extent, brushed by the Law and went on digging for other prizes. We demonstrate here that the Law holds under a much wider range of conditions, emphasize its application, and generalize its use.

The Fundamental Law relates three variables: your *skill* (call it c) in forecasting exceptional returns, the *breadth* (call it M) of your strategy, and the *value added* (call it VA) of your investment strategy. You can think of M as how often you play (number of times per year), and c as a measure of how well you play. The value added will be measured in terms of annual return. A strategy's value added will be proportional to the strategy's *Sharpe ratio* (call it SR).

The Sharpe ratio itself can be approximated as a simple function of the strategy's skill and breadth:[1]

$$SR = Mc^2. \tag{1}$$

The Sharpe ratio increases with the square of the skill level c and directly with the strategy's breadth. Like all laws in the social sciences, this is a rough cut at the truth, based on assumptions that are not quite true and simplified with some reasonable approximations. This law is not an operational tool; its purpose is to point out in broad terms the trade-offs involved in building an investment strategy.

To appreciate and understand the Law, we should step back and consider the strategic context of active money management. Our presumption throughout is that active management is conducted in the context of performance analysis. Both manager and client know before the fact how the outcomes of their decisions will be judged.

We look at performance relative to a benchmark or normal portfolio; this appears to make sense in today's world of specialized investment managers.[2] We shall also consider the normal to be, in a sense, efficient within the set of investment guidelines laid down for the manager. By this consideration, we are ruling out so-called tilt strategies where the active bets in the portfolio are permanent and are based on the presumption that the normal portfolio is less efficient than the portfolio the manager holds.

RICHARD C. GRINOLD is Director of Research at BARRA in Berkeley (CA 94704).

First, I define and discuss the concept of an information ratio. The information ratio is an important — perhaps the single most important — measure of investment performance. Investment managers will desire to have an investment strategy with the highest possible information ratio. The value added by the strategy will be proportional to the square of the information ratio.

Next, I present the Fundamental Law of Active Management. The Law shows how the information ratio for any strategy can be connected with two items: the skill and the breadth of the strategy. The skill of the strategy measures the strength of the link between the manager's forecasts of exceptional return and the realized returns. The breadth of the strategy measures the number of distinct investment bets made each year.

Given the Fundamental Law, I then discuss its implications for the active manager. The information ratio gives an upper bound on the value added by a strategy. The factors that limit our ability to implement the strategy fully are the strategy's depth and cost, and the aggressiveness with which we implement the strategy. In what follows, you will see how these aspects of a strategy limit our ability to enjoy the full benefit of our information.

INFORMATION RATIOS AND SHARPE RATIOS

The information ratio is a key concept in determining the value of an investment strategy. This section discusses the information ratio in detail, along with the square of the information ratio known as the Sharpe ratio. We must also distinguish between observed information ratios and forecasts of the information ratio.

We can think of the information ratio in two ways: after the fact (ex post) and before the fact (ex-ante). The ex post information ratio is the ratio of the realized return divided by the realized standard deviation of the return. The ex ante information ratio is the expected return divided by the standard deviation of the return. In the ex ante case, both the expected return and the standard deviation of the return are forecasts. Ex ante information ratios generally are positive: You do not want to play the game unless you think you are going to win. Ex post information ratios are about 50% positive and 50% negative; the average manager does not outperform.

The ex post information ratio is an important concept. Sponsors selecting and evaluating managers use it in historical tests of a strategy, and managers use it to make sure that their expectations have some connection with reality.

Let us now concentrate on the ex ante information ratio. We *assume* that our expectations of exceptional return are valid, which is a big assumption. We are assuming that our money managers know where their particular skills lie, know how well they forecast (i.e., their skill level), and know where they have no particular skill. This requires humility and a constant follow-up and testing on the part of each manager.

Consider a portfolio whose excess (of risk-free) return, r(P), is broken down into normal or benchmark return, r(N), and exceptional or active return, r(A). The portfolio's excess return is simply the sum of the normal's excess return and the active return.

$$r(P) = r(N) + r(A), \qquad (2)$$

where:

  r(P) is the portfolio's excess return,
  r(N) is the normal portfolio's excess return, and
  r(A) is the portfolio's active return.

The information ratio of the active return is

$$IR[r(A)] = E[r(A)]/Std[r(A)], \qquad (3)$$

where:

  E[r(A)] is the expected active return on the portfolio. This is sometimes called the portfolio's alpha,

and

  Std[r(A)] is the standard deviation of the portfolio's active return. This is called the level of active risk or aggressiveness.

The Sharpe ratio is the square of the information ratio, or

$$SR[r(A)] = IR[r(A)]^2 = E[r(A)]^2/Var[r(A)]. \qquad (4)$$

In a technical supplement to this paper, I show how an investor with mean variance preferences would behave depending on both the information ratio and the level of risk aversion.[3,4] The first finding is that the value added, VA, is proportional to the square of the information ratio:

$$VA[r(A)] = (0.25/\phi)(SR[r(A)]) = (0.25/\phi)(IR[r(A)]^2, \qquad (5)$$

where:

  VA[r(A)] is the value added by the active return r(A). This is sometimes called the certainty equivalent return. It is measured in annual percentage return,

and

φ is the investor's risk aversion. The risk aversion parameter establishes the trade-off between the expected active return and the active variance.

The information ratio has two important properties.[5] The first important property is that *all* investors who have mean variance objectives will prefer to have the portfolio with the highest information ratio possible. That is evident from Equation (5). The investors differ only in their aversion to risk. Investors with high risk aversion will not be aggressive in exploiting the information and will have lower value added. Nevertheless, Equation (5) demonstrates that the investor will always prefer the strategy that has the highest information ratio.

Second, the information ratio does not depend on how aggressively you pursue a strategy. If you double your aggressiveness by doubling your active bets on the assets, then both the expected active return and the standard deviation of the active return will also double, so the information ratio will remain constant. This property of the information ratio is the reason that all investors will prefer higher information ratios to lower. Once the investor has found the strategy with the highest information ratio, then she can tune the aggressiveness to suit her own level of risk aversion.

As the information ratio does not depend on how aggressive we are, we can standardize the information ratio either by using a convenient level of active risk (Std[r(A)]), of, say, 5% per year, or a standard level of alpha, say, 1% per year.

Although the information ratio does not depend on how aggressively we pursue our strategy, it does depend on our planning horizon. Notice that expected returns will grow proportionally with the length of the forecast period; fifty basis points per month is the same as 6% per year. The variances of the returns will also grow proportionally with the length of the period.[6] This means that the standard deviations of returns will grow as the square root of the length of the period. The information ratio will also grow as the square root of the length of the period, because we have something growing linearly with time in the denominator. Thus, the information ratio based on annual returns will be 3.46 (the square root of 12) times larger than the information ratio based on monthly returns. This paper will use the one-year standard.

You can see how the information ratio contributes to value added through Equation (5). A little pencil pushing will show how different information ratios and different levels of risk aversion, φ, interact to give us different values added. Table 1 shows three levels of risk aversion for the columns, and three possible information ratios for the rows.[7] The table is included to provide a feel for reasonable values of the information level and risk aversion. The entry in each cell is the value added annually.

TABLE 1

Value Added (In Annual %)

IR	Risk Aversion (φ)		
	0.0375	0.05625	0.075
0.5	1.66	1.11	0.83
1.0	6.66	4.44	3.33
1.5	15.00	10.00	7.50

The manager with an information ratio of 0.5 and risk aversion of 0.05625, for example, will have an expected active return of 2.22% and an active standard deviation (peek ahead to Table 2) of 4.44%. The value added is just $2.22 - (0.05625) (4.44)^2 = 1.11$.

Table 1 presents some very optimistic numbers. Observed information ratios, based on actual rather than predicted performance, cluster around zero. Only 20% or 30% of managers have an observed information ratio above 0.5 for any length of time (say, three years). An observed information ratio above 1.5 is rare indeed. Only 5% of active managers would have an observed information ratio of 1.5 over three years; 0.5 is good, and 1.5 is extremely good.

The levels of risk aversion in Table 1 run from aggressive (0.0375) to conservative (0.075). The optimal level of aggressiveness for the manager will depend upon both the information ratio and the manager's risk aversion. The relationship, derived in the supplement, is

$$\text{Std}[R(A)] = \text{IR}/[2.0(\phi)]. \qquad (6)$$

The more risk-averse managers will take less risk, and the higher information ratio managers should take more risk.

Table 2 shows the optimal levels of active risk for the combinations of information ratio and risk aversion in Table 1.

For an information ratio of 1.0, we see that a risk aversion of 0.05625 corresponds to an active risk

TABLE 2

Optimal Level of Aggressiveness (Std in Annual %)

IR	Risk Aversion (φ)		
	0.0375	0.05625	0.075
0.5	6.66	4.44	3.33
1.0	13.33	8.88	6.66
1.5	20.00	13.33	10.00

163

of 8.88% per year, which is consistent with the level of active risk for traditional active managers.

The situation is summarized in Figure 1, with active variance plotted on the horizontal axis and ex-

FIGURE 1

ACTIVE RISK MEAN VARIANCE POSSIBILITIES

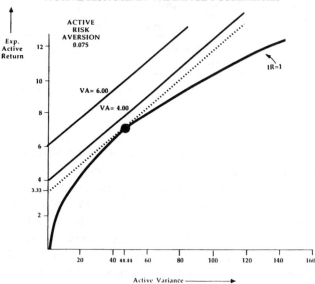

pected active return on the vertical axis. The curved line shows the choices available to the manager if the information ratio is 1.0; this line is merely a plot of the line $E[r(A)] = IR(Var[r(A)]^{1/2})$, where IR is a constant (in this case 1.0). The straight lines are lines of equal value added for the manager. We have taken the case of the risk-averse active manager, $\phi = 0.075$.

We can see clearly from Figure 1 that all managers who measure value added as expected return less a penalty for variance will agree that a higher information ratio is better than a lower information ratio. We also can see how varying levels of risk aversion can make the manager more or less aggressive in implementing the strategy.

The Sharpe ratio gives us only an upper bound on the value we can add. In deriving the ratio, we presume that we can pursue our information without any limitations. In fact, restrictions on portfolio holdings, a reluctance to incur transaction costs, and other considerations will restrict our ability to take advantage of the information at hand. In that case, we can look at Equation (5) as an upper bound on our ability to turn information into value added.

In the following sections, we will look at some simple determinants of the information ratio in order to find which attributes of an investment strategy will tend to make it successful.

THE FUNDAMENTAL LAW

The previous section shows that the informa-

tion ratio is an important measure of the quality of an investment strategy. How can an investment manager prospecting for investment strategies derive some idea of the quality of those strategies? A simple and surprisingly general formula can give us an approximation to the Sharpe ratio. The result is derived in the supplement. It is

$$SR[r(A)] = Mc^2, \qquad (7)$$

where:

M   is the number of independent forecasts of exceptional return we make per year, and

c   is the correlation of each forecast with the actual outcomes. Note that c is the same for all forecasts.

We can give two straightfroward examples of the Law in action.

First, a gambling example. Take a roulette wheel with eighteen red spots, eighteen black spots, and one green. The house's expected return per $1.00 bet on red or black is 1/37, or 2.7027%. The standard deviation of the return is 99.9634%. If there is a single $1.00 bet in a year, the information ratio will be 0.027038 and the Sharpe ratio 0.00073, or $(1/37)^2$. If we consider one million sequential bets of $1.00 in a year, then the expected return on the $1 million bet will remain at 2.7027%, but the standard deviation drops to 0.0996%, for an information ratio of 27.038 and a Sharpe ratio of 731.05 — exactly one million times the earlier value. In this example, M is the number of bets per year, and c is the house advantage, 1/37.

As a second example consider the monthly specific return on a collection of 200 assets as u(n).[8] We will assume that the specific returns are independent across stocks, have zero expected return, and have a monthly standard deviation of 10%. Suppose, in addition, that we have a forecasting procedure that can forecast u(n) with an R^2 of 0.01 (1%). That means the correlation between our forecasts and the subsequent specific returns will be 0.01.

One way to picture our situation is to imagine that the specific return itself is comprised of 100 independent terms, u(n,j) for j = 1,2,...,100.[9] That is,

$$u(n) = \Sigma j\ u(n,j). \qquad (8)$$

If each u(n,j) is equally likely to be +1.00% or −1.00%, then each will have a mean of zero and standard deviation of 1.00%. Note that that is consistent with u(n) having a standard deviation of 10%. Our forecasting procedure tells us u(n,1) and leaves us in the dark about u(n,2) through u(n,100). We know very little.

In this case, we will have 200 pieces of information per month for twelve months, a total of 2400 per year. Our skill level, the correlation of u(n,1) and u(n), is 0.1. According to the Fundamental Law, the Sharpe ratio should be 24 = 2400[(0.1)^2]. The question is: Can we fashion an investment strategy that will achieve a Sharpe ratio that high?

In order to build a portfolio strategy that exploits this information, we need a simplifying assumption. Let us assume that the normal portfolio is equal-weighted with 0.50% in each stock. In each month, we will expect to have about 100 stocks with a forecasted specific return for the month of +1.00% and 100 stocks with a −1.00%. If we hold the good ones at equal weight (1.00%), and do not hold the bad, then we have an expected active return of 1.00% per month and the active standard deviation is 0.703% per month.[10] The information ratio will be 24.24. Note that this ratio is greater than the 24 predicted by the formula, because there is a slight reduction in uncertainty due to the knowledge of u(n,1).

This example does more than show the formula at work: It shows how little information one needs to be highly successful. In fact, a correlation of 0.02 (an R^2 of 0.0004) between forecasted asset return and realized return over 200 stocks each month for twelve months will produce a highly desirable information ratio of 1.00.

Recall that the Law is based on a host of assumptions that are not quite true. We discuss some of those assumptions below. The basic insight we can gain from the Law is clear, however. The important thing is to play often (high M) and to play well (high c). In choosing between strategies, or in modifying a strategy, the Law will give us a rough guide in relating the choices to the value added as investment managers.

The Fundamental Law is designed to give us insight into active management; it is not an operational tool. You want to know the trade-offs between increasing the breadth of your strategy, M, by either covering more assets or shortening the time horizons of your forecasts, and improving your skill, c. Thus, we can see that a 50% increase in the breadth of our strategy (with no diminution in skill) is equivalent to a 22% increase in our skill (if we maintain the same breadth). A quick calculation of this sort may be valuable before launching a major research project.

Figure 2 shows the trade-offs between breadth and skill for two levels of the information ratio. We can see the power of the Law by evaluating two general strategies. In both strategies, we want to have an information ratio of 1.00. Start with a market timer who has information about market return each quarter. The market timer needs a correlation of 0.5 (1 = 4 [0.5^2]) in order to attain an information ratio

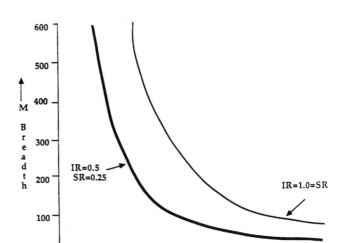

FIGURE 2

TRADE-OFFS BETWEEN SKILLS AND BREADTH

The Fundamental Law

of 1.00. As an alternative, consider a stock selector who follows 200 companies and revises each company's assessment each quarter. The stock selector makes 800 bets per year and needs a correlation of 0.035 (1 = 800 [0.035^2]) in order to obtain an information ratio of 1.00. Another stock selector, more specialized, may follow three companies and revise the bets on a daily basis, say, 267 times per year; this specialist will also make 800 bets per year and require a skill level of 0.035. The first selector achieves breadth by looking at a large number of companies intermittently, and the second selector does so by examining a small group of companies constantly. We can see from these examples that strategies with similar information ratios can differ radically in the requirements they place on the investor.

Notice that the forecasts should be independent. This means that forecast 2 should not be based on a source of information that is correlated with the sources for forecast 1. For example, suppose our first forecast is based on an assumption that growth stocks will do poorly, our second on an assumption that high-yield stocks will do well. These pieces of information are not independent; growth stocks tend to have low yields, and not many high-yielding stocks would be called growth stocks. We have only picked out two ways to measure the same phenomenon. An example of independent forecasts is a quarterly adjustment of the portfolio's beta from 1.00 to either 1.05 or 0.95 as a market timing decision based on new information each quarter.

165

In a situation where analysts give recommendations on a firm-by-firm basis, it is possible to check the level of dependence among forecasts by first quantifying the recommendations and then regressing them against attributes of the firms. It may be that the analysts like all the firms in a particular industry; their stock picks actually are a single industry bet. It could be that all the stocks have a high earnings yield; they have made a single bet on e/p ratios. Finally, it could be that the analysts like all the firms that have performed well in the last year; instead of a firm-by-firm bet, we have a single bet on the concept of momentum. More significantly, the residuals of the regression actually will be independent forecasts of individual asset return. Regression analysis gives us the opportunity both to uncover consistent patterns in our recommendations and to remove them if we choose.

The same masking of dependence can occur over time.[11] If you reassess your industry bets on the basis of new information each year, and your portfolios are rebalanced monthly, you should not think that you make twelve industry bets per year; you just make the same bet twelve times.

A simple example shows how dependence in the information sources will lower our overall skill level. Consider the case where there are two sources of information. If we look at each of them separately, we see that they both have a level of skill, c — that is, the forecasts have a correlation of c with the eventual returns. If, however, the two information sources are dependent, then the information derived from the second source is not entirely new. Part of the second source's information will just reinforce what we knew from the first source, and part will be new or incremental information.

We have to discover the value of the incremental information. As one can imagine, the greater the dependence between the two information sources, the lower the value of the incremental information. If g is the correlation between the two information sources, then the value of the two sources combined will be

$$c^2 + c^2 [(1-g)/(1+g)]. \qquad (9)$$

When there is no correlation between sources (g = 0), the value is $2c^2$. As g increases toward 1, the value of the second source is diminished.[12]

The Law is based on the assumption that each of the M active bets has the same level of skill. In fact, the manager will have greater skills in one area than another. The technical supplement shows that the Sharpe ratio is the sum of the value added from each information source, and Figure 3 demonstrates this

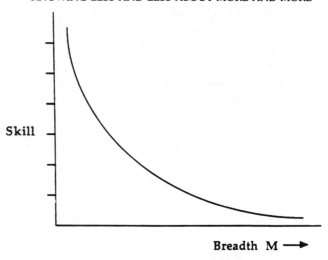

FIGURE 3

KNOWING LESS AND LESS ABOUT MORE AND MORE

Skill

Breadth M ⟶

phenomenon. If we order the information sources from highest skill level to lowest, the total value added is just the area under the "skill" curve. Notice that the Law assumes that the skill curve is horizontal — we replace the sum of the skill levels by the average skill level.

The strongest assumption behind the Law is that the manager will gauge the value of information accurately and build portfolios that use that information in an optimal way. This requires insight, self-examination, and a skill level in the investment manager that may be rarely achieved, no matter how admirable the goal.

The Law seems to push managers toward an eclectic style. If a manager can find some independent source of information that will be of use, that information should be exploited. The manager's style may represent a stew rather than a distinct ingredient. It is the manager's need to present a clear picture of the chosen style to the client that inhibits the manager from adopting such an eclectic style. At the same time, we can see that the sponsor who hires a stable of managers has an incentive to diversify their styles in order to insure that their bets are independent. The way investment management is currently organized in the United States, the managers offer the distinct ingredients, and the sponsor makes the stew.

So far we have laid out the building blocks of a successful active investment strategy; they are skill and breadth. In the next section we address the question of implementation.

IMPLEMENTATION

There are three important dimensions to implementation: depth, cost, and aggressiveness.

The depth of a strategy is related to the amount

of money invested in the strategy. Depth for a strategy is analogous to liquidity for an asset. Let us continue the examples of the market timer and the stock picker who follows 200 names, assuming that we have $1 billion to invest in the strategies.

Which of the strategies can absorb $1 billion? The market timing strategy surely can. The stock selection may or may not; it depends on the capitalization and liquidity of the stocks as well as the turnover.

Suppose our $1 billion is invested in an active fund that follows small capitalization stocks. The fund follows 200 companies with an average capitalization of $200 million and holds 100 of them at any time. There will be $10 million (on average) invested in each of the companies. If a company goes at the end of a quarter from buy to sell or sell to buy, then we have to sell or acquire 5% of the company's capitalization. About 100 firms should change status each quarter, so we have a considerable problem of too much money chasing too few assets too often. This strategy is beyond its depth. If we apply the same strategy to the 200 largest capitalization assets, our active positions would be less than 1% of each firm's capitalization, and we should not find any great difficulty getting into and out of our positions each quarter.

Here is an example of how depth can influence a strategy. Suppose we have restrictions that say we cannot own more than 4% of a company's stock, and that we will not take an active position larger than, say, three times the daily average trading activity in the stock. These restrictions on our level of holdings and our active holdings become tighter and tighter as more money flows into the strategy.

One way to see this is first to build an ideal portfolio that you would like the strategy to follow, and then see how close (minimal tracking error) you can get to the ideal when holdings and liquidity constraints are imposed. The results for one such experiment are shown in Figure 4, where money invested in the strategy (in billions of dollars) is plotted along the horizontal axis, with tracking error between the ideal portfolio and the actual portfolio on the vertical axis. As you would suspect, the more money in the strategy, the more tracking error between the ideal and the actual. The tracking error is in fact a measure of the strategy's inability to absorb more assets.

Cost is the second important implementation issue. There are two parts to the cost issue — costs of generating the information and costs associated with investments. For example, compare two ways of generating information: the labor-intensive traditional investment management and the computer-intensive process-driven strategy. In the traditional

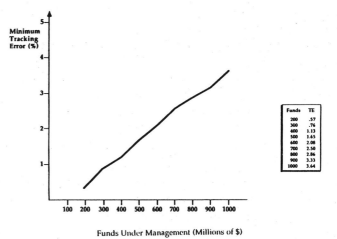

FIGURE 4

THE IMPACT OF LIQUIDITY RESTRAINTS

Funds Under Management (Millions of $)

Funds	TE
200	.57
300	.76
400	1.13
500	1.45
600	2.08
700	2.50
800	2.86
900	3.33
1000	3.64

approach, analysts examine company financial statements and conduct comparative analyses within economic sectors. Then portfolio managers integrate the analysts' outputs and build portfolios. In the process-driven approach, a research team looks for common factors or themes in the market that are useful in identifying mispriced securities. When what appears to be a successful theme is found, the execution of the strategy tends to be computer-driven with few if any judgmental overrides. With today's costs, the process-driven strategy is certainly less expensive than the traditional approach.

Turnover costs are another significant cost associated with conducting the strategy. High turnover means higher transaction costs and a larger and more active trading staff.

Aggressiveness is the last major implementation issue. In an ideal world, the investment manager (agent) would reflect the risk aversion of the plan sponsor (principal — although acting as agent for the corporation or beneficiaries). The sponsor should urge managers who have a smaller fraction of total assets under management to be more aggressive. On the other hand, aggressiveness creates a large element of business risk for the manager. Even the most effective active managers will experience significant runs of negative active return. If they are more aggressive than the other managers employed by the sponsor, they risk being fifth out of five — and a candidate to be dropped. If we consider Table 2 again, we see that managers with high information ratios in general should be more aggressive. Nevertheless, the high level of aggressiveness may threaten the success of the manager's business. This tension probably will result in less than optimal levels of aggressiveness among skillful managers.

167

Aggressiveness also limits our ability to implement the strategy. As the portfolio becomes more aggressive, we run into restrictions on short sales and prudence restrictions on concentration in certain assets or sectors.

CONCLUSION

We have shown how the value added by active investment strategies can be broken down into two components: the skill of the investment manager, c, and the breadth of the strategy, M. These are related to the value added by the strategy using Einstein's famous formula.

Three main assumptions support this result. First and foremost, we assume that managers have an accurate measure of their own skills and that they exploit their information in an optimal way. Second, we assume that the sources of information are independent, so that the manager does not bet twice on some repackaged form of the same information. Third, we assume that the information content, c, of each source is the same.

The first assumption, call it competence or hyper-competence, is the most crucial. Investment managers need a precise idea of what they know and, more significantly, what they do not know. Moreover, they need to know how to turn their ideas into portfolios and gain the benefits of their insights. The second two assumptions are merely simplifying approximations that can be mitigated by some of the devices mentioned above.

We also mentioned some difficulties in implementing strategies. These are depth (the strategic analogue of liquidity), cost, and the level of aggressiveness of the manager.

Now, how do you take information, evaluate it, and turn it into portfolios? This is the subject for a whole other article.

[1] Similarity with a more famous formula is coincidental.

[2] It is possible to repeat the analysis and look at performance residual to a market portfolio. We should also point out that performance relative to the normal and performance relative to the market will be identical as long as there is no market timing component of the active strategy.

[3] Readers who are interested in the technical details can obtain a copy of the supplement by writing to the author at BARRA, 1995 University Avenue, Berkeley, CA 94704.

[4] I refer to investors who like higher expected returns and dislike higher variance. Their objective can be written as $E(r) - \phi Var(r)$, where ϕ is a measure of their risk aversion.

[5] See the technical supplement.

[6] We are assuming that the returns are serially independent. In practice, serial correlations in asset or portfolio returns tend to be very small.

[7] The risk aversion here is the investment manager's aversion to active risk. As the performance of the active portfolio and the business risk of the investment management firm are closely linked, the level of active risk aversion is generally high. See Rudd (1987) for a discussion of investment and business risk.

[8] Specific return is the return unexplained by a multiple-factor model. As the multiple-factor model is designed to control for common factors of correlation, the specific returns will be, by assumption, uncorrelated across stocks.

[9] I learned this from Barr Rosenberg.

[10] We are assuming that no incidental bets are created by this procedure.

[11] Recall that our ground rules have outlawed permanent bets that are based on a perceived source of inefficiency in the benchmark.

[12] Note that a small negative correlation ($g < 0$) will make the second information source more valuable. Note also that it is not possible for the information sources to be perfectly negatively correlated ($g \approx 1$) and still both have a positive correlation c with the actual returns.

REFERENCES

Ferguson, Robert. "Active Portfolio Management." *Financial Analysts Journal*, May-June 1975, pp. 63-72.

———. "The Trouble with Performance Measurement." *Journal of Portfolio Management*, Spring 1986, pp. 4-9.

Fisher, Lawrence. "Using Modern Portfolio Theory to Maintain an Efficiently Diversified Portfolio." *Financial Analysts Journal*, May-June 1975, pp. 73-85.

Rosenberg, Barr. "Security Appraisal and Unsystematic Risk in Institutional Investment." *Proceedings of the Seminar on the Analysis of Security Prices*, University of Chicago, November 1976, pp. 171-237.

Rudd, Andrew. "Business Risk and Investment Risk." *Investment Management Review*, November-December 1987, pp. 19-27.

Sharpe, William. "Mutual Fund Performance." *Journal of Business*, January 1966.

Treynor, Jack, and Fischer Black. "How to Use Security Analysis to Improve Portfolio Selection." *Journal of Business*, January 1973, pp. 68-86.

The Sharpe Ratio

Properly used, it can improve investment management.

William F. Sharpe

WILLIAM F. SHARPE is professor of finance at the Graduate School of Business of Stanford University in Stanford (CA 94035).

O ver twenty-five years ago, in Sharpe [1966] I introduced a measure for the performance of mutual funds and proposed the term *reward-to-variability ratio* to describe it (the measure is also described in Sharpe [1975]). While the measure has gained considerable popularity, the name has not. Other authors have termed the original version the Sharpe Index (Radcliff [1990, p. 286] and Haugen [1993, p. 315]), the Sharpe Measure (Bodie, Kane, and Marcus [1993, p. 804], Elton and Gruber [1991, p. 652], and Reilly [1989, p. 803]), or the Sharpe Ratio (Morningstar [1993, p. 24]). Generalized versions have also appeared under various names (see, for example, BARRA [1992, p. 21] and Capaul, Rowley, and Sharpe [1993, p. 33]).

Bowing to increasingly common usage, this article refers to both the original measure and more generalized versions as the Sharpe Ratio. My goal here is to go well beyond the discussion of the original measure in Sharpe [1966] and Sharpe [1975], providing more generality and covering a broader range of applications.

THE RATIO

Most performance measures are *computed* using historic data but *justified* on the basis of predicted relationships. Practical implementations use ex post results while theoretical discussions focus on ex ante values. Implicitly or explicitly, it is assumed that historic results have at least some predictive ability.

For some applications, it suffices for future values of a measure to be related monotonically to past values — that is, if fund X has a higher historic measure than fund Y, it is assumed it will have a higher future measure. For other applications, the relationship must be proportional — that is, it is assumed that the future measure will equal some constant (typically less than 1.0) times the historic measure.

To avoid ambiguity, we define here both ex ante and ex post versions of the Sharpe Ratio, beginning with the former. Elsewhere, however, we focus on the use of the ratio for making decisions, and hence are concerned with the ex ante version. The important issues associated with the relationships (if any) between historic Sharpe Ratios and unbiased forecasts of the ratio are left for other expositions.

Throughout, we build on Markowitz's mean-variance paradigm, which assumes that the mean and standard deviation of the distribution of one-period return are sufficient statistics for evaluating the prospects of an investment portfolio. Clearly, comparisons based on the first two moments of a distribution do not take into account possible differences among portfolios in other moments or in distributions of outcomes across states of nature that may be associated with different levels of investor utility.

When such considerations are especially important, return mean and variance may not suffice, requiring the use of additional or substitute measures. Such situations are, however, beyond the scope of this article. Our goal is simply to examine the situations in which two measures (mean and variance) can usefully be summarized with one (the Sharpe Ratio).

The Ex Ante Sharpe Ratio

Let $\tilde{R}_F$ represent the return on fund F in the forthcoming period and $\tilde{R}_B$ the return on a benchmark portfolio or security. The tildes over the variables indicate that the exact values may not be known in advance. Define $\tilde{d}$, the *differential return*, as:

$$\tilde{d} \equiv \tilde{R}_F - \tilde{R}_B \qquad (1)$$

Let $\bar{d}$ be the *expected value* of $\tilde{d}$ and σ_d be the predicted standard deviation of $\tilde{d}$. The ex ante Sharpe Ratio (S) is:

$$S \equiv \frac{\bar{d}}{\sigma_d} \qquad (2)$$

In this version, the ratio indicates the expected differential return per unit of risk associated with the differential return.

The Ex Post Sharpe Ratio

Let R_{Ft} be the return on the fund in period t, R_{Bt} the return on the benchmark portfolio or security in period t, and D_t the differential return in period t:

$$D_t \equiv R_{Ft} - R_{Bt} \qquad (3)$$

Let $\bar{D}$ be the average value of D_t over the historic period from t = 1 through T:

$$\bar{D} \equiv \frac{1}{T} \sum_{t=1}^{T} D_t \qquad (4)$$

and σ_D be the standard deviation over the period:[1]

$$\sigma_D \equiv \sqrt{\frac{\sum_{t=1}^{T} (D_t - \bar{D})^2}{T - 1}} \qquad (5)$$

The ex post, or historic, Sharpe Ratio (S_h) is:

$$S_h \equiv \sqrt{\frac{\bar{D}}{\sigma_D}} \qquad (6)$$

In this version, the ratio indicates the historic average differential return per unit of historic variability of the differential return.

It is a simple matter to compute an ex post Sharpe Ratio using a spreadsheet program. The returns on a fund are listed in one column and those of the desired benchmark in the next column. The differences are computed in a third column. Standard functions are then used to compute the components of the ratio. For example, if the differential returns are in cells C1 through C60, a formula would provide the Sharpe Ratio using Microsoft's Excel spreadsheet program:

AVERAGE(C1:C60)/STDEV(C1:C60)

The historic Sharpe Ratio is closely related to the t-statistic for measuring the statistical significance of the mean differential return. The t-statistic will equal the Sharpe Ratio times the square root of T (the number of returns used for the calculation). If historic Sharpe Ratios for a set of funds are computed using the same number of observations, the Sharpe Ratios will thus be proportional to the t-statistics of the means.

Time Dependence

The Sharpe Ratio is not independent of the time period over which it is measured. This is true for both ex ante and ex post measures.

Consider the simplest possible case. The one-period mean and standard deviation of the differential return are, respectively, $\overline{d}_1$ and σ_{d_1}. Assume that the differential return over T periods is measured by simply summing the one-period differential returns, and that the latter have zero serial correlation. Denote the mean and standard deviation of the resulting T-period return, respectively, $\overline{d}_T$ and σ_{d_T}. Under the assumed conditions:

$$\overline{d}_T = Td_1 \tag{7}$$

$$\sigma_{d_T}^2 = T\,\sigma_{d_1}^2 \tag{8}$$

and:

$$\sigma_{d_T} = \sqrt{T}\,\sigma_{d_1} \tag{9}$$

Letting S_1 and S_T denote the Sharpe Ratios for 1 and T periods, respectively, it follows that:

$$S_T = \sqrt{T}\,S_1 \tag{10}$$

In practice, the situation is likely to be more complex. Multiperiod returns are usually computed taking compounding into account, which makes the relationship more complicated. Moreover, underlying differential returns may be serially correlated. Even if the underlying process does not involve serial correlation, a specific ex post sample may.

It is common practice to "annualize" data that apply to periods other than one year, using Equations (7) and (8). Doing so before computing a Sharpe Ratio can provide at least reasonably meaningful comparisons among strategies, even if predictions are initially stated in terms of different measurement periods.

To maximize information content, it is usually desirable to measure risks and returns using fairly short (e.g., monthly) periods. For purposes of standardization it is then desirable to annualize the results.

To provide perspective, consider investment in a broad stock market index, financed by borrowing. Typical estimates of the annual excess return on the stock market in a developed country might include a mean of 6% per year and a standard deviation of 15%. The resulting excess return Sharpe Ratio of "the stock market," stated in annual terms, would then be 0.40.

Correlations

The ex ante Sharpe Ratio takes into account both the expected differential return and the associated risk, while the ex post version takes into account both the average differential return and the associated variability. Neither incorporates information about the correlation of a fund or strategy with other assets, liabilities, or previous realizations of its own return. For this reason, the ratio may need to be supplemented in certain applications. Such considerations are discussed in later sections.

Related Measures

The literature surrounding the Sharpe Ratio has, unfortunately, led to a certain amount of confusion. To provide clarification, two related measures are described here. The first uses a different term to cover cases that include the construct that we call the Sharpe Ratio. The second uses the same term to describe a different but related construct.

Whether measured ex ante or ex post, it is essential that the Sharpe Ratio be computed using the mean and standard deviation of a *differential return* (or, more broadly, the return on what will be termed a zero investment strategy). Otherwise it loses its *raison d'être*. Clearly, the Sharpe Ratio can be considered a special case of the more general construct of the ratio of the mean of any distribution to its standard deviation.

In the investment arena, a number of authors associated with BARRA (a major supplier of analytic tools and data bases) have used the term *information ratio* to describe such a general measure. In some publications, the ratio is defined to apply only to differential returns and is thus equivalent to the measure that we call the Sharpe Ratio (see, for example, Rudd and Clasing [1982, p. 513] and Grinold [1989, p. 31]). In others, it also encompasses the ratio of the mean to the standard deviation of the distribution of the return on a single investment such as a fund or a benchmark (see, for example, BARRA [1993, p. 22]). While such a "return information ratio" may be useful as a descriptive statistic, it lacks a number of the key properties of what might be termed a "differential return information ratio" and may in some instances lead to wrong decisions.

For example, consider the choice of a strategy involving cash and one of two funds, X and Y. X has an expected return of 5% and a standard deviation of 10%. Y has an expected return of 8% and a standard deviation of 20%. The riskless rate of interest is 3%. According to the ratio of expected return to standard deviation, X (5/10, or 0.50) is superior to Y (8/20, or 0.40). According to the Sharpe Ratios using excess return, X (2/10, or 0.20) is inferior to Y (5/20, or 0.25).

Now, consider an investor who wishes to attain a standard deviation of 10%. This can be achieved with fund X, which will provide an expected return of 5.0%. It can also be achieved with an investment of 50% of the investor's funds in Y and 50% in the riskless asset. The latter will provide an expected return of 5.5% — clearly the superior alternative.

Thus the Sharpe Ratio provides the correct answer (a strategy using Y is preferred to one using X), while the "return information ratio" provides the wrong one.

In their seminal work, Treynor and Black [1973] define the term "Sharpe Ratio" as the *square* of the measure that we describe. Others, such as Rudd and Clasing [1982, p. 518] and Grinold [1989, p. 31], also use such a definition.

While interesting in certain contexts, this construct has the curious property that all values are positive — even those for which the mean differential return is negative. It thus obscures important information concerning performance. We prefer to follow more common practice and thus refer to the Treynor-Black measure as the *Sharpe Ratio squared* (SR^2).[2]

We focus here on the Sharpe Ratio, which takes into account both risk and return without reference to a market index. Sharpe [1966, 1975] discusses both the Sharpe Ratio and measures based on market indexes,

such as Jensen's alpha and Treynor's average excess return to beta ratio.

SCALE INDEPENDENCE

Originally, the benchmark for the Sharpe Ratio was taken to be a riskless security. In such a case, the *differential return* is equal to the *excess return* of the fund over a one-period riskless rate of interest. Many of the descriptions of the ratio in Sharpe [1966, 1975] focus on this case.

More recent applications use benchmark portfolios designed to have a set of "factor loadings" or an "investment style" similar to that of the fund being evaluated. In such cases, the differential return represents the difference between the return on the fund and the return that would have been obtained from a "similar" passive alternative. The difference between the two returns may be termed an "active return" or "selection return," depending on the underlying procedure used to select the benchmark.

Treynor and Black [1973] cover the case in which the benchmark portfolio is, in effect, a combination of riskless securities and the "market portfolio." Rudd and Clasing [1982] describe the use of benchmarks based on factor loadings from a multifactor model. Sharpe [1992] uses a procedure termed *style analysis* to select a mix of asset class index funds that have a "style" similar to that of the fund. When such a mix is used as a benchmark, the differential return is termed the fund's *selection return*. The Sharpe Ratio of the selection return can then serve as a measure of the fund's performance over and above that due to its investment style.[3]

Central to the usefulness of the Sharpe Ratio is the fact that a differential return represents the result of a *zero-investment strategy*. This can be defined as any strategy that involves a zero outlay of money in the present and returns either a positive, negative, or zero amount in the future, depending on circumstances. A differential return clearly falls in this class, because it can be obtained by taking a long position in one asset (the fund) and a short position in another (the benchmark), with the funds from the latter used to finance the purchase of the former.

In the original applications of the ratio, where the benchmark is taken to be a one-period riskless asset, the differential return represents the payoff from a unit investment in the fund, financed by borrowing.[4] More generally, the differential return corresponds to the payoff obtained from a unit investment in the fund, financed by a short position in the benchmark. For example, a fund's *selection return* can be considered to be the payoff from a unit investment in the fund, financed by short positions in a mix of asset class index funds with the same style.

A differential return can be obtained explicitly by entering into an agreement in which a party and a counterparty agree to *swap* the return on the benchmark for the return on the fund and vice versa. A *forward contract* provides a similar result. Arbitrage will insure that the return on such a contract will be very close to the excess return on the underlying asset for the period ending on the delivery date.[5] A similar relationship holds approximately for traded contracts such as stock index futures, which clearly represent zero-investment strategies.[6]

To compute the return for a zero-investment strategy, the payoff is divided by a *notional value*. For example, the dollar payoff for a swap is often set to equal the difference between the dollar return on an investment of $X in one asset and that on an investment of $X in another. The net difference can then be expressed as a proportion of $X, which serves as the notional value. Returns on futures positions are often computed in a similar manner, using the initial value of the underlying asset as a base. In effect, the same approach is utilized when the difference between two returns is computed.

Since there is zero net investment in any such strategy, the *percent* return can be made as large or small as desired by simply changing the notional value used in such a computation. The *scale* of the return thus depends on the more-or-less arbitrary choice of the notional value used for its computation.[7]

Changes in the notional value clearly affect the mean and the standard deviation of the distribution of return, but the changes are of the same magnitude, leaving the Sharpe Ratio unaffected. The ratio is thus *scale-independent*.[8]

THE INFLUENCE OF A ZERO-INVESTMENT STRATEGY ON ASSET RISK AND RETURN

Scale independence is more than a mathematical artifice. It is key to understanding why the Sharpe Ratio can provide an efficient summary statistic for a zero-investment strategy. To show this, we consider the case of an investor with a pre-existing portfolio who is considering the choice of a zero-investment strategy to augment current investments.

The Relative Position in a Zero-Investment Strategy

Assume that the investor has $A in assets and has placed this money in an investment portfolio with a return of $\tilde{R}_I$. She is considering investment in a zero-investment strategy that will provide a return of $\tilde{d}$ per unit of notional value. Denote the notional value chosen as V (e.g., investment of V in a fund financed by a short position of V in a benchmark). Define the *relative position*, p, as the ratio of the notional value to the investor's assets:

$$p \equiv \frac{V}{A} \qquad (11)$$

The end-of-period payoff will be:

$$A(1 + \tilde{R}_I) + Ap\tilde{d} \qquad (12)$$

Let $\tilde{R}_A$ denote the total return on the investor's initial assets. Then:

$$\tilde{R}_A = \tilde{R}_I + p\tilde{d} \qquad (13)$$

If $\overline{R}_A$ denotes the expected return on assets and $\overline{R}_I$ the expected return on the investment:

$$\overline{R}_A = \overline{R}_I + p\overline{d} \qquad (14)$$

Now, let σ_A, σ_I, and σ_d denote the standard deviations of the returns on assets, the investment, and the zero-investment strategy, respectively, and ρ_{Id} the correlation between the return on the investment and the return on the zero-investment strategy. Then:

$$\sigma_A^2 = \sigma_I^2 + 2\rho_{Id}\,\sigma_I\,p\sigma_d + (p\sigma_d)^2 \qquad (15)$$

or, rewriting slightly:

$$\sigma_A^2 = \sigma_I^2 + 2\,\sigma_I\,\rho_{Id}\,(p\sigma_d) + (p\sigma_d)^2 \qquad (16)$$

The Risk Position in a Zero-Investment Strategy

The parenthesized expression $(p\sigma_d)$ is of particular interest. It indicates the risk of the position in the zero-investment strategy relative to the investor's overall assets. Let k denote this *risk position*

$$k \equiv p\sigma_d \qquad (17)$$

For many purposes it is desirable to consider k as the relevant decision variable. Doing so states the magnitude of a zero-investment strategy in terms of its risk relative to the investor's overall assets. In effect, one first determines k, the level of risk of the zero-investment strategy. Having answered this fundamental question, the relative (p) and absolute (V) amounts of notional value for the strategy can readily be determined, using Equations (17) and (11).[9]

Asset Risk and Expected Return

It is straightforward to determine the manner in which asset risk and expected return are related to the risk position of the zero-investment strategy, its correlation with the investment, and its Sharpe Ratio.

Substituting k in Equation (16) gives the relationship between 1) asset risk, and 2) the risk position and the correlation of the strategy with the investment:

$$\sigma_A^2 = \sigma_I^2 + 2\,\sigma_I\,\rho_{Id}\,k + k^2 \qquad (18)$$

To see the relationship between asset expected return and the characteristics of the zero-investment strategy, note that the Sharpe Ratio is the ratio of $\overline{d}$ to σ_d. It follows that

$$\overline{d} = S\sigma_d \qquad (19)$$

Substituting Equation (19) in Equation (14) gives:

$$\overline{R}_A = \overline{R}_I + pS\sigma_d \qquad (20)$$

or:

$$\overline{R}_A = \overline{R}_I + kS \qquad (21)$$

which shows that the expected return on assets is related directly to the product of the risk position times the Sharpe Ratio of the strategy.

By selecting an appropriate scale, any zero-investment strategy can be used to achieve a desired level (k) of relative risk. This level, plus the strategy's Sharpe Ratio, will determine asset expected return, as shown by Equation (21). Asset risk, however, will depend on both the relative risk (k) and the correlation of the strategy with the other investment (σ_{Id}). In general, the Sharpe Ratio, which does not take that correlation into account, will not by itself provide sufficient information to determine a set of decisions that will produce an optimal combination of asset risk and return, given an investor's tolerance of risk.

ADDING A ZERO-INVESTMENT STRATEGY TO AN EXISTING PORTFOLIO

Fortunately, there are important special cases in which the Sharpe Ratio will provide sufficient information for decisions on the optimal risk/return combination: one in which the pre-existing portfolio is riskless, the other in which it is risky.

Adding a Strategy to a Riskless Portfolio

Suppose first that an investor plans to allocate money between a riskless asset and a single risky fund (e.g., a "balanced" fund). This is, in effect, the case analyzed in Sharpe [1966, 1975].

We assume there is a pre-existing portfolio invested solely in a riskless security, to which is to be added a zero-investment strategy involving a long position in a fund, financed by a short position in a riskless asset (i.e., borrowing). Letting R_c denote the return on such a "cash equivalent," Equations (1) and (13) can be written as:

$$\tilde{d} = \tilde{R}_F - R_c \qquad (22)$$

and

$$\tilde{R}_A = R_c + p\tilde{d} \qquad (23)$$

Since the investment is riskless, its standard deviation of return is zero, so both the first and second terms on the right-hand side of Equation (18) become zero, giving:

$$\sigma_A = k \qquad (24)$$

The investor's total risk will thus be equal to that of the position taken in the zero-investment strategy, which will in turn equal the risk of the position in the fund.

Letting S_F represent the Sharpe Ratio of fund F, Equation (21) can be written:

$$\overline{R}_A = R_c + kS_F \qquad (25)$$

It is clear from Equations (24) and (25) that the investor should choose the desired level of risk (k), then obtain that level of risk by using the fund (F) with the greatest excess return Sharpe Ratio. Correlation does not play a role since the remaining holdings are riskless.

This is illustrated in the Exhibit. Points X and Y represent two (mutually exclusive) strategies. The desired level of risk is given by k. It can be obtained with strategy X using a relative position of p_X (shown in the figure at point PxX), or with strategy Y using a relative position of p_Y (shown in the figure at point PyY). An appropriately scaled version of strategy X clearly provides a higher mean return (shown at point MRx) than an appropriately scaled version of strategy Y (shown at point MRy). Strategy X is hence to be preferred.

The Exhibit shows that the mean return associated with *any* desired risk position will be greater if strategy X is adopted instead of strategy Y. But the slope of such a line *is* the Sharpe Ratio. Hence, as long as only the mean return and the risk position of the zero-investment strategy are relevant, the optimal solution involves maximization of the Sharpe Ratio of the zero-investment strategy.

Consider, for example, a choice between fund XX, with a risk of 10% and an excess return Sharpe Ratio of 0.20, and fund YY, with a risk of 20% and an excess return Sharpe Ratio of 0.25. Assume the investor has $100 to invest and desires a level of risk (here, k) equal to 15%.

The optimal strategy involves investment of $100 in the riskless asset plus a zero-investment strategy based on fund YY. To make the risk of the latter equal to 15%, a relative position (p) of 0.75 should be taken. This, in turn, requires an investment of $75 in the fund, financed by $75 of borrowing (i.e., a short position in the riskless asset). The net position in the riskless asset will thus be $25 ($100 − $75), with $75 invested in Fund YY.

In this case the investor's tasks include the selection of the fund with the greatest Sharpe Ratio and the allocation of wealth between this fund and borrowing or lending, as required to obtain the desired level of asset risk.

Adding a Strategy to a Risky Portfolio

Consider now the case in which a single fund is to be selected to complement a pre-existing group of risky investments. For example, an investor might have $100, with $80 already committed (e.g., to a group of bond and stock funds). The goal is to allocate the remaining $20 between a riskless asset ("cash") and a single risky fund (e.g., a "growth stock fund"), accepting the possibility that the amount allocated to cash might be positive, zero, or negative, depending on the desired risk and the risk of the chosen fund.

In this case the investment should be taken as the pre-existing investment plus a riskless asset (in the example, $80 in the initial investments plus $20 in cash equivalents). The return on this total portfolio will be $\tilde{R}_I$. The zero-investment strategy will again involve a long position in a risky fund and a short position in the riskless asset.

As stated earlier, in such a case it will not necessarily be optimal to select the fund with the largest possible Sharpe Ratio. While the ratio takes into account two key attributes of the predicted performance of a zero-investment strategy (its expected return and its risk), it does not include information about the correlation of its return with that of the investor's other holdings (ρ_{Id}). It is entirely possible that a fund with a smaller Sharpe Ratio could have a sufficiently smaller

EXHIBIT
MUTUALLY EXCLUSIVE INVESTMENTS

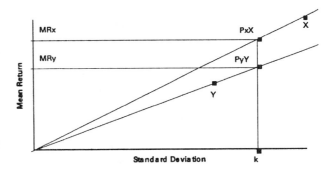

175

correlation with the investor's other assets that it would provide a higher expected return on assets for any given level of overall asset risk.

However, if the alternative funds being analyzed have similar correlations with the investor's other assets, it will still be optimal to select the fund with the greatest Sharpe Ratio. To see this, note that with ρ_{Id} taken as given, Equation (18) shows that there is a one-to-one correspondence between σ_A and k. Thus, for any desired level of asset risk, the investor chooses the corresponding risk position k given by Equation (18), regardless of the fund to be employed.

But, as before, the expected return on assets will be:

$$\overline{R}_A = \overline{R}_I + kS_F \qquad (26)$$

which can be maximized by selecting the fund with the largest Sharpe Ratio.

The practical implication is clear. When choosing one from among a group of funds of a particular type for inclusion in a larger set of holdings, the one with the largest predicted excess return Sharpe Ratio may reasonably be chosen, if it can be assumed that all the funds in the set have similar correlations with the other holdings. If this condition is not met, some account should be taken of the differential levels of such correlations.

THE CHOICE OF A SET OF UNCORRELATED STRATEGIES

Suppose finally that an investor has a pre-existing set of investments and is considering taking positions in one or more zero-investment strategies, each of which is uncorrelated both with the existing investments and with each of the other such strategies. Such lack of correlation is generally assumed for residual returns from an assumed factor model and hence applies to strategies in which long and short positions are combined to obtain zero exposures to all underlying factors in such a model.

In particular, this is assumed to hold for the "non-market returns," which are the residual returns in one-factor "market models" of the type employed in Treynor-Black [1973]. It is also assumed to hold for the "active returns" that constitute the residual returns in a model of the type used by BARRA (described, for

example, in Grinold [1989]).

Most germane, perhaps, for selecting funds, this is assumed to hold for the "selection returns" that constitute the residuals from the asset class factor model used in the style analysis procedure described in Sharpe [1992]. Note, however, that the key results apply to all three cases.[10]

Under the assumed conditions, the counterpart to Equation (13) is:

$$\tilde{R}_A = \tilde{R}_I + \sum_i p_i \tilde{d}_i \qquad (27)$$

where p_i represents the relative position taken in strategy i, and $\tilde{d}_i$ represents its return.

Letting σ_{d_i} represent the risk of position i, asset risk is given by:

$$\sigma_A^2 = \sigma_I^2 + \sum_i p_i^2 \sigma_{d_i}^2 \qquad (28)$$

and expected asset return by:

$$\overline{R}_A = \overline{R}_I + \sum_i p_i \overline{d}_i \qquad (29)$$

Adding subscripts to Equations (21) and (18), and substituting the results, gives:

$$\overline{R}_A = \overline{R}_I + \sum_i k_i S_i \qquad (30)$$

and

$$\sigma_A^2 = \sigma_I^2 + \sum_i k_i^2 \qquad (31)$$

Now, assume that the investor's goal is to maximize a standard risk-adjusted expected return of the form:

$$\overline{R}_A - \tau^{-1} \sigma_A^2 \qquad (32)$$

where τ represents risk tolerance (the marginal rate of substitution of variance for expected return). Substituting Equations (30) and (31) in (32) gives:

$$\overline{R}_I + \sum_i k_i S_i - \tau^{-1} \left(\sigma_I^2 + \sum_i k_i^2 \right) \qquad (33)$$

Since the terms involving the initial investment will be unaffected by the decisions (k_is) concerning the zero-investment strategies, it suffices to maximize:

$$\sum_i k_i S_i - \tau^{-1} \sum_i k_i^2 \qquad (34)$$

To do so, the partial derivative with respect to each decision variable (k_i) should be set equal to zero:

$$S_i - 2\tau^{-1} k_i = 0 \qquad (35)$$

The optimal risk position in strategy i is thus:

$$k_i = \frac{\tau}{2} S_i \qquad (36)$$

Hence the risk levels of the strategies should be proportional to their Sharpe Ratios. Strategies with zero predicted Sharpe Ratios should be ignored. Those with positive ratios should be "held long," and those with negative ratios "held short." If strategy X has a positive Sharpe Ratio that is twice as large as that of strategy Y, twice as much risk should be taken with X as with Y. The overall scale of all the positions should, in turn, be proportional to the investor's risk tolerance.

An interesting application occurs when long and short positions can be taken (e.g., via financial futures) in the asset classes that underlie a style analysis model of the type described in Sharpe [1992]. In principle, funds should be selected only on the basis of their selection returns, with the respective amounts of selection risk set in proportion to the funds' selection return Sharpe Ratios. The net exposures to asset classes required to implement this mixture of zero-investment strategies can then be compared with the investor's desired passive asset mix to determine needed net positions.

SUMMARY

The Sharpe Ratio is designed to measure the expected return per unit of risk for a *zero-investment strategy*. The difference between the returns on two investment assets represents the results of such a strategy. The Sharpe Ratio does not cover cases in which only one investment return is involved.

Clearly, any measure that attempts to summarize even an unbiased prediction of performance with a single number requires a substantial set of assumptions for justification. In practice, such assumptions are, at best, likely to hold only approximately. Certainly, the use of unadjusted historic (ex post) Sharpe Ratios as surrogates for unbiased predictions of ex ante ratios is subject to serious question. Despite such caveats, there is much to recommend a measure that at least takes into account both risk and expected return over any alternative that focuses only on the latter.

For a number of investment decisions, ex ante Sharpe Ratios can provide important inputs. When choosing one from among a set of funds to provide representation in a particular market sector, it makes sense to favor the one with the greatest predicted Sharpe Ratio, as long as the correlations of the funds with other relevant asset classes are reasonably similar. When allocating funds among several such funds, it makes sense to allocate funds such that the selection (residual) risk levels are proportional to the predicted Sharpe Ratios for the selection (residual) returns. If some of the implied net positions are infeasible or involve excessive transaction costs, of course, the decision rules must be modified. Nonetheless, Sharpe Ratios may still provide useful guidance.

Whatever the application, it is essential to remember that the Sharpe Ratio does not take correlations into account. When a choice may affect important correlations with other assets in an investor's portfolio, such information should be used to supplement comparisons based on Sharpe Ratios.

All the same, the ratio of expected added return per unit of added risk provides a convenient summary of two important aspects of any strategy involving the difference between the return of a fund and that of a relevant benchmark. The Sharpe Ratio is designed to provide such a measure. Properly used, it can improve the process of managing investments.

ENDNOTES

[1]We use the formula for the standard deviation of a population, taking the observations as a sample. When the value of T is the same for all the funds being measured, the standard deviation of the historic data (in which the denominator is T rather than T − 1) can generally be used instead, as the relative magnitudes of the resulting measures would be the same.

[2]Treynor and Black show that if resources are allocated optimally, the SR^2 of a portfolio will equal the sum of the SR^2 values for its components. This follows from the fact that the optimal holding of a component will be proportional to the ratio of its mean differential return to the square of the standard deviation of its differential return. Thus, for example, components with negative means should be held in negative amounts. In this context, the product of the mean return and the optimal holding will always be positive. For completeness, it should be noted that Treynor and Black use the term *appraisal ratio* to refer to what we term here the SR^2 of a component and the term *Sharpe Ratio* to refer to the SR^2 of the portfolio, although other authors have used the latter term for both the portfolio and its components.

[3]This type of application is described in BARRA [1992, p. 21].

[4]In this context, maximization of the Sharpe Ratio is the normative equivalent to the separation theorem first put forth in Tobin [1958] in a positive context.

[5]To see this, note that by borrowing money to purchase the underlying asset, one can obtain precisely the same asset at the delivery date. The ending value of such a strategy will be perfectly correlated with the value of the forward contract, and neither will require any outlay. If the payoffs at the end of the period differ, one could take a long position in one combination (e.g., the forward contract or the asset/borrowing combination) and a short position in the other, and obtain a guaranteed payment at the end of the period with no outlay at any other time. This is unlikely to be the case in a market populated by astute investors. In practice, transaction costs limit the precision of this relationship.

[6]Futures contracts are often not protected against changes in value due to (for example) dividend payments. They also generally require daily marking to market. For these reasons, they differ from forward contracts with dividend protection, for which the arbitrage relationship will hold within the bounds of transaction costs. Futures contracts generally require that margin be posted. However, this is not an investment in the underlying asset.

[7]Despite this drawback, once a notional value has been selected, the actual rate of return can be used for comparison purposes.

[8]Indeed, a Sharpe Ratio can be computed without regard to notional value by simply using the mean and standard deviation of the distribution of the final payoff.

[9]To see the advantages of concentration on the risk position of a strategy, consider two funds. One (X) invests directly; the other (Y) borrows money at the riskless rate and invests in X, with a leverage ratio of 2 to 1. Let k_x be the optimal position in fund X. Clearly the optimal position in fund Y will be half as large. However, the standard deviation of return on fund Y will be twice that of fund X. Thus the optimal risk position in Y will be the same as that in X.

[10]In fact, the basic relationship on which this section builds was first obtained by Treynor and Black [1973].

REFERENCES

BARRA Newsletter, September/October 1992, May/June 1993, BARRA, Berkeley, CA.

Bodie, Zvi, Alex Kane, and Alan J. Marcus. *Investments*, 2d edition. Homewood, IL: Richard D. Irwin, 1993.

Capaul, Carlo, Ian Rowley, and William F. Sharpe. "International Value and Growth Stock Returns." *Financial Analysts Journal*, January/February 1993, pp. 27-36.

Elton, Edwin J., and Martin J. Gruber. *Modern Portfolio Theory and Investment Analysis*, 4th edition. New York: John Wiley & Sons, 1991.

Grinold, Richard C. "The Fundamental Law of Active Management." *Journal of Portfolio Management*, Spring 1989, pp. 30-37.

Haugen, Robert A. *Modern Investment Theory*, 3d edition. Englewood Cliffs, NJ: Prentice-Hall, 1993.

"Morningstar Mutual Funds User's Guide." Chicago: Morningstar Inc., 1993.

Radcliff, Robert C. *Investment Concepts, Analysis, Strategy*, 3d edition. New York: HarperCollins, 1990.

Reilly, Frank K. *Investment Analysis and Portfolio Management*, 3d edition. Chicago: The Dryden Press, 1989.

Rudd, Andrew, and Henry K. Clasing. *Modern Portfolio Theory: The Principles of Investment Management*. Homewood, IL: Dow-Jones Irwin, 1982.

Sharpe, William F. "Mutual Fund Performance." *Journal of Business*, January 1966, pp. 119-138.

——. "Adjusting for Risk in Portfolio Performance Measurement." *Journal of Portfolio Management*, Winter 1975, pp. 29-34.

——. "Asset Allocation: Management Style and Performance Measurement." *Journal of Portfolio Management*, Winter 1992, pp. 7-19.

Tobin, James. "Liquidity Preference as Behavior Toward Risk." *Review of Economic Studies*, February 1958, pp. 65-86.

Treynor, Jack L., and Fischer Black. "How to Use Security Analysis to Improve Portfolio Selection." *Journal of Business*, January 1973, pp. 66-85.

The Invisible Costs of Trading

Trading is an adversary game — and a zero-sum game at that.

Jack L. Treynor

JACK L. TREYNOR heads
Treynor Capital Management, Inc.,
in Palos Verdes Estates (CA 92074).

I believe in active securities management. My only complaint is that some active managers seem to have a narrow understanding of what the game is. This is particularly true of what I will call the invisible costs of trading. Managers rarely mention them in discussions of trading cost; conventional measures of that cost omit them.

A view of trading that excludes these costs leads to the conclusion that bad performance is due to bad research. But this is impossible: The purpose of research is to forecast price movements. Worthless research makes worthless forecasts. A worthless forecast is equally likely to be followed by a price increase or a price decrease. Worthless research leads to unnecessary risk and unnecessary trading — but, in terms of its average contribution to return, gross of the visible trading costs, bad research cannot be worse than no research.

Most of the return in a diversified portfolio is the broad impact of economic and market news on the categories of assets held. This impact is the same whether the assets within these categories are traded or merely held. For active portfolios, therefore, the meaningful measure of performance is not total return, but the (algebraic) increment in return due to trading.

For long-term, average experience in diversified portfolios, we have the crude equation:

Return from Trading = Research − Trading Cost

in which the return from trading is often negative, but the research term never is. In such portfolios, consistent underperformance cannot be explained by bad research. The culprit must be trading cost. But the visible trading costs — commissions plus dealer spread — are too modest for listed stocks to explain any significant underperformance.

KEY ELEMENTS IN INVESTMENT PERFORMANCE

The explanation for costs of trading lies in two facts:

1. Trading is a zero-sum game (before dealer spread and commissions). For every trade, there will be one winner and one loser (relative, of course, to not trading).
2. In its motivation, the great majority of securities trading is adversarial.

Broadly speaking, active investors contemplate two kinds of price movement:

1. Changes in equilibrium price.
2. Changes in the discrepancy between trade price and equilibrium price.

The difference in trade prices between any two points in time is always some combination of these two kinds of price movement. All active investing is motivated by forecasts, implicit or explicit, of one kind or the other.

The information trader, for example, believes he knows something other investors don't know. It isn't in equilibrium price yet, but it will be when knowledge spreads to enough other investors. The information trader is betting on a change in equilibrium price. He or she relies on research to dig up information with potential market impact that isn't widely known — i.e., on *investigation*.

The value trader, on the other hand, believes he has identified a discrepancy between trade price and equilibrium value. He believes such discrepancies are only temporary. He is betting that, given market pressures toward equilibration, the observed discrepancy is more likely to diminish than increase. He relies on research to provide an estimate of equilibrium value he can compare to trade price — i.e., an *analysis* of the facts and figures in the public domain.

The distinction between information and value traders cuts across the distinction between buyers and sellers. Information traders can be motivated by either good news (in which case they are buyers) or bad news (in which case they are sellers). Value traders can be motivated by a trade price above what they think a security is worth (in which case they are sellers) or by a trade price below what they think a security is worth (in which case they are buyers).

To the layperson, a bargain price is a price below true (i.e., equilibrium) value. But value traders can be motivated by either a trade price above their perception of equilibrium or a trade price below it. Both price discrepancies represent potential profitable trading opportunities — i.e., bargains. In this symmetric sense of the word, we shall refer to value traders as *bargain hunters*.

ACTIVE INVESTING INCURS TRADING, AS WELL AS HOLDING, RISKS

We have noted that the information trader is betting on a change in equilibrium, while the value trader is betting on a change in the discrepancy between trade price and equilibrium price. There are risks for both, however. Even if the value trader has estimated equilibrium price correctly and identified a true bargain, equilibrium price may change before he can close out his position. Even if the information trader has uncovered information that correctly anticipates a change in equilibrium price, he may be forced to buy and sell (or sell and buy) at trade prices different from equilibrium. (See Exhibits 1 and 2.)

The key question for the active investor is whether these risks are merely random risks. If so, then the information trader is probably justified in focusing on the potential change in equilibrium price. If so, then the value trader is probably justified in focusing on departures of trade price from the estimate of equilibrium. Is the active investor as likely to gain as lose from these risks?

Consider the information trader. In order to justify ignoring discrepancies between the prices he trades at and equilibrium prices at the times of his trades, he needs to be able to assume that these discrepancies are random. But in order for him to transact with a value trader on the other side, for example, the latter must be motivated — must perceive a discrepancy between

EXHIBIT 1
HOW THE VALUE TRADER SEES
TRADING OPPORTUNITY

EXHIBIT 2
HOW THE INFORMATION TRADER SEES
TRADING OPPORTUNITY

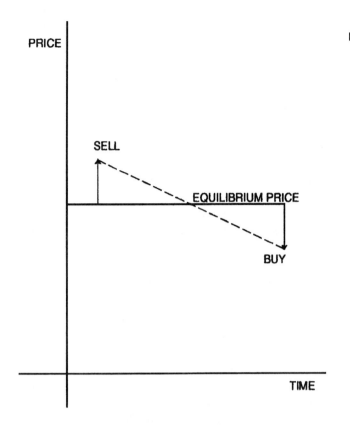

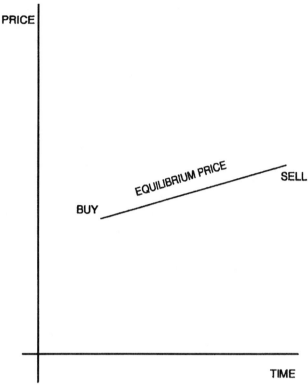

trade price and equilibrium that offers a bargain. The discrepancy cannot be good for the value trader on the other side without being bad for the information trader. The trade price discrepancies the information trader is ignoring in his focus on potential changes in equilibrium price are not random.

Or consider the value trader. In order to justify ignoring the possibility of changes in equilibrium price between the trade that opens the position and the trade that closes it, he needs to be able to assume that these changes are random — as likely to help as to hurt. But in order for him to transact with an information trader on the other side, for example, the latter must be motivated — must expect a change in equilibrium value. The change cannot be good for the information trader on the other side without being bad for the value trader.

If trading risks are not random, then it is dangerously oversimple to view value trading as searching for bargains, or information trading as scooping the consensus. (See Exhibit 3.)

INVISIBLE TRADING COSTS DEFINED

The oversimple view leads to a conception of active investing as a game that can be won, but not lost. Curiously, this view accords nicely with the old academic notion of efficient markets; if information gets into the consensus instantly, the value trader has noth-

EXHIBIT 3
TRADING ON GOOD NEWS

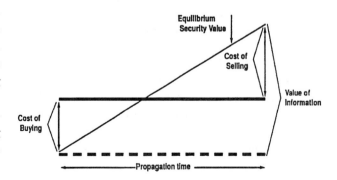

ing to worry about. If trade price never departs from consensus price, the information trader has nothing to worry about.

But if, contrary to the old academic view, securities markets aren't perfectly efficient, then today's consensus price is no longer an unbiased estimate of the future consensus price. And today's trade price is no longer a good proxy for today's consensus price. The value trader can get bagged, and the information trader can pay an exorbitant price for trading quickly.

In fact, markets are not perfectly efficient. Departures from perfect efficiency are unavoidable, because, without them, the party on the other side of the transaction would have no motive to transact. Because these departures provide the necessary motivation, *they are costs of transacting*.

These costs are orders of magnitude bigger than the ostensible costs of transacting — brokerage commissions and market impact. We call them the invisible costs of trading. Why invisible? The value trader won't know what information made his bargain possible until it bags him. The information trader won't know how much his trade price departed from consensus price until the trading pressure generated by his information abates.

It is hard to understand how an active investor can consistently lose big if the only costs are brokerage commission and market impact. But it's easy to understand when one allows for the invisible costs of trading.

EXCHANGING PRICE FOR TIME

We have noted that these two modes of active investing call for different kinds of research. They also call for different kinds of trading:

1. The value trader is interested in trading only if a perceived price discrepancy gets big enough to make it worth the while. Because he uses publicly available information, he is under no pressure to trade quickly. Time is unimportant compared to price.
2. The information trader wants to trade before his non-publicly known or non-consensus information gets into the consensus, hence into price. Price is unimportant compared to time.

Because information traders are highly unlikely to arrive in the market at precisely the same time, they are rarely able to accommodate each other's trades. And, unless one or both errs in his estimate of equilibrium value, a trade price cannot simultaneously be a bargain (in the symmetric sense noted) to both a value-motivated buyer and a value-motivated seller. But a trade won't occur unless both sides are motivated. Thus the transaction of greatest practical interest has an anxious information trader on one side and a bargain-hunting value trader on the other.

Adversarial transactions in individual securities typically involve the exchange of time for price: One transactor is making a price sacrifice in order to trade at a time of his choosing; the other is forgoing the time initiative in the transaction in order to trade at a price of his choosing.

In every completed transaction, there is one party who would have been better off not trading. There is no information so important its worth cannot be exceeded by the cost of trading quickly. There is no price bargain so big that it cannot be exceeded by the value of new information adverse to the bargain hunter.

On every trade, time is either worth more than it costs, or less. If the former, the transactor buying time (e.g., the information trader) will win, and the transactor selling time (e.g., the value trader) will lose. If the latter, the transactor selling time will win, and the transactor buying time will lose.

The active investors who lose consistently are those who buy time for more than it is worth or sell time for less than it is worth. Although couched in specific security transactions, what active investors are really buying and selling is time.

By "time," of course, we mean the right to transact quickly. What information traders, anxious to trade before their information gets impounded in price, are willing to pay for this right determines its worth. What they actually pay is the bargain — the difference between trade price and equilibrium price — demanded by bargain-hunting value traders. In order to know what "time" costs, one must have a good estimate of equilibrium price with which to compare trade price.

ACTIVE INVESTING IS A GAME OF ODDS

In practice, the value trader knows (or thinks he knows) the cost of time, because he can compare trade price with his estimate of consensus price. But he doesn't know what time is worth. Because he has new information, the information trader knows what time is worth, but, because he is in too much of a hurry to estimate consensus price, he doesn't know what time costs.

A problem occurs because the active investor's *research* fails to supply both sides of the worth- versus cost-of comparison. In fact he looks to the *trading desk* to supply the missing side. The value trader hopes his trading desk can smoke out the information that is creating the bargain his research identifies. The information trader hopes his trading desk can estimate the cost of trading quickly, including the price effects of other investors' anxious trading.

But, of course, even a sophisticated trading desk is dealing with fragmentary information. Even if active investors are dealing with hard information on one side of the equation, they are dealing with soft information on the other.

The situation is reminiscent of a card game in which you know your cards but not your opponent's. You know your research motive, and the transactor on the other side knows his. But you don't know his research motive, and he doesn't know yours. The outcome depends on the value of your research, the value of his research, and the trade price.

Negotiations on trade price are loosely analogous to betting in poker, or bidding in contract bridge. The fund manager's contribution to performance derives from skill in these negotiations — skill in ferreting out information about the other transactor's research motive while concealing information about his own.

It should be obvious that the task of negotiating securities transactions cannot be conducted in a vacuum. In particular, it isn't logical to decide to make a trade and then try to figure out how to execute it. Nor is it logical to give the responsibility for decisions to one party (i.e., the fund manager) and the responsibility for executions to another (i.e., the trader).

Such arrangements would be analogous in poker to giving the responsibility for deciding whether or not to pass to one party and the responsibility for deciding how much to bet to another. Or, in bridge, giving the decision whether to bid the contract to one party and the responsibility for bidding to another.

In these card games, knowing when to play and when not to play is vital. It is also vital in active investing. Like these card games, *active investing is a game of odds.* Research deals the cards, but it can't decide when to raise and when to fold.

HOW WE THINK ABOUT THE NATURE OF THE GAME AFFECTS OUR PERFORMANCE

Consider an example. Most of the price distortions detected by the value trader are caused by anxious information traders. If their information is impounded in the price *after* the value trader trades, he experiences an adverse price move equal to the value of the information. But, as noted, information traders have no easy way of knowing whether their information is already in the price. So many of the so-called bargains perceived by the value trader are caused by information that won't result in an adverse price movement.

If the value trader had his way, he would trade only on those price bargains created by information that is already in the price at the time of his trade, since he can't get bagged by this information.

The media are an obvious clue: Is there a big story in the media that could generate some anxious information trading? Does the stock appear to be mispriced even when the value implications of the story are taken into account? If the answer to both questions is "yes," then the opportunity for the value trader falls in the upper left quadrant in Exhibit 4. (The table applies only when the value investor has identified a price discrepancy.)

A story in the media (consistent, of course, with the observed discrepancy) increases the likelihood that the information causing the discrepancy is already in the price. But, as the joint probability in the upper right of Exhibit 4 suggests, the story doesn't guarantee it: There may be *another* story, not in the media, that is not yet in the price.

But if there is *no* story in the media, then the information is much less likely to be in the price. The story *might* have disseminated broadly through the population of investors without ever getting into the media. But this case is unlikely; hence the low joint probability in the lower left in Exhibit 4.

The value trader is not interested in joint prob-

EXHIBIT 4
Joint Probabilities (bargain price only)

	In Price (P)	Not in Price (P′)	Probability
Story in Media (S)	0.4	0.1	0.5
No Story in Media (S′)	0.2	0.3	0.5
	0.6	0.4	

abilities. He wants to know whether the information causing the price discrepancy he observes is in the price. If it is, he wants to trade. If it isn't, the price discrepancy may not be big enough to compensate him for getting bagged. In other words, he wants to know the *conditional* probabilities of the information's being already impounded in the price, given that there is, or is not, a story in the media.

Bayes' theorem tells the value investor how to calculate those probabilities. If the story is in the media, the probability that the information is already in the price is the joint probability that the story is both in the price and the media, divided by the sum of the probabilities in the "story in media" row — i.e., the sum of the respective probabilities that the story is in the price as well as the media and that the story is not in the price although in the media.

We have

$$PIS = \frac{PS}{PS + P'S} = \frac{0.4}{0.4 + 0.1} = 0.8$$

If the story is not in the media, the probability that the information is already in the price is the joint probability that the story is in the price though not in the media, divided by the sum of the probabilities in the "story not in media" row — i.e., the sum of the respective probabilities that the story is in the price though not in the media and that the story is in neither the media nor the price.

We have

$$PIS' = \frac{PS'}{PS' + P'S'} = \frac{0.2}{0.2 + 0.3} = 0.4$$

If, on the other hand, the value trader ignores the media, then the probability that the information is in the price is simply the sum of the joint probabilities in the "In Price" column (since these cases exhaust all the ways the information can be in the price). We have

$$0.4 + 0.2 = 0.6$$

The probability of getting bagged is the probability that the information is not in the price, or one minus these probabilities.

The numbers in our table are merely illustrative, but they do suggest that a value trader can reduce trading cost by playing the odds. If he ignores the media, for example, his probability of getting bagged is one minus 0.6, or 0.4; the expected cost of getting bagged by the information is 0.4 times the value of the information. If he breaks even before brokerage commissions and dealer spread, his invisible trading cost just offsets the value of his research:

Price Discrepancy − 0.4 (Bagging Information) = 0

If value traders are consistently winning at the expense of information traders, some of the latter will leave the game even as more value investors are drawn into the game. The bargains required to equilibrate value and information trading will shrink. The adjustment will continue until the two kinds of investors are again "breaking even." The reverse will happen if information traders are gaining at the expense of value traders.

Thus our example is not chosen idly: It represents the equilibrium bargain in departures of trade price from equilibrium price. If on average the price bargains motivating trades are worth 20% of the consensus value of the stock, then break-even for a value trader requires

0.2 − 0.4 (Bagging Information) = 0

Bagging Information = 0.2/0.4 = 0.5

or 50% of the value of the stock.

If our value trader trades only when a story is prominent in the media, then, as we calculated, the story would be in the price of the stock 80% of the time, but he would get bagged 20% of the time, and his gain per trade would be

20% − (1 − 0.8) × (50%) =

20% − 10% = 10%

According to our hypothetical table, media stories occur half the time (i.e., half the time that our active investor identifies a bargain). Assume his research has been identifying bargains at a rate sufficient to generate 100% per year turnover. Then his new turnover

EXHIBIT 5
Shared Beliefs of Active Managers

What you hold is more important than how you trade.

Trading costs are measured by commissions and short-term "market impact" (i.e., visible costs).

Other side of must securities trades is a dealer.

Market inefficiency is measured by what it takes to motivate the dealer.

Research is more important than trading.

Portfolio decisions and the costs of executing are separate problems.

If an active investor loses consistently, it is because of faulty research.

Since, before commissions and dealer spread, trading is as likely to gain as lose, research ideas are pure gravy. The object of the game is to trade on as many as possible.

---

rate will be half that, or 50% per year. His abnormal return per year, before commissions and dealer spread, will be

$$50\% \times 10\% = 5\%$$

Assuming round-trip visible costs of trading of 2%, we have

$$50\% \times (10\% - 2\%) = 4\%$$

for his net gain from active investing. For his former losses to brokerage and dealer spread we have

$$100\% \times 2\% = 2\% \text{ per year}$$

The total improvement is 600 basis points. Since public news stories are, after all, public, no additional research is involved.

For most active investors, 600 basis points is a substantial improvement. Why don't value traders invest this way?

Exhibits 5 and 6 summarize active investors' beliefs about active management. Why do active investors think this way?

1. Out of sight, out of mind. The invisible costs of trading are not easily measured, much less seen or visualized.

2. Because they trade with dealers, rather than each other, active investors forget that theirs is an adversary game — and a zero-sum game at that — before commissions and dealer spread.

3. If the average investor underperforms the market, his trading costs exceed the value of his research. Yet he devotes most of his time and effort to research. He rarely thinks about the motives of his trading counterpart.

4. Lacking a clear picture of the other transactor's trading motive, he sees his task as buying and selling securities, rather than buying and selling time.

5. Because he doesn't see active investing as buying and selling time, he doesn't realize that his task is comparing what time is worth to what it costs — and that his research supplies only one side of this comparison. He doesn't see active investing as a game of odds — about knowing when to trade and when not to trade.

CONCLUSIONS

Trades are not executed; they are negotiated. Conducting these negotiations, which will jointly determine which trades are actually made and the price of those trades, is the line function in portfolio management.

EXHIBIT 6
Contrasting Beliefs

Information Managers	Value Managers
Departures from equilibrium price are small.	Departures of trade price from equilibrium create bargains.
I get my information before it is impounded in price.	New information is impounded quickly.
The generation of private information is key to effective research.	Analysis of published financial data is key to effective research.
In trading, price is more important than time.	In trading, time is more important than price.

Research is a necessary, even critical, input to the negotiating process, but by itself it can never be sufficient.

Thus the research function stands in a staff support relation to the negotiator. The trading desk also stands in a staff support relation to the negotiator; its main function is not merely to execute but to supply that support.

ENDNOTES

Reprinted, with permission, from the proceedings of an AIMR conference in Toronto in November 1992 entitled *Execution Techniques, True Trading Costs, and the Microstructure of Markets.*

The author gratefully acknowledges the many valuable questions and criticisms raised by James R. Vertin, Chairman, AIMR Council on Education and Research, and Donald L. Tuttle, Senior Vice President, AIMR. He especially appreciates the open-minded consideration of what is still a very controversial stance.

PART FOUR
Real Estate

Although investors in Europe and Asia have long considered real estate an essential investment asset, the idea of including real estate in a portfolio of stocks, bonds, and cash took hold in the United States only as inflation concerns intensified throughout the 1970s. While inflation fears were fanning the interest of practitioners, finance theorists were discovering a new area that encompassed a great many interesting features.

Real estate is a hard asset and an illiquid one, but outside financing of real estate is imperative. The linkage to finance makes real estate returns negatively correlated with interest rates, but the nature of real estate leased-based income makes real estate returns positively correlated with inflation. As a consequence, the correlation between real estate and equity returns is complex and variable. Furthermore, the historical performance measurement data for real estate—primarily appraisal-based valuations—suggest that real estate values had remarkably low volatility, which appeared to give real estate superiority over other asset classes in the risk/return tradeoff matrix; this apparent superiority subsequently vanished in the real estate crash of the later 1980s. Yet risk in real estate is complicated. As compared with equities and bonds, where systematic risk predominates and most issues move up and down together, real estate investments have a high degree of specific risk. That is, the choice of the individual holding often counts for more than movements in the real estate market as a whole.

During the 1970s and 1980s, the *Journal* carried a significant number of articles on real estate and portfolio management, most focusing on these kinds of issues. The single representative included here was among the best for illustrating all of these considerations and for explaining the linkages between the world of finance and the real economy.

Real estate: The whole story

We allocate too little to it and pay too little heed to real estate diversification.

Paul M. Firstenberg, Stephen A. Ross, and Randall C. Zisler

Investors traditionally have thought of equity real estate as an inefficient market in which the key to success is in the skill with which an individual investment is selected and negotiated. The general approach seems to be to buy properties when they become available if they look like "good deals," with little regard for the equally important issue of how the acquisition fits with the other holdings in the portfolio and what effect, if any, it will have on the overall risk and return objectives of the portfolio. Only recently have some investors begun to think of the aggregate of their real estate investments as a *portfolio,* with its own overall risk and return characteristics, and to adopt explicit strategies for achieving portfolio goals.

This article takes the view that investors should examine equity real estate investments not only on their individual merits but also for their impact on the investor's overall real estate portfolio. In addition, investors need to assess how the real estate segment fits into their entire portfolio. In turn, this means:
- setting risk and return objectives for the equity real estate portfolio as a whole that are compatible with the goals for the investor's entire portfolio,
- devising a strategy for achieving these objectives, and
- evaluating the extent to which individual transactions conform to the strategy and are likely to further portfolio objectives.

These processes are, of course, familiar to anyone in the business of managing security portfolios. By contrast, there has been a nearly complete neglect of such theory and techniques in the management of real estate portfolios and in their integration into institutional portfolios. This, in turn, has deprived managers of the modern tools that they now employ when considering other financial decisions. Often, for example, the pension fund asset allocation process that results in a decision to "put 10% of the portfolio into real estate" seems governed at least as much by hunch as by any rational mechanism.

Again by way of contrast, probably there is not a single major institutional portfolio in the common stock area that does not make serious use of modern portfolio techniques to continually monitor overall portfolio risk and to assess portfolio performance. These techniques are often the central mechanism for determining management strategy and selecting managers.

While some funds rely much more heavily on quantitative techniques than others do, the implementation of these procedures clearly has moved well beyond the cosmetic and lip service stage. Furthermore, a good general rule is that the larger the portfolio, the greater the reliance on such techniques. This is no doubt a consequence of the realization that even a few good stock picks will have less of an influence on the performance of a $5 billion portfolio than over-

PAUL M. FIRSTENBERG is Executive Vice President of the Prudential Realty Group in Newark (NJ 07101). STEPHEN A. ROSS is Sterling Professor of Economics and Finance at the Yale School of Management in New Haven (CT 06520) and consultant to the Real Estate Research Group at Goldman Sachs & Co. RANDALL ZISLER is Vice President of Goldman Sachs & Co. and director of their Real Estate Research Group in New York (NY 10004). The authors are grateful to William N. Goetzmann of the Yale School of Management for his fine assistance.

189

all structuring decisions will. These decisions include how much to put into different categories of assets or stocks and the overall risk level of the portfolio.

Moreover, within an asset category, the selection of sectors in which to invest is likely to have more impact on results than the choice of individual investments. These types of decisions for real estate are likely to be as critical for performance as a few good individual property "investments" and individual property asset management will be.

Our intention is to show how pension funds and other large investors can use modern portfolio techniques both to construct real estate portfolios and to allocate funds to asset categories including real estate. Our concern, however, is not with a cookbook application of some handy formulas to the real estate market.

Because the real estate market is not an auction market offering divisible shares in every property, and information flows in the market are complex, these features place a premium on investment judgment. Managers who want to own some of IBM simply buy some shares. Managers who want to participate in the returns on, say, a $300 million office building must take a significant position in the property. One alternative is to purchase a share of a large commingled real estate fund, but that does not relieve the fund's managers from the problems of constructing their portfolio.

Our aim is not to eliminate the analysis of each individual property acquisition, but rather to supplement it with a thorough consideration of its contribution to overall portfolio performance. Modern portfolio analysis provides the tool for examining the risk and return characteristics of the overall portfolio and the contribution of the individual elements. The result of its application is a method for selecting properties whose inclusion in the portfolio is of overall benefit.

Before we consider this point in more detail, we examine how real estate performance results compare with those for stocks and bonds. In this analysis, the absence of the large and continuous data record available in the securitized markets presents some special problems.

TOTAL RETURN AND REAL ESTATE DATA

In all modern investment work, the focus of interest is on the total rate of return on assets, that is, the return inclusive of both income and capital gain or loss. The logic underlying this is the basic philosophy of "cash is cash." An investment with a total return of 10%, all from capital gains, is equivalent to one with a total return of 10%, all from income, be-

cause the sale of 9% of the shares in the investment that has risen in value will realize for the holder the same cash as the all-income investment provides. This basic truth, though, does not deny the possibility that, for some holders, there may be an advantage to receiving the return in one form or another.[1]

A real estate fund might rationally have an income as well as a total return objective, yet the transaction cost of selling appreciated property to realize income is particularly severe for real estate. While we recognize that this is an important issue, space considerations do not permit us to deal with it explicitly. Fortunately, too, this is not a serious limitation to our analysis, because the income component of large real estate funds is relatively insensitive to the decision as to how to allocate the funds across different types of real estate.

To determine the total return on real estate or any other asset, we just add the income component and the capital gain or loss. The income component of an asset's return is relatively straightforward to determine, as it is just a cash flow, and good data generally are available for the computation.

The price appreciation component, however, is much more difficult to assess. If an asset is traded in a continuous auction market, like the common stock of a major company, price quotes in the market provide a good method for valuing the asset. Most real estate assets trade infrequently, however, and valuation is more problematic. For some of the commingled funds, appraisals are the only source of property valuations.

The appraisal process merits a paper of its own, but a few points are sufficient for our purposes. Appraisals usually are conducted annually and are based on one of two methods or a combination of the two. If comparable properties have recently been bought or sold, then the appraisal can use their prices as benchmarks for estimating the value of properties that have not been traded. Comparability is increasingly difficult to achieve as the number and complexity of leases increases. Alternatively, the property can be valued by the discounted cash flow (DCF) method of discounting the projected net cash flows at some discount rate determined by prevailing market conditions. Neither of these methods can be as accurate as an actual market price, but there is also no reason to think that they will be biased in the long run. Furthermore, even if appraisals are biased, the appreciation computed from appraisals will not be biased as long as the bias is constant over time.

Although appraisals are not necessarily biased, there is evidence of considerable sluggishness or inertia in appraised values. By any of the common measures of the volatility of returns, real estate returns from appraisals appear to vary far less over time than other asset return series. Standard deviation is a measure of the spread or volatility of investment returns, and we will use the standard deviation also as a measure of the riskiness of real estate returns.[2]

The data below reveal that the standard deviation of stock returns, for example, is over five times greater than that of real estate returns. The extent to which this difference is a consequence of real estate returns actually being far less volatile than stock returns or a consequence of the use of appraisal values is not really known. In the data that follow, we make a correction that raises the volatility of the real estate returns to a level that seems more reasonable to us.

The major sources of data on real estate returns come from commingled funds. We have made use of three series of aggregate real estate returns and a separate series of the returns on different subcategories of real estate. For comparison purposes, we also use returns on other assets such as stocks and bonds. The data and the sources appear in the Appendix.

Table 1 describes how real estate returns have compared with the returns on stocks and bonds and with inflation. As the Frank Russell (FRC) and Evaluation Associates (EAFPI) series are based on appraisals, they might move more sluggishly than a true

market value series — if one were available. The two adjusted series under the FRC heading report the result of alterations in the FRC data designed to recognize this weakness. The "cap-rate adjusted" series estimates the change in value from a DCF model, and the "appraisal adjusted" series adjusts the standard deviation of the series upward.[3]

Even when the standard deviation of real estate returns is adjusted upward, both the return and the standard deviation make real estate an attractive asset category in comparison with stocks and bonds. Its lower risk and its comparable return partially offset the lack of liquidity inherent in real estate investments.[4]

We turn now to the issues involved in managing an equity real estate portfolio and the implications of modern portfolio analysis for real estate.

REAL ESTATE PORTFOLIOS: THE BASIC PRINCIPLES

In an imperfect real estate market, the skill with which individual assets are acquired, managed, and disposed of will be a major determinant of total return. Portfolio management is not a substitute for, nor should it divert attention from, property-specific management. Nevertheless, the composition of the portfolio as a whole will impact both the level and the variability of returns.

The twin considerations of individual property-specific management and portfolio analysis require different human skills and make use of different information. This leads naturally to a two-tiered approach to management:

- A macro analysis that employs portfolio management concepts and focuses on the composition and investment characteristics of the portfolio as a whole, identifying major strategic investment options and their long-run implications. Each property that is a candidate for acquisition or disposition should be analyzed for its impact on overall portfolio objectives.
- A micro analysis that employs traditional real estate project analysis, and focuses on the selection of the individual properties that make up the portfolio, evaluating a property's specific risk–reward potential against the investor's performance targets.

We will not have much to say here about the micro analysis; it is the traditional focus of real estate analysis. We make suggestions for it, but we do not propose changing it. Our interest is in the macro analysis.

Macro analysis derives the characteristics of risk and return for the portfolio as a whole from different combinations of individual property types and

TABLE 1

Real Estate Series and Other Assets

Index	Total Return (%)	Annualized Standard Deviation (%)	Series Begins (*)
Real Estate			
FRC	13.87	2.55	6/78
FRC (cap-rate est.)	13.04	11.28	6/78
FRC (appraisal adj.)	13.87	4.37	6/78
EAFPI	10.78	2.80	3/69
EREIT	22.26	19.71	3/74
Other Assets			
S&P 500	9.71	15.35	3/69
Small Stocks	14.51	23.90	3/69
Corporate Bonds	8.38	11.29	3/69
Government Bonds	7.91	11.50	3/69
T-Bills	7.51	0.82	3/69
Inflation	6.64	1.19	3/69
Risk Premium (spread over T-Bills)			
EAFPI	3.27	2.43	
FRC	4.36	1.29	
S&P 500	1.48	17.54	
Small Stocks	7.38	18.04	

* All series end in December 1985. For details and full titles of each series, see the Appendix.

geographic locations. It establishes the trade-off between the given level of return and the volatility of return that result from different mixes of assets. Selecting the particular risk–return trade-off that best meets an investor's requirements is the most crucial policy decision one can make and is one of our major concerns.

The macro policy is implemented only through the individual selection of properties at the micro level. A thorough analysis of a property should involve an analysis of its marginal contribution to overall portfolio return, volatility, and risk exposure. The difficulty in conducting such an analysis at the individual property level is what gives rise to the separation between the micro and macro analyses. In general, the macro goals are implemented at the micro level by choosing categories of properties to examine with the micro tools, rather than by examining each individual property's marginal effect on the portfolio.

We will employ some familiar principles from modern portfolio theory as guides in portfolio construction:

- To achieve higher-than-average levels of return, an investor must construct a portfolio involving greater-than-average risk. An investor whose risk tolerance is lower than that of the average investor in the market must expect relatively lower returns. Risk may be defined as the variability or dispersion from the mean of future returns or, simply put, the chance of achieving less-than-expected returns. The variability of returns usually is measured by the standard deviation.

- It is possible and useful to measure risk and return and to develop, in an approximate manner, a portfolio strategy that balances the trade-off between these two performance criteria. Because of the difficulty and costs of transacting in the real estate market, and because of the resulting lack of precise "marked-to-market" prices for real estate, it is unrealistic to attempt to fine-tune actual investment decisions in response to risk–return estimates. Even if an investor specifies a preference for a mean return of 15% with a standard deviation of 3%, to a 14% mean return with a standard deviation of 2.5%, translating that preference into a precise strategy is probably not feasible. Broader relationships between risk and return must guide real estate investment strategy.

- The total risk on any investment can be decomposed into a systematic and an unsystematic component. Unsystematic risk will largely disappear as an influence on the return of a well-diversified portfolio. To the extent that the return on an individual property is influenced by purely local events, it is unsystematic and washes out in a large diversified portfolio.[5] A regional shopping center, for example, might find its sales adversely affected by a plant closing. A chain of shopping centers spread across the country, however, would find total revenues unaffected by such local influences. Its revenues would depend on the overall economic conditions that affect costs and consumer demand. An investor who owned many such centers would not be subjected to the ups and downs of individual industries and markets and would be affected only by the general economic conditions that influence all retail businesses simultaneously.

- The risk from changes in economic conditions throughout the country is systematic and will influence any portfolio, no matter how large and well-diversified, because it influences each of the parts. For example, a downturn in consumer demand and a rise in wages will probably adversely affect all business, which means that even a conglomerate would suffer a decline in profits. Systematic risk can be lowered only by lowering long-run average returns. A conglomerate might attempt to lower such risks by implementing a strategic decision to sell some businesses and invest the proceeds in cash securities. The resulting revenues will have less sensitivity to the business cycle but also will have a lower average return. An investor could do the same.

In the sections that follow we will illustrate how investors can apply these principles in portfolio construction by examining how different combinations of property types and economic regions affect the risk and return characteristics of a portfolio.

Investors can reduce the unsystematic and, therefore, the overall risk level of the portfolio without sacrificing return by diversifying real estate investments among property types that have non-covariant returns and across geographic areas or leaseholds that are not subject to the same macroeconomic variables. Diversification also protects the investor from overemphasizing a particular asset class or area of the country that then falls victim to unforeseen, or more often unforeseeable, negative developments.

Spreading assets geographically has been a commonly used rough proxy for selecting areas that are economically non-covariant. A more detailed analysis, however, is required to determine whether geographically separate areas are actually subject to the same macroeconomic variables. The economic base of a particular geographic area may be broad-based, with multiple and widely diversified sources of revenues, or its economy may be largely dependent on a single economic activity. The latter is obviously a riskier area in which to invest, but much of its risk is unsystematic.

As a consequence, a diversified portfolio of areas, each of which is influenced by a different industry-specific risk, can avoid such risk at no cost in returns. For instance, the economies of Houston, Denver, and New Orleans were all highly vulnerable to one variable — oil prices; San Jose, California, Austin, Texas, and Lexington, Massachusetts, are all vulnerable, to a lesser degree, to the fortunes of the high-tech industries. A portfolio made up of properties in these cities is diversified geographically, but subject to significant systematic risks. By contrast, a portfolio made up of properties in Lexington, New Orleans, and, say, New York and Reno would have less overall risk.

This line of reasoning explains the power of diversification across geographic areas whose economies are independent. Within a given city, the same economic forces that influence the business demand for industrial and office space also affect the demand of workers for residential space, the demand of customers for hotel room nights, and the demand of retailers who sell to the workers. Too often, casual real estate market research leads to a claim of urban or regional diversification without an adequate analysis of the inter-industry and inter-occupational linkages affecting returns. Diversifying across different areas lowers risk to the extent to which the economies of the areas are independent of each other. Ultimately, the goal of diversifying a real estate portfolio should be to diversify across leaseholds.

Intuition also suggests that international diversification would be a powerful tool for accomplishing this goal. The question of whether a portfolio with London and New York properties is more economically diverse than a portfolio of Boston and New York is really the question of whether the underlying economy of Boston will move more or less with that of New York than will London.

REGIONAL DIVERSIFICATION

Figure 1 illustrates the trade-off between risk and return that is available when we break real estate investment into different regions and examine various portfolio possibilities for diversifying holdings across the regions. The four regions are the East, the Midwest, the South, and the West.[7] Figure 1 displays all the possible combinations of return and risk available from the different combinations of holdings across these four regions.

The expected return is graphed on the horizontal scale in Figure 1, and the vertical scale gives the standard deviation. The data are all historical.

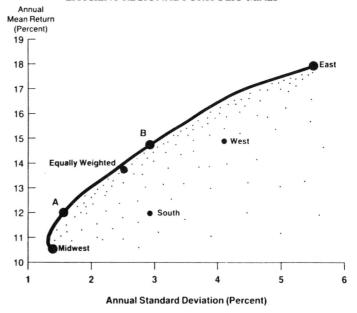

FIGURE 1

EFFICIENT REGIONAL PORTFOLIO MIXES

History is a guide to the future, but this is not to say that the next ten years will mimic the last ten. Rather, we are asking how different portfolios would have performed in the past. We contend that an intelligent look at past risk and return patterns is necessary for an understanding of the future. This, of course, is a weakness of all analysis, whether quantitative or not, but what else can we use to study the future if not the past?

By choosing different combinations of the four regions, all the points in the shaded part of Figure 1 are available. The labeled points describe the four pure regional portfolios. The East alone, for instance, shows a return of 17.9% and a standard deviation of 5.6%. The equally weighted portfolio in Figure 1 gives the return and the risk of a portfolio that puts one-quarter of its investment in each of the four regions.

Table 2 gives the background data underlying Figure 1. Here we have listed the return and standard deviation for each of the regions as well as the correlations in the returns across the four regions. Correlations are interpreted in the usual fashion. A positive correlation between two regions indicates that the returns tend to rise and fall together, and, as the table shows, all the regional correlations are positive. A zero correlation means that the returns tend to move independently of each other. All the correlations are low, and the correlation between the Midwest and the South is nearly zero. Combining asset categories that are only weakly correlated with each other greatly lowers overall portfolio risk. Figure 1 certainly reveals that this is the case for regional diversification.[8]

TABLE 2
Returns by Region, 1978-1985

Region	Annualized	
	Mean Return (%)	Standard Deviation (%)
East	17.91	5.58
Midwest	10.49	1.44
South	11.96	2.92
West	14.83	4.11

Region	Regional Correlation Matrix			
	East	Midwest	South	West
East	1.00	0.16	0.25	0.32
Midwest	0.16	1.00	0.04	0.14
South	0.25	0.04	1.00	0.46
West	0.32	0.14	0.46	1.00

TABLE 3
Efficient Portfolio Mixes by Region (Proportions, %)

East	Midwest	South	West	Mean (%)	Portfolio Standard Deviation (%)
	99		1	10.50	1.43
0%	81	18%	1	10.80	1.31
5	74	17	5	11.30	1.36
9	66	15	9	11.80	1.49
14	59	13	13	12.30	1.67
19	52	12	18	12.80	1.89
23	45	10	22	13.30	2.14
28	38	8	26	13.80	2.41
32	31	7	30	14.30	2.70
37	23	5	35	14.80	2.99
41	16	3	39	15.30	3.30
46	9	2	43	15.80	3.60
51	2	0	47	16.30	3.91
64			36	16.80	4.28
80			20	17.30	4.80
96			4	17.80	5.43

Using Figure 1, we can show that investing the entire portfolio in any single region is unnecessarily risky. For three of the regions, there is a superior alternative that involves combining the regions. The only exception is the all-East portfolio. As it had the highest return in the period used to construct Figure 1 (see Table 2), putting the entire portfolio into the East would have been the best choice, but, of course, we have no basis for assuming that the next ten years would still put the East on top.

As for the other three choices, take, for example, the South. The South had a mean return of 11.96% and a standard deviation of 2.92%. Compare these results with those of Point A, directly above the South on the curve that bounds the possible combinations of return and risk. This point has the same standard deviation of 2.92% as that of the all-South portfolio, yet its return is nearly 15%, or 300 basis points, greater than that of the all-South portfolio. Similarly, Point B, just to the left of the South, is also superior to the all-South portfolio. It has the same return of 11.96% as the all-South portfolio, but its risk level is about 1.5%, or nearly half that of the all-South portfolio. The points on the curve of Figure 1 are called efficient portfolios, because they give the best possible returns for their levels of risk. The points between A and B are efficient portfolios that dominate the all-South portfolio.

Table 3 lists the efficient regional portfolios for each level of return and shows their risk level. These portfolios are the ones that give the returns and standard deviations on the curve in Figure 1. Table 3 provides a great deal of valuable information on the optimal regional diversification of a real estate portfolio.

As we move from low returns to high returns — and higher risk — we see that in the range from an 11.3% return with a 1.4% standard deviation to a

15.8% return with a 3.6% standard deviation, the efficient portfolios diversify to include all the regions. In other words, as we avoid the extremes of the highest returns and risks and the lowest returns and risks, a characteristic of the efficient portfolios is that they are fully diversified. Indeed, as Figure 1 shows, the equally weighted portfolio that puts exactly the same investment into each region is essentially an efficient portfolio with its return of 14% and its standard deviation of 2.3%.

This is as far as this quantitative analysis can take us. At this point judgment takes over. The quantitative analysis can weed out the inferior choices, but, in the end, it cannot make the final choice for the manager. The manager is left with the central question: What combination of risk and return should be chosen and, therefore, which efficient portfolio.?[9] Each investor will have particular requirements for establishing the trade-off between risk and return.

We offer here only some broad considerations. For a publicly-held fund, the basic issue is one of marketing; the combination of return and risk and, therefore, the regional diversification should be chosen according to an evaluation of the clients' demands. For a pension fund, the decision should be based on how the real estate portfolio is expected to contribute to the overall objectives of the fund. We will look at this matter more closely when we consider allocating funds across asset classes, including real estate. When regional diversification and property type diversification are combined, the resulting reduction in risk is considerable.

PROPERTY TYPE DIVERSIFICATION

Figure 2 illustrates the trade-off between risk and return that is available from forming portfolios of the five different property types, and Table 4 gives the data underlying Figure 2. The properties are classified into five major property types: apartments, hotels, office buildings, retail properties including shopping centers, and industrial properties such as warehouses. This classification corresponds both to the available data and to an a priori sensible breakdown into non-covariant business groupings. As we would expect, the efficient portfolios are diversified by property type, but here the results are different from those obtained when we consider regional diversification.

As Table 5 reveals, the efficient portfolios can have as few as two asset types in them. For returns above 16.3%, the efficient portfolios are dominated by hotels and office properties. For the low-risk alternatives, apartments, industrial properties, and retail dominate. At all levels of risk and return, though, some diversification is appropriate.

It is difficult to say to what extent these results predict future patterns and to what extent they are the consequence of the relatively short statistical history. There is reason to believe, though, that we should depend less on the property diversification results than on the regional analysis. For one thing, the numbers themselves are less reliable. The hotel category, for example, is based on a relatively small number of properties, and they are unduly concentrated in New York City. For another, it may well be

TABLE 4
Returns by Property Type, 1978-1985

	Annualized	
	Mean Return (%)	Standard Deviation (%)
Apartments	15.29	3.97
Hotels	18.25	12.08
Industrial	13.63	2.27
Office	15.38	4.72
Retail	11.56	2.19

Property Type Correlation Matrix					
	Apartments	Hotels	Industrial	Office	Retail
Apartments	1.00	0.56	0.41	0.21	0.13
Hotels	0.56	1.00	0.17	0.11	−0.01
Industrial	0.41	0.17	1.00	0.65	0.59
Office	0.21	0.11	0.65	1.00	0.21
Retail	0.13	−0.01	0.59	0.21	1.00

TABLE 5
Efficient Portfolio Mixes by Property Type
(Proportions, %)

Apartments	Hotels	Industrial	Office	Retail	Mean (%)	Portfolio Standard Deviation (%)
4		4		92	11.80	2.10
9		20		71	12.30	1.97
13		36		51	12.80	1.94
18		50	1	31	13.30	2.01
23		61	3	13	13.80	2.18
30		61	9		14.30	2.43
41	2	34	24		14.80	2.81
53	3	7	38		15.30	3.29
38	16		46		15.80	4.03
15	33		53		16.30	5.23
	49		51		16.80	6.67
	67		33		17.30	8.40
	84		16		17.80	10.29
	98		2		18.20	11.88

that some of these returns reflect the economics of relatively tight leasing markets in the late 1970s and early 1980s. Furthermore, fundamental changes in the tax laws since 1986 probably will affect these property types differently.

For these reasons, we would advocate using Table 5 as a rough guide and tend to give greater weight to the middle region where all property types are represented. The final choice of a risk and return trade-off, as with regional diversification, rests with the manager and is governed by the same considerations as affect the regional choice.[10]

IMPLICATIONS FOR PORTFOLIO MANAGEMENT

We conclude from the foregoing analysis of the risk–return characteristics of portfolios constructed with different mixes of property types and geographic regions that:

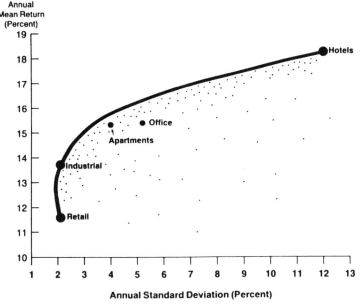

FIGURE 2

EFFICIENT PROPERTY TYPE MIXES

- There is a trade-off between the riskiness (as measured by standard deviation) of a real estate portfolio and the total expected return it generates. Consistent with experience with financial assets, the degree of risk an investor is willing to assume will be the single most important factor in determining return.
- Diversifying the composition of a portfolio among geographic locations and property types can increase the investor's return for a given level of risk. Diversification among holdings with non-covariant returns will reduce risk without sacrificing return. To construct such a portfolio, each investment category identified as offering diversification potential should be represented; the goal should be to have a substantial minimum threshold investment across property types and geographic regions (e.g., no property type or region should be below, say, 15% of the total portfolio).
- There are at least two alternative strategic approaches to diversifying a real estate portfolio. One approach calls for all investments to be made in strict accordance with diversification criteria, even though the assets allocated to different categories may exceed the minimums necessary to gain significant benefits. Under such a strict policy, an investor would not shift allocations because of perceived future changes in the payoffs from different allocations. The investor would modify the initial diversification slowly and generally only in response to some sort of significant long-term change in the marketplace. The assumption underlying this approach is that such modifications always create additional risk and that the investor lacks the forecasting ability to earn sufficient additional return to compensate for the risk.

  The second approach allows for strategic deviations from the strict plan, provided that the threshold minimum allocations are met. Such an approach could reflect an investor's confidence in the ability to project changes in the risk–return differential of various geographic areas or property types. Or it could stem from pursuing a high risk–return strategy of, say, investing in development projects or in less than fully leased properties in currently out of favor markets in the hope of producing results outside of the efficient frontier of Figures 1 and 2. In such cases, the portfolio will reflect the strategic investment selections that deviate from a strict diversification policy, with the expectation that the added risk will be compensated for by additional return. One way to implement such a strategy is to divide the portfolio into a strictly diversified component (a core portfolio) and a higher risk/higher return portion (an opportunity portfolio), with the blend between the two reflecting an overall risk–return target.

  In sum, an investor can target a real estate portfolio to lie at any point along the risk–return continuum; the crucial step is to articulate and explicitly adopt an investment strategy that fits this goal and that both the investor and the investment manager fully understand and agree upon. The strategies to be pursued in managing a real estate portfolio should be explicit, not unspoken.
- We need to learn a good deal more about the factors that, in fact, produce genuine diversification (i.e., non-covariant returns). Present categories of broad geographic regions or property types provide only crude guidelines for achieving efficient mixes. This lack of the proper economic classifications and the accompanying data are the most serious weaknesses of our analysis.

ASSET ALLOCATION: STOCKS, BONDS, AND REAL ESTATE

In principle, the same considerations that govern the construction of the all-real estate portfolio apply to the asset allocation decision. Table 1 gives the basic return and risk information, while Table 6 gives the correlations between real estate and other asset categories.

TABLE 6

Correlations Among Asset Classes*

	FRC	EAFPI	EREIT	S&P 500	Government Bonds	T-Bills	Inflation
FRC	1.00	0.71	−0.14	−0.26	−0.38	0.30	0.38
EAFPI	0.71	1.00	−0.20	−0.28	−0.10	0.54	0.48
EREIT	−0.14	−0.20	1.00	0.78	0.36	−0.23	0.03
S&P 500	−0.26	−0.28	0.78	1.00	0.49	−0.43	−0.15
Government Bonds	−0.38	−0.10	0.36	0.49	1.00	−0.09	−0.35
T-Bills	0.30	0.54	−0.23	−0.43	−0.09	1.00	0.41
Inflation	0.38	0.48	0.03	−0.15	−0.35	0.41	1.00

* For details and full titles of each series, see Appendix.

196

In constructing Table 6, we have treated real estate as a single category, even though different regions or property types will have different relations with other assets. Whenever we aggregate asset classes and consider their relationship with each other as classes, we always lose some of the fine detail. This is true of stocks as well as real estate. As these asset categories are managed as individual classes, however, the separation of management forces the separation of our analysis.[11]

From a portfolio perspective, the great attractive feature of real estate is its lack of correlation with other assets. Even if real estate risk is understated, the lack of correlation makes real estate a particularly attractive feature of a well-diversified portfolio.

Look first at the correlations among the three real estate indexes FRC, EAFPI, and EREIT. The two appraisal-based indexes, FRC and EAFPI, are highly correlated with each other, and both are negatively correlated with the stock market-traded REIT index, EREIT. This striking difference points up the difficulty with the real estate data. Indeed, both FRC and EAFPI are negatively correlated with the stock market as well, while EREIT with a 0.78 correlation with the S&P 500 actually looks like a stock index rather than the other two real estate indexes. (A closer look reveals that individual REITs can behave like the other real estate indexes; it all depends on the particular REIT.) Presumably, the truth lies somewhere between these two, and we can conclude that real estate returns, if not negatively correlated with those on stocks, are at least far from perfectly correlated with them.

One point with which all of the real estate indexes agree, however, is that real estate hedges against increases in inflation. All three indexes are positively correlated with changes in inflation. By contrast, the S&P 500 index has responded negatively to inflation.

Our argument for including real estate as a substantial portion of an overall investment portfolio is, thus, based on its significant diversification value in reducing risk, whatever the goal for returns.

Using the correlation data from Table 6 and the return data from Table 1, we created the efficient frontier of real estate, stocks, and bonds displayed in Figure 3 and tabulated in Table 7. We used the upward adjustment in the standard deviation of real estate in constructing Table 7 so as to avoid any possible underemphasis of its risk. The efficient portfolios in Table 7 display the same characteristics as the efficient portfolios of the real estate categories. In the middle ranges of return and risk, the portfolio is evenly diversified among the three categories, although real

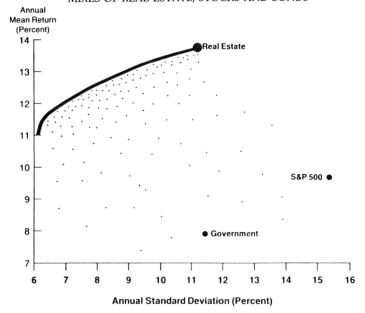

FIGURE 3

MIXES OF REAL ESTATE, STOCKS AND BONDS

TABLE 7

Efficient Portfolio Mixes of Real Estate, Stocks, and Bonds.
Real Estate Standard Deviation 'Cap-Adjusted' = 11.28%
(Proportions, %)

Real Estate (FRC Index)	Stocks (S&P 500)	Government Bonds	Mean (%)	Portfolio Standard Deviation (%)
49	11	40	11.00	6.16
52	12	36	11.20	6.20
55	13	32	11.40	6.29
58	14	28	11.60	6.44
61	15	24	11.80	6.65
65	16	19	12.00	6.91
68	17	15	12.20	7.22
71	18	11	12.40	7.56
74	19	7	12.60	7.94
77	20	3	12.80	8.35
80	20		13.00	8.79
85	15		13.20	9.30
90	10		13.40	9.89
95	5		13.60	10.56
100	0		13.80	11.28

estate has the major share. Insofar as the risk of real estate is still understated by the 11.3% standard deviation, these numbers will overstate real estate's role in an efficient asset allocation.

To examine this matter further, we raised real estate's standard deviation to be the same as that for the S&P 500, 15.4%. The resulting efficient portfolios are given in Table 8. Although the increase in the risk level of real estate lowers its contribution to the efficient portfolios and raises the proportion of bonds, the amount of the change is surprisingly small. For example, the efficient portfolio with a 12% mean return has a 61% holding in real estate when real estate

197

TABLE 8

Efficient Portfolio Mixes of Real Estate, Stocks, and Bonds.
Real Estate Standard Deviation = Stock Standard Deviation = 15.35%
(Proportions, %)

Real Estate (FRC Index)	Stocks (S&P 500)	Government Bonds	Mean (%)	Portfolio Standard Deviation (%)
38	13	49	10.40	7.05
41	15	44	10.60	7.09
44	17	39	10.80	7.19
47	18	35	11.00	7.37
50	20	30	11.20	7.61
53	21	26	11.40	7.91
56	23	21	11.60	8.26
58	25	17	11.80	8.66
61	26	12	12.00	9.10
64	28	8	12.20	9.57
67	30	3	12.40	10.80
71	29		12.60	10.61
76	24		12.80	11.22
80	20		13.00	11.92
85	15		13.20	12.70
90	10		13.40	13.54
95	5		13.60	14.42
100	0		13.80	15.35

is assumed to be as risky as stocks and a 65% holding when real estate is assumed to have a risk level below that of stocks but above its measured level. Of course, this result is dependent upon the limitations of the data and our model.

The important conclusion to draw from this analysis is that, even with an upward risk adjustment, real estate belongs in efficient portfolios at significantly higher levels than the 3.6% allocation for the top 200 public and private funds in 1986. Taking a pragmatic perspective, we feel that pension funds should seek initial real estate asset allocations of between 15 to 20%.

A second level of consideration in choosing among these possible asset allocations makes use of the additional data presented in Table 6, the correlations between asset returns and inflation and interest rates. Similar data can be collected for other major economic variables that influence asset returns, such as real productivity and investor confidence (see Chen, Roll, and Ross, 1986). We can see from Table 6 that real estate is positively correlated with inflation and, at least for the FRC and the EAFPI indexes, it is also positively correlated with interest rates. This is in marked contrast to stock returns, which are negatively correlated with the inflation variable and with interest rates.

This means that real estate returns have been a superior hedge against an increase in inflation or in interest rates, as compared with the experience of the stock market. As inflation or interest rates have risen, the stock market historically has tended to fall, and

real estate returns have tended to rise. Of course, this will depend on the source of the increase in inflation and interest rates. The Monday, October 19, 1987, crash in the stock market produced the opposite result, where sellers of stock ran to the bond market, pushing these prices up. Rather, we are primarily concerned here with a change in stock prices accompanied by a change in inflationary expectations. This differs from a once-and-for-all shift in prices, such as a jump in commodity prices because of formation of a cartel.

A corporate pension fund that is funded ultimately by the earnings of the company would find real estate a relatively attractive asset category if its earnings tend to be negatively related to inflation. For example, suppose that a manufacturing company believes that an increase in inflation brings about a more rapid rise in its wage and material costs than in the prices of its products. A fund with a tilt toward real estate would tend to offset this profit squeeze by rising when corporate earnings fell off.

This does not mean that companies whose earnings rise and fall with inflation should shun real estate. For example, a natural resource company with relatively fixed costs would find its earnings down in a period of low inflation. But the analysis of Tables 7 and 8 is still relevant, and the pension fund of such a company should still hold a significant proportion of its assets in real estate, simply to take advantage of the return and risk diversification characteristics. The proper conclusion to draw is that such a company should hold relatively less real estate than the manufacturing company.

In the end, the allocation decision among the three categories we have studied involves a judgment that is associated with the particular needs of the fund being considered. If, in addition to the considerations of risk and return on which we have focused, there is also a concern for liquidity, this will tend to push the fund toward marketed assets such as stocks and bonds and out of real estate.[12] There is no single answer that is best for all portfolios, only a range of desirable choices. Modern portfolio analysis limits this range to the manageable alternatives presented in Tables 7 and 8.

CONCLUSION

We have shown how modern portfolio analysis can be used both to optimally diversify a real estate portfolio and to allocate overall fund assets among real estate, stocks, and bonds. Real estate is an enormous percentage of world assets, and, as our final tables show, even with an upward risk adjustment, it may belong in efficient portfolios at significantly higher levels, such as 15 to 20%, compared to the 3.6% allocation in 1986 for the top 200 public and private pension funds.

REFERENCES

The two modern portfolio techniques used in the paper are the Capital Asset Pricing Model (CAPM) and the Arbitrage Pricing Theory (APT). Expositions of these approaches can be found in most textbooks on corporate finance. Two references are:

Brealey, Richard, and Stewart Myers. *Principles of Corporate Finance,* 2nd ed. New York: McGraw-Hill Book Company, 1984.

Copeland, Thomas, and J. Fred Weston. *Financial Theory and Corporate Policy,* 2nd ed. Reading, Mass.: Addison-Wesley Publishing Company, 1983.

The following article outlines the APT approach to strategic planning:

Roll, Richard, and Stephen A. Ross. "The Arbitrage Pricing Theory Approach to Strategic Portfolio Planning." *Financial Analysts Journal,* May/June 1984.

Other articles of interest include the following:

Chen, Nai fu, Richard Roll, and Stephen Ross. "Economic Forces and the Stock Market." *Journal of Business,* July 1986.

Hoag, J. "Toward Indices of Real Estate Value and Return." *Journal of Finance,* May 1980.

Miles, M., and T. McCue. "Commercial Real Estate Returns." *Journal of the American Real Estate and Urban Economics Associations,* Fall 1984.

Zerbst, R. H., and B. R. Cambon. "Historical Returns on Real Estate Investments." *Journal of Portfolio Management,* Spring 1984.

[1] Regulatory and accounting conventions may lead to a preference for income over capital gains. Tax issues also influence this preference. Furthermore, some funds may be precluded from realizing income through sales, and, even if they can sell appreciated assets to generate income, the transaction costs of doing so will detract from the return. On the other side, some investors actually may prefer capital gains to income (ignoring tax effects) to avoid being faced with the need to reinvest the cash.

[2] A rule of thumb is that two-thirds of the returns tend to fall within one standard deviation of the mean return and 95% of the returns fall within two standard deviations. The higher the standard deviation, the greater the range of the effective returns, and the greater the probability or likelihood of loss.

[3] The first correction uses a "cap-rate" proxy in place of appraisal returns. Net operating income is a commonly used yardstick for the valuation of real estate. By treating changes in the current income stream as indications of changes in the market value of the asset, we can estimate an appreciation return. Although this approach has a number of problems, at least it allows us to base the estimate of appreciation on known data. The result is an FRC series with an annual standard deviation of 11%.

We generated a series of appreciation returns on the change of an estimated value of the real estate index, where the value is given by the present value of a perpetual stream of income flows. The income flows are taken to be the current period income, and the discount rate can be modeled either as a spread over T-bills, or simply as a fixed rate.

$$Cr_t = \frac{(Ve_{t-1} - Ve_t)}{(Ve_{t-1})},$$

$$Ve_t = D_t/r_t,$$

where:

Cr = cap-rate return

Ve = cap-rate value

D = income per invested dollar

r = discount rate

Y = income return

I = appreciation index value

This simplifies to:

$$Cr_t = \left[\frac{I_t}{I_{t-1}} \cdot \frac{Y_t}{Y_{t-1}} \cdot \frac{r_{t-1}}{r_t} \right] - 1.$$

This method may have some validity, insofar as a similar procedure on the stock market produces estimates near the true value for volatility.

The appraisal-adjusted series is derived from an analysis of the appraisal process and estimates a volatility of returns based on the reported data. This method is an attempt to correct returns by removing any inertia or sluggishness inherent in the appraisal process. True rates of return should be uncorrelated with each other across time. Insofar as there is excessive correlation in the FRC returns, they will not accurately reveal the true return on real estate.

To model the appraisal process, we assumed that a property's appraised value is a mixture of the series of previous appraised values and the appraiser's estimate of the current market price the property would bring if sold. In other words, the appraiser incorporates past appraisals into the current appraisal.

The basis of this estimation is as follows. An estimated mean return can be expressed as the true mean, M_t, and some random error term, e_t:

$$M_t = R_t + e_t,$$

where the standard deviation of e_t is the true standard deviation of returns.

The appraiser can be thought of as combining the true mean return with a lagged return to make the following estimation:

$$E[R_t] = (1 - A)M_t + AR_{t-1}.$$

More generally, the process might use a whole year's worth of past returns in combination with the true mean to produce the current estimation:

$$E[R_t] = (1 - A)M_t + a_1R_{t-1} + a_2R_{t-2} + a_3R_{t-3} + a_4R_{t-4},$$

where

$$A = a_1 + a_2 + a_3 + a_4.$$

A linear regression based on this model yields the following information:

$$R_t = b_0 + b_1R_{t-1} + \ldots + b_4R_{t-4} + z_t,$$

where z_t is the residual error term.

Combining these two equations, we can solve for the true mean and standard deviation from the estimates of b_1, b_2, b_3, and b_4 as follows:

$$b_1 = a_1, \ b_2 = a_2, \ b_3 = a_3, \text{ and } b_4 = a_4,$$

and, therefore, the true mean:

$$M = b_0/(1 - A), \ b_0/(1 - A),$$

where

$$A = b_1 + b_2 + b_3 + b_4,$$

and the true standard deviation of returns is given by:

$$\sigma = \sigma(z_t)/(1 - A),$$

where $\sigma(z_t)$ is the standard deviation of the regression residual, z_t.

[4] We know very little about the effect of illiquidity on investment returns beyond the intuition that liquidity is certainly no worse than illiquidity. As we do not know much more than this, we will adopt the sensible policy of not saying much more.

[5] In practice, real estate managers spend most of their resources investigating local market conditions and negotiating terms of sale. Little if any attention is directed toward the role of a property in the overall portfolio. This is not as misdirected as it might seem. While diversification removes individual and unsystematic property risk, it does not help portfolio returns if misunderstanding the local markets results in overpaying for every property. Nevertheless, without understanding the marginal contribution that properties make to overall portfolio goals, the whole can be less than the sum of the parts.

[6] It is important that property returns be noncovariant, that is, that they not move together, or the risk will be systematic and the advantages of diversification will be lost. For example, a $100-million stock portfolio with 100 holdings of $1 million each will not be terribly well diversified if all of the stocks are utilities.

[7] Data are reported by the Frank Russell Company on a quarterly basis.

[8] We have used the appraisal based returns and have not adjusted the resulting standard deviations in Table 2 and Figure 1, but the possible low volatility of appraisal returns has no effect whatsoever on our analysis. If we were to increase all of the standard deviations by, for example, a factor of two, then this would double all of the numbers on the vertical scale of Figure 1, but all of the points would remain in the same position relative to each other. The analysis of Figure 1 would change only if the appraisals distort volatility by different amounts in the different regions. However, that seems unlikely (not to mention unknowable.)

[9] This is probably a good place to dispel another notion that sometimes surfaces in discussions of risk and return. Often a manager will say that "Risk is important, but over the long run, the risk will wash out and all that will matter is the expected return." This is a misunderstanding of risk and its relation to return and, in fact, both the return and the risk increase over time. The exact form this takes depends on various technical features, but generally over very long periods, the greater the standard deviation of a portfolio's returns, the more likely it is that the value of the portfolio will fall below a given level.

[10] It might have occurred to the reader that we should consider breaking real estate into twenty classifications according to both property type and region. For example, hotels in the West would be one of the twenty classes. This is possible, but we have chosen not to do so because of the small number of properties in some of these classes and the resulting lack of reliability of the figures.

[11] A subtle technical point arises from our focus on constructing efficient real estate portfolios. Because of the different interactions between individual stock categories and real estate, we are not assured that an efficient portfolio of stocks and real estate will make use of an efficient real estate portfolio. In practice, though, the difference will be small and the data are not accurate enough to discern the difference.

[12] Liquidity concerns, however, generally should not be a cause to forgo the diversification of benefits of real estate, because real estate constitutes a small percentage of most portfolios. Other assets can better serve as sources of ready liquidity.

APPENDIX

Data Series and Sources

Source	Data Description
Frank Russell Company (FRC Indexes)	A quarterly time series of equity real estate returns extending from 1978 to the present. The series is broken down by income and capital gains and also by region and property type. Currently, the data base has approximately 1000 properties owned by real estate funds with an average value of about $10 million per property.
Evaluation Associates (EAFPI)	A quarterly time series extending from 1969 to the present. It is an index constructed by an equal weighting of the returns on a number of largely all-equity real estate funds. The data base currently includes about thirty-three tax-exempt funds with a total asset value of about $25 billion.
Gs & Co. Equity REIT Returns (EREIT)	A monthly time series extending from 1974 to the present. It is an equally-weighted index constructed from thirty-three REITs holding more than 80% equity assets. In comparison with the FRC index, EREIT is more heavily concentrated in shopping centers and apartments and less in office properties.
Stock, Bond, and Inflation Data	Ibbotson and Associates provide a comprehensive monthly data base that begins in 1926.

PART FIVE
Fixed Income Portfolio Management

Prior to the 1970s, fixed income securities were simple investment products. Leaving aside the possibility of default by the issuer, the investor knew how much interest would be received periodically and when the amount borrowed would be repaid. This changed in the 1970s with the introduction of mortgage-backed securities. At the same time, the development of option pricing theory highlighted the need to assess these securities in terms of their call option component in a period of volatile interest rates.

Against this background, fixed income managers began to follow the practices of their counterparts in the equity management area and pursue active strategies. Half of the articles published in the Spring 1975 issue of *The Journal of Portfolio Management* (the third issue published) were devoted to fixed income portfolio management. Two of those articles, reprinted in this section, emphasized the dividends from actively managing bond portfolios and the issues that had to be addressed. The article by Madeline Einhorn highlighted a little-known concept

at the time—duration, or exposure to interest rate risk. Subsequent articles carried in the *Journal* elaborated on duration as a measure of interest rate risk, its limitations, and its uses in immunization strategies.

While there was research on term structure theory being published in pure academic journals, these journals did not devote space to the benefits of active bond portfolio strategies and how to control interest rate risk. Since its inception, *The Journal of Portfolio Management* recognized the importance of fixed income portfolio management and devoted considerable space to articles that are now viewed as classics. A good number of articles published by the *Journal* in the 1970s became the core material for the *Chartered Financial Analyst* examination.

The thirteen articles selected for this section constitute only a small fraction of the classic articles published by the *Journal* in this area. Some of the articles included cover topics that also are the focus of other sections—topics such as performance measurement and evaluation and portfolio strategies.

Breaking tradition in bond portfolio investment

If we can identify bonds that are more sensitive than others to interest rate changes, we can achieve improved control of risk in bond portfolios.

Madeline W. Einhorn

All portfolio managers try to minimize the consequences of their bad forecasts and maximize the consequences of their good ones. Not all portfolios, however, can readily absorb the full consequences of bad forecasts, which explains why variability in returns and degrees of risk are now the focus of increasing attention throughout the investment community. But if investors move from stocks to bonds in a search for greater stability in their portfolios,* how certain can they be that their bond portfolio will in fact provide the level of stability they seek? How can they differentiate bonds that are more sensitive to changes in interest rates from bonds that are less sensitive? How can they maximize their bond returns or minimize the risks of bond ownership by selecting bonds that are undervalued in relation to the prevailing interest rate level and structure? In short, is there such a thing as an aggressive bond portfolio in contrast to a defensive bond portfolio?

THE DATA

In an attempt to answer these questions, BEA Associates selected a group of ninety seasoned bonds whose composition would roughly parallel that of the public secondary corporate bond market. The relative proportion of lower rated debt was increased beyond its true existence in the secondary market. For example, bonds rated B and lower constitute only 1% of the total secondary market, but this lower rated group was increased to 4% to establish a better focus. The resulting bond universe, which excluded Canadians, rails, and banks, had the following composition:

Aaa	19 issues	Utilities	47 issues
Aa	30 issues	Finance Companies	10 issues
A	25 issues	Industrials	32 issues
Baa	8 issues	Transportation	1 issue
Ba	4 issues		90
B/CCC	4 issues		
	90		

Each issue in the group had at least $50 million par value outstanding, and all are known names although there was no attempt to select a preponderance of names that trade exceedingly well.

We used July 14, 1972 through March 29, 1974 as our time frame, and we got once-a-week "hard" prices (dealer bids or actual trades) for each bond in the group — ninety weeks of data on ninety bonds. An outside research firm[2] performed statistical tests to analyze the sensitivity of the ninety bonds to changes in the long-term interest rate, using Aa utilities, a traditional benchmark, as a surrogate for the long-term rate. Our aim was to regress or derive the relationships between the bonds based on class and rating.

The most difficult aspect of this study was getting real prices that represented actual trades or dealer bids for size. Many dealers were helpful,[3] but unfortunately they do not all price on the same day of the week. In establishing the data base for each bond of the ninety, interest rate changes on Aa utilities were extracted to conform with the given price changes of the individual bond so there was coincidence in the time periods for pricing and interest rate changes. Observations on price changes that were statistically large or abnormal were filtered out. We found and eliminated only fourteen such observations out of 2,200, indicating that our sample was accurate. Additionally, on the analysis of class and rating, price change observations for periods of time when call protection was inadequate were excluded.

THE CONCEPT OF DURATION

The theoretical backbone of the entire study was the relationship derived by Frederick Macaulay[4] in 1938 which relates the sensitivity of bond price changes to changes in interest rates. Macaulay related

changes in prices to changes in interest rates by a factor he called Duration, developed from the maturity, coupon, and yield characteristics of the bond. Price volatility has a relationship to the length of time of the bond contract, but it is not so much related to the maturity of the contract, which is the date of the final payment, as it is to the series of all payments over the entire life of the contract. The concept of Duration regards the regular coupon payments of a bond as, in a sense, zero coupon serial maturities (equal to the coupon in amount and payment date), with the largest payment occurring at the maturity of the contract (the final payment). The time of each payment is weighted by the present value of that payment; so the concept of Duration is essentially that of present value — weighted time. Duration, described in years, is the sum of the present values of all N coupons of a bond payable at six-month intervals over the length of time to maturity plus the final payment, with each coupon's present value weighted by the period of time it is to be outstanding prior to its payment and related to the present price of the bond.[5]
Where

P_1 = Present value of the first coupon =

$$\text{Coupon} \times \frac{1}{\dfrac{(1 + \text{yield to maturity})}{2}}$$

P_2 = Present value of the second coupon =

$$\text{Coupon} \times \frac{1}{\dfrac{(1 + \text{yield to maturity})^2}{2}}$$

$$P_N = (100 + \text{Coupon}) \times \frac{1}{\dfrac{(1 + \text{yield to maturity})^N}{2}}$$

$$\underset{\text{(in years)}}{\text{Duration}} = 0.5\frac{(P_1)}{P} + 1.0\frac{(P_2)}{P} + 1.5\frac{(P_3)}{P} + \ldots + \frac{\frac{N}{2}(P_N)}{P}$$

The formula that uses Macaulay's Duration to express price sensitivity to interest rate changes is expressed:

$$\frac{\Delta P}{P} = -D\Delta i$$

Where ΔP is the change in the weekly price of the bond
P is the price of the bond
D is Duration
Δi is the change in the interest rate continuously compounded

BETA VERSUS DURATION

We found a few surprising relationships and nonrelationships. First, in structuring a portfolio for sensitivity, the class of the issue, whether utilities, industrials, or finance issues, is relatively unimportant. Column 4 of Chart I shows the average interest rate sensitivity of the bonds by industry type. This beta or sensitivity alone is unrevealing as we know from the yield book that larger price swings in response to an interest rate change occur at longer maturities. Therefore, it is critical to look at sensitivity relative to Duration. The last column of Chart I shows the ratio Sensitivity/Duration, where beta is the measure of sensitivity, and Duration, stated in years, is the

CHART I

SECONDARY MARKET CORPORATE BONDS

Analysis of Interest Rate Sensitivity by Class

Theoretical Relationship: $\dfrac{\Delta P}{P} = -D\Delta i$

Regression Model: $\dfrac{\Delta P}{P} = \alpha + \beta \Delta i$

Class Description	Number of Issues	Average Correlation Coefficient	Average Interest Rate Sensitivity, β	Average Duration, D (years)	Total Variability	Sensitivity Duration Ratio $(-\beta/D)$
Utilities	47	0.554	−3.84	11.24	8.08	.341
Finance	10	0.552	−3.06	8.67	5.93	.353
Industrials	32	0.538	−3.07	10.35	8.65	.296
Transportation	1	0.457	−2.84	7.15	6.21	.398
Total	90	0.547	−3.47	10.59	8.02	.327

time factor weighted by the present value of each payment of a stream of payments. It can be seen that the Sensitivity/Duration ratios are quite similar to each other, although industrials appear to be very slightly cushioned. A relative scarcity of industrial names during our period of study, mid-1972 through the first quarter of 1974, probably contributed this cushioning effect.

SENSITIVITY VERSUS RATING AND CALL FACTORS

We corroborated another thesis that had been only intuitive: sensitivity declines with a decline in rating, especially for the Ba and B categories. Looking at column 6 of Chart II, it can be seen that the B rated bonds had the greatest total variability, i.e., the ratio of the standard deviation of the change in price to the standard deviation of the change in the interest rate. We can say that that portion of variability related to interest rate changes diminishes while total variability increases.

We tested the impact of call protection on price sensitivity and found, as we had expected, that a price to call price ratio of greater than one has a significant dampening effect on price movements in response to interest rate changes. However, what is surprising is that while price/call price is critical, the factor of *time* to call apparently has no effect on sensitivity.

Chart III shows price to call versus years to call for 2,300 observations. This chart enabled us to divide the ninety bonds into classes to analyze call protection. The bonds were divided into six classes; the first three classes have price/call price ratios greater than one as follows:

Class I: less than one year to call
Class II: one to three years to call
Class III: more than three years to call

From a regression analysis of these classes it turns out that Classes I, II, and III are insensitive to interest rate changes. Before this study we would have expected bonds with little call protection to have little sensitivity, and we would therefore have assumed that Class I would be insensitive. But we would not have expected Classes II and III, which have longer call protection, to be insensitive. It might be surmised that bonds in Classes II and III could be found to be sensitive to short-term interest rates rather than to changes in the long-term interest rate, but this would imply a strong assumption of a decline in long rates of such magnitude that many of the bonds in Classes II and III would be refunded at the end of their respective call protection periods.

Class IV has a price/call price ratio of 0.8-1.0 with less than one year to call.
Class V has a price/call price ratio of 0.9-1.0 with one to three years to call.
Class VI contains all else.

CHART II

SECONDARY MARKET CORPORATE BONDS

Analysis of Interest Rate Sensitivity by Rating

Theoretical Relationship: $\dfrac{\Delta P}{P} = -D \Delta i$

Regression Model: $\dfrac{\Delta P}{P} = \alpha + \beta \Delta i$

Rating	Number of Issues	Average Correlation Coefficient	Average Interest Rate Sensitivity, β	Average Duration, D (years)	Total Variability	Sensitivity Duration Ratio $(-\beta/D)$
AAA	20	0.608	-4.12	11.50	6.85	.358
AA	30	0.609	-4.22	10.77	7.25	.392
A	25	0.507	-3.04	10.45	8.00	.291
BAA	7	0.459	-3.51	10.79	8.64	.325
BA	4	0.353	-2.07	7.22	7.10	.287
B	4	0.125	1.47	8.65	19.65	-.169
Total	90	0.547	-3.47	10.59	8.02	.327

Chart III

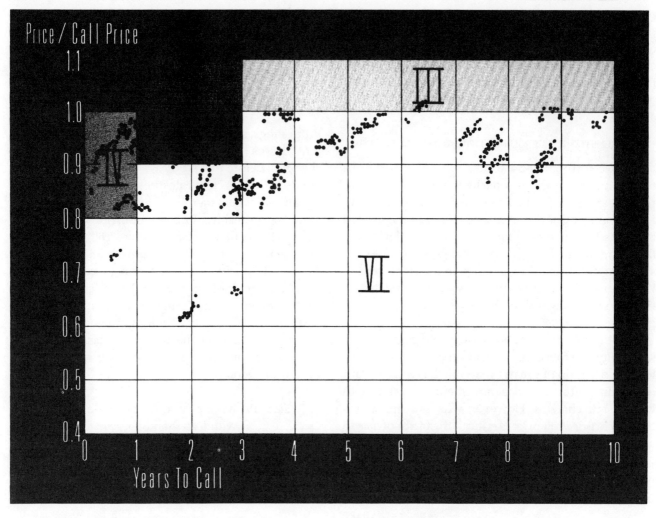

Chart IV shows the regression of interest rate sensitivity computed from price changes against theoretical sensitivity computed from the formula which uses Macaulay's Duration. The sensitivities should be roughly equivalent to minus average Duration. Looking at Chart IV, bonds with a Duration of twelve years should have a sensitivity of −12, but it can be seen that this is not the case. Correlation is about 51%, which is not as high as we would expect but it is meaningful, suggesting that interest rate sensitivities are indeed proportional to Macaulay's Duration. Macaulay's Duration efficiently integrates yield, coupon, and length of maturity in the appraisal of the sensitivity of prices to interest rate changes.

THE ELUSIVE INTEREST RATE BENCHMARK

It follows from this study that our traditional benchmark for long interest rates, the long Aa utility rate, should be scrapped because it is plagued by imprecision. The Aa utility rate is an estimate of the long-term interest rate, and it changes primarily because of inflation expectations with concomitant leads and lags of greater and lesser variation dependent on constantly shifting economic, political, and social values.

There must certainly be errors in the reporting of the Aa rate. Firstly, how many times have we known a deal was "hung up" only to read the next morning in the newspapers that the issue was 85-90% sold! Secondly, errors in the independent variable, the Aa utility rate in our study, cause systematic downward biases in slope estimates in regression analysis. The systematically lower slopes, i.e., about one-third expectations in large numbers, indicate substantial error in the *observed* (reported) Aa utility rate as a surrogate for "the" interest rate.[6]

This bond sensitivity study confirmed certain precepts we knew intuitively. When gearing for total return performance in the secondary corporate bond market, it makes almost no difference whether we structure a portfolio in terms of rating or industry class — what is important is to be fully invested or to open-end the portfolio. For total return it is not relevant how long a bond's call protection period is when the price and call price are within 20% of each other; what is important is the absolute price level.

CHART IV

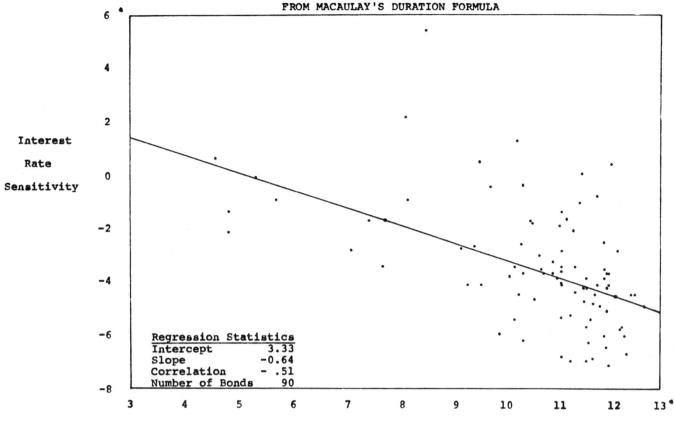

REGRESSION OF INTEREST RATE SENSITIVITY COMPUTED FROM
PRICE CHANGES AGAINST THEORETICAL SENSITIVITY COMPUTED
FROM MACAULAY'S DURATION FORMULA

Interest
Rate
Sensitivity

Regression Statistics
Intercept   3.33
Slope   -0.64
Correlation   - .51
Number of Bonds   90

Duration   (Years)

Consequently, it is apparent that we need a proxy for "the" long-term interest rate. We plan to use the existing data base on the ninety bonds of this study, add long U.S. Treasury bonds and long U.S. Agency bonds, and schematize a system of several long issues which might more closely approach a satisfactory proxy for "the" interest rate than any specific benchmarks or long rates used heretofore. Using the system already designed for this study, we plan to divide the bonds in groups which will enable us to test our derived scheme of rates during a lengthy observation period.

CALCULATING RELATIVE VALUATION

In recent years, much credibility has been attributed to yield spread analysis, and large volumes of trading in corporate bond portfolios occurred as a result of the analysis of what were regarded as typical yield spread relationships. After the Arab oil embargo in October, 1973, the question arose whether Aa and A utilities would ever again experience their traditional relationship to Aaa telephone bonds and Aaa-A industrial bonds. With inflation rampant in the economy, the question of an operating utility's yield level status *vis-à-vis* other publicly traded debt issues

became a sharper one.

In a chaotic environment for all financial markets, historical precedents and traditional relationships lose their lustre. If the fundamentals of an industry are known and understood and if a portfolio manager understands the strengths and weaknesses of a specific bond issue in an industry, then it is desirable to try to establish that bond's price movements in relation to interest rate movements. Any bond's Duration can be calculated, and if we assume that our surrogate scheme of rates is relatively close to the true interest rate in the marketplace, we can assess whether a bond is trading at fair value in the market. Since the price sensitivity of a bond equals minus Duration, again referring to the formula which incorporates Macaulay's relationship:

$$\frac{\Delta P}{P} = -D\Delta i$$

we can see if a specific bond is overvalued or undervalued with respect to interest rate changes.

If in one week Δi = + 10 Basis Points or +0.10%
Duration of a Bond = 10
$\therefore \Delta P$ should = −1%

207

The use of the concept of Duration would enable a portfolio manager to avoid many of the vogues and possible pitfalls inherent in historical yield spread analysis. However, fundamental analysis in bond selectivity is just as crucial.

Using a schematized group of rates which might more closely approximate the true rate, it may be possible to establish historical sensitivities for certain actively traded issues, and we might then start to deal in preliminary fashion with the ultimate solution to the problem of volatility in bond portfolios.

* Experience does justify this expectation. For the five years 1970-74, the Salomon Brothers High Grade Corporate Bond Performance Index and the two BEA Associates, Inc. Indices showed standard deviations ranging from 40% to 48% of the standard deviations of the S&P 500 and the NYSE Composite Index. See also footnote 1.

[1] The Salomon Brothers High Grade Corporate Bond Index is a total return index comprised of 100 long-term bond issues, rated Aa-Aaa, each with a minimum of $25 million par value outstanding. The index is weighted by market value.

The BEA Associates Industrial Bond Index is a total return index comprised of twenty long-term industrial bond issues rated Baa-Aaa, each with a minimum of $70 million par value outstanding. The BEA Utility Bond Index is a total return index comprised of fifteen long-term utility bond issues, rated Baa-Aaa, each with a minimum of $65 million par value outstanding ($45 million on pipeline issues). The composition of the two BEA Indices is approximately 80-85% A-Aa; the indices are unweighted.

[2] Dennis A. Tito of O'Brien Associates, Inc., Santa Monica, California, designed the system for the study.

[3] Miss Emily L. Meschter of BEA Associates provided invaluable assistance in this study. She gathered the prices from participating dealers and was responsible for codification of all input data. The Chemical Bank of New York contributed needed price histories. Dealers who participated by providing prices included:

Bear, Stearns & Co.
A. G. Becker & Co., Inc.
Blyth Eastman Dillon & Co., Inc.
Dillon, Read & Co., Inc.
Drexel Burnham & Co., Inc.
The First Boston Corporation
Goldman, Sachs & Co.
Kuhn, Loeb & Co.
Lehman Brothers, Inc.
Loeb, Rhoades & Co.
Mabon, Nugent & Co.
Merrill Lynch, Pierce, Fenner & Smith, Inc.
R. W. Pressprich & Co.
Smith, Barney & Co., Inc.
Wertheim & Co., Inc.

[4] Frederick R. Macaulay, *Some Theoretical Problems Suggested by the Movements of Interest Rates, Bond Yields and Stock Prices in the United States since 1856* (New York: National Bureau of Economic Research, 1938).

[5] Because of the infinite number of terms, it can be seen that the Duration of a perpetual bond approaches a number equal to one divided by the coupon. For example, a perpetual bond bearing an 8% coupon would have a Duration of 12½ years (1 ÷ 8). For a zero coupon bond, Duration equals maturity. For bonds other than zero coupon, Duration must be less than maturity.

[6] Using the X-axis to plot the independent variable (the reported values of the Aa utility rate), to the extent that the reported values contain error the plot points will "stretch" or expand horizontally the line of best fit (the least squares regression line), so that the entire slope will be lowered. This would be the case even if the Aa rate were overstated or understated, since the independent variable is concerned with changes in the Aa rate, not the level of the rate.

The dividends from active bond management*

The path to stable bond returns lies neither in principal protection nor in income lock-ups, but in active alternation between them.

Kenneth R. Meyer

The pension fund industry is experiencing a staggering amount of change brought on by a complex array of events. New demands from the recently enacted pension fund legislation, significantly higher levels of pension fund costs, new issues of portfolio accounting, and newly perceived liquidity requirements are just a few of the factors forcing corporate trustees and investment managers alike to reassess long established investment philosophies and objectives.

Manager recognition of the long-term nature of the pension fund liability is dictating extended time horizons for fund performance evaluation. Mediocre manager performance in disastrous equity markets has forced trustees to revaluate return objectives that stressed maximization of total return without regard to any stated minimum required return. Indeed, fund managers may now be shifting their priorities to insure that the fund can meet all current actuary requirements and, only *within* that constraint, seek to reduce costs (or increase benefit levels) by assuming higher levels of portfolio risk.

To some the fixed income security has become the panacea for all problems. These securities have not only provided far more pleasant rates of return than equities in recent years; they also appear to fit so neatly into this new orthodoxy of pension fund management objectives. This is particularly true with current coupons of 8% and more on long and even intermediate bonds. The coupons are contracted for at the time of purchase, they are currently comfortably in excess of most actuarial requirements, and active bond management may even be able to achieve some incremental return that would go a long way to reducing corporate pension costs.

But, alas, the world is just not that simple. Since interest rates are seldom stable for very long, the de-velopment of fixed income strategy for a pension fund is no simple matter. This article will analyze four fixed income management alternatives, attempt to point out serious inconsistencies in the application of three of them, and, most importantly, suggest a fixed income approach that is consistent with the developing changes in corporate pension fund objectives.

THE FIXED INCOME SECURITY

The value of a fixed income security is simply the sum of its coupon payments and the principal payment at maturity discounted back at some rate or series of rates over time. Equation 1 mathematically expresses the present value of a fixed income security.

$$P_1 = \sum_{i=1}^{n} \frac{c/2}{(1 + r)^i} + \frac{P_n}{(1 + r)^n}$$

P_1 = Present Value of Bond (Market Value)
C = Coupon (c/2 = semiannual coupon payment)
P_n = Principal Payment at Maturity
n = Maturity (number of years)
r = Discount Rate
i = Time Period

If one were to buy a bond and hold it to maturity, an analysis of this equation yields an interesting result. At the time of purchase, all factors in the equation are fixed except the discount rate "r." The coupons (c) are fixed at time of purchase; P_n will equal the par value of the bonds purchased; "i" and "n" are fixed time periods.

If this same bond is not expected to be held to maturity, P_n does become a variable. However, changes in P_n for a specified time period "n" are relatively insignificant when discounted back to present value over a long period of time. By comparison,

* This article was developed from a speech delivered by Mr. Meyer to the Second Institutional Investor Bond Conference, October 8, 1974.

changes in the discount rate "r" will have a very significant impact on the present value of the bond.

The most familiar definition of "r" is yield to maturity or, more generally, the level of interest rates at time of purchase. At the time of purchase, it is the discount rate that determines the present value of the expected coupon and principal payments. This yield to maturity figure is often taken to mean the equivalent of the expected total rate of return from the bond. In fact, the total rate of return of a bond held to maturity will equal the initial yield to maturity (r) only if all coupon payments are reinvested at "r."[1] Thus, "r" is also the reinvestment rate or series of reinvestment rates that exist at each coupon payment date.

At maturity or at the time of sale when all factors in the equation are known, "r" quantifies the total rate of return experience of the bondholder.

Thus, the very definition of a corporate bond reasserts the obvious but often forgotten conclusion that the actual investment return experience of any given bond or portfolio of bonds and its contribution to the attainment of the stated pension fund objective are directly related to the level of interest rates over time.

SHORT AND INTERMEDIATE MATURITIES

The first alternative would be to invest the portfolio primarily in cash equivalents and/or intermediate maturities. Essentially, this portfolio might be invested entirely in five-year instruments or shorter. As a result of the short average life of the portfolio, the fund is very well insulated from the impact of market risk for a specified period of time. In addition, the investment return of the fund can be reasonably well predicted over its average life. Given recent market experience, it is no surprise then that some pension funds have adopted this alternative.

However, the apparent "risk-averse" nature of this alternative is illusory at best if it is evaluated within the context of the real time horizon of the pension fund. The inconsistency between the average maturity of the short-term portfolio and the long-term pension fund objective creates a significant amount of reinvestment risk. Large segments of the fund assets will be reinvested at frequent intervals in the future at unspecified interest rate levels. The magnitude of this risk is illustrated in Table I.

If, for example, a fund generates an 8% investment return for a five-year period and then must reinvest all proceeds at the end of the fifth year at 6% for the next fifteen years, that fund will experience an investment return of only 6.5% compounded annually for the twenty-year period. Clearly, the reinvestment risk implied by investing all or substantially all of the

TABLE I

PRINCIPAL REINVESTMENT RISK

Average Return Experience First 5 Years	Average Return Experience Next 15 Years			
	4	6	8	10
4	4.0%	5.5%	7.0%	8.5%
6	4.5	6.0	7.5	9.0
8	5.0	6.5	8.0	9.5
10	5.5	7.0	8.5	10.0

assets of a pension fund at frequent intervals is significant and is directly related to the future levels of interest rates. By its very nature, this investment approach implies a very basic, fundamental investment decision that interest rate levels are going to remain constant or increase over time. Yet, in many instances, the funds that have adopted this alternative are those which want to eliminate the market risk of interest rate fluctuations.

THE LOCK-UP CONCEPT

Another portfolio alternative would be to "lock-up" a rate of return by buying long-term bonds with the intention of holding them to maturity at yield levels in excess of the current actuarial assumption. In fact, the lock-up concept is being considered by some as a convenient way to increase their plan's actuarial assumption.

But, again, the world is not that simple. The primary uncertainty or risk centers around "r," here defined as the reinvestment risk related to the reinvestment of the coupon stream. In order to realize an effective total rate of return over the life of the bond equal to the yield to maturity at the time of purchase, the stream of coupons must be reinvested at that yield to maturity.

The magnitude of this reinvestment risk is large and increases as the level of interest rates increases. This is indicated in Table II.

TABLE II

INCOME REINVESTMENT RISK

30-Year Par Bond with Coupon of:	% of Total Return Represented by Interest on Interest*
7%	69.5%
8	74.8
9	79.3
10	83.0

* All coupons reinvested at coupon level.

A 10% thirty-year corporate bond can be purchased at par in the market today. Over the life of this bond, a surprisingly large 83% of the total dollar income is generated by the reinvestment of the coupon stream

1. Footnotes appear at the end of the article.

alone. Expressed in broader terms, the largest proportion of the total dollar return of a bond will be determined by future levels of interest rates not known at the time of purchase.

Obviously, then, the future level of interest rates will dramatically impact the total rate of return of a particular bond or portfolio of bonds. Again using the example of the 10% thirty-year bond purchased at par, the total rate of return over the life of the bond will equal 10% only if the reinvestment rate (r) is 10% (Table III). If the reinvestment rate were to decline to 8%, the real return over the thirty-year period would be reduced to 8.7%.

TABLE III

IMPACT OF THE REINVESTMENT RATE
ON TOTAL RETURN

Assumed Reinvestment Rate	Total Rate of Return	
	8% 30-Year Bond at 100	10% 30-Year Bond at 100
4%	5.8%	6.4%
6	6.8	7.5
8	8.0	8.7
10	9.3	10.0
12	10.6	11.4

In addition to the reinvestment risk associated with the income stream, principal reinvestment risk also exists in the "lock-up" portfolio. The existence of call features on most high coupon long bonds could produce a significantly shorter average portfolio maturity if interest rates decline. The existence of a sinking fund would have a similar impact. This call risk and its impact on future realized portfolio return is similar to the principal reinvestment risk discussed in Alternative I.

In summary, the lock-up alternative of buying long bonds with the expectation of holding to maturity also implies an inconsistency. It has been shown here that future levels of interest rates are prime determinants of portfolio investment return. Yet the very definition of "lock-up" at time of purchase and the inflexibility of a buy-and-hold strategy do not recognize the uncertainty of future interest rate levels.

ACTIVELY MANAGED LONG-TERM PORTFOLIO

The third alternative would be to actively manage a long-term bond portfolio. Its proponents generally believe that interest rate cycles cannot be accurately forecast on a consistent basis, and therefore rate anticipation swapping would, at best, be unproductive. Rather, the portfolio manager should concentrate his or her analytical effort and trading activity in the long-term market to take advantage of recurring value disparities.

This strategy approach is the most glaringly deficient of the three. The income reinvestment risk inherent in any long-term fixed income security exists in the actively managed long-term portfolio. It cannot be reduced or eliminated through trading activity. Ostensibly, this trading activity can produce incremental rate of return extraneous to general interest rate movements. Examples of bond trading activity that might fit within this definition are listed below:

LONG BOND
TRADING ALTERNATIVES

Coupon Differentials
Quality Spreads
Types of Issuer
Differential Call Features
Sinking Funds

Upon proper analysis, one must conclude that although the types of trading activity indicated here can be productive, the rate of return contribution of each will be primarily a function of the beginning and ending level of interest rates. Again, a serious inconsistency exists. This investment philosophy attempts to isolate the portfolio from cyclical movements in interest rates by investing in long maturities. Yet, its primary contribution to incremental rate of return is generated by trading activities that are sensitive to short-term changes in interest rate levels.

TOTAL FIXED INCOME MANAGEMENT

For purposes of discussion, the fourth alternative might be termed Total Fixed Income Management. Total Fixed Income Management can be defined as an active bond management philosophy which requires that: 1) major asset shifts be made between maturity sectors in response to the cyclical movement of interest rates, and 2) all sector analysis and trading activity be assessed within a specific interest rate environment. Simply stated, all portfolio activity is directly related to expected interest rate changes. It is the only alternative in which the development of investment strategy is consistent with the level of portfolio risk implied by future changes in interest rate levels.

Consistently accurate forecasting of interest rate changes and effective translation into portfolio strategy would obviously produce spectacular investment returns for such a fortunate bond manager. The inverse would be equally disastrous for the particularly inept manager. Neither case is likely to occur. In all likelihood, some combination of these experiences would be the most reasonable assumption. Accordingly, in order to test the rate of return and risk implications of Total Fixed Income Management over a wide spectrum of possible outcomes, a simple bond portfolio simulation model was developed.

The composition of the model portfolio is indicated in Table IV.

TABLE IV

MODEL PORTFOLIO COMPOSITION

1975 – 1978
   ABC — 5-15-77

1979 – 1988
   DEF — 5-1-84
   American Telephone & Telegraph Co. 4⅜% 4-1-85

1989 – 1997
   JKL — 5-1-94
   Caterpillar Tractor Co. 5.30% 4-1-92

1998 & Over
   XYZ — 5-1-04
   American Telephone & Telegraph Co. 5⅛% 4-1-84
   Standard Oil of California 7% due 4-1-96
   Weyerhaeuser Company 8⅝% 10-1-00

The yield curve was segmented into four maturity groups. The portfolio consisted of nine individual bond issues, four of which are theoretical bonds. Each theoretical bond was assigned a coupon equal to the starting yield level of each simulation. The yield levels of the theoretical bond within each maturity category were priced off the basic long-term current coupon bond (XYZ-04), reflecting a reasonable yield curve formation. Initial yield levels from 6% to 10% on the long-term bond were analyzed in order to assess the impact of changing yield levels on bond portfolio performance. Market changes of 0, ±100, and ±200 basis points over one, two, and three-year time horizons were hypothecated.

Five possible portfolio weightings were used in addition to a market weighted portfolio. These portfolio weightings are outlined in Table V.

TABLE V

PORTFOLIO ALTERNATIVES
(Including Cash)

	Market Weighted	A	B	C	D	E
1974	1%	60%	55%	40%	25%	5%
1975 – 1978	20	10	10	10	10	5
1979 – 1988	23	15	10	15	10	5
1989 – 1997	35	5	10	15	35	20
1998 & Over	21	10	15	20	20	65

The market weighted portfolio was derived from *The Anatomy of a Secondary Bond Market In Corporate Bonds.*[2]

It excludes government debt with maturities less than three years and is weighted by par value. The five portfolio weightings represent what was thought to be a reasonable progression of portfolio decisions over a complete interest rate cycle. Within this time framework, the Total Fixed Income manager would be capable of moving from a 60% short position to a portfolio 85% invested in maturities ≥ 15 years.

Because of the complexity of the model, the discussion of the results will necessarily have to be simplistic. The results generated on the 8% starting yield level model are reasonably indicative of the overall results of the study and will eliminate the need to wade through the large number of calculations and portfolio return possibilities.

The results of the 8% market simulation model for the two extreme portfolio structures (A = 60% cash equivalents, E = 85% long maturities) are summarized in Table VI. Incremental compound annual rates of return measuring the total rate of return of the particular portfolio against the market weighted portfolio are summarized in the table. These results exclude any contribution from the cash equivalent position.

TABLE VI

TOTAL RATE OF RETURN VARIANCE
(8% Starting Yield Level)

	Portfolio A vs. Market			Portfolio E vs. Market		
	1 yr.	2 yr.	3 yr.	1 yr.	2 yr.	3 yr.
−200	−2.0	(−0.9)	−0.6	5.3	[2.7]	1.8
−100	−0.9	−0.5	−0.3	2.6	1.3	1.0
—	—	—	0.1	—	0.2	0.3
+100	0.9	0.5	0.4	−1.6	−0.7	−0.4
+200	1.6	[0.8]	0.5	−3.2	(−1.6)	−1.0

If one assumes an interest rate cycle of four years in duration with interest rates increasing from 8% to 10% over the first two years and decreasing 200 basis points to 8% over the last two years, perfect portfolio strategy would require owning portfolio A as interest rates rose and then shifting to portfolio E at the end of the second year. The compound annual rate of return generated by portfolios A and E respectively are boxed in. For the four-year cycle, perfect portfolio strategy would have produced a 1.8% compound annual rate of return in excess of the market portfolio. The particularly inept portfolio manager would have generated a −1.3 incremental return to the market as indicated by the circled numbers. In the latter case, the negative spread to the market portfolio would be moderated to the extent that the cash equivalent position generates some investment return.

The results of the simulation model indicate that a consistent application of a portfolio strategy that responds to changing interest rate levels will produce rate of return experiences within acceptable limits of variation. The spreads of +1.8 and −1.3 represent the extreme points of expected return variation. In fact, the normal inefficiencies of policy implementation, the expectation that investment decision making will not be perfect and that normal fixed income decision making patterns take the form of numerous decisions rather than the extreme A-E and E-A type, would imply smaller return variations than those in Table VI.

Based on this initial analysis, one must conclude that the consistent application of Total Fixed Income Management would:

1. Create the potential for incremental rate of return by recognizing the need for portfolio strategy flexibility in a dynamic interest rate environment.
2. Produce a level of portfolio risk that would allow for accurate corporate pension fund planning and useful long-term projections of portfolio return.

SUMMARY

If interest rates could reasonably be expected to remain constant or increase or decrease in a straight-line pattern, the fixed income security would indeed be the panacea for all of the pension fund manager's problems. The future investment return stream of the bond portfolio would be highly predictable; the fund's ability to meet current actuary requirements would be immediately measurable; and a true consistency between the predictable investment return and the calculated cost requirements of the fund would result.

Unfortunately, interest rates are not stable over time, a fact that has more than adequately been demonstrated in the past five to six years. Unless this un-certainty of future rate levels is integrated into a fixed income management philosophy, a fundamental inconsistency will exist.

The short-term investment alternative is widely accepted as a risk-averse strategy that isolates the portfolio from interest rate movements. Yet, it was shown earlier in this article that future levels of interest rates can significantly impact the investment return of the short-term portfolio over a long period of time.

The long-term investment alternatives subject the bond portfolio to both principal and income reinvestment risks, the magnitude of which is a function of unknown future levels of interest rates. Yet neither of these long bond alternatives allows sufficient flexibility for the manager to react to changing levels of interest rates.

These inconsistencies can be resolved only through an investment philosophy that recognizes the uncertainty of future interest rate levels and requires that all investment activity be made within the context of a specific interest rate framework.

One can hardly conclude, then, that fixed income securities provide a simple solution to the attainment of long-term pension fund objectives. The very definition of a corporate bond implies the need for the fixed income manager to make an unending series of value decisions among a complex array of fixed income alternatives in a dynamic interest rate environment.

[1] For a more complete discussion of this topic, see *Inside the Yield Book*, Chapter 1, Sydney Homer and Martin L. Leibowitz, Ph.D., Prentice Hall, New Jersey, 1972.
[2] Henry Kaufman, *The Anatomy of a Secondary Bond Market In Corporate Bonds*, Salomon Brothers, New York, 1973.

Duration as a practical tool for bond management*

By explicitly timing the investor's cash returns, this concept provides superior measures of risk and return for individual bonds and bond portfolios.

Richard W. McEnally

In 1938 Frederick R. Macaulay presented the concept of duration as a measure of a bond's life and suggested it might be superior to more conventional measures for purposes of fixed income security analysis.[1] Since that time others have discovered a number of additional applications for the concept in bond portfolio management.[2] Its practical use to date has been minimal, however.

Two factors appear to account for this situation: the lack of familiarity of duration and its applications and the inability to calculate duration values quickly and at a low cost. The recent advent of comparatively inexpensive hand-held calculators with programmable capabilities has obviated the latter problem. The purpose of this article is to attack the former difficulty by reviewing the concept of duration and its applications in bond portfolio management.

THE BASIC IDEA

The most common measure of the time dimensions of a debt instrument is its term of maturity, but this measure is flawed for many purposes. Its major weakness is its concentration on the timing of the single last cash payment without any consideration whatsoever to all others.

By way of example, consider two loans of the same life, one with no repayment prior to maturity and the other with a repayment schedule that results in retirement of 90% of the loan prior to final maturity. The lender is likely to have a much different view of these loans in assessing his exposure to adverse events over their life. Term to maturity ignores the rate at which the original principal is returned to the lender. To cope with this problem some lenders, such as life insurance companies active in the private placement market,

routinely compute a weighted average term to maturity, which scales the time of each repayment by the proportion of the original loan the repayment constitutes.

A similar but somewhat more subtle problem arises with the rate of return of value on bonds even when there is no sinking fund provision. The two bonds in Table 1 illustrate this issue. Here we have two bonds, each with a twenty-year term to maturity and each selling to yield 8% per annum to maturity. Bond A is priced at par while Bond B sells at a substantial discount because its coupon is only 4%. As the table shows, much more of Bond A's total present value or current price than B's (78% versus 65%) is associated with the value of coupons received along the way.

Table 1

Price Determination of Two Twenty-Year Bonds

	Bond A – 8% coupon YTM of 8.0%		Bond B – 4% coupon YTM of 8.0%	
Present Value of Coupons	$785.44	78.5%	$392.72	64.7%
Present Value of Repayment at Maturity ($1000)	214.56	21.5	214.56	35.3
Total Present Value = Present Price	$1000.00	100.0%	$607.28	100.0%

Note: Based on annual discounting and coupon receipt.

Correspondingly, the value of the $1000 repayment at maturity is much more important for Bond B than for Bond A (35% versus 22% of total value). Therefore, in a very real sense, Bond A has the shorter maturity, the present value of its cash flows being weighted much more heavily towards the near term.

We have all had it pointed out to us at one time

1. Footnotes appear at the end of the article.

* The author gratefully acknowledges the interest and support of members of the N.C. Institute for Investment Research.

or another that, other things being equal, the prices of low coupon (or deep discount) bonds are much more sensitive to interest rate changes. This illustration shows why: they are effectively longer-term bonds. Moreover, it is evident from this example that the same probability of default prior to maturity is more serious with the deep discount bond because a larger proportion of the investor's outlay is riding on the more distant cash receipts. Therefore, we might expect to find the low coupon bonds displaying more than average price sensitivity to changes in perceived risk.

HOW TO CALCULATE DURATION

Macaulay proposed the concept of duration as a measure of a bond's life that explicitly considers the timing of the return of value. In essence, duration is simply a weighted average maturity stated in present value terms; the number of years into the future when a cash flow is received is weighted by the proportion that flow contributes to the total present value or price of the bond.

For ease of exposition, let us assume annual compounding and one bond coupon payment per year. Then, algebraically, duration (D) is defined as

$$D = \sum_{t=1}^{n} t \left\{ \frac{\frac{C_t}{(1+r)^t}}{\sum_{t=1}^{n} \frac{C_t}{(1+r)^t}} \right\} \qquad (1)$$

where n is the life of the bond in years, C_t is the cash receipt at the end of year t — equal to the annual coupon except for the last year, when it is equal to the annual coupon plus the maturity value — and r is the yield to maturity.[3] The numerator of the expression within the brackets is the present value of a single year's cash receipt; the denominator is the sum of all these present values, which is equal to the total present value or price of the bond. Therefore, the entire expression within the brackets is the weight given to the tth receipt. The "t" outside the brackets is simply the number of years from the present when the cash is received, equal to 1, 2, 3, and so on. The number of years into the future of a receipt, multiplied by its weight and summed over all receipts, is the bond's duration.

Table 2 contains an example that should make this measure considerably more comprehensible. It shows the computation of the duration of an 8% coupon bond with five years to maturity priced at par. Here the operation of the weighting scheme is fairly evident. For instance, at maturity after five years this

Table 2

Duration of an 8% Coupon
Five-Year Bond Priced at 100

(1) Year	(2) Cash Flow	(3) P.V. of $1 @ 8%	(4) P.V. of Flow	(5) P.V.÷ Price	(6) (1)X(5)
1	$80	.9259	$74.07	.07407	.07407
2	80	.8573	68.59	.06859	.13718
3	80	.7938	63.51	.06351	.19053
4	80	.7350	58.80	.05880	.23520
5	1080	.6806	735.03	.73503	3.67515
Sum			$1000.00	1.00000	4.31213
Price			$1000.00		
Duration					4.31 years

bond is expected to pay off $1080, which accounts for about 73.5% of its current value. Multiplying the five years by 0.735, we find that this receipt contributes approximately 3.68 years to the duration of this bond of 4.31 years.

Notice that the 4.31-year duration of this bond is less than its term to maturity of five years. The duration of a bond can never exceed its term to maturity and will be less than the term to maturity except for single-payment bonds — bonds that make no coupon payments over their life, such as Series E Savings Bonds. While there is not much difference in the duration and term to maturity of this bond, the disparity increases substantially for bonds of longer life, provided the coupon rate is at all close to prevailing yield levels. For example, continuing the assumption of an 8% coupon and 8% yield to maturity, a ten-year bond would have a duration of 7.25 years, a twenty-year bond a duration of 10.60 years, and a fifty-year bond a duration of 13.21 years. Even such a bond with an infinite life would only have a duration of 13.50 years. The reason is that the more distant coupons contribute very little to the value of these bonds. The length of the term to maturity of these longer maturity bonds tends to give a misleading picture of their effective lives.

Returning to the bonds in Table 1 for a moment, Bond A has a duration of 10.60 years while the duration of B is 12.26 years. Duration does appear to capture the difference in the effective lives of these bonds.

DURATION AS A MEASURE OF INTEREST RATE SENSITIVITY

If duration were nothing more than a superior measure of the life of a bond, it would hardly be worth the attention it has received. In fact, the measure has several very useful but not readily apparent properties.

One is that the elasticity of a bond's price with respect to a change in the discount factor is equal to its duration with the sign reversed.[4] In other words, if we know a bond's duration, we know how much its price will change as its yield changes without needing to resort to trial and error experiments with a bond book or calculator. Algebraically, the relationship is

$$\frac{\frac{\Delta P}{P}}{\frac{\Delta (1 + r)}{(1 + r)}} = -D, \qquad (2)$$

where P is the initial price of the bond.

As an example of this relationship, consider again the bond in Table 2, initially priced at par to yield 8% to maturity. Let its discount factor, 1.08, rise by 1% to 1.0908 (or 1.08 × 1.01). When the bond is revalued at this rate, its price drops to $958.98, a decline of $41.92 from par. This change, −4.19%, is approximately equal to the negative of the bond's duration, 4.31, times the discount factor change of +1%. The accuracy of the relationship improves for smaller changes — for instance, an increase in the discount factor by one tenth of 1%, to 1.08108, will reduce the price by 0.429% to $995.71 — and for infinitely small changes, it will be exact.

Many bond people will find the notion of changes in the discount factor a bit unhandy. Two modifications in the formula may therefore be useful. Rearranging, recognizing that $\Delta (1 + r)$ is equal to Δr, and multiplying each side by 100%, we have

$$\left(\frac{\Delta P}{P} \right) 100\% = \Delta r \, 100\% \left(\frac{-D}{1 + r} \right) \qquad (2a)$$

which says that the percentage change in price is equal to the *percentage point* change in the bond's yield times the negative of the duration divided by the initial discount factor. We could call this latter term the adjusted duration (D'),

$$D' = \frac{-D}{1 + r} \qquad (3)$$

To see this simplification in action, let's assume that the yield on the bond in Table 2 goes to 8½%. The adjusted duration is −3.99 (or −4.31/1.08), so we would expect the price to decline by 1.995% (equal to ½% × 3.99). The actual change is −1.932% to $980.68, and once again, the match would be perfect for an extremely small change in the rate.

As a further simplification, for many practical purposes it should not even be necessary to adjust duration by the discount factor, especially for longer-term bonds or when making inter-bond comparisons. For example, we saw that the duration of Bond B in Table 1 was 12.26 years. No serious inaccuracy would be caused by using this figure rather than the adjusted

duration of 11.35 years for most purposes. And, of course, the ratio of the adjusted durations of one bond to another will be identical to the ratio of the unadjusted durations when their initial yields are the same, and nearly identical provided their yields are at all alike.

DURATION AS A MEASURE OF REINVESTMENT RATE RISK

Suppose a bond portfolio is being managed with an eye toward its value at some point in the future, with all coupon and principal repayments being reinvested as received — a situation that would characterize many life insurance and some individual and pension fund portfolios. Under these circumstances, the performance of the portfolio is very sensitive to the interest rates at which the intermediate cash receipts are reinvested.

Table 3 provides an illustration of this phenomenon. Here we have the two twenty-year bonds from Table 1, but instead of looking at their present values, we are examining the value of our initial investment at the end of twenty years, assuming all coupons are reinvested at 8% per annum — the yield to maturity of both bonds — 6%, or 10%. Since the bonds have different prices, the table also shows the dollars of future value per dollar of initial investment under each alternative.

Table 3

Effect of Reinvestment Rates on Terminal Values

	6% Reinvestment Rate		8% Reinvestment Rate		10% Reinvestment Rate	
	Bond A − 8% Coupon	Bond B − 4% Coupon	Bond A − 8% Coupon	Bond B − 4% Coupon	Bond A − 8% Coupon	Bond B − 4% Coupon
Future Value of Coupons	$2942.84	$1471.44	$3660.95	$1830.48	$4582.00	$2291.00
Repayment at Maturity	1000.00	1000.00	1000.00	1000.00	1000.00	1000.00
Total Future Value	$3942.88	$2471.44	$4660.95	$2830.48	$5582.00	$3291.00
Present Price	$1000.00	$ 607.28	$1000.00	$607.28	$1000.00	$ 607.28
Future Value/Present Price	3.943	4.070	4.661	4.661	5.582	5.419

Note: Based on annual compounding and coupon receipt.

If the reinvestment rate is equal to the yield to maturity of 8%, investment in either bond will return $4.66 in twenty years per dollar of initial outlay. At the higher reinvestment rate of 10%, both bonds return relatively more, while at the reinvestment rate of 6% they return less. This sensitivity to future interest rates is usually referred to as "reinvestment rate risk"; it has recently received fairly widespread attention because of historically high interest rates and the publication of Homer and Leibowitz's monograph, *Inside the Yield Book.*[5] Because of reinvestment rate risk, even a default-free bond held to maturity cannot be regarded as completely riskless, provided all coupons are to be reinvested.

The table also shows that the future value of

Bond A, the 8% coupon bond selling at par, is more sensitive to changing reinvestment rates than Bond B, the 4% coupon bond selling at a discount. A look back at Table 1 will suggest the reason: for Bond B, a larger proportion of the initial outlay goes to acquire the right to $1000 at maturity, a value which is completely unaffected by the reinvestment rate. Therefore, purchase of Bond B has the effect of locking in more of the total initial investment at its yield to maturity.

Bond B also has a duration that is closer to the twenty-year length of the investment horizon, 12.26 years versus 10.60 years for A. And in general it will be the case that, at any specific time, reinvestment rate risk is smaller the closer a bond's duration is to the number of years remaining to the investor's horizon date. In fact, Fisher and Weil have shown both theoretically and as a practical matter (considering brokerage fees, etc.) that the reinvestment rate risk of a bond portfolio can be neutralized or "immunized" almost completely if its weighted average duration is adjusted to equal the horizon period after each coupon payment date.[6] The most severe problem is that, with long horizons, bonds of sufficiently long duration may simply not be available.

DURATION AND TERM STRUCTURE

Fixed income portfolio managers customarily devote much attention to the term structure of interest rates, or the schedule of yields on bonds of different maturity expressed in years. This is fine if the object of the exercise is to evaluate the pure price of time. If interest centers on the price of risk exposure, however, either to changes in yield or changes in default probabilities — as usually seems to be the case — then it may be useful to restate the numbers in terms of yield versus duration.

A bit of what economists call "anecdotal evidence" may serve to make the point. In the spring of 1975, one of the author's former students who now manages several large bond portfolios observed that, according to his calculations, under the conditions then prevailing, the volatility of a thirty-year maturity bond's price to yield changes was not substantially greater than the volatility of a ten-year bond's price. Therefore, in view of the large yield sacrifice one had to make at that time to buy intermediate rather than long-term bonds (many people were then expecting interest rates to rise, and yield curves sloped steeply upward), he was concentrating his purchases in the long maturities.

His point, which was not well-received among more experienced bond managers, can be readily seen via duration. At that time, new issue, lower medium grade industrials with a ten-year maturity were selling to yield approximately 9.5% while the yield on otherwise equivalent issues with thirty years to maturity was around 11.25%. At these rates, the ten-year bonds had a duration of 6.88 years and the thirty-year bonds had a duration of 9.49 years; therefore, the price volatility of the medium grade bonds with respect to changes in their yields should be about 72% (or 6.88/9.49) of the volatility of the long-term issues.

The more experienced bond managers were probably thinking back to days gone by when interest rates were much lower and thus intermediate- and long-term bonds were much different. For example, consider a 4% ten-year bond and a 4.75% thirty-year bond. The ratios of the yields are about the same (11.25/9.50 = 1.18; 4.75/5.00 = 1.19), yet the durations are much different. The ten-year 4% bond would have a duration of 8.44 years and the thirty-year 4.75% bond a duration of 16.57 years. Under these conditions, the intermediate-term bonds would have only about 51% as much (8.44/16.57) yield sensitivity. The level of interest rates as well as the term to maturity influences interest rate sensitivity. Rising yields reduce the duration of long-term bonds more than intermediate- or short-term bonds, and "long-term" bonds are effectively much less long in term than they were years ago.

In any event, a number of economists, beginning with Macaulay himself, have suggested that it might be useful to derive yield curves with respect to duration rather than to maturity.[7] And, while one swallow doesn't make a summer, long-term bonds did have much the better performance in the market rally over the next twelve months.

DURATION AS A MEASURE OF PORTFOLIO RISK

Duration is useful at the aggregate portfolio level for the same reasons that it is useful when dealing with individual bonds. But duration has another attraction that results from what might be called its *additivity*. While we can compute a weighted average of almost any bond characteristic for a portfolio, in many cases the usefulness of the resulting number would be unclear.

For example, suppose we were to compute a weighted average term to maturity, weighting the term to maturity of each bond by the proportion that bond represents in the total portfolio; this would be useful information, and we could almost surely make some interpretations of it. However, it is not an unequivocal measure; a portfolio with, say, a twenty-year average term to maturity composed of all twenty-year bonds will behave differently from a portfolio composed of half ten-year and half thirty-

217

year bonds. With duration, circumstances are different. Any portfolio with a weighted average duration of twenty years should behave about the same as any other portfolio with the same duration in circumstances where duration is relevant regardless of the duration of the member bonds.[8]

Table 4 illustrates this additivity. Here three bonds that differ with respect to coupon, yield, and term to maturity combine to make up a $1000 portfolio with a weighted average duration of 4.31 years, the same duration as the bond in the Table 2 example. The discount factor on each bond is then increased by 1%, which is the same as an increase of 1% in the weighted average discount factor of the entire portfolio. This action reduces the value of the portfolio by $41.51 to $958.49, virtually the same as the decrease of $41.92 the bond in Table 2 experienced when its discount factor increased by 1%.

Table 4
Duration and Price Change of a Portfolio

(1) Bond	(2) Initial - Yield	(3) Initial - Price	(4) Duration	(5) Portfolio Proportion	(6) (3)X(5)	(7) (4)X(5)	(8) Subsequent - Yield	(9) Subsequent - Price	(10) (5)X(9)
1 year, 6% coupon	.06	$1000	1.00 yr.	.297	$297	.30 yrs.	.0706	$990.10	$294.06
5 year, 8% coupon	.08	1000	4.31 yrs.	.300	300	1.29 yrs.	.0908	958.08	287.42
10 year, 10% coupon	.10	1000	6.76 yrs.	.403	403	2.72 yrs.	.1110	535.50	377.01
Duration						4.31 yrs.			
Total Portfolio Value					$1000				$958.49

Because of this additivity characteristic, the weighted average duration of a portfolio could be very useful for assessing its potential loss of value in the face of large interest rate increases, sensitivity to changes in default probabilities some years out, and exposure to reinvestment rate risk.

HOW CAN YOU GET DURATION NUMBERS?

There are no published sources of bonds' durations at this time. Technically, the formula or variants of the formula given in Equation 1 and illustrated in Table 2 can be used to compute duration with only the aid of a simple calculator, but the procedure is so tedious that not many bond analysts are apt to attempt it. Durations can be computed readily with virtually any batch or time-shared computer, but access to suitable equipment may be a problem.

Comparatively inexpensive (under $500 in at least one case) mini-calculators with limited programming capabilities have come on the market, and it should be possible to quickly program almost any of these to compute duration. The manufacturers of most of these calculators can also provide a library of finan-

cial programs that typically will handle bond price and yield calculations. Therefore, an instrument can serve a variety of purposes in bond portfolio management, making the effective incremental cost of duration calculations inconsequential.[9]

[1] Frederick R. Macaulay, *Some Theoretical Problems Suggested by the Movements of Interest Rates, Bond Yields and Stock Prices in the United States since 1856* (New York: National Bureau of Economic Research, 1938), pp. 44-53.

[2] A useful review is provided by Roman L. Weil in "Macaulay's Duration: An Appreciation," *Journal of Business* 46 (October, 1973), pp. 589-92.

[3] The assumption of annual compounding and one coupon receipt per year is maintained throughout this paper. The practical impact of this assumption versus semi-annual compounding and coupon receipt is limited. For example, the duration of the bond in Table 2 would be shifted from 4.312 years to 4.218 years. A memorandum available from the author, "Computational Notes on Duration," presents formulas which can accommodate semi-annual compounding and coupon receipt, partial coupon periods, etc., and discusses their interpretation.

[4] A proof is provided by, among others, Michael H. Hopewell and George G. Kaufman, "Bond Price Volatility and Term to Maturity: A Generalized Respecification," *American Economic Review* 63 (September, 1973), pp. 749-53, especially p. 751.

[5] Sidney Homer and Martin L. Leibowitz, *Inside the Yield Book* (Englewood Cliffs, New Jersey: Prentice-Hall, Inc., 1970).

[6] Lawrence Fisher and Roman L. Weil, "Coping with the Risk of Interest-Rate Fluctuations: Returns to Bondholders from Naive and Optimal Strategies," *Journal of Business* 44 (October, 1971), pp. 408-431. It should be noted that the theoretical proof is only valid for a specific pattern of yield curve fluctuation over time. However, the empirical evidence leads to the conclusion that as a practical matter, this restriction is unimportant.

[7] e.g., Hopewell and Kaufman, "Bond Price Volatility . . .," p. 752, and J. L. Carr, P. J. Halpern, J. S. McCallum. "Correcting the Yield Curve: A Re-Interpretation of the Duration Problem," *Journal of Finance* 29 (September, 1974), pp. 1287-1294. For a contrary view, see Miles Livingston and John Caks, "A Note Regarding a 'Duration' Fallacy," forthcoming in the *Journal of Finance*.

[8] Fisher & Weil, "Coping . . .," p. 419. In an unpublished paper Ian Cooper has shown that this additivity will be less reliable at the short end of the maturity spectrum because of large changes in the shape of the yield curve in this maturity range.

[9] Professor Richard J. Rendleman of the Graduate School of Business, Northwestern University, has prepared a package of bond problems for the Texas Instruments SR-52. With the duration program in this package, a bond's duration is obtained in less than fifteen seconds simply by entering its coupon rate and term to maturity.

Goal oriented bond portfolio management

The "Baseline" method for relating short-term performance to long-term goals.

Martin L. Leibowitz

Managers of fixed-income portfolios have recently found themselves coming under increasing pressure from various forms of performance monitoring. Primarily, this monitoring has taken the form of total return measurement of portfolio results over relatively short-term measurement periods — *i.e.*, quarters or years. The manager's results are then compared with the returns achieved by general market indices, by short-term investments, or by other portfolios believed to be part of a "peer group." These comparisons increasingly play a major role in the evaluation of the portfolio manager's skills and services.

It is clear that performance monitoring can be helpful in many areas of investment management, especially when the monitoring is based upon objective, concrete measurements. However, the sole reliance upon total return comparisons over short-term periods is subject to a number of criticisms. Total return measurements do provide a useful yardstick of the extent to which the portfolio manager took advantage of general market opportunities during the measurement period. But this is only one factor in the complex process of portfolio management. A fundamental problem seems to arise when a *single* yardstick — total return measurement over short-term periods — is taken as *the sole* yardstick for all management activity.

This concentration on the single yardstick of total return can force dangerously simplistic comparisons among portfolios that may actually differ widely in function and purpose. In fact, the same level of achieved return may represent a very satisfactory result for one portfolio while having quite dismal implications for another portfolio with a different set of goals.

Moreover, even within a given portfolio, an over-emphasis on short-term return can lead to conflicts with the long-term goals of the fund. For example, it could lead the portfolio manager into concentrating his activity on catching short-term swings in interest rates. In turn, this could lead to a frequent series of major portfolio shifts, thereby introducing considerable timing risk into the overall management process. The resulting volatility risk might be in direct contradiction to the original purpose of placing the funds into a fixed-income portfolio in the first place. This is just one instance of how an exclusive focus on maximization of total return over short periods can violate a fund's policy constraints and cause deviations from the fund's true long-term objectives.

These problems are particularly acute for fixed-income portfolios because of certain distinctive characteristics of the bond market. Much of the institutional investment in bonds is motivated by long-term, risk-avoidance purposes. These long-term purposes typically overshadow any specific requirement for total return over short-term periods. Another important characteristic of the bond market is the structural clarity of its asset classes. This clarity enables the return/risk relationships among the different market sectors to be relatively well defined, especially over longer term horizons. The longer-term motivation of investors and the market's structural clarity obviously fit hand-in-glove, allowing for the identification of market sectors that are particularly well suited for serving the specific goals of a given fund.

By taking advantage of these special characteristics of the bond market, we believe that a *practical* technique can be developed for relating performance measurements over short-term periods to the fund's long-term goals.

THE BASELINE PORTFOLIO

In theory, the portfolio management process can be viewed as consisting of the four major steps shown in Figure 1. The first step is to identify the

FIGURE 1
OVERVIEW OF THE PORTFOLIO
MANAGEMENT PROCESS

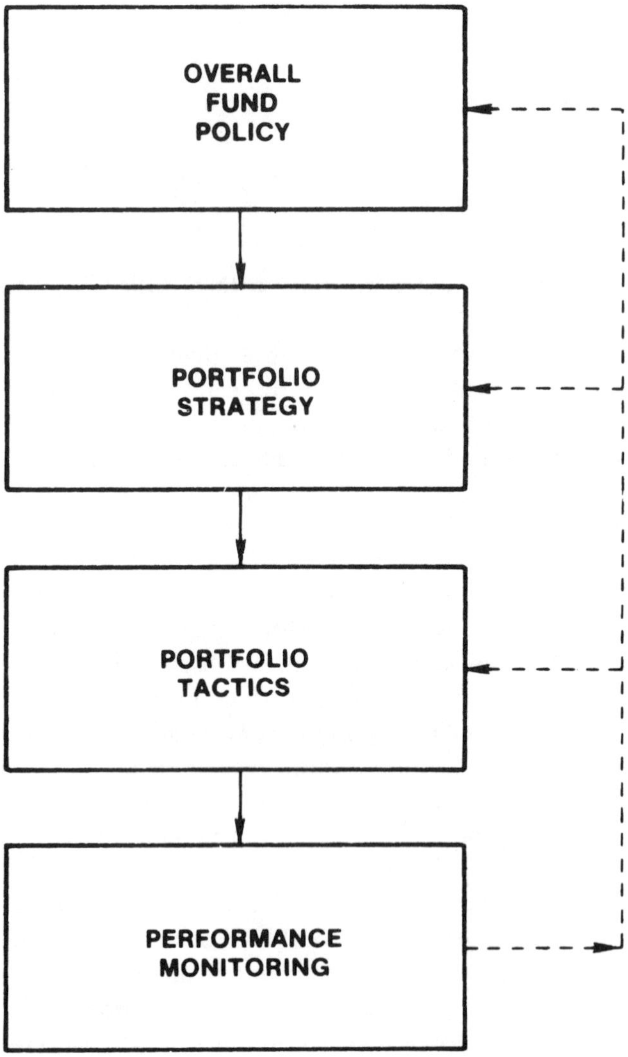

long-term objectives of the fund. The second step commences with the manager's judgments regarding market prospects. At this point, the manager must make the broad decisions that relate to portfolio strategy, *i.e.*, to determining the portfolio's maturity structure. Once this has been done, the third step consists of deciding upon the detailed portfolio tactics to be employed. These consist of selecting specific sectors to take advantage of perceived market oppor-

tunities. The fourth step then consists of a continuing performance monitoring (in the most general sense) to ensure that the portfolio objectives are being fulfilled.

The first step is far more difficult than generally believed. It is no simple matter to identify a full set of portfolio objectives and then to define these objectives in *a useful way*. Such efforts tend to lead to either a frustratingly vague description of the objectives or to lead to an impossibly long collection of goals which mix the minor considerations in with the major ones.

For example, Figure 2 illustrates only a partial

FIGURE 2
PORTFOLIO OBJECTIVES

MAXIMUM LONG TERM NOMINAL RETURN

MAXIMUM LONG TERM REAL RETURN

MATCH PRESCRIBED LIABILITY SCHEDULE

RESERVE AGAINST UNCERTAIN LIABILITIES

EARNINGS CONTRIBUTION

EARNINGS MANAGEMENT

TAX LIABILITY MANAGEMENT

LIQUIDITY WAREHOUSE

STABILITY OF PRINCIPAL

STABILITY OF INCOME OVER TIME

FACILITATE CORPORATE FLEXIBILITY

CORPORATE COMPLIANCE

AURA OF BALANCE AND PRUDENCE

list of the many objectives that could be ascribed to fixed-income portfolios. Moreover, any set of objectives is closely intertwined with an associated set of risk factors. (In this connection, risk is being defined in a far broader sense than the single volatility measure which has become traditional in many modern analyses. In the sense used here, risk entails all those potential events that could interfere with the portfolio being able to fulfill its long-term objectives.) When there are a large number of potential objectives and associated risk factors, it is no easy task to generate concrete guidelines for portfolio managers.

The purpose of the "Baseline Portfolio" is to provide a practical procedure for articulating the fund's long-term objectives in a concrete and useful fashion. The underlying idea is to take advantage of the relatively well-defined sector structure of the bond market. By selecting market sectors to match the fund's objectives and associated risk factors, one should be able to develop a portfolio structure that best suits the fund's long-term goals. This is called the fund's "Baseline Portfolio."

Since the Baseline Portfolio structure should be determined primarily by the long-range considerations, it should be relatively independent of the active manager's day-to-day market judgments. Thus, the Baseline Portfolio could be defined as the most balanced possible fulfillment of all of the fund's complex objectives and goals in the absence of an active market-related management activity.

AN EXAMPLE OF A BASELINE PORTFOLIO

Development of a Baseline Portfolio for an actual fund is certainly not a simple task. However, in order to provide a concrete illustration of the baseline approach, we shall show how one might try to develop a highly simplified Baseline Portfolio for a growing pension fund.

For this example, assume that the fixed-income portion of a pension fund is intended to provide a source of long-term nominal-dollar income that can be counted upon under virtually any economic conditions. The pension fund is a growing one, and is expected to experience a positive cash flow for the next 20 years. The fixed-income portion of the fund is envisioned as a nominal dollar "anchor to the wind" — to be relatively free from the volatility and economic risks entailed in the sizable equity portions of the fund. Because of the highly risk-averse nature of this fixed-income portion, the fund might be invested in a diversified portfolio of high-grade securities. This risk aversion would also apply to the maturity structure of the fund. We shall presume that the primary concern here is the risk related to maintaining a long-term income stream with some assurance, rather than the risk associated with volatility of market value. Consequently, it would seem that the Baseline Portfolio should consist primarily of long-term bonds. More-

over, the insistence upon assured long-term income flows would suggest that a high level of call protection be provided to the Baseline Portfolio. There are a number of ways to achieve this call protection. We shall assume that in this case it is to be achieved by excluding the "higher-coupon" cushion bonds. The resulting Baseline Portfolio might therefore consist largely of long-term high-grade corporate bonds, all with market prices below some modest premium above par.

Such a portfolio would behave very differently from a general market index, e.g., the Salomon Brothers Composite Rate-of-Return Index. This Baseline Portfolio would exhibit far more price volatility than the Index. Because of the sacrifice of the higher coupon bond component of the marketplace, it would have a lower overall yield rate. The price departure from the general market would be most evident under major moves in either direction. Under a major market deterioration, this Baseline Portfolio would fall off more in market value than the general long-term market. In contrast, under a major market improvement, there would be a greater price appreciation of the Baseline Portfolio than of the call-vulnerable general market. These performance characteristics of the Baseline Portfolio are intrinsically related to the fund's stated objectives of trying to assure long-term nominal income.

SHORT- VERSUS LONG-TERM RETURN/RISK PROFILES

Figure 3 illustrates how the return/risk profiles over a short-term period can be almost completely reversed over the long-term. Figure 3 is based upon the

FIGURE 3
RETURN PROFILES OVER LONG TERM HORIZONS

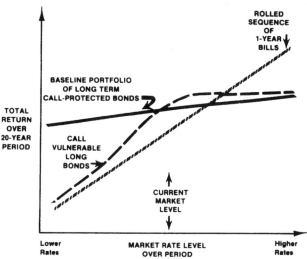

221

(admittedly artificial) assumption that the market moves to a flat yield curve at the indicated level and remains there for the next 20 years. The curves in Figure 3 then depict the resulting total return resulting over this 20-year period, incorporating the sizable effects from reinvesting coupons, maturity redemptions, and the proceeds from refunding calls. Over this 20-year period, the greatest variability in returns would be derived from a policy of rolling one-year Bills. The Baseline Portfolio of call-protected bonds would provide the greatest stability, while long-term call-vulnerable bonds would fall somewhere in between.

Figure 3 demonstrates that a higher level of volatility risk as measured by most modern analyses would actually have been necessary in order to provide the most assured approach to long-term return, free from the vagaries of intervening interest rates.

Indeed, for the stated objectives of this portfolio, investment in totally short-term cash instruments would represent the greatest level of true risk — risk here being defined in terms of threats to achieving the fund's long-term objectives.

For many long-term funds, total return analyses such as Figure 3 actually tend to *understate* the problem. By their very nature, total returns only reflect the growth of the dollar value. For many fund purposes, however, a dollar may have different *values* under different interest rate conditions. For example, the ability of a given dollar-size portfolio to provide an annuity of consumable dollars varies widely with future interest rate levels. When interest rates are low, the annuity-producing value of each future $1 is clearly lower than when rates are high. Thus, each unit of long-term return achieved under low interest rate conditions may be far less valuable than the same unit of return achieved at higher rates.[1]

MANAGEMENT ACTIVITY RELATIVE TO THE BASELINE PORTFOLIO

From the vantage point of the Baseline Portfolio, one purpose of investment management is to take advantage of market opportunities. Active management can then be viewed as a series of strategic and tactical judgments that would lead to market-motivated departures from the Baseline Portfolio in an effort to achieve improved portfolio results. The resulting portfolio improvements — as well as the incremental risks incurred in achieving them — should theoretically be measured against the yardstick of the Baseline Portfolio itself.

To see how this measurement can be accomplished, suppose that the actual portfolio's market value could always be converted into immediate cash proceeds. (This concept of equating a fund's nominal market value with a literal cash opportunity value lies at the heart of the conventional rate-of-return measurement process.) Then, at any moment, the actual portfolio could be translated into cash and these proceeds used to purchase a Baseline Portfolio. Suppose that this would lead to a purchase of 100 units of the Baseline Portfolio. If this were done, the manager would have reverted to the best possible passive portfolio structure. In other words, he would have converted all his funds into the "currency" of the fund's long-term objectives, *i.e.*, the Baseline Portfolio itself.

In general, however, the portfolio manager will retain some portfolio structure other than that of the Baseline. During the course of the subsequent measurement period, this actual portfolio will provide a certain total return consisting of both income and principal appreciation: perhaps with a certain amount of reinvestment return as well. This total return may look very acceptable compared to either investment in a general market index, in short-term investments, or to the relative performance of peer portfolios. At the end of the measurement period, however, the actual portfolio could again be subjected to the test of a theoretical repurchase of the Baseline Portfolio. No matter how well the actual portfolio may have done in terms of the traditional comparisons, if it converts back into fewer units of the Baseline Portfolio than before, then the fund has lost ground relative to its long-term objectives.

The gain or loss from this hypothetical repurchase of the Baseline is, of course, directly related to the incremental return achieved by the actual portfolio relative to the Baseline.

For example, at the outset, the fund might have a market value of $100 million. Theoretically, this could be used to purchase 100 units of the Baseline Portfolio, where the units have been (arbitrarily) scaled to have a market value of $1 million. Based upon various market judgments, the manager could depart from this Baseline and structure his actual portfolio along somewhat different lines. During the course of the ensuing measurement period, the actual portfolio achieves a total return performance of +11%, resulting in the fund having a total market value of $111 million. Over this same period, however, the Baseline Portfolio has done better, turning in a return of +15%. One unit of the Baseline has thus appreciated in cost from $1.00 million to $1.15 million. Consequently, on a hypothetical repurchase of the Baseline, the fund's actual value of $111 million would only allow purchase of:

$$\frac{\$111\,\text{MM}}{\$1.15\,\text{MM/Unit}} = 96.5\,\text{Baseline Units}$$

If the fund had remained invested in the Baseline, it would, of course, have maintained the original 100 units, and appreciated by +15% to $115 million. In this case, the manager's departure from the Baseline proved to be counterproductive.

The portfolio manager, in selecting his actual portfolio, clearly took an incremental risk in departing from the Baseline Portfolio. By so doing, his intentions had to be to seek an incremental return above and beyond what could be achieved with the Baseline Portfolio. Therefore, it becomes clear that the benchmark for measuring the portfolio's return is the return that could have been achieved by simply holding the Baseline Portfolio. To the extent that the achieved return exceeded the Baseline return, to that extent did the portfolio manager add to the achievement of the portfolio results as denominated in the currency of the Baseline Portfolio itself.

The Baseline Portfolio also provides an interesting mechanism for relating short-term incremental returns to long-term measures of value. For example, an extra total return of 400 basis points realized over a one-year period might correspond to an additional 40 basis points of long-term yield over the maturity span of the Baseline Portfolio. In other words, the extra market value achieved over the year could buy an incremental cash flow equivalent to putting the funds to work at a long-term yield 40 basis points higher than the actual market yield. (The appropriate factor here is the Horizon Volatility of the Baseline Portfolio. For most long-term bond portfolios, this factor will generally lie between 9 and 12.)

EVALUATING PROPOSED DEPARTURES FROM THE BASELINE

The Baseline Portfolio can serve both prospective and retrospective functions. After a given investment period has been completed, the Baseline can help the manager to evaluate, retrospectively, the return achieved in terms of his contribution to the fund's long-term goals. At the beginning of each investment period, however, the Baseline can help the portfolio manager to gauge — in a quantitative, objective fashion—the incremental risk incurred *relative to these same goals*. This *prospective* application of the Baseline Portfolio may be the most important one of all.

Figure 4 illustrates a manager's *prospective* evaluation of the tradeoff between expected return (over a short-term horizon) and some measure of "interest rate risk." For example, if the manager was neutral on the market so that the expected case could be repre-

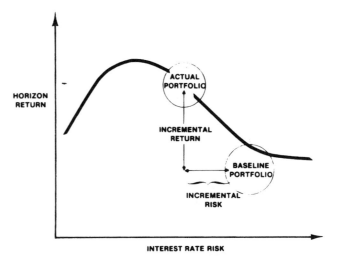

FIGURE 4
MARKET-MOTIVATED DEPARTURES FROM
THE BASELINE PORTFOLIO

sented as "no change in the yield curve," then the expected return would be the Rolling Yield.[2] On the other hand, if the manager's interest rate projections were more optimistic or pessimistic than the neutral case, then these judgments would be reflected in projected returns such as those plotted in Figure 4.

The horizontal axis in Figure 4 represents some measure of "interest rate risk" over the short-term investment period.

As noted earlier, the maturity structure is the most important decision made by an active portfolio manager. By varying the maturity structure, he can control the amount of "interest rate risk" contained in his portfolio. Various proxies for the "interest rate risk" of a portfolio have been proposed — average maturity, historical variability, percentage price volatility, Macaulay's duration, Horizon Volatility, Proportional Volatility.[3] For any of these measures, the Baseline can be viewed as the reference point. To the extent that the active manager departs from this Baseline level of interest rate risk, to that extent, he risks falling below the Baseline's performance.

This holds true for departures in *both directions*. As noted earlier, a defensive departure, while risk-reducing in terms of short-term volatility, runs the risk of an insufficient price appreciation to compensate for the lower income-productivity per dollar of market value under a move to lower yield levels.

Figure 4 illustrates the case of a manager undertaking just such a "defensive departure" from the Baseline's risk level. His motivation is clearly to obtain a sizable improvement in incremental returns. However, he is exposing his portfolio to a considerable shortfall in return relative to the Baseline in the event that interest rates move further downward than the

223

level embedded in his projected return curve.

One should take note of the apparent paradox in the situation portrayed in Figure 4. The greatest risk here is the prospect of a stronger-than-expected *downward* move in interest rates. This action would normally be viewed as "improving market." Yet, in this case, such a "market improvement" would lead to under-performance relative to the Baseline Portfolio, and hence would constitute the gravest threat to the fund's progress towards its long-term goals.

Figure 4 thus shows how a manager can gauge his incremental interest rate risk relative to the Baseline and, by implication, measure his more generalized risk relative to long-term goals. While there may be some controversy regarding what constitutes a satisfactory measure of interest rate risk, there is no disagreement that a greater level of risk consciousness needs to be introduced into the management process. Once any such volatility measure has been selected, the procedure implied in Figure 4 can be quantified, thereby providing the manager (and the sponsor) with a concrete, numerical indication of the incremental risk associated with a prospective portfolio strategy.

COMMUNICATION BETWEEN SPONSOR AND MANAGER

The Baseline Portfolio approach can facilitate the communication process between sponsor and manager.

At the outset, the Baseline Portfolio should itself be the result of discussions between the fund's sponsor and the manager. In these initial discussions, the sponsor must try to convey his sense of the fund's purpose, to define his overall objectives and their relative priorities, and to identify and delimit the risk factors that concern him. On the other hand, the manager contributes his knowledge of the behavioral characteristics of the various asset classes, along with his belief as to how they will function in the context of different portfolio structures.(At this point, the manager should try to put aside his perceptions of immediate market value, and concentrate on the general long-term characteristics of the various market sectors.)

In all too many instances, this interchange tends to remain at a rather fuzzy level of generality, with both parties espousing the obviously desirable "Nirvana points," *e.g.*, maximum return with minimum risk, highest yield without sacrifice of quality, minimum volatility with greatest stability of income, etc. If the discussion of goals ends at this point, then

neither party has communicated his sense of the appropriate tradeoffs. In a rather fundamental sense, no real understanding has been achieved.

A joint determination to specify a Baseline Portfolio can drive these discussions down to the concrete level. It will force the difficult choices to be made — and made *jointly* by both sponsor and manager. The sponsor must articulate the subtle priorities that can organize his many objectives, and he must develop a clear-cut structure by relating these priorities — with the manager's help — to choices between specific market sectors. The manager must rise above his active orientation to define the most balanced, passive portfolio structure matching his client needs. In this fashion, both parties are able to merge and consolidate their different points of view. In essence, by specifying a Baseline Portfolio, they have come to agree on a practical, passive alternative to active management.

As with any real process of communication, these interactions may prove painful and arduous at the outset. Once defined, however, the Baseline can prove a mutual vantage point for interpreting the actual returns achieved over time. The all-too-common confusion between conflicting short-term results and long-term goals will be reduced. Because of the sponsor's role in defining the Baseline, the manager will no longer find himself quite so vulnerable to criticism for the many portfolio effects that are (in reality) mandated by the nature of the fund. In particular, having the Baseline as a "baseline" may considerably reduce artificial pressures on a manager with regard to high volatility, yield give-ups, particularly high or low quality postures, having the portfolio balanced away from the general market structure, or for deviations from the performance returns achieved by general market indices or theoretical peer groups.

Moreover, by concentrating the objective setting in an initial phase shared with the sponsor, the Baseline approach should allow the investment manager to focus more clearly on his day-by-day market activities in the fund's behalf.

---

[1] For a more detailed discussion of this effect, see *The Horizon Annuity: An Investment Measure for Linking the Growth and Payout Phases of Long Term Bond Portfolios*, Martin L. Leibowitz, Salomon Brothers, 1976.

[2] See *The Rolling Yield: A New Approach to Yield Curve Analysis* by Martin L. Leibowitz, Salomon Brothers, April 21, 1977.

[3] For a more complete discussion, see *The Risk Dimension: A New Approach to Yield Curve Analysis* by Martin L. Leibowitz, Salomon Brothers, October 5, 1977.

The challenge of analyzing bond portfolio returns

If the client wants an accurate picture of the manager's ability, the interaction of maturity-sector-quality must be "decomposed."

Peter O. Dietz, H. Russell Fogler, and Donald J. Hardy

The decade of the 1970's has seen the rise of active or total return bond management, especially in regard to tax-free institutional portfolios. This approach to fixed-income management has created a wide variety of portfolios and results. The various techniques developed by institutional bond managers have left pension plan sponsors and other investors with the difficulty of analyzing performance results. While capital market theory has been widely used to address the issue of equity portfolio analysis, there has been no comparable "state of the art" development in the area of fixed-income measurement.

In this article we propose to discuss the rise of active bond management, the problems involved in analyzing the results of such management, and a methodology by which fixed-income portfolios can be more incisively analyzed. We have developed this method to isolate the impact of changes in the term structure of interest rates on portfolio results, the effect of sector and quality selection on the part of portfolio managers, and the impact of that portion of return unrelated to either interest rate shifts or sector/quality factors.

ACTIVE BOND MANAGEMENT

Traditionally, the measurement of bond returns to investors has been reflected in terms of yield. Prior to the 1970's most managers bought new issues and held them until maturity. In addition, many large public employee funds had restrictions on realizing losses. Thus, in periods of changing interest rate levels, these funds were often effectively precluded from trading bonds.

Gradually, restrictions on taking losses were removed, and two phenomena emerged. First, a new generation of bond managers now manages bonds on a total return basis — that is to say, the total of income flows plus capital changes. These managers are commonly called "active bond managers." Second, "swaps" have become more common. Historic spreads among bonds with similar (but not necessarily identical) characteristics are monitored. When a spread reaches an historic extreme, a manager will execute a substitution swap in the hope that the market is only temporarily imbalanced and will later return to normal. At that time the swap may be reversed, or a whole chain of swaps may be initiated. In any event, the manager's goal is to produce an incremental capital gain from a market inefficiency without compromising overall portfolio structure.

Another swapping tactic is the sector swap. Spread differentials are tracked between different market sectors as defined by maturity, quality, coupon, or issuer. When these spreads reach historically extreme points, a swap is executed with the expectation that it can be favorably reversed when the spread returns to normal.

Each of the tactics described above worked reasonably well until the 1973-1974 disruption of the financial markets. Price controls, the oil embargo, and double-digit inflation all combined to produce an inverted yield curve. This led to enormous differences in performance results among managers. Those managers in shorter term maturities not only protected principal, but also gained incremental income.

Substitution swapping and sector swapping were not able to protect managers from the damaging effects of being in long maturities during this latter period. As managers sought a strategy to protect themselves, the interest rate anticipation swap became the principal tool of many active managers. Primarily, this involves altering the maturity composition of a portfolio in order to take advantage of anticipated changes in interest rates. Additionally, the coupon level may be altered as a secondary method to position a portfolio for anticipated rate changes.

THE CHALLENGE OF ANALYZING BOND RETURNS

With the increase in the number of active bond manager strategies, measurement of their results has become more important — although not easier! To understand why the evaluation of bond managers has been so difficult, consider the following example: Suppose during the last quarter, the general level of interest rates rose; then, various widely followed indexes might appear as shown in Figure 1. Suppose,

FIGURE I
HYPOTHETICAL RESULTS WITH PRESENT TOOLS

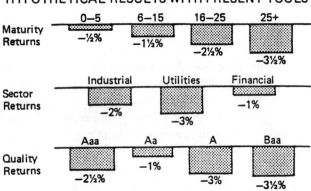

further, that a manager held only high-grade (Aaa) utilities, but of very short maturity. Since these maturities are less volatile, he produced a better return than either the utility average or the Aaa average.

Was he lucky to be short? What impact did his quality selection have on total return? Perhaps Aaa bonds declined more *on average* (for indexes such as in Figure I) than Aa bonds because they had a longer maturity! Similarly, his sector selection effect is not clearly delineated by average indexes — maybe the utility sector average return was lower because of a longer maturity, or because of its quality mix. To date, it has been impossible to develop incisive answers to these and other questions regarding the specific sources of total return.

If the client wants answers to these questions about a manager's ability, the *interaction* of maturity-sector-quality must be "decomposed." In other words, *each of these effects must be isolated* and the respective contribution to a manager's total return determined. Another example will clarify the need for such decomposition of the total return.

Assume that a position was held during the fourth quarter, 1978, in Philip Morris, Inc., 8.65% of 1984. This A-rated issue was priced at 99.63 at the beginning of the quarter and quoted at 95.63 on December 31, 1978. The quarterly total return on this

226

issue for the final quarter was −1.844, which included the beginning yield-to-maturity of 2.188.

The quarterly total return of −1.844 was the result of many capital market adjustments and expectations. Some questions that arise include the following: How significant was the manager's preference for high quality issues? How much was a result of a preference for Industrials versus Utilities or other sectors? How much was the consequence of a coupon of 8 5/8% that was below new issue rates? How much was due to call protection? These and other factors are all embedded in the total return figure.

To implement the decomposition of bond returns, total return must be broken out as shown in Figure II. While the return attributable to yield-to-

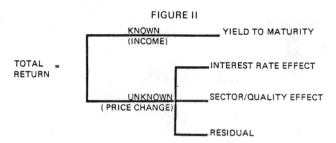

FIGURE II

maturity is known, the portions of return attributable to each of the other three components must be imputed. In order to explain how this might be done, let us return to the Philip Morris example.

THE METHODOLOGY

YIELD-TO-MATURITY. The methodology begins by asking, "What return would be expected if there were no changes in any capital market factors (i.e., interest rates, sector/quality differential, and so on)?" Then, the no-change assumption is loosened to examine the additional impact of interest rates and sector/quality preferences.

If no market changes occurred, the Philip Morris security in our example would have returned 2.188% quarterly, which is the quarterly yield-to-maturity based upon the beginning price. This yield-to-maturity resulted from: (1) accrued coupon payments; (2) price change to amortize the difference from par value; and (3) the "roll effect" which impacts the yield-to-maturity due to the slope of the yield curve as the bond matures. Even if a portfolio manager did nothing, this return would have been earned if no changes occurred in the capital markets. This quarterly return represents the payment required by investors based upon their expectation for future capital market events. Let us designated this return as

$$YTM = 2.188\%$$

INTEREST RATE EFFECT. Since yield-to-maturity is known in the short run and therefore precisely measurable, the first additional factor to be determined is the interest rate effect. The procedure is to hold all other factors constant and measure what the effect on each issue held in the portfolio would have been from changes in the term structure of interest rates during the quarter.

We use the U.S Treasury yield curve as a basis for determining changes in interest rates for two reasons:

1. This is the area of the bond market that is closest to the pure cost of money. All other sectors are priced off the Treasury yield curve.

2. It is the most efficiently priced sector of the market and there is no credit risk involved.

The Treasury yield curve is fitted for the beginning of the quarter, and each bond in the portfolio being measured is priced by the present value formula against the curve at its appropriate maturity. The difference between each portfolio holding and the comparable maturity Treasury issue is noted and expressed in basis points. Then, a Treasury yield curve is fitted for the end of the quarter. Each portfolio issue is then re-priced against this ending Treasury yield curve (after reducing maturities for the quarter that has elapsed), using the same basis point differential determined at the beginning of the quarter.

In the Philip Morris example, interest rates for a five-and-one-quarter year U.S. Treasury bond rose from approximately 8.45% to approximately 9.27% based upon the Treasury yield curves at the beginning and end of the quarter. Since the Philip Morris issue's beginning yield-to-maturity was 8.74% and a five-and-one-half year U.S. Treasury yielded 8.45%, then the beginning yield differential for all other factors was 0.29 basis points above U.S. Treasuries of comparable maturity. Assuming that this differential was maintained during the quarter because other capital market expectations were unchanged, the Philip Morris issue would be priced at 96.29 to yield 9.56% at the end of the period. Thus, this price decline represents the price loss due to a rise in the level of interest rates on U.S. Treasuries.[1] Let us designate this

$$INT = \frac{(96.29 - 99.63)}{99.63} = (3.347)$$

This procedure is illustrated in Figures III and IV.

SECTOR/QUALITY EFFECT. The next question is, "What effect have changes in the sector/quality differentials had on bond returns?" In order to analyze this question, we have developed an index of all bond issues on the Telstat pricing tapes with a minimum quality rating of Baa and a minimum of $50 million par value outstanding. This index (the "FRC Index") serves a dual purpose. First, it is decomposed into its con-

1. Footnotes appear at the end of the article.

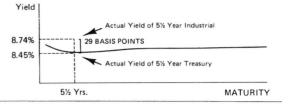

FIGURE III
BEGINNING TREASURY YIELD CURVE, FOURTH QUARTER, 1978

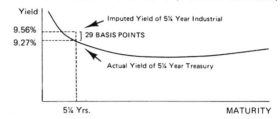

FIGURE IV
ENDING TREASURY YIELD CURVE, FOURTH QUARTER, 1978

stituent parts, thus providing a point of reference against which to compare each of the factors in the bond or portfolio being analyzed. In effect, this allows us to show how a managed portfolio of bonds performed during the period against a broad-based "unmanaged" index of institutional quality issues. Second, as will be demonstrated below, this index universe serves as the basis for a matrix to determine a manager's sector/quality selection effect.

In the process of analyzing each managed portfolio, the maturity, duration, coupon, quality, and yield-to-maturity of the portfolio is compared against the index, thereby showing structural differences. The positioning of a portfolio in terms of these very important characteristics may be reflected in favorable or unfavorable decomposition factors vis-à-vis the index. We have developed a quality scale that reads:

5.0 — U.S. Treasuries
4.5 — Government Agencies (including GNMA)
4.0 — AAA
3.0 — AA
2.0 — A
1.0 — Baa
0.0 — All others

The index derived from the Telstat pricing tapes is run through the model, and the yield-to-maturity and interest rate effect for each issue in the index is determined. This leaves an *additional return,* which is the difference between total return and the sum of yield-to-maturity plus the interest rate effect. This additional return is the basis for determining the sector/quality effect.

A matrix is established as shown in Figure V. The columns show quality designations from the Aaa level down to Baa, while the rows display major sectors such as Corporates, Utilities, . . . and Agencies. The *additional return of each issue is collected in its appropriate sector/quality cell.* The *average* of each cell becomes the sector/quality return for each issue of that classification held in the portfolio being measured.

227

FIGURE V   MATRIX FORMATION
SECTOR/QUALITY RETURNS (WEIGHTED)

	Aaa	Aa	A	Baa
Corporates				
Utilities				
Financial				
Telephone				
Foreign				
GNMA				
Agencies				

FIGURE VI
SECTOR/QUALITY RETURNS (WEIGHTED)

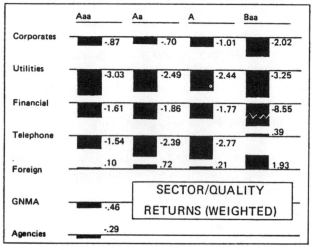

The sector/quality returns for the fourth quarter, 1978 are shown in Figure VI.

It is important to note that sector and quality are shown in relation to each other. Also, the computations for the excess returns in each cell are developed on a market value weighted basis.

Let us now return to the example of the Philip Morris issue. The previous price forecast of 96.69 for that security assumes that the 0.29 basis point beginning yield differential will not change. Such an assumption is unlikely. A sector/quality analysis of all single-A Industrials showed that, on average, they returned −1.013% less than would have been forecast based on just the change in U.S. Treasury yields. Thus, by holding a single-A Industrial, a portfolio manager would have expected to sacrifice about 101 basis points from the same maturity U.S. Treasury issue. Accordingly, let us designate this effect as

$$S/Q = (1.013)$$

(S/Q stands for sector/quality)

THE RESIDUAL RETURN. In the analysis of the Philip Morris issue, the final question is, "How much of the total return is left unexplained by the previous three numbers (yield-to-maturity, interest rate effect, and sector/quality)?" This is merely the "residual" between the total return and those three factors. It represents all other factors such as the call provisions or

possibly pricing tape abnormalities. Our tests indicate that such residuals are generally small and tend to cancel out on large unmanaged portfolios. In cases where the residuals are larger, the underlying reason usually provides significant insights into a manager's selection style. Let us designate the residual as

$$Residual = 0.328$$

The complete model for the analysis of a single bond return is

$$\text{Total Return} = \text{Yield-to-Maturity} + \text{Interest Rate Effect} + \text{Sector/Quality Effect} + \text{Residual}$$

If this model is applied to the Philip Morris issue, the effect is:

$$(1.844\%) = 2.188\% + (3.347\%) + (1.013\%) + 0.328\%$$

PORTFOLIO RESULTS

While the decomposition of returns for a single bond is interesting, the analysis becomes even more meaningful when applied to a portfolio. The factors in the model determine the extent to which a portfolio's results are due to interest rate anticipation, sector/quality selection, or the impact of individual features. This, in turn, permits the observer to make a judgment regarding how effectively a manager applies various active bond management techniques. To illustrate how such judgments are assisted, four additional figures are important:

Figure VII. The FRC Index developed from the Telstat pricing tape is decomposed into its constituent parts. In addition to serving as a data base to establish the sector/quality matrix, this index also provides a benchmark "unmanaged" portfolio against which managed portfolios may be compared. Figure VII is an analysis of index results for the final quarter of 1978; along with the beginning and ending U.S. Treasury yield curves for that period.

The FRC Index Analysis and Treasury yield curves clearly point out the negative environment during this period. The Treasury curve moved up and became more inverted; the sector/quality returns had a distinctly negative bias, with all sector/quality groups, except foreign, producing negative bias. Some of these "cells" were dramatically negative. For example, the Financial/Baa cell was heavily affected by the poor performance of Chrysler Financial Corporation issues. Overall, the sector/quality matrix implies that it did not pay to be aggressive in quality during this period and, indeed, that it was generally difficult to achieve any positive return increment over Treasuries.

Figure VIII. In the process of testing the model, we have evaluated a number of fixed-income portfolios. Figure VIII displays the performance results of three disparate portfolios for the fourth quarter of 1978. An examination of the respective beginning

Figure VII. FRC Index Analysis and U.S. Treasury
Yield Curves

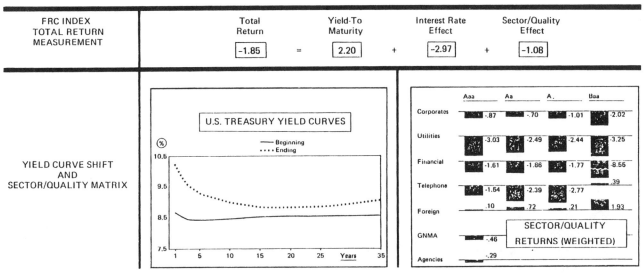

FRC INDEX TOTAL RETURN MEASUREMENT	Total Return		Yield-To Maturity		Interest Rate Effect		Sector/Quality Effect
	-1.85	=	2.20	+	-2.97	+	-1.08

YIELD CURVE SHIFT AND SECTOR/QUALITY MATRIX

U.S. TREASURY YIELD CURVES
—— Beginning
···· Ending

SECTOR/QUALITY RETURNS (WEIGHTED)

	Aaa	Aa	A.	Baa
Corporates	-.87	-.70	-1.01	-2.02
Utilities	-3.03	-2.49	-2.44	-3.25
Financial	-1.61	-1.86	-1.77	-8.55
Telephone	-1.54	-2.39	-2.77	.39
Foreign	.10	.72	.21	1.93
GNMA	-.46			
Agencies	-.29			

portfolio characteristics indicates that average maturities varied from short to long. Average coupon levels ran from slightly higher than the index to a 240 basis point discount from the index (i.e. Portfolio B). Finally, the universe quality level corresponds to roughly a AA+ level. Portfolios A and C were in very high quality instruments with heavy representation in Treasuries and Agencies. Portfolio B had an average quality level just above single A.

In the performance breakdown in Figure VIII,

Figure VIII. Beginning Portfolio Characteristics and Sources of Return

FRANK RUSSELL CO., INC.
FIXED–INCOME PORTFOLIO COMPARISON   FOURTH QUARTER
XYZ INVESTMENT MANAGEMENT CO.   1978

		PORTFOLIO A	PORTFOLIO B	PORTFOLIO C	FRC INDEX
BEGINNING PORTFOLIO CHARAC– TERISTICS	MATURITY	3.55 Yrs.	11.81 Yrs.	19.61 Yrs.	13.87 Yrs.
	DURATION	2.13 Yrs.	8.33 Yrs.	8.96 Yrs.	7.30 Yrs.
	COUPON	8.29%	5.42%	7.85%	7.82%
	QUALITY	4.35	2.19	4.88	3.58
	YIELD TO MATURITY	8.49%	7.40%	8.64%	8.80%
PERFORMANCE BREAKDOWN	YIELD TO MATURITY EFFECT	2.11%	1.86%	2.17%	2.20%
	INTEREST RATE EFFECT	-1.28%	-3.42%	-3.27%	-2.97%
	SECTOR/QUALITY EFFECT	-0.16%	-0.85%	-0.09%	-1.08%
	RESIDUAL	-0.13%	1.80%	-0.26%	0.00%
	STATIC PORTFOLIO RETURN	0.54%	-0.61%	-1.45%	-1.85%
	ACTUAL PORTFOLIO RETURN	0.61%	-0.55%	-1.71%	
	ACTIVITY FACTOR	0.07%	0.06%	-0.26%	

the same methodology is applied to develop the yield-to-maturity, the interest rate effect, the sector/quality effect, and the residual for Portfolios A, B, and C as was applied to the single bond example presented earlier in this paper. That is to say, each bond in a portfolio is decomposed and dollar-weighted portfolio effects are calculated.

Additionally, in Figure VIII the actual portfolio return reported is compared to the static portfolio return. This permits a judgment regarding the impact of a manager's activity during the period.

Figure IX. Figure IX shows the decomposed results for the three portfolios in a somewhat different

light. There are two columns for each portfolio. In the right hand column the *difference between the index and the static portfolio return* produces a management *differential*. For example, in Portfolio A the differential is 2.39%. In the left hand column the differential between that portfolio and the index for each of the components of return is shown. In Portfolio A the differentials for yield-to-maturity, the interest rate effect, sector/quality effect, and residual also add up to 2.39%.

Again, the impact of activity is measured by comparing the static return to the manager's reported return. This activity effect is expressed in the right hand column (e.g. Portfolio A is 0.07%) and added to the management differential. This results in a return attributable to the manager for the period. Portfolio A had a return of 2.46% attributable to this manager.

EVALUATION OF THE RESULTS

These statistics provide important information for assessing a manager's success.

Figure IX. Differential Management Effects Versus Unmanaged Index

FRANK RUSSELL CO., INC.
FIXED–INCOME PORTFOLIO COMPARISON   FOURTH QUARTER
XYZ INVESTMENT MANAGEMENT CO.   1978

	PORTFOLIO A	PORTFOLIO B	PORTFOLIO C
FRC INDEX RETURN	-1.85%	-1.85%	-1.85%
STATIC PORTFOLIO RETURN	0.54	-0.61	-1.45
RETURN DIFFERENTIALS:			
YIELD TO MATURITY	-0.09	-0.34	-0.03
INTEREST RATE EFFECT	1.69	-0.45	-0.30
SECTOR/QUALITY EFFECT	0.92	0.23	0.99
RESIDUAL	-0.13	1.80	-0.26
MANAGEMENT DIFFERENTIAL	2.39	1.24	0.40
MANAGER'S REPORTED RETURN	0.61	-0.55	-1.71
STATIC PORTFOLIO RETURN	0.54	-0.61	-1.45
EFFECT OF ACTIVITY DURING PERIOD	0.07	0.06	-0.26
RETURN ATTRIBUTABLE TO THIS MANAGER	2.46%	1.30%	0.14%

229

For example, Portfolio A with a short maturity and high average quality, achieved a positive static return of 0.54%. Figure IX shows that this manager achieved positive differentials over the index in both his interest rate effect and his sector/quality effect. Portfolio C had a high quality level, but his maturity was significantly longer than the other two portfolios and the index. Consequently, he had a static portfolio return of −1.45%, which included an unfavorable interest rate differential of −0.30% from the index. Nevertheless, his high quality orientation permitted a favorable sector/quality differential of 0.99% over the index.

By contrast, portfolio B is characterized by medium quality, lower coupon holdings. Although the interest rate effect of −3.42% was worse than either other portfolio or the index, the most striking effect was the high positive residual of 1.80%. This portfolio was heavily committed to discount industrial issues with active sinking funds, which was the principal reason for the large residual.

Although this methodology has proven to be useful in analyzing how managers apply different active bond management techniques to portfolio management, the client must recognize that informed judgments on a manager's abilities require continuous monitoring over an extended period of time, long enough to allow his "style" to work out in the market. Thus, see Appendix D.

Figure X. Here we have *hypothesized* a series of total and decomposed portfolio returns over a three-year period. The total return from the FRC Index has been set on the zero return line. The other lines represent the quarterly differential of the sample portfolio's return over the index's total return. Also, the differential between the sample portfolio's interest rate effect and the index's interest rate effect is plotted, as are the sector/quality and yield-to-maturity differentials. We believe that this form of presentation will effectively display those areas where a manager adds value to any actively managed bond portfolio.

Thus, in effect, Figure VII shows the environment in which managers had to operate during the final quarter of the year. Figure VIII displays important structural characteristics of three sample portfolios, along with the results of running each portfolio through the model. Figure IX offers insights into the value added to each portfolio over and above an unmanaged portfolio. And Figure X tracks the results over an extended period of time.

RISK CONSIDERATIONS

We believe that the foregoing methodology offers a promising approach for evaluating bond managers. One question has been left unaddressed, how-

230

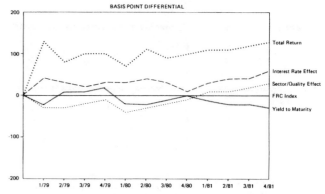

Figure X. Analysis Across Time

SAMPLE
SEGMENTATION OF FIXED-INCOME TOTAL PORTFOLIO RETURN
RELATIVE TO THE FRC INDEX

ever: How can the total returns from an actively managed portfolio be risk-adjusted? Both empirical and analytical results indicate that a bond's return may be a nonlinear function of most single-dimension risk measures. Also, such measures have difficulty in considering call risk, risk in conjunction with common stock portfolios, and so on. Presently, the theoretical state of the art does not provide a single linear bond risk measure, such as beta does for common stocks.[2]

On the other hand, the basic return equation presented here does imply a built-in risk adjustment. Over a full cycle in both the shape and the level of yield curves, the expected return should equal the yield-to-maturity (YTM) and the other effects should net out to zero, assuming an efficient bond market. Since managers repeatedly refer to such "cycles," it seems that this type of analysis provides an excellent risk adjustment against the general market yield-to-maturity, as reflected in the shape and level of the market's yield curve at any given point in time.

In conclusion, based upon our tests of actual portfolios, the methodology has proven valuable. In many ways, it simply parallels established practice by analyzing the breakdowns in bond performance results as anticipated by a manager as well as basing the analysis on the "default riskless" rate established in the Treasury market. Also, it provides fund administrators with an important communication tool for evaluating manager results and strategies over a market cycle.

---

[1] This explanation is provided for illustrative clarity. Actually, because of the slope of the beginning yield curve (with its resultant "roll" effect in the yield-to-maturity), the actual interest rate effect is priced on the difference of both the beginning and ending Treasury yield curves at the five-and one-quarter year range, after adjustment for the 29 basis points differential.

[2] For an extended discussion of this problem, see the sections on risk and risk-adjustment in the *Investment Manager's Handbook*, Chapter IX, Bond Management, by H. Russell Fogler, Dow Jones-Irwin, 1980.

The art of risk management in bond portfolios*

Duration matching immunization strategies outperform maturity matching strategies. Skill is critically important for the success of more active policies.

G. O. Bierwag, George G. Kaufman, Robert Schweitzer, and Alden Toevs

This paper demonstrates that risk, at least for default-free coupon bonds, is a function of the investor's planning period as well as of the characteristics of the security or portfolio itself. Thus, risk is more complex than is widely believed, and the accurate formulation of general risk measures applicable to all investors at all times is highly unlikely. We go on to demonstrate, however, that passive strategies are available in this area that can effectively reduce or even eliminate interest rate risk for most investors. In the process, we present empirical evidence on the success of such passive hedging strategies as well as of alternative active strategies that attempt to outperform the passive strategies.

Our arguments enlarge and elaborate on previous work on this subject provided by two articles in recent issues of this *Journal*. Both of these earlier articles emphasized the importance of the investor's planning period or investment horizon in formulating bond portfolio management policies and in measuring performance.

Seymour Smidt demonstrated that the same bond can have different risk-reward characteristics for different investors.[1] For a given change in interest rates, the greater the difference between the "duration" of a default-free bond (or bond portfolio) and the length of the planning period of the investor, the greater is the change in the return over the investor's planning period. If the duration of the bond were

equal to the investor's planning period, the change in interest rates would not reduce the return on the bond from that promised at the time the bond was purchased. Interest rate risk would have been effectively eliminated. Thus, a change in interest rates affects investors in the same bond differently when they have different planning periods. Smidt concludes that "the risk of an asset depends in part on the characteristic of the investor as well as the characteristics of the asset."[2]

Francis Trainer, Jess Yawitz, and William Marshall argue that the risk assumed by an investor in default-free bonds depends on the difference between the maturity of the bond and the investor's planning period.[3] They conclude that "the least risky security is the one whose maturity matches the length of the HP (holding period)."[4]

IMMUNIZATION THEORY

Investors could always realize the yields promised them at the time they purchase their bonds if they were able to purchase default-free zero coupon bonds with maturities equal to their planning periods. But what if zero coupon bonds do not exist for the required planning periods or cannot be constructed through short sales or option strategies? That is, what if markets are incomplete?

In an important article, Lawrence Fisher and Roman Weil have proven that it is possible, under restrictive assumptions, to devise a strategy that protects investors in default-free coupon bonds from unexpected changes in interest rates during the planning period in such a way that the yield realized will never be less than the yield-to-maturity for that period at the time they purchased the bond.[5] The assumptions re-

* An earlier version of the paper was presented at the Fall Seminar of the Institute for Quantitative Research in Finance in Hot Springs, Virginia, October 28-31, 1979.

1. Footnotes appear at the end of the article.

231

stricted the analysis to a one-time change in interest rates of equal magnitude for all maturities across the yield curve as well as zero taxes and transaction costs. In addition, Fisher and Weil used continuous compounding.

Under the Fisher-Weil strategy, the investor must calculate a weighted average of the periods in which the bond (or bond portfolio) is expected to make its coupon and maturity payments and must then select those bonds (or that bond portfolio) for which this weighted average is equal to the investor's planning period. In computing the average, the payment periods are weighted by the proportion of the present value of the corresponding payment to the overall present value of all payments (the price of the bond).

If the yield curve is flat, so that all one-period discount rates are equal, the equation for the weighted average of the payment periods is equal to the statistic developed more than forty years ago by Frederick Macaulay to measure the average life of a bond.[6] If the yield curve is not flat, the Fisher-Weil and Macaulay measures differ. Nevertheless, because of the similarity of the measures, Fisher and Weil adopted Macaulay's term "duration." For the flat yield curve, the duration of a bond is defined as:

$$D = \frac{\sum_{n=1}^{m} \frac{Cn}{(1+i)^n} + \frac{Am}{(1+i)^m}}{\sum_{n=1}^{m} \frac{C}{(1+i)^n} + \frac{A}{(1+i)^m}}, \qquad (4)$$

where: C = coupon payment,

A = maturity payment,

i = yield-to-maturity,

n = years to coupon payment,

m = years to maturity.

Fisher and Weil described their strategy for realizing no less than the yield promised for the planning period at the time of purchase as an "immunization" strategy.

Subsequent research by Bierwag, Kaufman, Khang and others has shown that immunization is possible for default-free coupon bonds under conditions less restrictive than those postulated by Fisher and Weil.[8] Portfolios may be immunized for discrete compounding, for more complex types of unexpected interest rate changes, for more than one unexpected change in interest rates during the planning period, and for multiple planning periods. However, the investor must predict the correct stochastic (random) process generating interest rate changes even though prediction of interest rates themselves is unnecessary. (Expected interest rate changes may be assumed to be already impounded in existing market yields.)

The stochastic generating process describes whether unexpected interest rate changes will affect all maturities equally, short-term maturities more than long-term, long-term more than short term, and so on. The nature of the stochastic process determines the exact weights in the formula for duration that provides for immunization. This duration is termed the immunizing duration or ID.

Although the formulas used to compute IDs become more complex than are given by equation (1), they remain weighted averages of the payment periods with the weights related to the proportional present value of the payments but not necessarily to the proportional present values themelves. Equations for IDs that are consistent with a number of reasonable stochastic processes are shown in the Appendix.[9]

We can illustrate how an immunization strategy works in a simple example of a single bond. Unexpected interest rate changes after the purchase of a bond or bond portfolio have two effects. One, they affect the prices of bonds. Two, they affect the interest rate at which the coupons and maturing bonds in the portfolio may be reinvested until the end of the planning period. The two effects work in opposite directions: An unexpected increase in rates, for example, will decrease bond prices but will increase the income from reinvestment during the planning period. Thus, these changes affect the overall return the investor will realize.

For a single bond, the annual realized return for a given planning period of length s that is equal to or shorter than the maturity of the bond is computed as follows:

$$h_s = \left[\frac{P_{t+s} + \sum_{n=1}^{s} C_n \prod_{q=n+1}^{s} (1 + i_q)}{P_t} \right]^{1/s} - 1, \qquad (2)$$

where:

h_s = annual return realized for s periods,

P_{t+s} = sale price at period t + s,

P_t = purchase price at period t,

s = length of planning period,

C_n = coupon payment in t + n,

i_q = one period interest rates in period t + q,

$\prod$ = product of a geometric series.

The equations for a single bond whose maturity is longer than the planning period and for bond portfolios are similar.

An unexpected increase in interest rates after purchase, on the one hand, will reduce the return from that promised at the time of purchase by reducing P_{t+s} in the numerator below its expected or amortized value. On the other hand, it will increase the return above that promised at time of purchase by increasing the income from coupon reinvestment income (the

232

second term in the numerator). The net effect on the total return depends on the relative magnitude of the two individual effects. These magnitudes, in turn, depend on the difference between the length of the immunizing duration of the bond and the length of the particular investor's planning period.

As already noted, when the appropriate immunizing duration of the bond is equal to the investor's planning period, the effects of interest rate changes on the price change and reinvestment components of return are approximately equal in magnitude. As they are opposite in direction, however, the two effects essentially offset each other so that the yield realized for the period cannot fall below the promised yield. The bond investor is immunized. When the length of the planning period and the ID are unequal, the two effects only partially offset each other and the realized return may fall below that promised at the beginning of the planning period.

If the ID exceeds the planning period, the downward price effect of an unexpected interest rate increase will outweigh the upward reinvestment effect, and the realized return will fall below the promised return. If the ID is shorter than the planning period, the reinvestment effect will outweigh the price effect, and unexpected interest rate increases will produce a return greater than that promised.[10] These outcomes would be reversed for unexpected interest rate decreases.

The above relationships are demonstrated numerically in Table 1 for the one bond case. We assume for simplicity that the yield curve is flat at 7½%, that there are no transactions costs associated with the reinvestment of coupons, and that an investor has a planning period of 10 years. All interest rate changes are assumed to be across-the-board, so that the yield curve will move up or down by the same amount for every maturity.

If the investor wishes to guarantee a return of at least 7½%, the immunization strategy requires that the investor select a default-free coupon bond with an immunizing duration of ten years as defined by equation (1). Such a bond is approximated by a 5% coupon, 15-year bond. If the investor wishes to attempt to better that return, he or she should choose a bond having a longer or shorter duration than the 10-year planning period, depending on his or her prediction of interest rates relative to the market consensus. Of course, the risk of realizing a lower return by following such an active policy is greater than that for the passive immunization strategy.

If interest rates do not change in the 10 years, the investor will realize an annual return of 7½% regardless of the duration of the bond selected. For example, when the market rate of interest is 7½%, the

TABLE 1

EFFECTS OF AN UNEXPECTED INCREASE IN INTEREST RATE
ON THREE BOND STRATEGIES PER $100

Given: Flat yield curve = 7½%
Coupon bond rate = 5%
Planning period = 10 years

	Maturity (years)		
	10	15	20
Duration (years)	7.8	10.1	11.6
Beginning bond price	82.63	77.71	74.31
Promised annual return (percent)	7.50	7.50	7.50
A. No change in interest rates:			
Bond price after 10 years	100.00	89.73	82.63
Coupons paid	50.00	50.00	50.00
Reinvestment of coupons semi-annually @ 7½%	22.54	22.54	22.54
Total value of investment	172.54	162.27	155.17
Realized annual return (percent)	7.50	7.50	7.50
B. Immediate increase to 9%:			
Bond price after 10 years	100.00	84.17	73.98
Coupons paid	50.00	50.00	50.00
Reinvestment of coupons semi-annually @ 9%	28.43	28.43	28.43
Total value of investment	178.43	162.60	152.41
Realized annual return (percent)	7.84	7.52	7.32
Loss in bond price	0.00	5.56	8.65
Gain in reinvestment income	5.89	5.89	5.89
Net change	+5.89	+0.33	−2.76

market price of the 5% coupon, $100 par value, 15-year bond with an approximate immunizing duration of 10 years is $77.71. Ten years later, at the end of the planning period, the price of the bond will have risen to $89.73 from the amortization of the discount. At the end of the period, the investor has also collected $50 in coupons in 20 equal $2.50 installments. If the coupons are fully reinvested at the end of each semi-annual period at 7½%, the interest income over the period will amount to $22.54. Substituting those numbers in equation (2) and solving for the annual return yields 7½%.

In another case, a 5% coupon, 10-year bond would be priced at $82.63 at the beginning of the period. This bond would have an initial duration of 7.8 years. Its value at the end of the period is $100.00. Coupons again would total $50, and their reinvestment income would produce $22.54 by the end of the 10 years. The annual return for that bond computed by equation (2) is also 7½%. As may be seen from Table 1, a 7½% return is also realized for a 5% coupon 20-year bond if interest rates do not change.

Now, let interest rates rise unexpectedly from 7½% to 9%, immediately after the purchase of the bonds and let them stay there for the remainder of the 10-year planning period. The price of the 15-year maturity, 10-year duration bond at the end of the period will be only $84.17, or $5.56 less than before. On the other hand, the reinvestment of the coupons at 9% will yield $28.43, or $5.89 more than before. The two changes approximately offset each other, and the annual return increases slightly to 7.52%.[11]

That, however, will not be the case for the other two bonds, including the 10-year bond whose maturity is equal to the planning period but whose ID is only 7.8 years. The price of the 10-year bond will rise from $82.63 to $100.00 as before, but the yield from the reinvestment of the coupons will now be $28.42, rather than $22.54. The total return thus increases to 7.87%. If the 5% coupon, 20-year maturity, 11.7-year duration bond had been purchased, its price at the end of the 10 years would be $73.98, slightly lower than the purchase price of $74.31. That is also $8.65 less than if interest rates had not changed. The price loss would more than offset the gain in coupon reinvestment income. The total annual return would be only 7.32%.

The ordering of the returns would be reversed if interest rates declined unexpectedly, but the 15-year bond would still generate at least a 7½% return. These results would differ if the investor's planning period were shorter (say, 7.8 years) or longer (say, 11.6 years) than 10 years. If it were 7.8 years, the 10-year bond would now be the bond that would guarantee at least the 7½% return.

If interest rates do not change unexpectedly, a default-free coupon bond generates a promised return to the end of the planning period that is known to the investor at the time the bond is purchased. Thus, the only risk the investor incurs is the risk that arises from unexpected interest rate changes that may reduce the realized return below the promised return.

It follows from the above analysis that, in a world of uncertainty, an investor can always realize at least the promised yield by purchasing one or more default-free coupon bonds whose appropriate immunizing duration is equal to the planning period. At this point, interest rate risk is effectively zero.[12] For bonds with durations either longer or shorter than the planning period, the risk of receiving less than the promised return is greater than zero and increases with the magnitude of the difference between the duration and the length of the planning period.

We can see from Table 1 that the difference between the realized return and the promised return is greater when the duration declines by 2.3 years from 10.1 to 7.8 years for the 10-year bond than when the duration increases by 1.5 years from 10.1 to 11.6 years for the 20-year bond, although the maturity change is 5 years for both bonds. Nevertheless, the differences in realized returns from the immunized return for these two bonds is proportional to the differences in their

duration from the immunized 15-year bond. Thus, the 10-year bond generates a return 32 basis points higher than the 7.52% immunized return; this is 60% greater than the shortfall of 20 basis points generated by the 20-year bond and is about the same percentage as its duration of 7.8 years is shorter than 10 years as the 11.6-year duration of the 20-year bond is longer than 10 years.

DURATION'S ATTRACTIONS

The determinants of the risk on a default-free bond may be expressed as:

$$\text{Risk} = f \, (\text{PL, ID}), \qquad (3)$$

where PL is the investor's planning period and ID is the appropriate immunizing duration. This formulation verifies Smidt's statement that bond risk depends on the characteristics of both the bond (ID) and the investor (PL). Furthermore, measures of risk computed for a given bond or bond portfolio, a given planning period, and a given stochastic process are not meaningful for investors with different planning periods, because the computation of the appropriate immunizing duration depends on the nature of the stochastic process that causes interest rates to change, because bond risk also depends on characteristics of the market and the ability of the investor to identify correctly the actual stochastic process, and, finally, because it is unlikely that all investors will have the same planning period. Consequently, universal risk measures cannot be estimated. At best, we can compute risk measures for a given bond and a given stochastic process for a range of planning periods; investors may choose those that correspond to their own particular situation.[13]

Thus, *risk is related to the difference between the length of an investor's planning period and the bond's duration as Smidt argued, not maturity as Trainer et al. argued.* As we can see in Table 1, equating maturity with the length of the planning period eliminates price risk but it does not eliminate reinvestment risk.

A coupon bond is in fact a series of zero coupon bonds having maturity values equal to the coupon payments and terms-to-maturity equal to the term of each coupon payment, plus one zero coupon bond having a maturity value equal to the par value of the coupon bond and a term-to-maturity equal to the maturity of the coupon bond. Because duration is an average of all these payment dates, it is always less than the final maturity of a coupon bond. Therefore, we may view an immunization strategy that matches the ID of a bond to the investor's planning period as a diversification strategy that uses bonds of different terms-to-maturity on each side of the investor's planning period. Duration matching approximately transforms a coupon bond into a zero coupon bond with a term-to-maturity (and thus also duration) equal to the planning period.

Duration analysis has important implications for formulating and evaluating bond portfolio strategies. It also improves significantly on traditional maturity analysis for these purposes, although the rules of thumb remain the same.

For example, investors in default-free bonds may pursue either passive or active policies. A passive policy locks in the current market interest rate for the investor's particular planning period. It is a hedging strategy for the investor who prefers not to try to out-guess and possibly outperform the market. The optimum long-term passive strategy is a duration matching immunization strategy.

On the other hand, an active strategy attempts to achieve a return greater than the current promised market return for the planning period. To be successful, the investor must predict interest rate changes that are different from those that are expected by the market, that are incorporated in the existing market term structure, and that will be realized if interest rates do not change unexpectedly. The expected return is higher but so also is the risk. As is demonstrated in Table 1, if an investor expects interest rates to be higher than the market does, the appropriate ID of an active portfolio would be one that is shorter than the planning period. The resulting return would be greater than the promised return. Conversely, if the investor expects interest rates to be lower than the market does, the appropriate ID of an active portfolio would be one that is longer than the planning period.

EMPIRICAL EVIDENCE

All of this may be fine in theory but does it work in practice? After all, the proof of the pudding is in the eating!

How well do these rules work in the real world? To find out, we simulated alternative strategies for the period 1925 to 1978 using annual interest rate data. Transactions costs and taxes are assumed to be zero for prime corporate bonds.[14] All coupons are assumed to be paid in full and compounded semi-annually. A 10-year planning period is assumed. We then constructed eight portfolios of bonds depicting two active strategies, five passive duration matching strategies, and one "yardstick" maturity matching portfolio. The five duration matching immunization strategies reflect five alternative assumptions about the nature of the stochastic process for interest rate changes.

The simplest strategy assumes a flat yield curve and equal interest rate changes for all maturities. The

corresponding ID is the Macaulay formulation shown in equation (1) and identified as ID1. The other four immunization strategies assume that the yield curve can have any shape.

The second strategy assumes further that any unexpected interest rate changes affect all maturities equally up or down by an amount λ, where λ represents the magnitude of the change as shown in Figure 1. Thus, the shape, although not the location, of the yield curve remains the same before and immediately after the shock. This strategy is referred to as an additive shock and is identified as ID2. (The ID equations for this and the next two shocks are shown in the Appendix.)

The third strategy assumes that the unexpected interest rate changes cause the rate on each maturity to be changed by an amount that is related to the product of the rate and λ, and is identified as ID3. This is a more complex shock to the term structure and is referred to as a multiplicative shock. The shape of the yield curve immediately after the shock relative to the yield curve before the shock depends upon the shape of the initial yield curve. If the initial yield curve was upward sloping, long-term rates would change more than short-term rates. If the initial yield curve was downward sloping, long-term rates would change less than short-term rates.

The final two immunization strategies assume that short-term rates always change by more than long-term rates. The two differ by the proportion that the short-term rates fluctuate more than the long-term rates. This is determined by the value of α in the ID4 equation in the Appendix Table. The greater α, the greater are changes in short-term rates relative to long-term rates. The relative magnitude of the changes in short- and long-term rates also depends on the slope of the term structure. For a moderately upward sloping structure, an $\alpha = 1$ indicates that the changes in the one-year rate are approximately three times as great as the changes in the 10-year rates; an $\alpha = 0.1$ indicates that the changes in one-year rates are approximately 1.3 times as great. The first strategy is labeled ID4(1.0) and the second ID4(0.1). It can be seen from the equations that, as the value of α approaches 0, ID4 approaches ID3. The five stochastic processes developed here do not exhaust all possibilities, but do appear reasonable.[15]

All of the immunization strategies select a portfolio of bonds whose appropriate ID is equal to the 10-year planning period.[16] All portfolios consist of combinations of two bonds, one long and one short. The long bond is a 20-year bond at the beginning of the planning period that is maintained in the portfolio, so that its maturity declines linearly to 10 years. The short

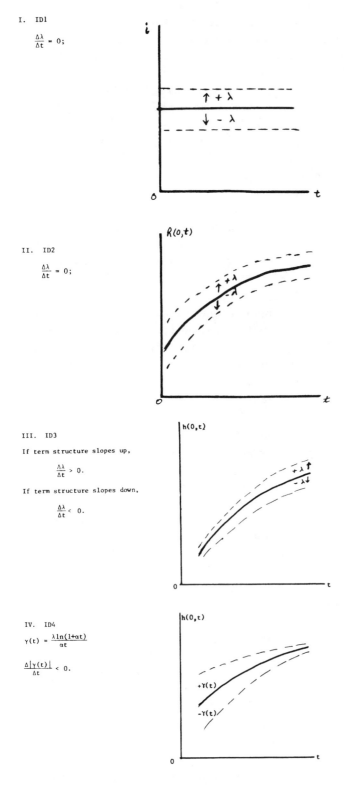

FIGURE 1

DIAGRAMATICAL REPRESENTATION OF INTEREST RATE SHOCKS

FOR IMMUNIZING DURATIONS

I. ID1

$$\frac{\Delta\lambda}{\Delta t} = 0;$$

II. ID2

$$\frac{\Delta\lambda}{\Delta t} = 0;$$

III. ID3

If term structure slopes up,

$$\frac{\Delta\lambda}{\Delta t} > 0.$$

If term structure slopes down,

$$\frac{\Delta\lambda}{\Delta t} < 0.$$

IV. ID4

$$\gamma(t) = \frac{\lambda \ln(1+\alpha t)}{\alpha t}$$

$$\frac{\Delta|\gamma(t)|}{\Delta t} < 0.$$

bond has an initial maturity of ten years, equal to the length of the planning period and is also maintained in the portfolio throughout the planning period so that its maturity is always equal to the remaining length of the planning period. Dollar amounts of the two bonds

are selected so that the initial ID of the portfolio is 10 years.

Because the passage of time does not reduce maturity and duration equally, the portfolio must be restructured at least annually to maintain the ID equal to the remaining length of the planning period.[17] The use of two bonds minimizes the number of bonds in the portfolio that need to be sold to achieve the annual restructuring, and we selected the initial 10- and 20-year bonds to reduce transactions costs. Most of the restructuring may be achieved through additional purchases of the short bond from the proceeds of the coupon payments.

Because duration is an average, there is an infinite number of portfolio compositions that are consistent with a specific value of duration.[18] However, because the relationship between interest rates and bond prices is not linear, all portfolio compositions do not generate the same results.[19] Theory and evidence suggest that the differences are not great if the investor correctly identifies the stochastic process and uses the correct ID.[20] The differences become more important if the stochastic process is not identified correctly and the incorrect ID is used. In these instances, the narrower the maturity spread of the portfolio, the smaller appear to be any returns below those promised. For zero coupon bonds with a maturity equal to the length of the planning period, a true "bullet" portfolio, the promised return is realized regardless of the stochastic process. The portfolio composition tested in this paper represents a "middle ground" barbell. More compressed portfolios may be expected to be better immunized against all possible stochastic processes and less compressed portfolios to be more poorly immunized.

One active policy involves "going short." That is, the portfolio consists of a series of one-year bonds that are successively rolled over each year. The second active policy involves "going long."[21] This portfolio consists of one initial 20-year maturity bond that is maintained in the portfolio so that its maturity declines to 10 years at the end of the 10-year planning period. In both of these active strategies, all coupon payments are used to buy the particular bonds involved in the respective strategy.

The "yardstick" portfolio consists of a single bond having an initial maturity equal to the 10-year planning period. Through time, all coupons in this portfolio are reinvested in bonds having a maturity equal to the remaining length of the planning period. Because, as noted earlier, the duration of a portfolio of coupon bonds is always less than the term-to-maturity, the maturity matching strategy belongs in the "go short" class. Nevertheless, this strategy is specified separately as a yardstick portfolio, because it has been widely used as an "immunization" strategy, e.g., by Trainer et al., and thus provides a convenient basis against which to evaluate all the other strategies with respect to immunization.

We evaluated the strategies both as passive and as active strategies. On the passive side, we evaluated each of the seven strategies on the basis of how close the yield realized over the planning period is to the associated promised yield. This is measured both by the frequency with which the realized yield is within plus or minus 5 basis points of the promised yield, and also by how often the realized yield is closer to the promised yield than the yield generated by the maturity strategy. As an active strategy, the portfolios are evaluated both by how often the generated realized yield is above the promised yield and how often the realized yield is the higher yield.

In order to examine the strategies under different market conditions, we divided the 1925-78 period into three approximately equal subperiods according to the movement in interest rates. In the first subperiod, 1925-49, interest rates decline and remained at low levels. In the second subperiod, 1940-63, interest rates began to climb slowly. In the third subperiod, 1954-78, interest rates became more volatile and increased sharply on average. The overlapping dates in the subperiods occur because of the assumed 10-year holding period. The last portfolio in each period is purchased 10 years before the end of the period. Thus, the last planning period began in 1939 in the first subperiod, 1953 in the second, and 1968 in the third. Because the overall period includes a severe depression, numerous recessions, a major world war, two smaller wars, and a severe peacetime inflation, one can expect the results to be robust and applicable to other periods. The results appear in Table 2. In addition to the measures described above, the average promised and realized yields are also shown.

We can readily see that the duration matching immunization strategies generate returns closer to the promised return than the maturity or the other non-immunization strategies. The ID1, ID2, and ID3 strategies produce very similar results. The results for ID4 differ somewhat, particularly when $\alpha = 1$. For the overall period, immunization strategies ID1-3 generated returns closer to the promised return than those generated by the maturity strategy about 90% of the time. For the individual subperiods, the success of these strategies ranges from 80% to 100%. Strategies ID1-3 also produce returns that are within 5 basis points of the promised return considerably more often than do those produced by the maturity strategy. Strategy ID4, with an $\alpha = 1$, which assumes that unex-

pected changes in short-term rates are much greater than those in long-term rates, immunizes less successfully. Indeed, in the 1954-78 subperiod, ID4 ($\alpha = 1$) fails to beat the maturity strategy in any year. In contrast, this strategy immunizes better than the maturity strategy in the 1925-49 subperiod and generates returns closer to the promised yield more often than do strategies ID1-3. When α is 0.1, the results are somewhere between those of ID4 ($\alpha = 1$) and ID3. In no period, however, are the results in favor of immunization improved over those of ID3.

The relatively poor results of ID4, which is the most intuitively pleasing, may be attributed in part to the use of annual average data. In these data, the greater variability observed in short-term rates for briefer intervals is averaged out. For the entire period, the standard deviation in one-year rates is only 10% greater than in 10-year rates and is only 50% greater in the most extreme subperiod. In contrast, the differences in variability are considerably greater for monthly observations.

The preliminary evidence in Table 2 suggests that, if the past is any guide to the future, portfolios structured on the basis of the simplest ID to compute — ID1, which requires only readily available promised yield data — have immunized almost as well as the more complex strategies and appear to be the most cost-effective. Although the duration matching immunization strategies come closer to realizing the promised returns than does the maturity matching strategy, contrary to theory, they generally produce returns somewhat less than those promised.[22]

As noted earlier, the above results are sensitive to the composition of the portfolios. If the width of the maturity spread in the barbell portfolios were widened to include, say, only one- and 20-year maturity bonds, all of the duration matching strategies fail in almost every instance to realize returns closer to the promised returns than those realized by the maturity matching strategy. This suggests that the "true" stochastic process may be too complex even in the Durand data to be captured adequately by the IDs tested. On the other hand, the investor can minimize shortfalls from the promised return by compressing the portfolio into a bullet or near bullet portfolio regardless of the stochastic process assumed.[23] Attempts to eliminate interest rate risk by duration matching immunization strategies appear to subject investors to a new "stochastic process risk." Thus, the potential gain from pursuing a duration matching immunization strategy depends on the relative magnitudes of the interest rate and stochastic process risks, and this strategy is desirable only if the latter is perceived to be smaller than the former.

TABLE 2

PROMISED AND REALIZED RETURNS FOR ALTERNATIVE PORTFOLIO STRATEGIES
10 YEAR PLANNING PERIODS 1925-1978

Strategy	Return							
	Promised (Annual Average)[c]	Realized (Annual Average)	Realized Minus Promised	Closer to Promised than Maturity Strategy	Within 5 Basis Points of Promised	Greater than Promised	Highest Realized	Lowest Realized
1925-1978[a]				(Percent)				
Immunization[d]								
ID1	3.364	3.286	−.078	86	48	9	0	0
ID2		3.289	−.075	89	48	9	0	0
ID3		3.289	−.075	89	48	9	0	0
ID4 (0.1)		3.270	−.094	82	27	2	0	0
ID4 (1.0)		3.236	−.128	52	34	11	2	0
Maturity		3.329	−.035	—	16	41	0	0
Rollover		2.927	−.437	2	7	48	50	48
Long Bond[b]	↓	3.194	−.170	9	7	45	48	52
1925-1949[a]								
Immunization[d]								
ID1	3.697	3.552	−.145	93	13	0	0	0
ID2		3.555	−.142	93	13	0	0	0
ID3		3.555	−.142	93	13	0	0	0
ID4 (0.1)		3.595	−.102	93	20	0	0	0
ID4 (1.0)		3.668	−.029	93	53	27	0	0
Maturity		3.465	−.232	—	0	0	0	0
Rollover		1.801	−1.896	0	0	0	0	100
Long Bond[b]	↓	4.749	+1.052	7	0	100	100	0
1940-1963[a]								
Immunization[d]								
ID1	2.257	2.214	−.043	79	50	14	0	0
ID2		2.214	−.043	86	50	14	0	0
ID3		2.214	.043	86	50	14	0	0
ID4 (0.1)		2.214	−.043	86	50	7	0	0
ID4 (1.0)		2.212	−.045	64	50	7	7	0
Maturity		2.214	−.043	—	36	29	0	0
Rollover		2.074	−.183	7	14	43	50	43
Long Bond[b]	↓	1.987	−.270	21	21	36	43	57
1954-1978[a]								
Immunization[d]								
ID1	4.064	4.026	−.038	87	80	13	0	0
ID2		4.027	−.037	87	80	13	0	0
ID3		4.027	−.037	87	80	13	0	0
ID4 (0.1)		3.930	−.134	67	13	0	0	0
ID4 (1.0)		3.759	−.305	0	0	0	0	0
Maturity		4.234	+.170	—	13	93	0	0
Rollover		4.848	+.784	0	7	100	100	0
Long Bond[b]	↓	2.767	−1.297	0	0	0	0	100

[a] The last portfolio in each period is purchased 10 years before the last year in the period.

[b] Maintained bond with initial maturity of 20 years.

[c] 10-year yield-to-maturity at date of purchase.

[d] Portfolio consists of initial 10- and 20-year bonds.

The evidence in Table 2 also indicates that the passive strategies performed less well than the active strategies in maximizing returns, if the investor had selected the "correct" active strategy. It is evident that the "correct" active strategy varied depending on the movement in interest rates during the planning period. Of course, in practice, selecting the "correct" active strategy requires that the investor accurately predict interest rates.

Because interest rates both increased and decreased in the 1925-78 period, the "go-short" rollover and "go-long" strategies performed about equally well. In the 1925-49 period, when promised yields declined sharply on average, the go-long strategy outperformed the promised yield and all other strategies in every year. In 1954-78, when interest rates increased sharply on average, the rollover strategy outperformed the other strategies 100% of the time. In 1940-63, when interest rates increased slowly from very low levels, the two strategies did about equally well on average. The maturity strategy did poorer than the rollover strategy when interest rates rose and better when rates declined.

Thus, the maturity strategy remains a hedging strategy, but one that is generally inferior to the correct immunization strategies. It is of interest to note that, on average, neither active strategy generated returns greater than the promised yields for the period as a whole or for the middle subperiod.

[1] Seymour Smidt, "Investment horizons and performance measurements," *Journal of Portfolio Management*, Winter 1978, 18-22.

[2] Smidt, p. 20.

[3] Francis H. Trainer, Jr., Jess B. Yawitz, and William J. Marshall, "Holding period is the key to risk thresholds," *Journal of Portfolio Management*, Winter 1979, 48-54.

[4] Trainer, et al., p. 53.

[5] Lawrence Fisher and Roman Weil, "Coping with the Risk of Interest-Rate Fluctuations: Returns to Bondholders from Naive and Optimal Strategies," *Journal of Business*, October 1971, 408-431. The promised yield-to-maturity is defined as the yield-to-maturity that would exist in the market on a zero coupon bond with the relevant maturity. The theory assumes that the implicit forward rates are unbiased estimates of the expected future rates for the same period.

[6] F. R. Macaulay, *Some Theoretical Problems Suggested by the Movements of Interest Rates, Bond Yields, and Stock Prices in the United States Since 1856* (New York: National Bureau of Economic Research, 1938).

[7] Duration has been previously discussed in this *Journal* by Richard W. McEnally, "Duration as a practical tool for bank management," *Journal of Portfolio Management*, Summer 1977, 53-57; D. Don Ezra, "Immunization: A new look for actuarial liabilities," *Journal of Portfolio Management*, Winter 1976, 50-53; and Madeline W. Einhorn, "Breaking tradition in bond portfolio investment," *Journal of Portfolio Management*, Spring 1975, 35-43. For a derivation of duration and its relationship to bond price volatility, see Michael H. Hopewell and George G. Kaufman, "Bond Price Volatility and Years to Maturity: A Generalized Respecification," *American Economic Review*, September 1973, 749-753.

[8] Reviews of recent developments appear in G. O. Bierwag and George G. Kaufman, "Bond Portfolio Strategy Simulations: A Critique," *Journal of Financial and Quantitative Analysis*, September 1978, 519-525; G. O. Bierwag, George G. Kaufman, and Chulsoon Khang, "Duration and Bond Portfolio Analysis: An Overview," *Journal of Financial and Quantitative Analysis*, November 1978, 671-681; George G. Kaufman, "Measuring Risk and Return for Bonds: A New Approach," *Journal of Bank Research*, Summer 1978, 82-90; G. O. Bierwag, "Immunization, Duration, and the Term Structure of Interest Rates," *Journal of Financial and Quantitative Analysis*, December 1977, 725-741; G. O. Bierwag, George Kaufman, and Alden Toevs, "Management Strategies for Savings and Loan Associations to Reduce Interest Rate Risk," *Proceedings of Conference on New Sources of Capital for the Savings and Loan Industry* (Federal Home Loan Bank of San Francisco, 1979); G. O. Bierwag, George Kaufman, and Alden Toevs, "Immunizing for Multiple Planning Periods," (Working Paper, University of Oregon, June 1980), and G. O. Bierwag, George Kaufman and Alden Toevs, "The Sensitivity of Immunization to Correctly and Incorrectly Identified Stochastic Processes," (Working Paper, University of Oregon, August 1980).

[9] Duration is frequently used also as a proxy for basis risk. Because the change in the price of a bond is determined by the change in all discount rates in the term structure up to the maturity of the bond, the duration to be used must be based on the correct stochastic process causing these rate changes. This will require the same IDs as required for immunization. Thus the Macaulay duration is an accurate measure of basis risk only for flat yield curves.

[10] For a single bond whose maturity is less than the planning periods, all the proceeds are assumed to be reinvested in a bond whose maturity is equal to the remaining length of the planning period. Thus, unexpected interest rate changes have no price effect; they affect only reinvestment income.

[11] The greater increase in reinvestment income than decrease in price and the resulting slightly higher return realized than promised occurs because changes in bond prices and interest rates are nonlinearly related.

[12] Interest rate risk is not precisely zero, as the realized return can be above but not below the promised return.
Although the above analysis refers only to default-free bonds, the theory is equally applicable to any security, equity as well as debt. When future cash flows and terminal values are uncertain, probabilities must be assigned to these values and the computed IDs become expected IDs. In order to achieve immunization with these securities, nonsystematic risk must first be eliminated through appropriate diversification. Some preliminary analysis appears in George G. Kaufman, "Duration Planning Period and Tests of the Capital Asset Pricing Model," *Journal of Financial Research*, Spring 1980, 1-9.

[13] Some of these arguments were made by Joseph Stiglitz in 1970: "If there are multiperiod bonds, returns will not in general be statistically independent over time; moreover which is the safe security and which is the risky depends on one's horizon, and as the individual grows older, this is likely to change . . . It is not correct to treat the long-term bond as a risky asset and the short-term bond as a safe asset. Since, from different horizons each are safe and from different horizons each are risky, at times each may act 'more' like a safe asset than the other."
Joseph E. Stiglitz, "A Consumption-Oriented Theory of the Demand for Financial Assets and the Term Structure of Interets Rates," *Review of Economic Studies* (July 1970), 349.

[14] For the sake of expediency and because of the roughness of the data, the yields-to-maturity are not adjusted to their zero coupon equivalents. To the extent that the Durand data are annual averages, they understate the variance in daily interest rates and bond prices. This may affect the results if the incorrect stochastic process and associated ID are selected

and if the individual trading prices fluctuate around the "true" price for that day.

[15] Other stochastic processes have been developed in Jonathan E. Ingersoll Jr., Jeffrey Skelton, and Roman Weil, "Duration Forty Years Later," *Journal of Financial and Quantitative Analysis* (November 1978); John C. Cox, Jonathan Ingersoll Jr., and Stephan Ross, "Duration and Measurement of Basis Risk," *Journal of Business* (January 1979), and Michael J. Brennan and Eduardo S. Schwartz, *Savings Bonds: Theory and Empirical Evidence* (New York: Salomon Brothers Center for the Study of Financial Institutions, New York University 1979).

[16] The duration of the portfolio of bonds is a function of the duration of the constituent bonds. See Appendix.

[17] The relationship between duration and maturity is discussed in Michael H. Hopewell and George G. Kaufman, "Bond Price Volatility and Term to Maturity: A Generalized Respecification," *American Economic Review*, September 1973, 749-53.

[18] Bierwag and Kaufman, "Bond Portfolio Strategy Simulations: A Critique."

[19] Because duration is a mean, portfolios having the same duration can have different second (variance) and higher moments.

[20] Bierwag, Kaufman and Toevs, "The Sensitivity of Immunization to Correctly and Incorrectly Identified Stochastic Processes."

[21] It may be noted that, to the extent the stochastic process is incorrectly identified and an incorrect ID used to immunize a portfolio, the investor has in effect pursued an active rather than passive strategy.

[22] The ability of the IDs to generate returns approximating the promised planning period yields is strong evidence that the imputed forward rates contain substantial information about expected future rates as suggested by the expectations theory of the term structures. The slightly lower than promised average returns suggest the possibility of liquidity premiums.

[23] Bierwag, Kaufman and Toevs, "Sensitivity of Immunization to Correctly and Incorrectly Identified Stochastic Processes."

APPENDIX

EQUATIONS FOR IMMUNIZING DURATIONS FOR SINGLE BONDS
(ANNUAL DISCRETE COMPOUNDING)

I. ID1 — Additive Shock, Flat Yield Curve $(1 + i_M + \lambda)$

$$ID1 = \frac{\sum_{t=1}^{m} tC(1 + i_m)^{-t} + mA(1 + i_m)^{-m}}{\sum_{t=1}^{m} C(1 + i_m)^{-t} + A(1 + i_m)^{-m}}$$

II. ID2 — Additive Shock $(1 + h(0,t) + \lambda)$

$$ID2[1 + h(0,ID2)]^{-1} = \frac{\sum_{t=1}^{m} tC(1 + h(0,t))^{-t-1} + mA(1 + h(0,m))^{-m-1}}{\sum_{t=1}^{m} C(1 + h(0,t))^{-t} + A(1 + h(0,m))^{-m}}$$

III. ID3 — Multiplicative Shock $(1 + \lambda)(1 + h(0,t))$

$$ID3 = \frac{\sum_{t=1}^{m} tC(1 + h(0,t))^{-t} + mA(1 + h(0,m))^{-m}}{\sum_{t=1}^{m} C(1 + h(0,t))^{-t} + A(1 + h(0,m))^{-m}}$$

IV. ID4 — Maturity Dependent Shock

$$(1 + \frac{\lambda \ln(1 + \alpha t)}{\alpha t})(1 + h(0,t))$$

$$Ln(1 + \alpha ID4)$$

$$= \frac{\sum_{t=1}^{m} \ln(1 + \alpha t)C(1 + h(0,t))^{-t} + \ln(1 + \alpha m)A(1 + h(0,m))^{-m}}{\sum_{t=1}^{m} C(1 + h(0,t))^{-t} + (1 + h(0,m))^{-m}}$$

Key

i_m = yield to maturity

$h(0,t)$ = zero coupon yield equivalent for period spanning 0 to t

C = annual coupon payment

α = indicator of ratio of change in short-term rate to change in long-term rate

λ = random interest rate shock

CALCULATION OF THE DURATION FOR PORTFOLIOS OF BONDS

In the formulas below, D_s is the duration of the bond with short maturity, D_L is the duration of the bond with the longer maturity, D is the duration of a portfolio of the two bonds where β_s is the proportion invested in the short bond.

I. ID1 and ID3:

$$D = \beta_s D_s + (1 - \beta_s)D_L.$$

II. ID2:

$$\frac{D}{1 + h(0,D)} = \frac{\beta_s D_s}{1 + h(0,D_s)} + \frac{(1 - \beta_s)D_L}{1 + h(0,D_L)}.$$

III. $\ln(1 + \alpha D) = \beta_s \ln(1 + \alpha D_s) + (1 - \beta_s)\ln(1 + \alpha D_L).$

The uses of contingent immunization

A new procedure for structured active management

Martin L. Leibowitz and Alfred Weinberger

The traditional motivation for bond investment was to secure a fixed cash flow over some appropriate time frame. The typical bond investor was highly risk averse. He was more than willing to sacrifice the excitement of potentially spectacular results in order to achieve a reliable pattern of return. Over time, a series of active management techniques evolved to take advantage of what were perceived to be market opportunities and/or to avoid the full impact of identifiable market problems. In the early years, active management was simply viewed as a way to enhance the basic return pattern available within the traditional fixed-income framework.

In recent years, however, the traditional role of bonds as an asset category has been buffeted by a series of dramatic changes in the marketplace. Surging interest rates and an explosion in volatility have characterized recent markets. At the same time, total return measurement has become an almost universally applied performance yardstick for bond managers. These measurements have highlighted the disastrous, and often negative, returns in many bond portfolios. When these short-term results are coupled with the unprecedented volatility and uncertainty that now seem to be a hallmark of the debt markets, it is little wonder that the traditional function of the fixed-income portfolio is being widely re-examined.

This environment imposes a harsh dilemma on the bond portfolio manager: How to pursue prudent active strategies and still provide his client with the comfort level that probably served as the primary basis for allocating funds to the fixed-income market in the first place?

THE ATTRACTIONS OF CONTINGENT IMMUNIZATION

It is this fundamental dilemma that motivated our development of the *contingent immunization* procedure. With this technique, the traditional purpose is served by specifying a minimum return target over an appropriate time frame. This minimum return target acts as the safety net — it provides a well-defined dimension of risk control. In essence, this safety net is woven out of the new developments that comprise the technique of bond immunization. This safety net is not binding, at least not at the outset, but it does place certain risk-control limits upon the management process. As long as the combination of portfolio structures and market circumstances remains within these risk-control limits, the manager can freely pursue enhanced return through active management.

Should a situation develop that threatens the fund's ability to reliably achieve its minimum return target, the portfolio is triggered into an "immunization" mode. In this eventuality, the portfolio is then restructured as an immunized fund designed to provide the minimum return target specified at the outset. Essentially, the portfolio will then have "fallen" into the safety net. Hence, our choice of the term contingent immunization.

A key ingredient in the contingent immunization approach is the development of an objective procedure for continually monitoring the portfolio over time so as to ensure that the safety net remains well placed. Furthermore, in addition to the analytic constraints, the portfolio must remain sufficiently liquid and the manager sufficiently alert so that any actions required to keep the program on track can be implemented on a timely basis. In particular, this presumes that the nature of market movements is consistent with the portfolio restructuring required should the immunization mode become necessary.

With this assurance, contingent immunization can provide a structural solution to the dilemma of the modern bond portfolio manager. On the one hand, the traditional comfort level sought by the fixed-income investor can be restored through an objective procedure with a reliable minimum return target. On the other hand, the manager remains free — usually surprisingly free — to exercise judgment in pursuit of the enhanced return that he and his client both desire.

THE TWO CHARACTERISTIC PARAMETERS

There are two parameters characterizing a given contingent immunization program that serve to define where on the risk/return spectrum the program will be positioned, as well as the degree of flexibility of the active management process. The two parameters are: 1) the minimum return target, or more specifically, the difference between the minimum return target and the immunization return then available in the market, and 2) the acceptable range for the terminal horizon date of the program. In other words, a limited horizon range is used to replace the rigidly fixed horizon date employed in conventional immunization programs. Thus, contingent immunization requires that the manager meet the minimum return target (which will be somewhat lower than the maximum rate currently available) over some investment period that falls within the specified horizon range.

As will become evident, it is the loosening up of the two characteristic parameters — minimum return and a fixed horizon date — that are the key sources of flexibility in a contingent immunization procedure.

In the subsequent discussion, we develop examples using the following values for the relevant variables:

immunization return	= 12%,
minimum return target	= 11%,
nominal horizon	= 5 Years,
acceptable horizon range	= 4-6 Years, and
initial portfolio value	= $100.

POTENTIAL RETURN PATTERNS

Figure 1 illustrates the potential rewards, and the risks involved, in contingent immunization relative to classical immunization. In the example, the portfolio manager is positive on the market and purchases a relatively long 30-year portfolio. Now, suppose an immediate favorable yield change occurs. The portfolio will jump in asset value. If the portfolio were liquidated and placed into a 5-year classical immunization mode, the resulting potential return would then reflect the increased return achieved over the entire 5-year period.

For example, suppose there was an immediate yield change of −3%, or a move from 12% to 9%. Then the portfolio would have a sufficiently large capital gain so that, if it were then immunized at the 9% level, the annualized compound return for the full 5 years would be about 14.7%. This type of result would

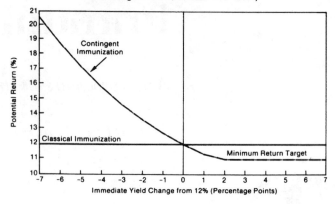

FIGURE 1.
30-Year Portfolio Under Contingent Immunization
(Immunization Return = 12%; Minimum
Return Target = 11%; Horizon = 5 Years)

be a positive consequence of the leeway afforded the portfolio manager in constructing the portfolio.

The risk side of the story in this example occurs if yields rise. Thus, an immediate market yield move of about +1.6%, from 12% to 13.6%, would make the potential return fall to the minimum target return of 11%. Under the contingent immunization program, this drop would result in the immunization of the portfolio in order to secure the 11% minimum return. In fact, this is precisely the type of contingency that leads to immunization under contingent immunization. Any additional yield increase beyond 13.6% would leave the potential return unchanged because the portfolio will have been immunized. (A reader familiar with the basic profit diagrams for options will immediately recognize their structural similarity to Figure 1.)

PORTFOLIO GROWTH OVER TIME

Figure 1 has demonstrated the nature of the rewards and risks in a contingent immunization plan for a single point in time. Figures 2, 3, and 4 use simulation results to illustrate these risk and reward patterns as they might unfold dynamically through time. By tracing these orbits of portfolio assets over the investment period, one can identify the critical events and the different patterns of realization that can occur with a contingent immunization program.

Figure 2 shows the results of a simulation where the efforts at active management have been unsuccessful. At the end of year 3, the portfolio had to be immunized in order to assure the minimum target return of 11% (to the outer limit of the horizon range). The short vertical lines descending from the portfolio growth curve at years 1 and 2 are a measure of how close the portfolio is to requiring immunization in order to assure the target return. In a sense, these lines represent the current latitude available to the portfolio manager. At year 3, this latitude is completely used up.

In contrast, Figure 3 shows the results of a simu-

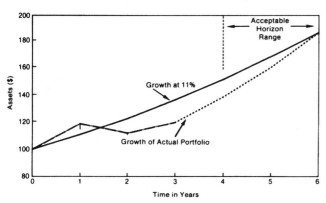

FIGURE 2.
Unsuccessful Active Management Under Contingent Immunization
(Immunization Return = 12%; Minimum Return Target = 11%)

lation of successful active management. The portfolio has grown considerably faster than would have been the case under strict immunization.

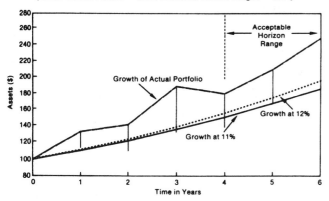

FIGURE 3.
Successful Active Management Under Contingent Immunization
(Immunization Return = 12%; Minimum Return Target = 11%)

Figure 4 is another way of looking at the preceding simulations of successful and unsuccessful active management. For each year of the simulations, the

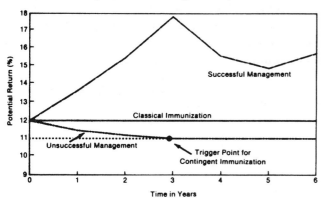

FIGURE 4.
Potential Returns if Immunized over Remaining Time to Horizon
(Minimum Return Target = 11%)

level of potential return is plotted. This is the return that would have been "locked in" if the portfolio had been immunized at that point. Years in which active management is successful (relative to an immunization mode) increase the potential return. Years in which active management is unsuccessful reduce po-

tential return. Finally, years where the portfolio is immunized for the remaining horizon leave the potential return unchanged.

CLASSICAL IMMUNIZATION

Let us now take a closer look at exactly why and how contingent immunization affords the portfolio manager greater flexibility than a classical immunization approach.

We begin with a quick review of some fundamental concepts of immunization. If we start with $100 and wish to realize a target return of 12% a year for 5 years, we would need to generate $176 at the end of 5 years. If the available investment yield level were other than 12%, we would need more or less than $100 to achieve $176 in 5 years. Figure 5 shows how much we would need today at various yield levels. The distinguishing feature of an immunized investment is

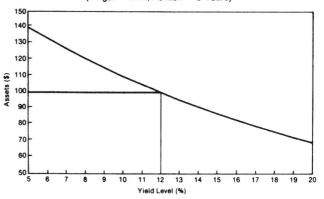

FIGURE 5.
Required Assets to Achieve Target
(Target = 12%; Horizon = 5 Years)

that, as yield levels change, we are always left with sufficient asset value to achieve, at the then-prevailing interest rates, the target amount at the horizon. Thus, if rates decline, the immunized portfolio must provide a capital gain sufficient to compensate for the reduced growth rate over time. For example, in a 10% interest rate environment, a portfolio value of at least $109 would be required. In other words, a value of $109 compounded at 10% for 5 years would grow to the $176 target value.

Figure 6 illustrates this point. Superimposed on the curve of Figure 5 is the price response of an asset for different yield levels. The price response does exactly what we would like. In fact, it does even slightly better. This asset is a bond with a *Macaulay Duration*[1] of 5 years at an initial yield level of 12%. If we purchase $100 of this bond, we see that any immediate shift in yields will always leave us with at least sufficient value to achieve the $176 at the end of 5 years. This would assure a realized return equal to the starting yield of 12%. If we choose an asset with a duration other than exactly 5 years, we would find our-

1. Footnotes appear at the end of the article.   **243**

selves with insufficient value to achieve the target under some yield moves. In particular, if the asset has a duration greater than 5 years, moves to higher yield levels would be troublesome. The opposite would hold for assets with duration less than 5 years.

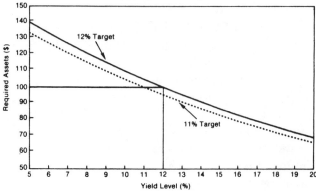

FIGURE 6.
Price Response and Assets Required
(Target = 12%; Horizon = 5 Years)

BUILDING FLEXIBILITY INTO IMMUNIZATION

Now let us see what happens when we start to loosen some of the rigid conditions of strict classical immunization. First, consider a reduction in the target return. Figure 7 shows the required assets at various yield levels for both the original immunization target of 12% and for the reduced target of 11%. Clearly, the reduced target requires a significantly lower asset value at all yield levels.

FIGURE 7.
Elements of Flexibility: Reduced Minimum Return Target
(Horizon = 5 Years)

Figure 8 now shows the increased flexibility available to a portfolio manager in asset selection. Along with the required asset curve at an 11% target return, we have the price responses of a 2-year bond (having a 1.8-year duration) and a 30-year bond (with an 8.6-year duration). Both these bonds have durations that differ widely from the 5-year horizon. Hence, neither one would fulfill the criteria for a strict immunization vehicle over the 5-year horizon. Yet both bonds have a degree of latitude such that their yields can change in either direction and there will still be sufficient assets to assure the 11% minimum return.

More specifically, if the portfolio manager were

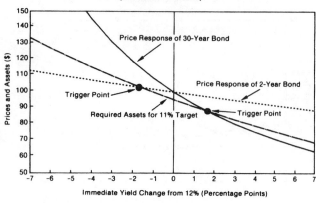

FIGURE 8.
Elements of Flexibility: Asset Maturity Selection
(Horizon = 5 Years)

expecting a decline in yield levels, he would want to position his portfolio in longer maturities, e.g., the 30-year instrument. If yields change in the expected downward direction, then the portfolio would have a value far in excess of that required to achieve the original target. Hence, the potential return of the portfolio will have increased.

On the other hand, if yields rise, there would still be sufficient assets to continue active management up to the point where the bond value fell below the curve depicting the asset level required to meet the 11% target. This corresponds to the yield level indicated by the trigger point at a yield move of +1.6%. At this level of yields, the manager would have to go into the immunization mode to assure the 11% target.

An active manager expecting higher yield levels could purchase the 2-year instrument. This would prove highly productive if yields rose as anticipated. If yields declined, the 2-year bond would continue to provide an adequate asset value up to the indicated trigger point at a −1.6% yield move.

TRIGGER YIELD CONTOURS

Figure 9 expands this concept of trigger yield moves to include the full range of available maturities. For all portfolio maturities between 0 and 30 years, it shows the yield level that would necessitate a shift into the immunization mode in order to assure the mini-

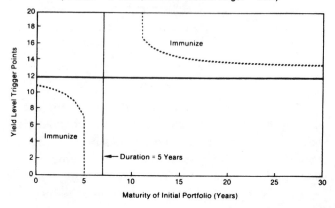

FIGURE 9.
Degree of Flexibility Achieved through Lower Target Return
(Horizon = 5 Years; Minimum Return Target = 11%)

mum target return. In other words, these are the trigger point yield levels of Figure 8, but for all maturities.

For portfolios where durations are longer than the 5-year horizon, the problems occur in a rising interest rate environment. Thus, the longer the duration, the smaller the adverse yield move that can be tolerated. For portfolios with durations shorter than 5 years, the shorter the duration, the smaller the yield decline to trigger immunization.

For portfolios with maturities between 5 and 11 years, there is *no immediate market move* that could force the portfolio into the "safety net."[2] In other words, within this range of maturities, there is *no way* to blow it in a *single* market event! On the other hand, there always exists some sequence of portfolio restructurings that, accompanied by repeated market fiascoes, would eat up the flexibility cushion and ultimately force the portfolio into the immunization safety net.

HORIZON RANGES

The discussion to this point has focused on the flexibility in portfolio management introduced by setting a minimum return target below the prevailing level of immunized returns. We now examine the effects of a second relaxation from the discipline of strict immunization. Figure 10 illustrates the effect of setting

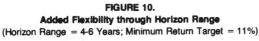

FIGURE 10.
Added Flexibility through Horizon Range
(Horizon Range = 4-6 Years; Minimum Return Target = 11%)

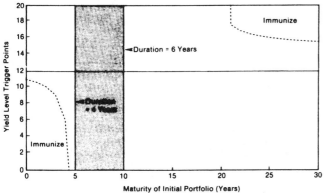

a horizon range in place of a fixed single-point horizon. In this figure, the minimum return target remains at 11%, but this return is promised for some point between 4 and 6 years in the future, rather than for exactly 5 years. The effect on management flexibility is dramatic:

1. The trigger point for a 30-year portfolio has moved from the 13.6% of Figure 9 to almost 16%.
2. The range of maturities for which there is no trigger point at all for immediate yield moves has expanded to 4.5 −20 years.

It is also noteworthy that the expansion in flexibility is most pronounced at the longer end of the maturity scale.

What happens when we change the target re-

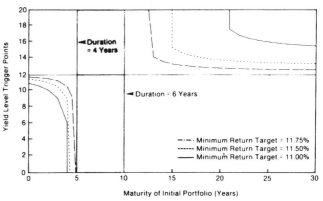

FIGURE 11.
Trigger Point Contours for Various Minimum Return Targets
(Horizon Range = 4-6 Years)

turn? Figure 11 demonstrates the effects of increases in the minimum return target from 11% to 11.5% and then to 11.75%. Not surprisingly, the range of management maneuverability begins to shrink as the minimum return target approaches our assumed immunization return of 12%.

MONITORING PROCEDURE

As was discussed earlier, the contingent immunization process has definite elements of risk control as an integral feature. This risk control must be exercised through close monitoring of the portfolio over time. The control procedures must ensure that the portfolio structure, in the context of prevailing market conditions, remains able to achieve at least the minimum return target. There exists a clear-cut mathematical procedure for establishing these control criteria.

Many facets of contingent immunization deserve further discussion, both in terms of the mathematical theory as well as the practical considerations involved in market applications. Our purpose here has been, in a general way, to offer for consideration an idea that blends different techniques into a new structured approach to the management process. The resulting synthesis of risk control and flexibility would appear to have special appeal to both portfolio managers and their clients — particularly in the volatile and uncertain markets of today.

---

[1] For a general discussion of classical immunization and the role of Macaulay Duration, see *Bond Immunization: A Procedure for Realizing Target Levels of Return*, Martin L. Leibowitz, Salomon Brothers, October 10, 1979. This article was reproduced in *Pros and Cons of Immunization*, Proceedings of a Seminar on the Roles and Limits of Bond Immunization, January 17, 1980.

[2] This effect is related to the minimum return concept for a fixed horizon date that was set forth by W. Marshall and J. Yawitz in "Lower Bounds on Portfolio Performance: A Generalized Immunization Strategy," Working Paper, Institute for Banking and Capital Markets, Washington University, January 1979.

Bond indexation: The optimal quantitative approach

Three algorithms for doing the job.

Christina Seix and Ravi Akhoury

Every technique for creating an optimal bond index portfolio begins by answering the same basic question: What are the sources of variability in bond portfolio returns? Each technique assumes that individual bond returns are generated by a number of underlying factors or sources of market risk plus an issue-specific idiosyncratic factor. All techniques strive to combine securities such that the issue-specific risk approaches zero in the solution portfolio.

Each of the construction algorithms discussed below requires an initial determination of the systematic risk factors that affect bond prices. The methods differ, however, in their approach to constructing the solution portfolio. One algorithm places exclusive reliance on current composition data. Another places little weight on composition but puts substantial emphasis on historic relationships.

The objective of each method is to construct a solution portfolio that will successfully track a specified index.

The three construction algorithms contrasted below are:
- the Cell Approach,
- the Linear Programming Method, and
- the Variance Minimization Method.

CELL APPROACH

The Cell Approach is the simplest method of establishing a portfolio that will mirror an index. It is based on 1) prespecifying the bond characteristics that govern its price behavior, 2) subdividing the market index into its component cells, and 3) replicating as many of the component cells as possible in the solution portfolio.

A typical construction algorithm might include the following subdivisions of index I:

s_1: maturity ranges

s_2: sectors

s_3: coupon ranges

s_4: quality ratings

s_5: call factors

s_6: sinking fund features.

We can express the total number of cells as the following product:

$$\prod_{r=1}^{6} s_r = s_1 \times s_2 \times \ldots \times s_6,$$

where each s_r represents a specific number of partitions.

The upper bound to this product is the number of issues in I. The *Census Method* is the broadest form of the Cell Approach. This method essentially includes most of the issues in I, based on the premise that the lowest tracking error (u) is generated when Πs_r approaches the number of issues in I.

The Census Approach is generally not practical

CHRISTINA SEIX is Managing Director of McKay Shields Financial Corporation in New York (NY 10176). RAVI AKHOURY is a Director of the same company. The authors wish to thank Robert Kuberek and Michel Houglet for their assistance.

246

for matching large bond indexes that can contain as many as 5,000 issues. Nevertheless, in both the Cell Approach and the Census Method, the same inverse relationship exists between the total number of cells (Πs_r) and the tracking error (u) of the solution portfolio.

In practice, the Cell Approach is efficient only in constructing large solution portfolios, because it requires a finer breakdown of the market than the other approaches, which have other constraints to insure an efficient matching of the index.

For large portfolios, the Cell Approach has generally produced an acceptable tracking error. It has limited flexibility, however, in solving more advanced index construction problems that require tilts or other forms of customization.

LINEAR PROGRAMMING METHOD

There are two sampling methods to solve the indexing problem: the *Stratified Sampling Method* and the *Linear Programming Method*. Both give control over the degree to which the index structure is replicated.

The indexing problem is essentially a linear programming problem with a special exclusivity property. Since the cells in the index are mutually exclusive and every bond is either in a cell or not, the Stratified Sampling Method is sometimes the more efficient way to construct the solution portfolio. On the other hand, the Linear Programming Method is an ideal solution to the bond indexation problem.

From a formal point of view, a linear programming problem seeks to find the maximum (or minimum) of an objective function, subject to a number of side conditions or constraints, which are the mathematical expressions of the restrictions on the problem. The alternatives appear as solutions to this system of relations. The problem should be such that the constraints can be expressed in the form of linear equations or inequalities.

The bond indexation problem quite naturally fits into the linear programming structure. The solution portfolio (P) is subject to linear constraints, which consist of various relationships that define the required composition of P, as well as side conditions that assist in the optimization process. There are various objective functions that we can use for the index problem, but historical experience suggests certain candidates that have led to optimal solution portfolios.

The process begins with a construction algorithm defined as a system of linear constraints. The number of linear equations depends on a K filter, where K is the minimum market weight that a cell must represent in the index portfolio (I), in order to

be included in the solution portfolio.

All cells of weight $<K$ are excluded from the system of linear constraints. Each cell $\geq K$ is defined as a linear equation as follows:

$$w_1 d_{11} + w_2 d_{12} + w_3 d_{13} + \ldots + w_n d_{1n} = G_1$$
$$w_1 d_{21} + w_2 d_{22} + w_3 d_{23} + \ldots + w_n d_{2n} = G_2$$
$$w_1 d_{m1} + w_2 d_{m2} + w_3 d_{m3} + \ldots + w_n d_{mn} = G_m$$

where

m = the total number of cells represented in the solution portfolio;

n = number of bonds in the universe;

G_i = weight of each cell in index;

i = 1, . . ., m;

$$\sum_{i=1}^{m} G_i \leq 1, \text{ where each } G_i \geq K;$$

w_j = weight in P of bond j;

j = 1, . . ., n; and

d_{ij} = 0 if bond does not classify in cell i; 1 if bond does.

Additional linear constraints to improve the optimization include: 1) setting the duration of P equal to the duration of I, 2) setting a diversification condition, and 3) setting a limit on transaction costs or turnover, etc.

The objective function for the solution portfolio can be defined as follows:

MAXIMIZE: the Average Outstanding Market Value of Solution Issues, subject to the above system of linear constraints.

Other objective functions might require that turnover be minimized, that yield to maturity on solution issues be maximized, or that current yield be maximized.

The solution to the Linear Programming problem will give the appropriate weight (w_j) for each bond (j) in P. It will create a solution portfolio that mirrors the index, by solving for the amount of each bond to be purchased.

Assuming the problem is feasible, there may be many portfolios that satisfy the system of linear constraints. The Linear Programming Method solves for the optimal portfolio in the sense defined by the objective function.

In its purest form, the Linear Programming Method is a sampling-oriented approach employing data that relate to the current composition of the index. The basic assumption is that the current composition of the index will best determine its price behavior; hence, the Linear Programming Method avoids dependence on historic data.

VARIANCE MINIMIZATION METHOD

In the Variance Minimization Method, one way to characterize the degree to which a solution portfolio tracks a specified index is to estimate the variance of the tracking error (V_u).

The approach defines the estimated price (P_j) of bond j, in terms of two sets of factors: a string of cash flows (C) discounted at different spot rates (R) throughout the life of the bond, and a set of other characteristics (G), such as sector, quality, and coupon, which influence the behavior of bond j. Specifically:

$$\widetilde{P}_j = \sum_{h=1}^{H_j} C_{jh} \cdot e^{-t_{jh}[R_{t_{jh}} + \sum_{k=1}^{K} b_{jk} \cdot G_k]} + \widetilde{e}_j,$$

where

$\widetilde{P}_j$ = price of bond j;

H_j = number of cash flows of bond j;

C_{jh} = h^{th} cash flow of bond j;

t_{jh} = time to the hth cash flow of bond j;

$R_{t_{jh}}$ = spot rates at times t_{jh};

K = number of distinct characteristics;

b_{jk} = 0 or 1 for most factors of bond j, depending on whether the kth factor is applicable to bond j;

G_k = special factors of bond j; and

$\widetilde{e}_j$ = issue-specific pricing error of bond j.

Once price is expressed as a multi-variate equation, the parameters can be estimated through the use of a statistical technique similar to a multiple regression analysis. (An actual multiple regression would require that the dependent variable be a linear function of the independent variables.) A large universe of bonds is used to estimate R and G at a particular point in time. The objective is to minimize the sum of the squares of the deviations of quoted prices and model prices that result from this equation.

The resulting R and G represent: 1) estimates of the spot rate curve ($R_1, \ldots, R_L$), where L is the total number of spot rates, and 2) estimates of the spread value of other defined characteristics ($G_1, \ldots, G_K$) at that point in time. The R and G can be estimated historically at each month-end for the entire universe of bonds. (We use discrete month-end points so as to correspond to index valuation dates.)

From this valuation model, we can develop a model of index composition that minimizes the variance of the tracking error.

In practice, as long as the portfolio matches the index in terms of exposure to R and G, all of the tracking error, which may be substantial, is attribut-

able to the issue-specific pricing error $\bar{e}$.

In forming the solution portfolio, which is our purpose, increasing the number of issues will diversify the issue-specific risk. For simplicity, therefore, we have omitted any reference to $\bar{e}$ in the presentation of the basic technique.

From the valuation equation above, we can now approximate the portfolio value and index value as follows:

$$P = \sum_j w_j \cdot P_j(R,G) = P(R,G,w), \text{ and}$$

$$I - I(R,C).$$

The portfolio and index returns can therefore be approximated as:

$$\frac{1}{P} \widetilde{dP} = \frac{1}{P} [\partial P/\partial R \ \widetilde{dR} + \partial P/\partial G \ \widetilde{dG}], \text{ and}$$

$$\frac{1}{I} \widetilde{dI} = \frac{1}{I} [\partial I/\partial R \ \widetilde{dR} + \partial I/\partial G \ \widetilde{dG}],$$

where the vectors are defined as:

$$\partial P/\partial R = [\partial P/\partial R_1, \partial P/\partial R_2, \ldots, \partial P/\partial R_L];$$
$$\partial P/\partial G = [\partial P/\partial G_1, \partial P/\partial G_2, \ldots, \partial P/\partial G_K];$$
$$\partial I/\partial R = [\partial I/\partial R_1, \partial I/\partial R_2, \ldots, \partial I/\partial R_L];$$
$$\partial I/\partial G = [\partial I/\partial G_1, \partial I/\partial G_2, \ldots, \partial I/\partial G_K];$$
$$\widetilde{dR} = [\widetilde{dR}_1, \widetilde{dR}_2, \ldots, \widetilde{dR}_L], \text{ and}$$
$$\widetilde{dG} = [\widetilde{dG}_1, \widetilde{dG}_2, \ldots, \widetilde{dG}_K].$$

The tracking error of the solution portfolio can then be defined as:

$$\bar{u}_P = \left[\frac{\partial P/\partial R}{P} - \frac{\partial I/\partial R}{I} \right] \widetilde{dR}$$
$$+ \left[\frac{\partial P/\partial G}{P} - \frac{\partial I/\partial G}{I} \right] \widetilde{dG}.$$

Let $A = \frac{\partial P/\partial R}{P} - \frac{\partial I/\partial R}{I}$, and

$B = \frac{\partial P/\partial G}{P} - \frac{\partial I/\partial G}{I}$;

then $\bar{u}_P = A \cdot \widetilde{dR} + B \cdot \widetilde{dG}$.

The optimal solution portfolio will minimize the variance $Var(\bar{u}_P)$ of the tracking error of P:

$$Var(\bar{u}_P) = [A_1, A_2, \ldots, A_L, B_1, B_2, \ldots, B_K] \cdot$$

$$\begin{bmatrix} Var(\widetilde{dR}_1) \ldots Cov(\widetilde{dG}_K, \widetilde{dR}_1) \\ \vdots \quad \ddots \quad \vdots \\ Var(\widetilde{dR}_L) \\ Var(\widetilde{dG}_1) \\ \vdots \\ Cov(\widetilde{dR}_1, \widetilde{dG}_K) \ldots Var(\widetilde{dG}_K) \end{bmatrix} \cdot \begin{bmatrix} A_1 \\ A_2 \\ \vdots \\ A_L \\ B_1 \\ \vdots \\ B_K \end{bmatrix} .$$

A quadratic optimization algorithm will then

solve for the weights of the securities in the solution portfolio, such that the estimated variance of the portfolio's tracking error is minimized for a given level of expected u, conditional on the estimated Variance/Covariance Matrix.

The key assumption in the Variance Minimization Method is that the Variance/Covariance matrix shown above is stable over time. This assumption is critical, as it enables the matrix to be estimated reliably with historic data. The assumption also allows us to have some confidence that these estimates will be valid in the future. While we have not tested this assumption directly, we have no reason to believe that it is invalid.

The Variance Minimization approach begins with the recognition that tracking error cannot be observed ex ante. Moreover, tracking error cannot be expressed as a function of any variables that can be expressed mathematically. As shown above, we can look at the estimated tracking error variance ex ante and express it in terms of the bond weights that we can control.

The Variance Minimization Method places little emphasis on the current composition of the bond market. Historic data are used to construct the Variance/Covariance matrix that provides the effect of certain characteristics relative to others in influencing the variability of bond returns. The approach is effective for medium-sized portfolios and for portfolios with tilts or other customized features, in that it represents a systematic way of trading off among candidates for the optimal solution portfolio.

CONCLUSION

We back-tested the Variance Minimization Method on a $50 million solution portfolio against the Shearson/Lehman Composite Index for a three-year period. The largest tracking error to develop in any particular month was -13 basis points. In most cases the tracking error was positive, and for the cumulative period it was positive. The matrix was found to be stable over the three-year period tested. Moreover, the method was flexible in permitting portfolio customization.

An important refinement to this construction algorithm is to weight current data more heavily than older data. When relying on the Variance/Covariance Matrix, this procedure uses the historic data, but minimizes its effect as the data get older.

The Linear Programming sampling method has some attractive structural features. Some of the constraints imposed in the Linear Programming approach should be applied to the solution portfolio of the Variance Minimization Method for optimal pragmatic results.

In the final analysis, the optimal approach depends upon the size of the solution portfolio and the desirability of a flexible construction algorithm for portfolio tilting or other portfolio customization. Naive strategies that exclude judgmental information can be combined successfully with standard bond indexation.[1]

---

[1] See H. Gifford Fong and Frank J. Fabozzi, "How to enhance bond returns with naive strategies," *The Journal of Portfolio Management*, Summer 1985, pp. 57-60, for a discussion of these applications.

Why invest in foreign currency bonds?

Their capabilities as diversifiers for US investors are singularly unappreciated.

Kenneth Cholerton, Pierre Pieraerts, and Bruno Solnik

Amerian investors should be making greater use of international bonds for purposes of diversification and for higher expected rates of return. These instruments are the most effective means of diversifying exposures to domestic monetary, budgetary, and other financial uncertainties.

Considering the large size of non-US dollar bond markets, it is surprising to see so little investment there by US institutions. For example, Intersec estimates foreign bond holdings of US pension funds to be less than $2 billion, as opposed to close to $15 billion in foreign equities. Yet the market capitalization of foreign bonds is much larger than that of foreign equities.

Indeed, non-dollar bond markets are growing rapidly. The Eurobond market is now comparable to the domestic US market in terms of new-issue volume, although it is still smaller in terms of market capitalization. The details appear in Table 1. We should also mention here that non-dollar bonds tend to have shorter maturities than US bonds have.

The following discussion analyzes diversification patterns provided by non-dollar bond markets and then explores the possibilities for forming optimal portfolios of both equities and bonds in both US and international markets.

RISK DIVERSIFICATION: THE RECENT PAST (1983-1985)

The recent past has seen a period of high monetary and financial uncertainties and dramatic US dol-

TABLE 1

SIZE OF MAJOR BOND MARKETS, AT YEAR-END 1984

Bond Market	Total Publicly Issued	As Per Cent of Public Issues in all Markets
	(billions)	%
US Dollar	$2,653.0	56.7
Japanese Yen	779.2	16.7
Deutschemark	299.1	6.4
Italian Lire	185.4	4.0
UK Sterling	152.0	3.2
Canadian Dollar	121.7	2.6
French Franc	110.5	2.4
Belgian Franc	78.1	1.7
Swedish Krona	75.7	1.6
Danish Krona	71.0	1.5
Swiss Franc	55.9	1.2
Australian Dollar	50.2	1.1
Dutch Guilder	48.0	1.0
TOTAL	$4,679.8	

Source: Salomon Brothers
The exchange rate at this writing was DM3.159/US$. A drop in the dollar value increases the relative size of non-dollar bond markets.

lar appreciation. In this period, the major bond markets exhibited a positive but rather weak correlation, as shown in Table 2, which reports the correlations of monthly rates of return from January 1, 1983 to April 30, 1985. Rates of return comprise accrued interest plus price movements in local currency.[1]

1. Footnotes appear at the end of the article.

KENNETH H. CHOLERTON is Director of Lombard Odier Internation Portfolio Management Limited in London (W1A 2AJ). PIERRE PIERAERTS is Mandataire Commercial at Lombard Odier in Geneva (1204 Switzerland). BRUNO SOLNIK is Professor at the Centre d'Enseignement Supérieur des Affaires in Jouy-en-Josas (78350 France).

TABLE 2

CORRELATION AND VOLATILITY OF MONTHLY RATES OF RETURN: 1 January 1983 – 30 April 1985
Lombard Odier — Domestic Government Bond Indexes, in local currency

	US Dollar	Swiss Franc	Deutschemark	Pound Sterling	Dutch Guilder	Japanese Yen	Mean Return % per month	Volatility % per month
US Dollar	1	0.28	0.44	0.39	0.38	0.47	0.63	2.18
Swiss Franc		1	0.54	0.17	0.27	0.54	0.13	0.61
Deutschemark			1	0.38	0.72	0.59	0.63	0.94
Pound Sterling				1	0.23	0.49	0.92	2.32
Dutch Guilders					1	0.55	0.57	1.10
Japanese Yen						1	0.73	0.81

In all cases, the domestic and Eurobond markets in the same currency are highly correlated (e.g. a correlation of 0.84 for the US government and Eurodollar bond markets), but the correlation across currencies is usually less than 0.5. For example the R^2 between domestic DM and US dollar bonds is 0.19, implying that the two markets have less than 20% of common price variation. Note, too, that the percentage of common price variation is always less than 50% between pairs of markets denominated in different currencies, and usually less than 25%. Table 2 also shows that the volatility (standard deviation) of non-US government bond markets tends to be much smaller than that of the US market, with the exception of the UK.

The correlation figures are even more striking if we calculate all rates of return in a common currency. A US-dollar-based investor would hope for a low correlation of the dollar returns on his various bond investments to provide for risk diversification. These correlation coefficients are shown in Figure 1. Clearly, the correlation between the various bond markets is low; monetary and budgetary policies and

long-term interest rates are not fully synchronized, giving ample potential for risk reduction.

Are these results confined only to the period under study? In the next section, we present long-term results for the period 1971-1984. The co-movement of each foreign bond market with the US market is less than 10% in all cases (R^2 less than 0.33). Thus, the markets' correlation has been very low in the recent past compared to the long-term figures.

Although the correlation of the US bond and stock markets indicates the well-known reaction of stock prices to movements in domestic interest rates, the correlation of foreign bonds with the US stock market is strikingly weak and sometimes negative (Figure 2). This is not a surprising result, given the independence between national economic and monetary policies. Clearly, foreign monetary and budgetary policies have little impact on US economic growth and on US share prices. Foreign bonds offer great diversification potential to a stock portfolio manager.

FIGURE 1

CORRELATION OF US AND NON DOLLAR
GOVERNMENT BOND INDICES (IN US DOLLARS)

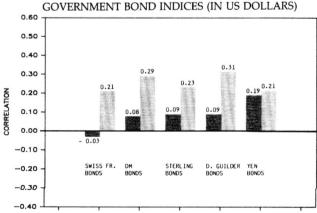

FIGURE 2

CORRELATION OF GOVERNMENT BOND INDICES
AND S&P 500 (IN US DOLLARS)

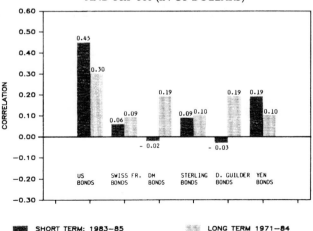

251

An important issue for investors is the relationship between interest rates and currency movements. It is often claimed in the media that a rise in national (real) interest rates leads to currency appreciation, and vice versa. This mechanistic relationship does not seem to hold.

Figure 3 might be interpreted as follows: The

FIGURE 3

CORRELATION OF BOND AND CURRENCY RETURNS

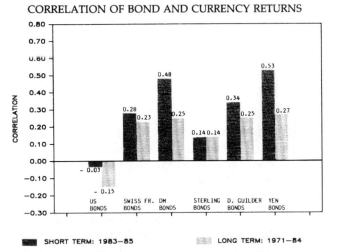

value of the dollar and US real interest rates do tend to be positively related, leading to a *negative* correlation between US bond returns and movements in the dollar. On the other hand, non-dollar bond prices are *positively* related to the value of *their* national currencies. In other words, a fall in the domestic currency influences the monetary authorities to raise interest rates to defend the currency, creating downward pressure on bond prices; conversely, a strong domestic currency induces an easing in policy.

This major difference between the US and other countries reflects the reserve asset and medium of exchange roles of the dollar in the international financial order. Even in the US, however, the relationship is much weaker, especially in the recent past, than is often claimed by commentators. This analysis, though, only addresses long-term interest rates, which may have weaker and different relationships with the dollar exchange rate than short-term interest rates.

RISK AND RETURN: THE LONG-TERM PERFORMANCE

Some statistics

It is important to look at both the recent experience and the long-term performance of assets.

The long-term performance — return and volatility — of the various government bond markets appears in Table 3.

Despite the recent dollar appreciation, the dollar performance of foreign markets has been better than that of the US bond market over the period 1971-1984. At the same time, while foreign bond markets have tended to be less volatile in local currency terms, currency volatility strongly increases the potential risk borne by a US investor, making each foreign bond market individually more volatile than the US bond market. The annual volatility of foreign markets ranges from 11.8% to 14.9%, while it is only 8.9% for the US government bond market.

Nevertheless, *the addition of foreign bonds to a US bond portfolio would have reduced the total risk of the domestic portfolio while improving its performance!* This excellent diversification benefit comes primarily from

TABLE 3

LONG-TERM PERFORMANCE (1/1971 to 12/1984)

RETURN AND RISK

	Mean Total Return % per yr.	Capital Gain % per yr.	Yield % per yr.	Currency Contribution % per yr.	Volatility in $ % per yr.	Volatility in Local Currency % per yr.
BONDS						
US Dollar	6.80	−2.70	9.50	0	8.92	8.92
Swiss Franc	9.41	0.41	5.10	3.89	14.90	4.48
Deutschemark	9.77	0.09	8.56	1.12	14.46	7.02
Pound Sterling	6.33	−0.45	12.54	−5.76	11.78	9.38
Dutch Guilder	9.29	0.01	9.18	0.10	13.57	7.11
Japanese Yen	12.60	0.86	8.91	2.82	14.48	6.15
US Stocks	7.96	3.18	4.78	0	15.43	15.43
HEDGED BONDS						
Swiss Franc	11.42	0.41	11.01	0	4.48	4.48
Deutschemark	12.56	0.09	12.47	0	7.02	7.02
Pound Sterling	9.86	−0.45	10.31	0	9.38	9.38
Dutch Guilder	12.09	0.01	12.08	0	7.11	7.11
Japanese Yen	12.54	0.86	11.68	0	6.15	6.15

the low correlations between markets and is illustrated in Figure 4, where we study the advantage of adding non-dollar bonds to a portfolio of domestic bonds.

FIGURE 4

RISK/RETURN TRADEOFF FOR INTERNATIONAL
BOND PORTFOLIOS

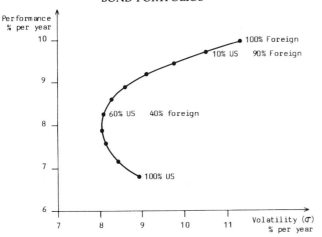

The indexes used here come from local publications in the various countries: They are either government bond indexes calculated locally or are reconstructed from published yield-to-maturity data on government securities.

We add non-dollar bonds by increments of 10%, equally distributed among the five major non-dollar markets (DM, Guilder, Sterling, Swiss Franc and Yen). The graph shows the performance and risk (standard deviation in % per year) of each combination or portfolio. Starting from a purely domestic portfolio with 100% in US bonds, for example, the substitution of 10% in non-dollar bonds increases the return from 6.80% to 7.18% and reduces the risk from 8.92% to 8.47%. The minimum-risk portfolio is obtained for a proportion of non-dollar bonds between 30% and 40%.

OPTIMAL INTERNATIONAL ASSET ALLOCATION

Solnik and Noetzlin (1982) have studied the performance of passive and active strategies for US investors over the period 1970-1980. They looked at the ex post efficient frontier, with no short-selling constraints on any investments, using a mean-variance Markowitz optimization.

The performance and risk of the ex post optimal investment strategy on the major stock and bond markets are given in Figure 5. The right curve indicates the optimal strategies when investments are restricted to stock markets. The left curve gives the optimal strategies in the universe of all stock and bond market indexes. All computations are performed from the viewpoint of a US dollar investor. The optimal strategies represent the portfolio of market indexes

FIGURE 5

EFFICIENT FRONTIERS — 12/1970 – 12/1980

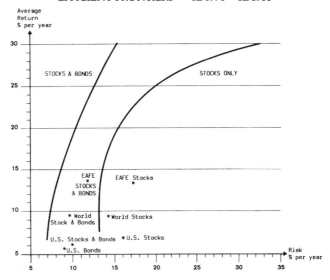

that would have maximized the dollar performance for a given level of standard deviation.

On the same exhibit appear some selected market indexes, especially the market-capitalization-weighted indexes combining both stocks and bonds. These indexes (US, EAFE and World) were calculated from the data base of domestic market indexes using the annually published market capitalizations. The EAFE index is the non-American index consisting of markets from Europe, Australia and the Far East.

Here are some conclusions on the risk-adjusted performance of the various strategies.

> It can be clearly seen that spreading investments over major foreign markets has reduced risk while enhancing return. Thus, even passive diversification along the lines of the Capital International World Stock Index has involved less risk than a purely US portfolio (14% instead of 16%) and provided a return more than 50% higher, even though US stocks made up more than half of this index.
>
> International diversification over stock and bond markets has offered substantially lower risk levels in spite of the volatility of bond returns. Accordingly, the world stocks-and-bonds index posted the same performance as the world stocks-only index with much less volatility (10% instead of 14%). The same conclusion applied for optimal strategies, as can be seen in Figure 5. Efficient portfolios made up of stocks only had a much higher risk (50% to 100% more) for the same level of return than efficient portfolios made up of stocks and bonds.

The results shown in Figure 5 suggest that there is scope for a profitable asset allocation strategy.

For a similar level of risk, an imaginative but passive asset allocation would have given a much higher level of return than the world stocks and bonds index.

While one cannot be sure that the same conclusions will always hold, these results argue strongly for a global management approach including both stocks and bonds to achieve higher risk-adjusted performance.

THE IMPACT OF CURRENCY

Currency movements appear to be a significant component of performance, especially in the short run. On the other hand, currency risk can be hedged. Currency hedging involves forward (futures or options) exchange contracts or a short-term swap with short-term borrowing in the foreign currency and simultaneous lending of dollars for the same maturity. In both methods, the cost (or additional return) is the interest rate differential for the appropriate term between the foreign currency and the US dollar.

The result of such a hedging strategy, with a systematic rollover of the foreign exchange hedge, is given in Table 3. In most cases, currency hedging would have improved the performance over the period, given the high level of short-term interest rates in the US and, in recent years, the strong dollar. On the other side, currency exposure is often a positive motive for foreign bond investment, as was the case in 1985.

A depreciation of the dollar might well also lead to a price appreciation of non-dollar bond markets. Foreign governments have very high real interest rates to underpin their currencies. A weakening of the dollar would allow a long awaited reduction in foreign real interest rates and hence bond market appreciation. Therefore, a foreign investor would enjoy both the currency and bond price movements. This is also suggested by the correlation numbers of Figure 3. It should be stressed that non-dollar bonds are more attractive than equities as a way to exploit currency opportunities.

Non-dollar bond markets have less implied risk than foreign equities. While currency variation is often the major source of return for non-dollar bonds, this is not necessarily the case for equities. Local equity market movements frequently offset currency gains, especially in more open economies where leading companies tend to be exporters whose profit margins are squeezed by a weaker dollar.

[1] This study uses Lombard Odier daily bond indexes, which have been published since 1982 and appear daily in the Wall Street Journal (Europe).

REFERENCE

Bruno Solnik and Bernard Noetzlin. "Optimal International Asset Allocation." *Journal of Portfolio Management*, Fall 1982.
The stock indexes come from Capital International.

Duration models: A taxonomy

Explaining price elasticity is not the same thing as explaining multi-factor returns.

G. O. Bierwag, George G. Kaufman, and Cynthia M. Latta

Duration analysis is now an accepted, if not a necessary, part of every bond portfolio manager's toolkit for analyzing interest rate risk. Most of the duration models currently in use are single-term models, but two- or more-term duration models have been attracting attention recently.

Unfortunately, there is considerable confusion about the meaning of these models and their proper uses. Academicians and practitioners alike often confuse the second- and higher-order terms in models that explain the instantaneous price elasticity of a security with respect to interest rates with the terms in multi-factor models that explain non-instantaneous bond returns.

This paper demonstrates that the higher-order terms in price elasticity models are not necessarily the same as the additional factors in bond return models, although they may at times look alike. Failure to recognize this difference may lead to poor predictions and possibly rejection of the usefulness of duration-based models. See, for example, Bierwag, Kaufman, Latta, and Roberts (1987) and Gultekin and Rogalski (1984).

DURATION AND CONVEXITY

Duration is related to the derivative of the price of a stream of future payments (F_1, F_2, . . ., F_n) with respect to the rates at which these flows are discounted. If the yield to maturity (i) is specified as the discount rate, so that the term structure is flat and any changes in interest rates are the same for all ma-

turities, the first derivative may be transformed into the common Macaulay duration (see Hopewell and Kaufman, 1973):

$$D = \frac{\sum[tF_t/(1 + i)^t]}{\sum[F_t/(1 + i)^t]} \qquad (1)$$

If the term structure is assumed to be generated by other stochastic processes, then this procedure derives other measures of duration.

By substituting duration as defined in Equation (1) in the first derivative of the price of a bond with respect to one plus the yield to maturity, and rearranging terms, the instantaneous percent price change due to a change in interest rates is approximated by the relationship:

$$\Delta P/P = -D\Delta i/(1 + i), \qquad (2)$$

where:

P = the bond price.

This price elasticity equation maps a straight line with duration as its slope. As the actual bond price–interest rate relationship for a bond of given coupon rate and term to maturity is curvilinear, Equation (2) provides a good approximation of the percent change in price for a given change in interest rates only for small changes in rates around the interest rate at which the straight line is tangent to the curve. Both the Equation (2) approximation and the actual price–interest rate relationships are plotted in Figure 1. Percent changes are equivalent to changes in log-

G. O. BIERWAG is Professor of Economics and Finance at the College of Business Administration at the University of Arizona in Tucson (AZ 85721). GEORGE G. KAUFMAN is The John F. Swift Professor of Finance and Economics at Loyola University of Chicago (IL 60611). CYNTHIA M. LATTA is Senior Financial Economist at DRI/McGraw-Hill, Inc. in Lexington (MA 02173).

FIGURE 1

SINGLE-TERM DURATION AND CONVEXITY

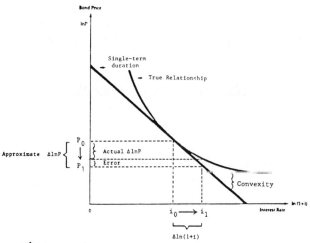

where:

$$\Delta \ln P = \frac{\Delta P}{P}$$

$$\Delta \ln(1 + i) = \frac{\Delta i}{(1 + i)}$$

arithms, so Equation (2) may be charted most easily by scaling the axes in logarithms.

As we can see from Figure 1, the larger the change in interest rates, the greater the distance between the actual curvilinear relationship and the straight line. The vertical distance between the two lines, or the "convexity" of the bond, represents the price prediction error for single-term duration models, such as given by Equation (2).[1]

This error can be reduced by expanding the Taylor series for the percent change in bond price around the initial interest rate and adding second- and higher-order terms as follows:

$$\frac{\Delta P}{P} = \frac{1}{P}\left(\frac{dP}{dh}\right)\Delta i + \frac{1}{2!}\left(\frac{1}{P}\right)\frac{d^2P}{dh^2}(\Delta i)^2$$

$$+ \ldots + \frac{1}{t!}\left(\frac{1}{P}\right)\frac{d^tP}{dh^t}(\Delta i)^t + \ldots, \quad (3A)$$

where:

h = (1 + i), and the derivatives are evaluated at the initial interest rate.

Taking the derivative yields:

$$\frac{\Delta P}{P} = \frac{-\Sigma tF_t(1 + i)^{-t}}{P}\left[\frac{\Delta i}{(1 + i)}\right]$$

$$+ \frac{\frac{1}{2}\Sigma t(t + 1)F_t(1 + i)^{-t}}{P}\left[\frac{(\Delta i)^2}{(1 + i)^2}\right] + \ldots. \quad (3B)$$

Substituting the definition of duration from Equation (1) yields:

$$\frac{\Delta P}{P} = -D\frac{\Delta i}{(1 + i)} +$$

$$\frac{1}{2}\left[D + \frac{\Sigma t^2(1 + i)^{-t}F_t}{P}\right]\frac{\Delta i^2}{(1 + i)^2} + \ldots. \quad (3C)$$

Duration now appears in every term in the equation. It is the only coefficient in the first term. In all other terms, duration comprises only part of the coefficient and is combined with progressively more information in progressively higher-order terms. As a result, the greater the number of terms, the closer the duration model approximates the actual relationship. This is shown in Figure 2 for a two-term duration expansion model.

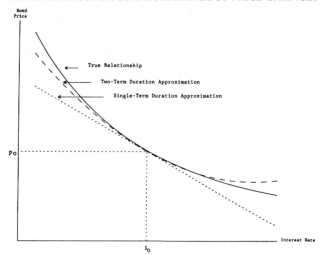

Single-factor duration may be viewed as a one-term or one-moment statistical summary of a series, such as a mean or median. Although the first-term summary measure provides important information about the series, it does not provide complete information. This requires the inclusion of second-, third-, and higher-moment measures, such as variance, skewness, and so on.

Knowledge of convexity and the additional information provided in higher-order terms is particularly useful when analyzing the price elasticity characteristics of different bonds having the same duration. Two bonds with the same duration but otherwise different characteristics are unlikely to experience precisely the same percent change in price for the same change in interest rates; the larger the interest rate change, the greater the difference. Differences in price responses may be progressively reduced by computing and sequentially matching the second- and higher-order terms in Equation (3C) for the two bonds.

256

The number of terms to be included in a duration price elasticity equation is determined by the benefit–cost trade-off for each user. The Table shows the percent of the actual price change predicted by one- and two-term Taylor series duration models for a series of bonds differing in term to maturity and coupon in different interest rate environments for selected changes in yields to maturity.

To focus on the basis point change in rates, the Macaulay durations frequently are divided by (1 + i). This measure is referred to as "modified duration." As we can see in the Table, one-term modified duration does not predict perfectly. The error varies in the different scenarios, depending on the characteristics of the bond and the market. One-term duration predicts better, the larger the coupon, the shorter the term to maturity, and the higher the market rate of interest; that is, the shorter the duration.[2] Addition of the second term of the Taylor expansion explains almost all of the price change not explained by the first term alone. Convexity is effectively eliminated. Thus, even if second-order terms are cost-effective relative to the first-order, higher-order terms are unlikely to be cost-effective. Note that, unlike the first-term approximation, which always overestimates actual price declines and underestimates actual price increases, second-term approximations can both over- and underestimate actual price changes.

The greater the convexity, as defined in Figure 1, the larger the increase in price of a bond will be when interest rates decline, and the smaller the price decrease when interest rates increase. This property is sometimes viewed as permitting riskless arbitrage profits among bonds of equal single-term durations. As is now evident, however, the existence of price convexity reflects only the incomplete specification of the measure of duration used.

In efficient financial markets, the properties of the bond that create a particular pattern are taken into account in its pricing. Two bonds with equal durations but different convexities should be priced differently, and riskless arbitrage profits should not exist. The perception of this possibility is a statistical artifact.

DURATION AND BOND RETURNS

Duration has also been found useful in explaining bond returns over finite periods of time. Duration return-generating models are constructed by differentiating the value of an investment fund accumulated over a particular planning period or time interval with respect to a change in the term structure during the period. Thus, the derived durations reflect the underlying stochastic process driving interest rate movements.

The number of factors necessary to explain the returns from any stochastic process is econometrically related to the number of interest rates or points on the term structure that can change, at least partially, independently. One-factor models assume that there is only one exogenous force driving interest rates. Thus, in effect, only one rate moves independently. Changes in all other rates along the term structure are assumed to be perfectly correlated with changes in this rate and move in lockstep fashion with it.

Knowledge of the stochastic process that describes changes in any one interest rate on the term structure can then describe changes in the entire term structure. Two-factor models permit two exogenous forces that drive two totally or partially independent rates. Changes in all other rates along the term structure will be combinations of changes in these two rates, or in functions of these two rates, and are perfectly correlated with changes in a weighted combination of these two rates or their functions. And so on for additional factors.

If one assumes a flat term structure and a stochastic process that changes all interest rates by equal amounts (additive shocks) so that the term structure remains flat, the stochastic process can be explained by a single factor whose coefficient is the Macaulay duration shown in Equation (1).

For example, return Equation (4) using Macaulay duration was derived by Babcock (1984):

TABLE

Estimated and Actual Decreases in Instantaneous Changes in
Bond Prices for Different Bonds and Yields to
Maturities when Interest Rates Increase 50 Basis Points

Coupon Rate	Term to Maturity	Modified Single-Term Macaulay Duration	Price Change		Actual
			Estimated*		
			1st Term	1st & 2d Terms	
(Percent)	(Years)			(Percent)	
YTM = 4%					
4	3	2.776	−1.388	−1.374	−1.374
	10	8.110	−4.055	−3.955	−3.956
	30	17.292	−8.646	−8.121	−8.144
16	3	2.556	−1.278	−1.266	−1.266
	10	6.566	−3.283	−3.209	−3.210
	30	13.816	−6.908	−6.549	−6.563
YTM = 12%					
4	3	2.564	−1.282	−1.271	−1.271
	10	6.934	−3.467	−3.389	−3.390
	30	9.228	−4.614	−4.416	−4.423
16	3	2.342	−1.171	−1.161	−1.161
	10	5.364	−2.682	−2.628	−2.629
	30	7.898	−3.949	−3.806	−3.811

* From Taylor series expansion using modified duration, annual coupon payments, and annual compounding.

$$E(i_j) = i_0 + \left(\frac{PL - D_j}{PL}\right)(\hat{i}_r - i_0), \quad (4)$$

where:

> $E(i_j)$ = expected annual interest return over investor's planning period for a default-free bond with duration D_j;
>
> i_0 = current market yield to maturity;
>
> PL = investor's planning period;
>
> D = Macaulay duration; and
>
> $\hat{i}_r$ = predicted reinvestment yield to maturity immediately after purchase.

As with price elasticity models, different assumptions about the stochastic process lead to different measures of duration.

If one assumes a non-flat term structure and a stochastic process that changes all zero-coupon equivalent interest rates (r_t) by amounts that are proportional to $(1 + r_t)$, the stochastic process is also a single-factor process but is associated with a different duration coefficient:

$$D = \frac{\sum[tF_t/(1 + r_t)^t]}{\sum[F_t/(1 + r_t)^t]} \quad (5)$$

where:

> t = points on the term structure so that $(r_1, r_2, \ldots, r_n)$ is the initial term structure.

This duration is referred to as Fisher–Weil duration (1971).

Single-factor models can describe the consequences of only a restricted set of term structure processes. Evidence from empirical term structure studies suggests that changes in actual term structures are more complex and require a number of factors to describe accurately. For example, the term structure of U.S. Treasury securities on August 27, 1987, is fitted well by a polynomial of degree 3:

$$r_t = 7.453 + 0.852 \ln t + 0.016 (\ln t)^2 - 0.023 (\ln t)^3. \quad (6A)$$

The method for estimating this equation is described in Bierwag, Kaufman, and Latta (1987). If on other dates the estimated coefficients, including the constant term, differ, the term structure may be driven by as many as four independent sources of interest rate movements. The evidence suggests that this may be the case. For example, the term structure on November 18, 1987, is fitted well by the following third-degree polynomial equation:

$$r_t = 7.342 + 0.984 \ln t - 0.128 (\ln t)^2 + 0.009 (\ln t)^3. \quad (6B)$$

All coefficients in this equation differ from those in Equation (6A).

Multiple-factor duration return-generating models may be developed in a number of ways. One method makes assumptions about both the number of factors and the nature of the stochastic process relating them. If, for example, the four coefficients in Equation (6A) represent four independent factors, the changes in the coefficients through time are predetermined by the nature of the stochastic process assumed.

Another method makes assumptions about the functional form of the term structures, assumes a number of factors equal to or less than the number of terms in the estimated functional form, e.g., in Equations (6A) and (6B), and derives durations from changes in the estimated coefficients for each factor in the different periods. Whether the number of factors assumed in either approach is sufficiently accurate is an empirical question to be determined by cost–benefit analysis similar to that for the appropriate number of terms to use in the Taylor expansion. An insufficient number of factors increases stochastic process risk.

Using the first approach, for example, Bierwag (1987a) and Bierwag, Kaufman, and Latta (1987) have developed a two-factor model based on a stochastic process that describes linear combinations of two independent interest rates (one a short-term rate and the other a long-term rate) and derives two durations:

$$D1 = \sum_{t=1}^{n} tF_t P(0,t)/A$$

$$(7)$$

$$D2 = \sum_{t=1}^{n} t^2 F_t P(0,t)/A,$$

where:

> A = value of the portfolio.

Note that the second duration is denominated in units of time squared. This term resembles the second term in the Taylor series expansion [Equation (3C)], which means that it and other similar duration measures are often confused for the second term in the Taylor expansion and given the same interpretation. These second factors are not measures of convexity, however, and the second-order terms derived from Taylor expansions are not useful descriptions of the stochastic processes driving term structures.

This can be easily demonstrated. For example, if the relationship between the two independent interest rates in the Bierwag model is specified in logarithmic rather than in linear form, the second duration measure will look like:

$$D2 = \sum_{t=1}^{n} t \ln t F_t P(0,t)/A. \quad (8)$$

The coefficient of the second factor is no longer a squared term and cannot be confused with the second term in a Taylor expansion.

Another approach to deriving multi-factor duration models was used by Chambers, Carleton, and McEnally (1988). They fitted term structures for Treasury securities to polynomials of various higher-order degrees. The equations resemble Equation (5), but are not in log form. They assumed that the motion in the term structures through time could be captured by changes in the coefficients of the first n terms of these equations and derived duration factors by differentiating the final accumulation value with respect to the assumed changes in interest rates. As they assumed the term structure to be described by a polynomial in terms to maturity, their higher-order terms resemble the higher-order terms from the Taylor expansion. Again, the resemblance is coincidental. A different functional specification of the term structure could yield different duration measures and eliminate the similarity.

Multiple-factor duration models also have been developed by Brennan–Schwartz (1983) and Nelson–Schaefer (1983), among others. As in the two models described above, the second-factor terms in these models need not be higher-order terms resembling those in the Taylor expansion.

CONCLUSION

Duration models are useful tools for security analysis only if they are fully understood and correctly specified. Multi-term models for approximating instantaneous price elasticities must not be confused with multi-factor models for estimating bond returns, even if they may look alike. That is, the presence of squared terms in duration equations need not indicate the existence of multiple factors, and multiple-factor models need not contain squared terms. To be useful and meaningful, duration must be used correctly.

REFERENCES

Babcock, Guilford C. "Duration As a Link Between Yield and Value." *Journal of Portfolio Management*, Summer 1984, pp. 58-65.

Bierwag, G. O. "Bond Returns, Discrete Stochastic Processes, and Duration." *Journal of Financial Research*, Fall 1987, pp. 191-209.

———. *Duration Analysis: Managing Interest Rate Risk.* Cambridge, MA.: Ballinger, 1987.

———. "Measures of Duration." *Economic Inquiry*, October 1978, pp. 497-507.

Bierwag, G. O., George G. Kaufman, and Cynthia M. Latta. "Bond Portfolio Immunization: Tests of Maturity, One- and Two-Factor Duration Matching Strategies." *Financial Review*, May 1987, pp. 203-219.

Bierwag, G. O., George G. Kaufman, Cynthia M. Latta, and Gordon S. Roberts. "Usefulness of Duration in Bond Portfolio Management: Response to Critics." *Journal of Portfolio Management*, Winter 1987, pp. 48-52.

Bierwag, G. O., George G. Kaufman, and Alden Toevs. "Recent Developments in Bond Portfolio Immunization Strategies." In George G. Kaufman, G. O. Bierwag, and Alden Toevs, eds., *Innovations in Bond Portfolio Management: Duration Analysis and Immunization.* Greenwich, CT.: JAI Press, 1983, pp. 105-157.

Bierwag, G. O., George G. Kaufman, and Alden Toevs. "Duration: Its Development and Use in Bond Portfolio Management." *Financial Analysts Journal*, July/August 1983, pp. 113-123.

Brennan, Michael J., and Eduardo S. Schwartz. "Duration, Bond Pricing, and Portfolio Management." In George G. Kaufman, G. O. Bierwag, and Alden Toevs, eds., op. cit, pp. 3-36.

Chambers, Donald, Willard Carleton, and Richard McEnally. "Immunizing Default-Free Bond Portfolios With a Duration Vector." *Journal of Financial and Quantitative Analysis*, March 1988, p. 89-104.

Diller, Stanley. *Parametric Analysis of Fixed Income Securities.* New York: Goldman, Sachs, June 1984.

Fisher, Lawrence, and Roman L. Weil. "Coping With the Risk of Market Rate Fluctuations: Returns to Bondholders from Naive and Optimal Strategies." *Journal of Business*, October 1971, pp. 408-431.

Goodman, Laurie S., and N. R. Vijayaraghavan. "Generalized Duration Hedging With Futures Contracts." *Review of Futures Markets* (Vol. 6, No. 1, 1986), pp. 96-108.

Gultekin, N. Bulent, and Richard J. Rogalski. "Alternative Duration Specifications and the Measurement of Basis Risk: Empirical Tests." *Journal of Business*, April 1984, pp. 243-262.

Hopewell, Michael H., and George G. Kaufman. "Bond Price Volatility and Term to Maturity: A Generalized Respecification." *American Economic Review*, September 1973, pp. 749-753.

Ingersoll, Jonathan E., Jeffrey Skelton, and Roman Weil. "Duration: Forty Years Later." *Journal of Financial and Quantitative Analysis*, November 1978, pp. 621-650.

Khang, Chulsoon. "Bond Immunization When Short-Term Rates Fluctuate More Than Long-Term Rates." *Journal of Financial and Quantitative Analysis*, December 1979, pp. 1085-1095.

Klotz, Richard G. *Convexity of Fixed-Income Securities.* New York: Salomon Brothers, October 1985.

Nelson, Jeffrey, and Stephen Schaefer. "The Dynamics of the Term Structure and Alternative Portfolio Immunization Strategies." In George G. Kaufman, G. O. Bierwag and Alden Toevs, eds., op. cit, pp. 61-101.

Roll, Richard. "Managing Risk in Thrift Institutions: Beyond the Duration Gap." Invited Research Working Paper, No. 60. Washington, D.C., Federal Home Loan Bank Board, October 1987.

Toevs, Alden L. "The Error Incurred By Using Duration as a Measure of Bond Portfolio Volatility." Research Report, Federal Research Foundation of Canada, 1982.

[1] In the academic literature, convexity is sometimes used to describe the property of some measures of duration (the Macaulay measure, for example) that, holding duration constant and regardless of the number of terms specified, generate returns that are positively correlated with the size of the coupon. This pattern suggests the possibility of riskless arbitrage from buying higher-coupon and selling lower-coupon bonds or portfolios of the same duration. Because these conditions are inconsistent with equilibrium in financial markets, duration measures that generate such patterns are disequilibrium measures for the assumed particular stochastic process generating interest rates; they represent inaccurate measures. Other duration measures exist that would not display this convexity and would be correct. The perception of riskless arbitrage opportunities actually is a function of the use of incorrect duration measures not of actual market conditions. Nor is it a valid criticism of duration measures in general; rather, it emphasizes the importance of using correct durations.

[2] For some long-term deep discount bonds, decreases in maturity may be associated with increases in duration so that the maturity relationship may not always hold.

Convexity and exceptional return

An application of return attribution analysis to fixed-income management.

Ronald N. Kahn and Roland Lochoff

Duration is the traditional measure of portfolio interest rate risk. It estimates the relative change in value resulting from small parallel shifts in the term structure.[1] As volatility has increased, however, duration has fallen short as the sole measure of risk. Convexity, which corrects the duration estimate for large parallel shifts, has recently been acclaimed the savior of duration. In fact, arguments based on the parallel shift worldview show that, beyond building a better risk measurement, more convexity is always better, ceteris paribus.[2] Whether the market moves up or down, high-convexity portfolios will always outperform low-convexity portfolios of equal duration and yield.

The argument that convexity can generate exceptional return assumes that the term structure always shifts in parallel. In fact, the term structure seldom, if ever, shifts in parallel. But is the deviation from the parallel shift assumption sufficient to negate the conclusion that convexity can generate exceptional return? This article examines this question in the U.S. Treasury market, using the technique of return attribution analysis, an approach long used to analyze equity returns. As we will demonstrate, return attribution analysis is also a powerful tool for investigating fixed-income returns.

THE ARGUMENT FOR CONVEXITY

The argument for convexity always begins with a price/yield curve such as the one illustrated in Figure 1 that shows the price/yield relationship for two dif-

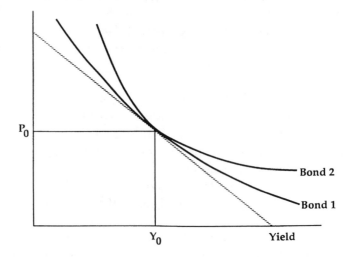

FIGURE 1

BOND PRICE/YIELD CURVE

ferent bonds (or bond portfolios). At the indicated yield, these bonds exhibit identical price and duration, but differing convexity. The duration is simply related to the slope of the curve, while the convexity measures the price/yield curvature:

$$\text{Duration} = -\frac{1}{P}\left(\frac{\partial P}{\partial y}\right) \qquad (1)$$

$$\text{Convexity} = \frac{1}{P}\left(\frac{\partial^2 P}{\partial y^2}\right), \qquad (2)$$

where P is the price and y is the yield to maturity. The convexity of Bond 2 exceeds the convexity of Bond 1. Hence, for any change in yield, Bond 2 will

RONALD N. KAHN is Manager of Special Projects at BARRA (Berkeley, CA 94704). ROLAND LOCHOFF is Manager of Fixed-Income Marketing at the same firm. The authors acknowledge benefiting from conversations with Richard Grinold, Andrew Rudd, Bob Fuhrman, Irwin Jones, and George Oldfield.

outperform Bond 1 because of the increased curvature of its price/yield relationship.

This result also follows from a Taylor expansion of the price/yield relationship:

$$P(y) = P(y_0) + \frac{\partial P}{\partial y} (y - y_0)$$

$$+ \frac{1}{2} \frac{\partial^2 P}{\partial y^2} (y - y_0)^2 + \text{higher order terms} \qquad (3)$$

$$= P(y_0) [1 - DUR (y - y_0)$$

$$+ \frac{1}{2} CON (y - y_0)^2 + \text{higher order terms}]. \qquad (4)$$

Assuming that these higher order terms are insignificant, the price difference between Bond 1 and 2 is:

$$P_2(y) - P_1(y) = P_2(y_0) \frac{1}{2} [CON_2 - CON_1] (y - y_0)^2 > 0. \qquad (5)$$

The weakness of this analysis lies in its dependence upon the simple price/yield relationship. In fact, bond prices depend upon a term structure of interest rates. Duration and convexity do not adequately capture the differing sensitivities of Bonds 1 and 2 to all possible movements of the term structure. If long rates rise while short rates fall, the yield of Bond 1 and the yield of Bond 2 may change by different amounts. Comparing the duration and convexity of two bonds makes sense only under the assumption that each bond's yield changes by an identical amount: the parallel shift assumption. As parallel shifts are seldom if ever observed, any conclusions arising from such analysis deserve careful examination.

RETURN ATTRIBUTION ANALYSIS

Return attribution analysis[3] assigns asset returns to a set of factors operating in the market. This analysis underlies multiple-factor models of the financial markets, and is entirely distinct from the statistical technique of "factor analysis."

At any given time, a cross-sectional analysis can use observed asset returns to determine the return to each of these factors. Historical study of these factor returns can determine how they depend upon excess market returns, and whether they exhibit excess return on average. This return attribution analysis is standard for equities, where valuation is difficult.

Bond analysis often concentrates on valuation: estimating the term structure of interest rates and the set of yield spreads in the market (e.g., Kahn [1989]). Returns to these factors follow from examining their change in value over time. Return attribution analysis estimates factor returns directly from bond returns,

never concentrating on bond values. As this analysis is rare for bonds, we outline the procedure here.

The idea is to attribute monthly bond returns to various factors in the market:

$$r(n,t) = \sum_{j=1}^{J} x(n,j,t) \, fr(j,t) + \epsilon(n,t) \qquad (6)$$

where:

$r(n,t)$ = excess return to bond n at time t;

= return to bond n at time t minus the risk-free return at time t;

$x(n,j,t)$ = bond n exposure to factor j at time t; and

$fr(j,t)$ = return to factor j at time t.

In matrix notation this becomes:

$$\tilde{r}(t) = \mathbf{X}(t) \, \tilde{fr}(t) + \tilde{\epsilon}. \qquad (7)$$

The factor exposures are standard statistics, rescaled appropriately. Consider, for example, the duration factor. A bond's exposure to this factor is related simply to its duration:

$$x(n,DUR,t) = \left[\frac{DUR(n,t) - DUR(market,t)}{SD(DUR)} \right] \qquad (8)$$

The duration factor exposure is the bond duration minus the duration of the market, and divided by the standard deviation of durations observed in the market. In general, the exposures to other factors follow this same pattern:

$$x(n,j,t) = \left[\frac{\xi(n,j,t) - \xi(market,t)}{SD(\xi)} \right] \qquad (9)$$

where:

$\xi(n,j,t)$ = unscaled exposure of bond n to factor j at time t.

This rescaling achieves three goals. First, the market exposure to each factor is zero. Second, a factor exposure of one corresponds to a portfolio whose exposure exceeds the market average by one standard deviation. In fact, exposure values are generally on the order of ± 1. Third, these factor exposures are dimensionless.

Return attribution analysis begins by running capitalization-weighted regressions[4] of monthly bond returns against their exposures to generate monthly factor returns:

$$\tilde{fr} = (\mathbf{X}^T \mathbf{W} \mathbf{X})^{-1} \mathbf{X}^T \mathbf{W} \, \tilde{r} \qquad (10)$$

$$fr(j) = \sum_n \left[(\mathbf{X}^T \mathbf{W} \mathbf{X})^{-1} \mathbf{X}^T \right]_{j,n} w(n) r(n) \qquad (11)$$

where the diagonal matrix W contains the capitalization weights for each return. These factor returns constitute returns to specific factor portfolios, as Equation (11) explicitly demonstrates. The factor return is simply a weighted sum of returns to specific bonds. The weights given above, therefore, describe a particular portfolio: the factor portfolio.

Straightforward analysis shows that each factor portfolio has zero net value (long and short positions cancel), unit exposure to the factor ($x(j,t) = 1.0$), and zero exposure to all other factors. In general, because the number of assets should exceed the number of factors, there will be a large set of zero net value portfolios with unit exposure to one factor and all other exposures perfectly hedged. The factor portfolio is the element of that set that exhibits the minimum return variance.

If the factors in the model are few and relatively uncorrelated, building portfolios with unit exposure to one factor and zero exposure to other factors should be straightforward. If a model includes many highly correlated factors, however, the associated factor portfolios may require strange weightings — large long and short positions in very similar assets — to generate unit exposure to one factor and zero exposure to other correlated factors.

These factor portfolios play an important role in tilt strategies. Tilting a portfolio toward a certain factor simply involves adding a multiple of the factor portfolio to the untilted portfolio.

Given a history of monthly factor returns, this analysis technique then investigates the dependence of the factor returns upon the overall excess market return. It also investigates whether each factor generates expected excess return.

Consider the following regression of historical factor returns against market excess return:

$$fr(j,t) = \alpha(j) + \beta(j) \times emr(t) + \mu(j) \qquad (12)$$

where:

$emr(t)$ = excess market return at time t, and

= market return at time t minus the risk-free return at time t.

The estimated factor beta, $\beta(j)$, captures the covariance of the factor return with the excess market return. The estimated factor alpha, $\alpha(j)$, captures the expected excess factor return when the market excess return equals zero. The excess market return is the capitalization-weighted mean excess return over the entire bond universe.

ESTIMATING RETURN TO CONVEXITY

The argument convexity's supporters make is that a higher-convexity bond or portfolio will out-

perform a lower-convexity bond or portfolio, assuming two bonds or portfolios of equal yield and duration. We can use return attribution analysis to investigate this assertion in a straightforward and quite general way.

Consider an analysis of observed bond returns based on three factors: yield, duration, and convexity. The convexity factor return describes the return to a portfolio whose yield and duration exactly match the market, but whose convexity lies one standard deviation above the market convexity. Such a portfolio should outperform the market, according to the argument presented earlier. In the language of return attribution analysis: The convexity factor alpha should significantly exceed zero.

We investigate these claims using monthly returns to U.S. Treasury bonds, notes, and bills between January 1980 and October 1986. We concentrate on the Treasury market for two reasons. First, the quality of Treasury market data is better than the quality of non-Treasury bond data. Second, Treasury returns are unaffected by changing sector spreads. We specifically exclude callable Treasury bonds from our sample, because option-adjusted durations and convexities are model-dependent, which could call our final results into question.[5]

The yield factor in the study is based on current yield. The analysis attributes returns to three factors in the market. The yield factor captures the return generated with no term structure movement over the return period. The duration and convexity factors capture the returns generated by term structure movements. As the return period for this study is one month, current yield is the natural choice for estimating returns generated in the absence of term structure movements.

RESULTS

The Table summarizes our results. The first line, for example, is interpreted to show that the monthly duration factor return estimates exhibited T-statistics with magnitude greater than 2.0 in 95% of the estimation months.

Figure 2 plots the duration factor return versus excess market return. The duration factor portfolio—whose duration exceeds that of the market by one standard deviation — outperforms the market when the market is up, and underperforms the market when the market is down. The duration factor has a beta of 1.22, not surprising, because the duration factor portfolio's duration exceeds that of the market. The duration factor does not exhibit a significant alpha. Duration is a significant factor in explaining return in 95% of the months observed. This does not

Factor	Alpha ± SE	Beta ± SE	R²	Percent Significant
Duration	−5.1 ± 4.2 basis points	1.22 ± 0.03	0.95	95
Convexity	3.2 ± 6.0 basis points	−0.35 ± 0.04	0.45	81
Current yield	2.1 ± 0.7 basis points	−0.02 ± 0.01	0.18	42

Notes: SE refers to the standard error of the estimate. The percent significant column lists the percentage of months in which the monthly factor return estimates were statistically significant.

FIGURE 2

DURATION FACTOR RETURN VERSUS
EXCESS MARKET RETURN

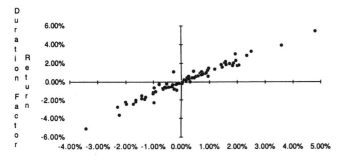

imply, however, that duration explains 95% of observed bond returns.

Figure 3 plots the convexity factor return versus excess market return. According to the arguments

FIGURE 3

CONVEXITY FACTOR RETURN VERSUS
EXCESS MARKET RETURN

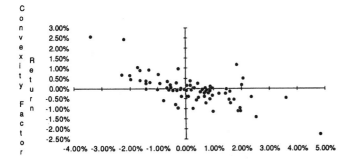

presented earlier, the convexity factor portfolio should outperform whether the market is up or down. Figure 3 shows no such behavior. Convexity, however, does appear to outperform in down markets. This is consistent with the estimated convexity factor beta of −0.34. The convexity factor does not have a significant alpha.

Figure 4 plots the current yield factor return versus excess market return. This factor estimates return generated in the absence of term structure movements, so it should be relatively independent of excess market return. In fact, the current yield factor beta is statistically indistinguishable from zero. The

FIGURE 4

CURRENT YIELD FACTOR RETURN VERSUS
EXCESS MARKET RETURN

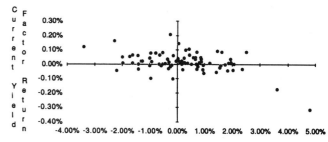

current yield factor alpha is distinguishable from zero, at 2.1 basis points per month. This factor alpha is still quite low, however, and current yield significantly helps to explain observed returns in only 42% of the months observed.

Figure 5 illustrates the adjusted R² figures for fitting this three-factor model to the monthly return data. In monthly fitting, the regression R² averaged 0.82 over the entire period, with a minimum of 0.23 and a maximum of 0.99.

Given that convexity and current yield are closely related to duration, especially for the non-callable universe, we examined this model for collinearity problems. Analysis of the X^TX matrix, which enters into the regressions, failed to detect a worrisome level of collinearity.[6]

More intuitively, we can construct a non-callable Treasury portfolio matching market duration and current yield, and exceeding the market convexity, without too much difficulty. Remember that the portfolio includes short positions (in fact the net value is

FIGURE 5

ADJUSTED R-SQUARE STATISTIC FOR THREE FACTOR MODEL

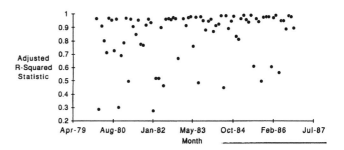

zero), and can use over a hundred different assets to hedge just two factors.

SUMMARY AND CONCLUSION

Overall, our results demonstrate that convexity has not generated excess return in the U.S. Treasury market. The claims for the value of convexity assume parallel term structure shifts. These are seldom observed. In fact, our analysis shows that deviations from the parallel shift assumption are significant enough to invalidate this argument.

Beyond refuting the claims about convexity, we have also demonstrated the power of return attribution analysis, which should become as standard for fixed-income analysis as it is for equity analysis.

[1] See the articles by Hopewell and Kaufman [1983], Kahn [1989], and Rudd [1988].

[2] Klotz [1985], however, argues that the risk generated by excess convexity may outweigh any excess return.

[3] The specific methodology presented here was developed by BARRA.

[4] In fact, the results we present below are unchanged if we run equal-weighted regressions instead of capitalization-weighted regressions.

[5] We have also run this analysis on the full Treasury universe, including the callable Treasury bonds. The results are unchanged.

[6] The ratio of largest to smallest eigenvalue in this matrix never exceeded 17 in any given month, and was often below 10. An infinite ratio, corresponding to an eigenvalue of zero, implies exact collinearity. Ratios greater than 30 generally signal significant collinearity as per Freund and Littell [1986].

REFERENCES

Freund, Rudolf J., and Ramon C. Littell. *SAS System for Regression.* Cary, North Carolina: SAS Institute, Inc., 1986, p. 81.

Hopewell, Michael H., and George G. Kaufman. "Bond Price Volatility and Term to Maturity: A Generalized Respecification." *American Economic Review*, September 1983, pp. 749-753.

Kahn, Ronald N. "Risk and Return in the U.S. Bond Market: A Multifactor Approach," in *Advances and Innovations in Bond and Mortgage Markets*, Frank J. Fabozzi, ed. Chicago: Probus, 1989.

Klotz, Richard D. "Convexity of Fixed-Income Securities." Salomon Brothers, 1985.

Rudd, Andrew. "Duration, Convexity and Multiple-Factor Models." *Investment Management Review*, September/October 1988, pp. 58-64.

Non-Parallel Yield Curve Shifts and Immunization

Why immunization need not, and often does not, work.

Robert R. Reitano

ROBERT R. REITANO is a Senior Investment Policy Officer and Director of Research at the John Hancock Mutual Life Insurance Company in Boston (MA 02117).

He gratefully acknowledges the technical assistance of Scott E. Navin and the support of the John Hancock in the development of the examples in this article.

A common goal for asset/liability managers is to maintain the modified duration of assets equal to a multiple of the modified duration of liabilities, where this multiple equals the ratio of liability to asset market values. Duration calculations are often made with respect to yield curves that reflect the average qualities of the respective portfolios. For more precision, each quality sector is valued on the appropriate yield curve, and the portfolio duration values are determined by taking weighted averages of the individual components. As is well-known, these weights reflect the relative market values of the individual components.

The principle underlying this duration management approach is that the asset and liability portfolio values will move in tandem as the underlying yield curves move in parallel. That is, each portfolio will change by approximately the same absolute amount for yield curve shifts for which each yield point moves by the same absolute amount. Consequently, the surplus or net worth position will remain relatively stable.

Put another way, this duration management approach assures that the duration of surplus will be zero. Subject to additional conditions on the respective portfolio inertias or convexities (Bierwag [1987], Grove [1974], Reitano [1990a, 1991b]), this surplus value will be "immunized." That is, parallel yield curve shifts will only stabilize or improve its value.

Another common management approach is to maintain the duration of assets equal to the duration of liabilities. Parallel yield curve shifts will then cause assets and liabilities to change by approximately the same relative amount. Consequently, the surplus or net worth position will also change by this common relative amount, and the net worth asset ratio, or ratio of surplus to assets, will remain approximately constant. Again subject to conditions on asset and liability inertias or convexities (see also Kaufman [1984]), the net worth asset ratio will in fact be immunized against parallel yield curve shifts.

Analyzed from the perspective of surplus management, these strategies disguise a number of risks. First of all, there are practical difficulties in maintaining perfect durational targets, and even small duration mismatches have the potential to create great surplus sensitivity (Messmore [1990]). In addition, managing duration values while ignoring convexities has the potential to "reverse immunize" the account, in that parallel yield curve shifts will only stabilize or decrease the value of surplus or the net worth asset ratio under the respective strategies.

As it turns out, the underlying yield curve shift assumption poses the greatest potential for risk. A series of articles (Reitano [1989, 1990b, 1991a, 1991c, 1992]) have analyzed the limitations of the parallel shift assumption and developed models that generalize the notions of duration and convexity to arbitrary yield curve shifts. In the process, it has become clear that the traditional measures can greatly disguise duration risk, as well as obscure the effects of convexity.

It is no surprise, therefore, that classical immunization theories, which rely on the parallel shift assumption underlying duration and convexity, can disguise risk and the potential for immunization to fail.

In this article, we explore this potential through the detailed analysis of an example of the immunization of a surplus position. For more generality and mathematical rigor, see Reitano [1990a, 1991b]. Although we focus on surplus immunization, the shortcomings of the traditional strategy to immunize the net worth asset ratio are comparable and readily illustrated with a second example, introduced in Reitano [1990b]. For an example of the immunization of future values of surplus, see Reitano [1991b].

AN EXAMPLE — SURPLUS IMMUNIZATION

Assume assets composed of a $43.02 million, 12%, ten-year bond, and $25.65 million, six-month commercial paper. The single liability is a $100 million guaranteed investment contract (GIC) payment in year 5. The current yield curve, on a bond yield basis, equals 7.5%, 9.0%, and 10.0% at maturities of 0.5, 5,

and 10 years, respectively. Yields at other maturities are assumed to be interpolated, and spot rates derived in the usual way. That is, they are derived as to price the various bonds suggested by the bond yield curve to par.

Given these assumptions, we then obtain:

	Market Value	Duration	Convexity
Assets	73.25	4.243	34.94
Liabilities	63.97	4.858	25.89
Surplus	9.28	0	96.85

It is easy to check that the asset duration equals the liability duration times the ratio of liability to asset market values.

This example is similar to one introduced in Reitano [1990b]. The difference here is a change in the mix of bonds and commercial paper to achieve the required asset duration. In the original example, the mix was chosen to reproduce the duration of liabilities.

HOW IMMUNIZATION WORKS

Let's denote by $S(\Delta i)$ the value of surplus if the yield curve moves in parallel by Δi. That is, using vector notation, the yield curve shifts as follows:

$$(0.075, 0.090, 0.100) \rightarrow$$
$$(0.075 + \Delta i, 0.090 + \Delta i, 0.100 + \Delta i).$$

Of course, $S(0) = 9.28$ as noted above. A standard calculation produces the approximation for $S(\Delta i)$:

$$S(\Delta i) \simeq S(0)(1 - D^S \Delta i + 1/2\ C^S(\Delta i)^2) \qquad (1)$$

where D^S is the duration of surplus, $D^S = -S'(0)/S(0)$, and C^S its convexity, $C^S = S''(0)/S(0)$ (see Reitano [1989, 1991a] for details).

It is clear from (1) that in order to have $S(\Delta i)$ no smaller than $S(0)$, we must have $D^S = 0$. This is because if D^S is positive, say, negative shifts would be favorable, but positive shifts unfavorable, and $S(\Delta i)$ could fall below $S(0)$. Although the C^S term could help, the $(\Delta i)^2$ factor significantly dampens its effect.

In addition to $D^S = 0$, we require C^S to be positive to assure immunization. The approximation in (1) then becomes:

$$S(\Delta i) \simeq S(0)(1 + 1/2\ C^S(\Delta i)^2) \qquad (2)$$

and the right-hand side of (2) can clearly be no smaller than S(0).

Consequently, we can be confident that the surplus value is immunized at least for moderate values of Δi. We say "moderate" because for very large values of Δi, the $(\Delta i)^3$ and higher powered terms ignored in (1) and (2) can become significant.

To implement this surplus immunization, we require relationships between D^S and C^S and the corresponding values for assets and liabilities. A calculation shows that D^S is a weighted average of D^A and D^L, while C^S is a weighted average of C^A and C^L:

$$D^S = w_1 D^A + w_2 D^L, \qquad (3)$$

$$C^S = w_1 C^A + w_2 C^L. \qquad (4)$$

Here, $w_1 = A/S$, the reciprocal of the net worth asset ratio, while $w_2 = -L/S$, or minus one times the financial leverage ratio.

From Equations (3) and (4), we see that in order to have D^S equal to 0, and C^S positive, we require that the duration of assets equal that of liabilities times L/A, and that the convexity of assets exceed that multiple of liabilities:

$$D^A = \frac{L}{A} D^L, \qquad (5)$$

$$C^A > \frac{L}{A} C^L. \qquad (6)$$

From the values for the example, we see that both (5) and (6) are satisfied. For this example, the approximation in (1) becomes:

$$S(\Delta i) \simeq 9.28 \, [1 + 48.43 \, (\Delta i)^2]. \qquad (7)$$

Calculating actual surplus values and those estimated by (7), denoted $S^e(\Delta i)$, we obtain the results in Table 1. Note that immunization against parallel shifts is successful, and that the estimates obtained with (7) provide good approximations to the actual resulting $S(\Delta i)$ values.

HOW IMMUNIZATION FAILS IN THEORY

The example illustrates an important point: Traditional immunization cannot fail in theory if the underlying assumptions are satisfied. To the extent it

TABLE 1
Actual and Estimated Surplus Values

Δi	$S(\Delta i)$	$S^e(\Delta i)$
-0.02	9.481	9.460
-0.01	9.327	9.325
-0.005	9.291	9.291
0	9.280	9.280
0.005	9.290	9.291
0.01	9.322	9.325
0.02	9.440	9.460

fails, it must fail because at least one of the assumptions underlying the model fails to hold. In practice, the assumption that fails is typically the assumption of parallel shifts.

Does this mean that immunization is impossible if yield curve shifts are non-parallel? The answer is: No, but you have to change the model, which will in turn change the conditions necessary for immunization.

Two approaches are in fact possible. First of all, one can change the yield curve shift assumption from parallel to another explicit shift type, and develop conditions under which immunization is then achieved. Second, the more general question of immunization against arbitrary yield curve shifts can be explored.

In this article, we examine the first approach because it represents a mathematically more straightforward generalization of the classical theory, yet provides deep insight into immunization theory and practice (see Reitano [1990a, 1991b] for more generality).

To this end, assume that $\mathbf{N} = (n_1, n_2, n_3)$ specifies the yield curve shift "direction" of interest. For the classical model, $\mathbf{N} = (1,1,1)$ is the assumed direction vector. In general, a shift of Δi "in the direction of $\mathbf{N}$" will mean that the six-month rate of 0.075 shifts by $n_1 \Delta i$, the five-year rate of 0.09 by $n_2 \Delta i$, and the ten-year rate of 0.10 by $n_3 \Delta i$.

Given this direction vector, one can define the notions of "directional duration" and "directional convexity" in the direction of $\mathbf{N}$. When $\mathbf{N} = (1,1,1)$, these notions reduce to the classical definitions of duration and convexity (see Reitano [1989, 1991a, 1992] for details).

As it turns out (see Reitano [1990a, 1991b]), denoting by $S_N(\Delta i)$ the surplus value given this shift of Δi in the direction of $\mathbf{N}$, Equation (1) still holds. The only difference is that the directional duration and convexity values, D_N^S and C_N^S, must be used. Analogous to the classical definitions, $D_N^S = -S_N'(0)/S_N(0)$, and $C_N^S = S_N''(0)/S_N(0)$. Further, Equations (3) and (4) still hold, as do (5) and (6) as the appropriate conditions for immunization. That is, if:

$$D_N^A = \frac{L}{A} D_N^L, \qquad (8)$$

$$C_N^A > \frac{L}{A} C_N^L, \qquad (9)$$

the directional duration of surplus, D_N^S, will be zero, and the directional convexity, C_N^S, will be positive. As in (2), therefore, surplus will be immunized against shifts in the direction of $\mathbf{N}$.

Consequently, the classical theory generalizes naturally to immunization against shifts of any specified direction. Unfortunately, structuring the portfolio so that (5) and (6) are satisfied does not generally imply that (8) and (9) will be satisfied for other direction vectors $\mathbf{N}$.

More generally, structuring the portfolio to satisfy (8) and (9) for a given $\mathbf{N}$ does not imply that these constraints are satisfied for other direction vectors. The reason for this is that both D_N and C_N can vary greatly as $\mathbf{N}$ changes, and can vary differently for assets and liabilities.

In theory, one can identify conditions under which "complete immunization" is achieved, that is, conditions under which immunization is achieved for every direction vector $\mathbf{N}$ simultaneously (see Reitano [1990a, 1991b]). Unfortunately, the condition on the durational structures of assets and liabilities is very restrictive and potentially difficult to implement, as is that for the convexity structures. Consequently, in practice some immunization exposure may be inevitable.

Returning to the example, which satisfied immunizing conditions for $\mathbf{N} = (1,1,1)$, we investigate the potential range of values for D_N^S and C_N^S, as the direction vector $\mathbf{N}$ changes. Because these ranges depend on the length of the vector $\mathbf{N}$ — that is, the square root of the sum of the squares of its components — it is necessary to restrict this value. Because we wish to compare the resulting ranges of values to the values produced in the classical model where $\mathbf{N} = (1,1,1)$, we restrict the length of $\mathbf{N}$, denoted $|\mathbf{N}|$, to equal $|(1,1,1,)| = \sqrt{3}$.

Given $\mathbf{N} = (n_1, n_2, n_3)$, the directional duration of the exemplified surplus function, $S_N(\Delta i)$, is given by:

$$D_N^S = 4.55n_1 - 35.43n_2 + 30.88n_3. \qquad (10)$$

The coefficients in Equation (10) are the "partial durations" of surplus, viewed as a function of the six-month, five-year, and ten-year bond yields. A calculation shows that for $\mathbf{N} = (1,1,1)$, the classical parallel shift assumption, we obtain $D_N^S = D^S = 0$ as expected.

For non-parallel yield curve shifts, however, the directional duration of surplus can be much different from 0. Specifically, restricting our attention to direction vectors of the same length as the parallel shift $(1,1,1)$, we have:

$$-81.78 \leq D_N^S \leq 81.78, \quad |\mathbf{N}| = \sqrt{3}. \qquad (11)$$

That is, the durational sensitivity of surplus can be as large as 81.78, and as small as -81.78, when yield curve shifts are allowed to be non-parallel. The v-shaped non-parallel shift, $\mathbf{N} = (0.167, -1.300, 1.133)$, has length $\sqrt{3}$ and produces the extreme positive duration, $D_N^S = 81.81$ (discrepancy due to rounding). Similarly, $-\mathbf{N}$ is an extreme negative shift.

As the referenced Reitano articles note, all extreme shifts are proportional to the "total duration vector," $\mathbf{D}^S = (4.55, -35.43, 30.88)$, made up from the partial durations used in (10). For example, the extreme positive shift $\mathbf{N}$ above is about 3.7% of $\mathbf{D}^S$.

Mathematically, the inequalities in (11) are produced using the Cauchy-Schwarz inequality for the size of an inner product or dot product. Because the expression for D_N^S in (10) equals an inner product of $\mathbf{D}^S$ with $\mathbf{N}$, the Cauchy-Schwarz inequality states that this value is less than or equal to the product of the lengths of these vectors, and greater than or equal to -1 times this value. In addition, the extremes of this inequality are achieved when the given vectors are parallel (see Reitano [1989, 1991a] for details).

Analogous to (10), the general formula for C_N^S is:

$$C_N^S = 7.14n_1^2 - 126.21n_2^2 - 127.64n_3^2 + \\ 2(-25.80n_1n_2 + 9.63n_1n_3 + 60.31n_2n_3). \qquad (12)$$

The coefficients in (12) are the "partial convexities" of

surplus. A calculation shows that when $\mathbf{N} = (1,1,1)$, $C_N^S = 96.85$, which equals the C^S value noted above.

For non-parallel yield curve shifts, the directional convexity value produced by (12) can be significantly different from this parallel shift value, and even negative. In particular, restricting our attention to direction vectors $\mathbf{N}$ of length $\sqrt{3}$, the length of $(1,1,1)$, we have:

$$-434.15 \leq C_N^S \leq 424.04, \quad |\mathbf{N}| = \sqrt{3}. \quad (13)$$

In addition, the yield curve shifts of extreme convexity are $\mathbf{N}_1 = (-0.306, -1.662, 0.379)$ and $\mathbf{N}_2 = (0.049, 0.376, 1.690)$.

A simple calculation shows that except for rounding, both shift vectors have length equal to $\sqrt{3}$, and using (12), $\mathbf{N}_1$ produces the negative lower bound in (13), while $\mathbf{N}_2$ produces the positive upper bound.

Mathematically, the inequalities in (13) are developed from (12) by noting that this expression for C_N^S is in fact a quadratic form in the vector $\mathbf{N}$. That is, this expression equals $\mathbf{N}^T \mathbf{C}^S \mathbf{N}$, where $\mathbf{C}^S$ is the matrix of partial convexities, or the "total convexity matrix."

Standard analysis techniques then reveal that this function is less than or equal to $|\mathbf{N}|^2$ times one constant, and greater than or equal to $|\mathbf{N}|^2$ times another constant. These constants are the largest and smallest eigenvalues of $\mathbf{C}^S$, respectively, and the function in (12) assumes these outer bounds when $\mathbf{N}$ is proportional to the associated eigenvectors (see Reitano [1991a] for details).

HOW IMMUNIZATION FAILS IN PRACTICE

In theory, it is clear from (11) that D_N^S need not be close to zero, even though it equals zero when $\mathbf{N} = (1,1,1)$. Similarly, from (13) we see that C_N^S need not be positive, even though it equals 96.85 when $\mathbf{N} = (1,1,1)$. Consequently, because we have as in (1):

$$S_N(\Delta i) \simeq S(0)(1 - D_N^S \Delta i + 1/2 \, C_N^S \, (\Delta i)^2), \quad (14)$$

it is clear that the surplus value need not be immunized in theory for general shift directions $\mathbf{N}$ other than $(1,1,1)$. That is, it need not be the case that $S_N(\Delta i)$ will equal or exceed $S(0) = 9.28$, in theory.

What about in practice, with actual observable yield curve shifts? Certainly, if yield curve shifts never

occurred that made D_N^S large, or C_N^S negative, the theory above would provide little insight into immunization practice.

To use a historic data base, we investigated monthly movements in the Treasury yield curve from the end of August 1984 to June 1990, at maturities of six months and five and ten years. Both one-month and overlapping six-month yield curve change vectors, $\mathbf{N}$, are analyzed. With sixty-five overlapping half-year change vectors, normalized to have $|\mathbf{N}| = \sqrt{3}$, we observe that:

$$-12.37 \leq D_N^S \leq 30.38,$$
$$-203.12 \leq C_N^S \leq 338.41. \quad (15)$$

Comparing the D_N^S values produced during this period to the theoretical range in (11), we conclude that while significant duration values are observed, the real world was relatively tame in this example compared to what theory suggests, covering only 26% of the potential range of values. Similarly, the observed C_N^S values, while clearly not all positive, are again somewhat tamely distributed compared to (13), although covering a larger percentage of possible values (63%) than did the associated D_N^S values.

Similar conclusions can be drawn from the seventy monthly change vectors, which produce the following somewhat larger ranges:

$$-20.53 \leq D_N^S \leq 35.69,$$
$$-228.80 \leq C_N^S \leq 368.73. \quad (16)$$

Turning next to the corresponding estimates of the surplus values using (14), the following range of values is produced using half-year change vectors:

$$8.25 \leq S_N^e(\Delta i) \leq 10.52. \quad (17)$$

The range for monthly change vectors is very similar, extending from 8.67 to 10.21. Both ranges compare unfavorably to the initial surplus value, $S(0) = 9.28$, implying that immunization was often not successful.

As for the distribution of results, Table 2 provides percentile data for the half-year change vectors. Almost half (thirty) of the sixty-five change vectors produce negative duration values, placing $D_N^S = 0$ when $\mathbf{N} = (1,1,1)$ at about the forty-sixth percentile of results. In addition, only four change vectors (6%) produce duration sensitivities lower than 2.0 in absolute

TABLE 2
Distribution of D_N^S, C_N^S, and $S_N^\varepsilon(\Delta I)$:
65 Overlapping Six-Month Periods,
August 1984 - June 1990

Percentile	D_N^S	C_N^S	$S_N^\varepsilon(\Delta i)$	$\frac{\Delta S}{S} \times 100\%$
1.5%	-12.37	-203.12	8.25	-11.1%
10	-8.56	-52.32	8.61	-7.2
20	-6.06	-15.37	8.76	-5.6
30	-3.82	17.10	8.95	- 3.5
40	-2.49	38.88	9.04	-2.6
50	2.05	61.79	9.15	-1.4
60	3.82	95.79	9.51	+ 2.4
70	4.24	137.62	9.69	+ 4.4
80	6.47	176.85	9.97	+ 7.5
90	8.94	212.49	10.06	+ 8.4
100	30.38	338.41	10.52	+13.3

Note: D_N^S and C_N^S are normalized so that $|\mathbf{N}| = |(1,1,1)| = \sqrt{3}$.

TABLE 3
Distribution of D_N^S, C_N^S, and $S_N^\varepsilon(\Delta i)$:
70 One-Month Periods,
August 1984 - June 1990

Percentile	D_N^S	C_N^S	$S_N^\varepsilon(\Delta i)$	$\frac{\Delta S}{S} \times 100\%$
1.5%	-20.53	-228.80	8.67	-6.6%
10	-16.10	- 70.60	8.86	-4.5
20	-9.27	-54.66	9.05	-2.4
30	-5.91	-30.19	9.16	-1.3
40	-2.44	2.48	9.22	-0.6
50	-0.35	52.32	9.30	+0.2
60	2.13	105.86	9.36	+0.8
70	4.26	131.68	9.41	+1.4
80	10.23	162.78	9.50	+2.4
90	12.52	206.92	9.54	+2.8
100	35.69	368.73	10.21	+10.1

Note: D_N^S and C_N^S are normalized so that $|\mathbf{N}| = |(1,1,1)| = \sqrt{3}$.

value, implying the extent to which the traditional value, $D^S = 0$, disguises surplus risk.

For directional convexities, only about 23% of the sample yield curve changes produce negative values, which may appear at odds with the symmetry of the theoretical interval in (13). However, the theoretical interval provides no information about the expected distribution of results; it only defines its possible range.

On the other hand, the yield curve shifts experienced during this relatively short period should not be interpreted as constraining those possible in other periods. The traditional value, $C_N^S = 96.85$ when $\mathbf{N} = (1,1,1)$, is seen to be at about the sixtieth percentile of this distribution.

From the distribution of estimated surplus values, $S_N^\varepsilon(\Delta i)$, we observe that the initial value, $S(0) = 9.28$, is at about the fifty-fourth percentile. That is, immunization was unsuccessful in a little more than half of the six-month periods studied. Also, the relative changes in surplus caused by these yield curve shifts are seen to be substantial, extending from -11.1% to +13.3%.

In general, these comments on the Table 2 distributions apply equally well to the distribution of monthly change vectors in Table 3. One exception relates to D_N^S, in that about 16% of the yield curve vectors produce duration sensitivities lower than 2.0 in absolute value, compared with 6% in the distribution

of half-year results. Also, almost 40% of the sample C_N^S values were negative, although skewness to positive values is still evident in this distribution. Finally, while still unfavorable about 50% of the time, the distribution of surplus changes is more tightly distributed, reflective of the shorter time frame used for yield curve changes.

It is natural to inquire into the accuracy of the surplus approximation in (14), which was used to evaluate the efficacy of immunization in Tables 2 and 3.

TABLE 4
Actual versus Estimated Values
Surplus Values After Yield Curve Changes
from Non-Overlapping Six-Month Periods

6 months beginning	$S_N(\Delta i)$	$S_N^\varepsilon(\Delta i)$	$S_N^\varepsilon(\Delta i)$ Percentile
1/1/85*	8.868	8.861	25th
7/1/85*	9.132	9.127	48th
1/1/86	10.529	10.517	100th
7/1/86*	8.382	8.383	5th
1/1/87	9.878	9.883	77th
7/1/87*	9.040	9.040	40th
1/1/88*	9.219	9.219	52nd
7/1/88	10.001	10.000	83rd
1/1/89*	8.899	8.896	27th
7/1/89	9.328	9.328	55th
1/1/90	9.508	9.509	60th

* Immunization unsuccessful: $S(0) = 9.280$

Table 4 provides actual and estimated values of $S_N(\Delta i)$ for eleven non-overlapping six-month periods between January 1985 and June 1990.

As can be seen, the approximation in (14) produced very good accuracy in all cases. In addition, we see that the range of resulting S_N values spans the range produced in Table 2. Finally, according to Table 4, immunization was unsuccessful during six of the eleven periods.

AN EXAMPLE — IMMUNIZATION OF THE SURPLUS RATIO

As noted in the introduction, the net worth asset ratio, $r^S = S/A$, can be immunized against parallel yield curve shifts by matching the asset to the liability duration, and maintaining more asset convexity:

$$D^A = D^L,$$
$$C^A > C^L. \tag{18}$$

As in the surplus immunization case above, immunization against shifts in the direction of **N** can be insured by (18), if directional durations and convexities are used in these constraints (Reitano [1990a, 1991b]).

Unfortunately, the problem here is the same as that illustrated so far. That is, structuring the portfolio to satisfy (18) for one assumption about **N** (for example, **N** = (1,1,1)) does not insure that such conditions are satisfied for other assumptions because of the potential for D_N and C_N to vary as in (11) and (13).

Consider the example above, except change the mix of assets to $50 million of the bond, and $17.48 million of the commercial paper, as in Reitano [1990b]. The duration of assets (4.857) then equals that of liabilities, while the convexity (40.41) exceeds that of the liabilities. The initial net worth asset ratio, r^S, then equals 0.12669.

While the same detailed analysis as above is possible, we present only the counterpart to Table 4. That is, in Table 5 are shown the values of the net worth asset ratios after actual six-month yield curve changes, $R_N(\Delta i)$, as well as those estimated by a formula comparable to (14).

As in Table 4, immunization was unsuccessful during six of the eleven periods. In addition, the actual net worth asset ratios were well-approximated by the approximating formulas over the full range of results.

SUMMARY AND CONCLUSIONS

Classical immunization strategies, which explicitly assume parallel yield curve shifts, cannot in theory be expected to provide immunization when the yield curve shifts do not cooperate with this defining assumption. However, these conditions readily generalize to conditions that insure immunization against any given yield curve shift assumption. Unfortunately, these conditions are not compatible in general. That is, immunization against a given type of shift will often create exposure to other types of shifts, causing immunization to fail as other shifts are realized.

TABLE 5
Actual versus Estimated Values
Net Worth Asset Ratios After Yield Curve Changes
From Non-Overlapping Six-Month Periods

6 months beginning	$R_N(\Delta i)$	$R_N^e(\Delta i)$	$R_N^e(\Delta i)$ Percentile
1/1/85*	12.140%	12.142%	23rd
7/1/85*	12.556	12.557	51st
1/1/86	14.267	14.272	100th
7/1/86*	11.434	11.436	3rd
1/1/87	13.480	13.478	78th
7/1/87*	12.325	12.324	35th
1/1/88*	12.626	12.624	52nd
7/1/88	13.760	13.752	89th
1/1/89*	12.206	12.208	26th
7/1/89	12.728	12.729	56th
1/1/90	12.964	12.963	60th

* Immunization unsuccessful: r^S = 12.669%

An ancillary benefit of the theoretical analysis, however, is that one can develop estimates of the degree of immunization risk. Inequalities such as in (11) and (13) provide the theoretical unit exposures to duration and convexity risk. These values are seen to capture much of the potential for immunization to fail, as the approximations for $S_N(\Delta i)$ in (14) and those for $R_N(\Delta i)$ accurately estimated actual values over a wide range of yield curve movements.

Of course, quantifying immunization risk is the first step toward reducing it.

REFERENCES

Bierwag, Gerald O. *Duration Analysis: Managing Interest Rate Risk.* Cambridge, MA: Ballinger Publishing Company, 1987.

Fisher, L., and Roman L. Weil. "Coping With the Risk of Interest Rate Fluctuations: Returns to Bondholders from Naive and Optimal Strategies." *Journal of Business,* October 1971.

Grove, M.A. "On 'Duration' and the Optimal Maturity Structure of the Balance Sheet." *Bell Journal of Economics and Management Science,* 5 (Autumn 1974), pp. 696-709.

Kaufman, G.C. "Measuring and Managing Interest Rate Risk: A Primer." *Economic Perspective,* Federal Reserve Bank of Chicago, January/February 1984, pp. 16-19.

Messmore, Thomas E. "The Duration of Surplus." *Journal of Portfolio Management,* Winter 1990, pp. 19-22.

Reitano, Robert R. "A Multivariate Approach to Duration Analysis." *Actuarial Research Clearing House,* Vol. 2 (1989).

——. "A Multivariate Approach to Immunization Theory." ARCH, Vol. 2 (1990a).

——. "Non-Parallel Yield Curve Shifts and Durational Leverage." *Journal of Portfolio Management,* Summer 1990b.

——. "Multivariate Duration Analysis." Transactions of the Society of Actuaries, Vol. XLIII (1991a).

——. "Multivariate Immunization Theory." TSA XLIII, 1991b.

——. "Non-Parallel Yield Curve Shifts and Spread Leverage." *Journal of Portfolio Management,* Spring 1991c.

——. "Non-Parallel Yield Curve Shifts and Convexity." Forthcoming, TSA, 1992.

Bond Yield Spreads: A Postmodern View

Another look at bond yield spreads.

Chris P. Dialynas and David H. Edington

CHRIS P. DIALYNAS is Managing Director and Portfolio Manager at Pacific Investment Management Company in Newport Beach (CA 92660).

DAVID H. EDINGTON is Executive Vice President and Portfolio Manager at the same firm.

One of the most important decisions bond investors make is allocation among the various classes, or sectors, of the bond market. Although a myriad of finer distinctions must be made, the essence of the sector decision is the choice between government bonds, whose fixed and reasonably certain cash flows are endearingly referred to as "riskless," and non-government bonds, whose cash flows are in many ways uncertain.

We address this basic sector decision, presenting four key determinants of the relative value of non-government bonds such as corporate bonds, mortgage pass-throughs, CMOs, and municipal bonds.

THE QUALITY SPREAD THEORY

Assessing the relative attractiveness of various classes of bonds generally begins (and too often ends) with a forecast of general economic conditions. The business cycle clearly impacts intermarket spreads, as illustrated in Exhibit 1.

This relationship is well motivated by the "quality spread theory." In tough economic times, earnings and cash flow of most debt servicers are reduced. Asset values that implicitly or explicitly collateralize debt are likely to deteriorate. Rational investors must demand an increasing premium to continue to hold "risky" non-government bonds, and yield spreads must widen. Conversely, in a strong economy, debt service capacity is enhanced, risk is diminished, and spreads must narrow.

Compelling intuition and strong empirical evidence validate the quality spread theory as a key determinant of relative value. Importantly, as we shall

EXHIBIT 1
**REAL GNP GROWTH VERSUS BOND YIELD
SPREADS**

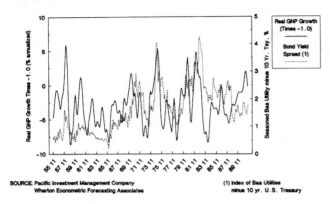

SOURCE: Pacific Investment Management Company
Wharton Econometric Forecasting Associates

(1) Index of Baa Utilities
minus 10 yr. U.S. Treasury

EXHIBIT 2A
**VOLATILITY VERSUS CORPORATE BOND
YIELD SPREADS**

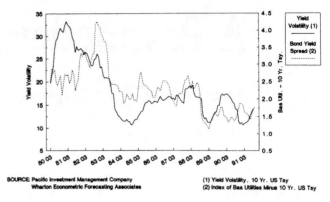

SOURCE: Pacific Investment Management Company
Wharton Econometric Forecasting Associates

(1) Yield Volatility, 10 Yr. US Tsy
(2) Index of Baa Utilities Minus 10 Yr. US Tsy

EXHIBIT 2B
**VOLATILITY VERSUS MORTGAGE PASS-
THROUGH SPREADS**

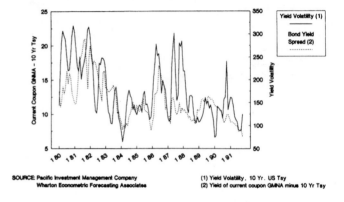

SOURCE: Pacific Investment Management Company
Wharton Econometric Forecasting Associates

(1) Yield Volatility, 10 Yr. US Tsy
(2) Yield of current coupon GMNA minus 10 Yr Tsy

demonstrate, it is not the only determinant.

THE IMPACT OF
INTEREST RATE VOLATILITY

Intermarket spreads are also closely related to interest rate volatility, as demonstrated by Exhibits 2A and 2B. In general terms, volatility reflects uncertainty; it's no surprise that volatility directly impacts the spread between government bonds, with certain cash flows, and other less certain classes of bonds. More specifically, the linkage between volatility and relative value occurs along several dimensions, relating to the behavior of embedded options, transactional liquidity, and the impact of volatility on the economic cycle.

Embedded Options

Students of option theory can easily motivate the linkage between interest rate volatility and yield spreads. The majority of non-government bonds include various attached state-contingent claims, or options. Many corporate bonds have cash call, refunding, or put provisions. Most sinking fund provisions have option-like characteristics because of the uncertainty of the sinking fund requirement. Substantially all mortgage pass-through securities have implicit call options, as mortgagors may elect to pay off or to refinance their mortgage. A majority of municipal bonds contain refunding provisions.

These embedded provisions represent a set of options granted by the holders of the instruments to the issuers — corporations, municipal entities, mortgagors. If investors expect an increase in interest rate volatility, they must demand higher yields to compen-

sate for the increased riskiness of callable and pre-payable securities, leading to a decrease in price. Importantly, this revaluation will occur in the complete absence of a change in the level of interest rates, a change in expectations for future interest rates, or changes in perceived creditworthiness — in this case, changing yield spreads are determined solely by changes in interest rate volatility.

Fortunately, option valuation technology allows the astute investor to isolate and quantify the value of embedded options, and to assess the effect of other determinants more accurately. Some caveats remain, however. One concern is that estimates of the value of embedded options are model-dependent. Differences in value result from differences in the nature of the interest rate distributions (lognormal, mean reverting, reflecting) used to model an unknown future and to a lesser degree from differences in implementation of a particular distribution (e.g., continuous versus discrete).

EXHIBIT 3
IMPACT OF VOLATILITY ON VALUE OF
CALLABLE BOND

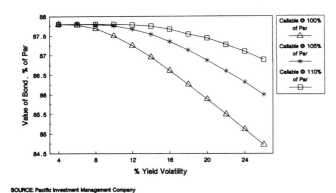

SOURCE: Pacific Investment Management Company

Another problem is obtaining a full term structure of market expectations for interest rate volatility. A typical callable corporate bond or prepayable mortgage pass-through security embodies options that have times to expiration of one to thirty years, and there are no liquid option markets of similar term to use for valuation purposes. A final problem is estimating the difference in expected volatility for bonds of various credit quality.

Exhibit 3 shows the impact of changing volatility on the price and yield of a typical corporate bond.

Volatility and the Business Cycle

The relationship between interest rate volatility and the business cycle creates a strong linkage between interest rate volatility and yield spreads. Violent changes in such a critical cost as interest charges impair the ability of productive entities to make investment decisions. Consumers likewise are likely to retrench in

EXHIBIT 4
IMPACT OF INTEREST RATE VOLATILITY ON REAL ECONOMIC GROWTH

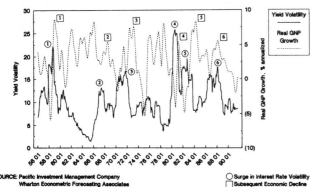

SOURCE: Pacific Investment Management Company
Wharton Econometric Forecasting Associates

○ Surge in Interest Rate Volatility
□ Subsequent Economic Decline

the face of uncertain real wealth and uncertain future income. As a result, high interest rate volatility often precedes periods of economic stagnation or contraction. This concept is supported in both the Keynesian and monetarist literature (see Hicks [1982] and Laidler [1990]) as well as empirically (see Exhibit 4).

Thus, surging volatility, or surging expectations for future volatility, must be associated with diminished expectations for economic growth, diminished perception of general creditworthiness, and a corresponding widening in yield spreads — even for bonds with no embedded options.

Volatility and Transaction Liquidity

Non-government bonds are generally less liquid than government bonds, as is seen in Exhibit 5. Liquidity also changes with market conditions. For bond brokers, an increase in volatility increases the risk associated with inventorying assets, long or short, and increases the hedging costs incurred in the course of making markets.

The more volatile the market, the wider the bid-ask spread must be. As bid-ask spreads increase, liquidity is impaired, and less liquid bonds such as corporates, mortgages, and other non-government bonds will be impaired more than government bonds.

At the same time, high expected volatility may be a reflection of dramatic changes in the economic landscape. At such times investors are more likely to choose to alter the duration, convexity, and quality characteristics of their portfolios. Demand for liquidity is likely to be unusually high, at the same time that liquidity supplied by those who broker bonds is scarce. In this environment, the value of non-government bonds will be impaired relative to highly liquid government securities, and spreads will widen.

EXHIBIT 5
Typical Bid/Offer Spreads

Investment	Spread
U.S. Governments	1–4 32nds
Mortgage Pass-Throughs	2–8 32nds
Mortgage Derivatives	4–16 32nds
Corporate Bonds	2–16 32nds
Municipal Bonds	2–16 32nds
Junk Bonds	16–64 32nds

Source: Pacific Investment Management Company.

EXHIBIT 6
Yield Ratios

Period	Average 10-Year Treasury Yield	Average BBB Utility Yield	Average Yield Spread (BBB Utility –10-Yr. TSY)	Average Yield Ratio (BBB Utility +10-Yr. TSY)
1955–1959	3.46	4.21	75	1.217
1960–1964	4.03	4.79	76	1.189
1965–1969	5.32	6.22	95	1.189
1970–1974	6.82	8.75	197	1.283
1975–1979	8.17	10.04	191	1.229
1980–1984	12.30	15.18	276	1.234
1985–1989	8.81	10.92	209	1.240

Source: Pacific Investment Management Company & Wharton Econometric Forecasting Associates.

THE YIELD RATIO THEORY

The yield ratio or relative yield theory suggests that the ratio of non-government bond yields to government bond yields will be more stable, and more useful to observe, than absolute yield spreads. This yield ratio theory identifies the importance of the level of yields as a determinant of yield spreads.

Exhibit 6 highlights the empirical consistency of the yield ratio and the relative inconsistency of the absolute yield spread.

As with the Quality Spread Theory, the intuitive appeal of this theory is straightforward. Investors are concerned with relative, rather than nominal, returns. The average seventy-five-basis point yield spread for a BBB utility bond during the 1955 to 1959 period represented a 22% increase in yield; in 1984, with Treasury yields in excess of 12%, the same seven-ty-five-basis point yield spread would have resulted in a paltry 6% increase in yield.

THE TERM STRUCTURE THEORY

This final theory suggests that yield spreads are influenced by the shape of the yield curve, independent of the general level of interest rates. Exhibits 7A and 7B illustrate the tendency toward narrowing spreads when the yield curve has a sharply positive slope, and the alternative tendency for yield spreads to widen when the yield curve is flat or inverted. As with volatility, the relationship between the term structure and intermarket spreads has multiple dimensions.

The Term Structure and the Economic Cycle

Two important factors in determining the shape

EXHIBIT 7A
THE TERM STRUCTURE VERSUS CORPORATE BOND YIELD SPREADS

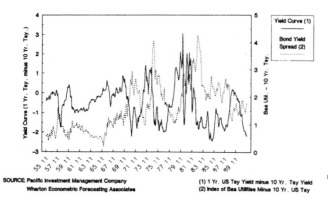

SOURCE: Pacific Investment Management Company
Wharton Econometric Forecasting Associates

(1) 1 Yr. US Tsy Yield minus 10 Yr. Tsy Yield
(2) Index of Baa Utilities Minus 10 Yr. US Tsy

EXHIBIT 7B
THE TERM STRUCTURE VERSUS MORTGAGE PASS-THROUGH SPREADS

SOURCE: Pacific Investment Management Company
Wharton Econometric Forecasting Associates
Kidder Peabody, Inc.

(1) Yield volatility, 10 yr US Tsy
(2) Yield of current coupon GNMA Minus 10 Yr Tsy

of the yield curve are Federal Reserve policy and investor expectations for the future direction of interest rates. Instead of adopting a true monetarist approach, monetary authorities have generally followed a counter-cyclical monetary policy. When a robust economy leads to heightened inflation expectations, the policy response is typically to constrain the money supply, which puts upward pressure on short-term interest rates. In time, this tight money policy will have the desired effect of curtailing inflation, at the expense of economic growth. As short rates rise, long rates may fall as investors begin to anticipate falling inflation and lower rates in the future.

Thus, a flattening yield curve is related to economic growth in two ways. A flattening yield curve, through the impact of higher short rates, may be a causal agent, leading to economic slowdown; alternatively, flattening via falling long-term rates reflects expectations of a slowing economy (or falling long-run inflation expectations, consistent with perceived weakness in collateral value). When evaluated in the context of the quality spread theory, the mechanics of the term structure, and its interaction with the real economy, dictate that a flattening yield curve must portend a widening of yield spreads.

Conversely, a steepening yield curve is the typical result of an accommodative monetary authority (falling short rates) combined with expectations for more robust economic growth and corresponding higher future interest rates. Thus, a positive yield curve would both contribute to, and reflect a general belief in, a more robust economic future. According to the quality spread theory, a positive yield curve must lead to narrowing yield spreads.

This relationship between the term structure and the real economy is also strongly supported empirically, as demonstrated by Exhibit 8.

CMO Arbitrage and the Impact of the Term Structure

Collateralized mortgage obligations exist because of "CMO arbitrage": Put simply, segmented tranches can be sold for more than the original pool of pass-throughs. The specific mechanics of CMO arbitrage are somewhat complex, but one important aspect is that CMO arbitrage is most pronounced in a positive yield curve, and virtually non-existent in a flat or inverted yield curve. In a positive yield curve environment, the opportunity for the brokerage community

EXHIBIT 8
U.S. INDUSTRIAL PRODUCTION VERSUS TERM STRUCTURE OF INTEREST RATES (LED 12 MONTHS)

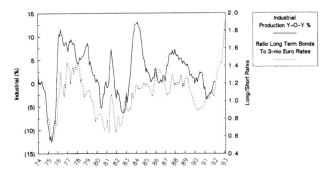

SOURCE: Pacific Investment Management Company
Wharton Econometric Forecasting Associates

to profit will dictate abundant CMO issuance, ensuring strong demand (and therefore narrowing spreads) for the underlying pass-through.

As various classes of non-government bonds are substitutes for one another, narrowing mortgage pass-through spreads will contribute to narrowing yield spreads of other non-government bonds as well.

THE UNIQUE 1985-1986 EXPERIENCE

The period from late 1985 through 1986 was marked by dramatic changes in the relative value of various classes of bonds, driven largely by strong disinflationary forces. In the first six months of 1986 long-term interest rates dropped a remarkable 2%, the yield curve flattened dramatically, and the implied volatility of options on bond futures more than doubled. These changes were influenced by the dramatic halving of the price of oil during this period.

During the latter six months of 1986, volatility expectations diminished, the yield curve steepened, and, once again, the relative value of particular sets of bonds changed substantially. Exhibit 9 summarizes the relevant data.

The ideas presented here are supported strongly by the 1985-1986 experience. First, widening spreads resulted (as our model would forecast) from a flattening yield curve and increases in volatility. Then, the reversal of these trends during the latter portion of 1986 predictably resulted in a substantial reduction in intermarket spreads. Exhibit 10 shows the magnitude of the relative changes.

EXHIBIT 9
1985-1986 Data

	12/1/85	6/13/86	12/1/86
Oil Price Per Barrel	29.35	13.20	18.00
Thirty-Year Bond Yield	9.93	7.52	7.42
Two-Year Note Yield	8.51	7.12	6.25
Implied Volatility on Thirty-Year Bonds	10.00	21.00	12.00
Thirty-Year Rate – Two-Year Rate	1.42	0.40	1.17
Thirty-Year Rate + Two-Year Rate	1.17	1.06	1.19

EXHIBIT 10
Comparative Spread Changes

U.S. Treasury 10.625 8/15/15 versus:

"A" Long Utility	Date	"A" Long Industrial
1.40%	12/1/85	1.25%
1.60%	6/13/86	1.60%
1.20%	12/1/86	1.45%

U.S. Treasury 9.50 11/15/95 versus:

"A" Prime Mtg. Municipal	Date	GNMA 8 1/2
-0.60%	12/1/85	0.32%
+0.20%	6/13/86	1.34%
-0.60%	12/1/86	1.12%

1985 had been a year of relatively slow growth. U.S. economic activity had been dampened by expensive oil, high U.S. and world interest rates, and the recent meteoric rise of the dollar. For the 1985 calendar year real GNP grew at a 3.6% rate, after growing at 5.1% in 1984.

By early 1986, however, the outlook had improved markedly. As of February, the dollar had fallen 30% against the yen from its peak in the first quarter of 1985. Oil prices fell by nearly 50% from 1985 levels. The combination of expectations for increased exports (based on the drop in the dollar), sharply lower energy costs, and falling interest rates in the U.S., Germany, and Japan formed an ideal backdrop for a cyclical upturn. Consumer confidence set record highs in March; most economists anticipated a return to 4% or 5% growth.

In spite of this consensus forecast for a strength-ening economy, the bond market was dominated by the strong disinflationary influences, and the first half of 1986 proved difficult for holders of non-government bonds. As interest rates fell, a variety of cash call and refunding provisions were exercised to retire expensive high-coupon debt early, reminding investors of the value of bond embedded options.

While long-term government bonds increased in price by 20%, corporate bonds lagged. In fact, long-term industrial bonds (those without event risk) increased in price by a modest 12% during this period in spite of general confidence.

The worst sector was the mortgage pass-through market, as mortgagors exercised their par prepayment option on a wholesale and unprecedented basis, in order to reduce financing costs. Current coupon GNMAs appreciated by less than 2%, and underperformed government bonds (on a total return basis) by an astounding 20%.

The second half of 1986 witnessed at least a partial reversal of the first half performance trends, as shown in Exhibit 10. As in the first six months, relative performance was driven almost exclusively by changing expectations for interest rate volatility and a changing yield curve shape. After peaking in June at 20%, implied volatility fell to 12% by December, fueling strong relative performance of the corporate and mortgage pass-through markets. Similarly, because the shape of the yield curve became very positively sloped during the period, corporate and mortgage bonds benefited.

As evidenced by the data in Exhibits 9 and 10, the relative performance of every sector of the bond market during the 1985-1986 period was consistent with the predictions that the proposed model would have provided, and quite inconsistent with the quality spread theory in isolation.

ANOTHER CASE STUDY: BOND YIELD SPREADS, 1990-1991

The 1990-1991 period is also useful in observing the impact of various causal agents on relative value. Once again, the factors we have identified had a critical impact on intermarket spreads.

The second half of 1990 was especially notable for two significant events. One was the onset of an economic recession, now officially recognized as having begun in July. The second was the invasion of

Kuwait by Iraqi forces under Saddam Hussein on August 2.

Immediately prior to the invasion, economic signals were mixed. Consumer confidence, as measured by various surveys, remained at robust levels, although it had declined modestly in the most recent surveys. Economic forecasts were also mixed, with those expecting continued moderate to slow growth slightly outnumbering those forecasting a recession. Implied volatility was close to a ten-year low. Corporate and mortgage spreads were also near historic narrows, reflecting the lack of volatility in the marketplace and the consensus, although tentative, forecast for continued economic growth.

The August 2 invasion changed the environment markedly. Implied volatility spiked in tandem with rapidly rising oil prices. Consumer confidence plunged sharply, and economic forecasts were generally revised downward, with predictions ranging from mild to severe recession. Intermarket spreads widened significantly in the face of increasing gloom and, especially, increasing volatility. Non-government bonds underperformed government bonds in the third and fourth quarters, reaching their widest spreads in November and December.

In the period from February to May of 1991, implied volatility in the marketplace fell dramatically. The stunningly successful military campaign against Iraq triggered a surge in national confidence, stabilized oil prices, and removed incapacitating uncertainty from the financial markets. The surge in confidence proved short-lived, however. The cyclical unwinding of the excesses of the 1980s, and the secular reversal of three decades of inflationary growth, quickly came to dominate the economic landscape. Consumer confidence resumed its steady downward trend, and the view that a bona fide recession was underway became more widespread.

This type of economic environment would not appear, on the surface of things, to bode well for the relative value of non-government bonds. Yet, driven by diminished volatility, an increasingly positive yield curve, and lower levels of interest rates, corporates and mortgages narrowed sharply, in many cases back to their preinvasion lows. Note the evidence in Exhibit 11.

A FINAL WORD

Investors must recognize the effect of the changing backdrop on which the theories presented here are overlaid. A changing regulatory environment or changes in the structure of the financial system may have a tremendous impact on relative value. Witness the impact of the development of the CMO market and its impact on the valuation of mortgage pass-throughs. The advent of the junk bond market, and the leveraged buyouts that it financed, gave rise to "event risk," which diminished the value of certain classes of industrial bonds (of course the unilateral ability of an issuer to downgrade itself through increasing leverage is itself an option).

Changing tax laws have direct and obvious implications for the value of municipal bonds, and may have more subtle impacts on corporate bonds in general, to the extent that preference for debt versus equi-

EXHIBIT 11
Corporate and Mortgage Spreads, 1990-1991

Corporate Bond	Relative to	Aug. 1990	Oct. 1990	Dec. 1990	Feb. 1991	Apr. 1991	Jun. 1991
Duke Power 9.625 2/20	30-Yr. TSY	105	121	135	122	119	112
Texas Utilities 9.75 3/20	30-Yr. TSY	89	101	107	92	90	85
GTE 9.875 4/20	30-Yr. TSY	135	161	180	160	145	135
Georgia Pacific 9.75 1/18	30-Yr. TSY	195	240	270	250	215	190
Ford 9.375 3/20	30-Yr. TSY	110	164	182	170	157	138
Mortgage Pass-Through	Relative to	Aug. 1990	Oct. 1990	Dec. 1990	Feb. 1991	Apr. 1991	Jun. 1991
Current Coupon FHLMC	10-Yr. TSY	104	116	125	108	107	96
Current Coupon GNMA	10-Yr. TSY	111	122	121	105	105	99

ty financing is altered. Bankruptcy court actions continually redefine the value of claims at various levels of corporate balance sheets; likewise, the unfolding of the bank and S&L bailout will affect valuation of debt instruments of the subsidiary bank, relative to debt of the parent bank holding company.

Perhaps the prevalence of institutional money management, and the accompanying focus on short-term performance, has created a structural change in relative value. Perhaps the increasing accessibility and liquidity of futures, options, swaps, and other hedging instruments have motivated a structural decrease in volatility by dampening the feedback between the productive economy and the financial markets.

Despite these and other substantial uncertainties, gains have been made in understanding relative value. The empirical evidence, intuitive concepts, and analysis presented here, combined with the 1985-1986 and 1990-1991 experience, point to the inadequacy of the quality spread theory in isolation. While certainly an important factor, the quality spread theory can be enhanced by observation of the impact of the level of interest rates, the term structure, and perhaps most importantly, market expectations for volatility.

The impact of changing volatility on bonds with embedded options can be isolated and evaluated (although not with complete precision) through the proper use of option valuation methods. More important, the impact of volatility on transactional liquidity and the economic cycle dictates that even the relative value of non-government bonds with "bullet" maturities (no embedded options) will still be significantly affected by changing expectations for future volatility.

REFERENCES

Black, F., and M. Scholes. "The Pricing of Options and Corporate Liabilities." *Journal of Political Economy*, 81 (1973), pp. 637-654.

Brimmer, A. "Credit Conditions and Price Determination in the Corporate Bond Market." *Journal of Finance*, 15 (September 1960), pp. 353-370.

Cox, J.C., J.E. Ingersoll, Jr., and S.A. Ross. "A Theory on the Term Structure of Interest Rates." *Econometrica*, 53 (1985), pp. 385-407.

Dialynas, C. "Bond Yield Spreads Revisited." *Journal of Portfolio Management*, 14, 2 (Winter 1988), pp. 57-62.

Fisher, L. "Determinants of Risk Premiums on Corporate Bonds." *Journal of Political Economy*, 67 (June 1959), pp. 217-237.

Hicks, J.R. *Money, Interest and Wages: Collected Essays on Economic Theory.* Cambridge, MA: Harvard University Press, 1982.

Kochan, James L. "Corporate-to-Treasury Yield Spreads: A Cyclical Analysis." In F.J. Fabozzi, ed., *Handbook of Fixed Income Securities.* Homewood, IL: Dow Jones-Irwin, 1987.

Laidler, D. *Taking Money Seriously and Other Essays.* Cambridge, MA: MIT Press, 1990.

Tobin, James. "Liquidity Preference as Behaviour Towards Risk." *Review of Economic Studies*, 26, No. 1 (March), pp. 54-63.

PART SIX
Options and Futures

With the introduction in the 1970s of options and financial futures ("pork bellies in pinstripes"), active and offensive-minded risk management, in its broadest sense, assumed a new dimension. A money manager now could achieve new degrees of freedom. It was now possible to alter the market risk profile of a portfolio economically and quickly. Options and futures offered portfolio managers risk and return patterns that were previously unavailable.

Much of the published literature on options from the inception of listed stock options in the early 1970s throughout the decade focused on two issues. First—most notably in the works of Fischer Black, Myron Scholes, and Robert Merton—was the pricing of these instruments. Second was return-enhancement strategies. The proliferation of published articles and advertisements about return-enhancement strategies led Fischer Black, in a 1975 article entitled "Fact and Fantasy in the Use of Options," published in the *Financial Analysts Journal*, to write, "For every fact about options, there is a fantasy—a reason given for trading or not trading in options that doesn't make sense when examined carefully."

The few articles on options published in *The Journal of Portfolio Management* from its inception to the end of the 1970s concentrated on the latter issue. The more high-powered mathematical articles focusing on option pricing models were left to the academic journals devoted to economic theory. The role of options in reshaping return distributions was not emphasized in the literature until the 1980s, and the most notable work on this subject was that by Richard Bookstaber and Roger Clarke in *The Journal of Portfolio Management*. Two of the five articles in this section reprint these classic studies. One of the five articles shows how to analyze options.

Although Treasury futures began trading in the mid-1970s, only one article on using these contracts was published in the *Journal* in the 1970s. The last two articles included in this section, both published in 1986, show how these contracts can be used to hedge a bond portfolio. While most practitioners commonly used Treasury futures to hedge corporate bond portfolios, the article by Robin Grieves shows how this can be done more effectively by using Treasury futures in combination with stock index futures.

Options can alter portfolio return distributions*

Many combinations of puts and calls can expand the available trade-off between risk and return.

Richard Bookstaber and Roger Clarke

One of the long-standing objections to the mean-variance approach to portfolio theory is its narrow definition of risk-return preferences. Investors choose between the mean and the variance of the portfolio returns, but they have no control over the higher moments of the distribution of returns. Hence, they will generally lock themselves into sub-optimal portfolio decisions.[1] The return characteristics of stock portfolios are at the heart of the problem: when stock returns are typified by a normal distribution, stock portfolios can only be manipulated along mean-variance lines.[2]

A number of authors have recognized that the option market provides a way to expand the set of investment alternatives by increasing the range of return characteristics the investor can control.[3] Potentially, the use of options in combination with stock portfolios can provide the investor with a portfolio containing almost any feasible set of return characteristics. The use of options allows the investor to "mold" the return distribution of the portfolio to fit his set of investment objectives. Indeed, the range of returns that can be created through the use of the option markets makes the two-dimensional trade-offs of conventional mean-variance portfolio theory obsolete.[4]

It has been well established theoretically that the use of options can substantially expand the state space spanned by available securities, thereby increasing the efficiency with which financial markets meet the return objectives of investors. But in practice the option market has greatly lagged in fulfilling this role. While many managers combine option positions with their stock portfolio, the full potential of the option market to alter returns and create return distributions that are consistent with the investor's preferences is far from being realized.

One problem that has limited the use of the wider range of possible strategies is that the exact effect of most strategies has remained unknown. The investor may understand how an option position will combine with the return on a single stock, but the result becomes complex for a portfolio that combines many stocks and options. While the formal mathematical solution for the return distribution of a stock portfolio combined with options is tedious, we have developed computationally efficient methods for doing these calculations. The purpose of this article is to apply these techniques to illustrate the effects of some popular option strategies on portfolio returns, and to indicate the vast range of option strategies available in portfolio management.

First, we will discuss some of the difficulties in evaluating the effect of options on portfolio returns. Then we will address three of the most frequently asked questions about the effect of options on portfolios: (1) How do various option positions affect the return distribution of the portfolio, (2) which option strategies are the best for various market conditions, and (3) how is the effect of option strategies related to the exercise price of the options used?

DETERMINING THE RETURN DISTRIBUTION OF OPTION PORTFOLIOS

A combined stock and option position can be plotted against the price of the underlying stock to

* This article is an excerpt from a book on options in portfolio management to be published by Addison-Wesley in 1982.

1. Footnotes appear at the end of the article.

283

trace out the familiar profit profile. The profit profile shows the value of the combined position as a function of the stock price and can be used to find the return distribution of the combined investment. Such a profile, however, is not as simple to determine when many options and stocks are combined. It is not enough just to know the return on the stock portfolio to determine the value of the total option position. The return on each individual stock conditional on the return to the other stocks in the portfolio must be known.

We can illustrate the complexity of the problem by considering the following examples.

Suppose an investor holds 100 shares of two stocks, each with one option written on it. Both stocks are initially at 45, and each option has an exercise price of 50. Assume the stock portfolio increases in value from $9,000 to $10,000 at the maturity date of the options. Table I shows that, if the increase in the value of the portfolio is due to one stock rising to 55 while the other stock remains at 45, then the investor receives only $500 of the $1,000 increase in the portfolio's value. On the other hand, if the increase in the portfolio results from both stocks rising to 50, then he receives the full $1,000 increase in value. Unless we know the value of each individual stock at the end of the period, therefore, we cannot know which options have been exercised and what the total return to the investor is.

EXPRESSING THE OPTIONED PORTFOLIO IN TERMS OF SHARE EQUIVALENTS

The previous example considered the return distribution for the period ending at the time of the options' expiration. We can calculate the return distribution of the combined portfolio for a time period ending before expiration by translating the option position into share equivalents through the use of the option hedge ratio.

The hedge ratio for the option tells how the op-

tion will move with a small change in the stock price. Thus, it tells the investor how many shares of stock will give the same amount of "play" as the option.

For example, if an option has a hedge ratio of .5, then it will move half a point when the stock moves by one point. The option therefore gives the same amount of play as holding 50 shares of stock. In terms of share equivalents, the option has a 50-share equivalent. By converting all of the options in the portfolio into their share equivalents, the investor can translate the current option position into a portfolio of stocks that has an equivalent risk and reward potential.

This technique will be valuable for examining the risk of the position over the very short term. It does not eliminate the difficulties of determing the return distribution of the portfolio over a longer holding period, however, because the hedge ratio, and hence the share equivalent, will vary as the expiration of the option approaches and as the stock price changes. In order to assess the return distribution of the portfolio over the next month, we must calculate the share equivalent for each option for each possible stock price that might exist in one month. Furthermore, that calculation must be made conditional on all the possible stock prices of all the other stocks held in the portfolio.

We can illustrate the limitations of the use of share equivalents by considering another example. Suppose an investor holds 100 shares each of stock A and stock B, which are both currently trading at $45 a share. The investor writes options on both stocks with an exercise price of $50. Assuming the options have four months to expiration, the riskless interest rate is 5% and the volatility of both stocks is .3, the hedge ratio for both of the options will be .37. In terms of share equivalents, each option will be equivalent to a short position of 37 shares of the underlying stock. In terms of *instantaneous return*, the optioned portfolio will have the same return characteristics as a portfolio containing 63 shares of each of the two stocks.

Unfortunately, a typical investor wants to know the return distribution for the portfolio over the next week or month, rather than just over the next instant. That investor will find considerable complexity added to the straightforward solution of the instantaneous problem.

The share equivalent of each option will change as its respective stock price changes. For any return for the portfolio of underlying stocks, any number of returns are possible for the optioned portfolio. In Table II, we present two possible returns for the optioned portfolio, given a particular return on the portfolio of the underlying stocks. Clearly, an unlimited number of returns are possible on the optioned portfolio for a given return on the underlying stock portfolio.

TABLE I

Own 100 Shares of Stock A and Stock B

When Purchased

Price of A = $45
Price of B = $45

Value of Portfolio = $9,000

Write Option on Both Stocks with E = $50

At Maturity

Value of Stock Portfolio = $10,000		Value of Combined Option and Stock Portfolio
Price of A = $55	Receive $500 from	$9,000 + $500 = $9,500
Price of B = $45	Stock Appreciation	
Price of A = $50	Receive $1,000 from	$9,000 + $1,000 = $10,000
Price of B = $50	Stock Appreciation	

TABLE II

Own 100 Shares of Stock A and Stock B

When Purchased

Price of A = $45
Price of B = $45

Value of Portfolio = $9,000

Write Option on Stocks with E = $50.
Hedge Ratio for Both Options = .37.
Share Equivalent for Both Option Positions = −.37 Share

In One Month

Value of Stock Portfolio = $10,000

Price of A = $55   Share Equivalent of Option A = 81 Shares.
Price of B = $45   Share Equivalent of Option B = 32 Shares.

The Share Equivalent Portfolio Is:
19 Shares of Stock A
68 Shares of Stock B

Price of A = $50   Share Equivalent of Option A = 60 Shares.
Price of B = $50   Share Equivalent of Option B = 60 Shares.

The Share Equivalent Portfolio Is:
40 Shares of Stock A
40 Shares of Stock B

Further, there are an unlimited number of returns possible on the underlying stock portfolio over any given time interval. This problem thus becomes even more complex than the first problem. Rather than partitioning each option above and below its exercise price, we must now consider its share equivalent for every possible value of the underlying stock conditional on the returns to every other stock in the portfolio. Computing the return distribution to an optioned portfolio over a finite time interval therefore becomes even more complex when the option position is considered before the maturity of the options.

There is a way around this problem, however. Although the analytical solution to the return distribution is complex, we have developed computationally efficient algorithms that give close approximations to the theoretical return distribution. The algorithms are based on the use of the expected value of the optioned portfolio conditional on the return to the stock portfolio. Asymptotically, these algorithms will approach the same distribution as the analytical solution and will take a computer seconds, rather than the hours that would be required to compute the returns by the analytical method. The results that follow are based on one of these algorithms.[5]

THE EFFECTS OF OPTIONS ON PORTFOLIO RETURNS

The return distribution for stock portfolios is generally assumed to be symmetric. But as options are added to the stock position, the distribution can be molded into a number of forms. The tails of the distribution may be truncated, leaving the investor with little risk of a loss or little possibility of a large gain, and a large portion of the probability mass may be centered in a particular range, giving a high probability of receiving that range of returns.

We have chosen three representative option positions to use as illustrations. Besides writing calls, we will consider buying puts, as well as a combined strategy of writing calls and buying puts in the same proportions.

In these strategies we use a representative portfolio of twenty stocks, and set the expected return and risk of the portfolio equal to that of the market.[6] The exercise price of the options is 15% above the current stock price for call options and just at the current stock price for puts. The option position is taken on all stocks in the portfolio in equal proportions. For example, if 600 shares of stock A and 1000 shares of stock B are held, then a 50% option position will involve three options on stock A and five on stock B, where each option is contracted for 100 shares of the underlying stock.

WRITING CALL OPTIONS

Figure I shows the return distribution for a portfolio with calls written on 0%, 25%, 50%, and 75% of the stocks.

The 0% portfolio is the reference case, since it is the return to the stock portfolio when no option position is taken. It has the characteristic symmetric distribution of stock portfolio returns.

By writing options on the portfolio, the upward potential is reduced. This is as would be expected, since any stock is limited to the 15% appreciation before it reaches the exercise price and is called away.

The distribution is further truncated when options are written on 100% of the stocks. The maximum

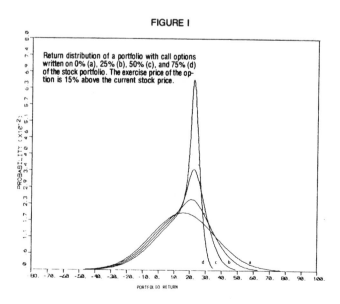

FIGURE I

Return distribution of a portfolio with call options written on 0% (a), 25% (b), 50% (c), and 75% (d) of the stock portfolio. The exercise price of the option is 15% above the current stock price.

PORTFOLIO RETURN

285

return is 21.2%, equal to the maximum possible appreciation in the stock price of 15% plus the premium received for the options.

Figure I illustrates some characteristics of call writing that are rarely acknowledged. While most investors recognize that the upward potential of the portfolio is reduced as the option position is taken, an additional cost of this position is a reduction in the expected portfolio return.

It is true that there is a higher probability of a moderate return, as indicated by the height of the density function in the range. This is the most discussed feature of the strategy. Nevertheless, many proponents apparently fail to recognize the low possibility of significant gains and the related drop in expected return. The recent history of the market has been one of few prolonged upturns, so this decreased expected return has not yet been found to be significant by many option traders.

BUYING PUT OPTIONS

In contrast to the strategy of writing calls, which truncates the right-hand tail of the distribution while maintaining downside risk, the put option strategy truncates the lower tail and maintains the upside potential. This is clearly a more attractive proposition. As would be expected, however, it also costs more. While the writer receives an option premium to add to his returns, the put buyer must release funds to initiate the position.

In effect, the put represents downside insurance — the put option provides insurance for the manager against dramatic declines in the value of the portfolio.

The return distribution for the put option appears in Figure II. The return for the stock portfolio (equivalent to an option position of 0%) is shown along with the return distribution when 25%, 50%, and 75% of the stock portfolio is covered by put options. The left hand tail of the distribution is truncated, while the right hand tail is left comparatively unchanged. The mode of the distribution is shifted to the left, indicating a large probability of receiving a moderate return. The bulk of the distribution is shifted further to the left than for the call writing strategy, indicating a greater chance of receiving a lower return. This would be expected since the writer adds the option premium to the portfolio, while the put buyer has to take the cost of the position out of the stock account.

When all of the stock is covered by put options, the minimum possible return from the stocks is 0%. When we add to that the cost of the put options, the minimum return is −5.0%. This will make the put option strategy valuable for the conservative investor, since it provides the ultimate downside protection. (Note that Figure I and Figure II are not directly comparable, since the exercise prices for the two differ.)

Current security regulations prohibit certain funds and trusts from using put options, although they do allow the writing of calls. The above discussion suggests that it is the call writer who faces the greatest probability of loss, while the use of put options presents a prudent strategy reducing the possible loss from adverse stock movements.

BUYING PUTS AND WRITING CALLS

Since puts reduce downside risk and calls reduce upside potential, logic tells us that a strategy that combines puts and calls should do both. As Figure III illutrates, this is exactly what the combined position does. The investor is given a high probability of a return within a given range, with that range determined

FIGURE II

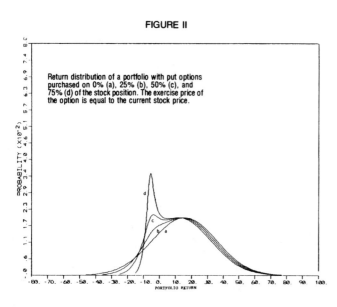

Return distribution of a portfolio with put options purchased on 0% (a), 25% (b), 50% (c), and 75% (d) of the stock position. The exercise price of the option is equal to the current stock price.

FIGURE III

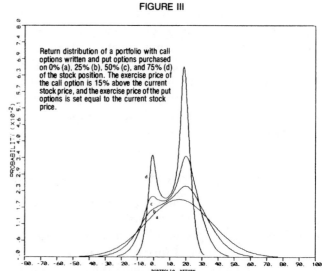

Return distribution of a portfolio with call options written and put options purchased on 0% (a), 25% (b), 50% (c), and 75% (d) of the stock position. The exercise price of the call option is 15% above the current stock price, and the exercise price of the put options is set equal to the current stock price.

by the exercise price of the options used. When all the stocks are covered by both the call and put, the return is certain to be no higher than 16.2% and no lower than 1.2%.

By altering either the exercise price and/or the relative proportions of the options used, considerable flexibility is possible in molding the shape of the portfolio's return distribution. To illustrate this, Figure IV contrasts the return distribution of the basic stock portfolio with two different alterations. The first alteration is done by using a 75% call option position with a 25% put option position. The second alteration uses a 25% call option position and a 75% put option position.

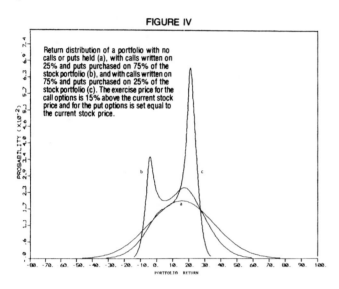

FIGURE IV

Return distribution of a portfolio with no calls or puts held (a), with calls written on 25% and puts purchased on 75% of the stock portfolio (b), and with calls written on 75% and puts purchased on 25% of the stock portfolio (c). The exercise price for the call options is 15% above the current stock price and for the put options is set equal to the current stock price.

Table III shows a further comparison of the three strategies. There we can compare the means and standard deviations of the various strategies, as well as the systematic risk of each of the strategies. It should be emphasized that the distribution is not fully described by these measures, since the higher moments are also altered. In this Table, α refers to the proportion of the portfolio covered by the option position.

TABLE III

	Mean Return	Standard Deviation	Systematic Risk
Pure Portfolio: $\alpha = 0$	15.0	19.8	1.0
Option Proportion: $\alpha = .5$			
Put	13.9	17.7	.87
Call	14.0	15.1	.74
Put and Call	12.9	12.7	.62
Option Proportion: $\alpha = 1.0$			
Put	12.8	15.9	.76
Call	13.0	11.4	.49
Put and Call	10.8	6.1	.27

THE RETURN OF THE OPTIONED PORTFOLIO AS A FUNCTION OF THE RETURN TO THE MARKET: VARIABLE BETA PORTFOLIOS.

As a second illustration of the effect of the various option positions on the portfolio returns, we present figures that plot the return to the optioned portfolio against the return to the market. These figures also give an indication of the return to the optioned portfolio as a function of the return to the underlying stock portfolio when the underlying portfolio is well diversified.

Figure V shows the return of the combined

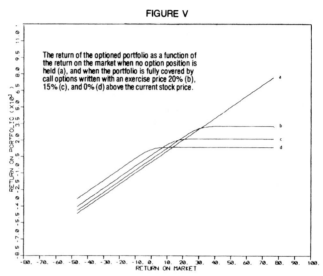

FIGURE V

The return of the optioned portfolio as a function of the return on the market when no option position is held (a), and when the portfolio is fully covered by call options written with an exercise price 20% (b), 15% (c), and 0% (d) above the current stock price.

portfolio when call options are written on 100% of the underlying shares of stock. Figure Va gives the return to the unoptioned portfolio, which is constructed to have a beta of 1. Figures Vb, Vc, and Vd give the return of the optioned portfolio when the exercise prices of the options are 0%, 15%, and 20% higher than the current stock price, respectively.

As we would expect, the downside risk is reduced for the optioned portfolios, because the option writer has the option premium as a buffer should the stock price decline. If the market goes up, the return on the combined portfolio is bounded by the exercise return plus the premium received in writing the calls.

In contrast to the call option strategy, Figure VI presents the returns from buying put options on 100% of the underlying portfolio. Figure VIa shows the return to the underlying stock portfolio, and Figures VIb, VIc, and VId show the return to the optioned portfolio when the exercise price on the puts option is -15%, 0%, and 15% higher than the current stock price, respectively.

It is evident in comparing Figure V and Figure VI that the put option provides better downside protection from adverse market changes, since the

FIGURE VI

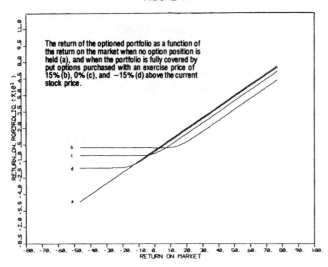

The return of the optioned portfolio as a function of the return on the market when no option position is held (a), and when the portfolio is fully covered by put options purchased with an exercise price of 15% (b), 0% (c), and −15% (d) above the current stock price.

FIGURE VII

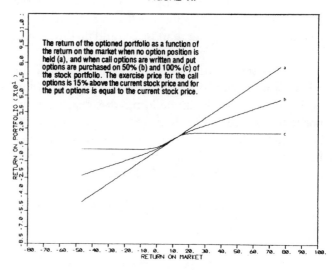

The return of the optioned portfolio as a function of the return on the market when no option position is held (a), and when call options are written and put options are purchased on 50% (b) and 100% (c) of the stock portfolio. The exercise price for the call options is 15% above the current stock price and for the put options is equal to the current stock price.

maximum loss is bounded by the exercise return plus the cost of buying the put option contracts. The upward potential shifts down by the cost of the put options, but is not bounded as it is with the call option strategy.

Figures V and VI bear a close resemblance to the profit profile that plots the value of one option against the underlying stock. The major difference is that the return in these figures curves up gradually near the exercise price of the option, while the return will exhibit a non-continuous change of slope for a position in a single option.

Several articles have appeared in the professional journals discussing the attractiveness of writing call options. As Figure V illustrates, the relatively high returns from such a strategy will exist only for moderate portfolio returns. Such moderate returns have persisted in the market over the past few years. In a market that is marked by high returns, however, writing call options will leave the investor worse off.

An investor can maintain some of the upward profit potential of the portfolio during periods of high market returns by covering a smaller percentage of the portfolio with calls. Figure VII contrasts the portfolio return when 50% of the portfolio is covered by both put and call options with the cases of having 0% and 100% of the portfolio covered. As we would expect during periods of high market returns, the return on the portfolio is reduced but not as much as if the portfolio were totally optioned. During periods of low market returns, the partial put option position provides some protection but not as much as when the portfolio is totally optioned.

This joint strategy provides some downside protection from a decline in the market but also limits the upward potential of the portfolio. When fully optioned, the premium received from the call options

will approximately offset the cost of purchasing the put options, and the investor will have a high probability of a moderate return regardless of the return on the market.

The slopes of the lines in Figures V, VI, and VII represent the beta of the portfolio in question. If the slope is forty-five degrees, then the portfolio return changes one-to-one with a change in the return on the market, and therefore has a beta of one. If the slope is flatter than forty-five degrees, the beta is less than one, approaching zero as the slope becomes horizontal. Similarly, a slope steeper than forty-five degrees indicates a beta greater than one.

Typically, the beta of a portfolio cannot be altered with changes in market return. A stock with a high beta will respond with a large increase in value should the market go up, but will also lose a great deal of value should the market decline. However, by using the proper option strategy, the beta of the portfolio can be varied according to the return of the market. The strategies discussed above are just a few of those available. Figure V illustrates how to have a beta of one for lower market returns while having a zero beta for higher market returns. Figure VI shows the opposite case, giving a zero beta if the return on the market is low and a beta of one if the return on the market is high. Obviously, these are just a few of the variations that are possible in altering the portfolio beta.

THE EFFECT OF OPTION EXERCISE PRICE ON RETURNS

A limitless number of types of option positions can be combined with a stock portfolio. The options can vary by number, by exercise price, and by time to expiration. In this paper, we have limited the analysis by assuming that all stocks have the same percentage of coverage by the option position. We have also assumed that all options have the same expiration date as investment horizon for the portfolio of stock. We now present the return distributions of optioned portfolios for various exercise prices.

Figure VIII shows the return distribution of

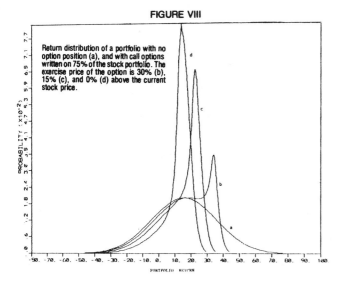

FIGURE VIII

Return distribution of a portfolio with no option position (a), and with call options written on 75% of the stock portfolio. The exercise price of the option is 30% (b), 15% (c), and 0% (d) above the current stock price.

writing call options on the underlying portfolio with 75% of the stock position being covered, and with the exercise price for the call option being set equal to the current stock price (VIIIa), 15% higher than the current stock price (VIIIb), and 30% higher than the current stock price (VIIIc).

As with alterations in the percent of the portfolio covered with options, an increase in the exercise price will reduce the amount of truncation in the right-hand tail of the return distribution. On the other hand, while increasing the proportion of the portfolio covered steepens the truncation, a change in the exercise price changes the point where the truncation begins.

This is also illustrated for the purchase of put options in Figure IX. As the exercise price of the put

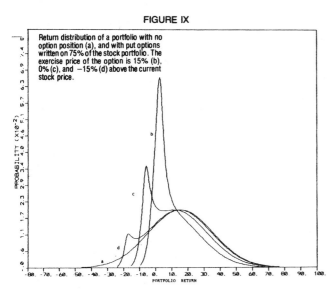

FIGURE IX

Return distribution of a portfolio with no option position (a), and with put options written on 75% of the stock portfolio. The exercise price of the option is 15% (b), 0% (c), and −15% (d) above the current stock price.

option drops from 15% above the current stock price (IXa) to the current stock price (IXb) and to 15% below the current stock price (IXc), the point of truncation also drops.

By combining the proper proportion of the portfolio covered with the proper exercise price for the options, the investor can control the probability of receiving returns below any given value. The proper exercise price determines the point at which low returns will be minimized while the percent of the portfolio covered will determine the abruptness with which low returns are prevented.

CLOSING THOUGHTS

While the methods used here can generate the return distribution for a given optioned portfolio, it would also be desirable from a practical standpoint to be able to start with a particular set of investor preferences and determine the portfolio that would best satisfy those preferences. While utility mazimization is easily characterized in the two-parameter world of mean-variance analysis, the characterization of the risk-return tradeoffs and the mathematical description of the utility maximizing portfolio is far more difficult in the expanded world of optioned portfolios.

The present paper provides insight into the effect of some popular options on portfolio returns. An important next step is to extend the methods discussed here to generate the optimal optioned portfolio for any given set of investment objectives.

[1] It is well known that maximization of a mean-variance criterion function is consistent with expected utility maximization for only the class of quadratic utility functions. Numerous authors have discussed the need to consider higher moments in characterizing risk preferences. Kraus and Litzenberger, and Simkowitz and Beedles, among others, have worked on extending the traditional mean-variable tradeoff to include the possibility of skewness preference.

[2] Some empirical research suggest that the return distribution for stock returns may be better represented by another family of distributions, such as the stable Paretian distribution function. The limitation of the possible distributions that the investor can generate still remains for these other functional forms.

[3] Ross, Hakansson, Banz and Miller, and Breeden and Litzenberger all discuss the increased spanning opportunities that are possible through the use of options.

[4] Leland shows that for a wide range of utility functions combining option positions with a stock portfolio will provide a return distribution that will lead to higher expected utility than is possible through trading in the strict mean-variance tradeoffs of a stock portfolio.

[5] A description of the algorithm is presented in Bookstaber and Clarke (1980). A second algorithm has also been developed by the authors to allow for correlation between the residuals. This algorithm is described in Bookstaber and Clarke (1979).

[6] We assume that the returns for each stock follow the market model

$$r_i = r_f + \beta_i r_m + u_i$$

where r_i is the return to the *ith* stock, r_f is the riskless rate, r_m is the excess return on the market index, and u_i is a random error term for firm i, with $E(u_i u_j) = 0$, $i \neq j$. In the figures we have generated, we assume that $r_f = 8\%$ and $r_m \sim N(.07, .04)$.

REFERENCES

Arditti, F. and Levy, H. "Portfolio Efficiency Analysis in Three Moments: The Multiperiod Case." *Journal of Finance*, 1975, 30, 797-809.

Banz, R. and Miller, M. "Some Estimates of Implicit Prices for State-Contingent Claims." *Journal of Business*, 1978.

Bookstaber, R. and Clarke, R. "Molding Portfolio Return Distributions with Option Strategies: Approximation and Simulation Results." Brigham Young University Working Paper Series #80-5, 1980.
——. "The Effect of Option Positions on Portfolio Return Distributions." Manuscript, 1979.

Breeden, D. and Litzenberger, R. "Prices of State-Contingent Claims Implicit in Option Prices." Research Paper No. 385, Graduate School of Business, Stanford University, 1977.

Black, F. and Scholes, M. "The Pricing of Options and Corporate Liabilities." *Journal of Political Economy*, 1973, 81, 637-659.

Hakansson, N. "Welfare Aspects of Options and Supershares." *Journal of Finance*, 1978, 33, 759-776.

Kraus, A. and Litzenberger, R. "Skewness Preference and the Valuation of Risky Assets." *Journal of Finance*, 1976, 31, 1085-1100.

Leland, H. "Who Should Buy Portfolio Insurance?" Working Paper No. 95, Institute of Business and Economic Research, University of California, Berkely, December 1979.

Merton, R. C. "Theory of Rational Option Pricing." *Bell Journal of Economics and Management Science*, 1973, 4, 141-183.

Merton, R. C., Scholes, M., and Gladstein, M. "The Return and Risk of Alternative Call Option Portfolio Investment Strategies." *Journal of Business*, 1978, 51, 183-243.

Ross, S. "Options and Efficiency." *Quarterly Journal of Economics*, 1976, 90, 75-89.

Simkowitz, M. and Beedles, W. "Diversification in a Three-Moment World." *Journal of Financial and Quantitative Analysis*, 1978, 13, 927-941.

Smith, C. W., Jr. "Option Pricing: A Review." *Journal of Financial Economics*, 1976, 3, 3-51.

Option portfolio risk analysis

How to use multiple-factor risk models to analyze the risks and returns of stock options.

Jeremy Evnine and Andrew Rudd

Over the past decade, sophisticated money managers have used multiple-factor risk models to aid investment decision making. They have most commonly used these models in the management of equities, although applications to fixed-income investment and other asset categories have also been developed.

Such models have a number of uses. They allow us to model the distribution of returns of an asset or of a portfolio of assets. In particular, we can compute the standard deviations of returns (total risk), the covariance of return with, say, a market portfolio (beta), and how the attributes of an equity portfolio would change if we cover the stocks with options. Risk models also allow us to do performance analysis. What kinds of bets did we take in our portfolio? Did these bets pay off? How much of our return was due to skill? How much to luck? There are also implications for the asset-allocation problem. How should funds be optimally allocated across a stable of managers that includes options managers? We can obtain information on these and other problems by utilizing multiple-factor models.

In this paper, we present a multiple-factor model for analyzing the risks and returns of stock options. We will first discuss multiple-factor models in general and the differences between such a model for stocks (which are fundamental assets) and options (which are derivative assets). We then describe the option risk model in detail. Finally, we discuss some applications of the model.

FACTOR MODELS

Multiple-factor models may be described mathematically by the following equation:

$$(2.1) \qquad r_s - r_f = x_1 f_1 + \ldots + x_n f_n + u_s,$$

where r_s is the return on an arbitrary asset in one asset class (e.g., common stocks); r_f is the return on the riskless asset; $f_1, \ldots, f_n$ are the returns on n marketwide factors of risk and reward that account for the commonality of returns among assets in the asset class; $x_1, \ldots, x_n$ are the exposures, or sensitivities, of a particular asset to the factors (determinable ex ante), and u_s is the "specific" return of a particular asset, the return that is residual to that accounted for by the factors, and which may be regarded as unique to each asset. The period over which returns are modeled is arbitrary but is typically set to one month.

An example is afforded by the Market Model (see, e.g., Rudd and Clasing [5]), which motivates this form of the factor model. In the Market Model, there is one factor (the excess return on the market), the exposure to which is the asset's beta:

$$(2.2) \qquad \beta = \mathrm{Cov}(r_s, r_m)/\mathrm{Var}(r_m),$$

with the asset's return given by:

$$r_s - r_f = \beta(r_m - r_f) + u_s.$$

More sophisticated models have multiple rather than single factors. For example, the BARRA equity risk model contains 68 factors, 13 of which are related to the fundamental characteristics of companies and 55 of which are industry groups. The factor exposures are determined directly from fundamental data reported on income statements and balance sheets.

Since the model is linear, we can compute the exposure to each factor of a portfolio (which is just a weighted collection of assets) by computing the weighted sum of the individual assets' exposures to

291

the factor. Similarly, the specific return of a portfolio is the weighted sum of the individual assets' specific returns.

We know that, say, the covariance of return between two stocks is not well predicted by a historical sample covariance, because the risk characteristics of the companies change through time. By contrast, if we define the factors in our factor model with care, it is not unreasonable to assume that their covariances are stationary over time and, hence, may be well predicted by historical sample covariances. We can then predict covariance between stock returns when we know the stocks' exposure to the factors. Changing stock covariance is now explained by virtue of the fundamental characteristics of the firms, and hence the stocks' factor exposures, changing through time.

With such a model in hand, money managers can compute the probability characteristics of their portfolios. They may shade their portfolios with respect to certain factors upon which they wish to place a bet. Or they may wish to bet on individual assets without altering "normal" factor exposures. Ex post, they may attribute their returns to the bets placed and can thus analyze their skill.

Even more sophisticated uses of an option risk model will be mentioned below.

The conceptual difference between a factor model for common stocks and one for stock options is that options are derivatives of stocks. In particular, we may view a stock as a call on itself, with zero striking price and infinite time to expiration. On the other hand, we may view an option as a combination of two assets: one is an appropriate position in the underlying stock; the other is a hypothetical "asset" that accounts for the nonequity-like nature of an option.

Consequently, an option factor model will be an extension of an equity factor model. As such, we seek to define only a "linked" model. That is, rather than trying to define a model of the form of (2.1), which implicitly involves modeling common stock returns, we will seek to construct a model of the form:

$$(2.3) \qquad r_c - r_f = \eta \cdot (r_s - r_f) + x_1 f_1^* \\ + \ldots + x_n f_n^* + u_c,$$

where r_c is the return on the call (or put); u_c is the return unique to the call; η (the Greek letter eta) is the "elasticity" of the call with respect to the stock, and $f_1^*, \ldots, f_n^*$ are common factors that account for the nonequity-like nature of options. We may then substitute, in place of $r_s - r_f$, any factor model for stock returns of the form of (2.1) to achieve a model of similar form to (2.1). Note that the form will not be identical to (2.1), because the nonfactor return will consist of:

$$(2.4) \qquad \eta u_s + u_c,$$

which is not unique to each option. In particular, we can see that all options on the same stock will be exposed to the specific return of the stock, as we would expect. Hence, ηu_s is a component of return that is neither due to common factors nor asset-specific, but somewhere in between. This is due to the linked nature of options.

THE OPTION FACTOR MODEL

Construction of the Model

In this section, we will outline intuitively the construction of the linked risk model. The technically oriented reader should be aware that rigorous mathematical derivation of the model proceeds with a Taylor expansion, which is discussed more fully in Evnine and Rudd [1].

The option return over the month is the ratio of month-end price to month-beginning price. As the latter is directly observable at the beginning of the month, let us discuss the determinants of the unknown month-end price. To this end, we define:

$$(3.1) \qquad BS(S, v, r)$$

to be the value of the Black-Scholes European (dividend-adjusted) call-pricing formula for a call, evaluated at stock price S, stock variance v, and interest rate r. For a put, let it denote the put value as determined from the call value and the European put/call parity formula (see Jarrow and Rudd [4]). We define r to be the 4½ month spot rate determined by fitting a term structure to all U.S. government bonds (see Houglet [3]). We define v, the fair variance of the stock, to be the variance implied by the middle maturity at-the-money call (for reasons that will become apparent later).

What are the factors of risk that determine the month-end option price and, hence, its monthly return? In a true Black-Scholes world, the only source of risk is stock risk, since v and r are assumed known and constant. Clearly, however, unanticipated changes in v and r will also cause unanticipated option return and, hence, they too must be regarded as sources of risk and reward.

The key word here is "unanticipated," since we can always predict option return, based on its fair value at month end, for any anticipated values of S, v, and r. Since returns are proportional price changes, let us define our unanticipated parameter changes in proportional terms also. In particular, denote the unanticipated stock price change by $r_s - r_f$, the excess return on the stock, and DELR to be the proportional interest rate surprise. Given a prediction of the term structure, we should expect the spot rate to realize the forward rate. (This is known as the expectations hypothesis.) To the extent that it may differ, we define DELR to be the proportional prediction error in the interest rate.

The variance factor, which we denote DEL-VAR, is slightly harder to develop. Since we have no model for variance changes, we should view any change in v as unanticipated. As a first pass, therefore, we might be tempted to define DELVAR to be the proportional change in stock variance. Unfortunately, this is a stock specific, rather than a market-wide factor. Therefore let us redefine DELVAR to be the proportional change in market variance, in some sense. We can either attempt to make this concept precise and define an exogenously determined value for this factor, or, alternatively, we can allow the outcome of DELVAR to be determined by the data from a cross-sectional regression, once we have defined an option's exposure to it. We have chosen the latter course.

We now turn our attention to the options' exposures to the three factors discussed above — namely, $r_s - r_f$, DELVAR, and DELR. The exposures x_i define a linear response to the factors. On the other hand, we know from the form of the Black-Scholes equation that option prices do not respond linearly to changes in S, v, and r. As far as DELVAR and DELR are concerned, this need not worry us, since (a) the nonlinearities are not of great magnitude, and (b) the realistic outcomes of DELVAR and DELR are not likely to be large, in practice. We can compute linear responses to DELVAR and DELR by manipulating the derivatives of the Black-Scholes formula, to obtain elasticities, which we denote by the Greek letters v (nu) and ζ (zeta), respectively.

The linear response of option return to stock return, which we denoted by η, is related to the option's hedge ratio Δ by:

(3.2) $$\eta = \Delta \cdot (S/C),$$

where C denotes option price. Notice that η is positive for calls and negative for puts. Its magnitude is always greater than 1 and gets larger as the option gets deeper out-of-the-money. η defines the notion of "stock equivalent" in a return sense, just as Δ defines it in a price sense.

Unfortunately, option response to stock return cannot be sufficiently captured by a linear function. It is precisely because options respond to stock movements in a nonlinear way that they are such interesting and useful vehicles. We can capture the vast majority of this nonlinearity by adding in an adjustment term that involves $(r_s - r_f)^2$. This is like approximating the Black-Scholes formula by a quadratic

equation. Unless the stock excess return is enormous, it will be a good approximation.

The effect of the nonlinear adjustment, which we denote ψ (the Greek letter psi), is related to option gamma, just as η is related to option delta. However, since the adjustment term involves $(r_s - r_f)^2$, which is stock-specific, we replace it by two factors. The first factor, β_s^2 MKTSQR, is the square of the stock's systematic return with respect to the S&P 500. The other factor, RES2, is an adjustment due to the stock's specific risk, σ_s^2.

Having exhausted the factors of return that we can deduce from a Black-Scholes perspective, we now define several factors that we clearly recognize as being common, marketwide factors of return, but for which Black-Scholes provides no explanation.

The first of these arises because the option's month-end price may not be its fair value. We hypothesize that systematic month-end mispricings occur because observed mispricings at the beginning of the month tend to persist. This is a reasonable hypothesis derived from our definition of fair variance, which is that implied by the middle maturity at-the-money call. That is, much observed mispricing at the beginning of the month (although clearly not all) may be attributed to striking price and maturity biases in the Black-Scholes formula. Over the month, maturities decrease by exactly one month, and stock prices will increase, in expectation, by a small amount, so we may expect these biases to persist — at least approximately. Hence, we define a factor exposure χ (the Greek letter chi) by:

(3.3) $$\chi = 1 - BS/C,$$

which measures the mispricing of an option relative to the middle maturity at-the-money call at the beginning of the month. This defines a factor (DVRG), determined from a cross-sectional regression, that measures the extent to which these biases persist (positive outcomes), vanish (0), or even reverse themselves (negative outcomes).

We can refine the effect of maturity and striking-price biases by adding in an autonomous option market factor (CONS), an out-of-the-money factor (OTM), a short-maturity factor (SHRT), and a long-maturity factor (LONG). We do not need an in-the-money factor, since the in-the-money options have much weaker option-like (higher) characteristics. The exposure of an option to these last four factors is 0 or 1, as appropriate.

Finally, several of the option factors were redefined separately for puts and for calls, to allow for the different characteristics of the call and put markets. For example, the factor model for calls in its final form is:

293

(3.4) $r_c - r_f = (\hat{r}_c - r_f) + \eta(r_s - r_f)$
$$+ \psi\beta_s^2 \text{MKTSQR} + \zeta\text{DELR} + \nu\text{DELVAR}$$
$$+ \text{CONS} + \chi\text{DVRG} + \psi\sigma_s^2 \text{RES2}$$
$$+ d_1\text{OTM} + d_2\text{SHRT} + d_3\text{LONG} + \epsilon,$$

where:

$$d_1 = \begin{cases} 1 \text{ for out-of-the-money options,} \\ 0 \text{ otherwise;} \end{cases}$$

$$d_2 = \begin{cases} 1 \text{ for short-maturity options,} \\ 0 \text{ otherwise;} \end{cases}$$

$$d_3 = \begin{cases} 1 \text{ for long-maturity options,} \\ 0 \text{ otherwise, and} \end{cases}$$

$\hat{r}_c$ represents the return that the option would achieve if all the other factors on the right-hand side of (3.4) realized zero return.

Estimation of the Model

We estimated the model over 59 months (January 1978 through November 1982), using a sample of options chosen by stratified random sampling, to represent the three striking-price bands (out-of, at- and in-the-money) and three maturity bonds (short, middle, and long) (see Evnine and Rudd [2]). The sample size was about four calls and three puts per optionable stock, on average.

We used two weighting schemes: a CAP-weighting scheme, based on each option's capitalization (defined as the product of open interest and price); and an optimal GLS-weighting scheme, based on a model for the variance of the residual (specific) risk, which is similar to a factor model (see Evnine and Rudd [1]).

Estimation was performed by regressing:

$$(r_c - r_f) - (\hat{r}_c - r_f) - \eta(r_s - r_f)$$
$$- \psi\beta_s^2 \cdot \text{MKTSQR} - \zeta \cdot \text{DELR}$$

against the exposures to the endogenously determined factors (shown for calls in (3.4)). A coefficient of determination for the entire estimation was computed, for which the denominator was the variance of total option return (as distinct from the dependent variable in the regression), and the numerator was the variance of fitted option return based on the regression estimates of the factors. The value obtained was 79% for GLS weighting and 70% for CAP weighting. By contrast, if we defined fitted return as:

$$(\hat{r}_c - r_f) + \eta(r_s - r_f),$$

ignoring the 15 "pure" option factors, we obtained a coefficient of determination of only 49%. Computed

on a year-by-year basis, the coefficients of determination were sharply increasing over the period 1978 to 1982, which we attribute to the increasing efficiency of the options markets over that period.

APPLICATIONS

One application that we mentioned earlier is risk analysis. For example, consider the following portfolios. Portfolio A is the Dow Jones 30 Industrials. Portfolio B consists of the Dow Jones 30 Industrials, with each of 25 of the 30 stocks covered by a middle-maturity at-the-money call. A risk analysis based on the BARRA equity risk model and the option model described in this paper obtained the following results.

Portfolio A had a standard deviation of total return of 19.69% annually, of which 19.23% was systematic with respect to the S&P 500 and 4.24% was residual. Portfolio beta was 0.94. Portfolio B had a total standard deviation of 10.92%, of which 10.34% was systematic and 3.52% was residual. Portfolio beta was reduced to 0.51 by virtue of the written calls. The only significant nonzero exposures to the option factors were:

MKTSQR: -1.16,

DELVAR: -0.02, and

CONS: -0.06.

There were no puts; no long, short, or out-of-the-money calls; insignificant interest rate risk, and the calls were, on the whole, fairly priced. The exposure to MKTSQR is a surrogate for the skewness of the portfolio return, since we anticipate MKTSQR to be the only factor with skewed distribution. In a sense, this is a measure of the downside protection and the upside limitation afforded by the written calls.

The coefficient of -0.02 to DELVAR means that if the market variance suffers a proportional increase of, say, 10%, the return on the covered call portfolio will decrease by $0.02 \times 10\% = 20$ basis points, due to the increase in value of the written calls. Similarly, if the call market has an autonomous return, over and above the return due to all the other factors, of 1%, then the portfolio return will decrease by 6 basis points, because -6% of the portfolio value is in calls.[1]

At month end, return may be attributed to the factor returns and the portfolio exposures. Residual return can be compared to residual risk to ascertain performance on a risk-adjusted basis — and so on.

Perhaps the most exciting potential use of the risk model lies in using it in conjunction with a math-

---

1. Footnotes appear at the end of the article.

ematical optimizer (quadratic optimization) to construct portfolios with desired risk characteristics. We give two examples of this.

First, suppose that a manager wishes to arbitrage stock index futures. Perhaps believing the future to be underpriced relative to the spot, he wishes to buy the future long and short the index. Shorting the index may be difficult for him to apply, so he may wish to substitute a portfolio of, say, 15 stocks that track the index as closely as possible. Even this may be hard, and he may wish to create synthetic shorts using long puts and short calls.

He can do this as follows. Having decided which stocks and options may enter his portfolio, together with any holding constraints, we can easily compute the exposure to the option risk model for his portfolio, for any chosen set of portfolio holdings. We may also compute the exposures of the index to be tracked. Hence, we may compute the exposures (and also specific risk) of the difference between his portfolio and the index. If we now choose, using quadratic programming, a set of holdings that minimizes the standard deviation of that difference (based on the computed factor exposures and specific risks), we will have a portfolio, easily purchased, whose return will deviate from that of the index as little as possible (in an ex ante probabilistic sense). This technique is already being used by arbitrageurs of index futures.

The second example involves the increasingly popular strategy of portfolio insurance. Suppose a manager has a portfolio valued at $110 million. He wishes to purchase a one-year 100 put on his portfolio. No such asset exists, of course, but since we can predict the volatility of his portfolio from the equity risk model, we can compute what the factor exposures of such a put would be to the option factor model. Hence, we can compute a set of hypothetical target exposures that are those of his put-protected portfolio. How can we produce a portfolio of real assets that tracks this target as closely as possible? We may

use the technique of quadratic optimization described above and include in the manager's universe the following assets:

i)   cash;
ii) all the stocks in his portfolio;
iii) long-maturity puts on, say, the AMEX MMI and the S&P 100, and
iv) options on individual stocks, particularly those whose portfolio weights differ substantially from their weights in the indexes.

If the manager's portfolio is well diversified, it will correlate highly with the indexes for which there exist listed puts. Corrections for the deficiencies in the protection afforded by index puts will be made automatically by the optimizer in adjusting the asset holdings. By revising the portfolio monthly, and rolling over the options as their maturities decrease, we can expect, ex ante, that by year's end, our strategy will produce returns that very closely replicate those that would have been achieved with the protective put.

---

[1] For a more in-depth discussion of the uses of the option factor model in portfolio risk analysis, see Rudd and Evnine [6].

REFERENCES

1. Evnine, J., and A. Rudd. "A Multiple Factor Risk Model for Stock Options Returns." Unpublished BARRA paper, 1983.

2. ———. "Option Return Indices." Unpublished BARRA paper, 1983.

3. Houglet, M. "Estimating the Term Structure of Interest Rates for Nonhomogeneous Bonds." Unpublished PhD thesis, University of California, Berkeley, 1980.

4. Jarrow, R., and A. Rudd. Option Pricing. Homewood, Ill.: Richard D. Irwin, Inc., 1983.

5. Rudd, A., and H. Clasing. Modern Portfolio Theory. Homewood, Ill.: Dow Jones-Irwin, 1982.

6. Rudd, A., and J. Evnine. Option Portfolio Risk Analysis: Case Studies. Unpublished BARRA paper, 1983.

The use of options in performance structuring

Molding returns to meet investment objectives.

Richard Bookstaber

During the first ten years of listed option trading, options were viewed as tactical, if not outright speculative, instruments. Investors purchased calls to gain leverage, bought puts to lock in gains or speculate on declines, and used covered writes to enhance yields on sluggish issues. The implications of options positions for the return characteristics of the overall portfolio were rarely a consideration; the concern in option trading was trade-by-trade profitability, not cumulative portfolio effects. As option markets have matured, however, and as new instruments such as index and interest rate options and futures have been introduced to address the major sources of financial risk, the emphasis has shifted toward using options strategically in portfolio management.

The purpose of this paper is to address the role of options in portfolio management; to explain the concepts behind option-related techniques for structuring portfolio returns and controlling financial risks, and to lay out both the opportunities and difficulties these techniques present.

The topic of options we will address is more general than it might at first seem. Broadly speaking, options are instruments with a payoff that is contingent on the value of another, underlying security. Listed options are traded on a number of exchanges, but options can also be traded over the counter and, most important, can be created synthetically through the proper set of transactions in other securities. Listed options, while the most visible option contracts, are only a small part of the picture.

When dealing with option strategies, the topic of portfolio management also covers a broad area. We can think of portfolio management as the management of overall investment or financial risk. Besides the management of equity and bond investment portfolios, portfolio management includes balancing asset and liability risk in banks and in savings and loans, creating payment streams to match obligations in insurance companies and pension funds, and constructing securities to satisfy the financing patterns required by corporations.

Portfolio management is typically approached as a two-dimensional tradeoff between the mean and variance of returns. The mix of risky assets and cash is the only tool that managers have at their disposal in adjusting the portfolio. The mix dictates the mean-variance tradeoff the portfolio will face.

Figures 1-A and 1-B illustrate this tradeoff. These figures depict portfolio returns with the familiar bell-shaped curve of the normal distribution. In this setting, a two-dimensional mean-variance tradeoff is a natural way of looking at returns, since the mean and variance completely describe the normal distribution. A more conservative manager will move funds from risky assets into cash, ending up with a return distribution such as Figure 1-B, with less vari-

RICHARD BOOKSTABER is Research Manager at Morgan Stanley & Co. Inc. in New York (NY 10020).

FIGURE 1-A

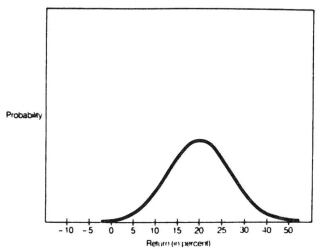

Return distribution of a stock portfolio. Mean return is 20 percent, with a standard deviation of 30 percent.

FIGURE 1-B

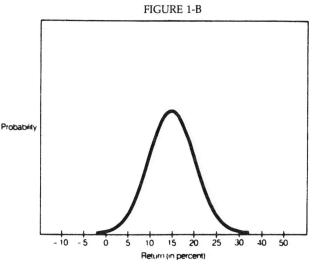

Return distribution of a stock portfolio. Mean return is 15 percent, with a standard deviation of 20 percent. Compared to the return portfolio of Figure 1-A, the investor has both lower expected return and lower risk. The returns continue to be normally distributed, however.

ance and a lower expected return. A more aggressive manager will go in the opposite direction, levering to achieve a higher expected return at the cost of higher variance. In either case, the manager can measure the alterations in the structure of returns simply in terms of mean and variance.

Comfortable and intuitive though it is, this two-dimensional tradeoff will not always result in a return distribution that meets portfolio objectives. A manager might prefer to control some other aspect of returns. For example, a manager may wish to achieve some guaranteed minimum return while retaining a portion of the upward return potential.[1] This objective would imply a non-symmetric return distribution such as that shown in Figure 1-C. This distribution

1. Footnotes appear at the end of the article.

FIGURE 1-C

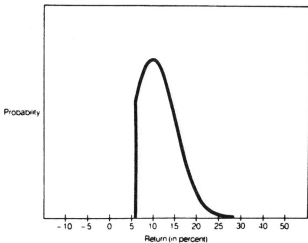

The return distribution that might be preferred by the portfolio manager. The probability of a large loss is eliminated.

truncates the downside risk while the right-hand tail still maintains some of the upside potential. Forming this return distribution requires more than mean-variance tradeoffs — it cannot be constructed using the conventional procedures of portfolio management.

The ability to form distributions of this type may have a value far beyond simply meeting subjective preferences. For example, the very pattern of liabilities may lead to a need for non-symmetric, non-normal returns. The obligation of a pension fund to meet a minimum actuarial payoff would lead to a return distribution like that shown in Figure 1-C. Other complex payoffs, such as those generated by the carefully tailored annuity products of the life insurance industry or the variable rate liabilities of many corporations and thrift institutions, will lead to return objectives that cannot be met by simple mean-variance adjustments.

Options are the building blocks for constructing the payoffs to meet these complex return objectives. We can use options to create the portfolio insurance depicted in Figure 1-C, or to mold returns to conform with virtually any other feasible distribution. This capacity for options to expand the set of contingencies has been established theoretically.[2] Here we will deal with the practical issues of how managers can implement these strategies.

THE INSURANCE FEATURE OF OPTION CONTRACTS

Let us begin by looking at an option as an insurance contract. The premium for the insurance is part of the option price. The variety of payoffs from option strategies comes from taking selective positions in the insurance — buying some insurance protection over one range of security prices, selling some insurance over another.

We can see the essential insurance feature of an option contract by constructing an option through an insurance-motivated transaction. Suppose an investor buys a security worth $1200 by investing $200 directly and borrowing the remaining $1000. The security is retained as collateral by the lender, to be released to the investor in one year upon repayment of the $1000 loan. Further, suppose the investor wishes to have protection should the security decline in value before the loan comes due and therefore arranges for the loan on a no-recourse basis. Then, if the investor fails to make the $1000 payment in one year, the lender will receive ownership of the security and will have no further recourse to the investor. This no-recourse feature amounts to giving the investor an insurance contract on the investment, with a deductible equal to the $200 initial investment.

At the end of the year, what will be the best strategy for the investor to pursue? Obviously, the investor will pay back the loan if the security value at the end of the year is at least as great as the $1000 necessary to gain clear ownership. The investor's profit in doing so will be the security value, S^*, less the loan payment, or $S^* - 1000$. If the security is worth less than the loan payment, the investor will be better off simply to walk away from the loan and let the lender take ownership, since the $1000 payment to claim the security will net the investor a loss. The payoff pattern from this insured loan is identical to that of a call option on the security with an exercise price of $1000. The call option gives the right to buy the security for $1000 and has a payoff that is the security price minus the exercise price, $S^* - 1000$, or zero, whichever is greater.

Using this no-recourse loan as a vehicle for analyzing a call option, we see the price of the call option can be broken up into three parts. First, there is the initial payment of $200. This payment, the difference between the security price and the $1000 exercise price, is called the *intrinsic value* of the option. Second, there is an interest carrying cost from holding the security in escrow. The investor pays the exercise price at the end of the year, but the lender has the $1000 tied up in the security over the loan period. Given an interest rate of r, this interest cost will be $(r/(1 + r)) 1000$. The third part of the option price is the insurance cost of the downside protection. Since the lender is absorbing the loss, there will be an insurance premium, P, implicit in the price of the call option.

Combining these three terms, and denoting the exercise price by E, we can express the call option as

$$C = (S - E) + E(r/(1 + r)) + P.$$

This expression shows the option price consists of intrinsic value, prepaid interest, and insurance against loss.

To gain more insight into the nature of the insurance premium, P, consider the contract the lender would need in order to overcome the risk from the loan's no-recourse feature. If the security is worth more than the exercise price at the end of the year, the lender will receive the $1000 payment and no other compensation will be necessary. If the value is less than the exercise price, the lender will have paid $1000 for a security that is now worth less than that; the lender will have lost $1000 - S^*$. The compensating contract, then, must give a payout equal to the difference between the exercise price and security price when the security price is less than the exercise price; it must give no payout when the security price is equal to or greater than the exercise price. This is exactly the payout given by a *put option*. A put option gives the right to sell the underlying security at the exercise price; its payout is the maximum of zero and $(E - S)$, the exercise price minus the security price.

Put and Call Options Redefined

The insurance premium for the no-recourse loan, P, is thus equal to a put option with one year to maturity and an exercise price of $1000. In this context, then, we can define a call option and a put option as follows:

Call option: A contract giving the holder the underlying security at maturity while insuring against any loss during the term of the contract beyond a deductible equal to the intrinsic value of the option.

Put option: An insurance contract that pays off to cover fully any security price decline below the face value of the contract, which is the put option's exercise price.

Some of the characteristics of option pricing are evident from viewing options in this insurance context. First, just as insurance premiums increase with an increase in riskiness, so option prices increase with an increase in the price volatility of the security. Second, call prices are an increasing function of interest rates, since higher interest rates increase the interest carrying cost. Third, just as insurance premiums decline as the amount of the deductible increases, so the insurance cost, P, drops as the intrinsic value of the call option increases. Fourth, the longer the term of the coverage, i.e., the longer the time to expiration of the option, the more the option will cost.[3]

Different patterns of returns are possible by properly selecting the option coverage. Indeed, given options at all exercise prices and all times to expiration, we could construct the entire range of attainable return structures.

To see this more concretely, consider a strategy of buying one option with an exercise price of $100, writing two options each with an exercise price of $101, and buying one option with an exercise price of $102. This position, called a butterfly spread, will lead to a payoff of $1 if the underlying security is at $100 at the time of option expiration, and a payoff of zero otherwise. Such a binary payoff can be used as the basic building block from any payoff schedule.[4]

TABLE 1

Security price	Value of option with exercise price of $49	Value of option with exercise price of $50	Value of option with exercise price of $51	Total strategy value
–	–	–	–	–
–	–	–	–	–
–	–	–	–	–
46	0	0	0	0
47	0	0	0	0
48	0	0	0	0
49	0	0	0	0
50	1	0	0	1
51	2	−2	0	0
52	3	−4	1	0
53	4	−6	2	0
–	–	–	–	–
–	–	–	–	–
–	–	–	–	–

Obviously, only a small part of this set of options are actually traded on the listed exchanges. These institutional limitations would seem to be a serious constraint for turning the great theoretical potential of performance structuring into a real opportunity. As we will see in the next section, however, we are not restricted to listed options. We can construct synthetic options of any exercise price and any time to expiration through the use of dynamic trading strategies.

THE CREATION OF OPTION POSITIONS USING DYNAMIC TRADING TECHNIQUES

The key difficulty in employing option methods is that the appropriate option contracts often do not exist in the market place. While a growing number of markets and securities are covered by option instruments, these may not match the terms of the option contract required for the portfolio strategy. For example, the maturity of the traded options may not match the manager's time horizon, or the security underlying the option contract may not match the asset mix of the portfolio. Fortunately, the principles of option theory can be applied to create the option contract synthetically even when the required option does not exist in the market. This is done by a dynamic reallocation of funds across sets of assets, or by a dynamic readjustment of positions in listed options and futures contracts.

To develop the dynamic strategy, we will concentrate on the creation of insurance provided by the protective put option. We can apply the same principles in forming other option positions and creating other return structures.

Dynamic Strategies as Multi-Point Stop-Loss Strategies

The simplest and most widely known technique for achieving downside protection is the stop-loss order. An investor can assure a $100 floor on a security price by stopping out of the security at a price equal to the present value of $100, $100(1/(1 + r))^T$, and putting the funds in the risk-free asset for the remaining time period, T. Once stopped out, the funds will accrue interest at the rate r and will be worth $100 at the end of the time period.

For example, if there is a year left in the holding period for the strategy and if r is 10%, then the security would be stopped out at $91. Putting the $91 in the risk-free asset at 10% would give the desired $100 return by the end of the year.

Figure 2 illustrates this stop-loss order. The figure overlays the security price with the percentage of

FIGURE 2

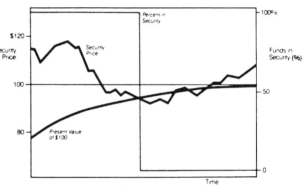

Investment pattern for a one-point stop-loss strategy

the portfolio invested in the security. Note that the level of the stop approaches the floor as the end of the holding period approaches, because the funds have less and less time to accrue interest. Once the security price drops below the stop, all funds are taken out of the security.

This insurance method is effective, but is also costly. It fails to take into account the possibility that the security may rebound from the decline, eliminating any possibility of sharing in later increases in the security price.

We can remedy this deficiency to a limited degree by allowing the stop to be reversible. Rather than pursuing this one-point stop-loss strategy, suppose we employ a two-point strategy where the investment is stopped out of the security when the price drops below the stop, and the security is bought when the price moves back through the stop-loss point. This will allow the required downside protection while no longer shutting the investor completely out of possible appreciation. This strategy is illustrated in Figure 3.

FIGURE 3

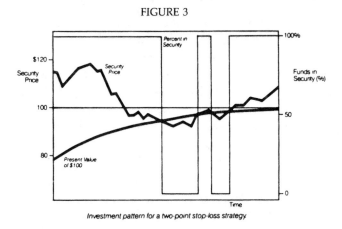

Investment pattern for a two-point stop-loss strategy

This two-point strategy, while superior to the simple stop-loss strategy, still imposes its own costs. In addition to imposing greater transaction costs, every reversal leads to a loss equal to the distance between the selling and buying point. Setting the points close together will not eliminate these costs. The closer these two points, the smaller the cost per reversal but the more frequently such reversals will occur. This cost will be greatest if the security vibrates around the breakeven point and will be smallest if the breakeven point is never hit.

Both the nonreversible one-point stop-loss strategy and the two-point stop-loss strategy will thus lead to a reduction in the expected return. This risk-return tradeoff is as expected, since the strategies provide a reduction of downside risk. The two-point stop-loss strategy will have the higher return, since it gives the opportunity to gain from price appreciation.

Given the results of the two-point strategy, we should logically consider the effects of extending the flexibility further. If we are confident the security in question will remain risky over the holding period — that is, if we believe the security will continue to be volatile — then there is no need to sell off completely when the security reaches the breakeven point of $100(1/(1 + r))^T$. Instead, we might move in or out of the security gradually as the security moves away from the breakeven point. This will lessen the chance of being whipsawed by repeated reversals.

Given the time left in the holding period, security volatility will make periodic moves around the breakeven point likely. Such moves will be more likely the longer the time left, the greater the volatility, and the closer the security price is to the breakeven point. Accordingly, the proportion of the security we stop out should take all of these factors into account. Furthermore, the breakeven point for the stop will change over time and with interest rates.

Thus, the rule we use for moving in and out of the security should be a function of the security price, the insured price, the holding period of the strategy, the interest rate, and the volatility of the security. Since these stop-loss strategies all mimic the sort of non-linearities common to options, it is not surprising these are the same factors we discussed above as determining the price of an option.

Obviously, an unlimited number of stop-loss adjustments are available to us with these factors in mind. Figure 4 shows the return to one particular strategy. With this alternative, we hold 50% of the funds in the security and 50% in the risk-free asset when we hit the breakeven point; we move completely in or out of the security only when the price has moved a significant distance away from the breakeven point. We let this strategy stop out completely at a point with twice the time factor as the breakeven point, $100(1/(1 + r))^{2T}$, stop out one half at the breakeven point, $100(1/(1 + r))^2$, and fully invest at $100 (1 + r)^T$. This three-point stop-loss strategy continues to give the required protection. Furthermore, by making finer adjustments and by retaining a partial holding over more of the range of the security price, the strategy will provide the protection for the least cost of the three strategies considered so far.

FIGURE 4

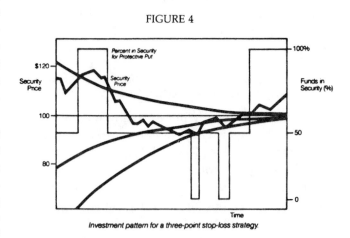

Investment pattern for a three-point stop-loss strategy

A Put Option as the Least-Cost Insurance Strategy

A cost is imposed by the insurance protection because the dynamic adjustments gradually pull funds out of the security as it declines and only gradually put funds back into the security as it appreciates.

Hence, the insured position cannot fully participate in the appreciation.

Our objective is to find the lowest-cost insurance contract. The best adjustment strategy will be the strategy that provides the downside protection while allowing the greatest sharing of security appreciation on the upside. We already know that the put option represents the ideal insurance contract for protecting against downside risk. If we could find a dynamic stopless strategy that replicated the behavior of a put option with a time to expiration equal to the investor's time horizon, and an exercise price of $100, we would have protection that precisely meets the insurance objectives, and, given efficient markets, that gives the protection at the lowest price.

All three stop-loss strategies considered above approximate a put option. They all give downside protection similar to that of a put option. And, like a put option, the two-point and three-point stop-loss strategies share in some of the upward potential of the security as well. On the other hand, they are not perfect replicas of a put option; they move in jumps as the security price changes, rather than in the smooth, continuous fashion of a put option. Nevertheless, they do suggest that an extension of the dynamic stop-loss strategy will move us closer to the pure put option protection desired.

Option pricing theory has shown this is in fact the case; we can create an option position by pursuing a strategy that dynamically adjusts the proportion of the underlying security and the risk-free asset.[5] Since an option can be replicated by such a strategy, this further implies the option price must always equal the cost of this replicating portfolio.

We can write the call option and put option equations as :

$$C = a_c - b_c B$$

and

$$P = -a_p S + b_p B,$$

where S is the security price, B is the price of the risk-free bond, and where the values of a_c, a_p, b_c, and b_p, are proportionality factors that take on values between zero and one.[6]

The call option is created by borrowing money at the risk-free rate (borrowing is implied by a negative value for b_c) and using it to purchase an amount a_c of the security. The borrowing leads to the leverage that is characteristic of a call option. The put is created by shorting the security (shorting is implied by a negative value for a_p) and putting an amount equal to b_p into the risk-free asset. When the put option position is combined with a long position in the security to form an insured position, the net effect of combining the initial long position in the security with the short position required to replicate the put option is a positive, but less than full, investment in the security.[7]

As was suggested by the three-point stop-loss strategy, the proportion of stocks and bonds in the option replication varies both over time and as the security price changes. The replicating portfolio must be continuously adjusted; hence, the dynamic nature of the strategy. The proportion terms a_c, a_p, b_c and b_p are not constants; rather, they are variables that will change with the time to the maturity of the holding period and with changes in the security price. As the three-point strategy further suggests, these terms will also be a function of the volatility of the security and the riskless interest rate.

Figure 5 illustrates the proportion of investment in the security when the investor follows the dynamic stop-loss adjustment of the protective put option strategy. This strategy provides the complete downside protection at the lowest cost. The strategy is overlaid on the three-point strategy described in Figure 4.

FIGURE 5

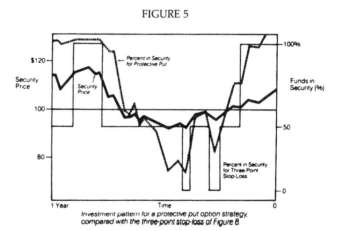

Investment pattern for a protective put option strategy, compared with the three-point stop-loss of Figure 8.

The naive one-point stop-loss strategy has been proposed in a number of insurance settings. For example, the original construction of the contingent immunization strategy for bond portfolios involves stopping out of an interest-sensitive bond position once a critical portfolio price or interest rate level is passed.[8] It should be clear from this discussion that such strategies, while providing the desired protection, are a more costly means of securing that protection than a strategy that more closely approximates the return structure of a put option.

VARIATIONS ON THE DYNAMIC STRATEGY: USING LISTED FUTURES AND OPTION CONTRACTS

As with any strategy, the dynamic strategy presents practical difficulties. These include:

1. The need for continuous adjustment.

   Theoretically, the option position requires continuous portfolio adjustments. The appropriate mix of the security and riskless asset changes over time and with changes in the security price. Discrete adjustments, by failing to account for the continuous nature of the movement of the security price and of time, will lead to a margin of error in the payoff of the option, as well as in its cost.

2. The accurate estimation of security price volatility.

   The appropriate portfolio mix will also depend on the volatility of the security. A highly volatile security will be more costly to insure, since the adjustments will catch less of each price swing. If the volatility of the security is forecast incorrectly, the result may lead to a higher cost or to less than complete protection.

3. The specification of the stochastic process driving security prices.

   The functional form of the proportionality terms in the option model depends on the nature of security price movements. The direction of the price movements has no bearing on the option model, but the way price movements tend to evolve does matter. For example, a security price that is typified by large periodic jumps will lead to a model specification, and hence to a different dynamic strategy, than a security whose price never experiences discrete jumps. Accuracy in the specification of the stochastic process is as important as accuracy in the estimation of the security price volatility emerging from that process.[9]

Just how critical these factors are to the successful implementation of the dynamic option strategies is an empirical question that cannot be answered here. Some of these problems are mitigated by using listed futures and option contracts in forming the dynamic strategy. We will discuss these variations on the dynamic strategy next.

Using Futures in Dynamic Strategies

The essential feature of the dynamic strategy is that the position in the security varies as the time to maturity and the security price vary. Obviously, one way to vary the size of the position is by transacting directly in the security itself. When there are futures on the security, we can also vary the position by leaving the actual security holdings unchanged and transacting in the futures contract instead.

For example, a put option on a well-diversified stock portfolio can be replicated by using a short position in an index future. As the portfolio value declines, requiring a smaller position in the portfolio, the short position will be increased. The short position will react in a direction opposite the portfolio position, leaving a net return to market movements that is essentially the same as if a portion of the portfolio itself had been sold off and transferred to the risk-free asset. The futures act as a damper on the effective portfolio position. The futures position is an alternative for the construction of dynamic strategies for any position that is highly correlated with the movement of traded futures, be they stocks, stock portfolios, bonds, foreign exchange, metals, or commodities.

Futures have a number of attractive features. First, because they combine a position in the asset with borrowing, they can lead to less costly transactions than the investor would incur with transfers between the security and cash. Second, execution is often better in the futures than in the cash market. This is particularly true when a single futures contract can be substituted for a portfolio-wide transaction, as in the case of stock or bond portfolios. Third, since futures are levered instruments, less cash is necessary to carry out the dynamic strategy.

The third point is especially important when the dynamic strategy is pursued separately from the portfolio holdings. For example, consider a pension sponsor with a number of outside managers, each managing a fraction of the fund. If the sponsor decides to pursue a dynamic strategy, the sponsor could conceivably have each manager restructure its management methods to incorporate the dynamic strategy.

There are obvious practical and administrative difficulties in doing this. And even if it were done successfully, the end result of having options on each of the individual portfolios would be an inefficient means of attaining the desired option on the overall pension fund investment.[10] On the other hand, the alternative of having the sponsor retain enough of the fund to make the market/cash adjustments itself would greatly reduce the amount retained under the outside managers, and would therefore change the character of the fund.

We can overcome these difficulties by using futures as the vehicle for making the dynamic adjustments. The pension fund sponsor, pursuing a dynamic strategy with futures, would need only retain enough cash to meet margin requirements. The sponsor could monitor its overall fund value, and, assuming its holdings are closely correlated with the overall market, use index futures to create a position that would be equivalent to selling off the necessary proportion of its holdings. The sponsor could do this without making any alteration in the managers' roles, without significant changes in the amount under management, even without the knowledge of the

302

managers. With protection against poor performance, any superior management performance will still lead to relative performance gains under the dynamic strategy.

Strictly speaking, the replication of a put or call option requires a proper balancing of positions in the riskless asset as well as risky security. The position in the riskless asset serves to make the position self-financing, i.e., the position neither requires further funding nor gives out payments from the time it is initiated until the expiration of the option contract. The self-financing feature is critical to the theoretical development of option pricing. Options are, after all, self-financing instruments: Once an option is purchased, no cash flow takes place until its exercise or expiration. Shifting between the risky security and the riskless asset maintains an economy in the development of the theoretical pricing argument since no other assets or transactions need to be tracked.

Nevertheless, when our attention moves from option pricing to hedging, and from theoretical development to practical implementation, the stringent requirements of maintaining a self-financing portfolio no longer apply. In practice, our concern is only with maintaining a position that gives a security payoff equal to that of an option. Failure to hold the proper proportion of funds in the riskless asset will not affect this essential return structure. It will affect only the ex post cost of the protection.

For example, if the manager chooses to place funds made available from the strategy into another risky asset rather than into the riskless asset, the overall cost of the dynamic strategy may now be thought to depend on the performance of that risky asset. But clearly that facet of the strategy can easily be separated from the insurance service the strategy is delivering.[11]

It is important to recognize this role of the riskless asset when using futures contracts in constructing dynamic hedges, because the most efficient use of futures may not maintain the theoretically correct position in the risk-free asset. Because they are levered, futures implicitly contain a short position in the risk-free asset, but this position will not necessarily equal that required for the strategy to be self-financing.

The most efficient use of futures may lead to periodic payments or cash requirements. When properly treated, these cause no difficulties for the construction or evaluation of the strategy. On the contrary, they may lead to important advantages over transactions in the security itself.

Using Options to Create Options

A second variation on dynamic strategies is the use of listed options. As with futures, listed options may exist on indexes and securities that are closely correlated with the security of interest. Obviously, if there is a listed option that is fairly priced and that exactly meets the time and contract specifications for hedging, then it will be preferred to constructing the option synthetically. Frequently, however, there is a listed option that only partially fits the hedging requirements. For example, the listed option may be on a slightly different underlying asset, perhaps on a Treasury bond futures contract when the underlying asset is a corporate bond portfolio, or on a stock index that does not exactly match the construction of the underlying stock portfolio, or the listed option may have too short a time to maturity or be at the wrong exercise price.

The first of these problems will not be unique to the use of the listed options. It will exist for futures and may also exist when a dynamic strategy is pursued directly through the underlying asset. Dynamic adjustments of stock or bond portfolios must be done piecemeal. The subset of securities to be adjusted will not exactly match the overall portfolio. As a result, it is possible the discrete adjustment of the dynamic strategy may induce more basis risk than the use of listed options that, although not perfectly correlated with the underlying asset, overcome the problems related to discrete adjustments.

The second problem of listed options — a time to expiration that is shorter than the time horizon demanded for the option protection — is probably considered the greatest barrier to using listed options. Listed options often cannot be found more than three months out, while the time horizon for dynamic strategies is typically one year or more. On the other hand, these short-term listed options can themselves be employed in a dynamic strategy for creating synthetic longer-term options. This strategy is similar to rolling over short-term futures contracts to create longer-term protection.

For example, suppose an investor were interested in a $100 floor for a security price for one year, and put options existed with three months to maturity. The investor might buy a three-month put with an exercise price of $100, and upon expiration of that put buy another three-month put with the same exercise price. The position would be liquidated at the end of six months, a new three-month option purchased, and the procedure would be repeated again at the end of nine months.

If the option expired out of the money, there would be no proceeds from the strategy, and more funds would be necessary to roll over the strategy. If the security dropped below the floor, the put option would return the difference between the floor price and the security price, covering the loss and providing the intrinsic value for buying the next contract.[12]

The actual cost of this technique depends on the path the security price takes. To see this, consider a security currently priced at $100 together with a call option purchased on the security with an exercise price of $100. Suppose a six-month option cost $10 while a three-month option cost $6. If the security is again at $100 when the three-month option expires, a second $6 option will have to be purchased, and the total cost of the rolling over strategy will be $12, or $2 more than the cost of the six-month option. If, on the other hand, the stock drops to $80 in three months, the price of the call option for the next three months will be far less, since the option is now $20 out of the money. The next option may cost only $1, leading the rolling over strategy to be less costly. The same will be true if the security rises substantially, to, say, $120. The first of the three-month options will then pay off $20 at expiration, and the second option, being in the money, will have a small premium above their intrinsic value, selling for, say, $21. The total cost of the rolling over strategy will then be $7, compared to the $10 cost for the straight six-month option.

This path dependence adds uncertainty to the cost of the strategy, and this may dampen its desirability. It also presents an opportunity to improve return potential by the selection of the options used each time the position is rolled over. For example, the investor can choose the time to roll over to maximize gain from mispricing between options, and can choose different exercise prices to alter the strategy if past performance warrants it.[13]

The use of listed options does have a number of particularly attractive features not shared by the other dynamic methods. First, the transaction costs and the timing of the transaction are known in advance. Second, like futures, the options are already levered, requiring less of a cash commitment than the straight security/bond strategy. And third, the option contract is protected against unforeseen jumps in the security price or changes in the security price volatility.

In a perfect market setting, the standard dynamic return structuring techniques using reallocations between the security and the riskless asset will replicate the desired option contract exactly. In practice, however, transaction costs, basis risk, capital constraints, and fundamental uncertainty about the return process and return volatility of the security make the proper choice of return structuring techniques more difficult.

We can, however, overcome some of the difficulties by making dynamic adjustments with the futures rather than the cash instrument, or by

constructing the return structuring by rolling over listed options. Furthermore, having a number of alternative routes to achieving the desired return structuring permits the exploitation of mispricing in the various instruments. For example, if listed options are considered to be underpriced, they may be preferred to the dynamic strategy on that basis alone. These methods are not always a practical alternative, however. Since listed options and futures may not exist on the underlying security itself, the problems of basis risk may be accentuated. These aspects of return-structuring techniques should be the subject of further empirical testing and comparison.

APPLICATIONS OF PERFORMANCE STRUCTURING

The flexibility of dynamic strategies allows the return distribution to be molded in a wide variety of ways. We can also apply such strategies beyond the creation of the portfolio insurance we have dealt with here to more complex and specialized applications ranging from hedging single-premium deferred annuities in the life insurance industry to asset-liability management for thrift institutions. In this section, I will present three examples intended to be more or less generic and to cover a range of possible strategies.

Cutting Losses: Protective Portfolio with Options

Protective puts are the best known and most widely used option-type strategy. There are a number of variations on portfolio insurance designed to adapt the basic concept of the protective put to particular markets and risks. For example, protective puts can be extended beyond the bond and equity markets to insure floor prices for commodities or foreign exchange, can be set to assure returns equal to a pension plan's actuarial interest rate assumptions, or can be modified to express the floor return as a fixed differential off the Treasury bill rate or other interest rates.[14]

Table 2 presents the results of creating the simple dynamic put option on an equity portfolio. The objective here is to achieve a floor return of 0% from the portfolio, while maximizing the share of any increase in the equity position. The strategy used here is repeated each year with an end-of-year horizon each year. That is, a new protective put with one year to expiration is constructed each January. Hence, we can look at the performance as a series of independent trials.

The table shows the annual results of this strategy for the years 1973-83. The first column of the table gives the returns to equity (the S&P 500 Composite). The next two columns relate to the performance of the synthetic option strategy. The first of these columns gives the annual return to the strategy, the second gives the capture of the strategy.

The capture is the return to the synthetic option

TABLE 2

PROTECTIVE PUT STRATEGY SIMULATION
COMPARISON OF ANNUAL RETURNS

		Dynamic Strategy			
Year	Equity	With Floor Exercise Price	Capture	With Variable Exercise Price	Capture
1973	−14.9%	−0.52%	Floor	−0.99%	Floor
1974	−25.2	−0.71	Floor	−0.99	Floor
1975	34.1	20.68	61%	31.20	91%
1976	23.0	14.99	65	22.42	98
1977	−7.2	−0.38	Floor	−1.02	Floor
1978	6.5	4.55	70	0.35	5
1979	18.5	16.62	90	18.48	100
1980	33.4	26.89	81	30.00	90
1981	−5.6	−0.38	Floor	−1.13	Floor
1982	20.8	11.30	54	1.96	9
1983	22.2	18.94	85	22.17	100

Cumulative Returns for 11 Years Compounded:

7.80%	9.76%	10.40%

- 52-week periods were used instead of exact calendar years.
- EQUITY: S&P 500 Stock Index adjusted for dividends
- Capture is the dynamic strategy return as a percent of the return to the equity portfolio when the equity portfolio return exceeds the 0% floor.
- Includes transactions costs of $25 per contract round trip.
- Assets are reallocated once every week.

strategy as a percent of the equity portfolio. Since replicating an option position involves a gradual shift into equity as the equity increases in value, only part of the equity performance will be shared by the option position. The incomplete capture is a direct implication of option price behavior; option prices move less than one-to-one with changes in the price of the underlying asset. The incomplete capture of potential gains can be thought of as a cost of pursuing the option strategy. This serves to emphasize that option-related strategies have tradeoffs consistent with market efficiency. Changes in return structure are met with commensurate costs. The cost for the repeated one-year protective put positions used in this example is greater than a single longer-term put option would be. The capture can be increased by taking a longer investment horizon in the performance structure.

It is evident from Table 2 that the portfolio performed as expected in providing the 0% floor return. In the four years that the equity market saw negative returns, the return to the structured portfolio was 0%. In the years of positive return, the structured portfolio shared to varying degrees in that return. In most cases, the protective put returned over 75% of the return to the equity portfolio. The capture was higher in years of higher equity return and was also higher the longer the equity sustained a high rate of return. This is an attractive and natural feature of option prices. The proportion of funds in equity is the average of proportions held over the annual period. In the simulation, these proportions were readjusted weekly.[15]

How much would it be worth to be able to receive a perfect stock-bond market timing service, a service that could always pick when holding stocks would do better than holding bonds? It is possible to create and price such a service through the simple option strategy of buying an index call option and placing the remainder of the portfolio in bonds.

To see this, select the call option to have an exercise price that equals the return possible through a bond investment. Then, if the option pays off, it will give a return equal to the stock market return less the bond price, while if the option expires worthless, the overall portfolio return will still equal the bond return. The net effect of this strategy will be to give a return equal to the equity or the bond, whichever is greater. This is the return that would be generated by following the advice of a perfect market timer. The cost of this strategy is the cost of the call option on the market.[16]

As this perfect market-timing example illustrates, options can perform a strategic as well as defensive role in portfolio management. The proper dynamic allocation between equities and bonds will replicate a call option on the market and provide a return equal to the greater of the two. Added onto an actively managed stock portfolio, such an allocation strategy can accentuate gains by increasing market participation during upswings while moving out of the market during downturns.[17] Table 3 shows the annual results of pursuing this strategy over the 1973-1983 period.

The gradual adjustments that constitute the dynamic technique lead the structured market-timing strategy to capture only a portion of the return of the better performing asset. As we discussed in the last example, this is a result of the core feature of option returns of reacting less than one-to-one with price changes in the underlying security.

In two instances, however, the option return actually is lower than either the bond or equity return. In 1976 the structured return was 16.6%, compared to 18.4% for bonds and 23% for equity; in 1981 it was −10.6%, compared to −1% for bonds and −5.6% for equity. This failure in the strategy is the result of employing only weekly adjustments in the historical simulation. While generally adjustments in the proportions of security holdings need to be made only infrequently, adjustments in the times of dramatic price movements may need to be made more than once a week to replicate the option position. These two years were marked by such price movements, and the inability of the simulation to make immediate allocation changes led to the inferior performance. This serves to emphasize the need for good monitor-

TABLE 3

MARKET TIMING STRATEGY SIMULATION
COMPARISON OF ANNUAL TOTAL RETURNS

Year	Bond	Equity	Dynamic Strategy	Capture
1973	0.83%	− 14.86%	− 5.96%	57%
1974	2.77	− 25.25	− 6.23	68
1975	6.96	34.15	26.34	71
1976	18.39	22.07	17.78	Floor
1977	− 0.64	− 7.20	− 4.44	42
1978	− 1.19	6.48	1.64	37
1979	− 1.58	18.48	14.21	79
1980	− 2.95	33.38	21.68	68
1981	− 0.98	− 5.58	− 7.74	Floor
1982	44.99	20.79	34.93	58
1983	1.03	22.17	16.32	75

Cumulative Returns for 11 Years Compounded:

5.41%	7.80%	8.94%

- 52-week periods were used instead of exact calendar years.
- For purposes of this study, the asset classes are defined as follows:
  BOND: 20-year Treasury Bonds
  EQUITY: S&P 500 Stock Index adjusted for dividends
- Capture is the absolute difference of the dynamic strategy return and the lower of the bond or equity return, divided by the absolute difference of the bond and equity return.
- Includes transactions costs of $25 per contract round trip.
- Assets are reallocated once every week.

ing and execution facilities in following dynamic strategies.

This market-timing strategy can be adapted to other portfolio management settings. For example, it can be used to accentuate the performance of a number of managers by creating an option that will lead to a return equal to the largest of the managers' returns. The same method could be used to focus in on the best of a number of investment themes. A manager who, for example, is interested in both energy-intensive industries and recreation-related industries could create options on each area to increase the leverage of the better performing area.

Combined Strategies: Extensions to Multiple Risky Assets

Having presented examples both for cutting losses through portfolio insurance and for accentuating gains through call option positions, the next logical step is to combine the two.[18] The resulting strategy will give the greater of the bond or equity return with a floor return equal to the short-term rate.

Table 4 presents the result of combining the two previous strategies in this way. Over the eleven-year period from 1973 to 1983, all three assets in the strategy came into use at some point. From 1973 to 1980, returns shifted between the floor of 0% and some capture of the equity rate. The capture was almost 100% in 1976 and 1979, and roughly two-thirds in 1975 and 1979. In 1982 the bond market had twice the return of equity and over three times the return

of cash, and the dynamic strategy shifted toward bonds. The stock-bond option in this strategy, which represents the market-timing aspect of the strategy, was sensitive enough to capture 81% of this return.

This strategy is easily extended to other risk-

TABLE 4

MULTIPLE RISKY ASSET STRATEGY SIMULATION
COMPARISON OF ANNUAL TOTAL RETURNS

Year	Asset Class		Dynamic Strategy	
	Bond	Equity	Floor Exercise Price	Capture
1973	0.83%	− 14.86%	0.44%	53%
1974	2.77	− 25.25	0.11	4
1975	6.96	34.15	16.39	48
1976	18.39	22.97	11.67	51
1977	− 0.64	− 7.20	0.01	Floor
1978	− 1.19	6.48	3.84	59
1979	− 1.58	18.48	13.20	71
1980	− 2.95	33.38	16.59	50
1981	− 0.98	− 5.58	− 0.04	Floor
1982	44.99	20.79	24.38	54
1983	1.03	22.17	13.74	62

Cumulative Returns for 11 Years Compounded:

5.41%	7.80%	8.81%

- 52-week periods were used instead of exact calendar years.
- For purposes of this study, the asset classes are defined as follows:
  BOND: 20-year Treasury Bonds
  EQUITY: S&P 500 Stock Index adjusted for dividends
- Capture is the dynamic strategy return as a percent of the return to the equity portfolio when the equity portfolio return exceeds the 0% floor.
- Includes transactions costs of $25 per contract round trip.
- Assets are reallocated once every week.

return considerations, and to more than two risky assets. One way to look at the combined strategy is as a call option on the best performing of the risky assets with a residual position in cash. The call option gives the leverage on the upside while giving out protection on the downside. Furthermore, the call option can be selected before the fact to act like a call option only on the asset that turns out to be the best performer. If one of the areas does well, the options will pay off for that area; if they all do poorly and the option expires out of the money, the cash position will still guarantee a floor return.

THE IMPLICATIONS OF PERFORMANCE STRUCTURING FOR PORTFOLIO EVALUATION

Care must be taken in evaluating portfolios with return distributions altered by option strategies. Methods of performance evaluation that depend on mean and variance measures of returns — as all of the common methods do — cannot be applied to portfolios resulting from dynamic strategies for the simple reason that those portfolios depend on more than mean and variance.[19] These strategies mold the return distributions, bringing the higher moments, such as skewness and kurtosis, into play.

For example, the protective put leads to a truncation of the left tail of the portfolio return distribution and a leftward shift of the distribution. The truncation reflects the protection from downside loss, and the shift reflects the cost of the insurance. Figure 6 shows the distribution of the underlying portfolio, with the familiar normal distribution and the distribution that

FIGURE 6

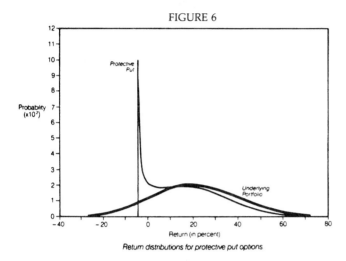

Return distributions for protective put options.

results when a put option is purchased on that portfolio.

In contrast to this strategy, consider the distributional effect of writing a covered-call option on the same underlying portfolio. The covered call has the opposite effect of the put option. It truncates the right tail of the distribution while shifting the distribution to the right. The truncation is the result of selling off the upward potential to the call buyer, and the shift reflects the premium received from that sale. Figure 7 compares the distribution of covered-call writing with that of the underlying portfolio.

Even a cursory reference to Figures 6 and 7 demonstrates that distributions resulting from option strategies cannot be understood by looking at the

FIGURE 7

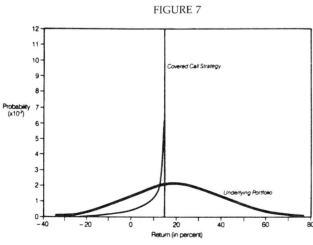

Return distribution for writing covered call options.

mean and variance alone. Indeed, in this particular case, an analysis based solely on expected return and variance of return will make call writing appear superior to put buying. The two strategies have much the same effect on expected return. The expected return drops from 18% for the underlying stock portfolio to 13.6% for the portfolio fully covered by a call option, and to 14.5% for the portfolio fully covered by the protective put. But the standard deviation of returns drops from 20% for the underlying portfolio to only 16.7% for the put strategy, while it is cut to 5.8% for the covered call strategy. The put strategy has a standard deviation that is nearly three times higher than for call writing. If standard deviation or variance is used as a proxy for risk, writing a covered call will be preferred to buying a protective put.[20]

Variance is not a suitable proxy for risk, however, since the option strategies reduce risk *asymmetrically*. The call truncates the right-hand side of the distribution and thereby reduces the desirable upside variance. The put, on the other hand, reduces the variance on the undesirable left-hand portion of the return distribution. It is natural, then, for a reduction in variance to be compensated differently for the two strategies.

This example illustrates the shortcomings of evaluation methods that rely on summary statistics such as mean and variance in dealing with option-related strategies. By trading off between the mean and the higher moments of the distribution, many unusual mean-variance relationships are possible.

For example, it is possible to construct a covered call strategy with both a higher expected return *and* a lower variance than the underlying portfolio. Or, by using far-out-of-the-money call options, it is possible to construct a portfolio insurance strategy that yields the same return floor as a protective put but with a higher expected return. (This strategy will give a high probability of achieving only the floor return and a small chance of receiving a very high return.) Such a strategy may not, in fact, lead to a desirable return structure. Strictly on a mean-variance basis, however, it certainly appears superior to the conventional insurance strategy of using a protective put.[21]

These two examples show the potential for misleading statements and inaccurate evaluations of alternative strategies. The incomplete state of performance evaluation may foster conflict between portfolio and management objectives. The strategies that lead to good measures of management success may not be those which best address the portfolio objectives. Given techniques that extend performance structuring beyond the two-dimensional plane of mean and variance, it is natural to expect that evaluation methods for these techniques must also break out of the mean-variance framework. We need a new set of performance techniques for the quantitative evaluation of portfolios engaged in these strategies.

Misinterpretations are also likely in the qualitative review of the performance of dynamically structured portfolios. For example, the portfolio insurance strategy requires selling off the security as the price declines and gradually buying it back as the price rises. Viewed outside the context of dynamic management, such a pattern of trading does not lead to favorable conclusions as to the manager's trading skills. Furthermore, most managers are evaluated by rankings based on realized return performance rather than on meeting distributional objectives. In these rankings, a manager's successful pursuit of a strategy for meeting a specified return objective may be overshadowed if a drop in realized return was a necessary cost of meeting that objective.[22] As with the misinterpretations inherent in applying the quantitative evaluation methods, the possibility of the manager pursuing a dynamic strategy may convey a mistaken impression that could keep these strategies from being correctly selected or effectively implemented.

CONCLUSION

The opportunities that option strategies present for molding the return distributions to meet investment objectives apply to a wide number of portfolio management and risk control problems. In their most general form, option strategies allow the manager to expand the set of insurable contingencies far beyond those available with static hedging methods. The use of dynamic hedging strategies to create the desired option-type payoffs allows returns to be structured even further than is possible with listed options; risks can be defined according to the specific asset/liability mix and risk preferences of management. The tools of option theory provide the technology for expanding the dimensions of risk management to meet the specialized demands of business.

We can summarize the technology of option theory as a payoff processor which reshapes return distributions.

The set of return distributions for the assets enter the processor, where the dynamic hedging technology remolds them to specification. The payoffs exit the processor with distributions of the desired shape.

Naturally, the benefits of dynamic return structuring are not gained without a cost. The protection of portfolio insurance is not free. Its cost, explicit in the price of a put option, is implicit in the dynamic strategy for replicating a put option, since, as we have seen, such a strategy leads only to partial participation in price increases. To state without qualification that a protective put strategy, or any other dynamic strategy, is superior to holding the uninsured portfolio

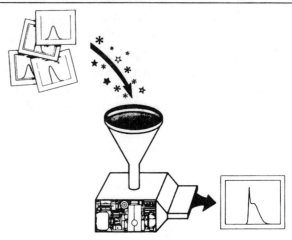

FIGURE 8
The Payoff Processor
Molding Returns to Meet Risk Management Objectives

ignores the risk-return tradeoffs that form the basis of asset pricing. While it is no doubt true that ex post the insured strategy will do better over some particular time period, ex ante the insurance will impose a cost. The same point applies to other strategies as well.[23]

The major issue we have addressed in this paper is how to minimize the cost of performance structuring, that is, how to find the dynamic strategy that best fulfills a given objective while still preserving the other features of the portfolio distribution. The least-cost dynamic strategy for meeting the objective of portfolio insurance will be the strategy which best replicates a put option. This conclusion flows over into a wide range of other portfolio objectives. In general, the least-cost means of return structuring can be represented through the appropriate set of put and call options on the underlying asset. This leads the goal of minimizing costs one step further, to finding the dynamic strategy which best replicates the required set of put and call options.

We have dealt with this and with the related issue of finding the most effective strategy, the strategy that gives the greatest chance of meeting the investment objectives under all possible market scenarios. We have addressed only indirectly a second vital issue of performance structuring: finding the strategy that meets the needs and objectives of the investor. Poorly written insurance policies can be formed just as easily with dynamic strategies as with more conventional insurance techniques. A strategy must not only meet its objectives, and do so at the least cost; the objectives themselves must also be intelligently conceived.

Like creating policies in insurance or contracts in law, creating the proper performance structure in finance is possible only when the nature of the risks and the objectives of the client are known. This requires more than an understanding of the tools of performance structuring. It requires a knowledge of the business being analyzed. The investment needs of the pension fund differ in scope and complexity from those of the insurance company, which in turn differ from those of the thrift institution. This is an area that is part art and part science, where judgment and experience are of key importance.

[1] The desirability of this type of insured portfolio is discussed in Leland, and in Brennan and Solanki. Skewness preference, i.e. a preference for a return distribution characterized by a degree of skewness as well as mean and variance, is discussed by Kraus and Litzenberger.

[2] See Ross, Breeden and Litzenberger, and Arditti and John.

[3] These characteristics, and a readable presentation of the nature of option pricing, can be found in Bookstaber. A more rigorous and detailed treatment can be found in Rubinstein and Cox.

[4] The creation of these binary payoffs, called primitive securities, through the use of option positions is covered in Breeden and Litzenberger (1978).

[5] The procedure for replicating an option through a dynamically adjusted position in the underlying security and risk-free asset is implied in the original work on option pricing by Black and Scholes (1973) and by Merton (1973). This procedure is discussed in simpler terms in Rubinstein and Leland, and in Chapter 4 of Bookstaber. The operaional considerations of these techniques are discussed in Platt and Latainer (1983a, 1983b).

[6] The exact functional form these factors take on depends on the assumptions of the model being used, particularly the distributional assumptions. If stock prices are assumed to be described by a lognormal distribution, the well-known Black-Scholes model will be appropriate. The binomial model of Cox, Ross, and Rubinstein will be an approximation for this same distribution. Merton has developed a model for a jump-diffusion process, a process that allows for discrete jumps in the security price. Cox has a model that allows the volatility of the security price to vary as a function of the security price. These models differ from the Black-Scholes model in terms of the functional form for a and b.

[7] The portfolio for replicating a put option is directly related to the replicating portfolio for a call option. This relationship can be expressed by the put-call parity formula presented in the first section of this paper:

$$C = (S - E) + E (r/(1 + r)) + P,$$

or

$$C = S - E(1/(1 + r)) + P.$$

As this formula shows, a call option can be created by holding the security, S, borrowing $E(1/(1 + r))$, and thus repaying E at expiration, and holding a put option. This creates a protective put on a portfolio that is similar to holding a call option on the portfolio. In fact, the only difference between the two is that a call option is levered through borrowing while the protective put position is not.

[8] For example, see Leibowitz and Weinberger.

[9] In particular, if there are sudden jumps in the underlying security while the Black-Scholes model is being used, the position will be subject to unexpected losses. The strategy will be unsuccessful in replicating an option position.

[10] This happens because an option on a portfolio of securities will not behave in the same way as a portfolio of options on each of the individual securities. The portfolio of options will be more expensive than the option on the portfolio. This is discussed in Merton (1973).

[11] The role of the riskless asset in creating a synthetic option is similar to its role in creating a synthetic forward contract for foreign exchange. The textbook method for creating a synthetic forward contract involves borrowing in one currency and converting it in the spot market into a second currency where the funds are then loaned out at the risk-free rate until the maturity of the contract. The result of these transactions is an obligation to deliver the first currency (to pay off the loan) and to receive the second currency. In practice, the funds need not actually be borrowed nor do they need to be loaned out as a riskless asset in the second currency. For example, the firm's own funds could be converted and the converted funds could be used for working capital needs. The end result of creating a forward contract will still be met, although the contract would be entangled with other transactions, and it would be more difficult to distinguish the nature of the forward contract. However, it is clear that creating the forward contract in this fashion might be more useful to the firm.

[12] If the exercise price of the synthetic option could not be matched by the listed options, it could still be constructed using the rolling over of listed options by following the proper hedge ratio. For example, if the hedge ratio or delta of the listed option is .5 while the hedge ratio of the desired synthetic option is .75, then .75/.5 = 1.5 of the listed option would be held for each of the synthetic options to be constructed.

[13] This problem of path dependence has occasionally been overstated. While path dependence does lead to uncertainty, it need not be an overriding concern. In practice, any strategy, including the straight dynamic approach, will face uncertainty, because the market and security price movement will not fit the assumptions of any model precisely. The key issue is whether the risk imposed by this uncertainty, and the cost of employing the strategies, is large in proportion to the benefit derived from being able to form a return that comes closer to meeting the portfolio objectives. Furthermore, rolling over positions can enhance returns if the investor has expertise in execution.

[14] Applications can be found in Platt and Latainer (1983a, 1984b, 1985), Tilley and Jacob, and Tilley (1984a).

[15] In practice, it is unlikely that weekly adjustments will actually be necessary. Depending on market conditions, in particular the degree of price movement, as few as four adjustments a year may be sufficient.

[16] The relationship between market timing and option valuation was first pointed out by Merton (1981). As put-call parity suggests, this relationship can also be looked at through a put option strategy. The market timing service can be created with a put option by holding the equity and buying a put option with an exercise price equal to the bond return.

[17] A variation of this strategy can be used to form a variable beta portfolio, a portfolio with a high beta, and thus high leverage, in strong markets, and with a low beta, and thus little reaction to the market, when the market declines. The variable beta strategy is presented in Chapter 6 of Bookstaber and Clarke (1983).

[18] Strategy is presented in Tilley and Latainer (1985). A theoretical discussion of this concept is presented by Stulz

(1982), and by Stapleton and Subrahamanyam (1984).

[19] Further discussion of the problems addressed in this section is provided in Bookstaber and Clarke (1984).

[20] This bias will appear for the Sharpe measure (which measures performance as the difference between the portfolio return and the risk-free rate, divided by the standard deviation of portfolio returns), the Treynor index (which measures performance as the difference between the portfolio return and the risk-free rate, divided by the portfolio beta), and the Jensen measure (which measures performance by the "alpha" of the security market line regression, i.e. by the vertical distance between the portfolio return and the capital market line).

[21] For this reason, care must be taken in using the expected return as the sole criterion for selecting the best portfolio insurance strategy. The protective put option may be the least-cost strategy in that it provides the desired protection for the lowest drop in expected return *while preserving the features of the underlying security return distribution*. But it will not be the least-cost strategy if no constraints are placed on alteration of the security return structure above the point of protection. The same is true of other option strategies. Unless the return structure is specified over the entire range of possible outcomes, there will be some strategies that fulfill the stated objectives at an apparently low cost but do so only by making unfavorable tradeoffs in other regions of the return distribution.

[22] The potential conflict of the manager between meeting the sponsor's objectives and maximizing relative performance suggests that the sponsor of the investment program might be better suited to the performance structuring role. We have discussed above how futures can facilitate this.

Morgan Stanley's approaches to product design take these differences into account at the outset. For example, strategies in the insurance area include hedging single-premium deferred annuities and universal life policies. For savings and loans, these techniques have been applied to asset-liability management and cash management. Other applications range from protecting investments in foreign currencies from adverse currency price movements to hedging the credit risk of high-yield bond portfolios.

[23] For other patterns of return structuring, the strategy may initially lead to positive inflows rather than costs as, for example, does the writing of covered call options. But in this case the cost balancing the initial inflow will be a reduction in the potential return from the later price movements.

REFERENCES

1. Arditti, F., and John, K. "Spanning the State Space with Options." *Journal of Financial and Quantitative Analysis*, 15 (March 1980), pp. 1-9.

2. Arditti, F., and Levy, H. "Portfolio Efficiency Analysis in Three Moments: The Multiperiod Case." *Journal of Finance*, 30 (June 1975), pp. 797-809.

3. Black, F., and Scholes, M. "The Pricing of Options and Corporate Liabilities." *Journal of Political Economy*, 81 (May 1973), pp. 637-654.

4. Bookstaber, R. *Option Pricing and Strategies in Investing*. Reading, Mass.: Addison-Wesley, 1981.

5. Bookstaber, R., and Clarke, R. "Options can alter portfolio return distributions." *Journal of Portfolio Management*, 7 (Spring 1981a), pp. 63-70.

6. ——. "An Algorithm to Calculate the Return Distribution of Portfolios with Option Positions." *Management Science*, April 1981b.

7. ——. *Option Strategies for Institutional Investor Management*. Reading, Mass.: Addison-Wesley, 1983.

8. ——. "Option Portfolio Strategies: Measurement and Evaluation." *Journal of Business*, 57 (October 1984), pp. 469-492.

9. ——. "Problems in Evaluating the Performance of Portfolios with Options." *Financial Analysts Journal*, 41 (January/February, 1985), pp. 48-62.

10. Breeden, D., and Litzenberger, R. "Prices of State-Contingent Claims Implicit in Option Prices." *Journal of Business*, 52 (October 1978), pp. 621-651.

11. Brennan, M., and Solanki, R. "Optimal Portfolio Insurance." *Journal of Financial and Quantitative Analysis*, 16 (September 1981), pp. 279-300.

12. Cox, J., and Ross, S. "The Valuation of Options for Alternative Stochastic Processes." *Journal of Financial Economics*, 3 (March 1976), pp. 145-166.

13. Kraus, A., and Litzenberger, R. "Skewness Preference and the Valuation of Risky Assets." *Journal of Finance*, 31 (September 1976), pp. 1085-1100.

14. Leland, H. "Who Should Buy Portfolio Insurance?" *Journal of Finance*, 35 (May 1980), pp. 581-594.

15. Leibowitz, M., and Weinberger, A. "Contingent Immunization, Part I: Risk Control Procedures." *Financial Analysts Journal*, 38 (November/December 1982), pp. 17-31.

16. Merton, R. "Theory of Rational Option Pricing." *Bell Journal of Economics and Management Science*, 4 (Spring 1973), pp. 141-183.

17. ——. "Option Pricing when Underlying Stock Returns are Discontinuous." *Journal of Financial Economics*, 3 (March 1976), pp. 125-144.

18. ——. "On Market Timing and Investment Performance. I. An Equilibrium Theory of Value for Market Forecasts." *Journal of Business*, 54 (July 1981), pp. 363-406.

19. Merton, R., Scholes, M., and Gladstein, M. "The Returns and Risk of Alternative Call Option Portfolio Investment Strategies." *Journal of Business*, 51 (April 1978), pp. 183-242.

20. ——. "The Returns and Risks of Put-option Portfolio Investment Strategies." *Journal of Business*, 55 (January 1982), pp. 61-67.

21. Platt, R., and Latainer, G. "Risk-return Tradeoffs of Contingent Insurance Strategies for Active Bond Portfolios." *Financial Analysts Journal*, 40 (May/June 1984), pp. 34-39.

22. ——. *Replicating Option Strategies for Portfolio Risk Control*. New York: Morgan Stanley Fixed Income Research, 1983a.

23. ——. *Replicating Option Strategies — Part II: Applications of Portfolio Insurance*. New York: Morgan Stanley Fixed Income Research, 1983b.

24. ——. "The Use of Synthetic Option Strategies in Fixed Income Portfolios." In F. Fabozzi, editor, *Winning the Interest Rate Game*, Chicago: Probus Publishing, 1985.

25. Ross, S. "Options and Efficiency." *Quarterly Journal of Economics*, 90 (February 1976), pp. 75-89.

26. Rubinstein, M., and Leland, H. "Replicating Options with Positions in Stock and Cash." *Financial Analysts Journal*, 37 (July 1981), pp. 63-72.

27. Rubinstein, M., and Cox, J. *Option Markets*. Englewood Cliffs, N.J.: Prentice-Hall, forthcoming.

28. Stapleton, R. C., and Subrahamanyan, M. G. "The Valuation of Multivariate Contingent Claims in Discrete Time Models." *Journal of Finance*, 39 (March 1984), pp. 207-228.

29. Stulz, R. M. "Options on the Minimum or the Maximum of Two Risky Assets." *Journal of Financial Economics*, 10 (July 1982), pp. 161-185.

30. Tilley, J. and Jacob, D. *Asset/Liability Management for Insurance Companies*. New York: Morgan Stanley Fixed Income Research, 1983.

31. Tilley, J. *Hedging Interest Rate Risk for Interest Sensitive Products*. New York: Morgan Stanley Fixed Income Research, 1984a.

32. Tilley, J. and Latainer, G. "A Synthetic Framework for Asset Allocation." *Financial Analysts Journal*, forthcoming.

Futures and alternative hedge ratio methodologies

You must segment the sources of interest rate risk.

Alden L. Toevs and David P. Jacob

This paper compares the major estimation techniques for calculating hedge ratios when the hedging vehicle is a fixed-income futures contract and the hedging objective is to minimize the variance of a target account for a fixed-income portfolio. We find that the sophisticated hedging techniques come from a common theoretical base, but they differ from one another in their estimates of the covariance between the hedging and target instruments and the variance of the hedging instruments. Their effectiveness often exceeds more naive approaches.

In practical applications, these sophisticated techniques normally do not produce widely different returns, but there are differences in computational costs among the sophisticated techniques. Based upon overall lower computational cost, ability to handle extreme or unique pricing relationships, and the possibility of more carefully modeling the basis, the conclusion of the paper is that a hedge ratio computed using an instantaneous price sensitivity (duration) measure bests regression-based hedging techniques.

The first section classifies hedge types by the target account of concern. We devote particular emphasis in the remainder of the paper to one of four types of hedges; this particular approach hedges the market price of a portfolio of fixed-income securities. This selection also maximizes the number of available hedging methodologies. The second section discusses the common theoretical base of the instantaneous price sensitivity hedge and two regression-based hedge ratio techniques. Next, we discuss some of the empirical realities associated with these theoretical bedfellows. Finally, we analyze the successes of the hedging techniques using data on several representative bonds for the period from mid-1982 to 1984. Our conclusions follow.

CLASSIFICATION OF HEDGE TYPES

Many analysts have wrestled with the problem of producing an all encompassing definition of hedging. We forego this problem by defining a hedge to be any activity that minimizes the variance of return. Risk minimizing hedges can be constructed for currently held or anticipated positions, and the hedge may be in place for a known or uncertain period of time. Furthermore, hedges may be applied to asset or liability positions. Given all these possibilities, it helps to categorize hedge types. Figure (1) provides such taxonomy for asset hedges; liability hedges are similarly classified.

The Inventory Hedge (Weak Form Cash Hedge) minimizes the price (market value) variance of an existing asset portfolio that is to be held indefinitely. The hedge placed on a bond dealer's inventory is an example of this type of hedge. As indicated in Figure (1), an inventory hedge uses a short position

ALDEN L. TOEVS is Vice President at Morgan Stanley & Co. in New York (NY 10020). DAVID P. JACOB is Research Manager at the same institution.

FIGURE 1

Hedge Classifications

	Time Uncertain	Time Certain
Currently Held Cash Position	**Weak Form Cash Hedge** (Inventory Hedge) Hedge Goal: Preserve capital on a daily basis. Hedge Strategy: Short the nearest-to-deliver futures contract.	**Strong Form Cash Hedge** (Immunization) Hedge Goal: Track daily the zero coupon bond due at the end of investment horizon. Hedge Strategy: Go long or short nearest-to-delivery futures contract.
Anticipated Cash Position	**Weak Form** (Anticipatory Hedge) Hedge Goal: Lock in currently available return or price at the uncertain cash inflow date. Hedge Strategy: Buy futures contract that expires nearest to the expected cash inflow date.	**Strong Form** (Anticipatory Hedge) Hedge Goal: Lock in currently available return or price at known cash inflow date. Hedge Strategy: Buy futures contract that expires nearest to the known cash inflow date.

in a futures contract. When interest rates rise, the cash position falls in value, but a short position has offsetting price variation. The futures contract or contracts selected should have the highest possible covariance in prices with the inventory. Usually, the nearest to delivery futures contracts on securities similar to those in inventory maximize this price covariance.

With a Strong Form Cash Hedge, the investor knows the time the portfolio will be held. The hedging goal is to minimize the variance in the expected total return on the portfolio for a given investment period. To immunize portfolio returns, the investor must create a cash and futures portfolio that has the same interest rate sensitivity as a zero coupon (pure discount) bond with an initial maturity equal to the investment period. As the "bogey" zero coupon matures, its interest rate sensitivity will decline more rapidly than the portfolio of cash and futures instruments. This tendency of the portfolio to become relatively too interest rate sensitive must be controlled by periodic rebalancing transactions.

Strong Form Anticipatory Hedges apply whenever a known amount of cash will be received at a certain future date and the portfolio manager wishes to minimize the variance of the acquisition prices of the cash securities. For example, suppose that the cash will be received on December 3, 1986 and the desire is to use this cash to purchase ninety-day Treasury bills. The forward price of such a bill is, say, $97.05. Based on this price, these bills have a bond equivalent yield of 12.19% from their delivery to maturity.[1] The hedging position chosen is the one that most closely realizes this market-forecasted price and yield. This hedge appears to require the acquisition of future delivery rights to as many dollars of bills as the anticipated cash inflow. On the other hand, margin calls on the long futures position must be financed, which means that the appropriate hedge ratio is not an exact dollar match. An added complication arises if the futures contract offers a deliverable bond other than that desired by the future investor.

In the Weak Form Anticipatory Hedge, the goal is to minimize the variance in an acquisition price (a rate of return for a specified holding period) on asset flows to be received at an unknown date. Like the Strong Form Anticipatory Hedge, this hedge requires the purchase of futures contracts with an interest rate sensitivity equal to that of the security to be purchased. The uncertain timing of the cash receipt reduces the effectiveness of this type of anticipatory hedge. Nevertheless the investor can use futures to narrow the range of possible outcomes.

The four-way classification in Figure (1) is incomplete. For example, an anticipatory hedge may be attempted when the cash to be received and the inflow date are both known with certainty, but the holding period for the investment is not. Alternatively, the cash inflow date and the holding period may be known with certainty but the amount of cash to be received may be uncertain. We will not dwell here on these complications. To do so obscures the goal of developing an analytical foundation for the construction of variance minimizing hedge ratios for the more frequently encountered hedges.

THE THEORY OF MINIMUM VARIANCE HEDGE RATIOS

With a general classification of hedges behind us, we now turn to the determination of "optimal" hedge ratios. As noted above, we view the hedging goal to be the minimization of the variance of either the price or total return of existing or anticipated cash positions. Since the minimum variance hedge ratios for any one hedge classification have substantial overlaps with other hedges, we will not discuss each hedge type in detail. We have chosen to critique the methods proposed for constructing minimum variance Weak Form Cash Hedges.[2] This type of hedge is instructive, because the others are special cases of it and because this one has had more proposed hedge ratio methodologies than the others.

We illustrate hedge ratio estimation techniques with a simple historical situation. On June 24, 1982,

1. Footnotes appear at the end of the article.

a trader had a $10 million face value position (10,000 bonds) in the U.S. Treasury bond maturing on November 15, 2010. This bond pays a 12.75% coupon rate and was priced on June 24, 1982 at 90.125, which gives a market value of $9.0125 million. The trader selected the T-bond futures contract for delivery in September 1982 as the hedging instrument. This contract traded at 59.3125 on June 24, 1982. The problem is to determine the number of futures contracts to sell in order to minimize the price variation of the cash position. Five methods with two additional variations have been offered for estimating the hedge ratio in this instance. The major techniques are: dollar value matches, conversion factors, regression analyses using price changes, regression analyses using price levels, and an approach based upon an instantaneous price sensitivity calculation. The following discusses the application of each technique to the situation existing on June 24, 1982.

Dollar Value Matches

A simple hedging strategy computes the hedge ratio using a dollar-valued exposure in futures contracts equal to the cash inventory market value. Since the trader was long $9.0125 million in cash securities on June 24, 1982, the short position selected with this method also was priced at $9.0125 million. Given a futures price of 59.3125, this requirement translates into a hedge ratio of 1.52.[3] In general, this hedge ratio methodology works well only when the interest rate characteristics of the cash bond closely match those of the futures market deliverable bond.

Conversion Factor Method

The conversion factor method extends the dollar value match when the futures exchange permits the short position holder to deliver several security grades to fulfill the futures contract. The conversion factor corrects the invoice amount covering the required par delivery of bonds for the difference between the coupon of the security being delivered and that of the standard coupon specified by the contract. For example, Treasury bond and GNMA futures contracts allow many coupon/maturity combinations to be delivered.

The 12.75% T-bond maturing on November 15, 2010 has a conversion factor of 1.50 on June 24, 1982. This value indicates that the hedger should sell 1.50 times the number of futures contract "bonds" as held in inventory. Essentially, the conversion factor method presumes that if the cash bond could be delivered tomorrow, the hedge position would have as many dollars in short contracts as the cash position has in long contracts to "deliver." The accuracy of the

conversion factor method increases when the delivery date nears and when the interest rate sensitivity of the cash bond approaches the interest rate sensitivity of the cheapest-to-deliver bond.

The above hedging techniques have convenience as their strong point. Neither method properly accounts for probable differences in the interest rate sensitivities of cash securities and futures contracts. Consequently, while there are circumstances when these naive approaches produce effective hedges, sophisticated hedging techniques more often provide better results. We will now examine these alternative techniques.

The following expression represents the change in value of a portfolio consisting of a cash bond and a short position of N futures contracts:

$$\Delta V = \Delta P_c - (N \times \Delta P_f) \tag{1}$$

where ΔV, ΔP_c, and ΔP_f are the changes in the value of the portfolio, the cash bond, and the futures contract, respectively. If we define the optimal hedge ratio as the one that minimizes the variance of changes in portfolio value, it can be shown that

$$N^* = \text{covariance } (\Delta P_f \text{ with } \Delta P_c)/\text{variance } (\Delta P_f), \tag{2}$$

where N^* is the optimal number of futures contracts to short. The mathematical proof is given in the Appendix.

The three remaining hedging methodologies considered in this paper are derived from Equation (2). Each in its own way accounts for differential interest rate sensitivities in cash and futures contracts. The methods differ only in how they use the available information to determine the covariance and variance terms in Equation (2).

Regressions of Price Changes

This estimation methodology has its roots in early academic work on commodity hedging. A representative series of daily changes in price for a cash bond and a closely associated futures contract are graphed in Figure (2). Regression analysis is applied to this scatter of points to find the best-fitting straight line. The equation used in the regression is:

$$\Delta P_c = a + b \, \Delta P_f + \text{error.} \tag{3}$$

The presumption in Equation (3) is that the changes in the cash and futures prices are linearly related to one another, subject also to random errors (basis risk). The estimated slope of the regression line, "b" in Equation (3), gives the change in the value of the cash price per dollar move in the futures price. That is, it represents the market dollar amount of the futures contract to short per market dollar amount of inventory.

Ederington (1979) showed that the value of "b" equals the minimum variance hedge ratio provided that: (1) The futures contract selected for the regression has the highest possible correlation with the cash security; (2) ΔP_c and ΔP_f are related in a linear fashion; and (3) the historical data used in the regression are consistent with the current variance and covariance characteristics needed for use in Equation (3). This proof is discussed in the Appendix. Any violation of these assumptions results in random or systematic basis risk. Representative data series have to be long enough to reflect true variance and covariance relationships, but they can also be too long if the relationship between the cash and futures prices changes through time.

FIGURE 2

Daily Change in Prices
U.S. Treasury 12.75's of 2010
vs.
Nearby T-Bond Futures Contract

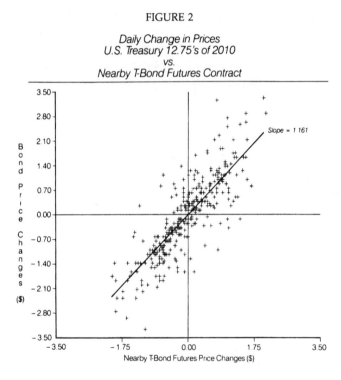

The data scatter in Figure (2) comes from daily price changes for the 240 trading days prior to 6/24/82 on the cash bond and the successively nearest-to-delivery T-bond futures contracts. The slope of the best fitting regression line is 1.16 and means that the hedger of the 12.75's of 11/15/2010 should short $1.16 in futures value per dollar of inventory.

Regressions of Price Levels

In a different regression approach, recently proposed, the regression fits a straight line to historical data series on cash and futures price levels rather than price changes. Figure (3) depicts the historical

relationship between the price levels on our cash bond and the successive nearest-to-deliver T-bond futures contracts. The estimated regression line for these data points is also graphed in Figure (3). (The scale differs significantly from Figure (2).) The regression equation that gives rise to this fitted line is:

$$P_c = s + t\,P_f + error. \qquad (4)$$

The slope of the line in Figure (3) is 1.43, which means that when P_f rises by one dollar, Pc rises by "t" dollars. Hence, the estimate of "t" can be thought of as a hedge ratio. (Note the substantial difference in this hedge ratio from that found using the same

FIGURE 3

Daily Price Series
U.S. Treasury 12.75's of 2010
vs.
Nearby T-Bond Futures Contract

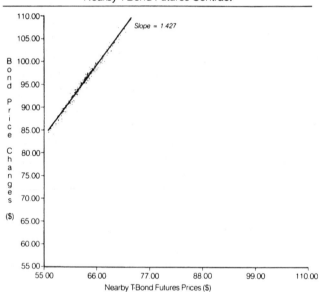

price data to run a regression of price changes.) The Appendix shows how "t" can be mathematically derived as a minimum variance hedge ratio.

Instantaneous Price Sensitivity Hedge Ratio

The price relationships depicted in Figure (3) can be exploited in a somewhat different manner. As shown by the broad, fuzzy line in Figure (4), a close but not precise price relationship exists between cash and futures prices. The fuzziness of the relationship exists between cash and futures prices. The fuzziness of the relationship occurs because of basis risk. Rather than fitting a straight line through observed data points lying in this fuzzy band, one might ask the question: Given the current price position, does financial theory indicate how this position would change with a slight change in interest rates?

314

Instantaneous Price Sensitivities

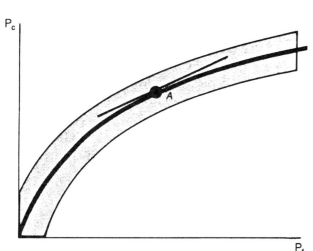

Slope of straight line estimates the hedge ratio

Slope is measured as in Equation (7) as $P_c D_c^*/P_f D_f^*$

Consider Point "A" in Figure (4). We chose this position to lie on the center line of the band, which indicates that current prices are such that futures are neither cheap nor rich to cash. The cash and futures prices are then reassessed after a small hypothetical movement in interest rates. This process is straightforward for cash bond prices, less so for futures prices. A futures price, however, implies a yield to maturity from the delivery date to the maturity date of the delivered bond. We vary this yield by one basis point, and then compute the new futures (deliverable) price. When we divide the instantaneous price change for the cash bond by that of the futures contract, we derive a hedge ratio.[4] This methodology produces the slope of the tangent to Point "A" in Figure (4). The Appendix shows this hedge ratio to be mathematically consistent with the minimum variance hedge ratio defined in Equation (2).[5]

It is more difficult to compute the price sensitivity of futures contracts that permit several securities to be delivered. First, the security that is expected to be cheapest to deliver must be identified. This bond's converted futures price (the quoted futures price times the conversion factor) coupled with its coupon rate, delivery date, and maturity date provide sufficient information to compute a yield to maturity from the delivery date to the maturity date of the cheapest-to-deliver bond. Vary this yield by one basis point and find the new price of the deliverable. Convert this new price back into a futures price by dividing it by the conversion factor. The new futures

price relative to the original price gives the price sensitivity of the futures price for a one basis point change in yields.

The instantaneous price sensitivity hedge ratio can be expressed in terms of the "durations" of the cash and deliverable security. A useful property of duration is that it can express the price sensitivity of a bond in a convenient and simple expression: Change in P per unit change in r equals $-D^* \times P$, where D^* represents the duration of the bond divided by the quantity $1 + (r/2)$, where r is the yield to maturity of the bond. (Some refer to D^* as the "modified" duration.) For a full explanation of duration and the above equation see Bierwag, Kaufman, and Toevs (1983).

The instantaneous price hedge ratio is the price sensitivity of the cash security divided by the price sensitivity of the futures contract. Thus, an estimate of the minimum variance hedge ratio, expressed in terms of durations, is:

$$N^* = P_c \times D_c^*/P_f \times D_f^*. \qquad (5)$$

The subscripts refer to the cash or futures securities.

The literature on interpreting Equation (5) has been unclear in two respects.

First, some writers have taken insufficient care to specify what hedging objective is being sought through the application of this equation. See the critical comments of Pitts (1985). We have addressed these comments in the Appendix, where we show that duration and regression hedges have a common theoretical base.

Second, there has been less than careful attention to the definitions of the prices and durations to be used in Equation (5).[6] For Weak Form Cash Hedges, P_c is the current market value of the cash securities in the portfolio. D_c^* is the current modified duration of the cash portfolio. When only one security is deliverable, P_f is the currently quoted futures price; otherwise, P_f is the current forward price of the cheapest-to-deliver security divided by the conversion factor of this security. D_f^* is the modified duration of the cheapest-to-deliver bond associated with P_f. It is calculated assuming the delivery date is today's date and using the cash flows associated with the deliverable bond from the delivery date to its maturity date.[7] Toevs and Jacob (1984) discuss the interpretations of prices and durations for other hedge classifications.

On June 24, 1982, the September T-bond futures price was 59.3125 and the Treasury 8 3/8 of 2008 was expected to be cheapest to deliver. This bond had a conversion factor of 1.0375, giving an estimated delivery price of $61.537. At this price the 8 3/8 of 2008 has a yield to maturity, calculated from its delivery date, of 13.88%. Using this yield and price, the duration of the cash flows from the delivery date to 2008 is 7.75 years, which gives a modified duration of 7.25 for use in Equation (5). The cash bond on June 24th had a price of 90.125 and a yield to maturity of 14.17%. This gives a duration of 7.34 years, 6.85 years in modified form. Substituting prices and durations into Equation (5) results in a hedge ratio of 1.38.

Some researchers have suggested adjusting durations for "relative yield volatilities." Rather than assuming that a one basis point change in the yield on a benchmark security implies a one basis point change in the yield on any other security, these researchers assume that the yield changes are related proportionally. For example, if the benchmark is a one-year Treasury bill, then a proportionality factor of 0.9 for a two-year Treasury note indicates that, when a basis point change in the bond equivalent yield occurs on the bill, the best guess is a 0.9 basis point change on the note.

We can construct the minimum variance hedge ratio obtained for situations when proportional yield changes occur in different securities by making a simple adjustment to the hedge ratio reported in Equation (5). It is:

$$N^* = P_c \times D_c^* \times R_c/P_f \times D_f^* \times R_f, \qquad (6)$$

where R_c and R_f are the relative yield volatility factors for the cash and futures positions, respectively. On June 24th, R_c/R_f was estimated to be 1.01.[8] This gives an adjusted hedged ratio of 1.39.

More comprehensive modeling of both duration and relative interest rate volatilities is possible. In the above, we have used a security's yield to maturity as the discounting rate for all cash flows associated with the security. Duration formulas exist that use individual discount factors (term structure rates). These formulas avoid having to make the assumption that yield curves are flat and change in a parallel fashion. Moreover, this approach allows the interest rate for each cash flow to have its own relative interest rate volatility. The needed substitution in the above formulas is the more correctly computed duration and relative yield volatility values.

AN EVALUATION OF HEDGE RATIO METHODOLOGIES

Dollar matching and conversion factor hedge ratio estimation techniques, while convenient, apply in limited circumstances. All three of the remaining methods are theoretically consistent with the mathematics of minimizing the variance of a portfolio of futures and cash securities. The merits of these three estimation techniques must, then, depend upon the empirical validity of their differing assumptions and the compromises that often arise in associated empirical analyses.

Let us begin by analyzing hedge ratios constructed from regressions of price *levels*. Consider Figure (5). Here the deliverable bond's interest rate sensitivity differs from the sensitivity of the cash bond. This is just the type of situation where non-simple-minded hedge ratio estimation methodologies are expected to add value. If interest rates have recently exceeded the interest rates giving rise to the current cash and futures prices (Point "A"), then the regression data are restricted to price combinations below those associated with Point "A." The estimated hedge ratio overstates the current interest rate sensitivity of the cash security relative to the deliverable security — too many futures contracts will be shorted given our current price environment. Just the opposite conclusion holds when the available data systematically lie above Point "A."

FIGURE 5
Regression of Prices
Historically Low Price Experience

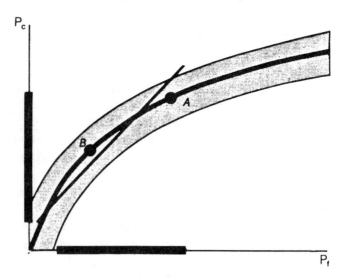

Slope of straight line estimates the hedge ratio

Hedge ratio too high

The regression-based hedge ratio can faithfully reflect the theoretically optimal hedge ratio only when a reasonable set of prices exists on both sides of the current prices of the cash and hedging instrument. This is unfortunate, because volatile and new price levels are normally situations when the correct execution of hedges adds the most value.[9]

The hedge ratio estimation technique derived

from regressions of price *changes* also suffers from the same potential problem noted in Figure (5). In addition, this regression technique assumes that the historical pattern of the average size of price changes will hold in the future. The importance of this assumption can be illustrated rather simply. Recall that the hedge ratio estimated for June 24, 1982 using a regression of price *levels* was 1.43, but using a regression of price *changes* we obtained a ratio of 1.16. If the cash and futures price *pairs* are randomly scrambled and new regressions are run, the regression of price levels still produces a hedge ratio of 1.43, as the same pairs of prices are being fitted by the regression line, but the regression of price changes now produces a hedge ratio of 1.42! For regression of price changes to provide theoretically defensible hedge ratios, one must assume both that the prior price levels and the prior daily average price changes reflect today's potential price change magnitude. Only the former assumption need be made when using the regression of price levels.

A final deficiency of regression hedge ratios relative to the instantaneous price sensitivity methodology helps make the transition from theory to practice. Advocates of regression techniques often ignore potential data problems of some importance. How would a bond portfolio manager deal with the data requirements needed to hedge a portfolio of 50 to 100 separate bonds? How can a regression be used to establish the hedge for a bond that has just been issued with a historically unusual coupon rate or maturity? How can regressions be conveniently performed for multiple bond portfolios? How can we rely upon them if an unusual new issue should become the cheapest-to-deliver security for existing futures contracts?

SOME EMPIRICAL RESULTS ON WEAK FORM CASH HEDGES

This section applies the hedge ratio estimation methodologies discussed above to recent market data. The time period analyzed starts in mid-1982 and continues to 1984. We use data for 1981 through mid-1982 (240 days) to run the initial regressions. Regressions are updated every twenty trading days by dropping the oldest twenty days in the data set and adding the newest twenty days. Such frequently run regressions help place regression-based hedge ratios in a favorable light.

We analyze four representative examples of Weak Form Cash Hedges. The first example hedges the 12.75% Treasury due in 2010. This security has an interest rate sensitivity during our sample period similar to that of the cheapest-to-deliver security as-

sociated with the T-bond futures contract. The second example hedges a Treasury note using the T-bond futures contract. The third and fourth examples examine the effectiveness of hedge ratio methodologies for single- and double-A rated long-term corporate bonds.

Example 1:
Hedging a bond similar to the
T-bond futures contract deliverable bond

We constructed daily hedges from June 24, 1982 to January 1, 1984 for the 12.75% Treasury of 2010, which ranged in price from 90 to 120. Table (1) reports the percentage of the cash security's variance reduced by the alternative hedge ratios. Take, for example, the dollar match hedge ratio results for a ten-day moving average.[10] The reported variance reduction of 92% comes from the following four steps:
1. Compute for each trading day from June 24, 1982 through December 31, 1983 the hedged and unhedged portfolio returns.
2. Average these two series using a ten-day moving average.
3. Compute the variances of these ten-day average returns over the entire period.
4. Find the percentage variance of the unhedged position reduced in the hedged position.

Similar calculations are made based upon a thirty-day moving average of daily hedging outcomes. Because the interest rate characteristics of the cash bond and the futures contract are similar, all hedge ratio techniques produce similar and excellent results.

TABLE 1

Percent Variance Reduced
Cash Security: U.S. Treasury 12.75 of 2010

	10-Day Moving Average	30-Day Moving Average
Dollar Matching	92%	96%
Conversion Factor	92	96
Change in Price Regression	90	91
Price Level Regression	92	96
Price-Sensitivity/Duration	92	96
Price-Sensitivity/Duration (corrected for yield volatilities)	93	96
Curvilinear Price Regression*	92	96

* The hedge technique labeled "Curvilinear Price Regression" is that derived using a regression discussed in footnote 9.

Example 2:
Maturity/Duration Mismatched Hedge

Inventory positions may have duration characteristics dissimilar to those associated with the deliverable security underlying the best available futures contract. After all, only three maturities are available in the Treasury futures contracts — the 90-day T-bill, the T-note, and the T-bond contracts.

This example studies a relatively severe mismatch in maturities (durations). The Treasury note paying 13% due in 1990 is hedged with the nearest-to-deliver T-bond futures contract. The results appear in Table (2). This example reveals the weakness of the naive hedging strategies that ignore the different interest rate sensitivities of the hedging and hedge instruments. As expected, the hedge performance for all hedge ratio methods falls below that experienced in Example (1), as no method perfectly estimates the influences of differential interest rate sensitivities.

TABLE 2

Percent Variance Reduced
Cash Security: U.S. Treasury 13% of 1990

	10-Day Moving Average	30-Day Moving Average
Dollar Matching	44%	68%
Conversion Factor	50	72
Change in Price Regression	78	84
Price Level Regression	76	86
Price-Sensitivity/Duration	80	87
Price-Sensitivity/Duration (corrected for yield volatilities)	77	88
Curvilinear Price Regression*	79	89

* See Table 1.

As in Example (1), a longer moving average offsets more of the random basis risk. All techniques remain tightly grouped, other than dollar matching and conversion factor methods. Note that the relative yield volatility correction in the price sensitivity hedge adds little value, because variations in long-term cash market security yields are relatively close to the variations in intermediate-term yields. The curved line regression of prices technique modestly improves the hedging efficacy of the standard regression of price levels methodology. This is expected, as the price relationship between the note and the T-bond futures contract has more distinct curvature — like that in Figure (5) — than is present in Example (1).

Examples 3 and 4:
Similar Maturity, Dissimilar Credit Quality Hedges

One can attempt to hedge inventories of long-term corporate bonds with T-bond futures contracts. In general, the greater the credit quality differential, the worse the hedge performance of T-bond futures contracts.[11]

Suppose the cash security to be hedged is the double-A rated GMAC 8% of 2007. While this bond is callable, the high price discount of this low-coupon bond considerably reduces the chances of a call. Effectively, the duration of the bond is nearly that of a non-callable bond.

Table (3) reports the relative performances of the various hedge ratios for the GMAC bond. Substantial portions of the variation in the naked position can be reduced by any means chosen to hedge. The convenience of dollar matching or price sensitivity hedge ratios argues for their use in practice. Given

TABLE 3

Percent Variance Reduced
Cash Security: GMAC 8's of 2007

	10-Day Moving Average	30-Day Moving Average
Dollar Matching	78%	89%
Conversion Factor	75	86
Change in Price Regression	75	80
Price Level Regression	75	86
Price-Sensitivity/Duration	78	88
Price-Sensitivity/Duration (corrected for yield volatilities)	78	89
Curvilinear Price Regression*	75	86

* See Table 1.

the poor performance of the naive dollar-matching strategy in other examples, however, price sensitivity hedge ratios provide a consistently superior methodology.

The next example examines the hedge effectiveness of alternative techniques when the corporate bond has a single-A credit rating. The cash security

TABLE 4

Percent Variance Reduced
Cash Security: Tenneco 8⅜s of 2002

	10-Day Moving Average	30-Day Moving Average
Dollar Matching	64%	65%
Conversion Factor	64	65
Change in Price Regression	64	69
Price Level Regression	64	69
Price-Sensitivity/Duration	64	69
Price-Sensitivity/Duration (corrected for yield volatilities)	64	70
Curvilinear Price Regression*	64	70

* See Table 1.

in this example is the Tenneco 8⅜% of 2002. This bond trades at a substantial price discount, which makes this callable bond effectively a long-term instrument.

The lower credit quality of this bond reduces the hedge effectiveness for any hedge technique chosen, relative to the GMAC bond. Proportionally, more systematic interest rate risk remains unhedged in this lower credit security than in the double-A rated bond examined above.[12]

The last two examples used deeply discounted callable securities. Hedge ratio construction for callable bonds priced at a premium, or bonds fluctuating between premium and discount prices, is fraught with difficulties. Consider regression-based hedge ratios. If interest rates have been falling during the recent period, the bond to be hedged may have recently been trading at a discount or near par but is now trading at a premium. At these prior prices, the threat of a call is much less than current expectations. Since these expectations fundamentally influence the interest rate sensitivity of the callable bond, the regression-based hedge ratios may be severely misestimated. Price sensitivity hedge ratios can suffer equally if they continue to be calculated to the maturity date. On the other hand, the duration of a bond can be continuously and efficiently adjusted for the interest rate influences of its call provision (see Toevs (1985)).

A final question can be raised about the above hedging examples. Given the problems with regression-based hedges discussed in Section III, why are these track records as good as they appear to be? First, great care was used to collect the data necessary to make the regression-based hedge ratios perform well. Second, call risk was minimized in our examples. Third, the data used in the regressions were from a time period when there were sufficient ranges in price and the size of price changes to minimize some of the weaknesses noted for regression-based methodologies. Fourth, the assumptions made in the price-sensitivity/duration-based hedge ratio approach are often violated in practice — yield curves are not flat, nor do they always shift in a parallel fashion. Thus, the simple Macaulay duration formula we used in the construction of these ratios is not strictly appropriate. More sophisticated duration formulas can add value. Fifth, the regression-based hedges captured any historical systematic basis risk, while our price-sensitivity/duration approach was not so modified.

CONCLUSIONS

Sophisticated hedge ratio estimation methodologies have a common root — the mathematical minimization of the variance in a portfolio's value. In practice, all estimation techniques face empirical realities that are inconsistent with their theoretical assumptions. Naive hedge strategies can work well in some but not all instances. Their deficiencies lie in

their assumption that the interest rate sensitivities of the hedging and cash instruments are equal.

We find that the duration hedge is more conveniently constructed than any regression-based hedge, because neither historical data series nor regression analyses need be used, and price-sensitivity/duration-based hedge ratios can be altered in numerous ways to increase hedging effectiveness, such as estimating relative *yield* volatilities, modeling the basis, and accounting for the influences of call provisions on interest rate sensitivities. By segmenting the sources of interest rate risk in the price-sensitivity/duration framework, we have increased our ability to model the residual risks of futures hedges. In practice, we find that simple price-sensitivity duration hedges perform as well as any currently available techniques. Thus, simply constructed duration-based hedges appear to dominate the more elaborately constructed regression-based hedges. Finally, although not formally discussed in this paper, the application of hedges to the other hedge types — Strong Form Cash Hedges and Anticipatory Hedges — often makes the use of naive and regression-based hedge ratios cumbersome if not impossible.

---

[1] The quoted price of Treasury bills is based on the discount yield for a 360-day year. A "price" of 88.21 implies a discount from 100 of 11.79. This discount yield can be used to compute the corresponding price as follows: Price = 100 − ((90/360) × 11.79). Given the price, a bond equivalent yield can be calculated.

[2] Detailed analyses of the other three hedges can be found in Toevs and Jacob (1984).

[3] This paper will report the hedge ratio as the market value of the futures contract selected per market value dollar of the security to be hedged. This measure avoids having to deal with the minor complications introduced by various futures contracts representing different principal value commitments.

[4] Most contracts have a delivery month rather than a delivery date, but we must use an expected delivery date in this case. A good rule of thumb is that delivery is expected to occur near the beginning (end) of the month when the yield curve is downward (upward) sloping.

[5] Under some circumstances, the futures price may not be fully arbitraged. The interest rate sensitivity of a mispriced contract can still be estimated using an assumption on what amount of the initial arbitrage premium remains after the interest rate shock.

[6] A number of papers by Chiang, Gay, and Kolb have contributed to the confusion on what prices and durations to use for the cash and futures contracts. This is surprising, because a clearer statement of the problem is found in an earlier piece by McEnally and Rice (1979).

[7] The duration of a security that only promises future cash flows is interpreted somewhat differently from the duration of a cash security. A futures position does not constitute an investment; rather, it represents an instantaneous exposure of wealth, through changes in the variation margin, to changes in market perceptions of the expected course of interest rates. The futures contract's duration indexes the volatility of the variation margin to changes in the interest rates expected to prevail on the delivery date of the associated security. The simplest duration of a futures contract to compute is that of the T-bill futures contract. The duration of a ninety-day Treasury bill at the delivery date of the contract equals .25 years. Thus, a T-bill deliverable in one month and a T-bill futures contract deliverable in twenty-one months have equal durations. This does not necessarily imply that the hedge ratio computed with Equation (5) would be the same if the hedging security were either of these bill contracts. First, the prices of these two futures contracts may differ. Second, their modified durations would reflect any unequal interest rates implied by differing prices of these contracts. Third, as will be discussed in a moment, hedge ratios may also be adjusted for relative yield volatility estimates.

[8] This was found by regressing the yield to maturity of the cash security against the yield from delivery to maturity of the cheapest-to-deliver security in prior periods.

[9] Remember that this criticism holds when the interest rate sensitivities of the cash and futures instruments differ from each other. If they did not do so, hedging is so simple that no sophisticated technique is required. In situations when the price relationship between cash securities and futures contracts is curved, as in Figure (5), a nonlinear regression equation might fit best. Toevs and Jacob (1984) examine this possibility, using a regression of the form $P_c = s + tP_f + vP_f^2 + error$. The empirical results for our example call for a hedge ratio of 1.53 as of June 24, 1982. In practice, we find the added complexity of this approach has little value.

[10] Short time span moving averages remove the basis risk that is purely random in nature.

[11] Note that it is more difficult to conduct regression analysis for corporate bonds than for Treasuries. Publicly available corporate bond price series have notable inaccuracies, making regression estimates for corporates much less accurate than those for Treasuries. We have minimized this problem here by using Morgan Stanley quotes on actively traded issues.

[12] A hedge methodology that takes into account the equity-like component of higher yielding bonds is discussed in Bookstaber and Jacob (1985).

REFERENCES

Bierwag, G. O., Kaufman, G. G., and Toevs, A. L. "Duration: Its Development and Use in Bond Portfolio Management." *Financial Analysts Journal*, July/August 1983.

Bookstaber, R. and Jacob, D. P. *The Composite Hedge: Controlling the Credit Risk of High Yield Bonds*. Morgan Stanley, 1985.

Ederington, Louis. "The Hedging Performances of the New Futures Markets." *Journal of Finance*, March 1979.

Gay, G. D. and Kolb, R. W. "The management of interest rate risk." *The Journal of Portfolio Management*, Winter 1983.

Kolb, R. W. and Chiang, R. "Improving Hedging Performance Using Interest Rate Futures." *Financial Management*, Autumn 1981.

McEnally, R. W. and Rice, M. L. "Hedging Possibilities in the Floatation of Debt Securities." *Financial Management*, Winter 1979.

Pitts, M. "Cross Hedging, Autocorrelated Errors, and the Trade-Off Between Risk and Return." Paper presented at the Financial Management Association Meetings, October 21, 1983.

——. "The management of interest rate risk: Comment." *The Journal of Portfolio Management*, Fall 1985.

Toevs, A. L. "Interest rate risk and uncertain lives." *The Journal of Portfolio Management*, Spring 1985.

—— and Jacob, D. P. *Interest Rate Futures: A Comparison of Alternative Hedge Ratio Methodologies*. Morgan Stanley, June 1984.

APPENDIX

DETERMINATION OF THE MINIMUM VARIANCE HEDGE RATIO

I. Minimum Variance Hedge Ratios

Let the unhedged position represent one unit of a cash security with a price of P_c. This price is a function of the maturity date and coupon rate of the cash security and of market determined interest rates. Let r_{c_o} represent the current market determined yield to maturity of the cash security. Let this yield change unexpectedly to $r_{c_o} + \lambda$, where $\lambda \gtreqless 0$. This unexpected change in interest rates causes the cash security price to change. Since the size of this price change depends upon the value of λ, the price change can be functionally stated as $\Delta P_c(\lambda)$. The variance of the change in price is represented by $var(\Delta P_c)$.

Now, consider the influence any hedging instrument has on this cash position. Let the price of the hedging security be P_h and let this price reflect a yield of r_{h_o}. An unexpected change in this yield to $r_{h_o} + \gamma$, where $\gamma \gtreqless 0$, produces a price change of $\Delta P_h(\gamma)$. The variance of the change in price is $var(\Delta P_h)$.

Given these variances, what is the variance of a portfolio of one unit of the cash security and N units of the hedging security? (The hedging security can be a cash, forward or futures contract.) Using standard statistical relationships, the variance of $\Delta P_c + Nx\Delta P_h$ is:

$$var(\Delta P_c + N\Delta P_h) = var(\Delta P_c) + 2 N\, cov(\Delta P_c, \Delta P_h) + N^2 var(\Delta P_h). \quad (A)$$

The number of units of the hedging securities that reduces this variance to a minimum is found by differentiating Equation (A) with respect to N and setting the result equal to zero. Thus,

$$N^* = -\, cov(\Delta P_c, \Delta P_h)/var(\Delta P_h). \quad (B)$$

This conclusion is similar to Equation (2) in the main text. In fact, Equations (B) and (2) are identical. If λ and γ are positively correlated, then ΔP_c and ΔP_h are positively correlated. The minus sign in Equation (B) indicates we should short sell N^* of the hedging security.

Note that N^* represents the optimal number of hedging contracts to short per cash contract only once the specific hedging contract has been selected. The optimal hedge requires that we first find the hedge security with highest net productive covariance and then establish N^* as the hedge ratio for this instrument.

The text notes that the regression of price levels and instantaneous price sensitivity/duration-based hedge ratio estimation techniques are all consistent with the concept of a minimum variance hedge ratio. This assertion is demonstrated here.

II. Regression of Price Changes

Louis Ederington (1979) first noted that the equation for N^*, which relates the covariance of cash and hedging securities price changes to the variance of the hedging security price changes, is statistically nothing more than the slope of a regression line. That is, if the regression $\Delta P_c = a + b\Delta P_f + error$ is run, the value the computer derives for "b" comes from dividing the sample covariance of the price changes by the sample variance of the price changes in the hedging security.

III. Regression of Price Levels

The value of a hedged portfolio can be represented as:

$$V_H = P_c + N \times P_h. \tag{C}$$

The initial value for P_c, related through the regression equation to the price of the hedge, is:

$$P_c = \hat{a} + b\hat{P}_h + error, \tag{D}$$

where the "$\wedge$" terms indicate regression estimates of an intercept and slope. If interest rates change then the new P_c relates to the new P_h through the above equation. Thus,

$$\Delta P_c = P_c^* - P_c = \hat{a} + \hat{b}P_h^* + error^* - \hat{a} - \hat{b}P_h - error;$$
$$\Delta P_c = \hat{b}\Delta P_h + (error^* - error). \tag{E}$$

The change in V_H derived from Equation (C) is, upon substitution of Equation (E):

$$\Delta V_H = (\hat{b} + N)\Delta P_h + (error^* - error). \tag{F}$$

The expected value of ΔV_H due to a change in interest rates is zero, and its variance becomes:

$$var(\Delta V_H) = (\hat{b} + N)^2 var\{\Delta P_h\} + var\{error^* - error\}. \tag{G}$$

To minimize this variance, select the value for N that drives the derivative of Equation (G) to zero. The required derivative is:

$$d\ var\{\Delta V_H\}/d\ N = 2(\hat{b} + N)\ var\{\Delta P_h\} = 0. \tag{H}$$

The only way this value equals zero is if $N = -b$. Thus, the minimum variance hedge ratio, N^*, equals the slope of the regression relating the price of the cash security to the price of the hedging instrument. If the hedging instrument is a futures contract, then the above analysis is not strictly correct. Portfolio value as expressed in Equation (C) becomes:

$$V_H = P_c + N(P_f - P_f'), \tag{I}$$

where P_f' is the futures price established when the hedge was first put into place. $N(P_f - P_f')$ represents total allocation to the margin account. The substitutions and derivatives as found in Equations (D) through (H) ultimately eliminate the fixed term $-NP_f'$, and the result is that $N^* = -b$ is maintained.

IV. Duration-Based Hedges

The duration-based methodology asserts that

$$\Delta V_H = \Delta P_c + N\ \Delta P_h; \quad \Delta r_c = k\ \Delta r_h + \epsilon;$$
$$\Delta P_c \cong -D_c\ P_c\ \Delta\ r_c/(1 + r_c/2); \text{ and}$$
$$\Delta P_h \cong -D_h\ P_h\ \Delta\ r_h/(1 + r_h/2).$$

Here k is the relative yield volatility factor, and ϵ is a random error term that permits imperfect price arbitrage.

The duration approach, therefore, begins with the equation:

$$\Delta V_h \cong -D_c^*P_c(k\ \Delta r_h + \epsilon) - ND_h^*P_h\ \Delta\ r_h, \tag{J}$$

where D_c^* and D_h^* are modified durations. For small changes in r_h, Equation (J) becomes exact.

Because Δr_h and ϵ are by definition uncorrelated and because the expectation of these two variables is zero, the variance of Equation (J) can be written as:

$$var\{\Delta V_H\} = \{(D_c^*P_ck)^2 + 2kND_c^*P_cD_h^*P_h + (ND_h^*\ P_h)^2\}var\{\Delta r_h\}$$
$$+ (D_c^*\ P_c^*)^2var\{\epsilon\}.$$

Minimizing this variance with respect to N produces:

$$N^* = -D_c^*P_ck/D_h^*\ P_h,$$

where k is the relative yield volatility factor, which may be equal to one.

Hedging corporate bond portfolios

Combinations of T-bond futures and stock index futures increase hedging effectiveness.

Robin Grieves

A corporate bond is a hybrid security: a combination of risk-free government debt and equity in the firm that issued the bond.

Weinstein [1985]

Changes in interest rates change both Treasury bond prices and corporate bond prices; changes in companies' prospects change stock prices and, by changing default risk, change corporate bond prices as well. If Treasury bond returns and corporate stock returns are results of different sets of forces, then we would expect a combination of T-bond futures and stock index futures to provide superior hedges for corporate bonds.

The purpose of this paper is to present the results from hedging portfolios of corporate bonds using a combination of Treasury bond futures and stock index futures. We have a priori reason to believe that such a hedge should be more effective than a hedge using Treasury bond futures alone.

A different but related problem has been considered by Bookstaber and Jacob [1985]. They devise a hedging rule for a *single* high-yield (in less polite circles, read "junk") bond. The rule involves shorting the common stock of the underlying company and shorting Treasury bonds. The proportions in the hedge are varied with market conditions, much like a synthetic put strategy used in equity portfolios. Bookstaber and Jacob's hedging technique is of primary interest to underwriters. The technique described in this paper is of primary interest to money managers.

METHODOLOGY

The method for determining the optimal hedge ratio and the effectiveness of hedging a portfolio is well established in the literature (see Ederington [1979], Hill and Schneeweis [1982], and Wilson [1984]). In short, we run a regression with price changes for the investment to be hedged as the dependent variable and price changes for the hedging instrument(s) as the independent variable(s). Regression coefficients are the optimal hedge ratios, and R^2 measures the variance reduction possible with the hedge.

Straightforward as this method sounds, there is still room for some question about how to measure price changes for the regression. In many instances, researchers compute time series differences in prices of the hedged and hedging instruments. When the processes generating price changes in the series are stable, it does not matter whether we look at price differences or percentage changes. The reason it does not matter is that the optimal hedge ratio in that case is a number of futures contracts, and those contracts generate price changes that are similar to the price changes in the cash position — independently of the price innovation process.

First consider bond price innovations. In general, we expect bond prices to be stationary. The next price change in newly issued, par value bonds is a surprise. Consequently, when we consider price differences for bonds and price differences for Treasury bond futures contracts, we are drawing from a single distribution, and what we would like to know is how many contracts will be optimal in the hedge portfolio.

Now consider stocks. Part of the return to the S&P 500 and to most other stock portfolios is expected capital gains. Therefore, we expect the price to grow over time. Price innovations come from a positive mean, multiplicative distribution instead of from a zero mean, additive distribution. Nevertheless, if we search for the optimal number of stock index contracts for hedging a stock portfolio by using price differ-

ROBIN GRIEVES is Assistant Professor of Finance at the College of Business Administration at the University of Nebraska in Lincoln (NE 68588). The author thanks Ramon DeGennaro, Richard McEnally, William McGuire, Rover Kutz, Clay Singleton, and an anonymous referee for helpful comments.

ences, we will again come close, because a constant number of contracts has the right amount of price innovation in it.

We encounter serious problems when the hedged and hedging instruments receive price innovations from different processes — as in our case. The economic meaning of not being able to use price differences to find the optimal hedge ratio is that *there is no constant number of stock index contracts that will effectively hedge a bond portfolio.* Instead, when we estimate the regressions in terms of percentage changes, we find the number of dollars of stock price variation and the number of dollars of T-bond price variation we need in our hedged portfolio to minimize the variance of returns to our bond portfolio. (For an example of using price relatives to determine optimal hedge ratios, see McEnally and Rice [1979].)

Several authors have investigated the effectiveness of various financial futures contracts for hedging bond portfolios (e.g., see Ederington [1979] and Hill and Schneeweis [1984]). These authors invariably find that basis risk persists. This basis risk is attributable to cross-hedging as well as to having too few maturity dates per year. They find that no *one* contract removes return variation. In addition, risk will remain even if the futures contract is for the investment in the portfolio, unless the investor's planning horizon matches the maturity date of the futures contract.

The next section reports my findings on the optimal ratios of Treasury bond futures and stock index futures for hedging corporate bonds.

DATA AND RESULTS

Bond yields, used to compute bond prices, were end-of-the-month yields by bond grade and bond type from *Moody's Bond Record.* All hedges and cash positions are evaluated over identical holding periods — as they ought to be.

I computed bond prices assuming a coupon rate equal to Moody's yield and a term to maturity of twenty years. All cash positions and all hedges began with bonds selling at par. While assumptions regarding the nature of the bonds in the portfolio influence the optimal hedge ratios, results concerning the effectiveness of the hedges and whether that effectiveness is enhanced by using stock index futures with T-bond futures are qualitatively invariant with respect to those assumptions.

The dependent variable in all regressions is the current price of last month's bonds divided by the beginning price of last month's bonds (always $1000).

The prices for Treasury bond futures listed on the Chicago Board of Trade are for the near-term contract extant at the end of the month. For example, the March contract is the hedging contract for December, January, and February. The June contract is the hedging contract for March, April, and May.

I also calculated T-bond futures price relatives for each hedging contract. The price relative for February, for example, is the February end-of-month price for the March contract divided by the January end-of-month price for the March contract. The price relative for March has the February end-of-month price for the *June* contract in the denominator. Every third month, then, requires two contract prices.

Stock index futures are S&P 500 futures traded on the Chicago Mercantile Exchange. They are prices for the near-term contract extant at the end of the month, just like the T-bond futures. Stock index futures price relatives are calculated in the same way as the T-bond futures price relatives.

All regressions cover the period July, 1982 through January, 1985, and contain 31 observations. The analysis begins shortly after the introduction of S&P futures contracts.[1]

As a benchmark, to see hedging effectiveness under ideal conditions, I considered hedging a portfolio of Treasury bonds. The data were end-of-the-month yields from Moody's U.S. Treasuries "longer" maturity — "longer" means bonds neither due nor callable in less than ten years. The yields were used to compute prices and price relatives just as with corporate bonds.

The results are in Table 1. H^* is the optimal hedge ratio for hedging with T-bond futures only and $H1^*$ and $H2^*$ are optimal hedge ratios for T-bond futures and S&P stock index futures when using both instruments to hedge. The numbers in parentheses under the hedge ratios are t-statistics with the null hypothesis that the associated coefficient equals zero.

The Treasury bond portfolio contains a variety of maturities. Since not all interest rate changes are parallel shifts in the yield curve, we would not expect the hedge to be perfect. It is not. Further, unless the portfolio contains only one bond, the cheapest-to-deliver in the futures contract, we would not expect the optimal hedge ratio to be one. It is not. Nevertheless, the usefulness of T-bond futures for hedging Treasury bond portfolios is confirmed.

Table 1 also displays the optimal hedge ratios and measures of hedging effectiveness for industrial and utility bonds by grade. The results are striking and confirm the efficacy of hedging with both contracts on industrial bonds. For example, with Moody's Aa bonds, R^2 increases from 0.58 to 0.64. This is accomplished by reducing the Treasury bond component of the hedge from 44 cents to 36 cents of current market value of T-bond futures per dollar of current market value of bonds, and adding 15 cents of current market value of stock index futures.

Continue with the results for industrial bonds

---

1. Footnotes appear at the end of the article.

TABLE 1

Bond Hedging Effectiveness and Optimal Hedge Ratios

Treasury Bond Contracts Only		Treasury Bond and Standard and Poor's Futures Contracts		

Treasuries

T-Bonds

R^2	H^*	R^2	$H1^*$	$H2^*$
0.98	0.92	0.98	0.90	0.04
	(37.44)		(33.06)	(1.47)

Industrials

Moody's Aaa

R^2	H^*	R^2	$H1^*$	$H2^*$
0.78	0.64	0.81	0.58	0.12
	(10.26)		(8.58)	(1.88)

Moody's Aa

0.58	0.44	0.64	0.36	0.15
	(6.32)		(4.92)	(2.22)

Moody's A

0.44	0.41	0.51	0.33	0.16
	(4.82)		(3.56)	(1.88)

Moody's Baa

0.36	0.38	0.51	0.25	0.25
	(4.05)		(2.66)	(2.87)

Utilities

Moody's Aa

R^2	H^*	R^2	$H1^*$	$H2^*$
0.86	0.71	0.86	0.67	0.07
	(13.10)		(11.10)	(1.20)

Moody's A

0.74	0.49	0.75	0.47	0.03
	(9.15)		(7.72)	(0.58)

Moody's Baa

0.78	0.50	0.80	0.46	0.08
	(10.22)		(8.53)	(1.59)

in Table 1. The increase in hedging effectiveness (change in R^2) increases as bond quality goes down. This is as we would expect. Aaa bonds trade at a small relative yield premium to Treasuries and that premium is subject to less basis risk than lower-grade bonds.

The proportion of stock index futures in the hedge portfolios increases as bond quality decreases. This, too, is as we would expect. Lower-grade bonds are more stock-like than higher-grade bonds.

The proportion of T-bond futures in the hedge portfolios decreases as bond grade decreases. Again, we have the plausible result that lower-grade corporate bonds are more stock-like and less T-bond-like than higher-grade corporate bonds. In fact, for Baa bonds the quantity of stock index futures in the hedge portfolio equals the quantity of T-bond futures.

The overall effectiveness of the hedge declines as bond quality declines, even though the contribution from stock index futures increases. This implies that some factors not reflected in Treasury bonds or corporate equities influence corporate bond prices. Improving these hedges is certainly one direction for future research.

Pure interest rate hedging effectiveness is uniformly higher for utility bonds than for industrials, while improvement in effectiveness is uniformly lower. Low t-statistics on the stock index futures raise doubts about whether there is any broad market component to utility bond returns at all. The results also provide evidence supporting the continued segregation of utility bond data from industrial bond data.

The results for utility bond hedging also lend credence to the hypothesis that Arbitrage Pricing Theory provides useful insights into hedging possibilities. The results imply the plausible view that the factor structure generating industrial bond returns is different from the factor structure generating utility bond returns. This difference is probably attributable to the utilities' regulators. Rate cases are, in part, decided so as to allow the utility to borrow and subsequently pay the interest on bonds. This should make them more like Treasury bonds and less like corporate stock.

CONCLUSIONS

Managers can hedge portfolios of industrial bonds more effectively using a combination of Treasury bond futures and stock index futures than they can hedge using Treasury bond futures alone. The improvement in effectiveness is greater for lower-quality bonds. Regrettably, these results do not extend to utility bonds. One direction for future research is to determine whether a utility stock index futures contract would significantly improve hedging possibilities in the utility bond market.

[1] Since each regression contains the entire data period, these are ex post hedging results. They represent the best results that could be obtained. When a longer series of S&P futures prices is available, it will be interesting to see how effective ex ante hedging can be. For these results, a regression including data to some date is run, the hedge ratio from that regression is used for the next month, a portfolio return is calculated, and the process is repeated for the next month. The variance of returns from these ex ante hedges is then compared with the variance from unhedged portfolios to determine hedging effectiveness.

REFERENCES

1. Bookstaber, R. and D. P. Jacob. *The Composite Hedge: Controlling the Credit Risk of High Yield Bonds.* Morgan Stanley, New York, March 1985.

2. Ederington, L. "The Hedging Performance of the New Futures Market." *Journal of Finance*, March 1979, pp. 157-70.

3. Hill, J. M. and T. Schneeweis. "The Hedging Effectiveness of Foreign Currency Futures." *Journal of Financial Research*, Spring 1982, pp. 95-104.

4. —— and ——. "Reducing Volatility with Financial Futures." *Financial Analysts Journal*, November/December 1984, pp. 34-40.

5. McEnally, R. W. and M. L. Rice. "Hedging Possibilities in the Flotation of Debt Securities." *Financial Management*, Winter 1979, pp. 12-18.

6. Weinstein, M. "The Equity Component of Corporate Bonds." *Journal of Portfolio Management*, Spring 1985, pp. 37-41.

7. Wilson, W. W. "Hedging Effectiveness of U.S. Wheat Futures Markets." *Review of Research in Futures Markets*, 1984, pp. 64-79.

Peter L. Bernstein is president of Peter L. Bernstein, Inc., economic consultants to institutional investors and corporations, and consulting editor of *The Journal of Portfolio Management*. He has also enjoyed a long career in managing both individual and institutional portfolios. In addition to teaching at the Graduate Faculty of the New School in New York, he has lectured widely throughout the United States and abroad and has published many articles in the professional and popular press. His books include *Capital Ideas: The Improbable Origins of Modern Wall Street* and *Against the Gods: The Remarkable Story of Risk*.

Frank J. Fabozzi, Adjunct Professor of Finance in the School of Management at Yale University, is editor of *The Journal of Portfolio Management*. He serves as an advisor to several major financial institutions in the United States, Japan, and Europe. Prior to joining the faculty at Yale, he was a Visiting Professor of Finance at MIT. He has authored and edited numerous books in investment management. His most recent books include *Investment Management* and *Bond Portfolio Management*.